Microsoft Exam Objectives
Exam 70-224: Installing, Configuring, and Administering Microsoft Exchange 2000 Server

Installing and Upgrading Exchange 2000 Server	Chapter(s)
Install Exchange 2000 Server on a server computer.	6
Diagnose and resolve failed installations.	14
Upgrade or migrate to Exchange 2000 Server from Exchange Server 5.5.	2, 16
Diagnose and resolve problems involving the upgrade process.	16
Manage coexistence with Exchange Server 5.5.	2, 11, 16
Diagnose and resolve Exchange 2000 Active Directory Connector problems.	14
Perform client deployments. Clients include Microsoft Outlook 2000, Outlook Web Access, POP3, IMAP4, and IRC.	7, 10, 17

Configuring Exchange 2000 Server. Types of servers include mailbox, public folder, gateway, virtual, Chat, and Instant Messaging.	Chapter(s)
Configure server objects for messaging and collaboration to support the assigned server role.	3, 4, 9, 13
Create and manage administrative groups.	4
Configure separate Exchange 2000 Server resources for high-volume access. Resources include stores, logs, and separate RAID arrays.	3, 15
Diagnose and resolve Exchange 2000 Server availability and performance problems.	14
Configure Exchange 2000 Server for high security.	1, 10, 12
Create, configure, and manage a public folder solution.	13, 15
Configure and manage system folders.	13

Managing Recipient Objects	Chapter(s)
Configure a user object for messaging.	8, 13
Manage user and information store association.	4, 5
Diagnose and resolve problems that involve user and information store placement. Problems include security, performance, and disaster recovery.	10, 15
Create and manage address lists.	8
Diagnose and resolve Recipient Update Service problems.	8

Monitoring and Managing Messaging Connectivity	Chapter(s)
Manage and troubleshoot messaging connectivity.	9, 10, 11, 14
Manage messaging queues for multiple protocols.	9
Monitor link status.	14
Configure and monitor client connectivity. Clients include Outlook 2000, Outlook Web Access, POP3, IMAP4, and IRC.	7, 17
Diagnose and resolve client connectivity problems. Problems include DNS structure, server publishing structure, DS Proxy/DS Access, address resolution, Instant Messaging clients, various connection protocols, and non–Windows 2000 environments.	11, 14
Manage public folder connectivity.	4

Managing Exchange 2000 Server Growth	Chapter(s)
Monitor services use. Services include messaging, Chat, public folder access, Instant Messaging, and calendaring.	14
Manage growth of public and private message store databases.	5, 15
Manage growth of user population and message traffic.	5, 15
Monitor the growth of client use. Clients include Outlook 2000, Outlook Web Access, POP3, IMAP4, and IRC.	14
Manage recipient and server policies.	8
Diagnose and resolve problems that involve recipient and server policies.	14
Optimize public folder and mailbox searching.	17

Restoring System Functionality and User Data	Chapter(s)
Apply a backup and restore plan.	3
Diagnose and resolve backup and restore problems.	3
Restore user data and System State data.	3, 14
Restore information stores.	3
Configure a server for disaster recovery. Configurations include circular logging, backup, and restore.	3
Diagnose and resolve security problems that involve user keys.	1, 12

MCSE™ Exchange 2000 Administration

Phillip G. Schein
Evan Benjamin

MCSE™ Exchange 2000 Administration Exam Prep
© 2001 The Coriolis Group. All rights reserved.

This book may not be duplicated in any way without the express written consent of the publisher, except in the form of brief excerpts or quotations for the purposes of review. The information contained herein is for the personal use of the reader and may not be incorporated in any commercial programs, other books, databases, or any kind of software without written consent of the publisher. Making copies of this book or any portion for any purpose other than your own is a violation of United States copyright laws.

Limits of Liability and Disclaimer of Warranty
The author and publisher of this book have used their best efforts in preparing the book and the programs contained in it. These efforts include the development, research, and testing of the theories and programs to determine their effectiveness. The author and publisher make no warranty of any kind, expressed or implied, with regard to these programs or the documentation contained in this book.

The author and publisher shall not be liable in the event of incidental or consequential damages in connection with, or arising out of, the furnishing, performance, or use of the programs, associated instructions, and/or claims of productivity gains.

Trademarks
Trademarked names appear throughout this book. Rather than list the names and entities that own the trademarks or insert a trademark symbol with each mention of the trademarked name, the publisher states that it is using the names for editorial purposes only and to the benefit of the trademark owner, with no intention of infringing upon that trademark.

The Coriolis Group, LLC
14455 N. Hayden Road, Suite 220
Scottsdale, Arizona 85260

(480)483-0192
FAX (480)483-0193
www.coriolis.com

Library of Congress Cataloging-in-Publication Data
Schein, Phillip G.
    MCSE exchange 2000 administration exam prep/Phillip Schein and Evan Benjamin.
       p. cm.
Includes index.
   ISBN 1-57610-919-4
   1. Electronic data processing personnel--Certification.   2. Microsoft software--Examinations--Study guides.   3. Microsoft Exchange server.   I. Benjamin, Evan. II. Title.
QA76.3 .S348   2001
005.7'13769--dc21
                                                    2001028260
                                                        CIP

Printed in the United States of America
10 9 8 7 6 5 4 3 2 1

President and CEO
Keith Weiskamp

Publisher
Steve Sayre

Acquisitions Editor
Lee Anderson

Development Editor
Deborah A. Doorley

Product Marketing Manager
Brett Woolley

Project Editor
Meredith Brittain

Technical Reviewer
James F. Kelly

Production Coordinator
Carla J. Schuder

Cover Designer
Jesse Dunn

Layout Designer
April Nielsen

CD-ROM Developer
Chris Nusbaum

The Coriolis Group, LLC • 14455 North Hayden Road, Suite 220 • Scottsdale, Arizona 85260

ExamCram.com Connects You to the Ultimate Study Center!

Our goal has always been to provide you with the best study tools on the planet to help you achieve your certification in record time. Time is so valuable these days that none of us can afford to waste a second of it, especially when it comes to exam preparation.

Over the past few years, we've created an extensive line of *Exam Cram* and *Exam Prep* study guides, practice exams, and interactive training. To help you study even better, we have now created an e-learning and certification destination called **ExamCram.com**. (You can access the site at **www.examcram.com**.) Now, with every study product you purchase from us, you'll be connected to a large community of people like yourself who are actively studying for their certifications, developing their careers, seeking advice, and sharing their insights and stories.

I believe that the future is all about collaborative learning. Our **ExamCram.com** destination is our approach to creating a highly interactive, easily accessible collaborative environment, where you can take practice exams and discuss your experiences with others, sign up for features like "Questions of the Day," plan your certifications using our interactive planners, create your own personal study pages, and keep up with all of the latest study tips and techniques.

I hope that whatever study products you purchase from us—*Exam Cram* or *Exam Prep* study guides, *Personal Trainers*, *Personal Test Centers*, or one of our interactive Web courses—will make your studying fun and productive. Our commitment is to build the kind of learning tools that will allow you to study the way you want to, whenever you want to.

Help us continue to provide the very best certification study materials possible. Write us or email us at **learn@examcram.com** and let us know how our study products have helped you study. Tell us about new features that you'd like us to add. Send us a story about how we've helped you. We're listening!

Visit ExamCram.com now to enhance your study program.

Good luck with your certification exam and your career. Thank you for allowing us to help you achieve your goals.

Keith Weiskamp
President and CEO

Look for these other products from The Coriolis Group:

MCSE Exchange 2000 Administration Exam Cram
by David Watts and Will Willis

MCSE Exchange 2000 Design Exam Prep
by Michael Shannon and Barry Shilmover

MCSE Exchange 2000 Design Exam Cram
by William Baldwin

MCSE ISA Server 2000 Exam Prep
by Kimberly Simmons and Masaru Ryumae

MCSE ISA Server 2000 Exam Cram
by Will Willis and David Watts

MCSE Migrating from NT 4 to Windows 2000 Exam Prep
by Glen Bergen, Graham Leach,
and David Baldwin

MCSE Migrating from NT 4 to Windows 2000 Exam Cram
by Kurt Hudson, Doug Bassett,
Deborah Haralson, and Derek Melber

MCSE SQL 2000 Administration Exam Cram
by Kirk Hausman

MCSE SQL 2000 Database Design Exam Cram
by Richard McMahon

To Harry—Baby, book, and tree; bell, book, and candle. Rest in peace.
—*Phillip G. Schein*

I dedicate this book to my wife, who knew I could write; to my parents, who just wanted me to be happy; and to a cat named Binoy. Oh, and to the class of 1981; well . . . now you know.
—*Evan Benjamin*

About the Authors

Phillip G. Schein (MCSE, MCT, MCP+I, MOUS, CNE, CTT, A+, i-Net+, and CIW-Site Designer) is an author/certified technical trainer specializing in Web application development, courseware design and publishing, and project management and in-house training. He recently wrote *MCSE Windows 2000 Security Design Exam Cram* and *MCSE Windows 2000 Security Design Exam Cram Personal Trainer* for The Coriolis Group. He has also written articles about the computer industry for more than 10 years. Phil has led corporate training seminars for Fortune 100 publishing companies, agricultural research firms, insurance reinvestment concerns, and business leaders in the insurance industry. You can reach Phil by email at **pschein@tchouse.com**.

Evan Benjamin (MCSE, MCT, A+, CNA, and Check Point's CIE) began life as a mathematician and somehow found his way into the thrilling world of computer networks. He has survived 18-hour days in New York City since 1997, working on everything from Windows for Workgroups to Windows 2000 Advanced Server systems to NetWare 5 systems. He became interested in Exchange Server after passing his first Microsoft exam. Evan has a B.S. in Mathematics from Washington University in St. Louis and an MBA from SIU, Edwardsville, Illinois. His main ambition in life is to have an operating system named after him. He lives in New York with his wife and can be reached by email at **ebtrain@yahoo.com**.

Acknowledgments

Books are not just a vicarious experience projected on some storage medium; for the writer, they are a daemon incarnate, a solitary hallucination that abides by its own rules of space and time. Unlike accessing The Matrix as a console cowboy in William Gibson's science fiction novel, *Neuromancer* (which we literally do when we use our browsers to answer email and enter chat rooms every day), an author's participation in the writing of a book is not always consensual once the initial contracts are signed. I jacked into my private mindscape to map out a virtual world of consumers and distributed service providers roaming the Net for two mutually exclusive reasons: to write about a fascinating topic and to memorialize a person. Many people have been my teacher and guide, my companion and critic. I am deeply in debt to them for choosing to help me during my journey. My personal participation, though, was far more nonconsensual than voluntary, driven by personal commitment and the faith people placed in me rather than by purely voluntary action or choice.

I want to thank Lee Anderson, acquisitions editor, for this second opportunity to add another contribution to the Coriolis collection of exam preparation material and for allowing me to work my tasks to their completion. Along with him, I wish to thank the following people for performing their roles in this project with quiet dignity and grace: Carla Schuder, production coordinator; Brett Woolley, product marketing manager; April Nielsen, layout designer; and Jesse Dunn, cover designer.

I owe yet again a debt of gratitude to Bonnie Trenga, copy editor, for teaching me greater precision in this craft. It has been 2 books and almost 12 months of work. I hear your voice as my words cascade onto a page, except that now, because of you, the words have better flow and wash crystal clear in the light of review. You have irrevocably altered my stream of consciousness. Thank you, Bonnie (yes, it *is* a nice name! <winK>). I want to thank Jim Kelly, technical reviewer, for very strong technical support, probing questions, and candid remarks. I wish we could have shared more between us in both content and style. Both you and Bonnie joined me in this hallucination throughout its production and pointed out where I should add structure and balance, and where there were only blurred images and a vague

Acknowledgments

outline of some possible virtualscape. I also want to thank Deb Doorley, development editor, for making insightful observations and helping me to deliver a more robust presentation of the material. I want to thank Bill Baldwin, who is authoring *MCSE Exchange 2000 Design Exam Cram,* for suggesting relevant topics and specific subject matter. Finally, I want to thank my parents for providing a green field for me and a tree for Harry.

I want to thank my co-author, Evan Benjamin, for working as hard as he has to help bring this project to successful fruition. It has been very rocky, but then again, I never promised you a green field deployment! Did I?

Finally, I acknowledge and especially thank one person for being a part of this nonconsensual hallucination. Though literally in different time zones and rarely using more than asynchronous communication, both of us have shared this intoxicating and all-consuming hallucination. I acknowledge you, Meredith Brittain, as a project editor who chose to join me a second time on what became a rather demanding and quite eventful journey. I hear Bonnie's voice but I feel your presence and know the awareness of it was essential in driving me to achieve closure with this project. Though this is the job you are paid to do, I need to say: Thank you, my friend, for your help, patience, support, and—what was most significant—your occasional silence. Once again, the horse and the horseman were one.
—*Phillip G. Schein*

There are multiple parties to be thanked, but like an Academy Awards victory speech, only the important people get acknowledged. Therefore, I must start with Phillip Schein, my co-author and fellow overachiever. Because of your confidence in me, I have done the unthinkable. There is no greater joy than to write and to communicate, and you have helped me do that. I can never thank you enough for opening up the doors for me, and for this I certainly owe you.

I also want to thank my editors at The Coriolis Group, especially Deb Doorley, Meredith Brittain, and Lee Anderson. Without their constant attention (and gentle prodding), these pages would be blank. I have never worked so hard as I did for this project, but in the end it was worth it. Let's just hope the next few years of therapy will more than justify my months of sleeplessness and anxiety.

I also acknowledge the constant support I got from my wife and family, who let me stay up every night until I finished. Thanks for passing food under my door and sustaining me. They keep asking me if I would do this over again, and I keep saying, "Yes!", but I hope the next few projects will be easier. To all the people who believed in me, you will never be forgotten. To all the people who didn't—well, as Jerry Seinfeld so eloquently stated, "The best revenge is to live well." I'm on my way.
—*Evan Benjamin*

Contents at a Glance

Chapter 1 Models and Methods 1
Chapter 2 Exchange Architecture 39
Chapter 3 Storage Services 71
Chapter 4 Administrative Services 109
Chapter 5 Planning and Deployment 145
Chapter 6 Installation 173
Chapter 7 Client Configuration 201
Chapter 8 Recipient Management 237
Chapter 9 Routing Management 273
Chapter 10 Interoperability 299
Chapter 11 External Connectivity 333
Chapter 12 Secure Communications 369
Chapter 13 Collaboration 405
Chapter 14 Troubleshooting and Monitoring 433
Chapter 15 Other Design and Support Issues 477
Chapter 16 Legacy System Issues 511
Chapter 17 Extending the Platform 559
Chapter 18 Sample Test 595
Chapter 19 Answer Key 613
Appendix A Answers to Review Questions 625
Appendix B Objectives for Exam 70-224 645
Appendix C Study Resources 649

Table of Contents

Exam Insights xxiii

Self-Assessment li

Chapter 1
Models and Methods 1

    The Knowledge-Management Paradigm   5
    What Is Knowledge?   7
    Windows DNA—A Management Model   8
        Common Management Information Services (CMIS)   9
        Generic Architecture for Information Availability (GAIA)   11
        Microsoft Operations Framework (MOF)   12
    Electronic Messaging Concepts   14
    Other Information-Management Models   17
        The X.400 and X.500 Message-Handling Models   17
        A Storage Technology—Microsoft Repository   22
        The First Wide Area Network (WAN)   23
        Online Information Services Beyond Email   24
    Exchange as Messaging Service Provider   25
        MS Mail and Sharing Information   27
        Exchange 4 and X.400   27
        Exchange 5 and the Internet   28
        Exchange 5.5   28
    Exchange as KM Information Broker   28
        Microsoft Exchange 2000 Server   29
        Microsoft Exchange 2000 Enterprise Server   29
        Exchange 2000 Conferencing Server   31

Expanded Functionality of Exchange 2000   31
Other Key Features of Exchange 2000   32
Chapter Summary   33
Review Questions   34

Chapter 2
Exchange Architecture 39

Business Objectives and TCO   41
Design   41
Administration   42
Legacy Exchange Overview   43
Why Legacy Issues Are Important   43
Legacy Structural Components   44
Other Helper Components   46
Transport Services   49
Legacy Internet Access Components   53
Comparing Features of Exchange Versions 4, 5, and 5.5   53
Workflow of Legacy Exchange   54
A New Perspective of Distributed Services   55
Storage Services—Messaging Infrastructure   56
Directory Services   59
Protocol Services—Physical Topology   61
Chapter Summary   64
Review Questions   65
Real-World Projects   68

Chapter 3
Storage Services 71

Design Objectives   73
Enhanced Administration   73
Storage Unification   74
Installable File System Features   76
The Collaborative Workspace   80
Database File Types   81

The Extensible Storage Engine (ESE)   83
    System-Related File Types   84
    Circular Logging   84
    Memory Management   85
    SGs   86
Indexing   91
Database Consistency   94
    Defragmenting Databases   95
    Using ESEUTIL   96
    Using Information Store Integrity Checker (ISINTEG)   97
    Using ESEFILE   98
Protocol Services   99
    EXchange InterProcess Communication Layer (EXIPC, or EPOXY)   99
    Distributed Architecture   99
Chapter Summary   100
Review Questions   101
Real-World Projects   105

Chapter 4
Administrative Services 109
Administrative Methods   110
    Microsoft Frameworks and TCO   112
Administrative Needs   115
    The Interplay of Roles   116
Recipient Management   118
    Domain Structure   119
    Administrative Models   120
    Administrative Tools for Recipient Management   121
    Permission Management   122
    Policies   124
Server Management   125
    Administrative Models   126
    Tools That Support Server Management   128
    System Policies and Groups   129

Other Administrative Areas   129
    Security and Distribution Groups   130
    Public Folders   130
    Evaluation and Performance Management   132
Chapter Summary   134
Review Questions   136
Real-World Projects   140

Chapter 5
Planning and Deployment 145

Planning Objectives   146
    Directory Service Components   146
    Corporate Objectives   147
AD Infrastructure   149
    AD Logical Structure   149
    AD Logical Components   155
Exchange Structure   158
    Physical Structure   158
    Recipient Management   160
    Server Configuration   164
Disaster Recovery Planning   165
Chapter Summary   166
Review Questions   167
Real-World Projects   170

Chapter 6
Installation 173

Managing Deployment   174
    Organization and Planning   175
    Proper Assignment of Tools   176
    Proper Tools: Terminal Services (TS)   176
The Installation Punchlist   177
Preparing a Working Environment   178
    Extending the AD Schema   178
    Creating Service Accounts   181

Deployment Plan 182
    Step 1: Gathering Information 183
    Step 2: Installation 187
    Step 3: Verification 191
    Step 4: Installing Supporting Software 191
Chapter Summary 192
Review Questions 193
Real-World Projects 197

Chapter 7
Client Configuration 201

The Range of Exchange Clients 202
    Microsoft Outlook 2000 203
    Microsoft Outlook Express 206
    Exchange Client 207
    Schedule+ 207
    Unix Clients 208
    Macintosh Clients 208
Installing Outlook Client 208
    Custom Installations 210
    Outlook 2000 Profiles 212
Outlook Web Access (OWA) 216
    Web Distributed Authoring and Versioning (WebDAV) Protocol 217
    OWA 218
    The Web Store 219
    OWA Administration 220
    Authentication of Accounts 221
    Requesting Exchange Services through OWA 222
    Internet Mail Protocols Supporting OWA 222
Legacy Features 227
    Remote Mail 228
    Scheduled Connections 229
    Configuring Remote Mail and Scheduled Connections 229
Chapter Summary 230
Review Questions 231
Real-World Projects 234

Chapter 8
Recipient Management 237

Recipient Types   238
Account Management   240
    Administrative Models   240
    Administrative Roles   240
    Mailbox Management   242
    Contact Management   243
    Group Management   243
Recipient Settings   245
    User Attributes   246
    Contact Attributes   255
    Group Attributes   257
    Address Lists   259
Policies   262
    Default Recipient Policies   262
    New Recipient Policies   263
    Maintenance and Support   264
    Basic Management Tools   264
Chapter Summary   265
Review Questions   266
Real-World Projects   270

Chapter 9
Routing Management 273

Historical Perspective   274
    RPCs and SMTP   274
    X.400 and SMTP   275
    MIME and S/MIME   277
    ESMTP   277
SMTP Services   279
    Transport Core   280
    How Components Work Together   281
    Processing Incoming Messages   283
    Categorization   285
    Outbound Mail   286

Routing Information in the AD and DNS   286
Routing Groups   287
Link State Routing   291
Chapter Summary   292
Review Questions   294
Real-World Projects   297

Chapter 10
Interoperability 299

Exchange 2000 Connectors   300
Installing Connectors   301
Basic Connector Properties   302
Exchange Connector Types   303
Exchange 2000 RGCs   304
Legacy Exchange 5.5 Site Connectors   304
SMTP Connectors   305
X.400 Connectors   307
Other Mail Systems   318
Lotus cc:Mail   319
Microsoft Exchange and Novell NetWare   320
MS Mail for PC Networks   321
Chapter Summary   326
Review Questions   326
Real-World Projects   330

Chapter 11
External Connectivity 333

Strategic Planning   334
Identifying a Foreign System   335
Performing a Structural and Functional Audit   335
Identifying Named Objects   337
Global Catalog (GC)   338
Recipient Policy   338
Connector Review   339
Exchange MS Mail Connectors   340
Exchange Lotus cc:Mail Connectors   341

Exchange Lotus Notes Connectors   347
Exchange Novell GroupWise Connectors   353
Mixed-Mode Environments   356
ADC   357
Routing in a Mixed-Mode Environment   357
Directory Synchronization with Mainframe Environments   359
Chapter Summary   359
Review Questions   361
Real-World Projects   365

Chapter 12
Secure Communications 369

Exchange 2000 Security   370
Security Policy   370
Defining Assets   371
Security Threats: Defining Vulnerabilities   373
Security Measures   375
Auditing   375
Security Controls   376
DNS Considerations   377
Bridgehead Servers   378
Firewall Technology   378
Exchange Server Security   382
The Key to Security   382
KMS   385
KMS and AD   390
Chapter Summary   398
Review Questions   399
Real-World Projects   402

Chapter 13
Collaboration 405

Collaboration Concepts   407
The Knowledge-Management Paradigm   407
Collaboration with Exchange Server   407

Instant Messaging 419
    IM and Domain Name System (DNS) 420
    Installing IM 421
    Managing IM Servers 423
    IM and Clients 424
Chapter Summary 424
Review Questions 426
Real-World Projects 430

Chapter 14
Troubleshooting and Monitoring 433

Looking for Trouble in All the Right Places 435
    Troubleshooting Tools Used with Exchange 2000 Server 435
    Additional Sources of Help 440
Monitoring Trends in Exchange Server 440
    Windows 2000 Monitoring Utilities 441
    Exchange 2000 Monitoring Tools 452
Disaster Recovery and Planning 459
    The Underlying Technology 460
    Backing Up Data Using Windows 2000 461
    Maintaining a Backup Schedule 465
    The Restore Process 466
Chapter Summary 468
Review Questions 470
Real-World Projects 474

Chapter 15
Other Design and Support Issues 477

The Design of Exchange 2000 Server 479
    The Four Phases of the MSF Infrastructure Deployment Process Model 479
    Assessing Project Risk 481
    Hardware Design Considerations 481
    FE/BE Servers 483
    Server Sizing Issues 490
Capacity Planning and Assessment 495
    Hardware and Topology Issues that Affect Capacity 496
    Other Factors that Affect Capacity 497

Assessing Client Traffic   498
Optimizing Capacity   499
Capacity and Design Troubleshooting Scenarios   501
Chapter Summary   503
Review Questions   504
Real-World Projects   508

Chapter 16
Legacy System Issues 511

Deciding to Upgrade   512
Preparing Your Environment   513
The Four Phases of Upgrading to Exchange 2000   520
Phase One: Preparing the Windows 2000 Forest   520
Phase Two: Installing the ADC   524
Phase Three: Preparing Your Windows 2000 Domains   528
Phase Four: Performing the In-Place Upgrade of Exchange Server 5.5   529
Post-Upgrade Procedures   532
Checking If the Upgrade Was Successful   532
Recovering an Exchange 5.5 Server after a Failed Upgrade   532
Removing Exchange 2000   534
Living in Harmony with Legacy Exchange   536
Using Site Replication Service (SRS)   537
Using the ADC Service   538
The Move Mailbox Utility   538
Mixed Mode vs. Native Mode   540
Connectors and Coexistence with Legacy Exchange   544
Chapter Summary   548
Review Questions   550
Real-World Projects   554

Chapter 17
Extending the Platform 559

Web Storage System   560
Extending Data Access   562
Web Store Events   565
Web Services   566
OWA Architecture   567
Requesting and Delivering Services   568

   Displaying Objects 568
   Server Access 569
   FE/BE Architecture 571
  Markup Languages 572
   Specific vs. Generalized Markup Languages 573
   Web Markup Languages 574
  Web Forms 579
  Web Solutions 579
   ODBC 580
   JDBC 581
   ColdFusion 581
   Active Platform 581
  Exchange APIs 583
  .NET Framework 585
  Chapter Summary 587
  Review Questions 589
  Real-World Projects 593

Chapter 18
Sample Test 595

Chapter 19
Answer Key 613

Appendix A
Answers to Review Questions 625

Appendix B
Objectives for Exam 70-224 645

Appendix C
Study Resources 649

Glossary 653

Index 671

Exam Insights

Welcome to *MCSE Exchange 2000 Administration Exam Prep*! This comprehensive study guide aims to help you get ready to take—and pass—Microsoft certification Exam 70-224, titled "Installing, Configuring, and Administering Microsoft Exchange 2000 Server." This Exam Insights section discusses exam preparation resources, the testing situation, Microsoft's certification programs in general, and how this book can help you prepare for Microsoft's Exchange 2000 Administration certification exam.

Exam Prep study guides help you understand and appreciate the subjects and materials you need to pass Microsoft certification exams. We've worked from Microsoft's curriculum objectives to ensure that all key topics are clearly explained. Our aim is to bring together as much information as possible about Microsoft certification exams.

Nevertheless, to completely prepare yourself for any Microsoft test, we recommend that you begin by taking the Self-Assessment included in this book immediately following this Exam Insights section. This tool will help you evaluate your knowledge base against the requirements for an MCSE under both ideal and real circumstances.

Based on what you learn from that exercise, you might decide to begin your studies with some classroom training or some background reading. You might decide to read The Coriolis Group's *Exam Prep* book that you have in hand first, or you might decide to start with another study approach. You may also want to refer to one of a number of study guides available from Microsoft or third-party vendors. We also recommend that you supplement your study program with visits to **ExamCram.com** to receive additional practice questions and get advice.

We also strongly recommend that you install, configure, and experiment with the software that you'll be tested on, because nothing beats hands-on experience and familiarity when it comes to understanding the questions you're likely to encounter on a certification test. Book learning is essential, but hands-on experience is the best teacher of all!

How to Prepare for an Exam

Preparing for any Windows 2000 Server-related test (including "Installing, Configuring, and Administering Microsoft Exchange 2000 Server") requires that you obtain and study materials designed to provide comprehensive information about the product and its capabilities that will appear on the specific exam for which you are preparing. The following list of materials will help you study and prepare:

➤ The *Exchange 2000 Server Resource Kit* CD includes comprehensive online documentation and related materials; it should be a primary resource when you are preparing for the test.

➤ The exam preparation materials, practice tests, and self-assessment exams on the Microsoft Training & Services page at **www.microsoft.com/ trainingandservices/default.asp?PageID=mcp**. The Testing Innovations link offers samples of the new question types found on the Windows 2000 MCSE exams. Find the materials, download them, and use them!

➤ The exam preparation advice, practice tests, questions of the day, and discussion groups on the **ExamCram.com** e-learning and certification destination Web site (**www.examcram.com**).

In addition, you'll probably find any or all of the following materials useful in your quest for Exchange 2000 Administration expertise:

➤ *Microsoft training kits*—Microsoft Press offers a training kit that specifically targets Exam 70-224. For more information, visit: **http://mspress.microsoft. com/findabook/list/series_ak.htm**. This training kit contains information that you will find useful in preparing for the test.

➤ *Microsoft TechNet CD*—This monthly CD-based publication delivers numerous electronic titles that include coverage of Exchange 2000 Administration and related topics on the Technical Information (TechNet) CD. Its offerings include product facts, technical notes, tools and utilities, and information on how to access the Seminars Online training materials for Exchange 2000 Administration. A subscription to TechNet costs $299 per year, but it is well worth the price. Visit **www.microsoft.com/technet/** and check out the information under the "TechNet Subscription" menu entry for more details.

➤ *Study guides*—Several publishers—including The Coriolis Group—offer Windows 2000 titles. The Coriolis Group series includes the following:

  ➤ *The Exam Cram series*—These books give you information about the material you need to know to pass the tests.

  ➤ *The Exam Prep series*—These books provide a greater level of detail than the *Exam Cram* books and are designed to teach you everything you need to know from an exam perspective. Each book comes with a CD that contains interactive practice exams in a variety of testing formats.

Together, the two series make a perfect pair.

- *Multimedia*—These Coriolis Group materials are designed to support learners of all types—whether you learn best by reading or doing:

  - *The Exam Cram Personal Trainer*—Offers a unique, personalized self-paced training course based on the exam.

  - *The Exam Cram Personal Test Center*—Features multiple test options that simulate the actual exam, including Fixed-Length, Random, Review, and Test All. Explanations of correct and incorrect answers reinforce concepts learned.

- *Classroom training*—CTECs, online partners, and third-party training companies (like Wave Technologies, Learning Tree, Data-Tech, and others) all offer classroom training on Exchange. These companies aim to help you prepare to pass the Exchange 2000 Administration test. Although such training runs upwards of $350 per day in class, most of the individuals lucky enough to partake find them to be quite worthwhile.

- *Other publications*—There's no shortage of materials available about Exchange 2000 Administration. The complete resource section in the back of the book should give you an idea of where we think you should look for further discussion.

By far, this set of required and recommended materials represents a nonpareil collection of sources and resources for Exchange 2000 Administration and related topics. We anticipate that you'll find that this book belongs in this company.

Taking a Certification Exam

Once you've prepared for your exam, you need to register with a testing center. Each computer-based MCP exam costs $125, and if you don't pass, you may retest for an additional $125 for each additional try. In the United States and Canada, tests are administered by Prometric (formerly Sylvan Prometric), and by Virtual University Enterprises (VUE). Here's how you can contact them:

- *Prometric*—You can sign up for a test through the company's Web site at **www.prometric.com**. Within the United States and Canada, you can register by phone at 800-755-3926. If you live outside this region, check the company's Web site for the appropriate phone number.

- *Virtual University Enterprises*—You can sign up for a test or get the phone numbers for local testing centers through the Web page at **www.vue.com/ms/**.

To sign up for a test, you must possess a valid credit card, or contact either company for mailing instructions to send them a check (in the U.S.). Only when payment is verified, or a check has cleared, can you actually register for a test.

To schedule an exam, call the number or visit either of the Web pages at least one day in advance. To cancel or reschedule an exam, you must call before 7 P.M. pacific standard time the day before the scheduled test time (or you may be charged, even if you don't appear to take the test). When you want to schedule a test, have the following information ready:

- Your name, organization, and mailing address.
- Your Microsoft Test ID. (Inside the United States, this means your Social Security number; citizens of other nations should call ahead to find out what type of identification number is required to register for a test.)
- The name and number of the exam you wish to take.
- A method of payment. (As we've already mentioned, a credit card is the most convenient method, but alternate means can be arranged in advance, if necessary.)

Once you sign up for a test, you'll be informed as to when and where the test is scheduled. Try to arrive at least 15 minutes early.

The Exam Situation

When you arrive at the testing center where you scheduled your exam, you'll need to sign in with an exam coordinator. He or she will ask you to show two forms of identification, one of which must be a photo ID. After you've signed in and your time slot arrives, you'll be asked to deposit any books, bags, or other items you brought with you. Then, you'll be escorted into a closed room.

All exams are completely closed book. In fact, you will not be permitted to take anything with you into the testing area, but you will be furnished with a blank sheet of paper and a pen or, in some cases, an erasable plastic sheet and an erasable pen. Before the exam, you should memorize as much of the important material as you can, so you can write that information on the blank sheet as soon as you are seated in front of the computer. You can refer to this piece of paper anytime you like during the test, but you'll have to surrender the sheet when you leave the room.

You will have some time to compose yourself, to record this information, and to take a sample orientation exam before you begin the real thing. We suggest you take the orientation test before taking your first exam, but because they're all more or less identical in layout, behavior, and controls, you probably won't need to do this more than once.

Typically, the room will be furnished with anywhere from one to half a dozen computers, and each workstation will be separated from the others by dividers designed to keep you from seeing what's happening on someone else's computer. Most test rooms feature a wall with a large picture window. This permits the exam coordinator to monitor the room, to prevent exam-takers from talking to one another, and to observe anything out of the ordinary that might go on. The exam coordinator will have preloaded the appropriate Microsoft certification exam—for this book, that's Exam 70-224—and you'll be permitted to start as soon as you're seated in front of the computer.

All Microsoft certification exams allow a certain maximum amount of time in which to complete your work (this time is indicated on the exam by an on-screen counter/clock, so you can check the time remaining whenever you like). All Microsoft certification exams are computer generated. The Exchange 2000 Administration exam is currently multiple choice; on other Microsoft exams, in addition to multiple choice, you may encounter select and place (drag and drop), create a tree (categorization and prioritization), drag and connect, and build list and reorder (list prioritization). The questions are constructed not only to check your mastery of basic facts and figures about Exchange 2000 Server Administration, but they also require you to evaluate one or more sets of circumstances or requirements. Often, you'll be asked to give more than one answer to a question. Likewise, you might be asked to select the best or most effective solution to a problem from a range of choices, all of which technically are correct. Taking the exam is quite an adventure, and it involves real thinking. This book shows you what to expect and how to deal with the potential problems, puzzles, and predicaments.

When you complete a Microsoft certification exam, the software will tell you whether you've passed or failed. If you need to retake an exam, you'll have to schedule a new test with Prometric or VUE and pay another $125.

Note: The first time you fail a test, you can retake the test the next day. However, if you fail a second time, you must wait 14 days before retaking that test. The 14-day waiting period remains in effect for all retakes after the second failure.

In the next section, you'll learn more about how Microsoft test questions look and how they must be answered.

Exam Layout and Design

The format of Microsoft's Exchange 2000 Administration exam is currently multiple choice. However, because many Microsoft tests contain questions in a format that differs from standard multiple choice, we discuss those question types here as well. For the design exams (e.g., 70-219, 70-220, 70-221, and 70-225), each exam consists entirely of a series of case studies, and the questions can be of six types. For the Core Four exams (70-210, 70-215, 70-216, 70-217), the same six types of questions can appear, but you are not likely to encounter complex multiquestion case studies.

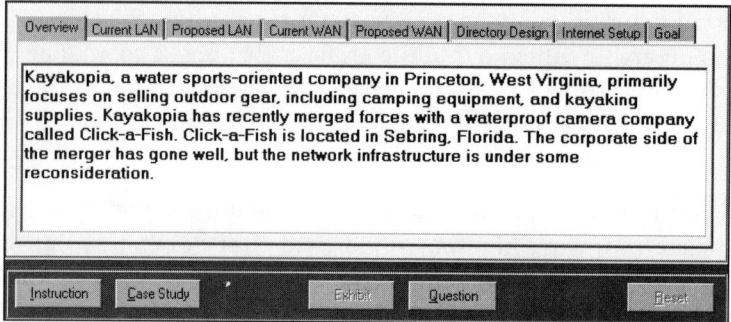

Figure 1 This is how case studies appear.

For design exams, each case study or "testlet" presents a detailed problem that you must read and analyze. Figure 1 shows an example of what a case study looks like. You must select the different tabs in the case study to view the entire case.

Following each case study is a set of questions related to the case study; these questions can be one of six types (which are discussed next). Careful attention to details provided in the case study is the key to success. Be prepared to toggle frequently between the case study and the questions as you work. Some of the case studies also include diagrams, which are called *exhibits*, that you'll need to examine closely to understand how to answer the questions.

Once you complete a case study, you can review all the questions and your answers. However, once you move on to the next case study, you may not be able to return to the previous case study and make any changes.

The six types of question formats are:

➤ Multiple choice, single answer

➤ Multiple choice, multiple answers

➤ Build list and reorder (list prioritization)

➤ Create a tree

➤ Drag and connect

➤ Select and place (drag and drop)

Note: Exam formats may vary by test center location. You may want to call the test center or visit **ExamCram.com** to see if you can find out which type of test you'll encounter.

Multiple-Choice Question Format

Some exam questions require you to select a single answer, whereas others ask you to select multiple correct answers. The following multiple-choice question requires you to select a single correct answer. Following the question is a brief summary of each potential answer and why it is either right or wrong.

Question 1

> What can you infer from the fact that EPOXY does not operate across remote links?
>
> ○ a. IIS must be installed on the server that hosts a Web Store.
>
> ○ b. EPOXY uses separate memory caches to manage data passed between IIS and the Store.
>
> ○ c. Davex.dll cannot use Hypertext Transfer Protocol (HTTP) to communicate across remote links.
>
> ○ d. The question is incorrect; EPOXY can operate across remote links.

Answer a is correct because EPOXY was designed to interface directly with IIS and thus minimize degradation in performance caused by context switches during interprocess communication. Answer b is incorrect because EPOXY uses shared memory to manage data. Answer c is incorrect because Davex.dll interprets HTTP requests and contacts the Web Store across EPOXY. Answer d is incorrect because the premise of the question is correct; EPOXY replaces the older RPC used in legacy versions but cannot operate across remote links.

> This sample question format corresponds closely to the Microsoft certification exam format—the only difference on the exam is that questions are not followed by answer keys. To select an answer, you would position the cursor over the radio button next to the answer. Then, click the mouse button to select the answer.
>
> Let's examine a question where one or more answers are possible. This type of question provides checkboxes rather than radio buttons for marking all appropriate selections.

Question 2

> Which of the following describe critical roles defined by the Generic Architecture for Information Availability (GAIA)? [Check all correct answers]
>
> ❑ a. A customer
>
> ❑ b. A broker
>
> ❑ c. A supplier
>
> ❑ d. A helper

Answers a, b, and c are correct. Customer, broker, and supplier are the three components of the Generic Architecture for Information Availability (GAIA) architecture. Answer d is incorrect because a helper component is independent of and complementary to the role of the broker. The other three components are required.

> For this particular question, three answers are required. Microsoft sometimes gives partial credit for partially correct answers. For Question 2, you have to check the boxes next to items a, b, and c to obtain credit for a correct answer. Notice that picking the right answers also means knowing why the other answer or answers are wrong!

Build-List-and-Reorder Question Format

Questions in the build-list-and-reorder format present two lists of items—one on the left and one on the right. To answer the question, you must move items from the list on the right to the list on the left. The final list must then be reordered into a specific order.

These questions can best be characterized as "From the following list of choices, pick the choices that answer the question. Arrange the list in a certain order." The following is a sample of a build-list-and-reorder question.

Question 3

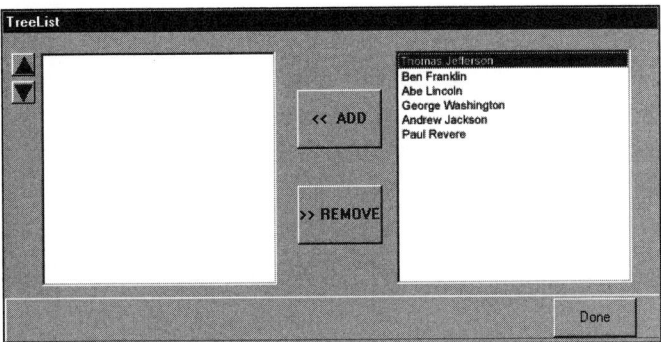

The correct answer is:

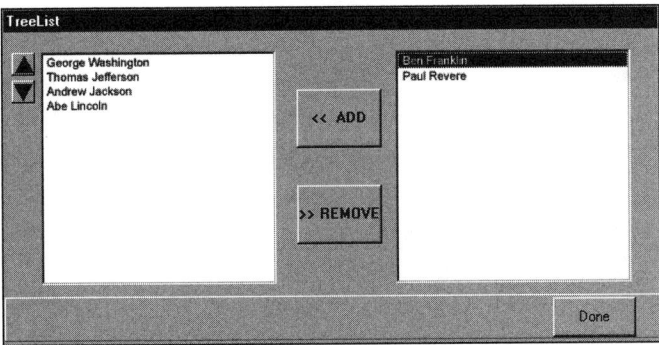

On an exam, the entire list of famous people would initially appear in the list on the right. You would move the four correct answers to the list on the left, and then reorder the list on the left. Notice that the answer to the question does not always include all items from the initial list. However, this may not always be the case.

To move an item from the right list to the left list, first select the item by clicking on it, and then click on the Add button (left arrow). Once you move an item from one list to the other, you can move the item back by first selecting the item and then clicking on the appropriate button (either the Add button or the Remove button). Once items have been moved to the left list, you can reorder an item by selecting the item and clicking on the up or down button.

Create-a-Tree Question Format

Questions in the create-a-tree format also present two lists—one on the left side of the screen and one on the right side of the screen. The list on the right consists of individual items, and the list on the left consists of nodes in a tree. To answer the question, you must move items from the list on the right to the appropriate node in the tree.

These questions can best be characterized as simply a matching exercise. Items from the list on the right are placed under the appropriate category in the list on the left, as shown in the following sample question.

Question 4

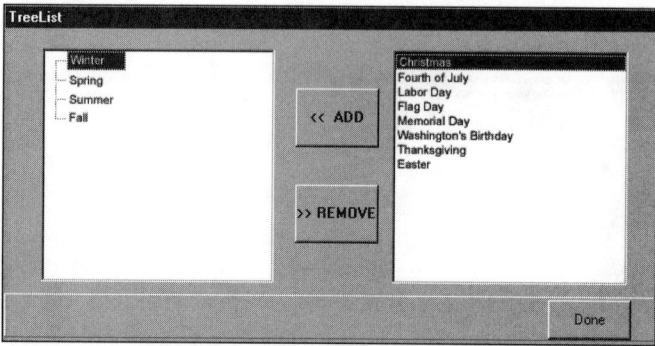

The correct answer is:

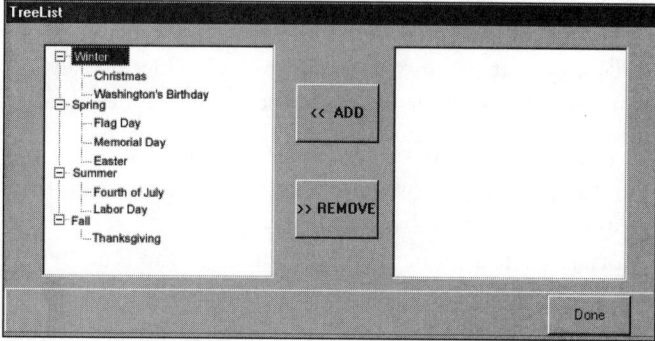

In this case, all the items in the list were used. However, this may not always be the case.

To move an item from the right list to its appropriate location in the tree, you must first select the appropriate tree node by clicking on it. Then, you select the item to be moved and click on the Add button. If one or more items have been added to a tree node, the node will be displayed with a "+" icon to the left of the node name. You can click on this icon to expand the node and view the item(s) that have been added. If any item has been added to the wrong tree node, you can remove it by selecting it and clicking on the Remove button.

Drag-and-Connect Question Format

Questions in the drag-and-connect format present a group of objects and a list of "connections." To answer the question, you must move the appropriate connections between the objects.

This type of question is best described using graphics. Here's an example.

Question 5

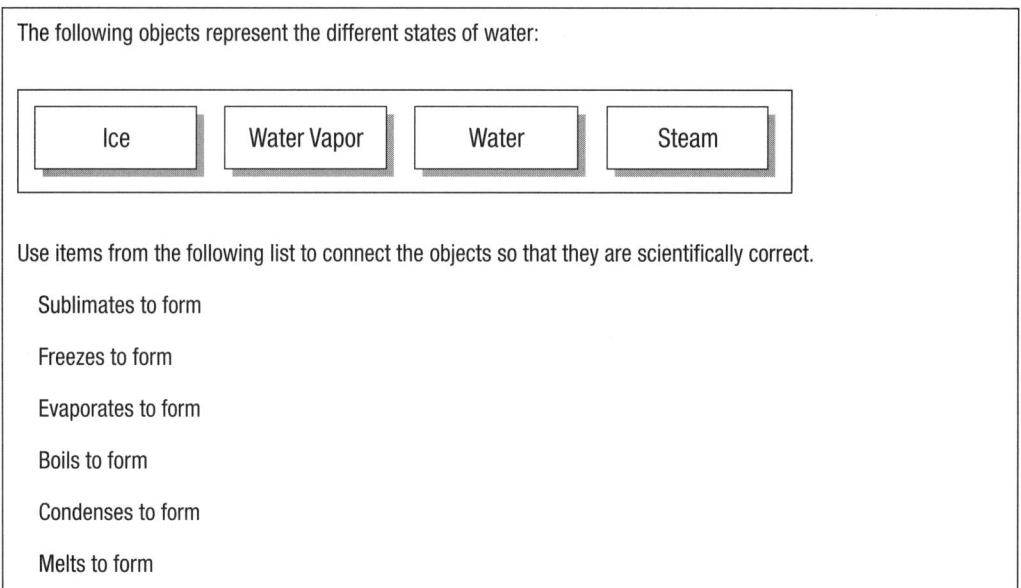

The correct answer is:

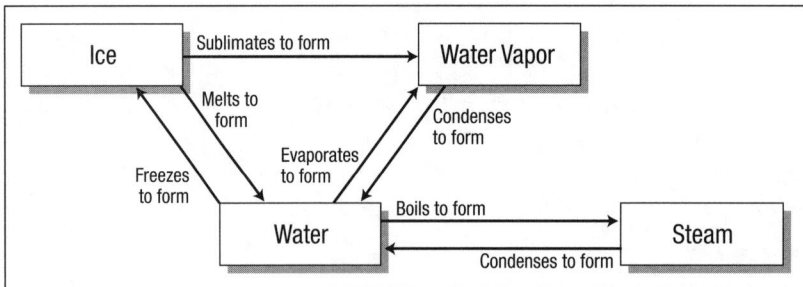

For this type of question, it's not necessary to use every object, and each connection can be used multiple times.

Select-and-Place Question Format

Questions in the select-and-place (drag-and-drop) format present a diagram with blank boxes, and a list of labels that need to be dragged to correctly fill in the blank boxes. To answer the question, you must move the labels to their appropriate positions on the diagram.

This type of question is best described using graphics. Here's an example.

Question 6

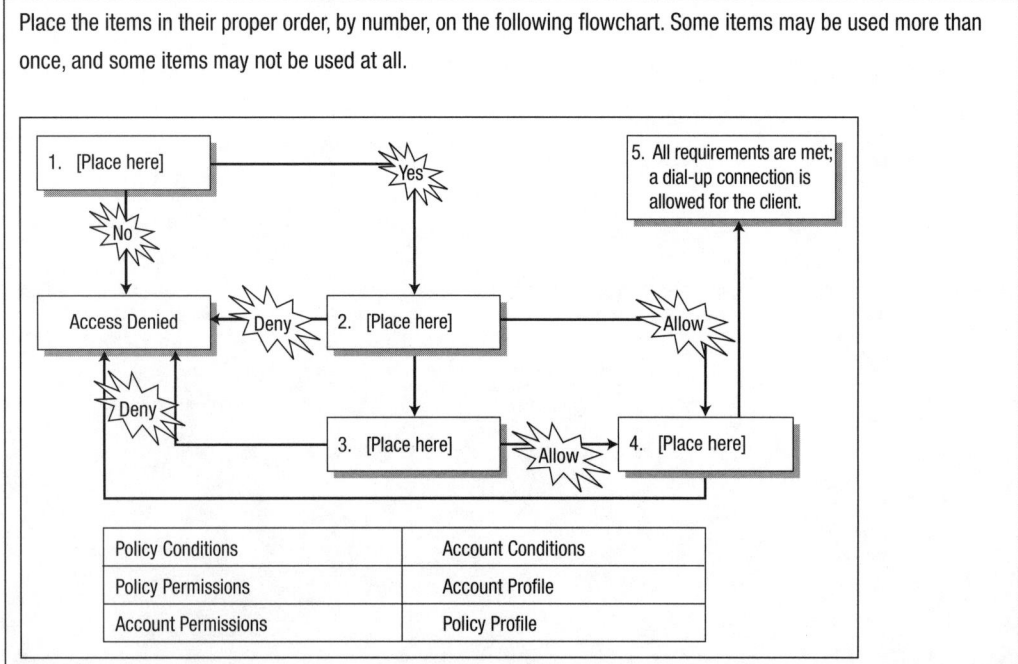

The correct answer is:

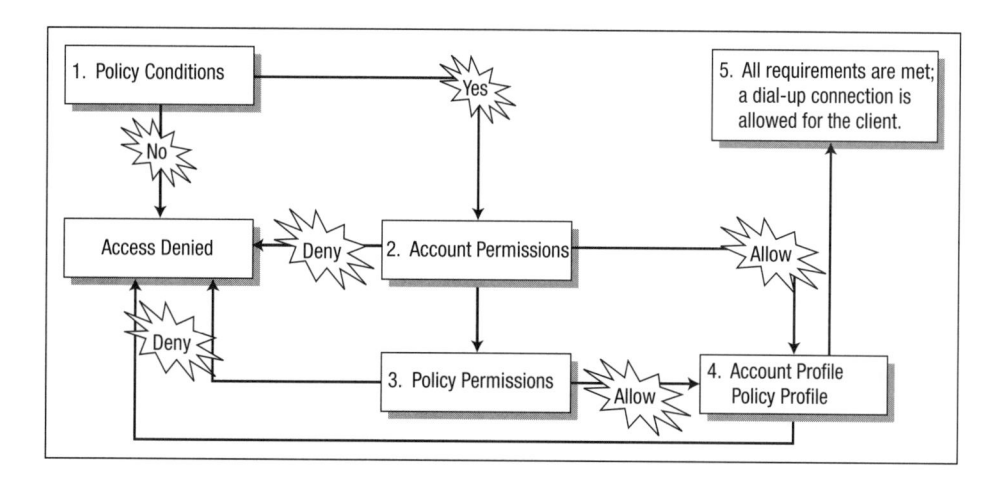

Microsoft's Testing Formats

Currently, Microsoft uses four different testing formats:

➤ Case study

➤ Fixed length

➤ Adaptive

➤ Short form

As we mentioned earlier, the case study approach is used with Microsoft's design exams. These exams consist of a set of case studies that you must analyze to enable you to answer questions related to the case studies. Such exams include one or more case studies (tabbed topic areas), each of which is followed by 4 to 10 questions. The question types for design exams and for Core Four Windows 2000 exams are multiple choice, build list and reorder, create a tree, drag and connect, and select and place. Depending on the test topic, some exams are totally case-based, whereas others are not. As mentioned previously, the Exchange 2000 Administration exam is currently all multiple choice.

Other Microsoft exams employ advanced testing capabilities that might not be immediately apparent. Although the questions that appear are primarily multiple choice, the logic that drives them is more complex than older Microsoft tests, which use a fixed sequence of questions, called a *fixed-length test*. Some questions employ a sophisticated user interface, which Microsoft calls a *simulation*, to test your knowledge of the software and systems under consideration in a more or less "live" environment that behaves just like the original. The Testing Innovations link at **www.microsoft.com/trainingandservices/default.asp?PageID=mcp** includes a downloadable practice simulation.

For some exams, Microsoft has turned to a well-known technique, called *adaptive testing*, to establish a test-taker's level of knowledge and product competence. Adaptive exams look the same as fixed-length exams, but they discover the level of difficulty at which an individual test-taker can correctly answer questions. Test-takers with differing levels of knowledge or ability therefore see different sets of questions; individuals with high levels of knowledge or ability are presented with a smaller set of more difficult questions, whereas individuals with lower levels of knowledge are presented with a larger set of easier questions. Two individuals may answer the same percentage of questions correctly, but the test-taker with a higher knowledge or ability level will score higher because his or her questions are worth more.

Also, the lower-level test-taker will probably answer more questions than his or her more-knowledgeable colleague. This explains why adaptive tests use ranges of values to define the number of questions and the amount of time it takes to complete the test.

Adaptive tests work by evaluating the test-taker's most recent answer. A correct answer leads to a more difficult question (and the test software's estimate of the test-taker's knowledge and ability level is raised). An incorrect answer leads to a less difficult question (and the test software's estimate of the test-taker's knowledge and ability level is lowered). This process continues until the test targets the test-taker's true ability level. The exam ends when the test-taker's level of accuracy meets a statistically acceptable value (in other words, when his or her performance demonstrates an acceptable level of knowledge and ability), or when the maximum number of items has been presented (in which case, the test-taker is almost certain to fail).

Microsoft also introduced a short-form test for its most popular tests. This test delivers 25 to 30 questions to its takers, giving them exactly 60 minutes to complete the exam. This type of exam is similar to a fixed-length test, in that it allows readers to jump ahead or return to earlier questions, and to cycle through the questions until the test is done. Microsoft does not use adaptive logic in this test, but claims that statistical analysis of the question pool is such that the 25 to 30 questions delivered during a short-form exam conclusively measure a test-taker's knowledge of the subject matter in much the same way as an adaptive test. You can think of the short-form test as a kind of "greatest hits exam" (that is, the most important questions are covered) version of an adaptive exam on the same topic.

Note: *Several test-takers have reported that some of the Microsoft exams can appear as a combination of adaptive and fixed-length questions.*

Microsoft tests can come in any one of these forms. Whatever you encounter, you must take the test in whichever form it appears; you can't choose one form over another. If anything, it pays more to prepare thoroughly for an adaptive exam than for a fixed-length or a short-form exam: The penalties for answering incorrectly are built into the test itself on an adaptive exam, whereas the layout remains the same for a fixed-length or short-form test, no matter how many questions you answer incorrectly.

Tip: The biggest difference between an adaptive test and a fixed-length or short-form test is that on a fixed-length or short-form test, you can revisit questions after you've read them over one or more times. On an adaptive test, you must answer the question when it's presented and will have no opportunities to revisit that question thereafter.

Strategies for Different Testing Formats

Before you choose a test-taking strategy, you must know if your test is case study based, fixed length, short form, or adaptive. When you begin your exam, you'll know right away if the test is based on case studies. The interface will consist of a tabbed Window that allows you to easily navigate through the sections of the case.

If you are taking a test that is not based on case studies, the software will tell you that the test is adaptive, if in fact the version you're taking is an adaptive test. If your introductory materials fail to mention this, you're probably taking a fixed-length test (50 to 70 questions). If the total number of questions involved is 25 to 30, you're taking a short-form test. Some tests announce themselves by indicating that they will start with a set of adaptive questions, followed by fixed-length questions.

Tip: You'll be able to tell for sure if you are taking an adaptive, fixed-length, or short-form test by the first question. If it includes a checkbox that lets you mark the question for later review, you're taking a fixed-length or short-form test. If the total number of questions is 25 to 30, it's a short-form test; if more than 30, it's a fixed-length test. Adaptive test questions can be visited (and answered) only once, and they include no such checkbox.

The Case Study Exam Strategy

Most test-takers find that the case study type of test used for the design exams (70-219, 70-220, 70-221, and 70-225) is the most difficult to master. When it comes to studying for a case study test, your best bet is to approach each case study as a standalone test. The biggest challenge you'll encounter is that you'll feel that you won't have enough time to get through all of the cases that are presented.

Tip: Each case provides a lot of material that you'll need to read and study before you can effectively answer the questions that follow. The trick to taking a case study exam is to first scan the case study to get the highlights. Make sure you read the overview section of the case so that you understand the context of the problem at hand. Then, quickly move on and scan the questions.

As you are scanning the questions, make mental notes to yourself so that you'll remember which sections of the case study you should focus on. Some case studies may provide a fair amount of extra information that you don't really need to answer the questions. The goal with this scanning approach is to avoid having to study and analyze material that is not completely relevant.

When studying a case, carefully read the tabbed information. It is important to answer each and every question. You will be able to toggle back and forth from case to questions, and from question to question within a case testlet. However, once you leave the case and move on, you may not be able to return to it. You may want to take notes while reading useful information so you can refer to them when you tackle the test questions. It's hard to go wrong with this strategy when taking any kind of Microsoft certification test.

The Fixed-Length and Short-Form Exam Strategy

A well-known principle when taking fixed-length or short-form exams is to first read over the entire exam from start to finish while answering only those questions you feel absolutely sure of. On subsequent passes, you can dive into more complex questions more deeply, knowing how many such questions you have left.

Fortunately, the Microsoft exam software for fixed-length and short-form tests makes the multiple-visit approach easy to implement. At the top-left corner of each question is a checkbox that permits you to mark that question for a later visit.

Note: Marking questions makes review easier, but you can return to any question by clicking the Forward or Back button repeatedly.

As you read each question, if you answer only those you're sure of and mark for review those that you're not sure of, you can keep working through a decreasing list of questions as you answer the trickier ones in order.

Tip: There's at least one potential benefit to reading the exam over completely before answering the trickier questions: Sometimes, information supplied in later questions sheds more light on earlier questions. At other times, information you read in later questions might jog your memory about Exchange 2000 Administration facts, figures, or behavior that helps you answer earlier questions. Either way, you'll come out ahead if you defer those questions about which you're not absolutely sure.

Here are some question-handling strategies that apply to fixed-length and short-form tests. Use them if you have the chance:

➤ When returning to a question after your initial read-through, read every word again—otherwise, your mind can fall quickly into a rut. Sometimes, revisiting a question after turning your attention elsewhere lets you see something you missed, but the strong tendency is to see what you've seen before. Try to avoid that tendency at all costs.

➤ If you return to a question more than twice, try to articulate to yourself what you don't understand about the question, why answers don't appear to make sense, or what appears to be missing. If you chew on the subject awhile, your subconscious might provide the details you lack, or you might notice a "trick" that points to the right answer.

As you work your way through the exam, another counter that Microsoft provides will come in handy—the number of questions completed and questions outstanding. For fixed-length and short-form tests, it's wise to budget your time by making sure that you've completed one-quarter of the questions one-quarter of the way through the exam period, and three-quarters of the questions three-quarters of the way through.

If you're not finished when only five minutes remain, use that time to guess your way through any remaining questions. Remember, guessing is potentially more valuable than not answering, because blank answers are always wrong, but a guess may turn out to be right. If you don't have a clue about any of the remaining questions, pick answers at random, or choose all a's, b's, and so on. The important thing is to submit an exam for scoring that has an answer for every question.

Tip: At the very end of your exam period, you're better off guessing than leaving questions unanswered.

The Adaptive Exam Strategy

If there's one principle that applies to taking an adaptive test, it could be summed up as "Get it right the first time." You cannot elect to skip a question and move on to the next one when taking an adaptive test, because the testing software uses your answer to the current question to select whatever question it plans to present next. Nor can you return to a question once you've moved on, because the software gives you only one chance to answer the question. You can, however, take notes, because sometimes information supplied in earlier questions will shed more light on later questions.

Also, when you answer a question correctly, you are presented with a more difficult question next, to help the software gauge your level of skill and ability. When you answer a question incorrectly, you are presented with a less difficult question, and the software lowers its current estimate of your skill and ability. This continues until the program settles into a reasonably accurate estimate of what you know and can do, and takes you on average through somewhere between 15 and 30 questions as you complete the test.

The good news is that if you know your stuff, you'll probably finish most adaptive tests in 30 minutes or so. The bad news is that you must really, really know your stuff to do your best on an adaptive test. That's because some questions are so convoluted, complex, or hard to follow that you're bound to miss one or two, at a minimum, even if you do know your stuff. So the more you know, the better you'll do on an adaptive test, even accounting for the occasionally weird or unfathomable questions that appear on these exams.

> **Tip:** Because you can't always tell in advance if a test is fixed length, short form, or adaptive, you will be best served by preparing for the exam as if it were adaptive. That way, you should be prepared to pass no matter what kind of test you take. But if you do take a fixed-length or short-form test, remember the tips from the preceding section. They should help you improve on what you could do on an adaptive test.

If you encounter a question on an adaptive test that you can't answer, you must guess an answer immediately. Because of how the software works, you may suffer for your guess on the next question if you guess right, because you'll get a more difficult question next!

Question-Handling Strategies

Based on exams we have taken, some interesting trends have become apparent. For those questions that take only a single answer, usually two or three of the answers will be obviously incorrect, and two of the answers will be plausible—of course, only one can be correct. Unless the answer leaps out at you (if it does, reread the question to look for a trick; sometimes those are the ones you're most likely to get wrong), begin the process of answering by eliminating those answers that are most obviously wrong.

Almost always, at least one answer out of the possible choices for a question can be eliminated immediately because it matches one of these conditions:

- The answer does not apply to the situation.
- The answer describes a nonexistent issue, an invalid option, or an imaginary state.

After you eliminate all answers that are obviously wrong, you can apply your retained knowledge to eliminate further answers. Look for items that sound correct but refer to actions, commands, or features that are not present or not available in the situation that the question describes.

If you're still faced with a blind guess among two or more potentially correct answers, reread the question. Try to picture how each of the possible remaining answers would alter the situation. Be especially sensitive to terminology; sometimes the choice of words ("remove" instead of "disable") can make the difference between a right answer and a wrong one.

Only when you've exhausted your ability to eliminate answers, but remain unclear about which of the remaining possibilities is correct, should you guess at an answer. An unanswered question offers you no points, but guessing gives you at least some chance of getting a question right; just don't be too hasty when making a blind guess.

Note: If you're taking a fixed-length or a short-form test, you can wait until the last round of reviewing marked questions (just as you're about to run out of time, or out of unanswered questions) before you start making guesses. You will have the same option within each case study testlet (but once you leave a testlet, you may not be allowed to return to it). If you're taking an adaptive test, you'll have to guess to move on to the next question if you can't figure out an answer some other way. Either way, guessing should be your technique of last resort!

Numerous questions assume that the default behavior of a particular utility is in effect. If you know the defaults and understand what they mean, this knowledge will help you cut through many Gordian knots.

Mastering the Inner Game

In the final analysis, knowledge breeds confidence, and confidence breeds success. If you study the materials in this book carefully and review all the practice questions at the end of each chapter, you should become aware of those areas where additional learning and study are required.

After you've worked your way through the book, take the practice exam in the back of the book and the practice exams on the CD-ROM. Be sure to click on the Update button in our CD-ROM's testing engine to download additional free questions from **ExamCram.com**! Taking tests will provide a reality check and help you identify areas to study further. Make sure you follow up and review materials related to the questions you miss on the practice exams before scheduling a real exam. Only when you've covered that ground and feel comfortable with the whole scope of the practice exams should you set an exam appointment. Only if you score 85 percent or better should you proceed to the real thing (otherwise, obtain some additional practice tests so you can keep trying until you hit this magic number).

Tip: If you take a practice exam and don't score at least 85 percent correct, you'll want to practice further. Microsoft provides links to practice exam providers and also offers self-assessment exams at **www.microsoft.com/trainingandservices/**. You should also check out **ExamCram.com** for downloadable practice questions.

Armed with the information in this book and with the determination to augment your knowledge, you should be able to pass the certification exam. However, you need to work at it, or you'll spend the exam fee more than once before you finally pass. If you prepare seriously, you should do well. We are confident that you can do it!

The next section covers the exam requirements for the various Microsoft certifications.

The Microsoft Certified Professional (MCP) Program

The MCP Program currently includes the following separate tracks, each of which boasts its own special acronym (as a certification candidate, you need to have a high tolerance for alphabet soup of all kinds):

▶ *MCP (Microsoft Certified Professional)*—This is the least prestigious of all the certification tracks from Microsoft. Passing one of the major Microsoft exams qualifies an individual for the MCP credential. Individuals can demonstrate proficiency with additional Microsoft products by passing additional certification exams.

▶ *MCP+SB (Microsoft Certified Professional + Site Building)*—This certification program is designed for individuals who are planning, building, managing, and maintaining Web sites. Individuals with the MCP+SB credential will have demonstrated the ability to develop Web sites that include multimedia and searchable content and Web sites that connect to and communicate with a back-end database. It requires one MCP exam, plus two of these three exams: "70-055: Designing and Implementing Web Sites with Microsoft FrontPage 98," "70-057: Designing and Implementing Commerce Solutions with Microsoft Site Server 3.0, Commerce Edition," and "70-152: Designing and Implementing Web Solutions with Microsoft Visual InterDev 6.0." Microsoft will retire Exam 70-055 on June 30, 2001 and the MCP+SB certification on June 30, 2002.

▶ *MCSE (Microsoft Certified Systems Engineer)*—Anyone who has a current MCSE is warranted to possess a high level of networking expertise with Microsoft operating systems and products. This credential is designed to prepare individuals to plan, implement, maintain, and support information systems, networks, and internetworks built around Microsoft Windows 2000 and its BackOffice family of products.

To obtain an MCSE, an individual must pass four core operating system exams, one core option exam, and two elective exams. The operating system exams require individuals to prove their competence with desktop and server operating systems and networking/internetworking components.

For Windows NT 4 MCSEs, the Accelerated exam, "70-240: Microsoft Windows 2000 Accelerated Exam for MCPs Certified on Microsoft Windows NT 4.0," is an option. This free exam covers all of the material tested in the Core Four exams. The hitch in this plan is that you can take the test only once. If you fail, you must take all four core exams to recertify. The Core Four exams are: "70-210: Installing, Configuring and Administering Microsoft Windows 2000 Professional," "70-215: Installing, Configuring and Administering Microsoft Windows

2000 Server," "70-216: Implementing and Administering a Microsoft Windows 2000 Network Infrastructure," and "70-217: Implementing and Administering a Microsoft Windows 2000 Directory Services Infrastructure."

To fulfill the fifth core exam requirement, you can choose from four design exams: "70-219: Designing a Microsoft Windows 2000 Directory Services Infrastructure," "70-220: Designing Security for a Microsoft Windows 2000 Network," "70-221: Designing a Microsoft Windows 2000 Network Infrastructure," or "70-226: Designing Highly Available Web Solutions with Microsoft Windows 2000 Server Technologies." You are also required to take two elective exams. An elective exam can fall in any number of subject or product areas, primarily BackOffice Server 2000 components. The three design exams that you don't select as your fifth core exam also qualify as electives. If you are on your way to becoming an MCSE and have already taken some exams, visit **www.microsoft.com/trainingandservices/** for information about how to complete your MCSE certification.

Individuals who wish to remain certified MCSEs after 12/31/2001 must "upgrade" their certifications on or before 12/31/2001. For more detailed information than is included here, visit **www.microsoft.com/trainingandservices/**.

New MCSE candidates must pass seven tests to meet the MCSE requirements. It's not uncommon for the entire process to take a year or so, and many individuals find that they must take a test more than once to pass. The primary goal of *Exam Prep* and *Exam Cram* test preparation books is to make it possible, given proper study and preparation, to pass all Microsoft certification tests on the first try. Table 1 shows the required and elective exams for the Windows 2000 MCSE certification.

▶ *MCSD (Microsoft Certified Solution Developer)*—The MCSD credential reflects the skills required to create multitier, distributed, and COM-based solutions, in addition to desktop and Internet applications, using new technologies. To obtain an MCSD, an individual must demonstrate the ability to analyze and interpret user requirements; select and integrate products, platforms, tools, and technologies; design and implement code, and customize applications; and perform necessary software tests and quality assurance operations.

To become an MCSD, you must pass a total of four exams: three core exams and one elective exam. Each candidate must choose one of these three desktop application exams—"70-016: Designing and Implementing Desktop Applications with Microsoft Visual C++ 6.0," "70-156: Designing and Implementing Desktop Applications with Microsoft Visual FoxPro 6.0," or "70-176: Designing and Implementing Desktop Applications with Microsoft Visual Basic 6.0"—*plus* one of these three distributed application exams—"70-015: Designing and

Table 1 MCSE Windows 2000 Requirements

Core

If you have not passed these 3 Windows NT 4 exams	
Exam 70-067	Implementing and Supporting Microsoft Windows NT Server 4.0
Exam 70-068	Implementing and Supporting Microsoft Windows NT Server 4.0 in the Enterprise
Exam 70-073	Microsoft Windows NT Workstation 4.0
then you must take these 4 exams	
Exam 70-210	Installing, Configuring, and Administering Microsoft Windows 2000 Professional
Exam 70-215	Installing, Configuring, and Administering Microsoft Windows 2000 Server
Exam 70-216	Implementing and Administering a Microsoft Windows 2000 Network Infrastructure
Exam 70-217	Implementing and Administering a Microsoft Windows 2000 Directory Services Infrastructure
If you have already passed exams 70-067, 70-068, and 70-073, you may take this exam	
Exam 70-240	Microsoft Windows 2000 Accelerated Exam for MCPs Certified on Microsoft Windows NT 4.0

5th Core Option

Choose 1 from this group	
Exam 70-219	Designing a Microsoft Windows 2000 Directory Services Infrastructure
Exam 70-220	Designing Security for a Microsoft Windows 2000 Network
Exam 70-221	Designing a Microsoft Windows 2000 Network Infrastructure
Exam 70-226	Designing Highly Available Web Solutions with Microsoft Windows 2000 Server Technologies

Elective*

Choose 2 from this group	
Exam 70-019	Designing and Implementing Data Warehouse with Microsoft SQL Server 7.0
Exam 70-056	Implementing and Supporting Web Sites Using Microsoft Site Server 3.0
Exam 70-080	Implementing and Supporting Microsoft Internet Explorer 5.0 by Using the Internet Explorer Administration Kit
Exam 70-085	Implementing and Supporting Microsoft SNA Server 4.0
Exam 70-086	Implementing and Supporting Microsoft Systems Management Server 2.0
Exam 70-222	Migrating from Microsoft Windows NT 4.0 to Microsoft Windows 2000
Exam 70-223	Installing, Configuring, and Administering Microsoft Clustering Services by Using Microsoft Windows 2000 Advanced Server
▶ Exam 70-224	Installing, Configuring, and Administering Microsoft Exchange 2000 Server
Exam 70-225	Designing and Deploying a Messaging Infrastructure with Microsoft Exchange 2000 Server
Exam 70-227	Installing, Configuring, and Administering Microsoft Internet Security and Acceleration (ISA) Server 2000 Enterprise Edition
Exam 70-228	Installing, Configuring, and Administering Microsoft SQL Server 2000 Enterprise Edition
Exam 70-229	Designing and Implementing Databases with Microsoft SQL Server 2000 Enterprise Edition
Exam 70-244	Supporting and Maintaining a Microsoft Windows NT Server 4.0 Network

This is not a complete listing—you can still be tested on some earlier versions of these products. However, we have included mainly the most recent versions so that you may test on these versions and thus be certified longer. We have not included any tests that are scheduled to be retired.

★ 5th Core Option exams may also be used as electives, but can only be counted once toward a certification. You cannot receive credit for an exam as both a core and an elective in the same track.

Implementing Distributed Applications with Microsoft Visual C++ 6.0," "70-155: Designing and Implementing Distributed Applications with Microsoft Visual FoxPro 6.0," or "70-175: Designing and Implementing Distributed Applications with Microsoft Visual Basic 6.0." The third core exam is "70-100: Analyzing Requirements and Defining Solution Architectures." Elective exams cover specific Microsoft applications and languages, including Visual Basic, C++, the Microsoft Foundation Classes, Access, SQL Server, Excel, and more.

▶ *MCDBA (Microsoft Certified Database Administrator)*—The MCDBA credential reflects the skills required to implement and administer Microsoft SQL Server databases. To obtain an MCDBA, an individual must demonstrate the ability to derive physical database designs, develop logical data models, create physical databases, create data services by using Transact-SQL, manage and maintain databases, configure and manage security, monitor and optimize databases, and install and configure Microsoft SQL Server.

To become an MCDBA, you must pass a total of three core exams and one elective exam. The required core exams are "70-028: Administering Microsoft SQL Server 7.0" or "70-228: Installing, Configuring, and Administering Microsoft SQL Server 2000 Enterprise Edition," "70-029: Designing and Implementing Databases with Microsoft SQL Server 7.0" or "70-229: Designing and Implementing Databases with Microsoft SQL Server 2000 Enterprise Edition," and "70-215: Installing, Configuring and Administering Microsoft Windows 2000 Server" or "70-240: Microsoft Windows 2000 Accelerated Exam for MCPs Certified on Microsoft Windows NT."

The elective exams that you can choose from cover specific uses of SQL Server and include "70-015: Designing and Implementing Distributed Applications with Microsoft Visual C++ 6.0," "70-019: Designing and Implementing Data Warehouses with Microsoft SQL Server 7.0," "70-155: Designing and Implementing Distributed Applications with Microsoft Visual FoxPro 6.0," "70-175: Designing and Implementing Distributed Applications with Microsoft Visual Basic 6.0," and two exams that relate to Windows 2000: "70-216: Implementing and Administering a Microsoft Windows 2000 Network Infrastructure" and "70-087: Implementing and Supporting Microsoft Internet Information Server 4.0."

If you have taken the three core Windows NT 4 exams on your path to becoming an MCSE, you qualify for the Accelerated exam (it replaces the Network Infrastructure exam requirement). The Accelerated exam covers the objectives of all four of the Windows 2000 core exams. In addition to taking the Accelerated exam, you must take only the two SQL exams—Administering and Database Design.

> *MCT (Microsoft Certified Trainer)*—Microsoft Certified Trainers are deemed able to deliver elements of the official Microsoft curriculum, based on technical knowledge and instructional ability. Thus, it is necessary for an individual seeking MCT credentials (which are granted on a course-by-course basis) to pass the related certification exam for a course and complete the official Microsoft training in the subject area, and to demonstrate an ability to teach.
>
> This teaching skill criterion may be satisfied by proving that one has already attained training certification from Novell, Banyan, Lotus, the Santa Cruz Operation, or Cisco, or by taking a Microsoft-sanctioned workshop on instruction. Microsoft makes it clear that MCTs are important cogs in the Microsoft training channels. Instructors must be MCTs before Microsoft will allow them to teach in any of its official training channels, including Microsoft's affiliated Certified Technical Education Centers (CTECs) and its online training partner network. As of January 1, 2001, MCT candidates must also possess a current MCSE.

Microsoft has announced that the MCP+I and MCSE+I credentials will not be continued when the MCSE exams for Windows 2000 are in full swing because the skill set for the Internet portion of the program has been included in the new MCSE program. Therefore, details on these tracks are not provided here; go to **www.microsoft.com/trainingandservices/** if you need more information.

Once a Microsoft product becomes obsolete, MCPs typically have to recertify on current versions. (If individuals do not recertify, their certifications become invalid.) Because technology keeps changing and new products continually supplant old ones, this should come as no surprise. This explains why Microsoft has announced that MCSEs have 12 months past the scheduled retirement date for the Windows NT 4 exams to recertify on Windows 2000 topics. (Note that this means taking at least two exams, if not more.)

The best place to keep tabs on the MCP Program and its related certifications is on the Web. The URL for the MCP program is **www.microsoft.com/mcp/**. But Microsoft's Web site changes often, so if this URL doesn't work, try using the Search tool on Microsoft's site with either "MCP" or the quoted phrase "Microsoft Certified Professional Program" as a search string. This will help you find the latest and most accurate information about Microsoft's certification programs.

Tracking MCP Status

As soon as you pass any Microsoft exam (except Networking Essentials), you'll attain Microsoft Certified Professional (MCP) status. Microsoft also generates transcripts that indicate which exams you have passed. You can view a copy of your transcript at any time by going to the MCP secured site and selecting Transcript

Tool. This tool will allow you to print a copy of your current transcript and confirm your certification status.

Once you pass the necessary set of exams, you'll be certified. Official certification normally takes anywhere from six to eight weeks, so don't expect to get your credentials overnight. When the package for a qualified certification arrives, it includes a Welcome Kit that contains a number of elements (see Microsoft's Web site for other benefits of specific certifications):

➤ A certificate suitable for framing, along with a wallet card and a lapel pin.

➤ A license to use the MCP logo, thereby allowing you to use the logo in advertisements, promotions, and documents, and on letterhead, business cards, and so on. Along with the license comes an MCP logo sheet, which includes camera-ready artwork. (Note: Before using any of the artwork, individuals must sign and return a licensing agreement that indicates they'll abide by its terms and conditions.)

➤ A subscription to *Microsoft Certified Professional Magazine*, which provides ongoing data about testing and certification activities, requirements, and changes to the program.

Many people believe that the benefits of MCP certification go well beyond the perks that Microsoft provides to newly anointed members of this elite group. We're starting to see more job listings that request or require applicants to have an MCP, MCSE, and so on, and many individuals who complete the program can qualify for increases in pay and/or responsibility. As an official recognition of hard work and broad knowledge, one of the MCP credentials is a badge of honor in many IT organizations.

About the Book

Career opportunities are available for well-prepared Exchange 2000 administrators. This book is designed to prepare you for Exchange 2000 Server Administration. Our goal is to help you develop a sufficient background for providing solutions rather than just configuring systems. Others who have prior experience with Exchange will find that the book adds depth and breadth to that experience. Also, the book provides the knowledge you need to prepare for Microsoft's certification exam 70-224, "Installing, Configuring, and Administering Microsoft Exchange 2000 Server." The exam is one of the available electives, and it is a crucial step in becoming a Microsoft Certified Systems Engineer.

We believe that Exchange 2000 Server is a major part of the Windows 2000 enterprise, as well as a fundamental part of any e-commerce business platform. It provides an extensible interface on which a corporate enterprise or Web-based e-commerce project can build a messaging infrastructure providing services related to communication, collaboration, and workflow control. The success of Exchange 2000 Server is reflected in the huge number of software vendors and developers who develop in this environment, or who have switched from other environments to Windows 2000 Server in order to use all the features available in Exchange 2000 Server. Many corporations run legacy Exchange Server and are planning to convert to Windows 2000 Server, Active Directory, and Exchange 2000 so that they leverage an extensible operating system with one of the most powerful messaging platforms available on the market today.

As you read this book, you will discover themes and ideas that can leverage the power of Exchange 2000 Server and advance your career in the area of information technology. This growing field offers ample opportunity for personal growth and for making a contribution to your business or organization. Our book is intended to provide you with knowledge that you can apply right away and a sound basis for understanding the changes that you will encounter in the future. It also is intended to give you the hands-on skills you need to be a valued professional in your organization.

The book is filled with real-world projects that cover every aspect of installing, managing, and configuring Exchange 2000 Server. The projects are designed to make what you learn come alive through actually performing the tasks. Also, every chapter includes a range of practice questions to help prepare you for the Microsoft certification exam. All of these features are offered to reinforce your learning, so you'll feel confident in the knowledge you have gained from each chapter.

Features

To aid you in fully understanding Exchange 2000 Administration concepts, there are many features in this book designed to improve its value:

- *Chapter objectives*—Each chapter in this book begins with a detailed list of the topics to be mastered within that chapter. This list provides you with a quick reference to the contents of that chapter, as well as a useful study aid.

- *Illustrations and tables*—Numerous illustrations of screenshots and components aid you in the visualization of common setup steps, theories, and concepts. In addition, many tables provide details and comparisons of both practical and theoretical information.

- *Notes, tips, and warnings*—Notes present additional helpful material related to the subject being described. Tips from the author's experience provide extra information about how to attack a problem, how to set up an Exchange 2000 Server for a particular need, or what to do in certain real-world situations. Warnings are included to help you anticipate potential mistakes or problems so you can prevent them from happening.

➤ *Chapter summaries*—Each chapter's text is followed by a summary of the concepts it has introduced. These summaries provide a helpful way to recap and revisit the ideas covered in each chapter.

➤ *Review questions*—End-of-chapter assessment begins with a set of review questions that reinforce the ideas introduced in each chapter. These questions not only ensure that you have mastered the concepts, but are written to help prepare you for the Microsoft certification examination. Answers to these questions are found in Appendix A.

➤ *Real-world projects*—Although it is important to understand the theory behind Exchange 2000 Administration, nothing can improve upon real-world experience. To this end, along with theoretical explanations, each chapter provides several hands-on projects aimed at providing you with real-world implementation experience.

➤ *Sample tests*—Use the sample test and answer key in Chapters 18 and 19 to test yourself. Then, move on to the interactive practice exams found on the CD-ROM. The testing engine offers a variety of testing formats to choose from.

Where Should You Start?

This book is intended to be read in sequence, from beginning to end. Each chapter builds upon those that precede it, to provide a solid understanding of Exchange 2000 Server. After completing the chapters, you may find it useful to go back through the book and use the review questions and projects to prepare for the Microsoft certification test for "Installing, Configuring, and Administering Microsoft Exchange 2000 Server" (Exam 70-224). Readers are also encouraged to investigate the many pointers to online and printed sources of additional information that are cited throughout this book.

Please share your feedback on the book with us, especially if you have ideas about how we can improve it for future readers. We'll consider everything you say carefully, and we'll respond to all suggestions. Send your questions or comments to us at **learn@examcram.com**. Please remember to include the title of the book in your message; otherwise, we'll be forced to guess which book you're writing about. Also, be sure to check out the Web pages at **www.examcram.com**, where you'll find information updates, commentary, and certification information. Thanks, and enjoy the book!

Self-Assessment

The reason we included a Self-Assessment in this *Exam Prep* book is to help you evaluate your readiness to tackle MCSE certification. It should also help you understand what you need to know to master the topic of this book—namely, Exam 70-224, "Installing, Configuring, and Administering Microsoft Exchange 2000 Server." But before you tackle this Self-Assessment, let's talk about concerns you may face when pursuing an MCSE for Windows 2000, and what an ideal MCSE candidate might look like.

MCSEs in the Real World

In the next section, we describe an ideal MCSE candidate, knowing full well that only a few real candidates will meet this ideal. In fact, our description of that ideal candidate might seem downright scary, especially with the changes that have been made to the program to support Windows 2000. But take heart: Although the requirements to obtain an MCSE may seem formidable, they are by no means impossible to meet. However, be keenly aware that it does take time, involves some expense, and requires real effort to get through the process.

Increasing numbers of people are attaining Microsoft certifications, so the goal is within reach. You can get all the real-world motivation you need from knowing that many others have gone before, so you will be able to follow in their footsteps. If you're willing to tackle the process seriously and do what it takes to obtain the necessary experience and knowledge, you can take—and pass—all the certification tests involved in obtaining an MCSE. In fact, we've designed *Exam Preps*, the companion *Exam Crams*, *Exam Cram Personal Trainers*, and *Exam Cram Personal Test Centers* to make it as easy on you as possible to prepare for these exams. We've also greatly expanded our Web site, **www.examcram.com**, to provide a host of resources to help you prepare for the complexities of Windows 2000.

Besides MCSE, other Microsoft certifications include:

➤ MCSD, which is aimed at software developers and requires one specific exam, two more exams on client and distributed topics, plus a fourth elective exam drawn from a different, but limited, pool of options.

➤ Other Microsoft certifications, whose requirements range from one test (MCP) to several tests (MCP+SB, MCDBA).

The Ideal Windows 2000 MCSE Candidate

Just to give you some idea of what an ideal MCSE candidate is like, here are some relevant statistics about the background and experience such an individual might have. Don't worry if you don't meet these qualifications, or don't come that close—this is a far from ideal world, and where you fall short is simply where you'll have more work to do.

➤ Academic or professional training in network theory, concepts, and operations. This includes everything from networking media and transmission techniques through network operating systems, services, and applications.

➤ Three-plus years of professional networking experience, including experience with Ethernet, token ring, modems, and other networking media. This must include installation, configuration, upgrade, and troubleshooting experience.

Note: *The Windows 2000 MCSE program is much more rigorous than the previous NT MCSE program; therefore, you'll really need some hands-on experience. Some of the exams require you to solve real-world case studies and network design issues, so the more hands-on experience you have, the better.*

➤ Two-plus years in a networked environment that includes hands-on experience with Windows 2000 Server, Windows 2000 Professional, Windows NT Server, Windows NT Workstation, and Windows 95 or Windows 98. A solid understanding of each system's architecture, installation, configuration, maintenance, and troubleshooting is also essential.

➤ Knowledge of the various methods for installing Windows 2000, including manual and unattended installations.

➤ A thorough understanding of key networking protocols, addressing, and name resolution, including TCP/IP, IPX/SPX, and NetBEUI.

➤ A thorough understanding of NetBIOS naming, browsing, and file and print services.

➤ Familiarity with key Windows 2000–based TCP/IP-based services, including HTTP (Web servers), DHCP, WINS, and DNS, plus familiarity with one or more of the following: Internet Information Server (IIS), Index Server, and Proxy Server.

➤ An understanding of how to implement security for key network data in a Windows 2000 environment.

➤ Working knowledge of NetWare 3.x and 4.x, including IPX/SPX frame formats, NetWare file, print, and directory services, and both Novell and Microsoft client software. Working knowledge of Microsoft's Client Service For NetWare (CSNW), Gateway Service For NetWare (GSNW), the NetWare Migration Tool (NWCONV), and the NetWare Client For Windows (NT, 95, and 98) is essential.

➤ A good working understanding of Active Directory. The more you work with Windows 2000, the more you'll realize that this new operating system is quite different than Windows NT. New technologies like Active Directory have really changed the way that Windows is configured and used. We recommend that you find out as much as you can about Active Directory and acquire as much experience using this technology as possible. The time you take learning about Active Directory will be time very well spent!

Fundamentally, this boils down to a bachelor's degree in computer science, plus three years' experience working in a position involving network design, installation, configuration, and maintenance. We believe that well under half of all certification candidates meet these requirements, and that, in fact, most meet less than half of these requirements—at least, when they begin the certification process. But because all the people who already have been certified have survived this ordeal, you can survive it too—especially if you heed what our Self-Assessment can tell you about what you already know and what you need to learn.

Put Yourself to the Test

The following series of questions and observations is designed to help you figure out how much work you must do to pursue Microsoft certification and what kinds of resources you may consult on your quest. Be absolutely honest in your answers, or you'll end up wasting money on exams you're not yet ready to take. There are no right or wrong answers, only steps along the path to certification. Only you can decide where you really belong in the broad spectrum of aspiring candidates.

Two things should be clear from the outset, however:

➤ Even a modest background in computer science will be helpful.

➤ Hands-on experience with Microsoft products and technologies is an essential ingredient to certification success.

Educational Background

1. Have you ever taken any computer-related classes? [Yes or No]

   If Yes, proceed to question 2; if No, proceed to question 4.

2. Have you taken any classes on computer operating systems? [Yes or No]

    If Yes, you will probably be able to handle Microsoft's architecture and system component discussions. If you're rusty, brush up on basic operating system concepts, especially virtual memory, multitasking regimes, user mode versus kernel mode operation, and general computer security topics.

    If No, consider some basic reading in this area. We strongly recommend a good general operating systems book, such as *Operating System Concepts, 5th Edition*, by Abraham Silberschatz and Peter Baer Galvin (John Wiley & Sons, 1998, ISBN 0-471-36414-2). If this title doesn't appeal to you, check out reviews for other, similar titles at your favorite online bookstore.

3. Have you taken any networking concepts or technologies classes? [Yes or No]

    If Yes, you will probably be able to handle Microsoft's networking terminology, concepts, and technologies (brace yourself for frequent departures from normal usage). If you're rusty, brush up on basic networking concepts and terminology, especially networking media, transmission types, the OSI Reference Model, and networking technologies such as Ethernet, token ring, FDDI, and WAN links.

    If No, you might want to read one or two books in this topic area. The two best books that we know of are *Computer Networks, 3rd Edition*, by Andrew S. Tanenbaum (Prentice-Hall, 1996, ISBN 0-13-349945-6) and *Computer Networks and Internets, 2nd Edition*, by Douglas E. Comer and Ralph E. Droms (Prentice-Hall, 1998, ISBN 0-130-83617-6).

    Skip to the next section, "Hands-on Experience."

4. Have you done any reading on operating systems or networks? [Yes or No]

    If Yes, review the requirements stated in the first paragraphs after questions 2 and 3. If you meet those requirements, move on to the next section. If No, consult the recommended reading for both topics. A strong background will help you prepare for the Microsoft exams better than just about anything else.

Hands-on Experience

The most important key to success on all of the Microsoft tests is hands-on experience, especially with Windows 2000 Server and Professional, plus the many add-on services and BackOffice components around which so many of the Microsoft certification exams revolve. If we leave you with only one realization after taking this Self-Assessment, it should be that there's no substitute for time spent installing, configuring, and using the various Microsoft products upon which you'll be tested repeatedly and in depth.

5. Have you installed, configured, and worked with:

   ➤ Windows 2000 Server? [Yes or No]

   If Yes, make sure you understand basic concepts as covered in Exam 70-215. You should also study the TCP/IP interfaces, utilities, and services for Exam 70-216, plus implementing security features for Exam 70-220.

Tip: You can download objectives, practice exams, and other data about Microsoft exams from the Training and Certification page at **www.microsoft.com/trainingandservices/default.asp?PageID=mcp**. Use the "Exams" link to obtain specific exam information.

If you haven't worked with Windows 2000 Server, you must obtain one or two machines and a copy of Windows 2000 Server. Then, learn the operating system and whatever other software components on which you'll also be tested.

In fact, we recommend that you obtain two computers, each with a network interface, and set up a two-node network on which to practice. With decent Windows 2000–capable computers selling for about $500 to $600 apiece these days, this shouldn't be too much of a financial hardship. You may have to scrounge to come up with the necessary software, but if you scour the Microsoft Web site you can usually find low-cost options to obtain evaluation copies of most of the software that you'll need.

➤ Windows 2000 Professional? [Yes or No]

If Yes, make sure you understand the concepts covered in Exam 70-210.

If No, you will want to obtain a copy of Windows 2000 Professional and learn how to install, configure, and maintain it. You can use *MCSE Windows 2000 Professional Exam Cram* to guide your activities and studies, or work straight from Microsoft's test objectives if you prefer.

Tip: For any and all of these Microsoft exams, the Resource Kits for the topics involved are a good study resource. You can purchase softcover Resource Kits from Microsoft Press (search for them at **http://mspress.microsoft.com/**), but they also appear on the TechNet CDs (**www.microsoft.com/technet**). Along with *Exam Crams* and *Exam Preps*, we believe that Resource Kits are among the best tools you can use to prepare for Microsoft exams.

---

6. For any specific Microsoft product that is not itself an operating system (for example, SQL Server), have you installed, configured, used, and upgraded this software? [Yes or No]

   If the answer is Yes, skip to the next section. If it's No, you must get some experience. Read on for suggestions on how to do this.

Experience is a must with any Microsoft product exam, be it something as simple as FrontPage 2000 or as challenging as SQL Server 7.0. For trial copies of other software, search Microsoft's Web site using the name of the product as your search term. Also, search for bundles like "BackOffice" or "Small Business Server."

> **Tip:** If you have the funds, or your employer will pay your way, consider taking a class at a Certified Training and Education Center (CTEC) or at an Authorized Academic Training Partner (AATP). In addition to classroom exposure to the topic of your choice, you get a copy of the software that is the focus of your course, along with a trial version of whatever operating system it needs, with the training materials for that class.

Before you even think about taking any Microsoft exam, make sure you've spent enough time with the related software to understand how it may be installed and configured, how to maintain such an installation, and how to troubleshoot that software when things go wrong. This will help you in the exam, and in real life!

Testing Your Exam-Readiness

Whether you attend a formal class on a specific topic to get ready for an exam or use written materials to study on your own, some preparation for the Microsoft certification exams is essential. At $125 a try, pass or fail, you want to do everything you can to pass on your first try. That's where studying comes in.

We have included a practice exam in this book, so if you don't score that well on the test, you can study more and then tackle the test again. If you still don't hit a score of at least 85 percent after this test, you'll want to investigate the other practice test resources we mention in this section.

For any given subject, consider taking a class if you've tackled self-study materials, taken the test, and failed anyway. The opportunity to interact with an instructor and fellow students can make all the difference in the world, if you can afford that privilege. For information about Microsoft classes, visit the Training and Certification page at **www.microsoft.com/education/partners/ctec.asp** for Microsoft Certified Education Centers or **www.microsoft.com/aatp/default.htm** for Microsoft Authorized Training Providers.

If you can't afford to take a class, visit the Training and Certification page anyway, because it also includes pointers to free practice exams and to Microsoft Certified Professional Approved Study Guides and other self-study tools. And even if you can't afford to spend much at all, you should still invest in some low-cost practice exams from commercial vendors. There are also exams on many topics that you can take online through the **ExamCram.com** Web site at **www.examcram.com**.

7. Have you taken a practice exam on your chosen test subject? [Yes or No]

    If Yes, and you scored 85 percent or better, you're probably ready to tackle the real thing. If your score isn't above that threshold, keep at it until you break that barrier.

    If No, obtain all the free and low-budget practice tests you can find and get to work. Keep at it until you can break the passing threshold comfortably.

Tip: When it comes to assessing your test readiness, there is no better way than to take a good-quality practice exam and pass with a score of 85 percent or better. When we're preparing ourselves, we shoot for 90-plus percent, just to leave room for the "weirdness factor" that sometimes shows up on Microsoft exams.

Assessing Readiness for Exam 70-224

In addition to the general exam-readiness information in the previous section, there are several things you can do to prepare for the Installing, Configuring, and Administering Microsoft Exchange 2000 Server exam. As you're getting ready for Exam 70-224, visit the Exam Cram Windows 2000 Resource Center at **www.examcram.com/studyresource/w2kresource/**. Another valuable resource is the Exam Cram Insider newsletter. Sign up at **www.examcram.com** or send a blank email message to **subscribe-ec@mars.coriolis.com**. We also suggest that you join an active MCSE mailing list. One of the better ones is managed by Sunbelt Software. Sign up at **www.sunbelt-software.com** (look for the Subscribe button).

Microsoft exam mavens also recommend checking the Microsoft Knowledge Base (available on its own CD as part of the TechNet collection, or on the Microsoft Web site at **http://support.microsoft.com/support/**) for "meaningful technical support issues" that relate to your exam's topics. Although we're not sure exactly what the quoted phrase means, we have also noticed some overlap between technical support questions on particular products and troubleshooting questions on the exams for those products.

Onward, through the Mist!

Once you've assessed your readiness, undertaken the right background studies, obtained the hands-on experience that will help you understand the products and technologies at work, and reviewed the many sources of information to help you prepare for a test, you'll be ready to take a round of practice tests. When your scores come back positive enough to get you through the exam, you're ready to go after the real thing. If you follow our assessment regime, you'll not only know what you need to study, but when you're ready to make a test date at Prometric or VUE. We wish you good luck and remind you to savor the excitement of living the adventure!

CHAPTER ONE

Models and Methods

After completing this chapter, you will be able to:

- ✓ Understand the shift in Microsoft design strategy and its impact on the role of the administrator in an enterprise environment
- ✓ Use network management models to describe management information services and Microsoft methodologies
- ✓ Understand the architectural origins of a messaging service provider
- ✓ Describe the key services that Exchange 2000 provides in a Windows 2000 enterprise
- ✓ Trace enhanced and changing features in the different versions of Exchange
- ✓ Compare various Exchange 2000 Server editions
- ✓ Understand the impact of new key features on areas such as storage and collaboration

This book is about Exchange 2000 and the bridging of a vast sea of computer resources to provide information readily accessible anytime, anywhere, through any digital device. It is also about a messaging and collaboration platform and a change in job description from networking technician to solution architect. Finally, it is about a change in paradigm—from data processing to knowledge management. A *paradigm* is a group of ideas that paint a mental picture and can provide a methodology or pattern of thinking about some aspect of our lives, our job, or our world. When the pattern of elements is so intrinsically bound together that its properties cannot be separated from its individual parts, we can describe it as a "gestalt" or "worldview." We describe here a new gestalt—a worldview of a vast array of distributed services in an enterprise namespace of millions of objects. Your job as an Exchange 2000 administrator is to manage a fundamental server platform that provides knowledge-related services within this vast enterprise namespace.

Theorists have suggested that the interpretation of a body of scientific evidence periodically changes through intellectual "revolutions" in some popular gestalt or cognitive worldview. These theorists say that it took an entire generation of "old" scientists to die before the "truth" (for example, that the earth revolved around the sun) was finally accepted as scientific fact by a younger, allegedly more open scientific community. Other theorists alternatively propose that the preponderance of new evidence simply contradicts older information measured in the laboratory or the real world to alter the worldview. People simply adjust their worldview to newly published facts. Although neither of these theoretical viewpoints about scientific revolutions have direct relevance to this book, both theories clearly depend upon the accumulation of data and its accessibility to increasing numbers of "knowledge" workers, which is not only relevant but at the center of the collaborative use of information. Furthermore, as technicians in the rapidly changing and highly competitive field of information technology (IT), we must understand and adopt a new worldview overnight or find some other means of supporting our families and ourselves.

This book is about learning how to function effectively in a new gestalt so that you can provide often mission-critical services to the user population. We will use this chapter to provide you with that critical, though at times theoretical, frame of reference. We will discuss the administration of Exchange 2000 Server and paradigm changes in handling information resources. More significantly, we will describe how the role of administrator has changed from managing data processing equipment to providing knowledge-management solutions. I introduce models that help describe the current paradigm, which I call the Knowledge-Management Paradigm. I then trace the origins of electronic messaging and cover key message-handling models that are the foundation for the Exchange Server product family. From this same service-oriented perspective, I briefly cover the issue of storage as it relates to the sharing of data across emerging management systems. Before delving into Exchange Server, I describe other kinds of online services, which have been incorporated beginning with Exchange 5.x as collaborative features. Then, I describe the specifics of Exchange—how it functions as a messaging service provider and also as a knowledge-management information broker. I conclude this chapter with introductory descriptions of features of Exchange 2000 that differentiate it from previous versions; these will be covered in more detail later in this book.

Figure 1.1 shows the functional layer of various Microsoft services providers, such as Commerce Server 2000, Internet Security and Acceleration (ISA) Server 2000, BizTalk 2000 Server, and so on. We show the provided services within the pyramid; these services are all accessible from the Internet. Thus, the entire collection of services is managed as a Web site even though some services, such as Exchange 2000 and SQL Server 2000, might be accessed from within the enterprise. Notice how we place Exchange 2000 Server at the base of the pyramid of services, where it can provide consumers, both on the Internet and in an organization's user population, with information-related services. Our figure suggests a change in emphasis of an administrator's job responsibility from that of technician/"plumber" to solution provider/"architect." This change in job role is a direct result of structural changes in the Exchange 2000 product itself, as well as in its functional role in the Windows 2000 enterprise.

The way we provide information stores will continue to significantly change the speed with which we formulate knowledge and arrive at new conclusions in the future, as well as the scope within which our conclusions can be based. Exchange 2000 as the foundation platform for messaging and collaboration plays a fundamental role in knowledge management. We use the term *paradigm* to describe how bits of evidence, observations, data, and events can be viewed, retrieved, and manipulated. Microsoft proposed its "Information at Your Fingertips" (IAYF) campaign in 1990. IAYF was marketed as "The right information at the right time for the right

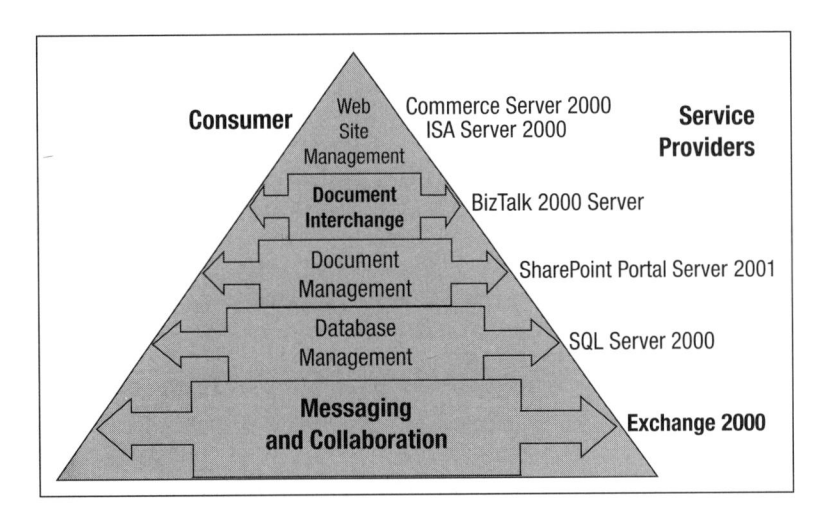

Figure 1.1 Business needs and solutions.

purpose." Microsoft's stated objective was to make finding and retrieving information easy and location-independent. This initiative, which stresses the functional change in how information is handled, parallels two other trends that forced a paradigm shift in the world of IT. Figure 1.2 shows how the original role of handling data processing systems has shifted from information systems to knowledge management.

Since the early 1960s, there have been three major paradigm shifts in how computers are used. In the 1960s through the 1970s, mainframe computers (referred to as Big Iron) were designed to process text and numerical data quickly, accurately, and efficiently; let's call this the Data-Processing Paradigm. From the 1970s through the 1990s, technologies have focused on workgroups and resource sharing; for our purposes here, we will call this the Information Sharing Paradigm. NT (Microsoft's New Technology), Novell NetWare, and Windows for Workgroups clearly demonstrated that personal computers rather than dumb terminals provided advantages through working in groups and sharing of files, folders, printers, and other resources. The idea of communication, collaboration, and control thus took root and forever changed the workplace.

This emphasis on knowledge management parallels structural changes in hardware and software. The progressive increase in hardware capacity has provided increasingly more complex operating systems to provide broader ranges of services to user populations. We can trace remarkable accomplishments beginning with the first Digital Equipment Corporation (DEC) Programmed Data Processor - 1 (PDP-1) in 1960. It was described as a general-purpose computer functioning as a building block in a wide class of high-speed digital systems. It was available to small and medium-size businesses because of its relative inexpensive

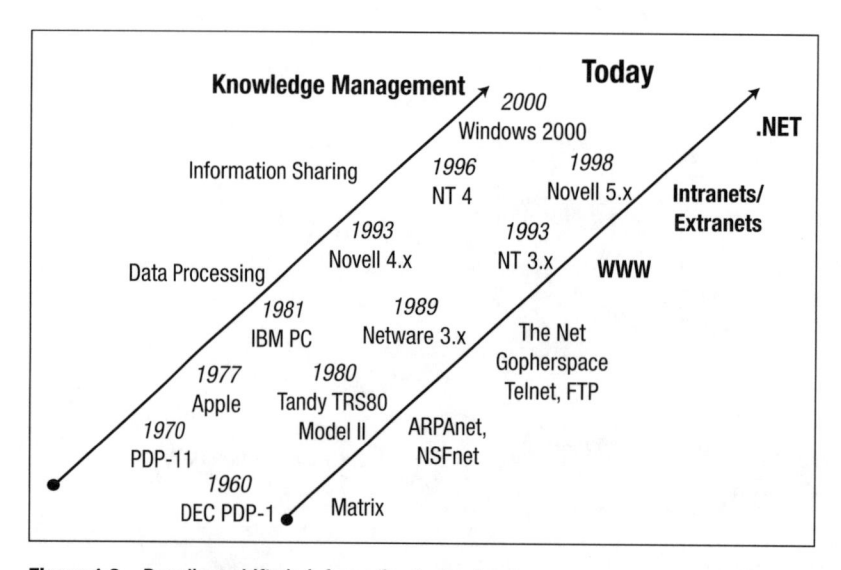

Figure 1.2 Paradigm shifts in information technology.

cost, and it could architecturally coexist with a variety of input/output devices without internal modifications. An offspring, the PDP-11, when compared to all other types of computing equipment, is probably one of the most successful computers ever manufactured. PDP-11 was significant because it was more microcomputer than minicomputer or mainframe. Around the same time as the release of the PDP-11, a myriad of personal-size computers were also made available in the marketplace, such as Apple (1977), Tandy (1980), and IBM (1981). Figure 1.2 shows these events in a time line. These landmark dates are shown alongside two other trends in the area of information technology, such as the explosive growth of communicating those services.

From the inception of an "internetwork of networks" in the early 1970s, the public network we call the Internet has grown at an explosive rate. This growth in communication thus allows the application servers and network operating systems to provide a greater range of distributed services. Tim Berners-Lee, a physicist at CERN in Switzerland, radically changed the way this information was shared by conceiving of the World Wide Web, a vast multimedia meshwork available from any network-enabled desktop. His communication concept leveraged both the vast distribution of personal computers as well as the emerging power of online communication over the Internet. The most recent paradigm shift toward information integration has arisen from this vast, virtual heap of multimedia data and communications, and the need for shared documentation. Although The Matrix was originally described as a unified, networked namespace to which any computer resource could connect, changes in Novell version 5 and Windows 2000 signal the final move toward the pre-eminence of TCP/IP protocol suite as the de facto protocol standard for all networking connectivity. As the digital economy continues to flourish, e-commerce will fuel the need to focus on more functional matters and distill the ever-increasing piles of factoids from this Matrix into a reusable and essential commodity—knowledge. The need for businesses and individuals to communicate, collaborate, and control the exchange of this commodity is the Knowledge-Management Paradigm. The Exchange administrator is in the middle of this paradigm shift and must adjust to it overnight.

The Knowledge-Management Paradigm

Your study of Exchange 2000 coincides with this current paradigm shift to knowledge management (KM) and is radically affected by it. In fact, the entire IT profession over the next few years will witness a subtle but significant change in job role—from IT "plumber" to IT "architect." This shift in focus parallels the change in management schemes brought about by emerging technologies such as Microsoft.NET Management Services, Microsoft's management software for Windows, and its new operating system initiative .NET platform. In the context of richer operating system services and management applications, less complexity in connecting applications across multiple platforms, and more rapid solution-development cycles, an Exchange administrator will be expected to create functional messaging solutions rather than to connect physical systems. In this chapter, to provide a conceptual framework, we will describe network-management models and architectures for information brokerage as well as messaging technologies. In future chapters, we will incorporate Microsoft's Enterprise Services Frameworks to help you analyze real-world and case study problems, as well as provide solutions using field-tested methodologies.

A discussion about how to locate and retrieve bits of knowledge amassed over the 30-odd years since the Internet began will range from email messages and public file sharing to Presence and Instant Messaging (IM). As an underlying technology, Exchange Server has often been relegated to "nothing more than" a messaging service provider. From its inception in 1996, however, this BackOffice product has been described as a platform for the "exchange" of data; today, it's called "information brokering." In fact, in Microsoft.NET, you will see that Exchange 2000, the first of the new breed of BackOffice products (now collectively called .NET servers), assumes a fundamental role as the premier platform for communication and collaboration across your business enterprise and beyond.

Note: In this book, the term "Exchange Server" refers to the generic Microsoft messaging product Exchange 2000 Enterprise Server. Any other versions or Exchange Server products will be specifically referenced as, for example, Exchange 2000 Server (the edition designed for small- to medium-sized organizations) or Exchange 5.5 Server (the legacy product). Sometimes, only the version number will be referenced, as in version 4 or version 5.5. When a reference is made to an actual server in, for example, a case study, the term "Exchange Enterprise server" will be used.

The drive behind both the architectural changes in Exchange 2000 and the .NET initiative is a result of the Internet's success and the digital economy's push for more efficient technologies that access increasingly broader, more diverse information infrastructures. Exchange 2000 is a software product that marks a change in business model, functional design, and architecture. For example, as an Exchange administrator managing a variety of data stores, the on-demand development of specialized business solutions may very likely dominate your working day. Information technologies are no longer monolithic, one-solution packages; they are distributed services that can be permuted in infinite ways. Your preparation, especially to be certified on Exchange 2000, is greatly affected by this change in design strategy and marketing plan. Microsoft, unlike companies like Sun, IBM, Novell, and Oracle, does not focus as much on providing technical services as it does on building software products and the solution frameworks that support them. In fact, its primary focus regarding these frameworks is on best practices related to architecture, development, and operations.

Beginning with Windows 2000 and products like Exchange 2000, Microsoft is shifting to a new, more encompassing technology with its .NET initiative. The stated goal of the .NET platform is to provide seamless interoperability with *any* Web-enabled resource. The adjective "any" in the paraphrased Microsoft slogan "access from any device, at anytime, from anywhere" is what makes this .NET initiative so challenging and the job description of an Exchange administrator more demanding than previous versions of the Exchange product. Beginning with the release of Exchange 4 in March 1996, Microsoft has continued to position this "messaging server" as the fundamental service provider of communication, collaboration, and workflow automation within and beyond the enterprise space. Exchange Server 2000, working synergistically with Active Directory (AD) and Internet Information Services, plays a major role in this new network operating system (NOS) initiative.

Microsoft's shift in technology paradigm changes the role of Exchange administrator from fixing, for example, bandwidth bottlenecks to applying solution frameworks within which "best-of-breed" technology snap-ins provide specific e-commerce business solutions. In many business situations, you will be expected to not just achieve, but to maintain "five 9" reliability (99.99999 percent uptime) for mission-critical, line-of-business (LOB) applications. There is no time for you to "reinvent the wheel" to manage a problem situation. The subtle but significant emphasis on IT "architect" rather than IT "plumber" is shaping the nature of the testing methods (from multiple-choice questions to case studies), the scope of the exam (Exam 70-224, "Installing, Configuring, and Administering Microsoft Exchange 2000"), and the skills necessary to function as a competent Exchange administrator. This book will provide you with both a useful framework within which to achieve competency and the information you need to design and deploy a reliable, enterprise-scale messaging infrastructure.

What Is Knowledge?

Knowledge in this book is defined in operational rather than philosophical terms. We use the commonly held definition of knowledge as accumulated data and information that we have in our conscious experience or that we have some method to retrieve. We extend this to KM, which refers to administering and manipulating the "collective experience" of an enterprise or organization. Although the concept of "knowledge" may have changed with paradigm shifts and improvements in technology through the history of humankind, the possessors of knowledge remain the same: people and the system they use to record data. Thus, any KM system includes both accessible data and some form of user collaboration in "interpreting" that data. Even the most sophisticated contemporary data mining yields nothing more than significant information; people make the final translation of information to knowledge. KM has come to the forefront as a paradigm because our current computer technology provides "connections" between people and digitized resources.

If knowledge is defined as the connection between people and information, then business organizations must incorporate new technologies to leverage this all-important communicative and collaborative "exchange" and to generate the greatest return on investment of their own data. Information through email, voice mail, office documentation, video, and any other forms of electronically encoded data must be accessible from anywhere at any time through any client device. Management of this kind of knowledge store also requires the need to administer, audit, and monitor the efficiency of processing this "business asset." The NET initiative calls for all .NET servers—which include Windows 2000, BizTalk 2000, SQL Server 2000, Exchange 2000, Commerce Server 2000, and the Internet Security and Acceleration Server 2000—to expose system-related events through Windows Management Instrumentation (WMI) so that as the enterprise expands, management of both NOS and service provider will scale with it.

Windows DNA—A Management Model

Microsoft's Distributed InterNet Applications Architecture (Windows DNA) describes tightly coupled Web-based applications as user (presentation) interfaces, business logic, and data services in a three-tier architectural model; see Figure 1.3. The .NET framework extends this structure by replacing these tightly bound applications with a more loosely coupled architecture of distributed services using, for example, cross-process communication protocols like Extensible Markup Language (XML) and Simple Object Access Protocol (SOAP). The User (Presentation) layer remains, however, typically separate from the Business Logic and Data Services layers. These multitier applications can request access to system services programmatically through well-known application programming interfaces (APIs) such as Microsoft Messaging API (MAPI), and, for example, the Component Object

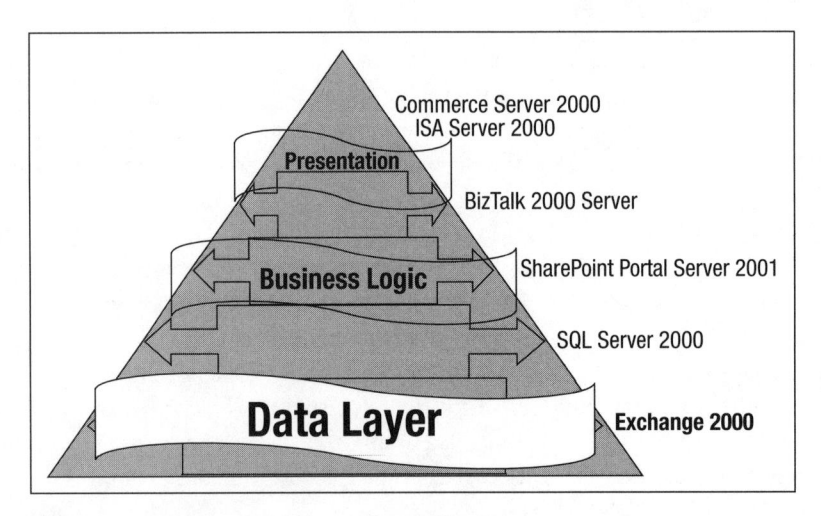

Figure 1.3 A functional multitier service architecture.

Model (COM). Standardized access to system or application services simplifies the design process and minimizes functional redundancy as well as coding errors.

The International Organization of Standardization (ISO) has defined a network management model called Common Management Information Services and Protocol Over TCP/IP (we use CMIS to refer to the management model and CMOT to refer to the network protocol) architecture—Request for Comments (RFC) 1095. This model, shown in Figure 1.4, describes the CMOT protocol stack and shows the layers from Application Entity down through Presentation layer to the Physical layer and actual network path or channel. We use this model as a frame of reference when we discuss Exchange architecture in future chapters. Pay particular attention to generic components and how they interact with each other in their respective models. These generic components and their functional roles create an operating system-independent, protocol-independent architectural context within which you can quickly analyze and understand most, if not all, contemporary service-providing software. As an IT "architect," you need to rapidly "assimilate" how new software products work and interact so that you can provide your employer with the appropriate business solutions at the lowest TCO.

Common Management Information Services (CMIS)

The venerable Open Systems Interconnection (OSI) Reference Model continues to help network administrators isolate functional areas within a networking framework. However, CMIS provides a generic architecture that focuses primarily on controlling and monitoring information exchanged between some "manager" and some remote "agent" in that networked environment. It also defines two different network protocols, CMOT and the more popular Simple Network Management Protocol (SNMP)—RFC 2959. The latter protocol is an important emerging standard in the IT literature, especially in areas of remote monitoring and administration.

The CMIS model, shown in Figure 1.5, defines five specific management functional areas (SMFAs) found in all 32-bit NOSs. The CMIS model categorizes these

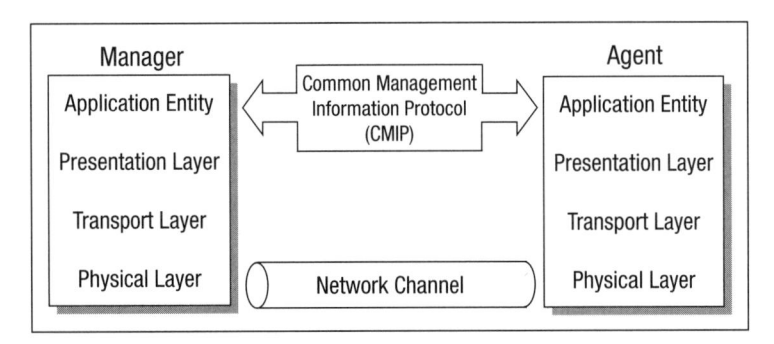

Figure 1.4 The CMOT protocol stack.

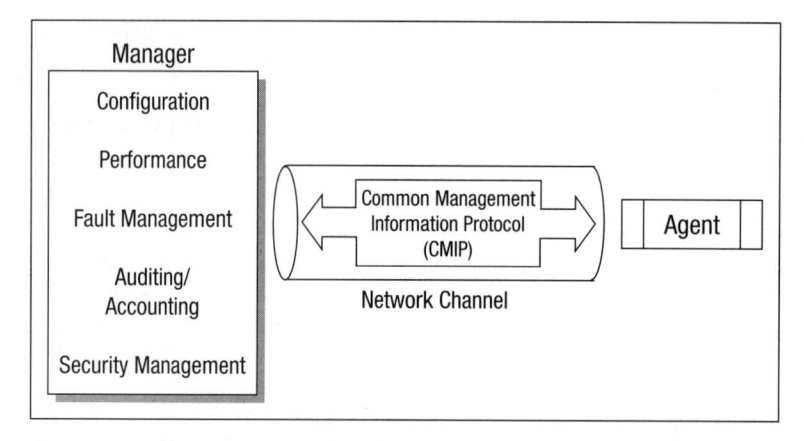

Figure 1.5 A listing of CMIS specific management functional areas (SMFAs).

functions but does not describe how they perform their specific roles to ensure their applicability across as many NOSs as possible. As an IT practitioner, you can use this model to differentiate functional roles in new service-providing software you encounter. In general, SMFAs can be described as the following:

- *Configuration-management services*—Where an event takes place
- *Performance-management services*—How an event takes place
- *Fault-management services*—What response takes place in response to a given action
- *Auditing/accounting-management services*—When an event takes place
- *Security-management services*—Who performs the event

In fact, the first two SMFAs have been present, at least in some rudimentary form, in even the earlier disk operating systems (DOSs), such as Digital Research's Control Program for Microprocessors (CP/M), Microsoft's Disk Operating System (MS-DOS), Digital Research's Disk Operating System (DR-DOS), and IBM's Personal Computer Disk Operating System (PC-DOS). Obviously, the key distinguishing factor between a DOS and a NOS is the inclusion of the last two SMFAs, auditing/accounting- and security-management services. Models like CMIS help us conceptualize how information technologies are built and interact in increasing complex digital environments. We distinguish between the roles of "management service" (sometimes shortened to "manager") and "agent" from that of a "client." An "agent" is preconfigured to perform some automated task for some specific management service without user intervention, whereas a "client" typically provides a broader feature set requiring user-defined configuration.

Generic Architecture for Information Availability (GAIA)

The CMIS model provides a network-management structure and was a useful resource to the IT "plumber" throughout the time of the Information-Sharing Paradigm. Windows 2000 with its distributed-services architecture, however, provides a new assortment of issues. In, for example, the world of Microsoft.NET, we encounter service-providing software that is multitier in structure and service oriented in function. In the Knowledge-Management Paradigm, there are new functional roles called consumers, brokers, and service providers. These generic roles of specific IT service providers are applicable at many different layers of the OSI Reference Model and help provide a necessary context to analyze complex events.

GAIA describes the roles and operations involved in locating, requesting, and receiving digital resources and services (collectively called "products") in a globally brokered distributed information environment. Figure 1.6 shows a model based on GAIA architecture; we use the roles of consumer, broker, and service provider to describe the environment. In addition to the three main roles (GAIA defines these roles as customer, broker, and supplier), there is a helper role, which can be described as an application software layer that assists in the mediation of the "service" transaction. These helpers are independent of and complementary to the role of the broker. In GAIA terms, helpers could provide functional support—such as global directory services, payment services, or authentication/authorization services—to the broker. Within any one service, we return to our CMIS model to define, in more molecular terms, in what SMFA the helper provides these particular services. Notice how our emphasis has shifted exclusively to function rather than structure.

We use the term "broker" because the GAIA model deals with discrete transactions called *actions*. In the Knowledge-Management Paradigm, you need to consider the more complex, distributed-services environment where one consumer contacts one or more brokers for some relatively simple "product" such as ordering a book online. In the Information-Sharing Paradigm, this product would most likely be a simple request for a service. In complex situations, the request for that service

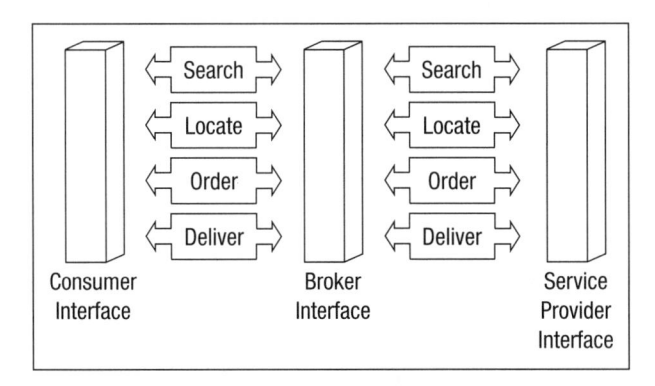

Figure 1.6 A model of GAIA-like roles and actions.

would be passed or "delegated" to a second, more appropriate service provider. In the Knowledge-Management Paradigm, however, the consumer can request a more complex "product," such as a Human Resources information file of some employee, which requires the contribution of many component services from many independent and physically distributed service providers. The broker mediates this transaction for the consumer.

GAIA transactions are composed of one or more specific actions defined in generic terms, such as search, locate, order, and deliver. The broker performs as a single front-end object for the consumer; it transparently coordinates all the back-end transactions, no matter how they are physically distributed. This front-end/back-end (FE/BE), distributed-services structure is a major architectural feature of Exchange 2000.

Microsoft Operations Framework (MOF)

Microsoft has described Exchange 2000 messaging and collaboration as three separate feature categories: messaging, messages, and messengers. These categories refer to messaging as the Exchange infrastructure (what are called management services in the CMIS and GAIA models), the messages as the information "product" held in data stores, and the messengers as the service-providing clients (what are called CMIS agents and GAIA consumers and service providers, described in later parts of this book). We use a different set of categories to distinguish functional roles from structural roles to better emphasize the overlapping perspectives that you must assume as an Exchange administrator.

The tightly-coupled, distributed-services architecture called Windows DNA has been conceived as a digital nervous system where many independent and physically separate processes run in concert to provide some computer-related service. We can use a similar biological metaphor for our study of Exchange 2000. To administer and maintain the proper functioning of the entire human body, you study physiology apart from anatomy. Exchange 2000 design allows us to similarly uncouple administrative services from the network infrastructure, which includes network topology and physical connectivity issues. The two complementary perspectives of function and structure are useful when you are working through Exchange 2000 service solutions and service-management issues, both on an exam and in the real world, because they reinforce the idea that an enterprise messaging infrastructure is an organizational "body" with a functional whole that is greater than the sum of its structural components. In fact, this analogy of these two complementary perspectives plays a prominent role in understanding the Microsoft Operations Framework (MOF), a support model that provides comprehensive guidance for achieving reliability, availability, supportability, and manageability of enterprise-based software products and technologies. This model uses concepts outlined in the IT Infrastructure Library (ITIL) of best practices for IT service management compiled by the Central Computer and Telecommunications Agency (CCTA) in the United Kingdom.

MOF, along with Microsoft Readiness Framework (MRF) and Microsoft Solutions Framework (MSF), form the Enterprise Services Framework (ESF), a collection that targets different aspects of the IT life cycle from preparation (MRF) through planning and building (MSF) to management (MOF). Figure 1.7 shows the Microsoft ESF and the IT Infrastructure Library. This book and the certification exam it prepares you for are most intimately involved with the operations framework. Our functional perspective corresponds to both Microsoft's service management concept and the ITIL, where problem management (PM) attempts to minimize the impact of failures through the accrual of information during incident resolution. PM consists of collecting information through three major activities:

➤ *Incident control*—The rapid restoration of normal service following disruption

➤ *Problem control*—The isolation of the root cause of the incident

➤ *Error control*—The subsequent activities necessary to prevent future disruptions of service

In addition to the above management areas, Microsoft includes several more service-oriented activities in its approach to PM, including:

➤ *Help desk support*—This is the interface between the IT team and the user community through first-line incident control in general PM.

➤ *Configuration management*—This provides details of configuration items that have been identified during the PM process as the cause of incidents and problems. The configuration management system also allows you to relate errors and change requests.

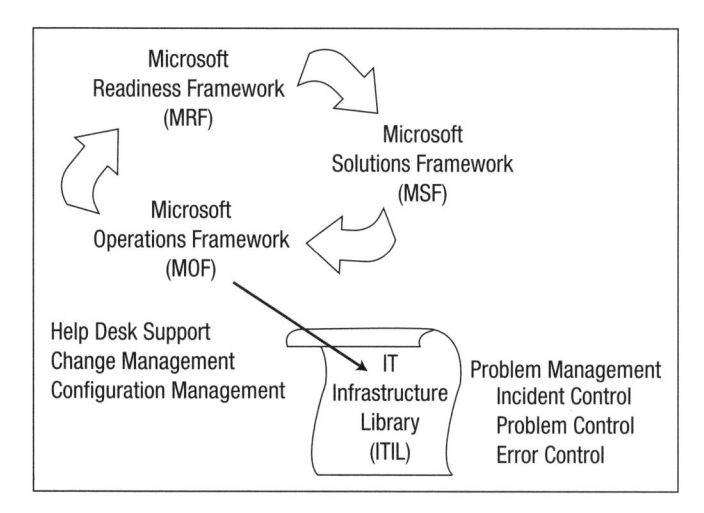

Figure 1.7 The ESF and the IT Infrastructure Library.

➤ *Change management*—This is similar to error control, mentioned earlier. This area covers the process of controlling changes, including those needed to correct errors that PM error control has identified.

Our discussions of the structural components of Exchange 2000, as well as our approach to Windows 2000, is from a service-oriented perspective. Exchange 2000 provides messaging and collaborative capabilities or business functions as service solutions, such as:

➤ LOB applications

➤ KM

➤ Messaging and data storage

➤ Archiving and information publishing

Recognizing what solution can be provided and how it is managed form an organic whole. As such, these are some of the skills Microsoft measures in its certification exam process. In addition to detailed discussions of Exchange 2000 infrastructure, this book will use the MOF methods and models in providing you with guidance in dealing with the operational interaction of people, process, and technology from a functional perspective.

We will show you how various hardware technologies ensure that mission-critical messaging services and "five 9" service level agreements (SLAs) run across a globally distributed enterprise. In fact, the administration of Exchange 2000 relies upon your understanding of Windows 2000 topology as well as AD directory services. Unlike with versions of Exchange that ran on legacy NT 4, the successful deployment of Exchange 2000 totally depends on a well-designed enterprise namespace and an efficiently functioning NOS platform. Beginning with Chapter 2, the real-world projects at the end of chapters provide exercises in real-world scenarios that demonstrate many of these points to you.

Electronic Messaging Concepts

You can think of electronic messaging as the simple delivery of information from point A to, at least, some single point B. In fact, a messaging system has specific characteristics, such as:

➤ A message source and one or more message recipients

➤ The delivery of messages as an asynchronous process

The dispatch of the message to target recipient, in other words, implies eventual delivery of the message or, after some reasonable period of time or number of attempts, notification of nondelivery. An *asynchronous process* here is defined as the independence between when the message is sent and when it is received. The design of an asynchronous messaging system has mutated with progressive changes in technology. Messaging products were historically shared-file systems where the message server hosted some shared folder called a mailbox for each named user known to the messaging system. These folder structures were passive repositories; the flow of messages depended on messaging-system clients to move mail to or from these central data stores. The host server or General Post Office (GPO) plays no active role in the flow of messages in products such as Microsoft (MS) Mail; it is strictly a data store.

With the specialization of function and the development of multitier architecture, the host server assumed a growing participatory role in providing messaging services. Exchange Server was, from its initial release, an example of a client/server messaging system. The host assumes an active role in providing the following services:

- Administering the messaging directory database
- Administering the messaging data stores
- Managing inbound and outbound message routing

In the simple two-tier client/server architecture most prevalent during the Information-Sharing Paradigm, you can begin to see the need for further differentiation of function to increase performance, improve scalability, and provide fault tolerance. As multitier architecture has taken hold, availability of new features and enhanced services has significantly increased.

In general and for the purposes of this book, the messaging system is considered in its entirety to be the collection of all messaging-related objects and includes client software, the communication infrastructure, the structure of the hosting servers, and the messaging software. With advances in hardware technology, differentiation of server architecture has coincided with differentiation of services the messaging software has provided. One hosting server can handle many client requests; services within the messaging software process these requests independently and in parallel. Though one process handles only one task, simultaneous multiprocessing within any one service on separate hosting platforms exponentially enhances capacity, performance, and reliability and improves upon even the best-of-breed legacy messaging architectures.

An *electronic message* refers to any kind of electronically transmitted data, such as text message, fax, video, or voice. *Electronic mail*, or *email*, is a single type of message; many other kinds of message types are now available to us in multimedia modalities other than text. An email message is a container object composed of the following four components:

- *Header*—This topmost section displays information about the email message to the message's recipient and is present in both incoming and outgoing messages. In a generic email message, both a destination in the form of a To: and a source in the form of a From: are necessary. When you compose a message, you are the source. Optional fields such as courtesy copy, Cc:, and blind copy, Bcc:, are available. Though also optional, a subject line, Subject:, is usually used to describe or summarize the contents or intent of the message.

➤ *Body*—This middle section component is the actual payload of the mail message that contains the message itself. Though not limited by default, best practices recommend that the common size limit for this part of the message should not exceed 1MB because of performance issues. A message over this size is more efficiently sent using File Transfer Protocol (FTP). Many mail systems and Internet Service Providers (ISPs) impose their own size limits that could prevent successful delivery of an oversized mail message.

➤ *Signature*—This bottom section of the message typically contains information that identifies the sender; the email program usually appends this to the message.

➤ *Attachment*—This external payload provides a method for transferring both documents and infectious viruses. It can be handled in many different ways or actually stripped from the message depending on the recipient mail server's policies.

Recipient is a term we use to describe the most basic administrative unit in the Exchange system. Recipient usually represents a mailbox. An administrator typically manages a collection of mailboxes, the final destination of a message. Messaging systems store messages in an area called the *message store*. Client software accesses the data stored in these message stores. A *directory* is a listing of recipients. In Exchange 2000, recipients are AD objects that include users, groups, and contacts. Recipients can be either mail enabled or mail aware. Windows 2000 AD has changed the way many recipients are managed in an enterprise. In fact, legacy systems like version 5.5 grouped recipients based on physical topology. However, Exchange 2000 has uncoupled the organization of recipients based on structural considerations and allows organizations to group the collection of Exchange servers and their objects in a more intuitive manner that more readily accommodates real-world needs. Thus, although Administrative Groups are collections of servers and objects that share some common administrative function or purpose, Routing Groups similarly describe a collection of servers in terms of network connectivity.

Connectors are software that provide gateway or funneling services between separate Routing Groups or to other email systems; they can be either internal managers or external helpers. An email system or service external to an Exchange organization is considered a foreign email system. The connector manages the translation of different mail formats across different systems. Active Directory Connector (ADC) is an example of the service that replicates information between a legacy Exchange 5.5 directory and AD directory services. This connector uses a connection agreement that defines the replication configuration.

Email addressing schemes refer to specific addressing formats of Internet mail. For example, a Simple Mail Transfer Protocol (SMTP) address is ***recipient@domain***. Though less common, other addressing formats like X.400 are still encountered on host-based email systems.

Communication between a client and a server is mediated through some interface called an application programming interface (API). You can also consider this software layer a helper service, though it is typically integrated with some underlying management function. Many APIs have been developed to promote interoperability. For example, Active Directory Services Interface (ADSI) allows COM-compatible programming languages to make directory calls to AD directory services. Another important API is MAPI, which is tightly integrated with both Windows and Exchange. Similarly, Collaboration Data Objects provide programmatic access to both SMTP and Network News Transfer Protocol (NNTP) running on Windows 2000.

Other Information-Management Models

Our discussion of information models has grown progressively more specific. We began with CMIS in describing specific functional areas within any network-management system. We then used the GAIA model—the roles of consumer, broker, and service provider—to suggest a more appropriate concept within the Knowledge-Management Paradigm. At the same time, we have explained that Exchange 2000 uncouples functional services from structural components, thereby providing further differentiation of both layers independent of the other. This dichotomy of function versus structure is important when you assume the role of Exchange administrator. You must somehow balance considerations of both physical architecture and function services with the needs of your client or your organization's corporate objectives. Though they are separate areas of medical science, physiology and anatomy equally contribute to the optimal functioning of the human organism.

The following models provide a historical perspective on how messaging systems have been conceptualized according to published standards. The original design of Exchange was based on the published X.400 standard and was mostly proprietary in nature, but it has since taken a more pragmatic turn in design toward greater network connectivity and broader standards-based protocol support. In fact, with the release of Exchange 2000, you see extensive Internet message support on top of an exposed, reliable, extensible, and scalable message store of enterprise proportions.

The X.400 and X.500 Message-Handling Models

This message-handling model is defined by the Telecommunication Standardization Sector of the International Telecommunication Union (ITU-T), formerly Comité Consultatif International Téléphonique et Télégraphique (CCITT). The ITU-T is the primary international body for telecommunications equipment and systems standards. The X.400 protocol model is proposed in a collection of publications ranging from X.400 to X.440; the actual protocol specifications are X.411, X.413, X.419, and X.420, whereas the most popular version is a revision of the 1984 standards jointly published by ITU-T and ISO in 1988. RFCs 1615 and 1616 discuss the deployment of X.400/88.

*Note: You can reference technical issues that specifically relate to Microsoft products from several Internet locations. A common source of technical references can be found at **www.microsoft.com/technet,** the online versions of Microsoft's subscription services, TechNet. Alternatively, Requests For Comments can be found at **ftp://ftp.isi.edu/in-notes/rfcxxxx.txt**, where xxxx is the RFC reference number. For example, RFC 1615 would be located using **ftp://ftp.isi.edu/in-notes/rfc1615.txt**.*

The three architectural components in an X.400 message handling system—User Agent (UA), Message Transfer Agent (MTA), and Message Store (MS), which Microsoft calls the Information Store (IS)—are shown in Figure 1.8 on the left side and center of the exhibit. Compared to the MS Mail design, you see that the UA was the original client software and that the MTA corresponds to the External or

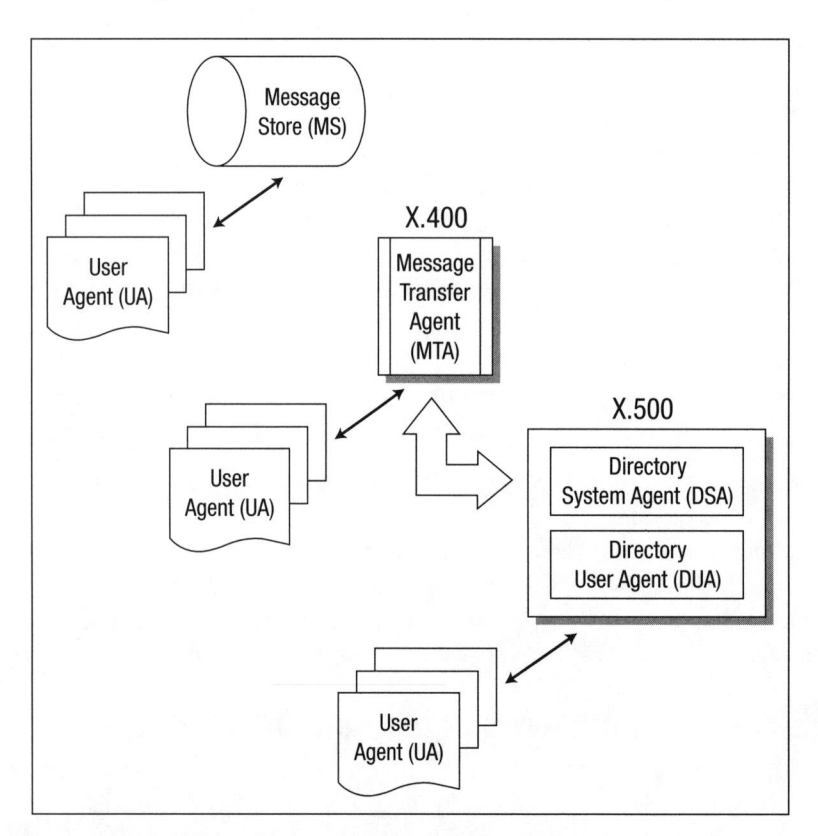

Figure 1.8 The X.400 and X.500 message-handling models.

Dispatch program that managed mail transfer outside the GPO. Unlike the GPO in MS Mail, the IS, composed of both a public and a private information store, services Exchange users within its own immediate namespace. The MTA is an Exchange service that processes messages outside the boundaries of the IS within the Exchange architecture. In addition, specialized connectors (sometimes called *gateways*) exchange messages across dissimilar protocols and between remote Exchange sites within an administrative grouping of servers called an *organization*. It is significant that the IS is an active component that manages its own namespace defined by the mailboxes it contains rather than a passive folder and file system. Furthermore, the messaging system is extensible and allows you to add connectors that attach to the system without making major structural changes to provide remote connectivity services.

X.400 has gained the acceptance of the standards community and provided the basic design for a messaging server. However, another protocol first defined in 1982—SMTP—is accepted as the de facto standard because it is simpler to use and has user interfaces in the public domain (RFCs 821 and 822). In fact, SMTP now installs automatically on all Exchange 2000 servers as a basic transport service. The importance of SMTP and Extended SMTP (ESMTP) as a substitute for remote procedure calls (RPCs) in server-to-server communications will be discussed in Chapter 10.

Figure 1.8 also shows two other architectural components: a Directory System Agent (DSA) and Directory User Agent (DUA), with the latter interacting specifically with the X.400 MTA on the right side of the exhibit. Another ITU-T standard cited in RFC 1330 describes the role of these two "directory" components within the concept of global directory services, collectively called the X.500 standard, which provide the following enhancements to the messaging model:

➤ Decentralized management

➤ Robust search capabilities

➤ A single namespace

➤ Structured information storage

The X.500 directory services model is standards based and provides a framework for developing an electronic directory of users in an organization collectively called a *namespace*. You can conceptualize this model—which has also been referred to as global White Pages, referring to the common listing of telephone numbers in some local region in any part of the world—as a "name" resolution service. The objective of publishing such a standard is to make these regional directories somehow accessible to a unified global directory listing of people, resources, and services. In the X.500 context, local directories are the DSAs mentioned above, which in turn reference different parts of some larger-scale Directory Information Tree (DIT).

DUAs, such as command-line utilities like Whois and Finger, request directory services through their "local" DSA. Although a single, unified global directory might be impossible to attain because of fundamental geopolitical differences, a more practical future goal is a standards-based, universal directory, or namespace that allows for you to commingle different proprietary namespaces (as in a federation of sovereign states).

There is an increasing trend toward the design of consolidated directory services to simplify requests for the resolution of "names" within and across networked systems. In fact, both Microsoft's AD and Novell's Novell Directory Services (NDS) have made this goal of providing this universal directory service their stated corporate objective. X.500 services were originally conceived as unifying X.400 messaging systems. Centralized directory access simplifies design of software that needs to resolve names, but it also promotes interoperability across messaging platforms. Exchange 2000, unlike its application server predecessors, is the first product in the BackOffice software suite that provides a streamlined design for the delivery of specialized services. It has delegated directory services to a more specialized NOS component—Active Directory—and thus has:

➤ Simplified the deployment of messaging services by reducing redundant directory functionality—specifically, Exchange Directory Services and AD directory services

➤ Provided for fault-tolerance of directory services by replicating directory information across the enterprise

➤ Enhanced NOS interoperability by consolidating this mission-critical information in an enterprise network service rather than a messaging service

Throughout your study of Exchange 2000, you will need to understand how messaging and collaborative services interact with three separate administrative areas: the Exchange 2000 administrative area, the Windows 2000 network substrate, and the ubiquitous AD directory services. Features and administrative responsibilities relating to directory services were conceptualized from four functional perspectives in the original X.500 specifications:

➤ *Information model*—What the information is

➤ *Functional model*—How the information is handled

➤ *Organization model*—How the information is organized

➤ *Security model*—Who can use the information

We will use similar reference models in describing the Exchange 2000 and network administrative roles throughout this book. Those people assigned administrative responsibilities involving Exchange, Active Directory directory services, and NOS support services in fact often conflict because of these groups have, in fact, different scope and service objectives. Exchange or messaging administrators typically scope the entire enterprise in terms of providing messaging services and benchmark the message flows against defined SLAs. Network administrators alternatively compare NOS performance against a different set of SLAs and literally orchestrate the interaction of many layered services provided by assorted servers with characteristically different workloads. Those who administer AD directory services have responsibilities that similarly fall somewhere between the two other support areas, messaging and NOS, though with a clear bias toward an enterprise-wide perspective. In fact, often a group of administrators handles all three areas at one time even though objectives may differ.

Figure 1.9 shows the dependency of many mission-critical services upon AD in a Windows 2000 enterprise environment. Exchange 2000, like all these other mission-critical services, including directory services, relies on mutual dependencies and linkages. In fact, not only does the SMTP service depend on Internet Information Server (IIS), Exchange IS, and the Exchange System Attendant (SA) but AD itself also uses SMTP for AD replication. Both of these systems, from a functional perspective, have grown complex.

Preparation for Exchange 2000 (prerelease code name Platinum) actually begins with Exchange 5.5. Understanding this still-popular version of Exchange will significantly impact your success in rapidly acquiring competency on Exchange 2000 and, in fact, will enhance your knowledge of Windows 2000 and AD. AD and the Exchange 5.5 Directory Store (DS) share so many architectural similarities that some consider AD to be an enterprise-wide DS or directory data store. The complexity of transitioning from version 5.5, which exclusively manages directory objects to enterprise-wide directory services, is discussed in Chapter 16.

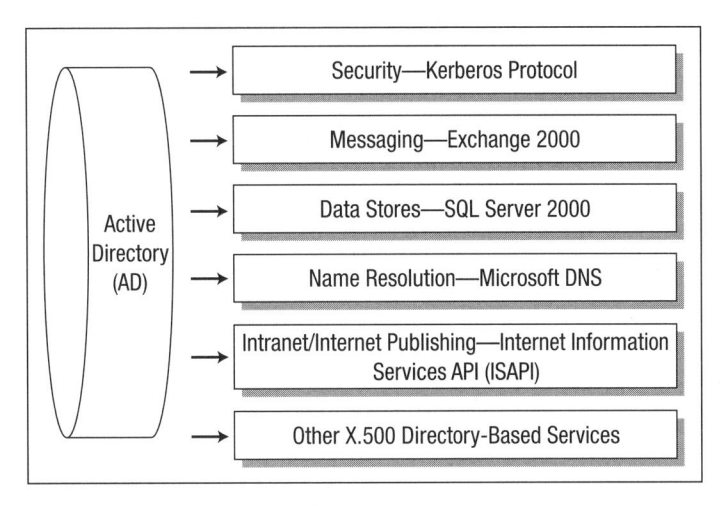

Figure 1.9 AD-dependent services.

A Storage Technology—Microsoft Repository

The design of .NET servers like Exchange 2000 reflects greater functional specialization than NT 4 service-providing applications because directory-related services are consolidated in the NOS. Identity and permission management in these software packages are either removed or left primarily for backward compatibility. In fact, the NOS handles mission-critical activities like authentication and authorization more efficiently than the specific service-providing software. You need to understand NOS directory services and storage management design and deployment before you install Exchange 2000 or any other service-providing packages on an enterprise production platform.

Before we delve into more architectural details, we'll cover another software product, Microsoft Repository, which will help you acquire a better understanding of the design changes involved in the transformation of Exchange 5.5 into Exchange 2000. Microsoft Repository is composed of two basic components:

➤ *A library of COM interfaces*—This provides access to what is called Open Information Model (OIM), a collection of standards-based programming conventions that deal with software development and warehousing issues. These conventions have facilitated the development of common tools such as the Unified Modeling Language (UML), the development of reusable software components, multidimensional online analytical processing (OLAP) databases, and semantic models.

➤ *A repository engine*—This provides the storage mechanism for these models. This engine is a key component of both Exchange 2000 and the legacy Microsoft Joint Engine Technology (JET) database systems, which include both system and application services like Exchange 5 (JET Blue) and Access (JET Red).

An information model is a catalog or schema of the types of data objects as well as the relationships among the objects with the application's universe. Microsoft Repository provides an extensible interface using COM, the older ActiveX interfaces, and the sharing of components developed by independent software vendors. As enterprises grow and merge, extensibility and flexibility are critical to maintain the flow of timely information. Microsoft Repository is a fundamental component of Microsoft's digital nervous system initiative. Managing metadirectories that consolidate directory access will provide the foundation for all future Microsoft initiatives, including Microsoft.NET. The repository technology provides yet another common software substrate with nonproprietary data structure and semantics in keeping with Microsoft's focus on functional interfaces—API, Transport Driver Interface (TDI), and Network Device Interface Specification (NDIS). As in many other areas of Windows 2000—Microsoft Cryptographic API (CAPI), Security Support Provider Interface (SSPI), and Public Key Infrastructure (PKI)—the use of the standards-based OIM positions a product like Microsoft Repository, or any other product that uses this technology, as a foundation upon which to base all future Web application development.

Note: *Acronyms such as API, TDI, NDIS, CAPI, SSPI, and PKI are common in the literature. Microsoft assumes that certification candidates have greater familiarity with its Windows 2000 products than in the past—one to two years of real-world experience, to be precise. Acronyms are not just common but essential in the real world.*

A repository-based service provider must be readily extensible in the application development and data warehousing areas. Access to and interchange with repository stores will incorporate COM, SQL, and Extensible Markup Language (XML) as standards-based forms of programmable data-store management. It is interesting that in July 1997, Microsoft, following the release of Microsoft Repository 1, began the collaborative development and marketing of Microsoft Repository 2. The name of its collaborative partner in the development of repository technology is PLATINUM technology, Inc.

The First Wide Area Network (WAN)

Before there were models describing how messages might be passed from server to server, and prior to development of technologies that stored these messages between routed hops from one system server to another, the first wide area network (WAN) was built. A connection between two California universities grew into an internetwork that spans the earth, and it provided services soon after its inception that embellished on the simple exchange of strings of text.

In 1962, the Rand Corporation released a secret report to the U.S. Military titled "On Distributed Communications Networks" that proposed a decentralized communication model. This networking scheme had no single central command or control center and thus was one of the first proposals of a fault-tolerant network. Beginning in the late 1960s, the Department of Defense, believing that any enemy attack would destroy only part of a "national network" but allow the remaining whole to continue to function, commissioned the Advanced Research Projects Agency to build such a network, called ARPAnet. The first two operational nodes were at the University of California at Los Angeles and Stanford Research Institute (SRI) in California in 1969. One of the first programs that was run on this prototypical WAN exchanged two characters, an L and an O, between the two linked sites before the system crashed. This was the first electronic messaging program. As the ARPAnet grew into the National Science Foundation network, NSFnet, researchers called the "inter-connecting" of networks "inter-networking"; this eventually was shortened to "the Internet." With the development of TCP/IP between 1974 and 1982, email programs were considered the network "killer app." In addition, more than any other software technology, it forced an exponential growth in the boundaries of what was then known as The Matrix and the transitioning from basic data processing to sharing information and collaboration across a network.

Note: Although the concept of a distributed and fault-tolerant (attack-proof) packet-switching network was considered by many parties here in the United States, the National Physical Laboratory in Great Britain was the first to establish a working packet-switching network prototype in 1968.

Email standards were formulated as email systems grew in popularity and bridged physical continents and logical operating systems. Unix-to-Unix Copy (UUCP) provided the transfer of text messages using the American Standard Code for Information Interchange (ASCII) character set. The 8-bit word length on which it was based was functional but unfortunately did not support non-English symbols (such as diacritical markings), images, sounds, or richly formatted text. As The Matrix spread to non-English-speaking countries, new standards arose. UUEncode/UUDEcode, another Unix utility, successfully transmitted non-ASCII, binary files (such as executable programs and images), but it wasn't until Multipurpose Internet Mail Extensions (MIME) was proposed in September 1993 as RFC 1521 that multiple character sets, images, and binary files could be sent across dissimilar mail systems.

Online Information Services Beyond Email

Microsoft, especially since Exchange 5.5, has consolidated many nonmail information-sharing services that have existed online for many years. X.500 (RFC 1580) actually supports data-management services like addition, modification, and deletion of data entries, as well as powerful search capabilities. Most literature refers to X.500 as a service that provides querying of information on people (principals) in some organization or namespace; in fact, it can broker other information-sharing services.

Many of the following services have been incorporated into the Exchange 2000 feature list:

➤ *LISTSERV*—An online service that provides distribution list management. It automates the one-way distribution of documentation (for example, a newsletter) to users with a common interest. Users elect to subscribe or unsubscribe to this communication system by notifying the LISTSERV "service provider."

➤ *NETNEWS (originally called Usenet in 1979)*—A bidirectional, worldwide message-sharing system that publishes messages, organized into newsgroups, in some standardized format. Published messages, categorized by their headers, can be both plain text and encoded binary information. Newsgroups can have a moderator who scans messages before they are distributed.

➤ *PROSPERO*—A global, distributed virtual file system that publishes virtual file structures, with user-defined names, mapped to physical file systems.

➤ *Internet Relay Chat*—A global, realtime, multichanneled, conversational system similar to the **talk** or **send** command on local area networks (LANs). The system is divided into separate "party lines" in which any one transmitted text-based message is seen by users who are on that same channel.

Exchange as Messaging Service Provider

As seen thus far in this chapter, several emerging trends and themes are reshaping your approach to and study of Windows 2000, and consequently Exchange 2000. Some of these trends are as follows:

- The driving force of e-commerce and the use of a common information infrastructure
- The extensibility and scalability of any NOS
- Consolidation of identity management in a metadirectory
- Integration of the online Internet services with NOS
- The growing prominence of distributed-services network architecture
- An emphasis on quantitative benchmarks like TCO, as well as SLAs

Each new version of the three major NOS "cultures"—Microsoft, Novell, and the Unix dialects—shows a greater ability to interoperate in an e-commerce environment, as well as communicate, collaborate, and control information exchanged across the Internet. To help you stay competitive in this rapidly changing profession, the remainder of this chapter identifies some key themes, emerging trends, and de facto standards. For example, the major NOSs now all use a common transport protocol: TCP/IP. Domain Name System (DNS), in general, is now the common form of name resolution. Specific functional management areas such as identity management, permission management, performance management, fault management, and auditing are now distributed both horizontally across the enterprise namespace, as well as vertically within the infrastructure of the specific NOS. The seven-layer OSI Reference Model, though over 30 years old, is still valuable in distinguishing the distinct conceptual layers at which a specific functional management area operates. For example, Windows 2000 Internet Protocol Security (IPSec) functions specifically at the OSI Network layer, whereas the Microsoft Kerberos protocol works at the OSI Application layer.

A second theme regarding the uncoupling of network topology from functional services is similar to the dichotomy of anatomy and physiology in the biological sciences. This separation, especially in Windows 2000, is fostering the emergence of specialties, each using new and different troubleshooting tools, techniques, and strategies. Although the NT 4 "general practitioner" encountered superficially similar problems, situations encountered in an e-commerce environment related to multitier application architecture are far more complex to analyze. Mission-critical services can extend not only horizontally across various hosting service providers throughout the enterprise, but also vertically down into the networking infrastructure of any single local machine. A Windows 2000 administrator may grapple with deploying and maintaining, for example, a Virtual Private Network

(VPN) and realtime collaboration. To perform their jobs competently, network administrators will require a thorough knowledge of how the horizontal and vertical dependencies within both networking dimensions impact the structural and functional aspects of their Windows 2000 enterprises and the financial (TCO) concerns of their employers.

Note: Your thorough understanding of TCP/IP is now a prerequisite in studying any popular NOS. Microsoft documentation that is supplied with core courses strictly adheres to this requirement. Topics such as the OSI Reference Model, the Department of Defense four-layer model, and Microsoft's four-layer model are typically part of this material. It is critical that you be familiar with all material covered in either the self-study or instructor-led courses that are commonly referred to as networking essentials.

Another noteworthy trend is the use of specialized APIs, standards-based "building materials" like Lightweight Directory Access Protocol (LDAP)-compliant directory structures, and the growing use of XML. As NOS cultures enhance their interoperability, multidirectory access, replication, and synchronization will grow into mission-critical functions across distributed services. As already mentioned, the Microsoft operating system initiative, called Microsoft.NET, is a new generation of software that will merge computing and communications through the use of programmable XML-based information architecture to accomplish this objective. Microsoft.NET will integrate services through what is termed a "universal canvas" or "digital dashboard" that unifies browsing, editing, and authoring seamlessly across both private enterprise and public Internet-based resources and services. Digital dashboards are actually specialized Outlook 2000 folders that provide access through a single interface to a variety of data stores. Exchange 2000 plays a major role in this initiative as Microsoft attempts to change the Internet from a patchwork quilt of individual Web-based host providers to expanding collections of interacting Internet workgroups.

Similarly, Outlook Web Access (OWA) and the Internet Information Services API (ISAPI) play important roles in this scheme by providing substrates that offer an extensible system interface. In fact, although able to run on a single server, both are optimized for FE/BE server support involving multiple server platforms. You again see the recurring theme of a distributed architecture implemented so as to ensure a consistent namespace, uncoupled from the physical servers and their mailboxes, and a scalable platform.

Note: In a mixed environment of both Exchange 5.5 and Exchange 2000, public folders are accessible only on the OWA-enabled Exchange 2000 servers.

Metadirectory services like AD and NDS support services like Exchange, GroupWise, Oracle, and SQL Server and will converge on some common scripting language that is nonproprietary, protocol-, and platform-independent. WMI will become the standard administrative medium, so it is likely that XML, a platform-independent scripting "lingua franca," will be recognized as the de facto standard for access to and control of distributed, multitier service providers both within and outside the boundaries of the enterprise. You will administer domains within your enterprise either locally through the Microsoft Management Console (MMC) or across an unsecure, public network through an XML-enabled-browser.

MS Mail and Sharing Information

Microsoft purchased an email product called Network Courier in 1991 and subsequently released it as MS Mail. This mail program was built on a series of shared files and directories, called a GPO, located on the disk drive of any designated server. MS Mail clients located on other workstations controlled the mail flow through the post office; the GPO was a passive file structure with few or no administrative tools and little or no security. Special executable programs like External and Dispatch, which moved and synchronized mail delivery among these passive GPOs, similarly managed mail delivery outside the GPO. It was tedious and time consuming to manage these outside "transfer agents" and to administer the GPO mail stores. The need for more efficient and powerful messaging systems was the first force driving Internet application development and continues to be a significant one.

Exchange 4 and X.400

From its initial release in March 1996, Exchange Server has been more than a program that sends and receives electronic messages or faxes, with or without attachments. In general, Exchange Server manages the transfer or "exchange" of all kinds of information. Compared to MS Mail, it manages the storage of those messages and other information in what is called a *message store* or *data store* that can be located on either local or networked drives. This change in design coincided with a shift in operating systems; version 4 ran on NT 3.51. These stores allow you to hierarchically arrange electronic messages and any other documents or files, such as spreadsheets, presentations, and so on, into folders. This storage component has grown in importance as the critical component that provides the platform for current and future collaborative initiatives. It is a messaging service, so it also has administrative tools that help you manage data by, for example, providing search features, filtered views, and custom rules that perform preprogrammed actions based on user-defined conditions. Another management tool is the directory of authenticated mail users in the system called an *address book* or *list*, depending on the version. The key features in version 4 were the rich-text email, folders, scheduling using Schedule+, Visual Basic–based forms, and connectors that included support for:

➤ X.400

➤ Dynamic Remote Access Service (DRAS)

- MS Mail
- Internet Mail (SMTP-based)

Exchange Server was implemented as separate NT services running on top of a fault-tolerant relational database engine. In its initial release, the X.400 model defined its messaging components.

Exchange 5 and the Internet

Although version 4 was Microsoft's first true client/server messaging product, its design was based on the standards-based, but unpopular, X.400 model, and its support for Internet protocols was weak. The major change in version 5 was support for additional Internet protocols like NNTP, Secure Sockets Layer (SSL), LDAP version 2 (only in query mode), Hypertext Markup Language (HTML), Hypertext Transport Protocol (HTTP), and Post Office Protocol 3 (POP3) for the first time. This emphasis on Internet connectivity was the beginning of a major shift in Microsoft marketing. The inclusion of support for HTTP, HTML, and especially POP3 also expanded the range of clients that could access an Exchange server, although POP3 doesn't recognize server-based directory structures like folders. Built-in support for NNTP provided both client and host capabilities in replicating newsgroups to intranet clients. A new component, Exchange Active Server, interfaced with IIS3 in translating HTML requests into MAPI before transmitting them to Exchange and supported SSL-encrypted transmissions of mailbox name and passwords. It is also noteworthy that Microsoft Outlook was included for the first time with the Exchange Server package.

Exchange 5.5

Released in 1997, version 5.5 has extended much of version 5 but has not added any fundamental changes to the feature set. Major themes among feature enhancements were structural changes that improved the server's ability to provide a mission-critical platform. Thus, the IS became limited only by available disk space and performance considerations. The speed of the backup was enhanced. Cluster Server support was added to the package. Secure MIME, Internet Mail Access Protocol (IMAP)4, and LDAP3 support was added to the protocols. New connectors and Chat Service were also added.

Exchange as KM Information Broker

We have mentioned that Exchange 2000 provides the platform for brokering complex information "products" called knowledge. Where does it fit into the average office setting? It was previously mentioned that Microsoft itself expects certification candidates to have administrative experience in medium-sized to large Exchange-based installations. But in fact, service-providing products are in development, which suggests that even Small Office/Home Office (SOHO) installations might consider running this important service.

Another product, SharePoint Portal Server 2001, delivers significant services to the Microsoft Office user, more commonly described now as a *knowledge worker*. SharePoint Portal Server 2001 will work with Exchange 2000 to provide enhanced document management, advanced search, and an intranet portal. It integrates Microsoft Office applications and Windows Explorer, through the digital dashboard framework. Together with SharePoint Portal Server 2001 working through the Web Storage System, digital dashboards use HTML to integrate within the user's workspace previously isolated software applications and the objects they hold. Both Outlook 2000 and Internet Explorer can provide both the SOHO end user and office worker in a medium-sized to large-scale installation with a richer, more integrated Web-based workspace where digital objects of all kinds will be accessible and easy to manipulate. The Web Storage System on which these products will run is part of the Installable File System inside Exchange 2000.

An Exchange administrator needs to recognize the inherent advantages of installing Exchange 2000, even in small office settings, as a way to enhance productivity. Even though SharePoint Portal Server 2001 may have its own limited run-time edition of the Web Storage System, the TCO in even a SOHO scenario may be offset by the possible long-term return on investment that such a set of features would provide. In fact, Microsoft offers several Exchange products scaled to different business scenarios. Microsoft distinguishes installations and products by the number of users, as detailed in the sections that follow.

Microsoft Exchange 2000 Server

Exchange 2000 Server is primarily a standalone server that provides a messaging and collaboration platform to the small-business scenario. This installation is limited to a 16GB database per server. It does not support clustering, a distributed configuration, or Chat Service. Microsoft considers the SOHO business scenario as the appropriate candidate for this Exchange product. In this scenario, there are 1 to 25 users, a simple LAN, automatic installation and configuration, and simple Internet connectivity.

Microsoft Exchange 2000 Enterprise Server

Exchange 2000 Enterprise Server is designed for business scenarios where multiple server access, unlimited message storage, and multiple stores per server are necessary support features. Microsoft considers the following business scenarios as appropriate candidates for this Exchange product:

► *Department/team*—1 to 250 users, backbone topology, access to corporate directory services, and remote administration

- *Enterprise*—250 to 1,000,000 users, 24x7 access with availability needs, distributed-services architecture, complex connectivity, legacy systems, and very large data stores

- *Hosted environments*—1,000 to 10,000,000 users, high availability, virtual server support, programmatic administration, and very large directories

The .NET server product line has been designed to fit these different environments based on type and size of business and the environment. These different products conform to the concept of TCO where resources are carefully matched to business needs to minimize the overall cost for installation, licensing, and support. Remember that TCO includes "hidden" costs such as ongoing maintenance, technical training of support teams, and end-user training.

Comparison of Exchange Server and Exchange Enterprise Server

Exchange Server and Exchange Enterprise Server both provide the following:

- Integration with AD
- Outlook 2000 Service Release (SR) 1
- Outlook for Macintosh 8.2.2
- Web Storage System
- Connectors to MS Mail, Lotus cc:Mail, Lotus Notes/Domino, and Novell GroupWise
- Internet POP3 and IMAP4
- HTTP Outlook Web Agent
- SMTP connector
- Instant Messaging

Table 1.1 shows feature differences between the two server products.

Table 1.1 Feature differences between Exchange 2000 Server and Exchange 2000 Enterprise Server.

Feature	Server	Enterprise Server
FE/BE configuration	No	Yes
X.400 connector	No	Yes
Unlimited message storage	No	Yes
Multiple stores per server	No	Yes
Windows clustering	No	Yes
Chat Service	No	Yes
Data conferencing	No	No
Multicast video conferencing	No	No

Exchange 2000 Conferencing Server

Another product in the Exchange Family, Exchange 2000 Conferencing Server, is designed for organizations of any size that need to provide data, voice, and video-conferencing services. This server is used in addition to the Exchange servers listed earlier. It exclusively provides data-conferencing and multicast video-conferencing services. Data-conferencing services, exclusive to this server product, include support for electronic conferencing, scheduling management, shared applications, and multicast video conferencing. The latter services require a T.120 client, such as Microsoft NetMeeting, to provide desktop services.

Expanded Functionality of Exchange 2000

Based on previous discussion in this chapter, it should be no surprise that Exchange 2000 includes *big* features because Windows 2000 is a platform designed to support an *enterprise*. Windows 2000 is fundamentally both extensible and scalable. These two features provide longevity to the NOS technology and encourage capital investment in this particular network culture as opposed to other systems like Novell or Unix. Exchange 2000—though still separate from the NOS—is nevertheless a critical part of any business design. Exchange 2000 provides communication, collaboration, and control to the entire Windows 2000 enterprise. We recommend that you maintain this particular service perspective as an Exchange administrator. Though many of these features, such as basic administration and protocols, are merely Exchange 5.5 enhancements, there are some important new services, such as those listed in this section. The remainder of this book will discuss in greater detail many of the enhancements Exchange 2000 provides in the delivery of messaging and collaboration services. Many of these services are already part of Exchange 5.5. Others are new features that are a result of design changes needed to provide scalability, reliability, and increased performance to the Exchange product in relation to changes in the underlying NOS, in Windows 2000, and in its new role as a KM service provider.

These new features include the following:

- *Fault-tolerance*—In Windows 2000 Advanced Server, Exchange 2000 Enterprise Server supports active/active clustering, an operating system feature where two physically separate machines support a virtual server that shares a common data store.

- *Multiple message databases*—Exchange 2000 Enterprise Server supports multiple message databases that provide for greater scalability, increased reliability through fault tolerance, and more efficient management through, for example, reduced backup and restore time.

- *Standardized interfaces*—The Exchange System Manager is an MMC snap-in that provides both a consistent management interface and enhanced customization of Exchange 2000 functions such as conferencing services, protocols, and connectors.

- *Data storage*—This storage and file-management technology provides a single repository and common infrastructure for structured and unstructured information. This technology is built on the synergy among local file systems, Exchange 2000 data stores, and Web-based services that provide accessibility.

- *Programmability*—Events (also known as *event sinks*) provide extensibility to any Exchange 2000 workflow processes through programmatic changes. Developers can add or modify developer-defined actions in response to system events that can extend the functionality of the messaging and collaboration services.

- *Presence and Instant Messaging*—This service provides instantaneous forms of one-to-one and one-to-many communication streams among users.

- *Organizational grouping*—A significant design change is the uncoupling of Administrative Groups, which are associated together for the purposes of permissions and policy management, from Routing Groups, which define mail transport. This change not only simplifies management but permits greater distribution of messaging and collaboration services independent of the network topology and physical constraints.

- *Full-text indexing and search*—Enabled through Exchange System Manager, full-text searches provide unified access to stored information through detailed searches of messages, attachments, documents, and Web content.

Other Key Features of Exchange 2000

Other key features need to be mentioned in more detail because of their significance. We present these features from a functional and structural perspective here. All features will be referenced at later times throughout the book.

Web Support

Web access to data has been vastly improved in response to the needs of e-commerce and the blurring between internally distributed and publicly accessible networked services. HTTP browser-based clients can access any object in the Web Storage System. As mentioned in the beginning of this chapter, Outlook Web Access with enhanced functionality will play a major client support role in increasing the access to enterprise resources for both the end user and the administrator. Exchange 2000 supports an extension to HTTP 1.1 called Web Distributed Authoring and Versioning (WebDAV) (RFC 2518); it allows you to manipulate remote servers as if they were local file systems. Database APIs like OLE DB and ActiveX Data Objects (ADOs) can also access these objects. Similarly, Exchange 2000 makes extensive use of XML, which, along with WMI and exposed system processes, allow the administrator more robust methods of remote administration. Furthermore, to support collaboration, new streaming technology allows a greater number of MIME message types. Using the same technology as IIS and SQL Server 7, you can index all content in a mailbox or public folder, including contacts, tasks, calendar items, and collaboration data.

Realtime (or Synchronous) Collaboration

An enhancement to collaboration and control is the delivery of that information to the desktop in realtime. Chat Service and Instant Messaging Service provide for the synchronous exchange of information as text messages. Exchange 2000 Conference Server, a separate Microsoft product, delivers data or videoconferencing from some messaging client. Although these features seem extravagant, TCO is again lowered when the expense of travel is factored into the delivery of these services to the corporate desktop. Integration of services such as the Conference Management Service reservation system, which directly accesses a desktop Outlook calendar, brings the Microsoft.NET vision of a universal canvas into better perspective.

An Extensible Development Platform

As mentioned at the start of this chapter, Exchange 2000 is providing the support features that will be the tools of WMI for years to come. In addition to programmable event sinks, developers can use enhanced Collaborative Data Objects (CDOs), OLE DB and ADO support, IIS, and Active Server Pages (ASPs) integration to provide libraries of COM+ components and workflow services based on both asynchronous and simultaneous, synchronous events. A good way to lower TCO is through automating workflows that currently require user intervention in realtime. Exchange 2000 includes CDO Workflow Objects, which are an enhanced library of prepackaged services that deliver secure and reliable application components based on the business logic of any organization. With the power of these tools and realtime collaboration, the only rate-limiting factor will be your network bandwidth (though for most of us it is insurmountable).

Chapter Summary

This chapter has discussed several different models that provide a frame of reference for the study of both NOSs and information-delivery services. These models were introduced in the context of a shift to the Knowledge-Management Paradigm and the effects this paradigm will have on both practical administration of Exchange 2000 and your successful completion of the certification Exam 70-224, "Installing, Configuring, and Administering Exchange 2000." Below are some particularly significant points to remember:

➤ The paradigm shift to KM will require a greater emphasis on architectural and functional matters rather than focusing on structural network issues. Similarly, the extensibility of Windows 2000 and Exchange 2000 will require a more eclectic background to provide business solutions that incorporate "best-of-breed" service-providing software that interoperates in an enterprise.

➤ CMIS and GAIA provide a context within which consumers request brokered services from specialized front-end software packages. These brokers seek and deliver requested products to the consumer anytime, anywhere, through increasing numbers of Web-based devices.

➤ Exchange 2000 is positioned as a KM broker in the .NET environment with its virtual server capabilities that can provide "five 9" reliability through clustering, unlimited data stores, FE/BE server configurations, and greater scalable client support that is mostly derived from its Web-based interfaces.

➤ X.400 provides a generic messaging model that consists of MTA, UA, and MS, which in Exchange architecture is called the IS. X.500 similarly provides a framework that describes decentralized directory stores, robust search capabilities, a structured IS, and a single namespace.

➤ The design changes and enhancements to Exchange version 5.x from Exchange version 4 were most significantly influenced by the growth of online services and the change in scale from the simple legacy domain model to enterprise-scale organizations. Microsoft Exchange 2000 is the first example of a Microsoft.NET server designed to support distributed-service architectures that span beyond the boundaries of an enterprise.

➤ Of the three Exchange Server products, Enterprise Server provides the most robust feature set; it includes greater fault-tolerance, reliability, and scalability. Exchange Conferencing Server complements these features with data- and video-conferencing capabilities. Exchange Server 2000 is designed for a SOHO business scenario.

Review Questions

1. What specific management areas are best understood in terms of their mutual dependency? [Check all correct answers]
    a. Identity management
    b. Permission management
    c. Directory services
    d. Network operating system (NOS)
    e. Network services

2. What will be common characteristics of future Microsoft server software? [Check all correct answers]
    a. A common set of screen interfaces
    b. Consolidated directory services
    c. Common dynamic link libraries
    d. NTFS
    e. FAT

3. Which theme is forcing different NOSs to more readily interoperate?
    a. E-commerce
    b. Consolidated identity management
    c. Standards-based protocols
    d. A common scripting language

4. What is a Microsoft benchmark for evaluating technology?
    a. Total cost of operating system
    b. Total cost of operation
    c. Total cost of ownership
    d. None of the above

5. Microsoft collectively refers to a network of personal computer-based services as what?
    a. Domain Name System
    b. Digital nervous system
    c. NOS
    d. LAN

6. What is the recommended prerequisite subject you need to be familiar with before you begin studying Windows 2000?
    a. DOS
    b. Windows NT
    c. TCP/IP
    d. Networking essentials

7. What components are specified in the X.4000 standard? [Check all correct answers]
    a. Message Transfer Agent (MTA)
    b. Message Store (MS)
    c. Information Store (IS)
    d. None of the above

36 Chapter 1

8. What new Microsoft initiative promises to create a "universal canvas" on client workstations?

    a. Microsoft.NET

    b. Microsoft Windows 2000

    c. **www.microsoft.net**

    d. Answers a and b

9. Which protocol plays the most significant role in messaging services?

    a. X.400

    b. X.500

    c. SMTP

    d. LDAP

10. Which of the following features would be associated with the X.500 standard? [Check all correct answers]

    a. Decentralized management

    b. Centralized management

    c. A single namespace

    d. An indexed namespace

11. Which of the following is not a service dependent on AD?

    a. Messaging

    b. Security

    c. Name resolution

    d. Network protocols

12. Which protocol provides an interface for messaging?

    a. MMP

    b. MAPI

    c. MIME

    d. MAIL

13. Which of the following does not provide a solution to identity management?

    a. ADC

    b. ADSI

    c. MSDSS

    d. API

14. Which protocols interface with the DS? [Check all correct answers]
    a. LDAP
    b. MAPI
    c. MIME
    d. ADSI

15. What are the basic components of Microsoft Repository?
    a. A storage engine and COM interface
    b. A search engine and file system
    c. A storage engine and file system
    d. A database management system

16. Which of the following best describes AD?
    a. Integration of online Internet services
    b. Extensibility of a NOS
    c. Consolidation of identity management
    d. Driving force behind e-commerce

17. When you are planning a project, what Microsoft methodology is especially useful?
    a. MSF
    b. MOF
    c. MSO
    d. MSS

18. What is a key feature of MSF?
    a. It is task driven.
    b. It is goal driven.
    c. It is milestone driven.
    d. None of the above.

19. Which step is not part of preparing a new installation?
    a. Create a plan.
    b. Conduct a gap analysis.
    c. Conduct a needs analysis.
    d. Conduct a goals analysis.

20. Which of the following messaging features raises TCO?
    a. Installing Exchange 2000 in native mode
    b. Installing Exchange 2000 in mixed mode
    c. Message routing
    d. Answers a and c

CHAPTER TWO

Exchange Architecture

After completing this chapter, you will be able to:

✓ Review legacy structural components and trace their counterparts in Exchange 2000

✓ Conceptualize Exchange 2000 architecture in terms of protocol, storage, and directory managers

✓ Compare feature differences among legacy Exchange versions

✓ Understand how Exchange 2000 management areas support new Microsoft operating system initiatives like .NET Servers

✓ Discuss the impact of multiple databases, distributed configurations, and clustering on performance, reliability, and scalability

According to Microsoft, two prerequisite technologies for knowledge management (KM) are a functional intranet structure and services providing messaging and collaboration. Figure 2.1 shows a block design of the idealized KM system. Exchange 2000 provides a messaging infrastructure, a universal Web Store, realtime collaboration, and integration with a complete intranet. The Exchange 2000 design is the first in a family of service providers that integrates deeply with Windows 2000. It delivers messaging and collaboration; its partner in this relation, Windows 2000, delivers an intranet structure that includes identity and permission management, or what is more commonly referred to as *directory services*. The combination of these systems thus provides the foundation depicted in Figure 2.1 and something more for Microsoft than a marketing strategy; it is a paradigm shift away from information processing toward KM.

With the change in paradigm comes new technology initiatives like Microsoft.NET and design changes like delegating directory services to the network operating system (NOS). .NET servers are architecturally more specialized than their earlier versions and have shed functionality common to other service providers in the enterprise. One such specific management functional area (SMFA), directory services, has differentiated in design and become a specialized part of the NOS called Active Directory (AD) directory services. This chapter will review legacy Exchange architecture as a foundation for understanding structural changes in Exchange 2000. It will also introduce the deep integration of Exchange in Windows 2000 and AD.

Microsoft's shift to this new Knowledge-Management Paradigm will require an Exchange administrator to understand the details of and rationale for architectural design changes in the enterprise and is the new format of certification examinations.

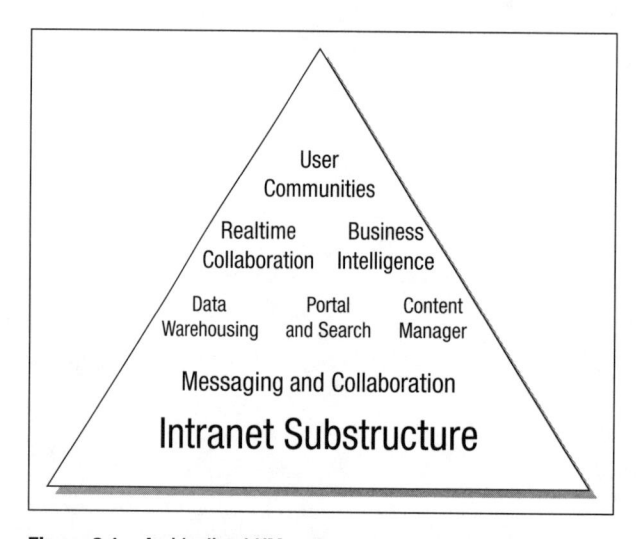

Figure 2.1 An idealized KM system.

Rationale is just as important in the listing of competencies for Exchange 2000 as understanding how to install client software. This chapter uses themes such as business objectives and total cost of ownership (TCO), consolidation of directory services, and the Microsoft .NET initiative to help you understand not just Exchange 2000, but also future releases of this fundamentally important messaging and collaboration software.

Business Objectives and TCO

In evaluating any service-providing software, the TCO is a major evaluation tool because it quantifies corporate benefits related to some corporate objective. The cost of client/server architecture, still applicable in the .NET world, includes more than just the initial capital investment of acquiring hardware and software. A corporate objective of reliable global messaging and collaborative services incurs the initial acquisition investment, as well as variable maintenance, support, and training expenses. In fact, over time, the capital expenditure very often dwarfs the operational expenses. The key factor in reducing TCO is thus controlling the expense involved in maintenance, support, and training. Design and administration are the two key facets in the management of these operational expenses, because both areas, if well defined and thoughtfully executed, can simplify and even enhance the user experience.

Design

Features that promote extensibility in a product reduce development time. One of the subtlest yet most significant characteristics of Windows 2000 over legacy NT is the extensibility of many SMFAs. For example, the audit/accounting and security managers—Security Support Provider Interface (SSPI) and Microsoft Cryptographic API (CAPI)—are fundamentally interfaces to which future add-in "helpers" can connect and perform complementary services. In fact, the rationale behind the original design of the hardware abstraction layer (HAL) was to uncouple the hardware from the NOS kernel and micro code, making network services portable and hardware independent. Using standards-based protocols and de facto application programming interfaces (APIs)—Open Database Connectivity (ODBC), ActiveX Data Object (ADO), and Messaging API (MAPI)—similarly increases the extensibility of the basic network structure and decreases development time and expense.

Exchange 2000 follows this same design strategy in an attempt to reduce TCO. The broadening range of clients and the Web exposure of its data stores increase its accessibility and minimize end-user training requirements. Products such as BizTalk Server 2000 foster rapid business application development through enterprise application integration (EAI) and are designed to interoperate with Exchange 2000 through standards-based protocols like Simple Mail Transfer Protocol (SMTP),

Hypertext Transport Protocol (HTTP), and Extensible Markup Language (XML). These design strategies directly address reduction in development, maintenance, and training expenses and thus improve the marketability of the .NET platform (Windows 2000, Exchange 2000, and so on) as well as reduce TCO. Capital investments in information technologies produced by software companies with the greatest market share of a specific industry best serve corporate objectives because their dominance over competitors theoretically suggests greater stability and implied longevity of their products. The longevity often translates into greater financial fortitude of that vendor over competitors, presumed longer-term support for versions of software, and greater research and feature development. Microsoft aggressively pursues new technologies, as well as builds extensive backward-compatibility features into its operating systems and application software.

Administration

The simplification of administrative support begins with instrumentation. Aside from maintenance and training expenses, training and support expenses increase TCO. One approach to minimizing this contribution is to simplify administration by centralizing management. Exchange has always provided a topological view of an organization that fostered simplified global management. The Exchange topology, though tightly coupled in legacy versions to the network infrastructure, was based on a logical, nested structure. The functional scope of this structure has been rooted in an all-encompassing organization within which well-connected Exchange servers populate physically separate sites.

Warning: The term "well-connected" when discussing servers is now commonplace and very significant. It connotes one-hop connectivity across permanent network connections running at least 10MB/sec. Overlooking this very important concept in designing a Windows 2000 enterprise or an Exchange 2000 site will lead to disastrous results for both your network throughput and your career.

Legacy messaging systems are often patchwork quilts of individual Exchange servers routing their messages through connectors that join geographically separate sites. However, these messaging servers provide communication and collaboration services to a single, unified namespace defined by a directory of recipients. The complexity of this network is usually transparent to consumers of messaging services; they insist on consistent levels of service throughout the namespace, no matter what the complexity or conditions. The Exchange administrator may, because of job roles or out of necessity due to the installation's size, have this single-seated global perspective, too! Centralized administration of an enterprise through the familiar and extensible Microsoft Management Console (MMC) is a major feature in Exchange 2000 design. In fact, Exchange 2000 comes with an assortment of snap-ins, including System Manager (discussed later in this chapter), Message Tracking Center, Public Folders, Security, and Conferencing Services.

Similarly, the initiatives that surround Web-Based Enterprise Management (WBEM) and Windows Management Instrumentation (WMI) and the use of XML will continue to reduce support expenses and TCO for some time in the future.

Legacy Exchange Overview

The legacy architecture and function often provide an understanding of the design rationale for current software products. Few ideas in any area of human knowledge are revolutionary; most are repetitions of some well-known or successful methodology, paradigm, or scheme. Exchange Server is a relatively new product. Since its release in the mid-1990s, the design has shifted from a standards-based, X.400 architecture to a modular, Internet-enabled, SMTP-driven, messaging platform. This shift occurred quickly in two generations of design. We will describe these historical origins so that you can better understand where Exchange is today and where it is going tomorrow.

Why Legacy Issues Are Important

Microsoft suggests that familiarity with version 5.5 is useful but not essential in preparing for the certification exams that cover either Exchange 2000 Administration or Design. We suggest that this reasoning is shortsighted due to the following:

➤ In real world situations, you will rarely encounter computer installations that are soft, beautiful "green fields"—that is, wide-open "spaces" of new Exchange servers free of "rocky" legacy resources sticking up out of the virtual landscape. Likewise, such "green field deployments" would rarely appear in certification exam case studies. Microsoft does not provide free software or free lunches.

➤ Exchange 2000 is a different class of service provider than Exchange 5.5, in that it is a .NET Server with a different architecture for a different paradigm, and a more differentiated and specialized design for a distributed services, e-commerce environment. Many of its features and functions, however, are not only recognizable but more easily understood because administrators are familiar with them in their legacy, Exchange 5.5 context.

➤ One strategy to prepare for the future is to study the immediate past.

Given the acceleration in software development and the prospect that a Mercury beta version (the legitimate spawn of Exchange 2000) will be released shortly after this book is published, it is advantageous for the certificate candidate as well as the IT practitioner to find technological patterns and follow functional themes in recent versions of software. This will prepare them for new changes in what are probably the most pivotal enterprise service management areas: messaging and collaboration, what is called corporate KM.

Legacy Structural Components

To appreciate the proposed modifications—such as 64-bit support, increased clustering capabilities, and enhanced backup strategies—in the next version of Exchange (code-named Mercury), you must first familiarize yourself with legacy architecture. When Exchange 4 was initially released in 1996, it was built according to X.400 specifications. Even version 5.5 is composed of the following four basic components:

- System Attendant (SA)
- Information Store (IS) (called a Message Store—MS—in the X.400 specifications)
- Message Transfer Agent (MTA)
- Directory Store (DS)

A committee made up of the International Organization of Standardization (ISO) and Comité Consultatif International Téléphonique et Télégraphique (CCITT), now known as the International Telecommunication Union (ITU), with representatives from more than 100 countries, actually created this X.400 design model. It was the first in a series of specifications that were collectively called Message Handling System (MHS).

System Attendant (SA)

The SA (mad.exe) performs specific management functions that include coordination of basic operations involving transport operations and database maintenance. It is the initial "loader" of Exchange services. The SA performs the following management functions:

- Builds the message routing tables and manages new recipient addressing
- Monitors link integrity messages from other Exchange servers
- Manages (monitors and attempts repairs) directory integrity in its own server
- Accumulates message transport data used to track a message's progress
- Generates foreign messaging addresses (such as X.400, SMTP, MS Mail, and cc:Mail) for recipients by interacting with attached connectors
- Interacts with the Key Management component when handling secure message exchanges that involve digital signatures and encryption

The SA maintains unseen activities such as link-state tables used for message delivery, which are vital to the proper functioning of Exchange Server. We recommend you familiarize yourself with the initial or "loader" programs of services in any NOS or application. If this program fails to load for whatever reason, all dependent programs will also fail. If you are troubleshooting some service on a host server, you typically confirm that the loader process is in fact running in the services list.

Information Store (IS)

This IS (store.exe) can manage one or two data stores: one private (priv.edb), which holds mailboxes, and the other public (pub.edb), which holds public folders. Although mailboxes are, by definition, restricted to private access, public folders provide access to many recipients in the namespace. Because you can characterize the legacy Exchange application as a single-instance store, you must restore the entire store to recover a single recipient object such as a mailbox. To support this need for organization-wide accessibility, the pub.edb data store is copied in part or completely to other Exchange servers within and across sites through a process called *replication*. This distribution of public stores helps balance the network load and reduce access costs across geographically separate sites. IS services represent the interface layering between the data stores and all other Exchange processes. Unlike the passive file structure found in MS Mail, the IS plays an active role in post office operations. Thus, the IS performs the following tasks:

➤ Delivers mail to local recipients

➤ Relays incoming and outgoing mail to the MTA

➤ Notifies recipients when new mail arrives

➤ Resolves names through directory lookups

➤ Manages the public folders

In addition to SA, store.exe is another key process that runs on the host server. Both store.exe and mad.exe can provide clues regarding an Exchange server's operational state. In fact, the store.exe process dynamically allocates memory space. This process, dynamic buffer allocation (DBA), proactively increases the database buffer cache to "reserve" enough memory space for paging and other input/output (I/O) activities. The success of this function has a major impact on maximizing Exchange Server performance.

Message Transfer Agent (MTA)

Like the independent programs dispatch.exe and external.exe in MS Mail, the MTA (emsmta.exe) routes mail between a local IS and other Exchange servers. It uses helpers like the legacy X.400 connector, Dynamic Remote Access Service (DRAS) connector, and the Site connector to route messages to other sites in the Exchange namespace or organization and other connectors to move messages between foreign messaging systems such as MS Mail and the Internet. Connectors are covered in more detail later in this chapter in the "Connectors (Protocols)" section.

When routing messages to other messaging systems on other NOSs like IBM Systems Network Architecture Distribution Services (SNADS), Professional Office System (PROFS), and Novell GroupWise, the MTA uses another breed of helper application called a *gateway*. The MTA internally converts messages from its default MAPI format to and from the standards-based X.400 format in keeping with its original design specifications in version 4. Because there are no external connectors through which to route messages in a single-server site, the MTA's sole function is to expand distribution lists (DLs).

Directory Store (DS)
Like the IS, Exchange DS (dsamain.exe) is both a service and a data store. It stores information about internal operations, such as synchronization and routing. This same information is provided to every other Exchange server within the site through replication. Thus, information about all sites within the Exchange namespace is shared among all Exchange servers. The DS controls the directory services; hence, other internal services (SMFA managers) and Exchange clients call upon it to resolve message address names.

The DS manages its own local address list or book, and identity management and permission management are closely integrated. Therefore, the DS also enforces security issues associated with the data stores. The integrity of directory information is critical to the messaging system's proper operation. The DS must therefore regularly send and receive directory updates from other DSs operating in other Exchange servers. The MTA transfers this directory information across sites. Compared to message exchanges between sites within an organization, more sophisticated (and optional) directory synchronization service providers pass information to foreign messaging systems.

Note: Terminology is important. The process of "freshening" or updating information within a namespace is called replication. The process of updating ISs across separate namespaces (such as with a foreign messaging system) is called synchronization. The two processes, though functionally similar, are not synonymous.

Other Helper Components
When you are studying legacy architecture, it is useful to categorize various helper components in specific management functional areas. As versions of software change over time, many of these helper components are internalized or, through differentiation, delegated to other service providers as a way to streamline design, remove redundancy, and simplify administration. As paradigms shift from Information-Sharing to Knowledge-Management, you will see a structural reorganization of many of these components into more logical functional areas. We categorize these helpers as directory services, MS services, and transport services.

Directory Services
Though issues of directory services are best left for discussions on planning and deployment, it is useful to briefly summarize how Exchange uses the directory services in Windows 2000. The AD refers all Exchange directory calls over a number of different protocols, including Lightweight Directory Access Protocol (LDAP) and its ICANN (Internet Corporation for Assigned Names and Numbers)-designated

TCP port, 389. Under AD, Exchange 2000 requires accessibility to the Global Catalog (GC) server for producing a Global Access List (GAL) of mail-enabled recipients, as well as for use with other directory services, such as DSProxy and DSAccess. Deploying redundant GCs is an important design consideration at the site level for both scalability and disaster recovery. An important maintenance routine is to monitor the service load on site GCs to proactively maintain the highest performance levels.

Outlook 2000 clients use DSProxy to facilitate access to AD data through this port. DSProxy handles AD directory requests on behalf of these MAPI clients through the Name Service Provider Interface (NSPI). Alternatively, legacy MAPI clients such as Outlook 97/98 and the Exchange client make MAPI Directory Service (MAPI DS) requests to an Exchange server using an older method, remote procedure call (RPC) connections. To minimize overhead, DSProxy NSPI forwards these RPC packets directly to AD without evaluating them. The GC replies to the DSProxy service, which, in turn, provides the results to the client.

Another DSProxy function, especially for Outlook 2000 clients, is a request, following the initial directory lookup, that all future directory calls be referred directly to the GC server. This service call referral not only facilitates name resolution (that is, the directory services provided), but also reduces the workload on the Exchange 2000 server itself. Another way to improve performance is to reduce these service calls through some directory access cache mechanism, which in Exchange 2000 is called DSAccess. Service calls are reduced because the cache holds recent lookup information so that the same directory service need not be repeated routinely over time. Increasing the cache size and holding latency significantly decreases DSProxy calls. Default cache parameters, changed through the Registry, are a maximum of 4MB for directory entries and up to 10 minutes for cache holding times.

Message Store (MS) Services

Exchange 2000 Server plays a central role in Microsoft's KM initiative. MS Mail was a legacy-messaging product, so helper programs were available to provide the communication and control. Exchange 2000 enhances old services and offers new features that provide the fundamental part of the KM foundation: collaboration. Primary areas of KM include organizational tools—specifically in the areas of search, categorization, and indexing—distributed processing, and accessibility through as broad a range of communication technologies as possible. Three initiatives are noteworthy in developing MS services that will provide the foundation for KM on an enterprise and distributed services basis:

> ➤ *Universal canvas*—The first digital dashboards (in their simplest form, a dynamic Web page running within the Microsoft Outlook 2000 client) provide both the accessible interface and the enhanced search features that will take full advantage of this unified messaging technology. Not only are many data types,

including collaborative objects, accessible on a common "canvas," but they also behave like any other Windows object. The interface provides the platform on which knowledge workers can select and manipulate different data forms in well-known, well-practiced ways of Windows application users.

- *Universal storage*—A core feature of Exchange 2000 is the Web Store, where any digitized item is accessible from both an intranet and Internet client for use on this universal canvas. The significance of Exchange Installable File System, the formal name for the Web Store, is that it is a common repository that can unify unrelated document types like collaboration objects (calendar, tasks, and contacts) with unstructured data objects like Word and Excel documents in one collaborative container that is easily accessible through a broad range of devices. This unified data store has the potential of providing information without limits or barriers.

- *Universal device interface*—The development of Windows CE for hand-held and palm computers leverages native support for Hypertext Markup Language (HTML) and XML as well as Wireless Application Protocol (WAP) and Wireless Markup Language (WML) in merging formats that are used on less conventional but increasingly more common mobile devices. Exchange 2000 provides services to this burgeoning population of end users. All these operating systems and languages are Web based and provide different degrees of data storage and information transfer. These common traits provide the population through which Microsoft will achieve its commitment of knowledge without limits anytime, anyplace, and anywhere.

Exchange Key Management

Exchange Key Management is responsible for securely transmitting messages using the Exchange Server option that relies on Data Encryption Standard (DES), CAST-40 or CAST-60 (both developed at Northern Telecom by Carlisle Adams and Stafford Tavares), or standard-based Secure MIME (S/MIME). This optional security-related service was introduced with version 5 and supports RSA public key encryption and digital signatures within and across separate Exchange namespaces. It does the following:

- Certifies and creates asymmetric encryption keys for authenticity
- Stores encryption keys for recovery purposes
- Manages digital signatures
- Certifies revocation lists of advance Exchange security users

System Management

The System Manager MMC snap-in is a legacy tool Exchange administrators need to connect to an Exchange Server to manage the messaging services. With delegation of directory services to AD, the information necessary to manage an Exchange organization is actually distributed and accessible from anywhere in the enterprise. Depending on the context within which you work, any administrative changes you make in the system can be replicated to all other servers throughout the organization. The System Manager snap-in is actually a default console file installed with Exchange Server; you do not have to construct it from scratch. This tool allows you to administer any Exchange service from any domain or domain controller through the same interface. In addition, you can:

➤ Organize administrative objects to simplify setting permissions and navigation

➤ Manipulate objects among Administrative Groups

➤ Handle server protocols and ISs

➤ Manage site replication, message tracking, and monitors

➤ Control public folders

For convenience, if you selected the Exchange System Management Tools component during the Exchange Server installation, Active Directory Users and Computers and System Manager will be installed on your server. In fact, you can also install these tools on any Windows 2000 Professional or Server system.

Other "helper tools" are Public Folders and forms that contain published information in specialized object containers that are stored in the IS. You can nest these objects and apply rules to them. You can also replicate them across sites. You create forms in the Exchange and Outlook Form Designer and store them for general access. You can use them to programmatically collect and process data in an automated workflow scenario. These specialized forms typically use MAPI to interface with various messaging components such as directory services supplied by Exchange Server.

Transport Services

Although a discussion of message flow and routing is outside the scope of this chapter, a basic understanding of transport architecture, as shown in Figure 2.2, is essential for putting Exchange components in perspective. Historically, inbound Exchange messages flowed into the Transport Core through the MTA, a component originally described in the standards-based X.400 architectural model. MTA support in Exchange 2000 now provides a legacy X.400 pathway through a *connector*. Foreign email systems, which have historically followed this X.400 standards-based architecture, still use either this connector or any customized connector using components from the Exchange Development Kit (EDK). Version 5.x began a shift away from the X.400 architecture toward a greater compatibility with Web-based protocols and de facto standards like SMTP. In fact, the default protocol and primary messaging service channel is now SMTP rather than the original remote procedure call (RPC)-based communications using the MTA. Exchange 2000 stores routing information in the configuration naming partition of

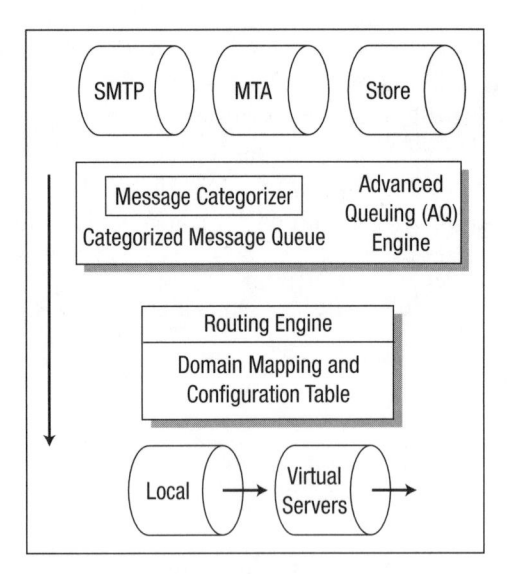

Figure 2.2 Exchange 2000 transport services.

the AD, which is replicated throughout an organization. Nevertheless, connectors still provide additional flexibility, especially in the customization of routing topologies. Another input method is direct submission of messages to the IS through legacy MAPI clients like Outlook or non-MAPI Outlook Web Access (OWA).

The SMTP service is composed of a protocol stack and a primary managing component called the Advanced Queuing (AQ) engine. The AQ is responsible for passing messages through several processing queues. SMTP messages are passed to an NT File System (NTFS)-based precategorization queue before being redirected to a message store.

The MTA accepts inbound messages across Transmission Control Protocol (TCP) port 102 and passes them through a local store queue to the SMTP-Out Store folder, which redirects them to the AQ. The messages are passed to a precategorizer queue. From this holding queue, the Message Categorizer (phatcat.dll) reads all messages one by one to determine, through a process called *name resolution*, the origin and destination address locations within the Exchange namespace. The categorizer also expands distribution lists (DLs) and retrieves operational specifications—such as forwarding instructions or size and delivery restrictions from the AD—that relate to the message. The processed message is then passed to a postcategorization queue the same way all other messages are handled; messages are passed back to the store for local delivery or back to the MTA for further routing and subsequent handling by the routing engine.

Outbound X.400 messages are passed to the AQ by a message store driver; one driver, sd_store.dll, passes messages to EPOXY (which is discussed later in this chapter), then to sd_iis.dll, and finally to AQ. AQ sends a message to the message categorizer, which resolves all recipient addresses, expands DLs, and so on. Once processed, the message returns to the AQ, which then queries the routing engine for "get_next_hop" information. Locally addressed messages are put into the Local Delivery queue in AQ. The AQ also creates destination message queues based on destination domain names from which SMTP services will route messages to the next appropriate services. The store driver picks up the message in the Local Delivery queue and submits it to the MTS-In queue in the IS. MTS-In is a MAPI system queue that holds converted messages with resolved addresses received from a connector ready for pickup. Its counterpart, MTS-Out, holds outgoing messages with unresolved addresses for a connector. Then, store.exe reads the message out of the queue and writes it to the local data store. Alternatively, store.exe submits the message to the MTA and then the MTA makes a call to the routing engine for additional address information, such as which outbound connector to use. MTA then delivers the message, just as it has done in earlier version 5 products.

Connectors (Protocols)

Exchange connectors link Exchange sites to one another to transfer messages and replicate directory information and the contents of public folders. Exchange 2000 includes three connectors:

- *Routing Group connector (RGC)*—Specialized software that exchanges messages exclusively between Routing Groups within an Exchange organization. This is the simplest and most common method for linking separate sites composed of groups of servers characterized by their own specific topology and underlying physical network properties. This connector must have a stable, permanent, high-bandwidth path between the two groups. Although it resembles the legacy Exchange 5.5 site connectors, the Routing Group connector relies on SMTP and message routing based on link state information rather than the legacy Gateway Address Routing Tables. In addition, RGC allows you to schedule and control message sizes.

- *SMTP connector*—Specialized software that exchanges messages between intra-organizational Routing Groups, across different organizations, or to third-party messaging systems. For example, it can connect two Exchange Routing Groups across a public network like the Internet. Simple Mail Transfer Protocol is the more common messaging protocol today designed specifically for server-to-server communication. Compared to RGC, SMTP has more flexible specifications and finer control in terms of authentication, scheduling, and permission management.

- *X.400 connector*—Specialized software that exchanges messages between intra-organizational Routing Groups, across different organizations, or to foreign X.400-based messaging systems. Within an Exchange organization, this connector is slower than RGC. The X.400 connector is especially well suited to connect with legacy systems.

Exchange gateways traditionally link Exchange sites to foreign messaging systems that run on non-Microsoft operating system platforms to transfer user messages and synchronize directory information. Examples of this kind of legacy helper software are Lotus Notes, SNADS, PROFS, faxes, pages, and voice mail. An Exchange 2000 server, because of performance issues, typically runs a single type of connector, as a Windows 2000 service, but can run any combination of the default connectors just mentioned as well as the following gateways:

➤ *Lotus Notes connector*—This software provides services that transfer message and directory information between Exchange Server and Lotus Notes.

➤ *Lotus cc:Mail connector*—This software provides access to non-MAPI legacy mail systems.

➤ *Novell GroupWise connector*— This software provides services that transfer message and directory information between Exchange Server and Novell GroupWise.

➤ *Legacy Microsoft Mail connector*—This software provides support for the old-fashioned store and forward MS Mail systems.

➤ *Internet Mail Service (IMS)*—Discussed in the "Legacy Internet Access Components" section later in this chapter to provide you with a foundation for understanding Exchange 2000 architecture.

In legacy Exchange, site and directory replication connectors are used for direct, synchronous links only within the same organization. They are the simplest form of intersite connectivity. DRAS connector, which is not supported by Exchange 2000, is similar to the legacy Site connector but operates asynchronously across lower-bandwidth plain old telephone service (POTS), integrated services digital network (ISDN), and X.25 lines. In Exchange 2000, separate internal connector directories or queues interface with the Extensible Storage Engine (ESE)—an enhanced version of the legacy Joint Engine Technology (JET) engine used in both Exchange Server and AD directory services—through SMTP services or the MTA. In fact, the MTA does not directly interface with SMTP services. The SMTP protocol provides connectivity over the Internet and, in Windows 2000 by default, a communication protocol between Exchange servers. The MTA similarly communicates with Exchange message categorization and routing components through dedicated holding areas. SMTP configuration information is stored in the IIS Metabase, a hierarchical database introduced with IIS 4 to hold information content about IIS services running on legacy NT 4. In Windows 2000, this configuration information is first written to the AD and is then applied to the Metabase through an update mechanism. This information is accessible through the Metabase Editor (MetaEdit) 2 utility, found in the Windows 2000 Server Resource Kit.

Connections are based on Routing Group topologies. You can connect Routing Groups in several different ways. Exchange Server improves upon legacy transport systems by introducing Routing Groups and link-state information as connection methods. Legacy Exchange used the Gateway Address Routing Table (GWART) for route selection, which was prone to routing loops. Exchange 2000 uses a link-state algorithm based on the current state of a network to provide a more reliable selection of the most efficient routing path. SMTP, as the default messaging transfer protocol connecting Exchange servers, offers additional advantages over legacy systems that rely on RPCs to exchange messages. For example, SMTP requires less bandwidth than RPC-based systems and is more tolerant to higher message latencies. It is also the de facto messaging protocol on the Internet.

Legacy Internet Access Components

There was a major shift in design focus between versions 4 and 5 that can best be characterized as Microsoft's change in approach to the Internet. Web-based access was suddenly viewed as a mission-critical method of communication and collaboration. There was also a major initiative in the development of interfacing with a wide range of Internet-based protocols. Some of the services included in Exchange 5.x that have been enhanced in Exchange 2000 are as follows:

➤ *Internet Mail Service (IMS)*—Originally called Internet Mail connector, this interface provides connectivity to SMTP mail systems. Changes have been made between versions 5 and 5.5 so that IMS can route Internet mail from non-Exchange clients and servers.

➤ *Internet News Service*—This service provides access to USENET, the bidirectional, worldwide message-sharing system that publishes messages organized into newsgroups, through native support for Network News Transport Protocol (NNTP).

➤ *Chat Services*—This component, in version 5.5, provides hosting services for Internet Relay Chat (IRC) sessions through specialized clients.

➤ *Outlook Web Access (OWA)*—Through the use of ActiveX Server, a layer of software that interfaces Exchange with IIS 4, applications and data can be transferred among HTTP, HTML, and MAPI. Active Server executes Web applications that conform to Microsoft's Active Server Pages (ASP) standards. Outlook provides the browser technology to use these ASP forms to access Exchange Server services.

Comparing Features of Exchange Versions 4, 5, and 5.5

The most significant differences in the evolution of Exchange services since its first release as version 4 have been in the storage services area and protocols. Beginning with version 5, database storage capacity is constrained only by the hardware platform on which the services are installed. Protocol services have continued to expand since Exchange's initial release. Beginning with version 5, Internet-related

Table 2.1 Comparison of features of Exchange versions 4, 5, and 5.5.

Feature	Version 4	Version 5	Version 5.5
Storage services	16GB	16GB	Unlimited
Protocols (network)	X.400, Site connector, DRAS, Internet Mail, MS Mail	X.400, Site connector, DRAS, Internet Mail, MS Mail, Lotus cc:Mail	X.400, Site connector, DRAS, Internet Mail, MS Mail, Lotus cc:Mail, Lotus Notes, PROFS, SNADS
Protocols (Internet)	SMTP	SMTP, POP3, HTTP, HTML, NNTP, LDAP3, SSL, ASP	SMTP, POP3, HTTP, HTML, NNTP, LDAP3, SSL, ASP, IMAP4, SASL, ETRN
Special features	Public Folders, scheduling, electronic forms	Public Folders, scheduling, electronic forms, Outlook Client, ASP, Active Messaging	Public Folders, scheduling, electronic forms, Outlook Client, ASP (renamed CDO), Exchange Scripting Agent, Chat, ILS

Note what the following acronyms stand for: CDO (Collaborative Data Objects), ETRN (extended TURN), ILS (Internet Locator Server), POP (Post Office Protocol), SSL (Secure Sockets Layer), and SASL (Simple Authentication and Security Layer).

connectivity has significantly broadened. Table 2.1 compares the features of the three versions of Exchange.

Workflow of Legacy Exchange

Exchange 5.5 messages are stored in IS. The IS service references addressing and routing information in the local directory service database (dir.edb) to determine local or remote delivery. The IS actively manages local message delivery, whereas the MTA performs all remote delivery functions. The DS also creates messages that are communicated to remote directory services through replication to ensure consistent directory information throughout an Exchange namespace.

The workflow of legacy Exchange involves a series of concurrent linear processes:

➤ The SA performs various administrative housekeeping tasks, such as monitoring servers and connections, and replicating directory information.

➤ The IS handles message storage.

➤ The MTA manages routing and message delivery.

➤ The DS controls access to MSs.

Now, let's leave legacy products and conceptualize a new paradigm. Borrowing from psychological literature, we adopt a *gestalt* or "world view" in which we reorganize the many messaging components and concurrent linear processes into three functional groups that we discussed earlier: directory service providers, message storage service providers, and transport service providers. We use the terms "service provider" and "specific functional area (loosely SMFA) manager" interchangeably. We also refer to identity management (which includes permission management) and the Windows 2000 directory service provider, Active Directory, interchangeably. We will refer to the Common Management Information Services (CMIS) model when dealing with infrastructure, and the Generic Architecture for Information Availability (GAIA) model when dealing from a more functional perspective with services in a .NET, multitier, distributed services architecture.

Furthermore, we have avoided the term "groupware" throughout this discussion because we will continue to emphasize the collaborative or messaging foundation of our operational definition of KM rather than conceptualizing KM as accumulative data warehousing. The most common example of groupware, Lotus Notes, is designed from this data-centric rather than messaging point of view. This difference in rationale is noteworthy and somewhat problematic in terms of Microsoft's .NET gestalt, which is moving away from monolithic, general-purpose applications (Lotus Notes + Lotus Mail, and so on) toward distributed service providers like Exchange 2000, SQL Server 2000, Windows 2000, and so on, working in synergy.

There has been a similar trend historically in network adapter local area network (LAN) drivers. The old monolithic Internetwork Packet Exchange/Sequenced Packet Exchange (IPX/SPX) Novell drivers were successfully replaced by more modular Open Data-Link Interface (ODI) LAN drivers, dinosaurs replaced by post-Ice Age smaller, more "efficient" flora and fauna that form a more robust, yet interdependent ecosystem. We will revisit this theme of differentiation and specialization leading to more efficient scaling when we deal with FE/BE distributed service architecture in the "Distributed Configuration" section later in this chapter and throughout distributed services environments in general.

A New Perspective of Distributed Services

If you imagine yourself as an architect of a .NET messaging service provider, how could you improve a legacy messaging system like Exchange 5.5? One recurring theme we have emphasized is differentiation through specialization. Windows 2000 has supplied us with a multimaster service provider of directory services, AD. Therefore, we can delegate DS control to the NOS and partition the remaining processes into two functional groups: protocol services (what the MTA manages) and storage services (what the IS manages). Helpers would most likely handle SA housekeeping. In fact, the entire protocol services layer has been delegated to another new part of Windows 2000 that was formerly IIS. You can see this layer at the top of Figure 2.3, labeled inetinfo.exe, which functions as an Internet Services API layer.

The interface separating Exchange storage services from protocol services is an area of shared memory called the EXchange InterProcess Communication layer (usually designated as EXIPC but pronounced EPOXY because it binds inetinfo.exe to store.exe). Protocol services, in another example of differentiation and specialization,

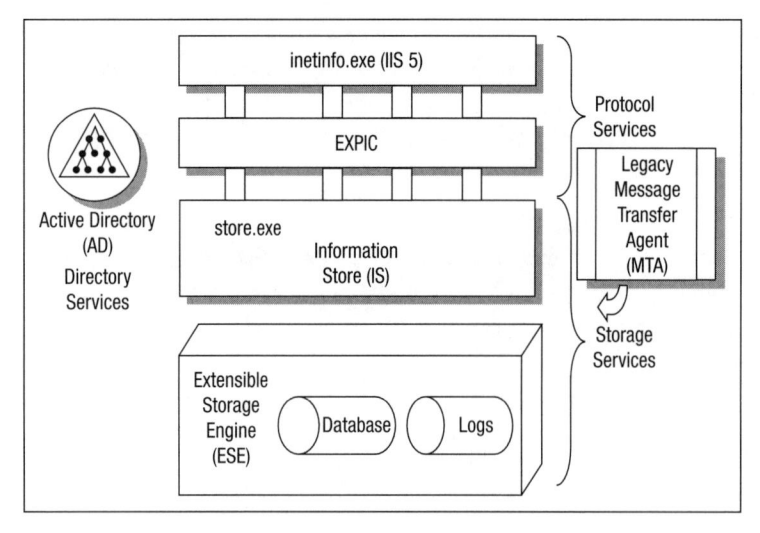

Figure 2.3 SMFAs in Exchange 2000.

are now managed by inetinfo.exe, a part of the former IIS 4 service provider. EXIPC is a helper application that provides a queue for communication flows between Exchange and the Internet engine that is now seamlessly embedded in the NOS. The delegation of identity management to AD in the NOS repeats the pattern of differentiating functional management areas. Directory services, depicted on the left side of Figure 2.3, as well as protocol services, are examples of consolidated services providing broad access to different service areas. This design change is in contrast to self-contained server applications like legacy Exchange and SQL Servers running in a local environment. The true distribution of these service areas is the beginning of a trend in Microsoft operating systems.

We will detail the architectural components of these three management areas—storage services, directory services, and protocol services—in the remaining sections of this chapter. As previously mentioned, Microsoft has categorized the Exchange 2000 feature set along three different dimensions: the messaging infrastructure, message storage, and the messengers. We will begin the discussion of Exchange 2000 infrastructure with the AD directory services and its role in identity management.

Storage Services—Messaging Infrastructure

Figure 2.4 shows a positive linear trend in the consolidation of directory services. Across the major NOS "cultures" (Microsoft, Novell, and Unix), you see differentiation and specialization of services that lead to the creation of specialized directory service providers. This trend in specialization lowers the cost of design and implementation as well as increases interoperability across NOS "cultures." Centralized directory access in the messaging infrastructure facilitates deployment of services by reducing redundant functionality and enhances NOS interoperability by

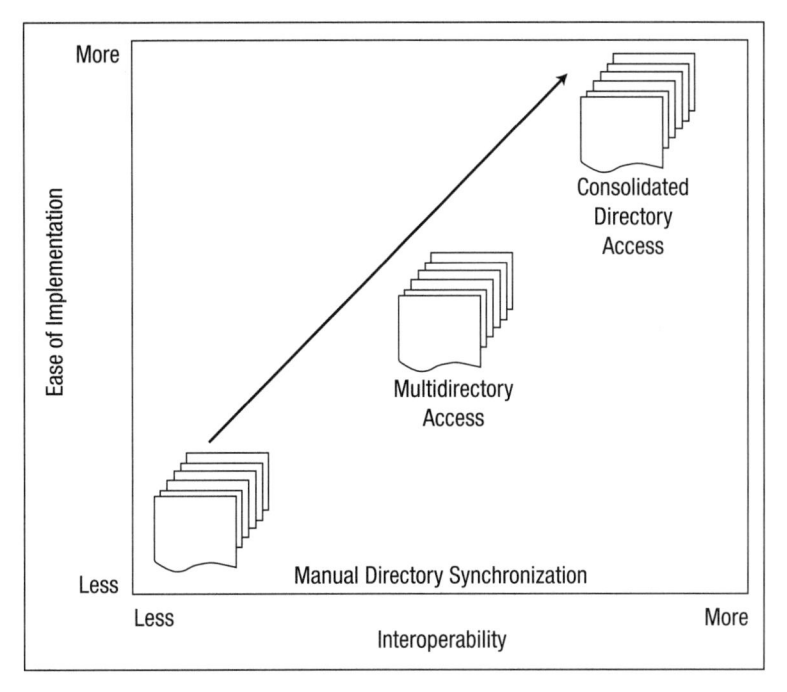

Figure 2.4 A major trend in directory services.

consolidating mission-critical services. Service-providing software packages like Exchange 2000 have been streamlined to reflect both specialized and differentiated function as directory services have been outsourced to the NOS. Identity and permission management in these service providers are becoming vestigial functions that remain functional primarily for backward compatibility; mission-critical activities like authentication and authorization (i.e., identity management) are, in fact, more efficiently handled by a NOS than a specialized service provider.

Typically, no single design solution exists as we transition from different legacy networks and their variegated services to a central identity management in a unified, distributed services architecture. Unfortunately, by definition, distributed implies a "rocky field" (as opposed to a "green field") of the newest hardware and software with no legacy systems or services to upgrade. Strategies to plow these fertile tracts populated with pockets of legacy systems without breaking the plowshare require a dedicated discussion of planning and deployment strategies, far outside the scope of this chapter.

Transitioning from Monolithic Legacy Environments

AD and the Exchange 5.5 Directory Store (DS) share so many architectural similarities that some consider AD to be an enterprise-wide DS or directory data store. The AD, though far more complex than the Exchange DS, is nevertheless based on its architectural design. Microsoft developed a successful field-tested product in Exchange DS. However, it faces many challenges when developing directory services for an enterprise. The simplest solution—a single domain model that holding all named users and resources, called *principals*—is unrealistic in all but mythical green-field deployments. Therefore, linking and mapping data stores across different directory services and databases are still primary concerns for most companies and administrators. Solving these problems of identity management includes using the following interfaces and technologies:

▶ *Active Directory Services Interface (ADSI)*—This is a set of extensible, Component Object Model (COM)-based programming interfaces that provide access to a variety of proprietary directory services, such as legacy NT 4 Security Accounts Manager (SAM), Windows 2000 AD, Novell's NetWare Directory Services, and any LDAP-based directory store.

▶ *Active Directory connector (ADC) and Microsoft Directory Synchronization Services (MSDSS)*—This helper synchronizes the data in different LDAP-compliant data stores, such as enterprise resource planning (ERP) applications like Service Advertising Protocol (SAP), with each other. MSDSS provides directory synchronization between Novell Directory Services (NDS) and Windows 2000 AD, and also support for legacy Microsoft Exchange versions 5 and 5.5.

▶ *Metadirectory technology*—This provides enterprise-wide identity management services to non-Microsoft platforms.

The trends in directory service consolidation where the internal data stores—previously managed as separate, internal data repositories—are replaced by a centrally located data store in AD or some other specialized service provider in retrospect seem obvious. Legacy Exchange Server has always stored details about mailboxes, DLs, and other messaging and configuration data in the DS. Consistent and reliable data has been very important; the DS has relied on multimaster replication to ensure that all Exchange servers in the organization that provided messaging services were current and consistent. Legacy DS provided email address validation and GAL management.

Based on metadirectory technology and directory consolidation, Exchange 2000 instead relies heavily on AD rather than its own DS for identity management. This design shift in Exchange 2000 away from an internal data repository is the first example in the BackOffice software suite of directory-service consolidation outside the server application and within the NOS platform. Microsoft states that this design is a new architectural standard. SMFAs within one host computer or across several different servers hosting the same SMFA are totally dependent on some common specialized function that is located somewhere else in the enterprise rather than on their own internal subsystems.

Directory Services

As indicated in Figure 2.4, AD directory services now support far more than authentication and authorization services, as NT LAN Manager (NTLM) authentication protocol did in legacy NT versions. Directory integration has a tremendous impact on the design, deployment, performance, and optimization of Exchange 2000. In fact, the optimal functioning of growing numbers of enterprise services collectively known as the digital nervous system will be far more dependent upon AD infrastructure than in any previous NT version.

As you begin to study AD directory services, you will discover, as Figure 2.5 shows, that AD and the Exchange DS share similar architecture. AD and DS provide an extensible API layer and storage engine, as would be expected of any repository-based technology.

The DS supports MAPI and standards-based LDAP, which are software layers on top of the ESE. Microsoft has stated that the repository engine in Microsoft Repository runs on top of both SQL Server 7 and the Microsoft JET database systems. The storage engine is based on a transactional logging model illustrated in Figure 2.6. A queue directory holds messages in various stages of routing until they are either written to a private or public database or sent to another server. This "holding" store is typically optimized for performance rather than capacity or reliability.

In summary, Exchange 2000 stores data in the following kinds of files:

➤ *Rich-text files*—Messaging API (MAPI) EDB data files that contain message headers, message text, and standard attachments

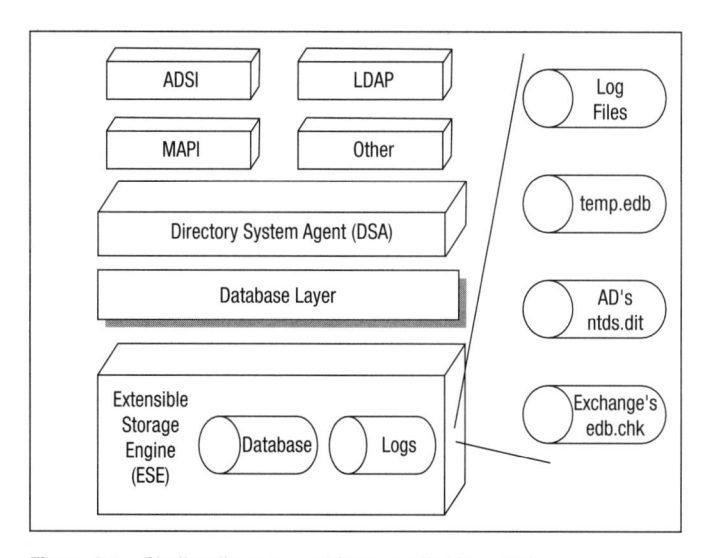

Figure 2.5 Similar directory architectures in AD and DS.

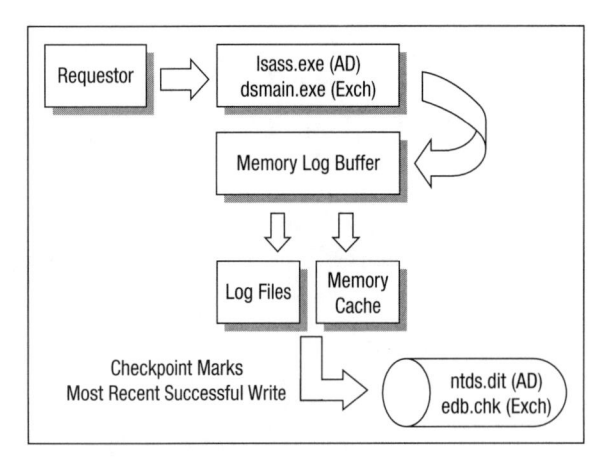

Figure 2.6 A transactional logging model.

- *Native streaming files*—Multipurpose Internet Mail Extensions (MIME) STM data files that contain multimedia content as MIME streams.

- *Sequential transaction files*—Log files that are especially optimized for reliability because they play a critical role in any disaster-recovery scenario.

Upon installation of Exchange, two data stores, each with their own EDB and STM data files, are automatically created: a mailbox (private) store and a public folder (public) store. These "storage" stores are optimized for capacity and reliability. When a message is delivered, it is written to a transaction log file, which is always 5MB in size. The database layer of both AD and DS handle self-contained, independent transactions, often described as *atomic transactions*. A transaction is considered a self-contained, independent set of changes to an object that include creations, deletions, and updates. The Database (DB) layer writes transactions to this current transaction log file and memory-resident cache.

Disk operations that support this logging process are sequential in nature because transactions are logged in sequence. The storage engine, after the transaction is finished and when the operating system allows, commits the transaction to the database store and advances a checkpoint to the beginning of the next uncommitted transaction. The efficiency in this storage system is in sequentially writing messages to the log file first and returning to the queue; searching for and writing to the specific data files located in randomly located stores are performed in an asynchronous and independent manner.

Both Exchange and AD use this storage system technology in the same way. The checkpoint always marks the most recent successfully committed database transaction and plays a critical role in file integrity and disaster recovery. The mechanism for handling either Exchange users or Windows 2000 principals is thus almost the same. Both use the granularity of NTFS Access Control Lists (ACLs) that control access at both the container (folder) and object (file) levels. Because Microsoft doesn't count on green-field deployments, Exchange 2000 includes an ADC that, as stated in the "Transitioning from Monolithic Legacy Environments" section earlier in this chapter, provides bidirectional replication between legacy Exchange and AD data stores.

Protocol Services—Physical Topology

Windows 2000 provides the context in which distributed-service architectures can flourish. .NET servers such as Exchange 2000 are designed to exploit this network environment by implementing partitioned services that can, like identity-management services, be hosted on physically separate machines. Although Exchange 2000 Server is actually designed for standalone Small Office/Home Office (SOHO) business scenarios, Exchange Enterprise Server is designed for enterprise environments that can accommodate more than a million users. This flexibility in architecture comes from the partition of protocol and storage services that can be hosted in a distributed configuration on FE/BE systems.

Administration of these multitier service architectures is uncoupled from the network topology and fault-tolerant hardware technology that transparently provides "five 9" reliability. It is thus easier to manage geographically distributed organizations through centralized maintenance and support using either customized MMC or Windows Management Instrumentation. For example, there are three administrative views of the enterprise through separate MMC snap-in tools—AD Sites and Services, AD Domains and Trusts, and AD Users and Computers—and an array of Exchange-specific snap-ins, including Exchange System Manager. The network topology is administered through Routing Groups. Hardware technology solutions that provide different mixes of capacity, performance, and reliability include Redundant Array of Independent Disks (RAID), Network Attached Storage (NAS), and Storage Area Networks (SANs). Alternatively, virtual server support is delivered through two-way (Windows 2000 Advanced Server) and four-way (Windows 2000 Datacenter Server) active/active clustering. (Clustering is an operating system feature where two active though physically separate machines share a common data store and take "turns" hosting a virtualized server that accesses that common data store at any given moment in time.) These technologies depend on the fundamental concept of partitioned services that can be separated from one another and run on physically separate hardware platforms. Exchange Server 2000 not only partitions its SMFAs but also the specific services within those areas. We will now discuss physical solutions that separate functional components from one another, such as multiple databases, distributed configuration, and clustering.

Multiple Databases

Every version of Exchange has relied on larger message databases as the functional scope of the provided services expanded. Exchange 2000 designed for an enterprise in the .NET gestalt theoretically supports up to 90 databases in 15 separate Storage Groups (SGs)—though this limit has been reduced, in the Release To Manufacturing

(RTM) distribution, to 24. The unlimited database size introduced in version 5.5 has been carried over into Exchange 2000. The hosting of massive data stores (over 100GB per database) is balanced by the ability to separate those data stores into smaller physical databases. This partitioning provides the scalability of spanning large data stores over several physical devices, as well as more practical administration of, for example, backups of more manageably sized physical drives.

Classic backup and restoration strategies can now realistically handle these new storage scenarios in SOHO situations. However, their importance in an environment that demands "five 9" reliability is significant but secondary to newer technologies like NAS and SAN that work transparently below the Open Systems Interconnection (OSI) Application layer and the end user's levels of perception. The strategies used in providing enterprise solutions differ in terms of capacity, performance, and reliability. A single storage solution for all types of data, especially on Exchange 2000, is typically not the most efficient business solution. Furthermore, the balance among the data type, file size, scalability, and manageability of data stores is also affected by corporate IT objectives and the perceived value of the data handled. Although log files and data files in general require different strategic planning to optimize their use as a resource, the most significant selection criterion for any one storage strategy is the corporate perceptions of these data stores in terms of asset value and risk tolerance.

Distributed Configuration

Partitioning specific management functional areas like protocol services, storage services, and directory services provides more than design efficiency. In a .NET gestalt, these services are distributed across different host servers. Similar to when we use a multitier architectural model, which separates presentation services from business logic and data storage, we can create a front-end server farm that is responsible for collecting incoming requests for Exchange 2000. This bank of front-end servers provides a unified namespace. For example, in an enterprise with multiple Exchange servers that host private stores, each client would have to specify its own host. A front-end bank of servers alternatively "presents" to the user population a scalable unified namespace, an easily configurable point of access into their mail system that will, in turn, relay requests to the appropriate host of the private stores.

Front-end servers also provide inherent network efficiencies such as load balancing. Load balancing, achieved through the Windows 2000 Network Load Balancing service or manipulation of Internet Protocol (IP) addresses (a DNS round-robin), means that incoming requests for service are balanced across a group of up to 32 servers acting as physically independent request queues. This front-end role, easily configured on a server's Properties sheet, provides scalable access and high levels of performance necessary to support an enterprise's messaging needs. When you enable this front-end server feature, service requests are automatically relayed to the back-end database storage services located on a different host server. It is important to remember that FE/BE technology provides load balancing but does not provide any fault-tolerance measures.

Clustering

Paralleling the separation of physiology from anatomy and function from structure, *clustering* is a technology that virtualizes a single service on multiple host servers. This feature, like directory services, is provided by the NOS through an easy-to-use graphical user interface called Configure Your Server. The server cluster is composed of individual nodes that share common storage. Clustering was introduced in version 5.5, but the technology was limited. In its first release, the service ran on only one node at a time in the cluster. In other words, one node was the active host; the other passively slept. If the active node failed, the passive node assumed its host role for the virtualized services. This active/passive version has been replaced by an active/active version in which the services can run on all nodes simultaneously. Current versions of Windows 2000 Advanced Server and Windows 2000 Datacenter Server provide this active/active cluster feature with two nodes and four nodes, respectively. The following coordinate the nodes:

➤ *Cluster Service*—Running on each node, it monitors performance and workload across the cluster.

➤ *Resource Monitor*—Running on each node, it interfaces with local resources on the node.

The virtualization of services is not associated with any one specific hardware platform. However, it is so "real" that the virtual service in fact has its own name associated with an IP network address (from its current host) published by the cluster service. Virtual services form resource groups that the cluster manages. A resource group is owned by one node at a time and moves as a unit. A node, hosting a resource group, knows where to move the resource group in case of failure. The cluster service moves the resource group and reassigns the IP address to correspond to the new hosting node. The cluster in itself is assigned a single IP address to which all service requests are addressed. Within the cluster, all nodes belong to the same subnet so that the cluster's primary IP address is within a common broadcast domain and thus can be redirected to the resource group on whichever host it currently resides. This technology leverages the use of multiple databases in separate Storage Groups to support a failover event, when one node in, for example, a two-node cluster fails and the resource group is automatically moved to the other node. Cluster technology delivers "five 9" reliability service levels to mission-critical operations with little impact on variable expenses for maintenance, support, or training.

Note: Do not confuse the virtual services in a resource group with another Exchange 2000 feature called Virtual Servers, which involves assigning virtual servers to different physical IP addresses bound to separate network adapters on the same physical machine.

Chapter Summary

This chapter addressed the infrastructure through which Exchange 2000 provides core scalability, reliability, simplicity, and lower TCO. The architecture was introduced from a historical point of view because the structure of version 5.5 is not only similar to Exchange 2000 but also still a viable messaging platform. Its broad embedded base increases the likelihood that you either will encounter it deployed as a production platform or will be faced with the prospect of upgrading its services and migrating its users to Exchange 2000. Below are some particularly significant points to remember:

- There is an increasing tendency among all three major NOSs to consolidate directory services as metadirectories. Exchange 2000 is one of the first application server products to use data stores located in the AD rather than in its own internal data repository.

- Microsoft has positioned Windows 2000 as an increasingly standards-based, scalable, and extensible NOS able to provide very large-scale support for Web-based organizations. Through the use of AD, Exchange 2000, and NOS-based IIS, it can expose data objects and provide developmental tools that can communicate, collaborate, and control the workflow of any network-based business.

- One can significantly reduce TCO by controlling maintenance, support, and training; capital investment is usually not the primary contributor to TCO. Exchange 2000 reduces TCO through extensibility of its functional areas of management, uncoupling of function from hardware and network topology, and use of standards-based protocols. Another approach to reduce TCO is to simplify administration by centralizing management.

- The legacy SA (mad.exe) is the initial Exchange loader and performs numerous tasks, including maintaining the routing tables and new recipient addressing; monitors link integrity messages from other Exchange servers; manages directory integrity; accumulates message transport data; generates foreign message addresses; and interacts with the Key Management component.

- The legacy IS (store.exe) manages one or two data stores: priv.edb and public.edb. The store.exe file delivers mail to local recipients, relays incoming and outgoing mail to the MTA, notifies recipients of incoming mail, resolves names through directory lookups, and manages public folders.

- The legacy MTA routes mail between the local IS and other Exchange servers. It uses helpers like the legacy X.400 connector and DRAS. The MTA internally converts MAPI messages to/from X.400 format and expands DLs.

- Like the IS, Exchange DS (dsamain.exe) is both a service and a data store. It stores data about internal operations such as synchronization and routing. It replicates this data across all other Exchange servers.

Review Questions

1. Which SMFA has been "outsourced" to Windows 2000?
   a. Identity maintenance
   b. Permission management
   c. Directory services
   d. Directory database
   e. Network services

2. What significant characteristic do Microsoft Windows 2000 interfaces provide?
   a. Backward compatibility
   b. Consolidated directory services
   c. Scalability
   d. Extensibility
   e. Security

3. Which of the following will not reduce TCO when you are implementing Exchange Server?
   a. Different HTTP client software
   b. Customized electronic forms on a Web site
   c. Standards-based protocols
   d. Installing Exchange 2000 in a NT 4 domain

4. Which is not a contributor to the TCO of IT?
   a. Maintenance
   b. Support
   c. Capital investments
   d. None of the above

5. What protocol does not interoperate with Exchange 2000?
   a. XML
   b. HML
   c. HTML
   d. HTTP

6. What is a major theme that significantly simplifies administration of a software product?

    a. Good documentation
    b. Clear graphical displays
    c. Good toolbars
    d. Good help screens

7. Which executables are X.400 standard components? [Check all correct answers]

    a. mad.exe
    b. external.exe
    c. store.exe
    d. ds.exe

8. What program helps the Message Transfer Agent (MTA)?

    a. X.400 connector
    b. X.500 connector
    c. RAS connector
    d. All of the above

9. What is the process that DS uses to send and receive directory updates from other mail servers? [Check the best answer]

    a. Synchronization
    b. Repopulation
    c. Replication
    d. Answer a or c

10. Which statement about Key Management is correct?

    a. It is not part of Exchange services.
    b. It provides Data Encryption Standard (DES) encryption services.
    c. It provides both DES and MIME encryption services.
    d. It provides both DES and Secure MIME (S/MIME) encryption services.

11. Which of the following provides asynchronous connectivity?

    a. Dynamic RAS (DRAS)
    b. Site connector
    c. X.400 connector
    d. None of the above

12. Which feature distinguishes Exchange 5.5 from earlier versions?
    a. X.400 connector
    b. MAPI
    c. Storage services
    d. Public folders

13. Which Exchange version introduced support for the Internet mail protocol SMTP?
    a. Version 4
    b. Version 5
    c. Version 5.5
    d. Exchange 2000

14. Which are not concurrent processes in the workflow of a legacy Exchange server? [Check all correct answers]
    a. DS controls access to MSs.
    b. MTA manages local messages.
    c. IS handles message storage.
    d. SA replicates messages.

15. How is Exchange different from Lotus Notes?
    a. Exchange does not provide collaborative services like Notes.
    b. Exchange is a messaging and collaborative service; Notes is just a collaborative service.
    c. Exchange focuses on messaging; Notes focuses on sharing data.
    d. Exchange provides integration with Access for data sharing.

16. Which statement is not correct?
    a. MTA manages protocols to provide routing services.
    b. IS references dir.edb to determine addressing information.
    c. IS is a data store and a service.
    d. SA is run only when it is necessary to perform housekeeping tasks.

17. To streamline the legacy Exchange design, which service is redundant?
    a. IS
    b. SA
    c. DS
    d. MTA

18. What software component is considered a transitional solution when you upgrade from legacy Exchange?

    a. ADSI

    b. AD

    c. ADC

    d. None of the above

19. Which technology would improve performance but not reliability?

    a. Clustering

    b. FE/BE distributed configurations

    c. Resource groups

    d. Load balancing

20. Which Exchange products support clustering? [Check all correct answers]

    a. Exchange Enterprise Server version 5.5

    b. Exchange Server 2000

    c. Exchange Enterprise Server 2000

    d. All of the above

Real-World Projects

Warning: This exercise assumes that a test Windows 2000 Server is installed. We strongly recommend that you read the instructions carefully and thoroughly *before* installing the product. Never perform a trial or practice installation on a production machine unless you understand the options presented and are willing to accept responsibility for the worst possible outcomes: total loss of data and reinstallation of a NOS. If you are unsure about an option, cancel the installation and consult, for example, **www.microsoft.com/technet** or **www.microsoft.com/exchange** about the option to be installed.

Two2Tango Inc. is an international online dating service. It has hired Terry Tulleridge to administer its Exchange 2000 messaging system. Terry earned her Windows 2000 MCSE last month and is very excited about working with Exchange 2000. She has experience running a 300-seat Exchange 5.5 installation and has concentrated her studies over the last two months on Windows 2000 AD design. Terry has read that Exchange 2000 provides global, single-seat control just like version 5.5 but uses a new interface called Exchange System Manager. System Manager manages all Exchange objects. She also knows that other complementary tools will snap into the MMC. She needs to consider delegating administrative responsibility to regionally located administrators all over the world. She will send each regional administrator his or her own specific "Exchange toolset." Terry sits down and begins to build a customized console for herself. She is curious to see how long the process will take.

Project 2.1

To build a customized console:

1. Click once on the Start menu.
2. Select Run.
3. Type "mmc /a".
4. On the Console menu in the upper-left corner of the window, select Add/Remove Snap-in. Note that the keyboard equivalent is Ctrl+M.
5. Click on Add and then select Exchange System.
6. Click on OK, click on Close, and then click on OK again.

This is easy to do and fast, she says to herself. She next decides to add more customization to the console so that each regional administrator will have only the tools he or she needs to get the job done. She has learned that this is a good procedure when delegating responsibility to operators at remote sites. She realizes that some "regionals" may not actually be "network people," so to simplify the tasks she needs them to perform, she uses the Taskpad icons. She believes this approach is less intimidating and more graphical than memorizing a series of dialog box responses.

Project 2.2

To create a console Taskpad:

1. On the console's menu bar, click on the Window button.
2. Select New Window and make certain it is maximized.
3. In the left pane, right-click on the Computer Management icon.
4. Select New Taskpad View.
5. Follow the wizard and take the time to read every panel. Accept the default settings.
6. At the wizard's conclusion, click on Finish.
7. Press the Hide Console Tree toolbar button.
8. In the View menu, click on Customize and select each option to Show/Hide.
9. When you are finished, click on OK.
10. Click on the Console button and select Save As.
11. Name your customized console and click on the Save button.

Having hidden unnecessary information and tested her ability to customize specific functions in a single console, Terry is confident she can send each "regional" his or her own customized "Exchange toolset" that will be easy to use even without a technical background. She will be able to delegate administrative responsibility without increasing training costs because most of the operations will be performed from the Taskpad. She congratulates herself for completing her task in much less time than she anticipated and for creating her own customized instrumentation.

CHAPTER THREE
Storage Services

After completing this chapter, you will be able to:

✓ Describe the design objectives for Exchange storage services

✓ Discuss specific features of the Web Storage System

✓ List the main areas of programming support for the Web Store

✓ Differentiate among Exchange database file types

✓ Explain how a transaction is processed

✓ Discuss how data is analyzed for full-text searches

✓ Recount different methods of establishing database consistency

✓ Distinguish the different roles of Exchange Storage Engine Database Utility (ESEUTIL), Information Store Integrity Checker (ISINTEG), and Exchange Storage Engine File Utility (ESEFILE)

✓ Define the role of the EXchange InterProcess Communication layer (known as EPOXY)

Microsoft's stated objective in collaborative services is to make information available anytime, anywhere, from any device. The Web Store as a concept is intuitively obvious. To make as many different data objects accessible to a collaborative workspace as possible, you need to use a common application programming interface (API) that is open to as many different kinds of clients as technically possible. This intuitive concept, however, requires a type of file system heretofore unknown. This universally accessible workspace must support devices that range from palmtops to desktops; protocols such as legacy Messaging API (MAPI) and Internet Mail Access Protocol (IMAP) 4; and data types such as email text with images, sound, video, collaborative calendaring, and contacts. Then, Exchange administrators need to add legacy application files from Microsoft Word, Excel, and PowerPoint. Administrators need a way to dynamically catalog these objects so that they can be systematically retrieved. Finally, administrators must provide a client interface that can show these different objects in one universal window with all the drag-and-drop functionality to which administrators have grown so accustomed. Knowledge workers (what were formerly called *end users*) will expect to seamlessly manipulate these displayed objects within and across universal windows in the same unified way as they do now across their desktop.

This is what the Web Store—technically called Exchange Installable File System (EXIFS)—provides for us through a unified messaging and collaboration platform called Exchange 2000. EXIFS runs in Exchange 2000 as a hidden service that allows file-level access to objects in mailboxes (which were formerly private) and public file stores through a system-generated M: drive created on the Exchange server (as shown in Figure 3.1). Beneath the M: drive you see a folder named for

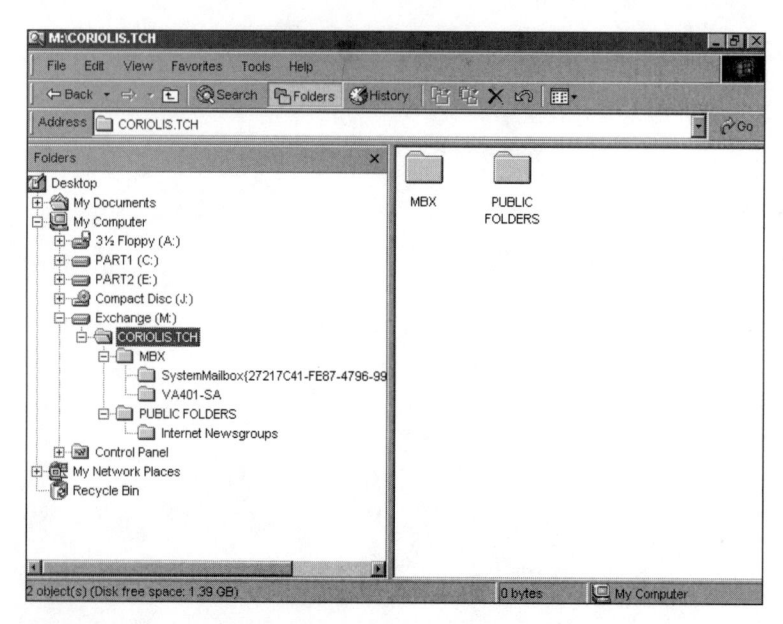

Figure 3.1 Windows Explorer view of the Exchange Installable File System.

the Active Directory domain in which the Exchange 2000 is installed, in this case, CORIOLIS.TCH (where TCH is an arbitrary top-level domain extension). The significance and functionality of EXIFS, especially in view of Microsoft's operating system initiatives, have yet to be fully realized, in terms of accessibility from beyond the legacy networked workstation.

This chapter covers storage services—specifically, design objectives, the Web Storage System, database file structure, the Extensible Storage Engine (ESE), and manipulation of public folders as fundamental storage service activities. The chapter describes how EXIFS provides greater capacity than legacy disk storage, increased reliability, and improved performance in an enterprise environment. It then describes how you can systematically retrieve information through indexing, which is a critically significant feature in both document management and knowledge management (KM) services. We conclude with a discussion of database consistency and protocol services as they relate to storage issues.

Design Objectives

Exchange 2000 storage services have been designed so that information barriers to collaboration are minimized or totally removed and so that heterogeneous file types can be stored in a container without limits to accessibility, capacity, and reliability. The Web Storage System provides many of these features through the functionality of a file system, the accessibility of the Web, and the structural characteristics of a centralized repository that can store and manage as many kinds of content as digital technology can provide. This system must also include specific management functional areas (SMFAs) responsible for content categorization and efficient search methods. Furthermore, such a file system that supports Microsoft's shibboleth of "knowledge without limits" must centralize administration as well as provide scalability, reliability, and security.

Enhanced Administration

EXIFS integrates heterogeneous content by providing a single repository for messaging-related data as well as other information resources within one common infrastructure. The integration of file system services, database services, and collaboration services provides the unified messaging platform on which knowledge workers need to perform their work. A single, unified KM system enables administrators of such a platform to reduce the total cost of ownership (TCO) of even the smallest Small Office/Home Office (SOHO) because using one storage engine to manage multiple applications and services helps improve production and decrease maintenance costs and training. Deploying one repository like the Web Storage System unifies both the storage engine and the shared storage space.

Administrative tools that are needed to manage SMFAs—such as configuration, performance, and fault management—and disaster-recovery functions like backup and restoration, are further simplified in this single-system scheme. A single storage repository similarly simplifies application development by reusing the same API used to access an even broader base of exposed data objects. The Web Storage System, because of its increased capacity, demands more elaborate content management features for data retrieval of heretofore-isolated Microsoft Office documents. The unstructured data stores of, for example, Microsoft Word and Excel, can now be commingled and assimilated into a larger, though still manageable, collaborative context of Exchange messages and, for example, Public Folder documents. Other management features include enhanced end-user access control through an extensible array of application interfaces ranging from a 21-inch PC desktop to 1.5-inch wireless cellular phone display window. Thus, Exchange 2000 provides greater scalability and centralized control over these data stores through storage unification.

Scalability and Control

New Exchange 2000 features (such as Storage Groups) impact on the administration and management of storage services, and all support enhanced scalability, reliability, and capacity. Individual service areas within the Exchange messaging system (protocol services and directory services) are uncoupled from storage services to offer greater flexibility and scalability across physically separate host servers than the monolithic architecture of legacy Exchange. Within storage services, you can partition Message Stores (MSs) in manageable databases of unlimited capacity. Although legacy Exchange MSs were based on only one database, you can now split Information Stores (ISs) across separate physical database files on the same host server or different servers. You can independently stop or start these databases for maintenance. The objective here is to approach year-round accessibility to online services that "five 9" reliability service levels demand. Within these MSs, Exchange version 5.5 divided data files into private mailbox stores and Public Folder stores. Exchange Enterprise 2000 specifically replaces these two data files with multiple stores within Storage Groups (SGs). An SG of multiple databases functions as a single administrative unit and shares a common transaction log. Different strategies exist for partitioning data files; a single SG on a host can have multiple databases or a host server can support multiple SGs.

Storage Unification

Probably the most important feature of Exchange storage services is EXIFS, commonly called the Exchange 2000 Web Store. The Web Store, by default, is mapped to a logical drive M: (called a *portal* into the store.exe process) on the host Exchange server as shown in Figure 3.1. The MBX subfolder under the folder named for the Active Directory domain is the logical root for all mailboxes on this particular server. The M: drive supports the same Win32 interfaces that you use to read and write data to any legacy object located on the familiar local or logical drives. A browser client can access data objects using Hypertext Transport Protocol (HTTP) and the Uniform Resource Locator (URL) **http://hostserver/username**. It is significant that the IS acts like a mounted file system so that both local and remote applications can address it through a mapped drive or universal naming convention to store their data. It is even more dramatic that these same objects are also accessible through an HTTP-based URL. Finally, it's a major departure from all previous versions of Exchange storage services that this same Web Store has built-in indexing to support content searches.

The relationship between Exchange 2000 and Windows 2000 at both the functional and structural levels is noteworthy. The exposure of MSs to Web-based clients through close integration with Internet Information Services (IIS), in addition to a reliance on Active Directory (AD) for identity and permission management, signals a significant departure from previous software designs.

From a solutions services perspective, the Web Store provides the following three services:

- *File system services*—These services expose both Office documents and audio and video streaming data to access by client software regardless of whether data is in the form of hierarchical collections (folder trees) or heterogeneous file types.

- *Database services*—These services retrieve data based on queries more complex than searches within the file system services. Views are kept consistent when updates change the values of data.

- *Collaboration services*—These services provide messaging, contacts, calendaring data support, and group and realtime collaboration.

The Web Store is basically a single repository for heterogeneous file types (including contacts and calendaring, email, and voice mail messaging) using consistent search and data categorization. This unified store supports the expanded use of not only Exchange Server 2000, but also Office 2000 and other BackOffice service providers.

From a services-management perspective, two other design objectives are critical, namely:

- *Fault tolerance*—Using multiple databases and SGs that can be independently managed minimizes losses through service failures.

- *Load balancing and scalability*—Partitioning databases and judiciously using SGs can increase capacity, performance, and reliability. For example, if a disaster occurs, faster restorations require less downtime of potentially smaller segments of the user population.

All these objectives have been achieved through Exchange 2000 design changes and promise to be incorporated into an entirely new operating system approach in all future Microsoft.NET servers. This new approach will involve a more loosely coupled enterprise of distributed, building block services that will depend on the above objectives.

Installable File System Features

Key concepts in exposing heterogeneous file types to such a broad range of clients lie in object storage and conversion using a file format compatible with any client that requests the object. We'll discuss Web-based support, public folders, native (streaming) data files, and other such concepts in this section.

In Exchange version 5.5, messages were maintained in Message Database Encapsulated Format (MDBEF). When a Web-based, non-MAPI client requested a message from the store, IS (now the *rich-text data store*) used the IMAIL process to convert the contents from MDBEF to the appropriate Multipurpose Internet Mail Extensions (MIME) or non-MIME format, depending on the client's characteristics. This conversion process consumed both time and resources. EXIFS alternatively includes two storage formats: a native content store (*.stm file) and a rich-text store (the legacy *.edb file). The native content store helps to minimize the overhead involved in file type conversions.

EXIFS now exposes all objects as normal files accessible through a network share point. Because EXIFS is a hidden service, you cannot see it in the Services applet within the Administrative Tools program menu. You can stop and start the EXIFS service, however, by issuing **net stop** and **net start** commands from the command line. Halting the service does not cause the drive mapping to disappear.

> **Warning:** Attempting to restart the EXIFS service may cause a System 2 error. This is a confirmed problem in Microsoft Exchange 2000 Server. Article Q246216 in TechNet (dated October 3, 2000) advises that you should execute **subst m: /d** from the command line before **net start exifs**.

Within the EXIFS portal is a domain folder named for the domain in which the Exchange server is installed. Within that container are two component EXIFS folders:

➤ A mailbox folder (MBX) root for all mailboxes on the Exchange server

➤ An All Public Folders folder that is the root of the default Public Folder tree

If you have the appropriate permissions, you can access these hierarchies using, for example, explicit folder names that correspond to mailbox alias names. In fact, each folder and object has a unique, text-based URL associated with it for HTTP Web access.

Web-Based Support

The most important feature of the Web Storage System is accessibility. The broadest range of clients are Web based, so EXIFS natively supports the HTTP protocol and is configured to integrate with IIS. Hypertext Markup Language (HTML) support is built into the system and, in fact, provides graphical HTML 3.2 support of folders and their contents. Internet Explorer provides the same view of folder hierarchies that a MAPI client like Outlook would display in the form of a file tree of network shares. In addition, Extensible Markup Language (XML) provides standards-based programmable access to the Web Store and its content. Native support for XML is a very important design addition because it provides remote access to this data and control of services through Web-based platform and protocol-independent scripting..

The Web Storage System is accessible through a set of HTTP extensions collectively called Web Distributed Authoring and Versioning (WebDAV). These extensions represent an additional standards-based software layer that rests on top of HTTP 1.1 as a helper. WebDAV provides read/write access to the data store over HTTP. It accommodates, for example, structured, relational database tables and objects as well as unstructured, word processing documents. In addition, you can synchronize the contents of WebDAV clients to their server-side counterparts, allowing offline usage of automatically updated data. WebDAV has made the use of Web folders almost identical to the use of network file server folders, except for the client and the HTTP protocol.

Public Folder Support

Public folders have similarly undergone changes from version 5.5 to Exchange 2000. You now administer them from a Microsoft Management Console (MMC) snap-in called Exchange Folders. Public folders stored in a hierarchical structure are referred to as a *Public Folder tree*. Each tree stores its data in a single folder store on each server. You can't create a Public Folder store without first creating a Public Folder tree. Regarding access, the default Public Folder tree, referred to as the MAPI Clients Tree in the System Manager MMC snap-in, is the only tree accessible to MAPI clients like Outlook 2000. Other Public Folder trees, referred to as *General Purpose Trees*, are currently accessible only to compliant Network News Transfer Protocol (NNTP) clients, Web browsers, and Windows applications through the EXIFS and WebDAV.

Public folders are important because they can replicate their contents to multiple Exchange servers. The process of copying folders produces multimaster replicas distributed across the Exchange namespace. This process not only improves workflow through better load balancing of servers but also improves chances of recovery from an unexpected system disruption due to server failure. Because there is no master replica, changes made to one replica are automatically replicated to all other replicas in the organization. It is best to choose a default Public Folder server that is located in the same Windows 2000 site and Exchange 2000 Routing Group as the home mailbox store to keep delays in replication acceptable.

Management of these folders has also been improved. Just as different Administrative Groups simplify the organization of recipients, you can now create multiple Public Folder trees separate from the default Public Folder tree. Furthermore, each public folder can have specific usage rules to maintain security. In fact, Public Folder trees have their own hierarchies and owner-defined access criteria. Although Public Folder trees are replicated to all Exchange servers in an organization, the content of those trees can be replicated only to designated servers.

Streaming Data Support

In the early 1970s, simple text files traveled across the Internet. Nowadays, users are sending messages with extremely large multimedia components. Though they enrich our digital experience, these multimedia messages place huge demands on bandwidth and the data storage capacity. EXIFS natively stores large messages and attachments. It services client requests for this data through data streams that are different from the older, but more common, rich-text format (RTF). Streaming technology also supports specialized applications like PowerPoint 2000 and NetShow. Because streaming media support comes directly from the Web Storage System natively storing the content, content management is treated the same way as any other data content.

Integration of the Web Storage System with Windows 2000

The Web Storage System is seamlessly integrated with Windows 2000 and leverages that association by using AD data stores. Windows 2000 Access Control Lists (ACLs) are used in the Web Storage System through its close association with AD. EXIFS uses configuration information and the security information to extend user access control to individual containers and their contents item by item. Security group assignments and tools (such as the Windows Explorer ACL editor, which modifies permissions) apply to objects in the EXIFS share just as they would in a Windows 2000 network file share. Because both are integrated with one another, using EXIFS does not increase the overhead associated with security management. Similarly, administrators already familiar with directory services will find little changed when they are managing objects in the Web Store.

Property Promotion

Emphasis on KM makes rapid document search and retrieval a mission-critical function. As more and more data is assimilated into the Web Storage System, identifiable properties that distinguish one unstructured Word document from another will assume a new level of significance. EXIFS can store these custom properties in its database to enhance future retrieval. In fact, Outlook's product leverage in the marketplace is that knowledge workers can use the same application to manage both shared and personal documents containing messaging, calendar, and contact information. This "unified canvas" (one of Microsoft's many buzzwords), on which any kind of data can be viewed and manipulated, is the digital dashboard that commingles messaging, collaborative, and Microsoft Office product data objects in, for example, a single Outlook interface. This unified window delivers to knowledge workers the promised vision of working in a common interface without information constraints or limits.

The Web Storage System, through a feature called *property promotion*, can automatically populate record fields (such as the document author's name, title, and so on) in a consistent view independent of the client who is accessing the information. You can truly consider the Outlook inbox to be universal when all object types are displayed as entries with their properties promoted to listable fields displayed in one of its windowpanes. End users will be able to search across objects of any object type or location across a vast data store. This integrated view extends across clients and different but compatible applications, increasing the productivity of almost every computer-related task.

Offline Folders

Although the emphasis has been on connected data objects, the Web Storage System also provides seamless offline, asynchronous integration with online resources. For some time, Outlook has provided the explicit synchronization of the same online/offline containers and their contents. The Briefcase data structure is another example of this specialized container. With EXIFS, Windows 2000 users have the benefits of a synchronized data store regardless of client without training or additional overhead. Thus, especially in view of the proliferation of laptop, handheld, and palmtop devices, EXIFS, in combination with Windows 2000, can provide an asynchronous, connection-independent workspace that can, on demand, automatically resynchronize itself with the online world whenever or wherever there is a connection or dial-up access.

Programming Support and Development

EXIFS provides automatic integration of key collaborative objects like messaging, contacts, and calendaring through the use of known Web technologies, development methods, and programming models such as Active Server Pages (ASP) and Component Object Model (COM)+. Key features of particular interest to developers are:

➤ *Win32*—This legacy API seamlessly integrates with EXIFS's leverage so that the sharing of EXIFS resources is functionally identical with the sharing of folders and files through a network share on a file server. Applications that use network-sharing features can be ported to EXIFS without design modifications. End users do not require training.

➤ *ActiveX Data Objects (ADOs)*—ADOs provide simplified APIs that access Web Store objects just as they do network-based objects. These ADOs also provide support for structured data found in products such as relational database management systems like Structured Query Language (SQL) Server, programming languages like Visual Basic, and Web application technologies like ASP.

➤ *Object Linking and Embedding Database (OLEDB)*—Like ADO, this COM API provides access to data objects. Unlike ADO, OLE DB is a low-level API that through an OLE DB provider installed with Exchange offers developers a richer set of object properties and methods. This interface is the method of choice for COM-based system-level development that integrates with other BackOffice products such as SQL Server.

➤ *Collaborative Data Objects (CDOs)*—CDOs are APIs that expose objects related to messaging, calendaring, and contact management for application development using programming languages. Exchange Server includes a library of workflow services that specifically leverage a distinguishing characteristic of this object class: the transactional, synchronous nature of events related to these objects.

These popular object models and APIs, in conjunction with development tools such as Visual Studio, provide rapid application development without programming that requires additional training. EXIFS and the Win32 API seamlessly integrate to create solutions that incorporate other unique software features and added functionality. EXIFS also supports Internet standards, so well-known tools (such as the end-user authoring FrontPage application) further expand the possibilities of using existing, well-tested Web-based applications as a substrate on which to attach new functionality and expand already existing business applications.

The Collaborative Workspace

A globally accessible, 24×7×365 Web Store, by definition, demands reliability because it must be accessed all the time. This operational requirement has changed the way administrators design and manage IT service-providing platforms. For example, fault tolerance hardware design provides reliable access. Similarly, partitioning of data stores allows periodic maintenance without a perceived interruption in service. There are now many reasons to provide such demanding levels of service. When assessing this operational need in relation to the scale of an enterprise with a known user population, most of us are overwhelmed. If you assess this same need in relation to the scope of an unknown population across the Internet, accessing objects in the same data store, you begin to see why support strategies used in a legacy NT 4 environment are no longer applicable. There is, however, still yet another dimension to this scenario. The nature of the data and how it is used have subtly changed. Since the 1970s, information technologies have been basically information processing. The growing emphasis on working with "knowledge" shifts our approach from this information processing to managing now-huge information and data stores. KM adds the collaborative dimension to this mix of digital resources. It demands the unlimited, simultaneous presentation of many kinds of content on one universal canvas—anytime, from anywhere, using any device. This presentation of content without barriers and the distributed services architecture that would support it are what Microsoft describes as Microsoft.NET. We will now better define the fundamental database file structure that can potentially provide this unlimited data store found in Exchange 2000.

Database File Types

An Exchange 2000 database consists of two kinds of files that accommodate different content:

➤ *Rich-text file (*.edb)*—This legacy file type contains mail messages and MAPI content.

➤ *Streaming file (*.stm)*—This native content file type is specially designed to store multimedia MIME content and specifically non-MAPI information.

Exchange 2000 treats rich-text and streaming files—along with Key Management Server files (*.kms) used for security encryption services and Site Replication Service files (*.srs) for backward compatibility—as record types collected in a single database. A pair of one *.stm and one *.edb file are together considered one message within that database; this message contains native content and space-usage information (the *.stm portion), and checksums (the *.edb portion). These file pairs are organized into 4K pages, though the structure of each file type and the content are different. Legacy Exchange stored *.edb data in 8K pages. Although *.edb files are organized as B-tree structures for indexing, *.stm files are grouped in clusterings of raw blocks to provide more efficient support for their streaming content.

An Exchange 2000 database in the Web Storage System supports three different file types: *.log files, *.stm files, and *.edb files. Mailbox stores, called private ISs in legacy versions, now consist of both priv1.edb and priv1.stm files. Similarly, a Public Folder store, called a public IS in legacy versions, contains pub1.edb and pub1.stm.

Though the file content has changed, the databases themselves still support version 5.5 features like the Single-Instance Store (SIS) feature, illustrated in Figure 3.2, where a message is stored once within a database. A single instance of a 1MB message is separately sent to 50 recipients in the Private Information Store labeled Mailbox Store 101 in Storage Group 1; another 1 MB message is sent to another 50 recipients in Storage Group 2. Any recipient of that message in that mailbox store is sent a pointer to that message content, not a copy of the original object. Thus, the message that is sent to 100 people occupies a combined total of only 2MB of storage space. With the introduction of multiple databases and SGs, however, the usefulness of this feature has changed; SIS can neither extend outside any one database, nor is it maintained in different databases in any one SG.

Changes to the database are stored in transaction log files. These files are a sequential list of every operation performed on the database in Exchange 2000 and are critical for restoring committed transactions that can be lost due to a disruption in service. The current log file is always named edb.log (for Exchange DataBase), where *edb* represents the actual base name of the file on the server. As the maximum 5MB

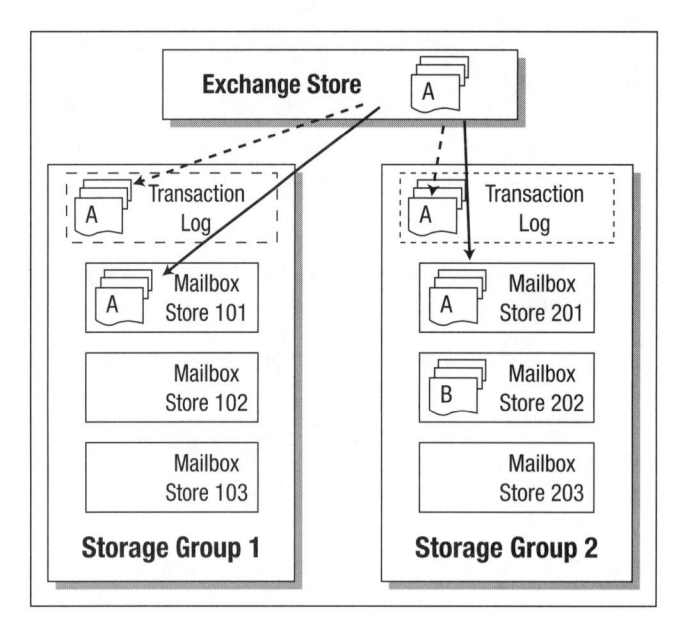

Figure 3.2 How SIS works.

size is reached, the edbtemp.log file is started. The log file is renamed edb*xxxxx*.log, where *xxxxx* is a five-digit hexadecimal equivalent of the number of the next transaction to be entered in the log file. The edbtemp.log file becomes edb.log, and the process repeats itself.

Rich-Text Files

Rich-text files hold messages from MAPI clients such as Microsoft Outlook. These are legacy file types from older Exchange versions and use transaction logging just like version 5.5. MAPI clients access messages from these data stores without converting them. If a non-MAPI client attempts to read a rich-text file, Exchange must convert the message to the file type of the requesting client. The process that converts messages to dissimilar clients is called *on-demand conversion*.

Exchange 2000, by default, avoids converting data because the native file format has changed from legacy rich text to the streaming file type. This deferred content conversion reflects the move toward Web-based client access and the richer content available across the Internet. Thus, the client request now determines whether a conversion occurs. If, for example, an Outlook client requests a message stored in a native content *.stm file, Exchange 2000 does not move the message out of its native content store. Rather, it converts it in memory (RTF/HTML converter) and passes it directly to the MAPI client. If, however, the Outlook client modifies the file and saves it, Exchange assumes the client will make subsequent requests for data. Upon receiving the updated message, Exchange converts the native content to rich text and writes it to the legacy rich-text file store. It then deletes the message in the native content store.

Streaming Files

Version 5.5 has only one data type—rich text—so it writes messages to the *.edb data store in MDBEF format. A non-MDBEF format from the Internet (e.g., MIME) first needs to be converted by the special IMAIL process to be written to the data store in MDBEF format. Exchange 2000 has changed the native content store and reversed this entire process so that HTTP and IMAP4 store the content directly without wasting time and resources. The native content file handles streaming data (which includes audio, video, voice, and other multimedia formats) without the unnecessary overhead of compression or B-tree indexing used in *.edb format. Specifically, *.stm pages are grouped in clustered block or run format, much like file allocation tables are used in NT File System (NTFS). These pages are clustered as 16 runs of 4K pages each or 64K blocks to facilitate more efficient input/output (I/O) processing. Thus, messages delivered from the native content file are "streamed" to the non-MAPI client. In a similar way, any non-messaging Win32-based client accesses the native content data over server message block (SMB) architecture. Local area network (LAN)-based clients thus share access to the native content as network file shares in addition to HTTP-based clients.

The Extensible Storage Engine (ESE)

The ESE has replaced Joint Engine Technology (JET)—JET Blue as distinguished from JET Red in Access—in version 5.5 as an efficient, self-tuning, transaction logging system that maintains data integrity and consistency in the Exchange data stores. ESE fundamentally manages database transactions and is used by the AD and other Windows 2000 system services. A *transaction* is a sequence of related tasks treated as an indivisible unit for the purposes of integrity. Either the transaction is completed (or committed) or it is deleted (or rolled back) as a single unit. Any transaction must satisfy the four following criteria, commonly referred to as the ACID test—described in International Organization of Standardization/International Electrotechnical Commission (ISO/IEC) 10026-1:1992 Section 4:

➤ *Atomicity*—All operations or tasks in a transaction are completed by the system in their entirety or none will be completed.

➤ *Consistency*—A transaction creates a new valid state of data in the system or returns the data to the previous state it was in before the transaction was applied.

➤ *Isolation*—A transaction remains independent of all other transactions or processes until it is committed by the system.

➤ *Durability*—Once a transaction is committed by the system, the data state created by that transaction is permanently available even if a system failure and restore occur.

Of the four criteria listed above, durability is the most significant. ESE uses transaction logs to ensure, upon restarting the Exchange service following a graceful or ungraceful shutdown, that the data stores are in the same state they were in immediately before the shutdown.

System-Related File Types

The ESE provides Exchange with flexible, high-performance transacted storage by using several key files. ESE writes specific operations in a sequential order to transaction logs (*.log), then to cached buffers, then to disk. This procedure minimizes I/O activity, increases performance, and provides integrity upon recovery from a shutdown. All "instances" of a database—that is, where multiple databases are run as an SG under a single ESE process—share a common log file. As Exchange writes transactions to the *.edb and *.stm data stores on disk, a checkpoint file (*.chk) advances through the log file, marking the last completed transaction. Thus, each SG has a *.log file that chronicles each consecutive database operation and a *.chk file that marks the last completed operation. During recovery, ESE uses the *.chk file when and where the last I/O operations were done.

During online backup procedures, Exchange copies database pages located on disk to a tape backup unit for either long-term, offline storage or as part of a disaster recovery. Patch files (*.pat) are used only during the backup and recovery procedures where one is created for each database file during a backup procedure. Exchange supports online backup and restore procedures, so user transactions continue to occur during the procedure. If one of these user transactions refers to a page that has not yet been copied to the tape, it is written to disk before that portion of the disk is backed up. If, however, the portion of the database has already been written to the backup tape, the transaction is recorded instead to a *.pat file. The *.pat file is then written to the backup tape.

Circular Logging

Database circular logging uses transaction log technology but automates the maintenance procedure of old log files by overwriting transaction logs after those transactions are committed to disk. In other words, only a few log files are active at any one time; others, arranged in order of seniority, are reused as new logs are written over the old ones. Circular logging reduces disk storage requirements and prevents wasted tape resources from accumulating. It does so at the expense of prohibiting the use of, for example, differential and incremental backup strategies that rely on collections of transaction log files accumulated over a predefined time frame for replay during a disaster-recovery process. In Exchange 5.5, circular logging was enabled by default; in Exchange 2000, it is disabled by default.

How a Transaction Is Processed

Data is read from a database file into memory as 4K pages. Each page, sequentially numbered, contains an assortment of information that includes, but is not limited to, timestamps, flags, checksums, and the actual data or pointers to pages that contain data. The transaction lists a series of tasks or operations to be performed on the data written to memory. Although the series of operations listed in the transaction is performed to the page in memory (but not yet written or committed to disk), the operations are also recorded in the version store in the memory cache. If an unexpected shutdown occurs, the list of recorded modifications is referenced, and partially completed ones are reversed or rolled back. When a transaction is completed (committed), the set of operations in the memory cache is written to the transaction log buffer before the operations are written to the transaction logs on the disk. The engine uses the memory cache to minimize the time required for processing requests and a transaction log buffer to minimize I/O delays while transactions are actually logged. ESE uses a "write-ahead" logging strategy, where it records actions in the log file before performing them. Here are the steps involved:

1. Data is written to a cached version of the log in the log buffer area.
2. The page in memory is modified.
3. The cached log entry is written to the log file on disk.
4. A checksum is calculated for the modified (or dirty) page, and it, along with the page, is recorded in the database on disk.

The checksum (sometimes called the *message hash*) is a derived string of 4-byte bits stored, along with the page number, in the header of the database page. Subsequent reading of the page will use this checksum to verify the read data's integrity.

Using a "write-ahead" strategy, cached changes are sometimes written to the log files "very much ahead" of data pages written to disk. Because transaction information is recorded in log files, however, the two processes run asynchronously without presenting a problem to the system's integrity. During normal operations, the asynchronous "write-ahead" strategy is advantageous because transactions are logged sequentially but tend to "batch" themselves among the contiguous data pages in memory, reducing I/O activity. If an ungraceful shutdown and the obliteration of "dirty" pages in memory occur, ESE can "replay" the log files upon startup and sequentially rebuild the missing committed transactions.

Memory Management

Caching plays a major role in reducing I/O activity and thus improving performance, so ESE manages memory allocation very carefully. In fact, Exchange has historically reserved memory space in advance for its own use. In legacy versions, Performance Optimizer modified cache sizes. Beginning with version 5.5 and in Exchange 2000, dynamic buffer allocation (DBA) actually increases memory buffer areas in advance. The Cache Size counter in Performance, under Administrative Tools, measures how much memory is reserved for store.exe. When evaluating this measure, you need to balance improved system performance (reduced paging, reduced I/O activity, and so on) with maximum memory utilization. Thus, Exchange allocates as much memory as it "expects" to use without adversely affecting the operation of the system and other applications.

A simple way to monitor memory allocation is through Windows Task Manager. Figure 3.3 shows memory allocation for both store.exe and mad.exe on the Processes tab of the Task Manager window. You can confirm both total memory usage and availability in the lower section of the Performance tab on the Windows Task Manager as well. Customize more sophisticated instrumentation through Performance, located under Start | Programs | Administrative Tools.

SGs

An SG of databases runs under a single process of store.exe. This process is now referred to as a *single instance* of the ESE. The SG specifically consists of the properties database file (*.edb), the streaming database file (*.stm), and the log files (*.log). Though beta versions supported up to 15 SGs, the current version of Exchange 2000 can contain a maximum of 4, each holding a maximum of 6 databases (24 databases per server). In actual practice, only five databases are used; the sixth database is reserved for temporary tables and large sort routines. You can independently stop, dismount, start, or mount databases without disrupting other database processing. Similarly, a corrupted database will not mount but likewise will have little effect on the overall processing of store.exe.

Multiple databases in multiple SGs provide greater flexibility in managing storage services than using fixed-disk assemblies when you are administering Exchange 2000. For example, you can perform multiple backups on multiple databases to multiple tape backup units simultaneously. Figure 3.4 shows an example of two

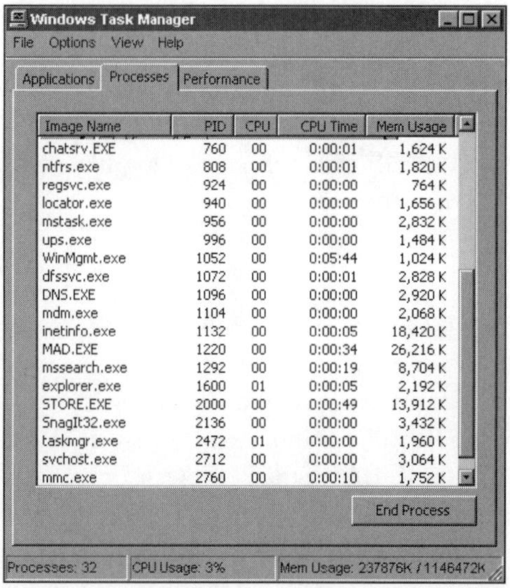

Figure 3.3 The Processes tab in Windows Task Manager.

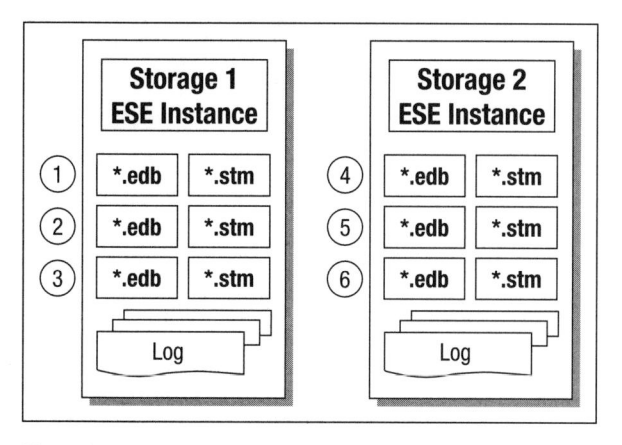

Figure 3.4 How Storage Groups are arranged.

SGs, each with a group of mailstores composed of an *.edb and an *.stm file. These groups are numbered 1 through 6 across the two SGs. If mailbox store 4 fails, only SG2 (which affects mailbox stores 4 through 6) needs to be repaired offline; the other SG will remain online and functioning. Each SG also reserves two log files, res1.log and res2.log, in the log directory as placeholders for reserve disk space if the service runs out of space. If a disaster occurs, you can perform multiple restores simultaneously. You can organize databases in SGs by location, department, or function that logically reflect the way your corporation operates. Thus, SGs greatly improve maintenance by partitioning the data stores; when distributed across hardware that supports server clusters, they provide near-perfect "five 9" reliability.

Managing SGs

SGs are actually a management rather than a physical entity. By definition, an SG is a collection of databases all controlled by a common policy. Use SGs only when you need databases with special configurations. Thus, you need this management tool only when, for example, you need to create a separate data store for inbound newsgroup feeds or public folders requiring some specialized settings or configuration. These data stores operate under different policies from, for example, mailbox stores.

Store.exe manages all SGs. Each SG runs in its own workspace inside Store with its own transaction logs and checkpoint file. Unlike legacy Exchange 5.5, which ran both the public and private data stores within a single instance of Store, Exchange 2000 provides fault tolerance by dividing mailboxes across SGs and thus across separate instances of Store.exe running on the Exchange server. Because there is no single Information Store, there is no single point of failure. Similarly, the workload is distributed so that the heavy I/O demands of a messaging server are balanced across SGs and the physical machines that host them, such as cluster resources. A *cluster* is a virtualized server that runs on several different hardware resources—that is, physical servers, each sharing in the hosting responsibilities. A failure of one hardware node in the cluster triggers a transition of the virtual server to a different physical host; there is no perceived disruption in delivered services. In a less elegant way, failure in one SG affects only the services provided to users with resources mapped to that one specific SG rather than the users of an entire community.

In a legacy Exchange system, the Store service failed to launch if either public or private data stores had detectable problems on startup. Exchange 2000, during startup, registers a troubled database as offline and proceeds to launch the remaining healthy databases. In a different scenario, if the EDB5 database in Storage Group 2 fails, using Figure 3.4 as an example, the administrator must repair just that SG, not Storage Group 1. The partitioning of databases across the two SGs, even when located on the same physical server, protects users whose mailboxes are located in Storage Group 1. Because all the databases in Storage 2 share a common transaction log, all services in Storage 2 are halted while repairs occur. The users on Storage 1, however, experience no disruption in services, no matter how badly the EDB4 database is damaged.

Legacy Exchange ran only one instance of the Store at any time and thus was severely constrained in the delivery of services if, for whatever reason, that service instance failed to operate properly. Because Exchange 2000 manages multiple databases, it provides more robust delivery of services as compared to older versions of Exchange. Databases, as mentioned previously, can assume various states of operation, such as:

- *Mounted*—This state of normal operations means the data store is online and available to Store.

- *Unmounted*—This offline state means the data store is inaccessible to the Store and Exchange clients. The administrator in the previous example would take the SG, in which the damaged EDB4 database is found, offline for maintenance.

An important operational difference between legacy Exchange and Exchange 2000 is that Exchange 2000 can launch SGs without mounted databases. The System Manager is a tool that can mount or unmount these data stores within an SG on demand. Figure 3.5 shows the context menu you use to perform this operation. Similarly, the Properties sheet of a data store provides several features, including the option not to mount a data store at startup, as shown in Figure 3.6. Thus, an administrator can control the functioning of the databases within the SG, as well as manipulate the SGs themselves.

In general, two categories of parameters control how the SGs are managed by the Store. These parameters are categorized as global and SG-specific configuration sets. Global parameters configure settings that apply to all SGs, such as cache allocation sizes. SG-specific settings however, affect specific databases. The administrator can partition his or her databases in specific SGs and then configure how the Store

Storage Services 89

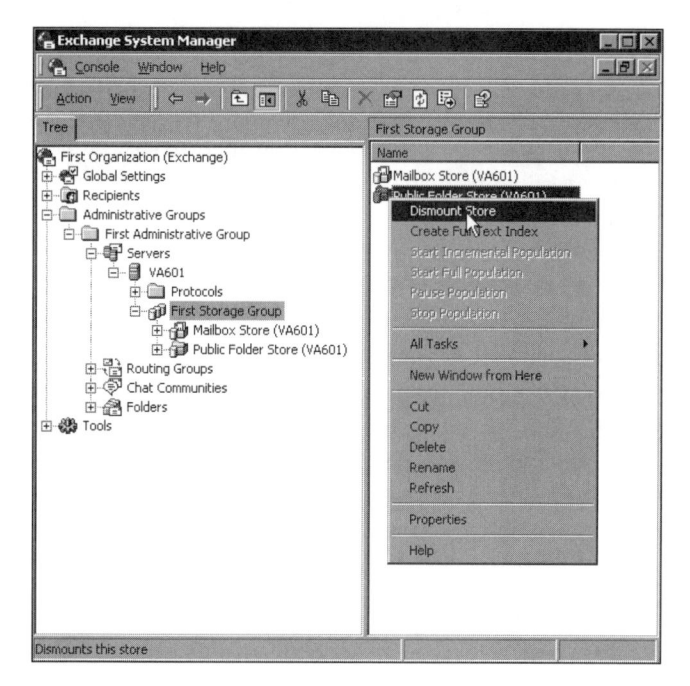

Figure 3.5 Using System Manager to dismount message stores.

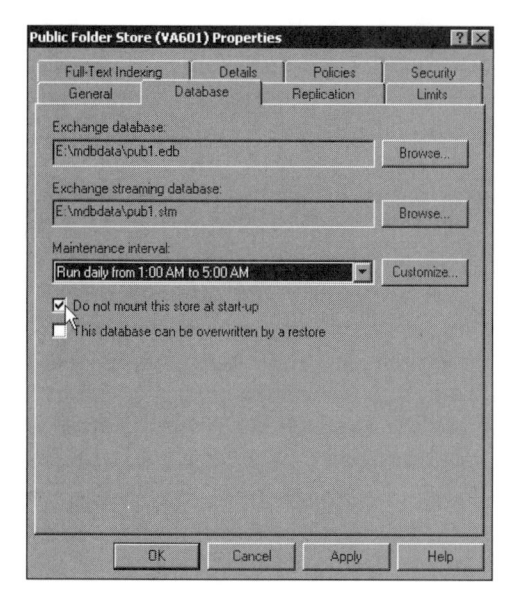

Figure 3.6 A data store Properties sheet showing specific maintenance options.

manages the specific SG during daily operations. Specific settings might include the location of the databases, the transaction logs, and other support files. This information is accessible from the Properties sheet of the SG object in System Manager.

Planning SGs

As stated in the previous section, you need to carefully consider creating an SG. It is important to plan the use of additional databases because of their subtle impact on TCO. The additional resources place greater demands on the capacity of your hardware, such as CPU, memory, and storage, as well as on maintenance time. Every new SG requires disk space not only for databases but also for transaction logs. Planning storage requirements includes not just adding capacity, but possibly different fault-tolerant configurations. A Redundant Array of Independent Disks (RAID) configuration can provide fault-tolerant solutions, such as mirroring (RAID 1) and striping with parity (RAID 5), but are falling short with respect to the demands of enterprise systems. The more robust fiber channel implementations of Storage Area Networks (SANs) are replacing RAID towers in large enterprise deployments. A SAN is a data storage solution that is actually a high-speed network of shared servers exclusively providing storage services. This arrangement of servers, providing storage services, is available to an entire organization or exclusively the Exchange organization as a backend.

On a smaller scale, having multiple Store instances running multiple databases means administering more copies of transaction logs during backup and disaster recovery procedures. The more complicated the backup sets, the greater the likelihood a recovery plan will fail due to simple user error. If you do create new data stores and excess capacity, you raise the possibility of needing to balance existing workloads through the migration of recipient objects. The steps required to optimize these newfound resources require careful planning and consideration because such procedures can impact accessibility to services and may run an unacceptable level of risk to data if not properly executed. Whether dealing with SANs or RAID 5 towers, the important themes in planning include the scalability of backend systems without interruption of mission-critical services, as well as "five 9" reliability, where uptime is measured as 99.99999 percent, and cumulative downtime caused by both scheduled and unscheduled events totals no more than 9 hours over 365 days.

Exchange database transactions use a two-phase commit, where data is first written to a memory cache and then to a transaction log. At some point later in time, the data stored in memory is actually written to the database. The speed in writing data sequentially to the transaction log in this two-step process has a more significant effect on performance than writing to the database because the database is uncoupled from the processing of information. If the transaction log entry is slow, the processing also slows down to stay synchronized with the writing of the log entries. For optimal performance, the transaction logs must be written to the most responsive drives in the system. This further affects TCO because best practices recommend locating an SG's transaction logs on a separate disk that is optimized for both speed and fault tolerance. The combination of both striping, for speed, and mirroring (or duplexing), for fault tolerance (hence RAID 0+1), provides the best possible hardware platform.

However, the storage of Exchange databases requires a different set of solutions because the I/O characteristics of storing messages are random. The parallel threading of Exchange Server software delivers multiple concurrent reads and writes to the storage devices. RAID 5, with its striping feature, provides the best possible throughput for this flow of data. In addition, the parity block, though stealing several machine cycles to write itself to disk, provides a valuable measure of fault tolerance through recoverability of data. Although RAID 5 currently delivers the most affordable storage solution for mission-critical data, the lowering of hardware costs, the partitioning of data through SGs, and the need for greater speed may soon shift the favored storage solution to RAID 0+1 configurations. This shift in architecture among smaller enterprises will occur because the striped mirror array is twice as fast as a striped array with parity. Larger enterprises will migrate all their storage services to SANs.

Indexing

The Web Store provides storage services and a single repository for heterogeneous content. Outlook users need to search for documents; they neither care about storage services nor know about the heterogeneity of content within a single repository. Retrieving information requires some systematic categorization of these separate objects so that these Outlook users can find their documents more easily. Content indexing to optimize retrieval in a heterogeneous population of objects must include:

> *Key attribute fields*—Attribute fields range from the sender, recipient, and subject line in email messages to the titles of documents in Word, Excel, and PowerPoint.

> *Object properties*—These properties on the "outside" of the object include, for example, the typically neglected user-defined, customized attributes in the Properties sheets of Office documents. Figure 3.7 shows the open document Properties sheet after selecting Properties from the File menu.

> *Object content*—Data here extends from the content of an email message and its attachment to phrases used to describe a slide in a PowerPoint presentation.

The corpus, or body, of material to be indexed is the entire data store, so considerable processing power and time are key factors. Features such as Single-Instance Storage, tempered by the use of multiple databases and SGs, significantly affect the efficiency of this process. Similarly, faster searches are performed because full-text indexing is routinely performed before the client-initiated search.

Another important feature in the retrieval of information is property promotion. Advance searches involving built-in, standard object properties (like author, subject, file type, and customized properties) are recognized and automatically promoted to the IS as part of the object's record in the database. This often-neglected feature, in

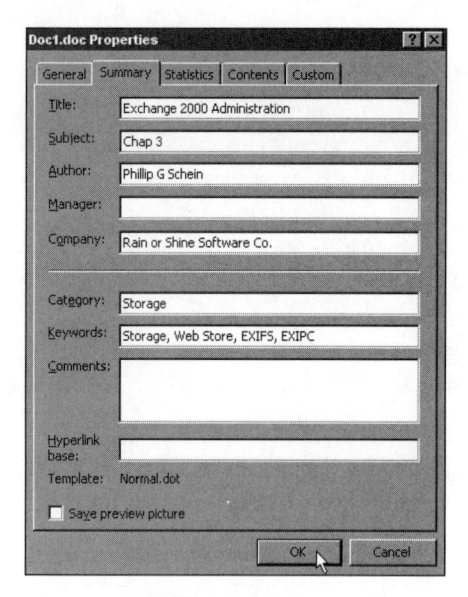

Figure 3.7 Properties sheet in an MS Word Document.

the Properties item in the File menu of all Office application products, increases the object's value because its systematic use over time provides enhanced granularity in cataloguing. It also offers a greater ability to associate that object with files with common or similar characteristics or origins.

Indexing is now word-based and limited to specific document types, including:

➤ HTML documents (★.html, ★.htm, ★.asp)

➤ Embedded MIME messages (★.eml)

➤ Word documents (★.doc)

➤ Excel documents (★.xls)

➤ PowerPoint documents (★.ppt)

➤ Text files (★.txt)

Messages and their text-based attachments are indexed; binary attachments are not. Full-text searches index data differently from character-based searches. Full-text indexing matches "computer" with "computers" because the *stemming process* indexes them as related words; however, this process does not match "comp" with "computer." Full-text searches run on the Exchange server rather than the client to provide greater performance and backward compatibility for legacy applications. If, however, full-text indexing is not enabled on the server for whatever reason, MAPI clients can perform their own character-based searches at the time of the query. The Microsoft Search service provides the indexing function, so both EXIFS and the Search service must be running to create and maintain the integrity of the index. You should also remember the impact that indexing has on system performance and system resources. Depending on the size of the body of material to be indexed, a full-text index consumes a disproportionately large amount of CPU time. In addition, an index is a separate file structure stored on a local disk. Although the index uses the same SIS feature found in the Exchange database, it still consumes disk space ranging from 10 percent to 30 percent of the corpus's size, depending on the nature of the context being indexed. For example, a corpus of approximately 5GB of disk space will generate approximately a 1GB index.

Despite Microsoft's stated objectives of access to services across any client application, full-text searches are currently client software dependent. Although Post Office Protocol (POP3) does not have search capabilities, online MAPI, IMAP4, and custom clients using WebDAV or Extended OLE DB can perform two types of searches: a full-text search using Microsoft Search services, and a query based on document properties provided by the ESE.

The Exchange 2000 Query Processor analyzes each search request to determine whether Exchange 2000 or Microsoft Search should provide the indexing services. This determination is based on whether the property is, in fact, indexed. Properties other than, for example, the default Subject, Body, To, and From, on which a particular request is made, are not included in the index. The Microsoft Search service builds the index that Exchange 2000 uses by identifying and logging searchable text within a corpus one folder at a time. You can configure the service to perform immediate or scheduled updates when subsequent changes to a folder within a data store occur. You can optimize these settings on the Full-Text Indexing Properties sheet in the data store's Properties sheet, as shown in Figure 3.8.

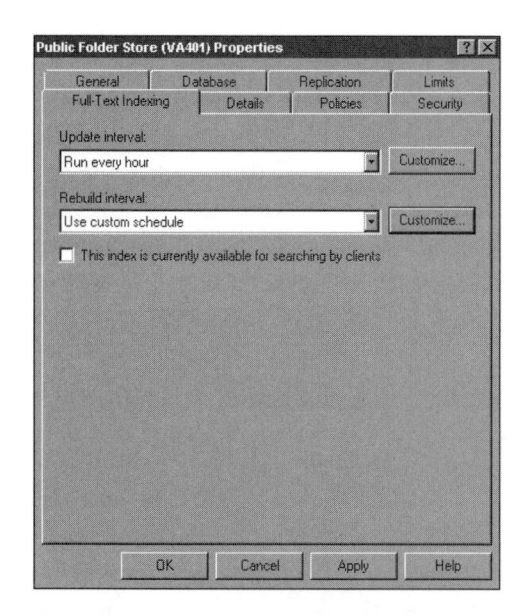

Figure 3.8 A Properties sheet that shows the Full-Text Indexing tab.

Control over updating indexes is a critical administrative feature because the process has a tremendous impact on CPU utilization and system resources. EXIFS changes are typically added to an index based on a predetermined schedule. Microsoft Search then performs an update or refresh of the index at a specifically scheduled time. It's always a difficult decision to maintain a balance among the availability of CPU resources (for example, during off-peak processing periods), the nature and turnover of the data, and your user population's need for refreshed indices; however, you need to routinely do so at least once a day.

Full-text searches are built from objects with specific file types. If a document file type does not match its extension, Microsoft Search does not include it in the index. This object omission is recorded as an error and logged in the Windows 2000 Application log in Event Viewer at the end of the indexing process. This error entry records the number of unsuccessfully indexed documents. A detailed list of these documents is included in a separate gather file that is also created during the indexing process. This text file, with a *.gthr extension, is located in the \Exchsrvr\ExchangeServer\GatherLogs folder. It records the subject or file name, the URL location, and an error number of the message or document that was dropped during the indexing process. You can use the gthrlog.vbs utility, located in \Program Files\Common Files\System\MsSearch\Bin, to decode the error number in the gather file using the following syntax at the command line

```
cscript gthrlog.vbs <file name>
```

where *<file name>* is the name of the *.gthr file.

Database Consistency

To optimize I/O activity, administrators expect ESE database files to never be totally up to date with changes to pages and logs in memory. A graceful shutdown implies that the most current changes to the state of the database have been gracefully flushed from memory structures and systematically applied to the database's files stored on disk. The flag in the data file header is set to indicate that there are no integrity problems with the data file; ESE does not have to replay transactions and roll back incomplete operations. Instead, a consistent state will have been reached before the user turns off power. This is the perfect-world scenario.

If a database is inconsistent because of the failure of files to open or checksums of pages to agree, treat your database folders as if they were single files. Check the following areas when you attempt to achieve database consistency:

- Defragmenting databases
- Soft recoveries
- Maintaining database integrity

Best practices recommend some guidelines for maintaining healthy database files including:

- Never arbitrarily modify the state or position of any file in a database folder.
- Never alter the contents of a file unless you know exactly what the object does and know it is safe to alter it.
- Never experiment with a database on a production platform.
- Always create a shadow installation of the production platform that exactly corresponds to the original installation and attempt to replicate production problems there first before testing possible solutions.

When you are troubleshooting either software design or network connectivity issues, your ability to replicate an event or condition on demand suggests that you sufficiently understand the casual relationships to force the effect. Only when you have established these relationships with certainty, is it prudent to provide a solution.

Defragmenting Databases

Defragmentation is the process of rearranging objects in such a way as to promote a more organized, efficient ordering or positioning of data pages to maximize some operation. Thus, you should defragment disk sectors written in a file allocation table (FAT) file structure so that they are logically contiguous and thus more efficiently read by a hard drive head as the disk revolves around its spindle. Similarly, you should rearrange data to efficiently fill database pages so that used data blocks are contiguous and unused storage space is minimized. You can accomplish this operation in two ways:

- *Online defragmentation*—This operation automatically detects and releases objects no longer in use within the defined space of the database. It is user controlled, listed in Database Maintenance on the Exchange Database tab, and is by default performed at 2:00 A.M. local time every day.
- *Offline defragmentation*—This operation creates a new database by copying all database components like records and tables to the new structure in a contiguous, defragmented order. This offline process requires sufficient free space to accommodate the size of the original database. ESE considers the new copy of the old database, following offline defragmentation, an entirely different database. You should perform a full backup and delete both the original database and its now useless log files. Given the draconian measures of deleting all traces of the former database following an offline defragmentation procedure, this process does recover storage space but is not recommended as a routine maintenance procedure.

Using ESEUTIL

The ESE utility, or ESEUTIL, is a database-level utility that extracts or dumps header information from databases, checkpoint files, and transaction log files in the EXIFS. The information in these headers can be valuable when you need information about the file's current state. Extracted output can include the DBSignature line, used to match the *.edb, *.stm, and *.log files; the State line, which indicates whether or not the file was consistent before shutdown; and signature information, which ESE uses to identify the file. Here are some examples of how to use it:

➤ To extract transaction log file header information, use **ESEUTIL /ML** followed by the name of the transaction file to determine if a failure to properly play back a transaction has occurred.

➤ To repair the structure of database tables and records with broken links, you can use **ESEUTIL /P** to attempt to restore links, though the process is slow and data loss is likely during the repair process, because ESEUTIL will repair the database by deleting corrupted pages.

➤ To check database integrity, use **ESEUTIL /G** to act in a read-only mode to check tables, rebuild indices in a temporary tempedb.edb database, and compare indices.

➤ To perform the offline defragmentation operation mentioned earlier in this chapter, use **ESEUTIL /switch**. Upon successfully copying all database structures, it discards unused pages and compacts the database file. Previous transaction log files are no longer useful to replay old transactions because new signatures in the header are created following the defragmentation.

➤ To force what is called a *soft recovery*, use a special property, **ESEUTIL /R /I**. A soft recovery is signified by the **/R** switch. The skipping of corrupted records in a missing database ("hanging attach" records) is necessary or the utility will stop running. If, for example, a single database were lost due to hardware failure, you force a soft recovery on the remaining databases and log files, skipping (the **/I** represents ignore) any logical references to the now-lost database. You would then restore the missing database from a previous backup. In this scenario, ESE performs every operation in the transaction logs until the most current entry in the log file (say, for this example, edb.log) is reached. If a commit operation is never read for an open transaction, ESE reverses or rolls back the previous operations to maintain database integrity. This particular rollback process is called *Log Transaction Redo*. Thus, **ESEUTIL /R /I** may at least salvage remaining databases through the replay of old transaction logs by returning them to a consistent state.

The complete list of the six **ESEUTIL /switch** modes of operation include defragmentation/compaction, recovery, integrity, file dump, repair, restore, and update (rarely used; it updates older databases, but has been largely replaced by the installation wizard). Each mode of operation typically has a large list of options that modify the selected operation according to the following syntax:

```
eseutil
 | /D database [/L logPath] [/S systemPath] [/B backupName]
     [/T tempName] [/P] [/O]
 | /G database [/T tempName] [/V] [/X] [/O]
 | /M[mode] fileName
 | /P database [/T tempName] [/D] [/V] [/X] [/O]
 | /R { /IS | /DS } [/L logPath] [/S systemPath] [/O]
 | /U database /D dllPath [/B backupName] [/T tempName] [/P] [/O]
```

Using Information Store Integrity Checker (ISINTEG)

Another useful utility, a built-in component of Exchange 2000, is ISINTEG. This comprehensive suite of tests determines and—if enabled—repairs integrity weakness in offline databases. Before you run this test suite, dismount your data store. Also remember to be selective; it is not advisable to run the entire suite on production platforms unless you can afford to remain offline for a long time. Consult Microsoft TechNet Article Q198788 (dated August 20, 1999) for a batch script that will allow unattended operation of this utility. Furthermore, to run, ISINTEG creates a temporary database and does not run on SGs with a sixth running database. The command line for running this utility is as follows

```
isinteg -? [-pri] [-pub] [-fix] [-l [logfilename]]
```

where the parameters have the following explanations:

➤ **-?**—Displays the usage.

➤ **-pri**—Checks the private IS (default).

➤ **-pub**—Checks the public IS.

➤ **-fix**—Repairs the IS.

➤ **-l [*logfilename*]**—Stores log information in *logfilename*. The default is isinteg.pri or isinteg.pub.

ISINTEG runs three times in either the default check-only mode or fix mode. It uses the following reference database in its test suite:

➤ *Pass 1*—A reference database is constructed and the test output is labeled Reference Table Construction. Each table has as many rows as there are in the original database with a single key field.

➤ *Pass 2*—The reference database constructed in Pass 1 is filled with test results.

➤ *Pass 3*—In this last pass, tables in the reference database originally constructed in Pass 1 are searched, fields are compared against the original database, and discrepancies are noted. If the utility mode is **-fix**, the discrepancies in integrity are corrected. This test output is labeled Reference Table Verification.

When you run ISINTEG, it confirms that the MSExchangeIS service is stopped. It then checks Registry settings on the server. It browses the offline database for errors, builds a database (refer.mdb) of reference counts, and checks all cross-reference tables in the database. It compares the counts found to those in the reference database. The **-fix** switch updates what it determines to be true values. Some of the tables it checks are ACL List, ACL Member, Attachment, Deleted Folders, and Deleted Recipients. Exchange 2000 Server no longer uses the **-patch** switch, which, in legacy versions, is the offline backup restore patch.

Using ESEFILE

ESEFILE is a utility included with Exchange Server version 5.5 Service Pack 3 (SP3) and Exchange 2000 Server. It is located in the Support folder on the Exchange Server 5.5 SP3 CD-ROM and in the Support\Utils\I386 folder on the Exchange 2000 CD-ROM. Use this utility on any version 5.x or Exchange 2000 databases.

The syntax for this utility is:

```
esefile [/C source destination] [/X file] [/S file] [/D file page number]
   [/U file]
```

where the parameters have the following explanations:

➤ **/C**—Copies the source to the destination

➤ **/X**—Is the edb.dll format checksum

➤ **/S**—Is the ese.dll format checksum

➤ **/D**—Dumps a page from a file

➤ **/U**—Deletes a file

ESEFILE has two main uses: copying large files and testing the checksums on an Exchange Server database. To copy files, type "esefile /c *source destination*" at the command line. Only one file can be copied at a time, and the destination must be a local drive. Database files are opened and copied in an uncached mode. Wildcards are not accepted nor are file timestamps preserved. The testing of checksums is especially relevant in restoring backups. Exchange Server, for example, automatically restores all the appropriate database files when you perform an online backup. If, however, you restore a backup offline, you must know what files are critical and therefore must be restored. An online backup checks page-level integrity of the database files as they are streamed onto tape. When performing operations offline, you must manually perform a consistency on the main database files (dir.edb, priv.edb, or pub.edb) using ESEUTIL and a page-level integrity check of the copied databases using ESEFILE.

Protocol Services

Each of the three service areas—database services, directory services, and protocol services—has contributed to Exchange messaging services in different ways yet supports the same enterprise-level needs of capacity, performance, and reliability. The uncoupling of a functional, service-providing layer from the "plumbing infrastructure" is critical when you are designing an enterprise-wide messaging system just on the basis of scope and scalability. The migration from a smaller domain concept to a larger enterprise namespace requires the ability to separate functional service areas and the physical components that support them from one another. These distributed services need to have specialized connective facilities that transfer the functionality and that glue one specific functional area to another. This metaphor apparently did not go unnoticed in the minds of the Exchange 2000 designers.

EXchange InterProcess Communication Layer (EXIPC, or EPOXY)

Decoupling one SMFA from another typically increases the reliability, flexibility, and scalability of a distributed service provider by allowing component processes to run separately in a redundant fashion. In the case of uncoupling protocol services from the Web Storage System, we see the services moved to a very fast intermediate layer necessary to transfer data between Exchange processes and the Web Store. Exchange 2000 uses a specialized queuing layer called EXIPC that interfaces with the IIS process, INETINFO.EXE, as well as with STORE.EXE. It has been nicknamed EPOXY (and the catchy name has stuck!) as a reference to glue that attaches Exchange to the Internet Information services running within the Windows 2000 NOS. This interface layer is also accurately referred to as a *protocol stub*. It is a high-performance, asynchronous, communication facility that uses a common memory heap to transfer data between these two service layers through specific protocol stacks like Simple Mail Transfer Protocol (SMTP), Hypertext Transfer Protocol Distributing Authoring and Versioning (HTTP-DAV), NNTP, IMAP, and POP3. A *heap* is a specially designated pool of memory reserved for temporarily storing data structures, the type and size of which are determined at runtime. EPOXY constantly obtains space from and releases memory space back to this pool on demand as it services client requests for data from the Web Store.

Distributed Architecture

Two subtle characteristics that have permeated Microsoft architecture since the early 32-bit Windows architecture have been the emphasis on interfaces and the associated modularity of the parts attaching to them. EPOXY is a special communication facility that interfaces two key service areas: the IIS area in Windows 2000 and EXIFS in Exchange 2000. Throughout this chapter and the literature, reference is made to front-end/back-end (FE/BE) configuration as a key in load balancing as well as distributed services architecture. FE/BE here separates the protocol services area from the storage area so that, fundamentally speaking, the two services can actually run on separate servers. Such a division enhances performance, capacity, accessibility, and fault tolerance. We would suggest that a more subtle significance is in the aspect of redesigning self-contained service areas such as storage or protocol services as more modular literally independent service providers. This trend has already led to a new design in best-of-breed servers and Exchange 2000, and a whole different approach to providing enterprise services. This distributed architecture is a first glimpse of the .NET world.

Chapter Summary

This chapter delineated design objectives and general features of Exchange storage services as well as specific features of EXIFS, commonly known as the Web Storage System. Below are some particularly significant points to remember:

- Storage service design objectives include enhanced administration through one global, single-seat point of administration; scalability and simplified control; and storage unification.

- The Web Store provides solution services in the form of file system, database, and collaboration services, and service management through fault tolerance, load balancing, and scalability.

- Within the default M: drive is a domain folder. Within that folder is the MBX and the All Public Folders folder for Public Folder trees.

- The default public tree, the MAPI Clients Tree, in the System Manager MMC snap-in is the only tree accessible by MAPI clients. Other General Purpose trees are accessible using non-MAPI, NNTP-compliant, Web browsers, and Windows applications through EXIFS and WebDAV.

- Some key features of EXIFS are Web-based client access and support, public folder support, streaming data support, integration with Windows 2000 directory services and security, property promotion, and offline folder synchronization support.

- EXIFS supports some important APIs and models for developing the interface to the data store, including Win32, ADO, OLE-DB, and CDO.

- Database file types include both legacy rich-text files (*.edb), native content streaming files (*.stm), Key Management Server files (*.kms), and Site Replication Service files (*.srs).

➤ SIS, where a message is stored once in a database, is a critical feature for using data stores efficiently; it thus increases the physical capacity of data stores.

➤ Other file types important for properly operating the ESE are transaction log files (*.log), used for tracking individual operations in a transaction; checkpoint files (*.chk), used to track committed transactions in the log file; and patch files (*.pat), used during backup and restore operations.

➤ Circular logging, disabled in Exchange 2000, is an automated maintenance procedure that systematically overwrites old transaction logs. It is disabled because the destruction of old log files prohibits the use of important backup strategies, such as differential and incremental procedures.

➤ The current version of Exchange 2000 can support 24 databases divided up into 4 separate SGs. Each SG has one log file and is treated as a single administrative unit. A sixth database in each SG is reserved for system use.

➤ Content indexing to optimize document retrieval must include key attribute fields, object properties, and object content. Indexing in Exchange 2000 is based on a full-text search of object content. Object properties are stored separately in the *.edb data file although content is typically stored in the streaming file.

➤ Database consistency is achieved through a variety of procedures, including defragmentation, soft recovery, and the maintenance of database integrity by using utilities like ESEUTIL, ISINTEG, and ESEFILE.

Review Questions

1. How does the Web Storage System enhance administration?
    a. One repository decreases storage requirements on a server.
    b. Windows Management Instrumentation (WMI) simplifies remote maintenance and monitoring.
    c. One repository unifies shared storage space.
    d. One repository eliminates the need to partition data stores.
    e. One repository simplifies a disaster-recovery plan.

2. What are the functional services that best describe Exchange 2000? [Check all correct answers]
    a. Protocol services
    b. Directory services
    c. Database services
    d. Storage services
    e. Messaging services

3. How are legacy MSs different from the stores in Exchange 2000?
   a. Legacy MSs were based on one database.
   b. Exchange 5.5 MSs were unlimited in size.
   c. Answers a and b.
   d. None of the above.

4. Which statement about the Web Store is incorrect?
   a. EXIFS is mapped by default to the M: drive.
   b. Win32 interfaces can read/write to **http://hostserver/username**.
   c. The Web store is accessible using HTTP.
   d. Exchange 2000 works with IIS to provide access to the Web Store.

5. Which services does the Web Store provide? [Check all correct answers]
   a. Exposure to both mailboxes and public folders
   b. Retrieval of data based on queries
   c. Access to CDOs
   d. Access to traditional MAPI objects
   e. Answers a, b, and c

6. What service-management features does the Web Store provide? [Check all correct answers]
   a. Exposure to both mailboxes and public folders
   b. Retrieval of data based on queries
   c. Access to CDOs
   d. Access to traditional MAPI objects
   e. None of the above

7. Which of the following statements are true? [Check all correct answers]
   a. Every time non-MAPI clients access Exchange 2000, the data they request undergoes conversion.
   b. Every time MAPI clients access Exchange 2000, the data they request undergoes conversion.
   c. When MAPI clients access Exchange 2000, their requests for data are sometimes converted to RTF.
   d. When non-MAPI clients access Exchange 2000, the data they request is never converted.

8. EXIFS includes what two storage formats?
    a. *.edp
    b. *.edb
    c. *.stm
    d. *.stb
9. What EXIFS-related directories are by default automatically created on the N: drive?
    a. A domain folder
    b. An MBX
    c. Answers a and b
    d. None of the above
10. Which of the following statements are correct? [Check all correct answers]
    a. Each object in EXIFS has a URL.
    b. You can stop and start EXIFS from the command line.
    c. You can stop and start EXIFS from the Services applet.
    d. You cannot stop or start EXIFS.
11. Which of the following statements is correct?
    a. EXIFS natively supports HTTP and is integrated directly with Exchange Server.
    b. WebDAV-based applications provide graphical support via HTML because WebDAV is a set of HTML extensions.
    c. Answers a and b.
    d. None of the above.
12. What features does WebDAV offer? [Check all correct answers]
    a. Read access to structured content in EXIFS over HTML
    b. Read access to unstructured content in EXIFS over HTTP
    c. Synchronization with server-side data stores
    d. Write access to all EXIFS data stores
13. What changes have public folders undergone in Exchange 2000 as compared to legacy versions?
    a. Administration is performed using an MMC snap-in.
    b. Public folders can now replicate their contents.
    c. Public folder access is controlled by an ACL on a folder-by-folder basis.
    d. Public folders now hold mail messages, document files, and forms.

14. What programming support does the Web Store provide? [Check all correct answers]
    a. Win32
    b. MAPI
    c. OLE
    d. ADO

15. What file types are collected in a single database? [Check all correct answers]
    a. *.edb
    b. *.stm
    c. *.srs
    d. *.kms

16. SIS has the greatest impact on what system feature?
    a. Performance
    b. Reliability
    c. Capacity
    d. Security

17. What is the maximum size that edb.log can reach before starting edbtemp.log?
    a. 4K
    b. 1MB
    c. 5MB
    d. 16MB

18. When is a message stored in native content moved out of a data store? [Check the best answer]
    a. When a MAPI client requests data
    b. When a MAPI client modifies and saves data
    c. When a non–MAPI client saves data in RTF
    d. None of the above

19. Which criterion does not apply to transactions?
    a. Transactions must create a new data state before they are committed.
    b. All transactions are independent of other transactions until they are committed.
    c. A transaction is either completed or not completed.
    d. When a transaction is applied, it is permanent.

20. In a full-text search, which of the following first terms of the pair would match the second terms in the pair? [Check all correct answers]
    a. Comp would match with computer
    b. Computer would match with computers
    c. Compute would match with computer
    d. All of the above

Real-World Projects

Theresa Threepenny wants to get accustomed to her new position as an Exchange 2000 administrator at her company's headquarters in Tres Arroyos, New Mexico. Her company has recently migrated to Windows 2000, and, because of her experience working in the Information Technologies department for three years, her superiors believe she can administer an Exchange 2000 organization. She was working with the network administrator managing a 330-user network prior to her change in responsibilities. In assuming her new job responsibilities, she has emptied out the drawers of the desk in her new office. The only thing she has found of value is a half-used bottle of Excedrin and a roll of Tums. She decides to keep them both. She needs to plan how she will assume the role of Exchange administrator in her new position.

Theresa's manager wants to use the M: drive for a special permanent project. She has asked Theresa if it is possible to change the M: drive now associated with the Web Store to another project and reassign the Web Store to the W: drive.

Microsoft Exchange Server 2000 defaults to drive M: for the EXIFS component. This component provides the administrator and users with access to the IS as if it were a file system. The default drive letter chosen to represent this file system is M; however, you can change this by making a Registry entry.

Warning: Using Registry Editor incorrectly can cause serious problems that may require you to reinstall your operating system. Microsoft cannot guarantee that you can solve problems resulting from incorrectly using Registry Editor. Use Registry Editor at your own risk.

Project 3.1

To change the Web Store drive identifier:

1. From Run, start Registry Editor by typing "Regedt32.exe" in the Run box.
2. Locate the following key in the Registry:

   HKEY_LOCAL_MACHINE\SYSTEM\CurrentControlSet\Services\EXIFS\Parameters

3. On the Edit menu, click on Add Value and then add the following Registry value:

   ```
   Value Name: DriveLetter
   Data Type: REG_SZ
   Value: W
   ```

   *Note: If the **DriveLetter** value already exists, double-click on the value and then change the drive letter.*

4. Quit Registry Editor. This example uses drive W:. When the Exchange server is restarted, drive W: will be used instead of drive M: to represent the IS by means of a file system.

Theresa is interested in viewing all the hidden system files. She is careful to disable the view after she is done.

Project 3.2

To view hidden system folders:

1. Start Exchange System Manager.
2. Expand Folders.
3. Click on Public Folders.
4. Right-click on Public Folders and then click on View System Folders.

The manager has also asked Theresa to add new Public Folder trees and create new folders within them for the Marketing department. This department is launching a new marketing program and needs to have all brochures reviewed by all persons involved in each project. The Marketing Department thought that dedicated Public Folder trees would be the most effective way to distribute information on a broad scale. To create a new Public Folder store, you must first create a new Public Folder tree.

Project 3.3

To create a new Public Folder tree:

1. Start Exchange System Manager.
2. Locate the Folders container.
3. Right-click on the Folders container, click on New, and then click on Public Folder Tree.
4. Choose a name for the Public Folder tree and type it in the Name field; it is the only required field.

Now that Theresa has created a Public Folder tree, she can create a new public folder.

To create a new public folder:

1. Start Exchange System Manager.
2. Click on the SG where the folder store will be stored.
3. Right-click on the SG, click on New, and then click on Public Store.
4. Choose a name for the public store and type it in the Name field.
5. Click on the Browse button to choose the selected Public Folder tree and then select the Public Folder tree.

If no associated Public Folder tree exists, you receive an error message when you attempt to create a new Public Folder store: "All the Public Folder trees already have an associated public store on this server. You will need to create a new Public Folder tree before creating this new public store."

CHAPTER FOUR

Administrative Services

After completing this chapter, you will be able to:

✓ Describe the functional and structural changes in Exchange 2000

✓ Identify administrative needs and objectives and relate them to total cost of ownership (TCO)

✓ Understand how to create customized instrumentation using the Microsoft Management Console (MMC)

✓ Delineate various models used in both recipient and server management

✓ Define various tools used to support both recipient and server management

✓ Identify key areas used to evaluate and measure system performance

✓ Define various metrics that you can use in performance management

This chapter describes ways to create tools to manage an enterprise-wide messaging service, what metrics you use to measure performance, and what administrative models facilitate the delivery of a highly reliable service to your user population. The chapter briefly discusses major issues you encounter while deploying a messaging system, as well as while managing an enterprise-level Exchange organization, because the operational success of an implementation lies mostly in understanding how to evaluate and manage performance levels. The chapter begins with tools that describe the functional organization of an Enterprise system, as well as underlying physical connectivity. Exchange 2000 architecture differs from that of legacy versions in mixing real-world concepts (such as flexible, organizational groupings of people) with a network infrastructure's physical limitations. Using flexible groupings of people independent of the network structure is advantageous because it allows an administrator to shape a messaging system in ways that reflect real-world needs and objectives rather than the limitations of underlying physical hardware. Such administrative flexibility has an immediate and dramatic impact on TCO in lowering costs of deployment and training because the business logic of the workflow remains unchanged.

Administrative Methods

Exchange 2000, one of the new breed of Microsoft.NET servers, has undergone both specialization in function and streamlining in architectural design. These functional and structural changes include:

➤ A new management model that uncouples function from structure and changes the way directory services are provided to the user population

➤ Internal separation or partitioning of protocol, storage, and directory services

➤ A shift in emphasis on protocols from Messaging Application Programming Interface (MAPI) and X.400 to Simple Mail Transfer Protocol (SMTP)

➤ Integration of knowledge management (KM) features such as a full-text search engine

➤ Use of a new, enterprise-wide routing engine

➤ Delivery of enhanced client-side functionality

A significant characteristic of .NET servers, as a group, is their close integration with the Windows 2000 operating system; many services, like Exchange's legacy internal directory service, are redundant in the Windows 2000 environment. .NET servers, such as Exchange 2000, now defer directory service requests to the Windows 2000 Active Directory (AD) and the Global Catalog (GC). In this chapter, we will introduce you to a method of management that is different from what might be appropriate in an Exchange 5.5 environment. Legacy Exchange was managed as a namespace separated from the Windows NT 4 operating system; Exchange 2000, and the tools that manage it, are a seamless part of the Windows 2000 network operating system (NOS). In the real world, it is likely that you will need to understand and manage an Exchange organization within this new *gestalt* or worldview, as well as deal with the structural eccentricities of older legacy services.

There has been a shift of emphasis in both planning and deploying an enterprise messaging system, especially in view of the uncoupling of the messaging function from the networking infrastructure. Messaging-related object attributes are more fundamental to the design of the enterprise fabric. Compare this scenario to that of version 5.5, where the administrator modifies messaging-related objects in the Exchange directory and optimizes workload characteristics of a "network of servers" running on top of structurally separate NT domains. Exchange 2000 administrators will more likely be forced into the role of architect and provider of messaging and collaboration solutions within a Windows 2000 enterprise rather than play the role of technician, because the nature of the administrative role has changed. Outlook and user interfaces like digital dashboards will raise more work-related possibilities in the minds of the end user; the Exchange administrator will be called upon to deliver services based on these possibilities.

In addition, management of recipients, for example, is through AD at the level of the NOS rather than legacy Exchange directory services. The roles of administering a network and a messaging system have become far more co-dependent. From an Exchange 2000 administrative perspective, you shape messaging and collaborative solutions not on a separate horizontal layer above the operating system but vertically down through the messaging layer to the NOS directory object itself.

Another significant dimension in administrative services relates to the nature of the services provided to the user population. In terms of the Microsoft Enterprise Services framework, there is a close relationship between solution-providing services and service-management services. Microsoft Solutions Framework (MSF) helps you focus on planning, building, and deploying, for example, messaging, collaboration, and KM solutions. Microsoft Operations Framework (MOF) addresses the ongoing operational aspects of the provided solution. The Central Computer and Telecommunications Agency (CCTA) of the United Kingdom has also published its own IT Infrastructure Library (ITIL) that extensively documents methodologies for problem management. Most employers expect an Exchange 2000 administrator to perform both functions at very high levels of reliability.

A Corporate Information Officer or Board of Directors measures the success of an Exchange 2000 implementation in terms of TCO and return on investment (ROI), not network utilization or bandwidth consumption. These particular metrics of success are not new to even legacy Exchange 5.5 administrators. However, the way you apply them in the context of an enterprise by using MSF and MOF gives them far greater focus and precision than when you used them in NT 4 domain models. Accountants and investment analysts can now assign some real variable cost value to operational definitions like service-level agreements (SLAs), problem management, and Help Desk professionals. The dimensional aspects and performance measures of an Exchange administrator, especially in a Windows 2000 enterprise system, have changed in subtle, though significant, ways.

Microsoft Frameworks and TCO

MOF emphasizes two separate but related functional areas: service solutions and service management. Thus, once a system is deployed, the "other side" of the IT job description deals with administering this newly installed "solution," heretofore called a *production platform*. Key service-management issues in Exchange 2000 are enhanced scalability, reliability, and capacity. These performance-related measures ensure that the solution delivers promised features at agreed service levels. The factors that affect performance are woven into the fabric of a solution not just during the planning stages of the messaging solution but also from the start of the design of the Windows 2000 enterprise itself. The close integration of Exchange with AD demands an optimally functioning Windows 2000 environment.

To assist you with designing and deploying an Exchange 2000 organization, messaging solutions have been partitioned or separated into specific management functional areas (SMFAs): protocol services, directory services, and storage services. This division of functional roles offers greater flexibility and scalability than the legacy monolithic design structure, and is a characteristic of a distributed services environment. The potential of this greater flexibility, however, can be realized only when the system design is well conceived and properly deployed. Thus, MSF efficiently provides the foundation on which the MOF process of providing business-specific service solutions through well-defined service-management practices will work at the lowest TCO.

Another point is more political in nature. MSF teams and projects come and go, depending on the nature of a business; for most, they come and go, never to be seen again. MOF operations teams, on the other hand, endure. The requisite skills these people possess must evolve continuously to meet the changing requirements of the corporation and the user population. The operations staff must be represented from the beginning of an MSF-based project. This is critical to assure that the solution and its deployment include MOF's operational requirements, standards, staffing, tools, processes, and, most significantly, their cooperation. Such involvement also allows for testing and validation by applying MOF to the target solution or environment during the MSF deployment phase and ensures a smooth transition to an ongoing operation.

Administration Objectives and TCO

Although initial capital investments in a properly conceived IT project can overwhelm even the largest corporation, the greatest reduction in TCO occurs over time. It's difficult to calculate these long-term, ongoing changes in costs, however, because, in most cases, ROI is difficult to assign to any one definable cost center.

Instead, you can talk of reducing soft costs (lowering TCO) in three general support and maintenance areas:

➤ *Hardware maintenance*—Costs related to upgrades, remote monitor services (RMON), and so on of local hardware

➤ *Application support*—Costs related to line-of-business (LOB) and complementary software applications

➤ *User support*—Costs related to end-user assistance in application use, configuration management, and disaster recovery

You need to structure your planning phase so that you easily control support, maintenance, and other soft-cost areas such as training. These administrative service areas are summarized under a variety of MOF service-management features, such as change and configuration management, problem management, and Help Desk. The MOF helps define these soft-cost centers that, even during the MSF planning stages, have a powerful impact on long-term TCO reduction. An example of the close interaction of MSF and MOF and the subtlety of soft costs could involve, for example, deploying a single Windows 2000 services "solution" like Terminal Services Architecture (TSA) in an enterprise. This service provides remote terminal access to a Windows 2000 server from a machine running any operating system that supports Windows Terminal Services client.

Terminal Services, for example, provides lower hardware maintenance costs as compared to regular maintenance methods by reducing the need to perform support operations at the user's workstation or prevent a user from working while PCs are repaired. Because neither the application nor data is locally maintained, the end user is not restricted to a specific machine. Similarly, you reduce costs associated with application deployment when you make applications available to users via Terminal Services. Finally, Terminal Services substantially reduces direct and indirect end-user support costs. Application software is installed and configured on the Terminal Services, so you reduce the requirement for support at a user's desktop. You also have the opportunity of providing users with less expensive, sometimes older hardware while still providing agreed-upon levels of service. In addition, because the software is centrally configured for all users, intermittent or isolated configuration problems do not exist. One fundamental "solution" cultivated in the design stages can radically change operational overhead and long-term TCO.

Deploying and Administering Exchange Server

IT management has evolved, especially in a Windows 2000 environment, from "tinkering and tweaking" to thorough analysis and methodical planning. You will see that uncoupling function from structure brings an entirely new freedom to administering a messaging system. On the other hand, the "five 9" reliability in service has simultaneously "raised the bar" in terms of definable SLAs and performance. You should not underestimate or ignore the subtle interaction a flawed

NOS design has on the most skillfully constructed Exchange deployment plans. Thus, we continue this chapter with a summarized "green-field" deployment plan and analyze the administrative and management features necessary to deploy and manage an Exchange organization on an ongoing basis. We define "green-field" deployments here as installations that do not have any legacy systems or configuration issues. Such installations are rare in the real world, especially because of the large embedded base of Exchange 5.5 installations and the robust nature of the legacy Exchange feature set. In the IT world, why fix something that performs well? Nevertheless, we use a "green-field" installation to simplify the discussion of how you model the management tools to satisfy the real-world needs of evaluating and measuring the messaging system's performance. The installation plan includes four phases:

1. *Create a deployment plan based on corporate objectives and user needs.* Deployment scenarios require you to assess user needs, name schemes, network and domain/site topology, and foreign connections, as well as validate and optimize the enterprise design.

2. *Deploy the NOS.* The structural aspects of the forest, domain, and site—as well as the forest schema; topology of domain controllers (DCs) and GC servers; and changes in client access, including address book lookups and changes in group design—all require the appropriate instrumentation. This phase is critical to the success of any Exchange deployment.

3. *Prepare directory services.* Prepare the Exchange 5.5 directory (if it's in mixed mode) and the AD through modifications in the enterprise schema necessary for deploying the messaging system.

4. *Deploy the first Exchange 2000 server.* With the deployment of the first Exchange server and the change in enterprise structure, you see the changeover from Microsoft Solutions Framework (MSF) to Microsoft Operations Framework (MOF).

An installation of a real-world system will most likely include running legacy systems. However, in an effort to keep descriptions simple, we do not cover it here. Although the four stages are universal, the remaining stages require additional attention to migrate existing legacy systems and services to a Windows 2000 native-mode platform:

5. *Merge the Exchange 5.5 namespace with AD.* Run the Exchange 2000 Delegation Wizard and create a bridgehead server to access the messaging platform.

6. *Upgrade the Information Store (IS) and other Exchange components.* Upgrade recipient objects like the mailbox store, Public Folder store, and connectors, and create new Administrative Groups.

7. *Switch to native mode.* Before switching to native mode, make final changes, if necessary, to reorganize your organization.

Although the first four stages are universal, the remaining stages require additional attention to migrate existing legacy systems and services to a Windows 2000 native-mode platform. Although an installation of a real-world system will most likely include running legacy systems, we do not cover these systems in this chapter in an effort to keep descriptions simple. For consideration of systems running legacy products, see Chapter 16.

Administrative Needs

In all the steps of planning deployment just mentioned, you must assess the needs of people in your target user population and processes in your target installation, as well as determine how these needs will be managed in an enterprise. Unlike legacy messaging platforms that were relatively separate from the administration of the underlying NOS, Exchange 2000 makes extensive use of Windows 2000 directory services. Tools necessary to manage these integrated administrative needs must support SMFAs involved in:

➤ *User management/directory services*—This management interface, providing different views of AD and other network-related resources, must support an administrative topology that handles permission management and administrative system policies.

➤ *Server/network/routing management*—Functionally separate from the administrative topology, network components and Routing Groups, in particular, need to be similarly viewed and managed, though as a separate administrative entity dealing with infrastructure and connectivity issues between groups and with foreign mail systems.

➤ *Storage services/public folder management*—You need to manage various aspects of storage services in the form, for example, of Storage Groups (SGs) and multiple databases. Similarly, the management of public folders, which can now form potentially complex, hierarchical trees, has been segregated and spun off as a possible separate, specialized area of administration.

➤ *Collaborative services management*—The addition of realtime collaborative services (RTCs) such as chat service, data- and videoconferencing, and presence management and Instant Messaging, require specialized areas of administrative management in order to support an already wide array of Exchange services.

➤ *Mixed-mode operations with legacy systems*—In Exchange 2000, each legacy site has one Administrative Group within which one or more Routing Groups are found. Active Directory Connector (ADC) maintains directory synchronization between legacy directory services and AD. This is necessary because you cannot install a legacy Exchange server in a native-mode Exchange 2000 organization.

The Interplay of Roles

You can manage each one of the above-listed management areas either from a single seat or as a separate branch of one messaging service that extends across an entire enterprise. The MMC is instrumentation you need to provide the extensibility of features and the scalability across an entire enterprise forest. This one-tool framework supports the addition of all or specific snap-in tool components that provide either single-seat global administration or a modular, customized toolset for managing SMFAs within the range of messaging and collaborative services.

The careful scoping of these SMFAs in terms of people, processes, and the underlying network infrastructure (sometimes called the *physical plant*) contributes to how well the instrumentation achieves its design objectives. Though this statement sounds somewhat circular, you create effective deployment plans the more you know about how to manage the system you are about to deploy. The trick to deploying systems is to mentally rehearse what you need to do, where you need to go, and what resources you need to accomplish the project *before* you actually start the project. Unfortunately, because every messaging system has unique characteristics that conform to specific corporate objectives, good instrumentation and methodologies derived from best practices come from working with fully deployed systems. The recursive nature of this relationship reinforces the concept mentioned earlier about the interplay between MSF and MOF. The key to successful reduction in TCO is to have operations people intimately involved and fully vested in developing proposed solutions. We thus start with the most basic of Windows 2000 management tools, the MMC.

Microsoft Management Console (MMC)

The MMC, though first introduced with IIS 4 on NT 4, is a fundamental part of Windows 2000 both in its ubiquitous nature within the NOS and in the theory on which Windows 2000 rests. This tool is nothing more than a featureless Windows Explorer–type interface that provides both extensibility and scalability. As in Explorer, windows are divided into two separate sections or panes: a Scope pane on the left side and a Details pane on the right. The left pane also contains two tabs:

➤ *Tree tab*—The Tree tab (sometimes called the *console tree*) shows a hierarchical display of items that are available within the specific console. You define the scope of any one item by selecting it in the left pane on this console tree; the right pane shows the details of your selection.

➤ *Favorites tab*—You can use the Favorites tab just above the left window to create shortcuts to items in the console tree. Toolmakers attach as few or as many snap-in tools to the tree within this console frame as they deem necessary to construct a complete toolset.

The MMC supports two types of snap-in components:

- *Standalone snap-in tools*—This instrumentation functions alone without additional support.

- *Extension snap-in tools*—This instrumentation augments the functionality of a parent snap-in tool and depends upon it.

This Component Object Model (COM)–based frame, like Windows 2000 itself, accommodates applications developed by third-party, independent software vendors (ISVs). The ISVs are encouraged to use it as a design substrate on which to assemble their own new, specialized combinations of network tools and utilities. Because it is a multidocument interface (MDI), the console implicitly enforces a design standard for all Windows 2000 snap-in tools—Windows-based applications with well-known user features such as hierarchical displays and drag-and-drop capabilities. Standardization of this interface minimizes end-user training and thus reduces TCO.

It is, in fact, just a tool frame, so it can accommodate as many or as few snap-ins as are necessary to complete some predefined task. Toolmakers or authors then secure the frame to prevent future unauthorized modification. This locking feature implicitly controls feature availability and access to end users. Finally, and most significant from an administrative perspective, the frame or console is a self-contained MSC (or management saved console) object file. Administrators/authors can delegate administrative responsibilities and email a saved console file for use on some remote Windows-based machine. The MMC runs on Windows NT 4, 2000, and 9x operating systems without additional assembly. This tool frame epitomizes the very network philosophy of Windows 2000: extensibility, scalability, modularity, and portability.

The MMC's Construction and Operation

You can find prebuilt Exchange management consoles on the Microsoft Exchange menu listed below the Programs menu. Management consoles in general have a user mode with three varying levels of access (full access, limited access multiple windows, and limited access single window). Alternatively, you can open consoles in author/creator mode when you create or modify a specific console frame. These two general modes—user and author—parallel how toolbars work in any Windows-based Office application when you use the Customize feature typically found in the Toolbars submenu under View. To create a new console frame, sometimes called a *console root container*, explicitly in author mode, type the following command-line information in the Run dialog box,

```
mmc path/filename.msc /a
```

where **path/filename.msc** is the proposed location and console file name, and **/a** explicitly confirms author mode (in which, as stated previously, modifications are allowed from the console).

You add snap-in components through the Add/Remove Snap-in feature selection on the Console menu (or by using the keyboard equivalent, Ctrl+M). If you choose to build your own console and want to include directory services, you can use several snap-in tools related to the functioning of directory services and the AD:

- *AD Sites and Services*—This snap-in specifically manages sites, subnets, forests, and DCs, the delegation of authority, and directory replication schedules. It conceptualizes your administrative workspace in terms of uniform distributed enterprise-wide Windows 2000 services.

- *AD Domains and Trusts*—This snap-in tool manages trust relationships between domains within a Windows 2000 forest and across forests, non-Windows Kerberized realms, and legacy NT 4 domains. It provides a Windows 2000 workspace that accommodates older legacy domain models and non-Microsoft systems.

- *AD Users and Computers*—This tool manages daily administrative tasks that relate to DCs, identity and permission management of users, computers, groups, organizational units (OUs), printers, and shared folders within an enterprise workspace.

- *Other specialized snap-in tools*—You can add more tools such as Active Directory Services Interface (ADSI) Edit, a powerful low-level editor that allows expert users to view, modify, create, and delete any object in the AD, and ADC Management, which handles connections to legacy Exchange 5.5 sites.

AD Sites and Services snap-in supports a Group Policy extension. AD Users and Computers includes Group Policy and Remote Access Services (RAS) Dialin - User Node Extension, and Terminal Services - Extension. Whether standalone or extension, all snap-ins conform to the MDI interface specification. You can get a feature list (now called the *context menu* instead of the shortcut menu) by right-clicking on an object. Administrators can use either user profiles or Group Policy settings to preserve the integrity of an MMC and prevent intentional or accidental changes to snap-ins. Windows 2000 automatically installs some management consoles; for example, all three directory services consoles—AD Users and Computers, AD Sites and Services, and AD Domains and Trusts—are installed on a DC in native mode.

Recipient Management

Solutions are the glue that Microsoft expects you to provide in your role as an administrator. Microsoft, unlike other major IT players like Sun, Novell, and IBM, is in the business of creating software and methodologies that use the software in some productive manner. TCO and ROI measure productivity. Thus, you shape Exchange Server to your organization's needs. As mentioned previously, you should propose solutions—using, for example, MSF—in the context of how you will provide ongoing maintenance and support. Exchange 2000 has changed how basic recipient objects are viewed because it no longer "owns" these objects; the NOS and AD do. Your effectiveness in managing a messaging environment depends upon how well you organize the objects within it. Because these objects are actually part of AD, the key to your organizational abilities lies in how well you understand the way AD manages the enterprise namespace.

Domain Structure

You need a methodology to organize and coordinate the providing of some service. AD now provides an object with attributes that, in fact, can be Exchange specific. Thus, the old legacy Exchange Directory Services mailbox and distribution list objects, which were separate from the named principal account in the DC's directory database, have been replaced by an AD user and group, respectively, that are both mail enabled. In the past, the user with the named principal account known by the legacy primary DC also had an assigned mailbox in the Exchange directory store. In Windows 2000, there is a consolidation of identity management; the same named principal or user has extensible attributes. You can mail-enable identity management, centralized in AD, by adding appropriate object attributes to the AD schema and assigning meaningful values to them. Any Windows 2000 named object or principal, with its collection of relevant attributes, is still, interestingly enough, known by DCs in Windows 2000 just like in the legacy NT 4 domain model—but now, all DCs share equal information and, generally speaking, equal power and responsibility within the native Windows 2000 enterprise.

Single-Master Domain Model

The single-master primary DC model of NT 4 has grown into a more robust, fault-tolerant, and scalable multimaster model in Windows 2000. All DCs within this larger enterprise domain namespace know each individually named object and its attributes. This is compared to the need for legacy domains to form trust relationships in NT 4. You need a more flexible administrative category—an OU—as an administrative container to compensate for this larger namespace and potentially greater number of objects. OUs, or OUs within an OU, provide more flexible boundaries than the more formal, and traditional, domain boundaries within which to apply permissions.

Organizational Units

You manage permissions within the boundaries of a domain or one or more of the flexible OUs within it. Legacy permission management works at two levels; it uses global and local groups to simplify the assignment of permissions to individual users. Microsoft suggests you assign users to global groups first and then assign those global groups to local groups in resource domains with access to those specific local resources. Groups as organizational containers are more stable objects than individual users in the namespace. Therefore, to control their inheritance of local resource permissions, it is easier to move users in and out of global groups located in some master domain than manage the many possibilities of their membership in numerous local groups throughout resource domains. In Windows 2000, OUs similarly help to organize named objects across broader namespaces. As in the legacy scenario with global group usage, Microsoft recommends delegating control through OUs because of their flexibility. Because function and structure are separated in Windows 2000, mailbox-enabled recipient objects and their Exchange server mailboxes do not have to be a part of the same OU or domain. Thus, administrators can design and delegate control over a messaging system in a manner that more readily reflects their corporation's organizational structure.

Administrative Models

Exchange, even in legacy versions, has followed the more intuitive model you now see in Windows 2000 native-mode enterprises. In its most fundamental sense, an "exchange" of messages occurs within the boundaries of some namespace or organization. This logical boundary defines recipients; those outside this defined namespace are foreign. Two different models, a centralized administrative structure and a delegated administrative structure, describe methods of managing Exchange 2000 recipients; a third model known as the messaging group administration of Exchange attributes is appropriate in a mixed-mode Exchange 2000 architecture that supports the older NT 4 domain structure and legacy Exchange 5.5.

Centralized Administration

Just as it is simpler to use global groupings to administer users in an NT 4 domain model, an Exchange administrator can group all recipient objects in one centralized OU. Centralizing objects in one container simplifies permission management by applying Group Policy, a fundamental management strategy Microsoft expounds upon in Windows 2000 design. For example, child groups inherit the policies and permission of the container group. Management is not only simplified within one centralized container of recipients, but the Administrator group who manages this container is also clearly defined as compared to the legacy concept of administering recipient objects distributed across several sites.

Delegated Administration

Delegated administration decentralizes the management responsibilities among separate groups of administrators and recipients. The focus on one centralized container shifts to a collection of separate containers, each possibly distinguished by any number of geopolitical or functional differences. Such a structure may actually simplify the administration of some organizations, especially those broken up into heterogeneous units. Yet the structure still provides the native-mode substrate for an Exchange 2000 deployment.

Legacy Issues

When you are dealing with heterogeneous messaging systems, a third model, which Microsoft calls the messaging group administration of Exchange attributes, provides support for the single domain structure of NT 4 and Exchange 5.5. By specifying attribute-level permissions, you can separately administer Exchange objects and integrate the two different directory databases. Although awkward as an ongoing administrative model because you lose many directory features in a mixed-mode Windows 2000 enterprise, this model is critical in providing messaging services while migrating systems to a fully enabled Exchange 2000 messaging and collaborative platform.

Administrative Tools for Recipient Management

You need various MMC toolsets to provide the necessary tools to manage any Exchange organization. To run Windows 2000 servers remotely, install Windows 2000 Administrative tools on, for example, a Windows 2000 Professional workstation. You can install the necessary administration tools by launching adminpak.msi, located in the I386 folder on the Windows 2000 Server Installation CD-ROM. Similarly, you can remotely manage Exchange 2000 using Windows Professional clients by selecting Exchange 2000 System Management Tools in the Exchange 2000 Setup Wizard. You can also install these tools using the Software Installation node of the Group Policy snap-in on a server running Windows 2000. You can publish programs in AD, as well as assign an application to a specific computer. Use Add/Remove programs, located in Control Panel, to install the tools.

Terminal Services

Another solution is to install Windows 2000 Terminal Services on any server that is running in remote administration mode. You should now consider this tool to be an important part of your administrator's toolkit. You should install Windows 2000 Terminal Services on Exchange servers that operate in remote administration mode for access through a console session across a local area network (LAN) or dial-up connection. If the user has the appropriate permissions, Terminal Services in Window 2000 Server automatically provides two user licenses for remote monitoring services and the following advantages:

➤ Remote control of all server-provided services over network or dial-up connections

➤ Access from any workstation that supports the Terminal Services client

It is recommended that you install Windows 2000 Terminal Services on all servers that operate in remote administration mode. Any workstation running Windows 2000 Professional should have both Windows 2000 Administration Tools and Exchange 2000 System Management Tools installed. By adding a Windows 2000 Terminal Services client to the set of management tools, an administrator can control any server from anywhere without loading a single client application rather than, for example, Exchange System Manager or predesigned MMCs on remote workstations.

Logical Organization

You need to combine these administrative tools with careful organization of recipients within your organization. OUs, unlike legacy recipient containers in Exchange 5.5, impose structure but do not affect the naming of objects in the Outlook Address Book. Similarly, the logical nature of the OU, as opposed to the nature of legacy recipient containers, does not impact on movement of mailboxes, as it formerly did between containers. The OU provides a logical structure within which object administration is simplified and the application of Group Policy more easily controlled. You again see an important theme: Exchange 2000 allows you to organize your namespace according to your business workflow without placing artificial constraints on address-book views or changes in mailbox locations.

Permission Management

Permission management in Windows 2000 encompasses two dimensions: vertically through access scoping of the Account Operator, Administrator, and Domain Administrators Group, and horizontally through inheritance or overriding permissions in the object hierarchy. To realize efficient and robust enterprise designs, you must completely understand the interaction of these two dimensions. Full control over AD objects now includes mailbox location and other messaging-related information. Using AD Users and Computers, like creating a published NetBIOS file share, restricts the access of some local administrator to create mailbox-enabled users or move mailbox containers unless the appropriate permissions, like Mailbox Manager rights, have been assigned. Always remember, though, that just as local logons will subvert any security measures imposed by a NETBIOS share on the access to local folders, the use of a command-line utility in the appropriate security context—such as AD Administration Tool (ldp.exe)—can also subvert security restrictions to accessing the AD. Use the AD Delegation Wizard to grant permissions to any AD group, including the built-in Account Operators Group; use the Exchange Administration Delegation Wizard to grant those special Mailbox Manager rights. The more centralized the model, the more simplified the organization is; combine management of both user accounts and mail-related administration roles into one central Administrative Group.

AD Delegation of Control Wizard

Another tool that helps in administrative tasks is the AD Delegation of Control Wizard, which grants a wide range of access rights to both domains and OUs. This wizard allows you to assign specific Read/Write properties to many levels of object classes, as shown in Figure 4.1. Given the level of control made accessible by a host

Figure 4.1 Active Directory Delegation of Control Wizard assigning permissions.

of tools and wizards, it is strongly recommended that you keep the delegation of authority and the assignment of permissions as simple as possible over the broadest and most flexible of objects, like, for example, OUs. The strategy is in many ways similar to the legacy approach to assigning users to global groups. Now more than ever, though, it is important not to specify different and possibly conflicting permissions among different objects at different class levels.

Exchange Administration Delegation Wizard

The Exchange Administration Delegation Wizard is like the AD Directory Delegation of Control Wizard in that it assists you with delegating responsibility for managing messaging configuration objects in AD. You can use the tool to assign to a group or individual one of three roles that are similar to those used in Exchange 5.5:

➤ *Exchange Administrator (View Only)*—All Exchange object configurations are Read Only.

➤ *Exchange Administrator*—All Exchange object configurations are Read/Write.

➤ *Exchange Full Administrator*—All Exchange object configurations are Read/Write and Change Permissions.

You assign these delegated roles to various groups that administer the Exchange organization, as shown in Figure 4.2. Just as in the legacy domain model, the actual rights and permissions are assigned to groups rather than individuals. You assign individuals instead to these general, or in legacy terms, global, groups. These groups simplify the assignment of administrative rights.

In the Windows 2000 distributed services environment, permission settings of different objects with different scopes can cause unpredictable and often undesirable

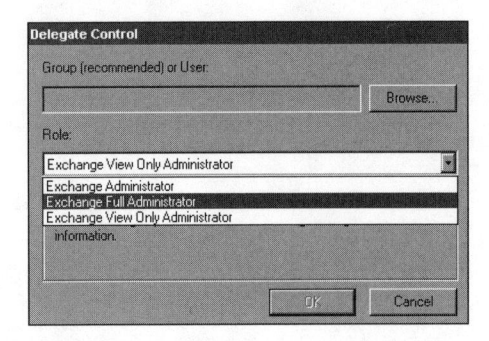

Figure 4.2 Exchange Administration Delegation Wizard assigning roles.

changes in an entire class of objects in an enterprise hierarchy. These effects may not only prove damaging but also very difficult to troubleshoot and correct. This wizard manages the Administrative Group and the right to create mailboxes. You should use this Administrative Group exactly the way global groups are used in legacy NT 4 systems; users are added to or removed from this all-powerful group that is delegated with the responsibility of managing the Exchange organization.

Policies

Exchange 2000 recipient policies are yet another form of scoping access, much like legacy Exchange site addressing. A *policy* is nothing more than a collection of settings applied to one or more objects found in the same class. You can thus control objects in the same class through a single set of configurations or policies. Exchange 2000 supports two kinds of policies, system policies and recipient policies.

System Policies

System policies are actually server-side collections of configurations. These include the mailbox store, the Public Folder store, and the server engine itself. After you configure an attribute through some policy change, the only ways to change it are to modify and reapply the policy or to delete the policy object itself.

Recipient Policies

Recipient policies are user-side objects that relate to users, contacts, and groups. The current version of Exchange 2000 supports a single recipient policy class: the policy that controls email address generation, similar to but more flexible than the legacy Exchange 5.5 counterpart. During installation, the "default policy" is placed in the Recipient Policies container under the Recipients node in the organizational tree.

A noteworthy characteristic of recipient policies is that they are not immediately applied but instead are associated with a collection of objects forming a Lightweight Directory Access Protocol (LDAP) query recordset from a built address list. The System Attendant (SA) service applies the recordset of LDAP specifications about every 10 minutes. Filter rules are applied to multiple address lists you create to implement policies. For example, different SMTP addresses could use recipient policies to control the conditions under which one address or another is used. The recipient policies update the recordset stored in the domain-naming context in the AD and replicate them throughout the forest. Thus, Exchange 2000 uses policy-driven settings to cause a specific output of data. This is an important theme, especially in the management of distributed services.

Server Management

The separation of function from structure affords the administrator greater freedom to mold the Exchange organization to the needs of corporate objectives and the user population without constraints imposed by a physical network. A second dichotomy, client-side as opposed to server-side management, has a similar impact on how a system is used because, generally speaking, the client never has access to server-side features. The administrator can, under some circumstances, totally automate installation and restrict the range of features to minimize the need for user intervention, maintenance, or training. Thus, server-side management can centralize control of the messaging platform and significantly reduce TCO. Microsoft categorizes server-side management for its new breed of .NET servers into three SMFAs of control and management:

➤ *Exchange 2000*—The specific, service-providing application

➤ *Active Directory*—The directory services provider

➤ *Windows 2000*—The system services platform

With the streamlining in design and specialization of function, service-providing platforms like Exchange 2000 and SQL 2000 have delegated internal directory services to the NOS and hence have greater integration with the operating system than legacy products. Unlike, for example, Exchange 5.5 running on NT 4, operating environment design and the performance of AD directory services affect how Exchange 2000 will run. This dependency can have an additional advantage in that the same Administrative Group can now vertically manage all three layers rather than separate the roles of Exchange administration from the operating system. It is noteworthy that the joint administration of both the NOS and Exchange was less likely in legacy NT 4, because the messaging and operating system services were horizontally arranged and functionally separate. Especially when migrating from an older messaging platform like Exchange 5.5, you need to address Exchange's *gestalt* change from horizontal to vertical management and, for example, AD directory services. Exchange 2000 will most likely be the first enterprise-wide system an organization deploys; merging administrative areas of responsibility in the technical services area can profoundly improve support services and the organization's ongoing operation.

Administrative Models

Just as with recipient management, there are three administrative models used to manage server-side services:

➤ *Centralized management*—As previously mentioned, centralized management is typically the simplest model to create and manage services and thus results in a lower TCO.

➤ *Distributed management*—In some situations, especially in organizations that are divided into geopolitical groupings, distributed management may more closely correspond to the actual way the corporation is arranged.

➤ *Mixed management*—In native mode, Exchange 2000 provides far more flexibility in design than legacy versions of the messaging product. You can implement different Administrative Groups that control message routing and recipients, as well as apply different policy levels to the server, user, or both.

The advantage of Exchange 2000 over legacy products is its ability to conform to the organizational needs of the corporation as an enterprise. Especially in a mixed-management model, you can manage large-scale deployments both horizontally and vertically, depending on corporate needs and the specific circumstances of any particular group of Exchange servers and DCs.

Centralized Management

A centralized management model divides Exchange servers into one or more Administrative Groups. Unlike with recipients, you cannot move servers among these groups once you have assigned them. In addition to these Administrative Groups, you can assign one or more Routing Groups to handle message transfer. A centralized model is most appropriate for small to medium-sized organizations with a central technical support group. Microsoft strongly recommends that you leverage both AD and Exchange Server scalability by minimizing the number of organizational layers. In other words, Exchange System Manager, by default, does not even suggest the existence of Administrative Groups. The system has been designed with the implicit assumption that you will not need or use separate administrative groupings. As you install servers, they are all added to a common group unless you create a new administrative grouping. To do this, you must first display this object in the console tree by selecting the General tab on the organization's Properties sheet. Two checkboxes, shown in Figure 4.3, allow you to Display Routing Groups, Display Administrative Groups, or both in the console tree. These options are available in all three management models.

You must display an Administrative Group before you can add new servers to it. If you subsequently clear these group display options, the group divisions will be lost and all servers will be grouped back into the same Servers node in the Exchange

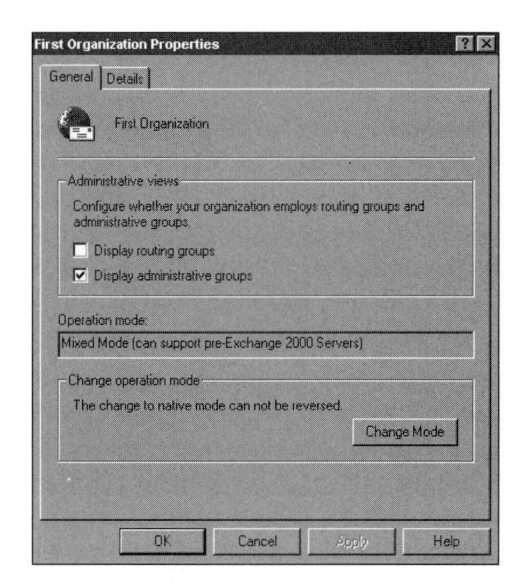

Figure 4.3 Enabling the Routing Group and Administrative Group nodes on the console tree.

System Manager console tree. If you re-enable the display of the Administrative Group node, servers are not restored back to prior settings.

Distributed Management

In the distributed management model, Exchange servers are assigned to Administrative Groups based on the corporation's needs or constraints. Though centralized management is chosen by default, "green-field" deployment, where no legacy systems are involved in the messaging installation, is rare. You will more typically find large installations with patches of legacy hardware and software. With a distributed management model, you have the flexibility to assign responsibilities and personnel to specific groups that are based on the existing corporate topology. It is noteworthy that when Exchange 2000 interfaces with legacy version 5.5 systems, flexibility is usually lost as groups reassume the more rigid constraints of the legacy version. In other words, an Exchange 2000 Administrative Group behaves like a legacy version 5.5 site when the two messaging systems coexist in one organization.

Mixed Management

The use of the term "mixed" in this description is misleading. The ability to mix different groups and manage routing in specific areas is based on the flexibility of Exchange 2000. The mixed-management model requires that the messaging organization be composed exclusively of Exchange 2000 servers. Mixed management does not work in a heterogeneous installation that mixes Exchange 2000 with legacy systems. Exchange 2000 provides the advantages of Administrative Groups, Routing Groups, and permission management of both server features and recipients.

Tools That Support Server Management

Administrative and technical support is predicated on both good organization and the proper tools. You can conceptualize the messaging and collaborative service platform as a collection of Exchange servers that together form a specialized layer of software that rests on top of the NOS and AD directory services. Thus, the features that you find in organizing the Windows 2000 enterprise are just as relevant when you are dealing with Exchange 2000. The integration of messaging platform with the NOS, especially in the areas of server management, is why it's important that you thoroughly understand the NOS and directory services design before you assume responsibility for designing, deploying, or managing an Exchange system.

Logical Grouping

The flexibility of Exchange 2000, combined with new Windows 2000 features like OUs, provides many good ways to organize people, processes, and machines. Structural solutions like creating resource domains in legacy systems have been replaced by logical groups that can more accurately reflect a corporate workflow.

Organizational Units

OUs are the best way to scope permissions and rights. In fact, Microsoft specifically states that it's a poor practice to create domains instead of OUs for the purpose of managing the delegation of rights and responsibilities because it wastes resources such as a DC, unnecessarily increases network utilization because of support traffic, and needlessly complicates an organizational structure. Creating an OU, alternatively, can more readily provide vertical resource management that extends from the messaging platform down through the directory services layer into the NOS. Thus, vertical management should, in fact, include an Exchange administrator's ability to start or stop services and install software within an OU. Such specific vertical control over system services is difficult to provide in legacy systems like Exchange 5.5.

Administrative Groups

Exchange servers may differ in terms of system policies, groups, public folders, or IRC chat communities. You can manage these SMFAs by assigning a collection of machines to an Administrative Group. Membership in an Administrative Group does not preclude membership in a Routing Group in some other Administrative Group. Once membership is assigned, however, you cannot move a server to another group. You can, however, by using the Exchange Tasks Wizard, move mailbox data stores between servers. Thus, in native mode, you can uncouple the Administrative Groups from Routing Groups to gain further flexibility. In mixed mode, however, many features drift back to their more limited legacy characteristics.

Routing Groups

You can create one or more Routing Groups, which handle message transfer within Administrative Groups. This additional organizational structure will help support differences in the quality of network connectivity within an OU. In native mode, you can assign servers to any Routing Group regardless of their Administrative Group membership. These groupings provide support for underlying infrastructure where:

➤ Servers are running different versions of Exchange software or have different connectivity characteristics

➤ A single Routing Group consolidates servers in different Administrative Groups for simplified management and control

Using Routing Groups can provide an organized, unified view of connectivity separate from a more complex but functional arrangement of people and processes.

System Policies and Groups

One of the advantages of Administrative Groups is a clear view of topology, membership, and relations among various components. Another benefit is that you can apply system policies easily and systematically. As mentioned earlier, policies are specific configuration settings applied to a specific grouping of system objects. You can create policies in one Administrative Group and apply them in other groups, thereby simplifying administration and consistency when applying server settings. In a distributed management model, you can easily administer organization-wide standards like mailbox size and message retention times through a common set of system policies located in some Administrative Group.

Other Administrative Areas

Managing recipients and servers is just one aspect of administering an Exchange system. In Exchange 5.5, you organized users by mail distribution lists (DLs) to simplify the simultaneous delivery of mail to many people; in Exchange 2000, you change an attribute in an AD group object to receive that mail. The legacy concept of mailbox is now, in Exchange 2000, a mailbox-enabled user. Similarly, the legacy custom recipient has been transformed into a mail-enabled user. Attributes associated with these objects are changed to produce some desired feature. Because these features are merely enabling some object attribute, changes such as a new phone number or mail address are performed through any DC. In legacy systems, such record modifications would have required access to a specific directory in a specific Exchange server, and they would have been far more complicated to perform as compared to Exchange 2000 and its enterprise-wide accessibility to users and features they need to perform their work. Thus, administration is simpler than in legacy products because concepts such as user have been consolidated in the more logical directory services of the NOS. From a similar administrative perspective, sharing information through public folders has always been part of the Exchange Server suite of features. It is a powerful method that facilitates collaboration among groups. Of the four basic types of recipients—namely, user, group, contact, and public folder—the administrative features of public folders have also been simplified.

Security and Distribution Groups

Groups in any network operating system are used to reduce administrative effort and enhance the management of users through simpler group changes. The two basic groups in Windows 2000 that serve this function are as follows:

➤ *Security groups*—In Exchange 2000, this group controls access to resources and can also be used for mail distribution. The mail distribution aspect is used to keep group members informed about changes to resources under the group's purview. Its mail-enabled capability makes creating a separate DL unnecessary.

➤ *Distribution groups*—As in previous versions of Exchange, this group is used exclusively for distributing mail. Because members of this group are not granted access to any resources other than mail, there is little opportunity to inadvertently grant access to a user.

Security groups are collections of security principals or named users within AD that simplify the assignment of special permissions to network resources. Distribution groups replace legacy distribution lists (DLs) in Exchange 5.5. In fact, legacy DLs have been merged into a combination of both of these groups; a new kind of mail-enabled group.

You typically use security groups. Use distribution groups exclusively for mailing lists, but they are also appropriate for nontrusted recipients. You can also use the universal group in native-mode Windows 2000 for viewing list membership; mixed mode requires DLs.

Public Folders

As an administrator, you may need to design public folder hierarchies to provide common access throughout the enterprise. AD directory services simplify the permission management of these messaging objects. Unlike legacy Exchange versions that control permissions to mailbox containers and users through internal directory services, Exchange 2000 provides access control in a unified manner through AD and the operating system.

Access Control

In legacy Exchange, you grant access to a public folder at the object level of the mailbox or user; you control mailbox access through the user account in the directory database located in the DC. The unification of objects within the AD namespace has not only simplified the security model but has also allowed an increase in the granularity or specificity of permission management at the object level, as shown in Figure 4.4.

In Exchange 2000, you grant access to public folders and all other messaging objects directly to the user and group object in AD. In a heterogeneous installation

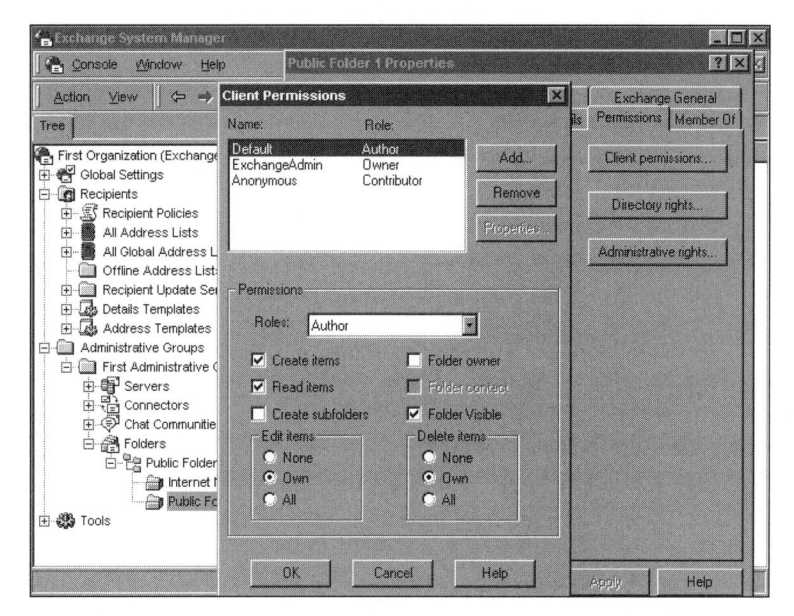

Figure 4.4 A public folder Properties sheet showing client permissions.

where Exchange 2000 coexists with legacy Exchange, group types involved in permission management are very important. ADC synchronizes legacy DLs with AD universal distribution groups but does not provide access control for Exchange 2000 public folders. You can convert universal distribution groups to universal security groups when you upgrade or replicate public folders from legacy Exchange to Exchange 2000 or when you use Outlook clients to assign access rights to public folders.

Public Folder Affinity

Public folder hierarchies can be an important addition to the feature list of a messaging and collaborative platform. These containers provide a highly visible central data store that is accessible across the enterprise. You can replicate a data store in one public folder to all the other folders throughout the enterprise. When users access a folder not located on their local server, the server can provide the Outlook client with a sorted list of servers that have replicas of the original stored material. Public folders replicate by default across all available connectors. Exchange 2000 can determine the location of the closest replica with information available through Routing Groups. In legacy Exchange public folder referrals, called *public folder affinity*, the server used these lists for routing to determine the order in which requests were referred to these remote servers. Unlike in Exchange 5.5, affinities in Exchange 2000 are transitive so that an affinity between a routing referral on server A and server B and between server B and server C provides a referral path from server A to server C. Thus, if all server locations are connected, all servers receive public folder request referrals by default.

Evaluation and Performance Management

Managing recipients and servers is part of day-to-day operations and has always been part of the Exchange administrator's scope of responsibilities. New concepts that have expanded this scope include:

➤ Uncoupling of administrative function from physical structure

➤ Greater extensibility of user interfaces and access to data objects, creating greater opportunity for messaging and collaborative solutions

➤ Integration of Exchange administration with network administration, requiring either greater sharing of management responsibilities or careful scoping of authorities

An administrator needs to assume a global perspective when dealing with messaging solutions. The role of architect, however, must be tempered by the responsibilities of monitoring and providing ongoing service and support. Here again, the scope of this technical support has expanded; Exchange is an enterprise-wide provider of mission-critical services. As administrator, you must constantly provide the highest levels of reliability and access. A subtle part of delivering these services is in planning short-term capacity and long-term growth. Problem management has grown into a collection of methodologies that both Microsoft and, for example, the CCTA have refined into SMFAs with their own performance metrics. The areas of maintenance and support in the context of 24×7×365 service levels are now just as much measured components of the profit equation in many ongoing financial concerns as gross and net sales figures themselves. These areas of concern include:

➤ *Capacity planning*—These system metrics predict how the component parts of the enterprise grow in relation to increases in the general corporation's size. If you want to anticipate subtle changes in resource capacity and performance, it's critical to identify and accurately measure the rate of growth and utilization of different components. In a "five 9" reliability scenario, capacity planning identifies the mean time between failures of the $0.35 fuse as well as the $35,000 Redundant Array of Independent Disks (RAID) tower. Failure of either hardware component can have a similar effect on the system's access and reliability.

➤ *Problem management*—These tools and methodologies work in both a preventative and curative mode. They work in both a proactive and retroactive way and when systematically performed, add to the system's future reliability.

➤ *Maintenance and support*—These systems focus on identifying, isolating, and correcting a problem as expeditiously as possible.

Your corporate objectives and agreed-upon service levels should be built into the design phase of your deployment. During both deployment and the quality assurance phase that follows, the monitoring and diagnostic information coming from your measurements should directly address the ongoing needs of your support team. Best practices recommend including support team personnel among those who handle deployment. It is especially important to monitor the Exchange "application" layer as actually a part of the NOS. For example, the proper functioning of DNS and DHCP is just as significant to the transfer of Exchange messages as it is to the network administrator building new client workstations.

Exchange 2000 Tools

Microsoft Exchange provides both reactive and proactive tools. Reactive tools evaluate and manage problems after they have occurred. Proactive tools forecast potential problems. They search continuously for some irregularity and take corrective actions when they are triggered. Three key tools are:

➤ *Exchange Monitoring and Status Tool*—Located under Tools in the Exchange System Manager, this tool replaces the Server Monitor and Link Monitor tools in legacy Exchange versions. Instead of registering information above some static threshold set by an administrator, it provides information related to the continued growth of queues. All servers and connectors are listed in the Status container. Baselines in the Default Exchange Services node are monitored. Some services included in this container are the ISs, Message Transfer Agent (MTA) stacks, routing engine, protocol services, and Web Publishing Service. You can add other services to this container.

➤ *Queue Viewer*—This tool, used to view the state of all message queues, is useful in troubleshooting problems after they have been identified in the Monitoring and Status Tool. Figure 4.5 shows how to set objects and categories for Exchange 2000 diagnostic logging of Access Control to mailbox datastores on Server VA401. Diagnostic events will be reported in Event Viewer logs.

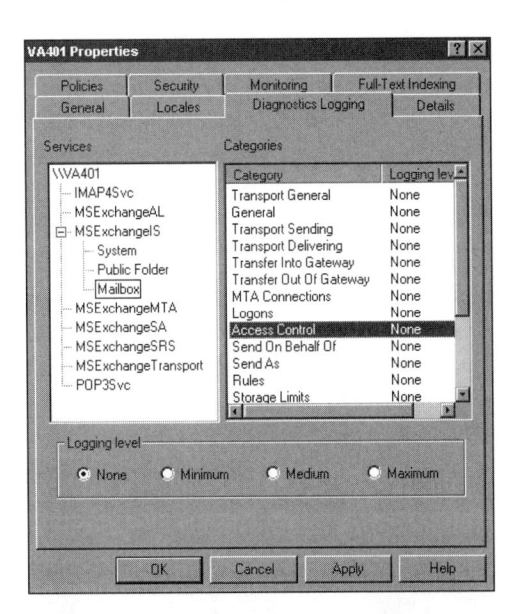

Figure 4.5 Diagnostic logging on a server Properties sheet.

▶ *Message Tracking Center*—This tool allows you to track a message from the sender to the recipient through the Exchange system.

In addition to message-tracking logs, these tools provide corroboration of reports about the user population. When you use the collection of baseline data proactively, it can help you forecast a problem before it escalates to a level that impacts the messaging system's overall performance.

Windows 2000 Tools

Tools that monitor the system layer or foundation on which Exchange services run are similarly categorized into both reactive and proactive. These tools are common across all application software and, in fact, provide a common interface to help technicians evaluate the nature of an irregular event or problem. Two noteworthy tools in common use are:

▶ *Performance Monitor*—System Monitor, available when you select Performance in the Administrative Tools folder, can chart ongoing activity in realtime or redirect information to a log file for future analysis. Realtime alerts triggered by selected conditions such as MTA Work Queue Length are of great diagnostic value when you are monitoring the MTA's health. Analysis of server activity can indicate the impending failure of some component as well as changes in system capacity.

▶ *Event Viewer*—All applications that run on the NT and Windows 2000 platforms log their error messages and warnings to the event log. You can view and filter these generated messages through Event Viewer in the MMC. This one tool, fundamental to the NOS, is probably the most important piece of instrumentation in your administrator's toolkit.

System and Exchange administrators typically formalize some daily procedure that scans the Event Viewer and a handful of favorite tools. It is imperative that data be collected for baseline purposes and as a daily maintenance task, as well as be carefully and thoughtfully analyzed. Very often, you can forecast serious problems by noticing subtle changes in a baseline or seemingly innocuous warning message from some application. It is also important to listen to an end-user report and systematically cross-check it with data collected from your instrumentation.

Chapter Summary

This chapter addressed a variety of management tools and methods used to efficiently administer an enterprise-scale Exchange 2000 messaging system. The following are some particularly significant points to remember:

▶ Key functional changes in Exchange 2000 include a new management model that uncouples function from structure; internal partitioning of protocol, storage, and directory services; a shift in emphasis on protocols from MAPI and

X.400 to SMTP; integration of KM features such as the full-text search engine; use of a new, enterprise-wide routing engine; and delivery of enhanced client-side functionality.

► In the Microsoft Enterprise Services Framework, there is a close relationship between solution-providing services and service-management services.

► Management tools necessary to manage integrated administrative needs must support SMFAs involved in user management/directory services, server/network/routing management, storage services/folder management, collaborative services management, and mixed-mode operations.

► The MMC supports two types of snap-in components: a standalone snap-in and an extension snap-in tool. Because the console uses the multidocument interface (MDI), a fundamental part of the Microsoft Windows architecture, it implicitly enforces a design standard for all Windows 2000 snap-in tools.

► Three snap-in tools are related to directory services functioning: AD Sites and Services, AD Domains and Trusts, and AD Users and Computers.

► Three models describe recipient management: a centralized administration using one container; delegated administration where management is decentralized across separate containers; and messaging group administration of Exchange attributes, where legacy systems are supported.

► Administrative tools for recipient management are primarily the Windows 2000 Administrative Tools (found in adminpak.msi, located in the I386 folder on the Windows 2000 Installation CD-ROM). You can remotely manage Exchange 2000 by using Windows 2000 Professional and selecting Exchange 2000 System Management Tools in the Exchange 2000 Setup Wizard.

► Use the AD Delegation Wizard to grant permissions to any AD group, including the built-in Account Operators; use the Exchange Administration Delegation Wizard with Mailbox Manager rights access. The AD Delegation of Control Wizard grants access rights to both domains and OUs.

► Server-side management is categorized into three SMFAs: Exchange 2000, AD, and Windows 2000. The three administrative models used to manage server-side services are centralized management with the lowest TCO; distributed management, where management more closely corresponds to the way a corporation is organized; and mixed management, where native-mode Exchange 2000 provides support for mixed central and delegated models.

► Tools that support server management use organizational objects found in Windows 2000, such as domains and OUs, as well as Administrative and Routing Groups, and system policies.

► The Exchange Administration Delegation Wizard is like the AD Directory Delegation of Control Wizard in that it assists you with delegating responsibility for managing the messaging configuration objects in AD. You can use this tool to assign three different roles: Exchange Administrator (View Only), Exchange Administrator (Read/Write), and Exchange Full Administrator (Read/Write/Change Permissions).

➤ Legacy DLs have been replaced by two kinds of mail-enabled groups: security and distribution groups.

➤ Public folders in Exchange 2000 have enhanced access control and transitive public folder affinities.

➤ Evaluation and performance management cover three specific areas: capacity planning, problem management, and maintenance and support.

Review Questions

1. What specific features have changed from Exchange 5.5 to Exchange 2000? [Check all correct answers]

    a. Identity management

    b. Permission management

    c. Directory services

    d. NOS

    e. Network protocol services

2. What metric category does top management now commonly apply when evaluating the job performance of an Exchange administrator?

    a. Bandwidth consumption

    b. Cost and financial return

    c. Design integration

    d. Reliability

3. What Microsoft methodologies are useful in dealing with maintenance and support issues? [Check all correct answers]

    a. MMC

    b. MSF

    c. MOF

    d. ITIL

4. What support and maintenance areas have the greatest impact on TCO? [Check all correct answers]
    a. Hardware maintenance
    b. Application support
    c. User support
    d. None of the above

5. What phases of installation are important in planning management instrumentation? [Check all correct answers]
    a. The Exchange deployment plan
    b. The NOS deployment plan
    c. The configuration of Active Directory
    d. Corporate objectives

6. What support areas can be included in Exchange 2000 administrative areas? [Check all correct answers]
    a. Application software
    b. Network connectivity
    c. Web development
    d. User (identity) management

7. During deployment, what is considered one of the recommended best practices?
    a. Have the MSF team design your management instrumentation before you deploy your system.
    b. Have the MOF team design your management instrumentation after you deploy your system.
    c. Have the MSF team and MOF team design your management instrumentation after you deploy your system.
    d. Combine as many MOF team members on the MSF team as possible.

8. What particular issue should you remember when using the MMC?
    a. The console runs only on Windows 2000 and NT 4.
    b. The framework must be locked before distribution.
    c. Answers a and b.
    d. None of the above.

9. What MMC snap-ins support user management? [Check all correct answers]
    a. ADSI
    b. AD Users and Computers
    c. AD Sites and Services
    d. AD Domains and Trusts

10. Legacy distribution lists have been replaced in Exchange 2000 by what object?
    a. Mailbox-enabled users
    b. Mail-aware users
    c. Mailbox-enabled groups
    d. Mail-aware groups

11. Which statement incorrectly describes Exchange 2000?
    a. The Exchange 2000 namespace uses a single-master model.
    b. Domain controllers in an Exchange 2000 namespace know each individual named object.
    c. OUs provide more flexible administrative boundaries in Exchange 2000 as compared to domains in Exchange 5.5.
    d. None of the above statements is incorrect.

12. What recipient model is most appropriate for a multinational company?
    a. Centralized.
    b. Delegated.
    c. Messaging group administration.
    d. There is not enough information to answer.

13. What is the name of the Windows 2000 administrative tool setup file?
    a. adminpak.msi in \I386
    b. adminpak.msi on the Windows 2000 Installation CD-ROM root directory
    c. adminpak.msi in \I386 on the Windows 2000 Installation CD-ROM root directory
    d. setup.exe in \Tools under \I386 on the Windows 2000 Installation CD-ROM root directory

14. For what two reasons would you consider installing TSA on Exchange servers?
    a. TSA delivers remote control of all server-provided services over both network and dial-up connections.
    b. TSA provides access to any workstation that supports the Terminal Services client.
    c. Terminal Services works automatically on any Exchange server.
    d. Terminal Services licenses need to be purchased for remote administration.

15. What tool does not require Mailbox Manager rights to create a mailbox-enabled user or move a mailbox container?
    a. ldp.exe
    b. ldd.exe
    c. lpd.exe
    d. lpp.exe

16. What administrative model is appropriate to manage server-side services in a mixed-mode environment?
    a. Centralized management
    b. Distributed management
    c. Mixed management
    d. Answer b or c

17. What happens to Administrative Groups when you disable the Administrative Group option in Exchange System Manager?
    a. Once the option is enabled, you cannot hide the Administrative Group node.
    b. Once the option is enabled and populated, you cannot hide the Administrative Group node.
    c. All servers are placed back in the default server group.
    d. None of the above.

18. Which statement is false?
    a. Although you can move data between servers in different Administrative Groups, once a server is assigned to a group, you cannot move that server to another group.
    b. Regardless of Windows 2000 mode or Exchange 2000 Administrative Group membership, you can assign servers to any Routing Group.
    c. Membership in an Administrative Group does not preclude membership in a Routing Group in a different Administrative Group.
    d. All the above statements are true.

19. Which statement is true?

    a. You can use the Exchange Administration Delegation Wizard to assign different attributes to administrator roles just like the attributed roles in Exchange 5.5.

    b. You must create system policies in the OU in which they apply.

    c. Both Routing and Administrative Groups are used to create security and system policy boundaries.

    d. None of the above statements is true.

20. Which statement is false?

    a. ADC synchronizes legacy DLs with AD universal distribution groups and access to Public Folder trees.

    b. In Exchange 2000, you can grant access to public folders and all other messaging objects in AD with increased granularity as compared to legacy versions.

    c. In mixed deployments where Exchange 2000 coexists with legacy systems, some conversion of mail-related objects occurs automatically.

    d. Unlike with legacy Exchange, public folder affinities in Exchange 2000 are transitive.

Real-World Projects

Harry Frasier works for the state government and is responsible for an Exchange system that currently covers four counties that surround Framingham, Virginia. Harry has worked for the state for over 12 years and has administered several Exchange 5.5 systems. His unit, the Department of Corrections, has recently migrated to Windows 2000, and the State Commissioner wants him to install and administer Exchange 2000 in a pilot study.

For now, Harry plans to distribute consoles to various locations in each of the four counties. His primary concerns are simplicity and security. His first objective is to create custom MMC snap-in tools using the MMC. He should apply various restrictions (such as restricting author mode and using various snap-ins) to those snap-ins. Finally, he wants to delegate various administrative tasks to different people. He wants to know the range of control he has over distributing these administrative tools.

Project 4.1

To create a custom console:

1. Run mmc.exe at the command line.

2. Click on the Add/Remove Snap-in on the Console menu.

3. Select Add to display the available snap-ins.

4. Select the Computer Management snap-in in the dialog box and click on the Add button.

5. Upon completing your selection, click on the Close button.

6. Click on OK.

7. Select Options on the Console menu.

8. Select the Console tab and choose Author Mode in the Console Mode box.

9. Click on Save As on the Console menu and specify a file name that will be saved with an .msc extension.

Harry can make specific setting selections and save the MMC file for distribution. He also knows he can restrict MMC features through Group Policy under Administrative Templates | Windows Components | Microsoft Management Console. He would like to see how this is done at the Registry level. Harry wants to restrict users from opening the MMC in author mode, from opening console files in author mode, and from opening any console files that open in author mode by default.

Note: Use Registry Editor at your own risk. Incorrect entries in the Registry can cause damage to your system configuration that may require you to reinstall your operating system. Create an Emergency Rescue Diskette before you attempt this lab.

For all the remaining labs, Harry had to create the following key in the Registry:

`HKEY_CURRENT_USER\Software\Policies\Microsoft\MMC`

He will populate this key with various string names and values to create the appropriate conditions. Before he can set string values in the Registry, Harry has to create the MMC key under Microsoft:

1. Run REGEDIT at the command line.

2. Expand HKEY_CURRENT_USER, Software, Policies, and Microsoft.

3. Right-click on the Microsoft key name and select New.

4. Select Key, type in MMC in the text box and press Enter. You will see the MMC key shown in the Registry path above. You will place all the strings and their values in this key during the remainder of these labs.

Harry wants to prevent people from opening the MMC in author mode, or using any console files that open in author mode by default.

Project 4.2
To modify the RestrictAuthorMode Registry key of the MMC console by using the Registry:

1. Right-click the MMC key and select New.

2. Select DWORD Value and type "RestrictAuthorMode" in the open textbox. Press the Enter key to confirm the string name. Notice the string is still selected.

3. Press the Enter key a second time and enter "1" to enable the feature. The Base section of the dialog box should indicate that you have entered a hexadecimal value.

This key stores the Restrict The User From Entering Author Mode Group Policy setting as "1" for enabled or "0" for disabled. If the setting is set to Not Configured, Group Policy deletes the entry from the Registry. If it is not configured or you delete the entry yourself, the system behaves as though the value is "0". The RestrictAuthorMode Registry key prevents users from opening the MMC in author mode or opening any console file that opens by default in author mode. This key value restricts the user workstation from possible alteration of any console file. When this key is disabled or not configured, users can open the MMC in author mode and create their own consoles. The users can, however, open MMC user mode console files such as those on the Administrative Tools menu.

4. To disable this feature, return to the string value and either double-click it or right-click it and select Modify.

5. Replace the hexadecimal 1 with a 0 and press Enter.

6. To remove this feature, right-click on the string value and select Delete.

Project 4.3
To modify the RestrictToPermittedSnapins Registry key of the MMC console by using the Registry:

1. Right-click the MMC key and select New.

2. Select DWORD Value and type "RestrictToPermittedSnapins" in the open textbox. Press the Enter key to confirm the string name. Notice the string is still selected.

3. Press the Enter key a second time and enter 1 to enable the feature. The Base section of the dialog box should indicate you have entered a hexadecimal value.

This Registry key stores the setting of Restrict Users To The Explicitly Permitted List Of Snap-Ins Group Policy. If you disable this key with "0" or set the key to Not Configured, all snap-ins are permitted, except those explicitly prohibited.

Note: *Snap-ins are explicitly prohibited when the **Restrict_Run** value in the Snap-ins Class ID subkey is disabled.*

A value of "1" prohibits users from running any snap-ins except those that are explicitly permitted for use. This value is best to use when most or all snap-ins are prohibited. Disabling this key (the default value) enables users to run snap-ins unless they are specifically prohibited from doing so.

4. To disable this feature, return to the string value and either double-click it or right-click it and select Modify.

5. Replace the hexadecimal 1 with a 0 and press Enter.

6. To remove this feature, right-click on the string value and select Delete.

Harry now has the choice of specifying the access level to any specific console file when an MMC snap-in is added through Group Polices or modifying the Registry of a machine to restrict the modification, running, or extension of any console by adding snap-ins.

CHAPTER FIVE

Planning and Deployment

After completing this chapter, you will be able to:

- ✓ Understand corporate objectives involved in deploying Exchange

- ✓ Describe various Active Directory (AD) components used by Exchange

- ✓ Identify key corporate area objectives when you are designing a deployment plan

- ✓ Discuss themes particularly relevant when you are designing a Domain Name System (DNS) namespace

- ✓ Describe the changes to domains and trust relationships as an enterprise grows

- ✓ Distinguish naming contexts that partition an AD

- ✓ Delineate best practices that pertain to recipient management

- ✓ Identify key issues in a deployment disaster recovery plan

This chapter uses a punch list approach in planning an Exchange 2000 deployment. With knowledge of architecture, key features, and management tools in hand, you need to systematically identify needs to formulate an effective deployment plan. Part of deployment is project management that is milestone driven to evaluate progress and to take compensatory or corrective action when necessary. Your ability to measure your progress will come from the quality of your instrumentation, which can range from a punch list to system performance monitoring.

Your deployment plan begins with the structure of your organization and its corporate objectives. Exchange 2000 architecture will vary depending on this structure, these objectives, and the current configuration of your network infrastructure (such as the distribution of GC servers, proximity of DCs to an installed Exchange server, and so on). It is rare to start from scratch in what is called a "green-field" deployment scenario. However, to simplify this presentation, we will assume in the main portion of this chapter that there are no legacy software or hardware issues. We discuss legacy issues as a subsidiary topic.

Planning Objectives

Successfully deploying Exchange depends, for the most part, on the design of an enterprise's underlying Windows 2000 and Active Directory (AD) infrastructure. The design of Microsoft.NET servers has so thoroughly integrated application services with the network operating system (NOS) directory services that a carefully balanced synergy among all three components—Exchange, Windows 2000, and AD—is critical. You need to identify critical dimensions in your enterprise to build an effective plan that not only guides implementation but also provides a benchmark against which you can measure your progress. These dimensions or perspectives often overlap. The domain structure reflects functional relationships whereas the site topology clearly delineates how areas functionally interconnect. Finally, the physical plant itself forms the plumbing through which all system traffic flows. Unlike with legacy systems, Exchange 2000 administration more likely cuts vertically through these functional layers than lies horizontally on top of or below another layer. The effectiveness of a messaging and collaborative system lies in this multilayer synergy with, fundamentally, some underlying Windows 2000 native domain, its controllers, and the hierarchical position it has in an enterprise.

Directory Service Components

AD defines the universe of named objects and fundamentally manages identity and permissions within the enterprise. These two specific management functional areas (SMFAs) shape the logical structure or namespace of the enterprise. Exchange or any other service provider within the enterprise must constantly interface with directory services to deliver whatever services they are programmed to provide. This logical structure has three basic components:

- *Naming contexts*—These logical constructs define information boundaries or namespaces within a specific database structure.

- *Global Catalog (GC) server*—These specialized domain controllers (DCs) store writable copies or replicas of the domain naming context for a local domain and the surrounding domains that together form a forest with a common schema naming context. These specialized controllers are, in fact, the local source for directory database information.

- *Groups*—Either security or a distribution AD group, these administrative units correspond to legacy distribution lists (DLs) with a scope attribute; they cover domain local, global, or universal areas of influence and control.

These components all contribute to the effective functioning of an organization's messaging and collaborative platform. You must shape each component to accommodate your corporate objectives, user requirements, and administrative constraints. It is important that the deployment team faced with the task of molding Exchange into a messaging "solution" be sensitized to the technical needs involved in supporting and maintaining that solution daily. You also need to identify and solicit information as well as support from various segments of your user population.

Corporate Objectives

These objectives come from various segments of your user population. The interests of decision-making management most likely have the greatest influence on the project planning and deployment processes. Nevertheless, you must carefully research the more mundane needs of your worker population. In fact, their work habits and attitude have just as great an influence on the "corporate" culture as top-level management objectives and goals. Part of a good deployment plan includes "marketing" a few favorite aspects of the new system. Any change in workflows integral to most deployment plans—no matter how beneficial—will, in the short term, upset people as well as disrupt jobs and procedures. The goodwill of your user population and a positive "corporate" culture can keep a project moving forward even in the worst possible scenarios.

From the corporate perspective, objectives include requirements divided into three areas:

- *Organizational*—This area covers corporate policies and standards that must satisfy corporate objectives, the business's mission, and legal and financial aspects of running a corporation or business concern. These requirements most likely come from top-level management or decision-making bodies within an organization. For the most part, your deployment plan is composed of definitions of scope and boundary areas, functional hierarchies, and key milestones in your deployment project.

- *User*—These requirements include the many necessary tasks that need to be performed daily as part of your workforce's job responsibilities. These "to do" lists make up the implementation steps within the broader deployment plan. Many of these implementation steps are interdependent and thus require careful execution. Communication with as many groups of people as possible is particularly important when you are collecting a comprehensive list of user requirements. The solution providers on the deployment team are expected to devise technical solutions that satisfy these user requirements. For example, the need to interact with coworkers on a particular project requires significant and relatively transparent collaborative methods. Technical solutions that leverage Exchange features are presence management and Instant Messaging (IM). You can rapidly distribute departmental data by systematically using public folders. Rapidly locating and easily retrieving archived data depend upon using full-text indexing in mailboxes, folders, or both.

- *Administrative or support*—Newly designated solution providers, originally charged with the daily responsibilities of support and maintenance, typically build technical solutions that easily conform to existing configuration and support requirements because they will inherit these systems once solutions are brought online. Microsoft, in its Solutions and Operations Framework, recommends that operations people be included as part of the solution provider team to firmly anchor proposed designs in the daily workflow. There are several ways to significantly lower total cost of ownership (TCO) during the design and deployment phase at the start of the deployment plan. Best practices include policy-based management and security (such as Group Policy for password security, System Policy for server and data stores, Recipient Policy for objects), carefully planned storage design (such as partitioning databases to promote easier backup and scalable growth), and creating users and group definitions that simplify the application of administrative policy. Although perceived as additional overhead once deployed, Terminal Services very often reduce support and maintenance costs. You need to address these and other support and maintenance issues as part of the design phase of an enterprise service-providing platform deployment.

Maintenance and support issues are important considerations when you are shaping the deployment plan's design. Other important areas are the capacity and growth of the underlying business concern, user population, and the network infrastructure (also known as the *physical plant*). You also need to consider new and changing technology that could seriously impact the delivery of mission-critical services to your enterprise. Due to the initial cost of many hardware and software systems, information technology (IT) systems are typically the most resistant to change over time. The desire to realize a return on capital investment often unconsciously subverts the introduction of new, efficacious technologies and postpones the retirement of legacy systems. For example, you will likely encounter a large-scale Exchange 5.5 messaging platform somewhere in your organization. These systems continue to deliver mission-critical services. The human and financial pain involved in installing them very often discourages migration to "more modern" systems. Increases in internal capacity and growth will include these legacy systems for some time to come. Similarly, consolidating foreign systems under a common directory system or migrating foreign systems to Exchange will also complicate an installation and must be considered as part of many typical installations.

AD Infrastructure

Designing an enterprise begins fundamentally with defining the namespace through AD directory services. Various new components, like tree domain structures and forests, dramatically alter the *gestalt* or worldview of an enterprise as compared to the older, simpler domain models of NT 4. New Windows 2000 administrative features like organizational units (OUs) and GCs, in addition to modifications to legacy features like trust relationships and replication, have significantly altered the messaging infrastructure's flexibility. An administrator can now more intuitively and naturally map procedural workflows to Exchange components in the workplace with only limited concern for underlying constraints of the physical infrastructure.

AD Logical Structure

AD is a distributed service that scales from a single domain functioning as a classic, legacy domain model to thousands of servers that provide support for a namespace that includes millions of named objects. The logical structure that provides this scalability is based on a new multimaster domain model and a hierarchical namespace. Both concepts have been fundamental designs of the Exchange organizational view from its earliest version. The design concepts and the logical structure they provide have differentiated into an SMFA that has seeped down to lower levels in the NOS itself. The separation of directory services at the application level and their consolidation at the NOS level are typical of other .NET servers like Structured Query Language (SQL) 2000. When you consider that both Exchange 2000 and SQL 2000 use AD, the advantage of the .NET single directory design in terms of simplified administration and a single replication mechanism is very clear.

The planning stages of deployment begin with definitions and the determination of project scope. The various steps involve the following:

➤ Defining a namespace by establishing naming conventions and organizational structures

➤ Planning an organizational topology

➤ Planning a network topology

➤ Creating the first domain

➤ Defining the relationships between trees and trusts when deploying additional domains

Defining a Namespace

A *namespace* is a logical boundary within which a collection of unique named objects exists. This concept is growing in popularity, especially in ITs, because networked computer systems are extending beyond their physical infrastructure and growing in size. The capacity of an AD namespace that defines an enterprise is well beyond a million objects. Collections of named objects of this magnitude are constrained only by the naming convention that uniquely identifies one member item from another. Since 1970, the universe of named objects or nodes that share Internet Protocol (IP) have been catalogued using DNS.

This naming system maps or resolves a unique 32-bit node address to a literal character string known as a Uniform Resource Locator (URL). The URL syntax, typically divided into three components, denotes a vertical tree or hierarchical structure organized around a set of top-level domains (TLDs) such as .com, .edu, .org, .net, and .mil. The other two components are host name and a registered domain name associated with a TLD such as mysite.com. The first URL component designates the host machine in that specific domain, as in mymachine.mysite.com. We will use .tld in this book as a placeholder for one of these well-known TLD branches. The fully qualified domain name (FQDN) is composed of a label or host name associated with a domain name that carries its TLD tag, as in **www.mydomain.com**. Although DNS, with its Unix background, is the most common namespace in view of its Internet role, it provides only one service: name resolution of IP node addresses to URLs. Microsoft, in designing an enterprise structure, required a more comprehensive management of objects than DNS provides. Thus, it adopted AD directory services to provide object identities within a Windows 2000 enterprise.

AD directory services provides identity management to all distributed services in a Windows 2000 enterprise. By default, it uses IP to communicate, so it relies on DNS to resolve AD object names to IP node addresses. In other words, AD is yet another Microsoft enhancement that leverages a well-known standards-based technology such as DNS with Microsoft's own directory services substrate. AD is fundamental to every SMFA in the NOS. Through synergy with this centralized directory service, basic services like Kerberos security and applied services like Exchange 2000 and SQL Server 2000 provide distributed services to a namespace that can extend literally around the earth.

The enterprise is organized into logical subunits of forests, trees, and domains, which, in turn, are composed of elements or AD named objects. You form a tree branch by linking domains using two-way, transitive trusts; domains are structurally based on the legacy model used in NT 4. Similarly, a forest is a collection of these domains that share a common object schema, configuration, and GC. The named objects within domains are, for the purposes of network connectivity, resolved to and identified by unique IP node addresses. Thus, all AD objects use a DNS-style naming convention as well as an AD moniker. The AD name is compatible with

NetBIOS (Network Basic Input/Output System), which remains one of the oldest parts of the Windows 2000 NOS. For example, a named object in a domain in New York State provides messaging services. Its NetBIOS name is NYCE2K23, which might translate to Exchange Server 2000 #23 in New York City. The DNS name is e2k23.ny.mycompany.tld, which translates to the e2k host in the New York domain of mycompany.

Organizational Topology

After carefully considering the NetBIOS names of servers, any naming scheme that clearly distinguishes Exchange 2000 from legacy Exchange 5.5 may be useful in terms of future design and deployment. Like a venerable Hewlett-Packard LaserJet 4 Plus, Exchange 5.5 servers mixed with Exchange 2000 servers will likely continue to deliver reliable service to an organization for many years to come. Consider using friendly NetBIOS names that help identify these legacy servers. Conversely, if a key corporate objective is secure installations, remember that an Exchange server is a strategic target for network attacks. Avoid any reference to its messaging and collaboration services.

The key to planning a namespace is formulating a design that efficiently resolves names. Unlike historic workgroups where broadcasting a name often yielded a response from a host machine, enterprise networks (because of their scale) will fail without name resolution, because a consumer will not be able to locate a service provider. Plan your DNS and AD namespaces so that naming conventions coexist without conflict, as well as easily scale as the namespaces increase in size and forests grow. Often, the DNS namespace already exists through a formal registration procedure. You must design AD as a separate namespace or subdomain under an existing TLD. Remember to research naming conventions carefully to avoid conflicts that your DNS namespace might have with currently existing naming schemes on the Internet.

Microsoft has the following suggestions for planning your DNS namespace:

➤ Register your domain to avoid current or future design conflicts.

➤ For security reasons and design flexibility, use different internal and external namespaces. One approach is to create a subdomain structure, especially if you have previously registered your external domain namespace. Once you create subdomains, you can partition your hierarchical namespace beneath these subdomains to better reflect functional, geopolitical, legal, or business concerns, or to simplify administration. Avoid overlapping internal and external namespaces anywhere in your enterprise.

➤ Create AD child domains immediately subordinate to their parents in the DNS namespace. Thus, you construct your domain tree just as you would build a folder structure on a file server to simplify administration. For example, based

> on corporate needs and objectives, you create child domains under appropriate parents, such as child2.child1.parent.mycomp.tld.

> ➤ From a security and administrative perspective, distinguish internal and external names on physically separate network nodes or servers. When you are dealing with a network environment, external servers are exposed to public networks like the Internet and must be protected from all forms of attack. By separating external from internal namespaces on physically separate machines, you build a firm foundation on which you can deploy your future security initiatives. Centralize name resolution of external servers on one key server and have all other internal DNS servers forward requests to it. This configuration simplifies the installation of firewall technologies.

The fundamental guideline to follow when you are planning a namespace is to systematically build a layered structure that distinguishes external from internal names. Both DNS and AD must coexist within this logical space to avoid naming conflicts, but you must also keep them separate for security reasons. External DNS namespaces are typically in the public record; internal namespaces can be secured through internal DNS name servers isolated from outside the enterprise through a form of firewall technology.

Domain Topology

AD directory services add functional "value" to DNS. Microsoft has taken several field-tested technologies like Public Key Infrastructure (PKI) and Kerberos authentication protocol and extended their features in Windows 2000. In PKI, Microsoft enhancements include support of Transport Layer Security (TLS) and smart cards and, in Kerberos, the addition of public key encryption into the authentication process, as well as auditing and permission management at the resource level. In a similar way, Microsoft has extended the DNS. The AD namespace defines the identity of objects rather than "just" resolving host names to IP addresses. An object's identity includes attributes that empower that object and, when combined with permission management, give it power to function within the enterprise. Identity management depends upon efficiently replicating services to deliver what Microsoft considers an essential network feature, Single Sign On (SSO) convenience; no matter where named principals log on to the network, you can quickly ascertain their identity and authenticate them when they log on. This accessibility is a major Windows 2000 theme; no matter how an enterprise and domain structure might change, named objects need the ability to use network resources and request services within a scope of authorization.

The most basic OU in Windows 2000, as in NT 4, is the domain, which is a collection of resources, managed as an administrative unit, that share a common identity and access management policy. Its autonomous character and structure in NT 4 have changed in Windows 2000 to better support AD directory services and the differences in potential scaling of an enterprise compared with a domain. A single domain as a logical unit can span many physical nodes. Unlike the legacy structure, though, AD uses a multimaster controller model where, instead of a single central or primary directory service provider, all DCs are equal in functional scope and authority. Any single controller can accept changes to the Directory Store (DS) and propagate those changes. Authentication responsibilities and database maintenance are now equally shared. Each controller now holds a replica of the domain-naming context to which it belongs as well as a replica of the configuration and schema-naming context for the forest that its domain populates. You use the Active Directory Installation Wizard (dcpromo.exe) to promote any member server to a role of DC. After the Wizard creates this controller, DNS is queried to determine the local configuration for name resolution. If queries are unsuccessful, this wizard configures the local computer to function as a DNS root server.

You can optimize, through various Registry settings, a Windows NT or 2000 server configuration to handle any one of three different workloads: a network file and print server, a dedicated application server, or a DC. These settings, in concert, change cache sizes, buffer space allocation, configuration refreshes, and response latencies across a myriad of SMFAs, as well as subtly change workload characterization. A Windows 2000 DC must have the basic server configuration to support directory services and its associated workload characterization. A domain is defined by the physical presence of at least one controller that holds a complete replica of the domain-naming context or directory database for the specific domain it defines. It is also defined by a complete replica of the configuration and schema naming contexts for the forest within which the domain is located. As mentioned earlier, dcpromo.exe can promote and demote a member server to or from this functional role.

The First Domain

Just as creating the first DC in an installation defines a domain, the first domain running AD establishes the root server of a forest. The forest name is based on the DNS name of this first domain. When you define this first domain, you need to consider two important factors. As with a legacy primary DC in NT 4, you can never remove the first domain from the forest it defines. Similarly, the hierarchical structure of a domain tree and root server in a forest precludes the possibility of representing other domains above the first domain in a domain tree. The first domain is the TLD; all subsequent additions to that domain tree are below this top level. In fact, a common design strategy is to create a TLD placeholder that exclusively contains only DC machine accounts. This TLD name is registered on the Internet and is freely published. You can then create child domains beneath it or separate internal domains that form other domain trees. A placeholder domain provides a unified hierarchical forest structure within which internal domains can be independently brought online without fear of complicating an enterprise design.

Sizing additional DCs depends on fault tolerance and network load considerations. Due to the dependence of distributed services like messaging and collaboration on Windows 2000 AD architecture, a standard design includes at least two DCs for each domain. If the domain spans multiple sites, you must consider how well the wide area network (WAN) connection will provide fail-over support. Site topology provides preliminary information that will help you determine DC deployment. However, you also need to collect baseline information that accurately portrays daily levels of client workload, such as creating new accounts, changing passwords, and monitoring periods of peak authentication activity. All DCs within the site share a characteristic "domain controller" workload rather than service loads for application servers or file/print servers.

Adding a Windows 2000 DC to an existing legacy NT 4 domain creates a mixed-mode environment. An AD domain in mixed mode is restricted by the legacy limitations of the NT 4 directory database, which can handle up to 40,000 objects. The first Windows 2000 DC assumes the role of primary DC in this single-master state. There is a one-time election, in which all DCs upgrade to Windows 2000, to change to native mode. The irreversible change to native mode forces configuration changes that provide scalability needed in an enterprise namespace. The Windows NT 4 clients access all these changes in the NOS without modification. Microsoft strongly recommends that the NOS operate in native mode to simplify the Exchange installation process.

Trees and Trust Relationships

Domains in Windows 2000 form special parent-child hierarchical domain trees. The first domain spawns child domains, which thereafter share its DNS name and create a contiguous namespace. For example, mycompany.com as the first domain in a tree has child domains that all share the same DNS root name. Thus, child1.mycompany.com can, in turn, be the parent of grandchild101.child1.mycompany.com, and thus extend the domain tree in a systematic function. Domains within a common forest with different domain names are by definition in different domain trees.

AD simplifies security administration across domains in the same contiguous namespace by unifying the authentication process and eliminating administrative overhead found in the legacy complete trust and master domain models. If a named principal is authenticated in one domain during an SSO, trust relationships between that trusted domain and other trusting domains support the recognition of this authentication without the need for additional validation. Permission management, as with the legacy domain model, remains a function of individual object-level access control entries (ACEs). The nature of these trust relationships, however, has changed in Windows 2000 native mode; each child domain automatically has a two-way transitive trust relationship established with its parent domain or other domain trees in the forest. A transitive trust is automatically applied through the

Kerberos security protocol to all domains. If a named principal is authenticated in a parent domain, access to resources in any child or grandchild domain is automatically made possible without additional administrative overhead. There are also shortcut trust relationships that reduce the nodes through which a DC in one domain tree needs to communicate with a DC in another domain tree regarding the attributes of a specific named principal. In general, transitive trusts unify all domains in an AD forest, whether they are children trusting parents or tree root domains trusting other noncontiguous tree root domains under the same forest root domain.

Unfortunately, there is no easy way to break trusts between domains in the same forest. When designing an AD enterprise, be especially careful of user accounts and groups within a forest that have rights to change that forest. The Exchange Administrators group is trusted across the forest and is a high-profile target for a security attack through, for example, impersonation. If, because of geographic or political reasons, transitive trust relationships are not acceptable, you should separate business entities into separate forests. It is always possible to create explicit one-way trust relationships among domains in separate forests that provide limited access to resources in specific domains.

AD Logical Components

The AD is organized into various logical structures that provide directory services throughout the enterprise. In general, these structures provide ways to partition objects into manageable administrative units by creating a naming context. Then, a specially designated DC called the GC server (discussed later in this chapter) globally catalogs and publishes these various contexts throughout the forest. Another AD component that helps to organize and facilitate the delivery of directory services is logical groupings of recipient objects for permission management and message distribution.

Naming Contexts

A *naming context* is a partitioned section of the AD hierarchy with specific properties that are distinguishable from those of other sections. These defined subspaces within the AD structure are categorized by domain, configuration, or schema data and form information units that are replicated among DCs. The specially designated GC server (discussed next) holds a fourth category of information: a limited set of attributes of every object in every domain in the forest. Multidomain forests have a common configuration and schema but unique domain data. Naming contexts include:

➤ *Domain*—This subspace is the collection of all AD objects (such as users, contacts, and groups) in a domain that are replicated to every other DC within, but not outside, the domain.

- *Configuration*—This information subspace contains, for example, information about the physical network. It is replicated to every domain in the forest in the Configuration container in the AD. Data in this partition of the AD is critical for creating replication connections with correct and consistent configurations among DCs in the forest.

- *Schema*—This subspace provides the information used to define data including the object classes and attributes that collectively make up the AD. Object classes are the kinds of named principals that populate an enterprise and must be consistent across all domains through representations in every DC in the forest.

The Configuration container in AD contains replication topology and related metadata for the entire enterprise. In addition, the Configuration container stores configuration information for service-providing servers like Exchange 2000. Thus, the configuration of distributed services is replicated along with other AD data among all domains in the forest. When the first Exchange 2000 server is installed in the forest, AD schemas are further extended to accommodate messaging and collaboration system data. This extension of the schema can include modifying existing attributes as well as adding new attributes. LDAP Data Interchange Format (LDIF) files are imported as part of this installation process. In fact, Exchange 2000 consolidates data about recipient objects, configuration, schema, and the Global Access List (GAL) as object attributes in the AD. The majority of the data is stored in the configuration naming context, which is replicated to every DC in the forest.

GC Server

In addition to domain, configuration, and schema data categories, there is a select set of object attributes that specially designated DCs share. This partial listing of object attributes includes the most frequently used search information to facilitate AD querying. A GC of named principals and their select attributes are stored strategically throughout the enterprise to enable you to efficiently locate an object from anywhere in the entire forest. This availability is critical to AD operations because, in a native-mode domain, logons require the lookup of, for example, a user principal name (UPN) to process a logon request. A local DC sends a query to a GC server to determine group membership of a named principal. The local DC must know everything about a user's group memberships to properly manage the permissions of its own resources. Without access to all of a user's security credentials through this lookup service, most logon requests are denied.

AD usage, as well as fail-over and load distribution, significantly impacts planning the deployment of GC servers. Outlook 2000 directly queries the GC server for addressing information by searching the GAL. Other clients use Exchange 2000 as a proxy to the GC server. Monitor usage, especially after adding, for example, an Exchange 2000 server, expands the schema and may significantly increase network consumption. If services are distributed across several servers, you can use Network

Monitor to view, for example, Lightweight Directory Access Protocol (LDAP) traffic that passes between the Exchange server and the GC server. These requests for address book searches and message routing are balanced across the closest GC servers. Depending upon the Exchange 2000 server configuration, a variety of factors affect sizing, including the hardware power of your servers, the number of users, the volume of messaging, and the kinds of messaging and collaboration objects exchanged among recipients.

Exchange 2000 servers typically request two AD services: address book searches and configuration data searches. Address book searches are performed on the closest available GC server. An Exchange server establishes several LDAP connections to both DCs and nearby GC servers. Routing and configuration data is obtainable from any DC within the local domain because the Configuration container naming context is replicated to all DCs in the forest. A recommended practice is to place a GC server near Exchange 2000 servers, especially in the same site. The Exchange 2000 server prefers to use the same DC to service these requests rather than poll different controllers.

AD Groups

AD contains two types of groups for organization purposes: security groups and distribution groups. Security groups can be mail enabled and, if you assign a Simple Mail Transfer Protocol (SMTP) address, can act as the equivalent of a legacy Exchange 5.x DL. Group membership can include assigned permissions to public folders. Distribution groups provide similar advantages for mass distribution of information through bulk message exchanges and can function as universal groups even in a mixed-mode domain where legacy NT 4 limitations are imposed on Windows 2000 servers. Unlike security groups, though, distribution groups cannot be assigned network resource permissions nor permissions to public folders.

AD groups are equivalent to legacy Exchange 5.x DLs. Each has a scope attribute that determines membership and usage within the organization. Depending on whether a domain is mixed or native, you can restrict a group scope to a local domain, a global group between domains, or a universal group that extends across a forest. When working with groups, you need to consider the following:

- *Naming conventions*—Mail-enabled groups should use a naming convention compatible with Windows 2000 naming standards.

- *Ownership*—Group ownership is typically assigned to the creator of the group.

- *Size of groups*—Microsoft suggests nesting groups that contain more than 500 objects while keeping total group membership to fewer than 5,000 named objects.

Group scoping is very flexible because membership is stored in the GC server and replicated throughout the forest. There is, however, a penalty for this flexibility because replication between GC servers impacts network utilization across the entire enterprise. Microsoft thus recommends that changes to universal groups occur as infrequently as possible. If you modify domain local and global groups, replication and its associated impact on available bandwidth are confined within the boundaries of the domain. The compromise here is that group membership is not published in the GC and hence is not visible to users in other domains. For example, Outlook users can view group membership of domain local or global groups within their own domain only.

Thus, you need to consider several factors when you are determining group scopes. For example, universal groups are necessary in enterprises with multiple domains. In a single-domain enterprise, a universal group is not necessary because all domain objects are local. If network connectivity exists among domains, static universal groups provide greater functionality than global groups. If connectivity is poor or membership is especially dynamic, domain scoping is more efficient than scopes that extend across the enterprise. Finally, if messaging originates from outside the domain, universal scoping again provides greater efficiency than global groups. The type and scope of groups depend on your corporate objectives and the needs of your user population.

Exchange Structure

Server sizing is a fundamental part of the design and planning process. You must consider scalability along both a horizontal and vertical dimension. Horizontal scalability deals with adding additional servers to deliver the same set of services, load balancing, and hardware solutions such as clustering. Vertical scalability is concerned with configuring a single machine to deliver several different messaging and collaboration components for a broader range of services. Microsoft Windows clustering and performance optimization through load balancing and front/backend servers can dramatically affect a messaging system's performance and scalability. As with previous discussions of sizing and deployment of DCs, fault-tolerance issues are also important considerations in your final plans for deployment.

Physical Structure

Just as you can optimize an NT or Windows 2000 server configuration to handle the characteristic workload of a DC, Exchange servers need to support characteristic application workloads and unique server-server interactions. Exchange 2000 organizations must support both horizontal and vertical scalability. Any single server in a messaging system may need to work with other servers supporting similar functions to balance service loads. This is horizontal scalability. It must also vertically support other functional components like the Web Storage System, mail connectors, and the Message Transfer Agent (MTA) if it functions as the only Exchange server in its own site.

The Exchange 2000 platform is actually composed of many server types that can perform specific management functions in isolation or in association with other servers online in the same network subnet or physically contiguous site. Depending on the size of your messaging and collaboration system and your budget, you might independently deploy many different types of servers to maximize performance, including the following:

- *Mailbox servers*—These servers are dedicated message stores that hold and provide access to messaging data through a variety of protocols such as Messaging Application Programming Interface (MAPI), Hypertext Transport Protocol (HTTP), Internet Message Access Protocol 4 (IMAP4), or Post Office Protocol 3 (POP3).

- *Public folder servers*—These servers provide public information stores to clients using the MAPI, HTTP, HTTP (or Web)-Distributed Authoring and Versioning (DAV), or IMAP4 protocols.

- *Connector servers*—These servers specifically perform a mail transfer function that runs one or more specialized connector types such as X.400, SMTP, Lotus Notes, or Novell GroupWise. You typically install these connectors to support existing foreign or legacy systems; where necessary, they may run as a dedicated service.

- *Front-end servers*—These servers optimize performance and simplify administration by providing centralized access to all clients. Service requests are consolidated and redirected to back-end servers where data stores are handled as a dedicated service. Partitioning of services provides greater opportunity to optimize the functioning of the host machine.

- Realtime collaboration servers, which are made up of the following:

    - *Data conferencing servers*—Exchange Data Conferencing Service (DCS), running on these dedicated machines, delivers online text-based conference, chat, and application and file sharing services.

    - *Video conferencing servers*—Exchange Video Conferencing Service (VCS), along with DCS, are conference technologies. VCS allows users to manage multiuser video and audio conferencing services.

    - *Instant Messaging (IM) servers*—These servers run the IM service as either a home server that hosts users or an IM router that manages routing requests.

    - *Chat (Internet Relay Chat [IRC]) servers*—These dedicated servers run the Chat or IRC service.

To optimize the performance of any of these servers, Microsoft recommends that you operate each messaging and collaboration component service on its own dedicated platform wherever possible. Distributing services has the advantage of simplifying software configuration and interoperability issues. Dedicating one server to one Exchange 2000 service component simplifies support and maintenance as well as improves stability, reliability, and horizontal scalability. For optimal AD performance, Microsoft also recommends dedicated DCs and GC servers. Because Microsoft Outlook clients and Exchange 2000 server components depend on access to the GC, we strongly discourage you from installing Exchange Server servers that provide DC services. Such recommendations, however, should always be tempered by corporate objectives and financial resources.

Recipient Management

When planning to deploy a messaging and collaboration system, you need to focus on organization, then users, and then support and maintenance. Organizational planning within the Exchange namespace involves defining users, resources, and even names of departments with standardized naming conventions and arranging recipients in groups. You can organize recipients either functionally or physically in Administrative and Routing Groups, respectively. Just as we suggested in the planning stages of the AD structure, recipient management within your Exchange organization will be simplified if you systematically deploy recipient objects in two separate stages. First you should define naming standards for users, groups, and contacts. Then, design and deploy public folders. You need to focus on naming standards, their inherent structure, and their organization within the enterprise.

Naming Standards

Exchange systems can grow to hundreds of thousands of users. Although you can use nested groups, it is still important to require unique names for objects—users, resources, and servers—especially when you are administering enterprise messaging systems. Exchange 2000 is a fundamental part of the NOS and is directly affected by any addition or migration of a foreign system to the enterprise. An Exchange administrator needs to review any recipient-related change to an enterprise for possible duplication or conflict in named objects when dealing with multiple messaging platforms. Areas of possible conflict include:

➤ *Organization names*—Though it's possible to create multiple organizations in a single enterprise, these names usually reflect the identity of the corporate entity they service. Such names can have a maximum length of 64 characters, but a best practice is to limit their length because users may often manually enter them as a part of an email or messaging address.

➤ *Routing Group names*—Naming conventions for these groups typically reflect distinct physical boundaries based on WAN links (such as geographical regions and network subnets) or functional workflows (such as departments and corporate divisions). Just like organization names, they have a maximum length of 64 characters, but you should limit their length because manual entry of the name may occasionally be required.

- *Server names*—You should establish naming conventions for servers before installing any NOS. These object names are fundamental to the installation process. In a Windows NOS, the server name for an application server is the same as its NetBIOS name registered with NOS system services. NetBIOS server names are restricted to a maximum of 15 characters and often cannot be changed after the installation process.

- *Recipient names*—Exchange 2000 categorizes recipients as users, contacts, groups, and public folders. A display name can have as many as 256 characters, though using this maximum length is discouraged. Using the common length restriction among legacy systems—eight characters—is considered a best practice among Exchange administrators.

It is also important to consider how the naming convention you choose will affect the addresses that outside messaging systems use to communicate with your recipients. Foreign systems, by definition, do not necessarily use similar addressing conventions. Exchange 2000 can resolve inbound messages from foreign messaging systems within separate address spaces designated for each system; foreign addressing schemes are translated and processed for delivery to Exchange recipients.

Thus, in association with good system administration, you must thoughtfully establish and carefully maintain naming conventions for primary objects. Standards for distribution groups and connectors, as well as users and contacts, are also important considerations in distributed administration models that include multiple administrators in different regions.

Public Folders

You configure public folders in Exchange 2000 as multiple trees, each of which contains any number of hierarchically arranged public folders. Users with the appropriate security context create top-level or root folders of each tree on their own home server. Lower-level, child folders are located on the same server as the folder in which they were created. You can store folder contents on a single server or replicate them to other servers in the Routing Group and organization. Thus, designing public folders is associated with planning Routing Groups. When reaching decisions regarding public folder storage and replication, you need to determine:

- *The number of Public Folder trees*—Will these trees be centrally managed as an enterprise-wide tree or independently managed in a decentralized fashion by, for example, separate departments or corporate divisions?

- *Patterns of replication*—Will stores remain on a single server or be replicated to other servers in the Routing Group? Will the contents of these stores replicate to remote Routing Groups?

- *Resource allocation*—Will a specific server contain only public folders or will a server manage both public and private message stores?

> *Permission management*—Will these public folders be accessible to all principals in the enterprise or to specific groups that require additional security overhead? Will access extend to the creation of top-level Public Folder trees or will the basic tree structure be secure?

Like naming conventions for other Exchange 2000 recipient objects, public folders can have names up to 256 characters long. As mentioned previously, excessively long names are discouraged because of the occasional need for manual entry. It is important to consider that the client software you use to display Public Folders typically truncates long names within the allocated space of their windowed interfaces. Put the characteristics on which information will be grouped at the beginning of the name rather than at the end. For example, in some situations 99 Financials Marketing is a better name than Marketing Financials 99 when there are other calendar or fiscal years published in the same folder tree. Shorter, more succinct names will make it easier for end users to view these important shared resources.

Hierarchies

From a user perspective, the public folder hierarchy organizes information so that it is easy to locate. From a support and maintenance perspective, this hierarchy is essential. You need to carefully plan and define the structure of Public Folder trees to simplify delegation of administrative tasks. Because public folders are a primary vehicle for mass distribution of information, you need to consider the following issues:

> *Target audience*—Who are the target users for this information? What is the distribution of the audience within and across sites?

> *Service level*—How often will this information be accessed?

> *Management*—Are there different required levels of access, such as Read Only, Read/Write, and Create/Read/Write?

> *Support and maintenance*—Should maintenance of the Public Folder tree be delegated to an interested party with a vested interest in the information, or should the trees be centrally administered?

Once you have considered levels of security access, you can easily add permissions and maintain folders delegated to end users or a group administrator if you carefully plan from the beginning.

Public Folder Affinities

In a broad context, public folders provide an inexpensive way to distribute massive amounts of information with little ongoing maintenance. Replication, although relatively automatic, does incur operational costs; it consumes bandwidth. One solution is to have isolated remote users across scattered Exchange sites preferentially access the Public Folder trees on, for example, a dedicated server located in a way that optimizes the distribution of information to the greatest number of users. Unlike in legacy Exchange 5.5, public folder affinities in Exchange 2000 are transitive. In other words, if there is an affinity between Site A and Site B and an affinity between Site B and Site C, there will also be an affinity between Site A and Site C. Thus, if one Routing Group is connected to another, all servers will receive public folder referrals. You can, however, configure Routing Group connectors to deny public folder referrals. In general, though, you determine an alternative public folder server based on the routing cost to reach that server across Routing Groups. Public folder affinity applies to all connectors, such as:

➤ *Routing Group connector*—Connects two Routing Groups.

➤ *SMTP connector*—Connects two organizations, or connects an organization to a third-party messaging system.

➤ *X.400 connector*—Connects two organizations, or connects an organization to a third-party legacy messaging system.

Upgrading to Exchange 2000 does not upgrade public folder affinities, so you need to carefully plan how deploying Exchange 2000 might affect user access to public folders within an enterprise.

Public Folder Replication

Public folders are a special messaging object because they can synchronize their contents across data stores located throughout an organization. Public folder replication involves the contents of the Public Folder trees and is based on user utilization of that data store and available bandwidth among folder trees. The penalty of replication within, and especially across, sites can be excessive. Therefore, you need to consider conserving network bandwidth by using public folder affinities rather than relying on the expensive process of creating replicas of data stores across physically separated Public Folder trees. Conversely, you can optimize high utilization of data stores if you distribute copies throughout an organization. Thus, a punch list of planning issues involved in public folder replication should include:

➤ *Use of replication*—Would replication optimize resource utilization or waste network bandwidth?

➤ *Folder content*—What data stores do you need to replicate? Are unnecessary data stores replicated?

➤ *Distribution of users*—What are the distances between sites and the user population with these remote sites?

It is also imperative that you regularly review all public folder sites. Examine what replicas are copied, how often they are replicated, changes in a site's effective bandwidth, and changing user needs. A best practice is to limit the amount of public folder replication because of its affect on network bandwidth utilization.

Server Configuration

Server configuration on a single machine involves several key operational components: processor, disk system, memory, and network configuration. We will discuss only server-configuration issues that relate directly to Exchange 2000: clustering and client access.

Clustering

Windows 2000 provides both a scalable and reliable operating system platform for mission-critical services such as application, storage, printing, directory, and security. Messaging and collaboration, though architecturally separate from the NOS, are fundamental services that drive mission-critical operations. Messaging system failures quickly impact the user population and can thus immediately disrupt workflows and generate lost revenue. Service level agreements (SLAs) now even minimize scheduled downtime for maintenance. When e-commerce systems exposed to public networks are involved, any downtime is unacceptable.

Concepts of fault tolerance are now complemented by concern for "five 9" or 99.99999 percent reliability in system accessibility and uptime performance. Hardware solutions like clustering achieve these levels of services by eliminating single points of hardware failure through the grouping of independent servers.

Clustering Services is a technology that increases system availability by reducing the chance that any single system component can halt system services. A Windows 2000 cluster connects two or more server platforms together in a physical resource group; this managed group supports one virtual server. Windows 2000 Advanced Server supports two-node active/active clustering, where each node shares part of the processing at all times. Through redundancy, a server cluster supports a common disk subsystem that behaves like a single, network-addressable virtual computer. The virtual server's configuration reflects each of the individual servers in the cluster. At any one moment, one server in the cluster is the active node while the other nodes passively stand by for service. From an end-user perspective, the virtual server hosting (for example) mailboxes is accessible at all times. Because the disk subsystem is common to all clustered servers, the location of the active node among the clustered machines at any given time is irrelevant to delivery of services. Clustering Services, which runs only on Advanced Server and Datacenter Server, controls all cluster activity. The current version of Windows 2000 Advanced Server runs two nodes. Exchange Server can use the active/active implementation of clustering. Not all the components are currently supported in a clustered environment.

Client Access

One of the advantages of Exchange 2000 is its accessibility through a wide range of client software. Microsoft has maintained backward compatibility with previous versions of Exchange, so deploying an Exchange 2000 server does not necessarily require simultaneously upgrading client software or retraining the user population on software. Client accessibility contributes greatly to lowering TCO when you are planning to deploy an Exchange 2000 system. Thus, all client software that accesses Exchange messaging services is compatible with Exchange 2000.

Outlook 2000, of course, takes full advantage of the design changes in Exchange 2000. For example, it is currently the only client that can access the GC directly; legacy Outlook clients access Exchange Server, which relays address list information. Furthermore, Outlook 2000 is more functionally integrated with Office 2000 and AD directory services than with the monolithic structure of legacy versions of Exchange. It thus provides greater collaborative support through extensibility of customized digital dashboards, filtered offline synchronized data storage, and personal management features than either legacy Office or Exchange versions. These client features are discussed in Chapter 7.

Exchange 2000 has significantly enhanced another client feature, Outlook Web Access (OWA). Access to data resources works in almost exactly the same way as it does in other Office products when you view data stores through Internet Explorer (IE) 5 except that you are on the Internet and using a browser client. Microsoft has designed OWA so that browser access and features such as drag-and-drop object manipulation, toolbar operations, menus, and rich-text Hypertext Markup Language (HTML) editing function exactly the way they do in a local Office application. Thus, deployment plans are simplified because the user population more than likely already uses client software such as Outlook or IE. The most important information you need to collect concerns the version of client software and any special client configuration necessary to access specialized services.

Disaster Recovery Planning

A recommended best practice is to include members of your technical support team in the planning stages so that any proposed solutions are conceived in a strategic framework compatible with the levels of ongoing support and maintenance. Similarly, when you are planning to deploy a messaging system, you must formulate contingency plans for a critical system failure that occurs either during installation or during daily ongoing operations. In most deployment scenarios, some form of messaging system is already in operation. Migrating recipients to Exchange 2000, even when performed in stages, rarely runs to completion without an unforeseen event disrupting an aspect of service. Issues you need to consider during your planning for deployment include:

➤ *Formal action plan*—Is there a formal, well-documented, and perhaps even partially tested disaster plan in place designed especially for this deployment project?

➤ *Chain of command*—Who is responsible for deciding when contingency plans need to be executed and in what order they need to be performed?

> *Ancillary support procedures*—Have all backup and support systems been confirmed before actual deployment?

The deployment team must carefully consider various disaster scenarios and contingency plans because any migration plan should be conceptualized as a "cut over" from one system to another, not a less obtrusive redirection of workflows. A very important aspect when you are formulating these contingency plans is meaningfully estimating realistic downtime. When you are dealing with a mission-critical system like a messaging platform, business decisions are based on quantifiable amounts of lost revenue due to disrupted services. You choose alternative plans during a disaster based on these projected recovery times. Rehearsing even parts of a disaster recovery plan provides more reliable downtime and recovery estimates than listing them as possibilities on a piece of paper. If accurate, these estimates are often critical when you are choosing a proper course of action and want to minimize the loss due to a critical system failure. In actual practice, however, you can, in a number of ways, foster a user perception that in fact migration and upgrade processes are almost self-running wizards. You can integrate Exchange 2000 servers in mixed-mode environments, maintain compatibility with legacy Exchange 5.5 systems and client software, and efficiently deploy GC servers.

Chapter Summary

This chapter addressed many of the issues involved in designing a deployment plan for implementing an Exchange 2000 server. Here are the particularly significant points to remember:

- Exchange 2000 interfaces with three basic components of the AD: naming contexts (or partitions), the GC server, and AD groups.

- Corporate objectives are typically categorized as related to organizational concerns, user issues, and administrative and support issues.

- When you are planning a namespace, it is particularly important to register the TLD, use different internal and external namespaces, create AD child domains subordinate to parent domains in the DNS namespace, and partition the internal and external namespaces on physically separate servers.

- The fundamental theme when you are planning a namespace is to systematically build a layered structure that distinguishes external from internal namespaces without conflict or overlap.

- In Windows 2000 native mode, trust relationships are transitive. In general, transitive trusts unify all domains in an AD forest, whether they are in the same domain tree or not.

- Service providers like Exchange 2000 store their configuration information in the Configuration container in the configuration-naming context of the AD.

- Exchange 2000 servers request two AD services: address book searches and configuration data searches. The former is performed on the closest GC server; the latter is obtained from the closest DC.

Review Questions

1. What specific Active Directory components does Exchange 2000 interact with? [Check all correct answers]
   a. Naming contexts
   b. Domain Controllers
   c. Global Catalog servers
   d. Groups
   e. Naming standards

2. What key areas categorize corporate objectives when you are planning Exchange 2000 deployment? [Check all correct answers]
   a. Organizational
   b. User
   c. Structural
   d. Administrative
   e. Security

3. What kind of design model is Active Directory based on?
   a. Single-master model
   b. Multimaster model
   c. Multiple domain model
   d. Master domain model

4. Which of the following statements characterizes the DNS namespace?
   a. DNS was developed by Microsoft to resolve host names to IP addresses.
   b. DNS resolves host names.
   c. DNS is the default NetBIOS name-resolution method in Windows 2000.
   d. None of the above.

5. Which of the following does Windows 2000 directory services use for name resolution?
   a. Domain Name System
   b. Active Directory
   c. Answers a and b
   d. Sometimes answer a and sometimes answer b, depending on the naming convention

6. What logical components can a Windows 2000 enterprise be organized into? [Check all correct answers]
   a. Tree
   b. Branch
   c. Forest
   d. Leaf

7. With what protocol is the AD name component specifically compatible?
   a. NetBEUI
   b. NetBIOS
   c. TCP/IP
   d. None of the above

8. Which statement is true?
   a. The key to planning a namespace is efficient address resolution.
   b. The key to planning a namespace is well-defined groups.
   c. The key to planning a namespace is efficient name resolution.
   d. Answers a and b.

9. Which statement is not a best practice when you are planning DNS namespaces?
   a. Register your top-level domain as soon as possible.
   b. Use consistent naming conventions throughout your enterprise.
   c. Create child domains immediately subordinate to their parent domains in the DNS namespace.
   d. Where possible, partition your namespace on physically separate servers.

10. What is the best configuration for an Exchange 2000 server?
    a. Exchange 2000 on a GC server
    b. Exchange 2000 on a DC
    c. Exchange 2000 on IIS 5
    d. None of the above

11. Which naming context is particularly relevant to Exchange 2000?
    a. Domain
    b. Configuration
    c. Schema
    d. GC

12. What process are LDIF files part of?
    a. Installation of Active Directory in Windows 2000
    b. Installation of Exchange 2000 Server
    c. Modification of the Active Directory schema during Exchange 2000 installation
    d. Modification of Exchange 2000 during installation setup

13. Which of the following is a best-practice recommendation?
    a. Deploy an Exchange server close to a domain controller.
    b. Deploy an Exchange server on a domain controller.
    c. Deploy an Exchange server close to a GC server.
    d. Deploy an Exchange server on a GC server.

14. When you are working with AD groups, what factors should you consider? [Check all correct answers]
    a. Naming conventions
    b. Group size
    c. Naming contexts
    d. Ownership

15. When you are considering using universal groups, which of the following is true?
    a. You should use universal groups in a single-domain enterprise.
    b. You should use universal groups when there is network connectivity among domains.
    c. You should use universal groups when membership is especially dynamic.
    d. None of the above.

16. Which of the following are examples of horizontal scaling? [Check all correct answers]
    a. Clustering
    b. Front/back-end servers
    c. Web Store
    d. Load balancing

17. What factors are relevant when you are planning public folder storage and replication? [Check all correct answers]

    a. Number of trees

    b. Number of branches

    c. Replication patterns

    d. All of the above

18. When you are considering public folders, which statement is incorrect?

    a. Replication consumes more network bandwidth than public folder affinities.

    b. Public folder affinities consume more network bandwidth than replication.

    c. Exchange 2000 public folder affinities are transitive; legacy Exchange affinities are not transitive.

    d. You can configure Routing Groups to deny public folder referrals.

19. What key components contribute to standalone server performance? [Check all correct answers]

    a. Processor

    b. Memory

    c. Network connectivity

    d. All the above

20. When you are describing ongoing system accessibility, what measure is most relevant?

    a. Fault tolerance

    b. MTBF

    c. Uptime performance

    d. Redundancy

Real-World Projects

Pierce Finger is the new Exchange administrator for Hands-On Training Corporation. He wants to introduce himself to the other employees in the firm by sending out a personalized message to all key managers at Corporate Headquarters. He decides to create a mail-enabled group to simplify his task.

Project 5.1

To create security and distribution groups:

1. Start Active Directory Users and Computers.

2. Right-click on the container in which you want to place the group.

3. Select New and then Group from the context menu.

4. In the Group Name text box, type the name of the group you want to create. Notice that the first 20 letters are used to create the pre–Windows 2000 group name.

5. Select the appropriate group scope from the option box on the left side.

6. Select the appropriate group type from the option box on the right side.

7. Click on the Next button. If extensions are installed properly, you can determine whether the group should have an email address, Exchange alias, and Administrative Group.

8. Click on the Next button, and then click on Finish to create the group.

Pierce can now add members to the group, add this group to another group, assign a manager as a point of contact, set message size restrictions, and limit the users who can send messages to the group.

Project 5.2

Pierce mentions in his letter of introduction that he intends to create a newsletter for internal use. He decides to use a public folder to distribute this document.

To create public folders in System Manager:

1. Start System Manager.

2. Expand the Folders object.

3. Right-click on the Public Folder tree in which you want to create the public folder, select New, and then click on Public Folder.

4. In the Properties dialog box, type the name you want to create in the Name field and then enter a description in the Public Folder Description field. The name you specify will set the email address for the public folder.

5. Click on the Replication tab to list folders on other servers to which you wish to replicate your data store.

6. Click on OK.

Pierce has finished creating his public folder. He sends his email message to his new group and begins designing his newsletter.

CHAPTER SIX

Installation

After completing this chapter, you will be able to:

✓ Select tools appropriate for managing specific services

✓ Identify specific tasks that you need to complete before you install Exchange

✓ Understand the conditions and tools that prepare an environment for Exchange installation

✓ Identify key information you need before the installation process

✓ List physical and organizational specifications required for an installation

✓ Evaluate configuration strategies that optimize the delivery of Exchange services

✓ Identify the various server components that you can select during an Exchange installation

✓ List post-installation tasks that you must do to verify the successful installation of server software

Windows 2000 has introduced changes in philosophy, design, and technology. The concept of enterprise and distributed services has replaced the legacy NT 4 domain model and the monolithic design of application servers. Microsoft's philosophical shift in marketing strategy with the introduction of Windows 2000 and Microsoft.NET servers has been cleverly described in the technical press as sticking the E for "enterprise" between the N and the T to produce .NET, a new operating system platform. From a design viewpoint, we would also suggest the E stands for "extensibility," where services are differentiated into specialized functional areas loosely distributed throughout the organization.

Exchange 2000, as compared to legacy versions of the mail server, reflects a similar change in gestalt or worldview. The change is from a collection of physically linked sites to an enterprise-wide organization, from a messaging system to a collaborative foundation for knowledge management (KM). Installation of new server products like Exchange and SQL Server thus begins with more than just a superficial installation of a network operating system (NOS) platform. This chapter begins with a discussion of the style of managing an Exchange installation in relation to these philosophical, functional, and structural changes in the NOS. We then outline four simple steps in the implementation of what might be considered a "greenfield" installation, where Exchange 2000 is deployed in an organization unfettered by legacy hardware and software constraints and complications. We approach the installation systematically so that the punch list of steps can apply whether an organization has an intranet with 25 users or 2,500 users. In addition, as we describe the general steps in installing an Exchange 2000 system, we also show you how the major themes of scalability and extensibility in Windows 2000 design are mirrored in the uncoupling of function from structure.

Managing Deployment

An important key to the efficient management of any project is carefully planning and the use of proper tools. Exchange 2000 depends on efficient management and a well-running network operating system to support the 24×7 service levels that are often associated with a messaging platform. This dependency on the NOS, unlike with any other legacy version of this application server, is primarily due to the partitioning of services that characterize Exchange 2000 and other .NET servers from their predecessors. Active Directory (AD) is a fundamental part of the NOS, so installing Exchange is based on properly installing that NOS and efficiently running it. To confirm that Windows 2000 is functioning properly, you must look beyond legacy authentication, file, and print services. Approach an Exchange installation by first assembling a suite of tools that will provide information pertaining to the configuration and performance levels of the NOS.

Organization and Planning

Windows 2000 is very different from NT 4, especially in the separation of function from structure, so you need to access and use a broader range of instrumentation. In monolithic service environments such as Exchange 5.5 and SQL Server 7, instrumentation is predictable and therefore easy to standardize. Windows 2000, however, needs a highly extensible tool like the Microsoft Management Console (MMC) to accommodate a broader, more eclectic suite of tools. Exchange administrators are provided with the Exchange System Manager MMC snap-in, but will more likely fashion their own management console from more personalized choices. As an administrator, you need to have a thorough knowledge of the following management areas and to assemble an appropriate collection of tools before you begin a formal Exchange 2000 installation:

- *Directory services*—This is the suite of tools that manage the AD directory services, including recipient management, organizational design, Group Policy, replication, and synchronization among stores that provide the directory services. Recipient management includes creating user, contact, and group accounts. In addition, Exchange 2000 offers mailboxes, address lists, and special features such as instant messaging (IM). The AD-related MMC snap-ins—AD Users and Computers, AD Domains and Trusts, and AD Sites and Services—are critical tools. In mixed-mode environments, the Active Directory Connector (ADC) provides synchronization services for legacy Exchange sites.

- *Transportation/protocol services*—Network management includes designing and deploying transport, communication, and name-resolution services like Windows 2000 Dynamic Domain Name System (Dynamic DNS) and Dynamic Host Configuration Protocol (DHCP), as well as Windows Internet Name Service (WINS) for backward compatibility to legacy systems. This area tends to be structural in orientation. It also includes designing and managing connectors and Routing Groups. Tools here include Internet Services Manager, the DNS console, and Exchange System Manager.

- *Storage services*—Managing data stores includes both NT File System (NTFS) and Web Store architectures implemented in ways that optimize performance and fault tolerance. These services must protect the integrity of the data and transaction logs, provide disaster-recovery solutions, and include reliable backup and restore strategies. Tools here include Exchange System Manager.

- *Administrative services*—Exchange system management includes all the services that support the messaging and collaborative platform. Exchange server management includes the integrative management of Storage Groups and databases, public folders and connectors, as well as administrative and Routing Groups. Operating system server management includes monitoring process and performance as well as creating and reviewing system service logs. Integrating Exchange with other services like Internet Information Server (IIS) is also important. Tools here include Computer Management and Performance.

In legacy versions of Exchange, this broad range of service areas was managed from a single administrative tool wielded typically by a small, specialized user group. Windows 2000 instead separates functional areas—a physical, server side and a more functional, user management side. Windows 2000 leverages the extensible framework of the MMC to administer these various functional management areas. When preparing for an examination or problem management in a real-world corporate organization, you should mirror this same separation of physical structure versus function.

Proper Assignment of Tools

Administrative management is divided into user-oriented tasks, performed by the AD Users and Computers snap-in, and server-oriented tasks, performed by the more familiar Exchange System Manager snap-in. You can no longer connect simultaneously to several Exchange organizations through the Connect To Server option available in the Exchange 5.5 administration program. You can use various combinations of snap-ins, along with Exchange System Manager, to customize your management environment or the toolset of those to whom you delegate administrative responsibilities. Thus, the same tool framework accommodates both user-oriented and server-oriented functionality within different scopes of authority—local machine, domain controller (DC), Exchange organization, and so on. Additional snap-ins provide other functionality, such as Advanced Security (encryption key management), chat and conferencing, folders, and message tracking. Although the Exchange System Manager console comes prebuilt, you can customize new consoles in minutes.

Proper Tools: Terminal Services (TS)

Although Exchange 2000 management tools do not function properly on legacy Windows workstations, you can install the management tools on Windows 2000 Professional. You can install the Exchange System Manager snap-in in combination with the messaging and collaboration services, or by itself. The minimum installation of Exchange Server installs the services without the management and collaboration tools.

The inclusion of TS has significantly improved Windows 2000 remote management. In fact, installing the Exchange System Manager snap-in and other administrative tools on a Windows Professional workstation for remotely supporting and maintaining servers is no longer the only way to provide remote technical support. The TS client has distinct advantages over, for example, the Exchange System Manager snap-in when you are installing and managing Exchange 2000 Server. Although TS must be configured and running on a target server before you can connect to it with the TS client, it runs a wide selection of tools needed to support and maintain the operation system once it's installed. Exchange System Manager or a customized version of the MMC that includes the Exchange snap-in is still restricted to whatever predetermined administrative functions it is designed to perform. Although network connections are preferable, TS can support and maintain a server across a dial-up connection even at transmission speeds as slow as 28.8Kbps. Best practices recommend that you use 640×480 screen resolutions, especially over non-networked connections, to improve general performance. In fact, TS outperforms an Exchange 5.5 administrative program over these dial-up connections because it does not depend upon remote procedure calls (RPCs) to transmit information between client and host. A Windows 2000 server supports two concurrent TS connections without requiring a license. It is important to remember that port 3389 must be accessible if the TS connection passes through a firewall.

The Installation Punchlist

In part due to design changes that have increased the dependency of Exchange 2000 on its platform operating system, you cannot "just" install Exchange 2000. Beyond basic prerequisites of hardware and operating system software, AD must not only be "active" but efficiently providing services throughout the enterprise. Properly configuring network services such as DHCP and Dynamic DNS is also critical to a successful deployment. For example, Exchange 2000 depends on Dynamic DNS to resolve the names of other Exchange 2000 servers in an organization. Without these network services running properly, Exchange 2000 replication and routing will, at best, fail. A far worse scenario is when these services run sporadically and cause more subtle, seemingly random, system errors.

Actually installing the software is relatively simple. Nevertheless, you should not underestimate the differences between acquiring technical knowledge and providing messaging and collaborative solutions. The fundamental concept behind Exchange 2000 as a .NET server is its extensibility to loosely couple with other Internet-based applications in providing distributed services to network consumers. Installing any single layer of services, especially one as fundamental as enterprise messaging, depends on how well other layers already function. Furthermore, legacy Exchange products provide a broad range of services such as Simple Mail Transfer Protocol (SMTP) servers, mailbox servers, public folder servers, and bridgehead servers. Exchange 2000 has added new capabilities to this repertoire, including front-end servers, conferencing servers, and IM and presence management servers. These services can have complicated relationships with AD as well as impact server subsystems like storage, network bandwidth, and processor utilization. Your flexibility in providing future solutions depends on where and how you install this server software.

Preparing a Working Environment

After you gather information and do the virtual walkthrough of setup steps, you must perform tasks that prepare the environment for the Exchange 2000 installation. Make certain the NetBIOS name of the server is the correct name, for example, for the first Exchange server in an organization. This is a simple task to perform before the application software is installed. You do so by, for example, accessing the Network Identification tab on the Properties sheet of Network Neighborhood. After you install Exchange 2000, this task will no longer be simple. In fact, the installation of the first Exchange server radically changes system objects. Users receive new attributes to handle Exchange-related characteristics like mail boxes and special feature permissions. Security groups and designated uses must be created. The entire structure of the NOS and AD must be prepared for the addition of an entirely new layer of distributed services.

Extending the AD Schema

For both political and security reasons, most organizations do not want administrators of an application server to have privileged rights at either the level of domain or enterprise. Exchange 2000 uses the AD to function, so its setup procedures appear more complex than those of previous versions of the server software. To install Exchange 2000 Server, you must extend the structure or schema of the AD to accommodate Exchange-specific class objects and data. The easiest way to update the AD schema is to simply run the installation utility, setup.exe. Two utilities, ForestPrep and DomainPrep, perform these specialized tasks.

ForestPrep

When you run setup.exe with specific switches from the command line interface (CLI), two utilities, ForestPrep and DomainPrep, perform specialized tasks that prepare Windows 2000 for the Exchange messaging infrastructure without necessarily installing Exchange Server. Together, these tools modify AD to accommodate new messaging objects and attributes. The user account, under which these utilities are run, must have sufficient privileges to change AD structure and add messaging objects to the configuration naming context. Figure 6.1 shows these feature switches in the setup.exe usage menu.

Both ForestPrep and DomainPrep run automatically during setup, but only if:

- ➤ The security context under which setup is run (the logon account) has the high-level permission access of both EnterpriseAdmin and SchemaAdmin
- ➤ The first Exchange server installation is in the parent or root domain of a forest

The root domain is necessary because setup/ForestPrep needs to run in the same domain as the Schema Master. Quite often, you find these conditions in small-business

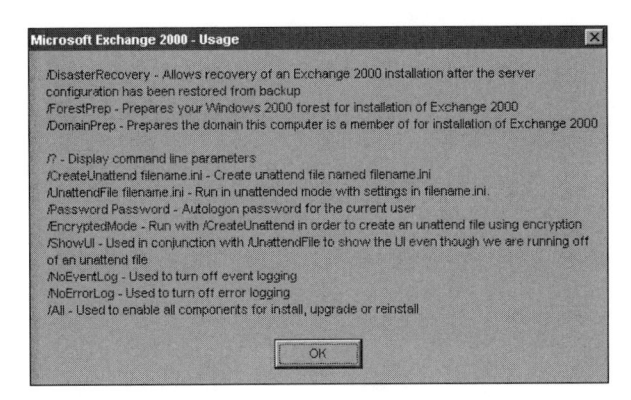

```
Microsoft Exchange 2000 - Usage

/DisasterRecovery - Allows recovery of an Exchange 2000 installation after the server
configuration has been restored from backup
/ForestPrep - Prepares your Windows 2000 forest for installation of Exchange 2000
/DomainPrep - Prepares the domain this computer is a member of for installation of Exchange 2000

/? - Display command line parameters
/CreateUnattend filename.ini - Create unattend file named filename.ini
/UnattendFile filename.ini - Run in unattended mode with settings in filename.ini.
/Password Password - Autologon password for the current user
/EncryptedMode - Run with /CreateUnattend in order to create an unattend file using encryption
/ShowUI - Used in conjunction with /UnattendFile to show the UI even though we are running off
of an unattend file
/NoEventLog - Used to turn off event logging
/NoErrorLog - Used to turn off error logging
/All - Used to enable all components for install, upgrade or reinstall

        OK
```

Figure 6.1   The setup usage menu showing options for ForestPrep and DomainPrep.

settings. In larger corporate settings, however, a different set of conditions may arise. If an Exchange administrator does not have high-level permissions, two separate groups must participate in the installation. Both ForestPrep and DomainPrep allow you to separate setup tasks that require privileged NOS access from more basic administrative operations necessary to manage an Exchange organization. This privileged access, assigned to Enterprise administrators and schema administrators, provides a security context within which you can modify AD. Another reason for separating the updating of the AD schema from the basic Exchange installation, especially in an enterprise environment, is the time it takes to replicate the AD changes across a forest. Full schema replication, even in isolated networks with few domains, can take several hours. It is best to provide sufficient time for this replication to take place so that you can successfully install Exchange. Separating the schema replication from the installation of the server application helps ensure that the installation goes quickly and properly.

ForestPrep extends the object definitions of the AD to accommodate Enterprise-specific information, creates the Exchange organization name and object in AD, and creates an Exchange container in the configuration naming context. It also assigns sufficient privileges to an administrator account to access these objects. This administrator account has sufficient privileges to install the first Exchange server in an organization. Although the account has the same rights as an administrator created by the Exchange Administration Delegation Wizard, best practices recommend that, when ForestPrep creates the first user administrator, the actual installer of the Exchange server, whatever his or her security level, should use the wizard to create all subsequent administrator logins. In fact, you should run ForestPrep only once in any Windows 2000 forest. Figure 6.2 shows the setup screen when you run ForestPrep.

Aside from knowing the name of the Exchange 2000 organization and the account name of the designated person or group who will install the first Exchange server in your organization, the following must be true for you to run ForestPrep:

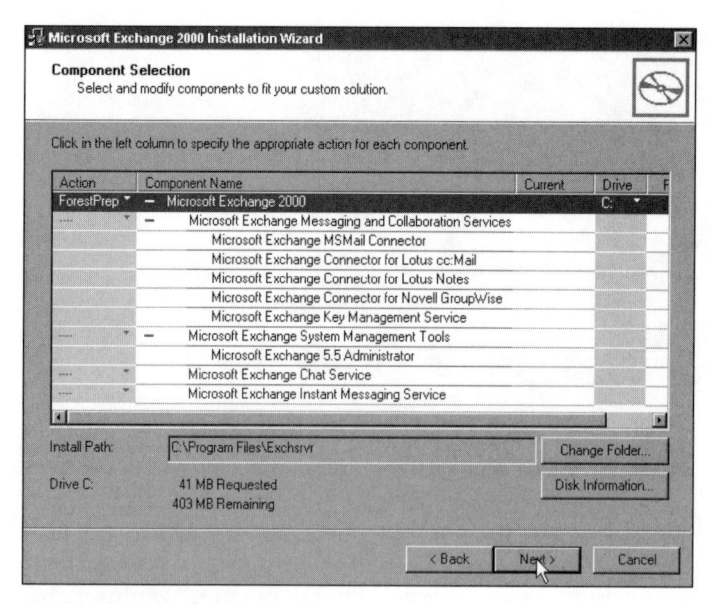

Figure 6.2 The ForestPrep setup screen.

- You must run the utility in the same domain as the Schema Master, which by default is your parent domain.

- The user account used to log in and run ForestPrep must have both EnterpriseAdmin and SchemaAdmin permissions.

- If you are joining an Exchange 5.5 site, you must run ForestPrep in a security context that has administrator access rights for both the Exchange 5.5 site and the container beneath it.

When you run ForestPrep, you extend the AD schema to include Exchange-specific information that affects the entire forest. Depending on the topology of the enterprise and the size of AD, schema changes may take a considerable amount of time to replicate throughout the forest. The utility creates an Exchange 2000 organization name and object in AD. When you run DomainPrep in each domain where Exchange 2000 is to be installed, the Installation Wizard queries AD for this configuration information, simplifying the deployment of Exchange 2000 throughout the forest. This is why it is critical to allow the replication process to finish before installation. It also assigns Exchange Full Administrative permissions to the user account that you specify when the utility runs. This account has sufficient privileges to install Exchange 2000 throughout the forest. After the first installation of Exchange 2000, best practices recommend that you use this account to run the Administration Delegation Wizard, which, in turn, configures Exchange-specific roles for administrators across the forest. If you run ForestPrep in a forest that is running legacy Exchange Server 5.5 or earlier, the utility similarly extends AD, creates the Exchange 2000 organization object in the AD schema based on configuration information from your Exchange Server 5.5 organization, and assigns Exchange Full Administrative account permissions just like when you install Exchange 2000. Best practices recommend granting the existing Exchange Server 5.5 administrator these permissions.

The **/DomainPrep** switch is an option that runs at the domain level in which the Exchange server will be located. It requires the privileges of a domain administrator because it creates global groups used to administer Exchange. When you run DomainPrep, you are prompted for the address list server that is responsible for the catalogue of named objects found through Lightweight Directory Access Protocol (LDAP) searches and located in this domain. An *address list server* works with the System Attendant to maintain catalogues of objects compiled during the running of LDAP queries. These search queries build the address lists that are directory and lookup services for Outlook clients. The DomainPrep utility creates the global and security group, Exchange Domain Servers; the domain local security group Exchange Enterprise Servers; and the All Exchange Servers group. It also adds the Exchange Domain Servers group to the All Exchange Servers group. It also grants appropriate rights to the address list server.

Creating Service Accounts

ForestPrep creates an administrator account with sufficient permissions to only install Exchange 2000. This account, by default, cannot perform basic administrative functions such as creating accounts or assigning mailboxes to users unless the account is manually assigned membership in the Account Operators Group. Thus, another important task is to create specialized service accounts through AD. Like legacy server applications such as Exchange 5.5 and the SQL Server family, Exchange 2000 consists of many component functions that execute within the security context of a common named Windows 2000 service account. This named account provides distributed services by communicating with other platforms that run similar or complementary services within the common context of a Routing Group. Best practices recommend creating a service account and assigning it appropriate security privileges before the setup procedure. Name this account when you run ForestPrep.

The next recommended step is to log on to the server on which you plan to install the application software with the service account to confirm that the account is properly established. When you begin the installation procedure, the setup wizard typically queries you for a specific service account. In fact, it provides, as a default response, the username used to boot the physical server. If, in fact, this is the newly created service account, this setup step is simple and foolproof. Alternatively, you can use the specially designated account that the ForestPrep utility assigned permissions. Very often though, administrators mistakenly use either a regular user account or an administrator account assigned to install application services. Assigning the service account privileges to a widely used account introduces security problems in terms of unauthorized access and is very difficult to correct.

You need two specialized service accounts during the installation phase. The first account is the standard site service account used during installation. Another account functions as an alternative administration account to distribute administrative responsibilities. Create these accounts directly in AD Users and Computers in the domain in which you plan to install the Exchange 2000 server. Best practices recommend selecting both the User Cannot Change Password and Password Never Expires options on both these accounts to avoid later authentication problems. The required site service account must have membership in several security groups (Domain Admins, Enterprise Admins, and Schema Admins) to perform both installation and subsequent maintenance and support. After you have added these named accounts to AD, best practices recommend creating or updating an Emergency Repair Disk through the Windows 2000 Backup utility so that you have an updated version of all configuration changes in your server.

Finally, a common administrative practice is to perform a full system backup using the Windows 2000 Backup utility just before installing any major software application. It's impossible to reverse preparatory steps that involve altering the AD structure (such as the ForestPrep and DomainPrep options in the Exchange 2000 Setup utility) using ordinary means because they alter the schema or data definition of objects in AD. A full system backup procedure simplifies restoring a server to its original operating state if the installation is problematic. In any deployment plan, you must provide for as many alternative options as possible in case a system disaster occurs.

Deployment Plan

It's critical to have a good deployment plan in place when you set up an Exchange server. This applies even when you install Exchange 2000 Server (rather than Exchange 2000 Enterprise Server, which we describe in this book) in a Small Office/Home Office (SOHO) environment. A necessary first step in any deployment plan is gathering information, platform resources, installation materials, and tools. The second step—the process of installing Exchange 2000—is usually automated, requiring only simple data entry of identification information. This relatively simple, self-contained, and self-working operation is all that is required for installing such complicated software because of the increasing sophistication of wizard programs. The third step, quality assurance, is far more complicated than Steps 1 and 2. Verifying that services are running properly requires systematic and coordinated testing that extends beyond installation to ongoing maintenance. Using baselines in establishing system benchmarks for future comparison is a critical tool in this process. The last step includes creating a post-production checklist of tasks that add additional layers of support and services to the core messaging system. These include additional service upgrades and third-party applications that add functional areas such as remote management services, backup, and virus protection.

Step 1: Gathering Information

Most steps in a deployment plan involve creating specific checklists that you can easily incorporate into a project-management system. Although building lists of things to do seems like extra work, it very often helps to structure a project and expose potential problems. Constructing such punch lists also provides a virtual walk-through of the steps you need to take to successfully achieve a goal. Documenting this walk-through with appropriate modifications and annotations is an important part of a support and maintenance archive because it serves as a blueprint for future projects that more than likely will have many similar tasks in common. The main goal of Step 1 is to gather as much information and compile as many resources as possible before you actually implement the system in Step 2.

Best practices suggest that you need to consider the following questions before you install Exchange 2000 in Step 2:

➤ *Physical requirements*—Have hardware and software requirements been met?

➤ *Structural (organizational) requirements*—Has the logical structure of the organization been defined?

➤ *Exchange-specific configuration requirements*—Has the system configuration been optimized for the future installation of Exchange 2000? Have appropriate services and accounts been created to support the installation?

Physical Requirements

Before you install any software, it is critical to determine whether your hardware meets more than published requirements. It is common for published minimum requirements to seriously underestimate the material needs in a real-world deployment project. This is because the published requirements are, in fact, the hardware and software specifications that a product requires to successfully launch itself, not run efficiently. From a real-world perspective, we strongly suggest that you budget resources based on configurations that exceed Microsoft's recommended hardware configuration, because even these specifications provide only a minimum footprint within which the application server can operate. Table 6.1 shows minimum and recommended configurations according to Microsoft.

These specifications are only part of the hardware configuration. Physical compatibility of the software with the hardware is also an important issue. Microsoft tests

Table 6.1 Minimum and recommended Exchange 2000 configurations.

Hardware	Minimum	Recommended
Processor	300MHz Pentium	400MHz Pentium
Memory	128MB	256MB
Storage	2GB for Exchange; 500MB available on the system drive	Space for messages and public folders; configuration as RAID 1 or RAID 5

its software products on many hardware components. The omission of a manufacturer or a particular piece of hardware from this published list does not necessarily mean that a certain component will not work with Microsoft software; it means only that Microsoft has not included that item in its testing procedures. The Microsoft "Designed for Windows" logo identifies hardware and software products that have been tested to meet Microsoft standards for compatibility with its products. Microsoft can provide support for the installation or maintenance of any of these products, but not for any omitted items. You should consult the Microsoft Hardware Compatibility list before you consider investing time and resources in a deployment project. This list is available at **www.microsoft.com/hcl**.

Another compatibility issue is the currency of your version of software. Microsoft typically provides free software updates or service packs online, through subscription services, or upon request on CD-ROM (for a minimal shipping fee). These service packs apply updating information to the application and/or supporting operating system platform. It is important that you regularly update your system with these service packs. However, if possible, apply service packs to nonproduction platforms first. Given the potential level of integration and customization of your enterprise system, you need an opportunity to carefully evaluate what the proposed and actual effects of applying the service pack will be in your environment. Read all documentation that accompanies a service pack carefully. It is your responsibility to understand whether a service pack includes the contents of previous service packs, includes recent hot fixes, or makes desirable or undesirable changes to software on your system.

Unlike service packs, hot fixes or software patches are special updates that address specific weaknesses in an existing version of software. These hot fixes are available from a variety of online Microsoft areas, including its FTP site, **ftp://ftp.microsoft.com/bussys**. These patches are usually included in the next service pack. As with service packs, carefully evaluate the effects of a hot fix before you apply it to software running on a production platform. It is especially important that you consult readme files that accompany a patch because of the patch's very specific nature in resolving a particular system weakness.

Structural (Organizational) Requirements

The .NET environment is fundamentally an operating system framework that supports loosely coupled services distributed across an enterprise. Installing Exchange 2000 weaves an additional thread into this distributed services blanket. When you installed legacy Exchange products, you placed a monolithic server application on a hardware platform that met minimum hardware and software requirements, and you configured your messaging system. Legacy Exchange services created their own virtual space in the NT 4 domain model. Alternatively, Exchange 2000 provides services that are a seamless part of the enterprise namespace. From an administrative perspective, Exchange's functional working space is synonymous with the entire AD enterprise; messaging and collaborative infrastructure and AD namespace are a unified whole.

Installing Exchange 2000 is based on the enterprise services you will provide your user population. The performance of your messaging organization will be integrally involved with how that enterprise system balances network bandwidth and service loads. As with NT 4, each physical server has a characteristic load: file/print server, DC, or application server. You optimize the local system based on this characteristic service load. This methodology applies in Windows 2000, although some concepts, such as the role of DCs, have changed. A Windows 2000 DC primarily supports enterprise-wide directory services, so best practices recommend running application services, like Exchange 2000, on a separate physical machine in close proximity to a DC. Adding application services to a physical machine characterized as a DC obviously requires that you make significant changes in the physical specifications of the machine—in processor, storage, memory, and network bandwidth.

In Windows 2000, you will also encounter new organizational issues. For example, running Exchange 2000 on a DC means that administrators have privileges on all DCs in the enterprise that are running Exchange Server! The scope of responsibility is significantly different in an enterprise environment than in the legacy NT 4 domain environment and must be carefully considered during the planning stages of deployment.

Exchange 2000 services integrate with the Windows 2000 architecture, so you must install an Exchange 2000 server in a domain with a Windows 2000 DC with an AD Global Catalog (GC) Server. You can install the Exchange 2000 Server software only on Windows 2000 Server products, not on Windows 2000 Professional or legacy Windows or NT products. Furthermore, each Exchange server must be able to access this DC and Dynamic DNS services to communicate with other Exchange servers. Integration of Exchange services with the NOS architecture now includes network-level services like IIS, which you need to include in deployment plans because of additional demands on memory and processing resources. Depending on the extent of provided services, any one Exchange server may need additional physical resources to provide, for example, FTP in addition to SMTP and Network News Transfer Protocol (NNTP) services to a user population. From an organizational perspective, you need to define the role of an Exchange server in providing services. Based on the menu of services, you compile necessary hardware and software resources. The workload characterization of an application server like Exchange 2000 must not only provide for typical messaging and collaborative loads, but also resource-intensive services like the Web Store and online services (especially in a Windows 2000 enterprise environment).

In your deployment plan, when you install the first Exchange server in your organization, you will be creating a new messaging organization, Administrative Group, and Routing Group. The administrative concept of *domain* is fundamentally the same as it was in the NT domain model, so creating these organizational structures within a single Windows 2000 domain is a practical first step in an initial installation. If you create a Routing Group that crosses domain boundaries, however, you must establish appropriate security policies before you begin your setup phase or risk failures in various setup procedures due to a lack of access rights across the domains.

Exchange-Specific Requirements

When you are planning deployment, you define organizational roles in relation to the structure of your enterprise. You then need to optimize network and hardware configurations both within the context of a domain and at the level of the local machine. Optimizing the local machine balances performance with reliability within the physical constraints of the hardware. Thus, separate physical disks allow you to separate your operating system files from your pagefile. Best practices recommend similarly separating your Exchange information stores from your transaction log file, especially because the former store is randomly accessed, whereas the latter is a sequential write operation. In addition, separating the logs provides greater chance of recovery if a system failure such as a database disk crash occurs. The combination of backup copies of data and current log files typically restores a system to the working state it was in just immediately prior to the time of failure. Locate these small log files (5MB storage space each) in, for example, a FAT file structure formatted in partition sizes of no greater than 500MB; read/write operations in a FAT file system outperform those in NTFS within these lower partition ranges.

Another configuration alternative to optimize the delivery of services at the local machine level is using hardware and software Redundant Array of Independent Disks (RAID) technologies. Using RAID 0, often called *stripe sets*, requires multiple physical disks. A stripe set significantly boosts access to data, although it doesn't provide improved reliability. The same technology with an added fault tolerance feature—stripe sets with parity (RAID 5)—especially when provided through hardware rather than software, boosts access times over a non-RAID drive assembly. It also provides the added feature of online recovery of message information stores and other mission-critical data. RAID 1 technology, involving *mirroring* and *duplexing*, is best suited for optimizing the transaction log files. This is because the overall storage configuration of 500MB compensates for the loss of physical storage a disk will provide; RAID 1 uses only 50 percent of available storage space for data.

Exchange 2000 provides other features that optimize 24×7 delivery of services. For example, Storage Groups organize different kinds of data stores across disk subsystems to facilitate regularly scheduled maintenance procedures. For example, you can create a mailbox store for messaging or a Public Folder store for the mass distribution of information. A Storage Group in the Exchange system is a collection of six databases that use the same transaction log file, though one of the six databases is reserved exclusively for system use. As we discussed in Chapter 3, the store process, store.exe, manages an Exchange 2000 database, composed of a rich-text file and a streaming file, as one administrative unit. Organizing data in a Storage Group, much like assigning data across RAID disk assemblies, requires careful planning to facilitate both regular maintenance backups and recovery from a disk failure.

Exchange 2000 Server includes support for many Internet protocols, including SMTP, NNTP, HTTP, and FTP. All these protocols require configuration in terms of network connectivity and security access. IIS 5 is a required service on the physical server running the Exchange Server application. When IIS is installed, you also need to install the NNTP protocol stack, which is not a default protocol for these services (as are, for example, SMTP and HTTP); rather, it is necessary for the Exchange 2000 messaging components. Use the **IPCONFIG /all** command to confirm proper configuration of the basic Transmission Control Protocol/Internet Protocol (TCP/IP) protocol suite. Finally, Exchange 2000 provides its own management of security in the form of the optional Key Management Service (KMS). This service integrates with AD and Microsoft Certificate Services to manage encryption keys, specifically used to encrypt mail messages. Directory services like AD, name resolutions services like DNS, and security providing-services like Certificate Server must be working properly to facilitate the Installation Wizard's programmed operations.

Step 2: Installation

You can run the installation of Exchange 2000 directly from a CD-ROM or through a shared directory located on a networked distribution server. The typical installation folders for a server running on an Intel processor are located in the \Setup\i386 subfolder. Remember to close all applications before beginning the installation process because many applications are mail enabled and make background requests of messaging services. These requests will disrupt the installation process. It is also important to install the application software using a user account to which you intend to assign administrative privileges. This service account, as noted in the "Preparing a Working Environment" section earlier in this chapter, must have sufficient access rights to perform all the administrative tasks necessary to install and maintain an Exchange server.

The installation process begins with a splash screen that welcomes you to the Microsoft Exchange 2000 Installation Wizard, as shown in Figure 6.3. You are asked for a 25-digit key to begin the setup procedure. (Evaluation copies have the key already preconfigured.) The Installation Wizard then searches for Exchange Server components already installed on your machine. If legacy Exchange 5.5 is installed, the wizard prompts you about performing an upgrade to Exchange 2000. You then see the Component Selection screen, shown in Figure 6.4. Using the drop-down menu adjacent to the Exchange component listing, you can select from three choices:

Figure 6.3 The Microsoft Exchange 2000 Installation Wizard splash screen.

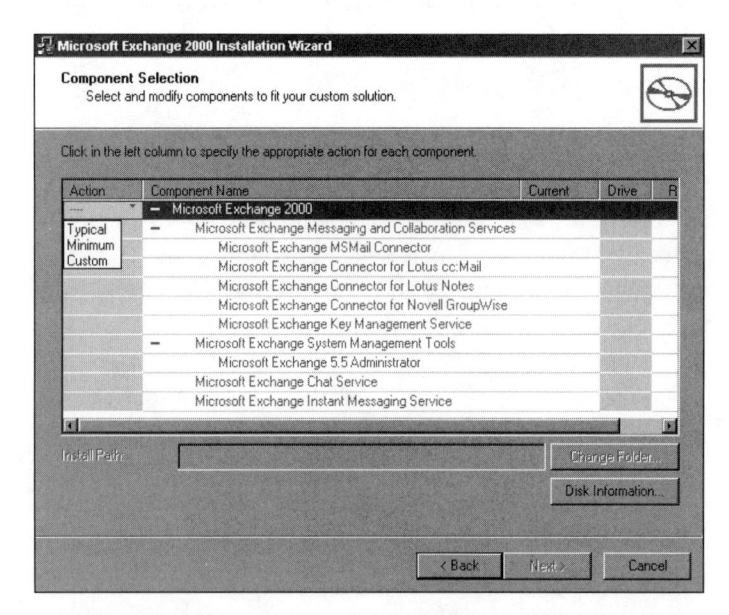

Figure 6.4 The Component Selection screen provides choices during installation.

- *Typical Mode*—This default selection installs all available Exchange components.

- *Minimum Mode*—This selection installs the main components and messaging services. It does not, however, install System Manager or any collaborative services.

- *Custom Mode*—This selection, as in most setup wizards, provides a listing of all installable features.

After you select components and calculate the required storage space for the installation process, you are prompted for the designated storage location for all the component system files. These files are stored in one location; components cannot be stored on separate drives. Components are listed in hierarchical fashion during the Exchange 2000 installation as follows:

- *Microsoft Exchange 2000*—This is the primary selection item for installing all the messaging application components.

- *Microsoft Exchange Messaging and Collaboration Services*—Selecting this item selects and installs all basic messaging components. Use this item to individually deselect specific messaging and collaborative component services. NNTP must be running for you to install these services.

- *Microsoft Exchange MSMail Connector*—This item, under Messaging and Collaboration Services, installs support software for legacy Microsoft Mail for PC networks.

- *Microsoft Exchange cc:Mail Connector*—This item, under Messaging and Collaboration Services, installs support software for the Lotus cc:Mail system.

- *Microsoft Exchange Connector for Lotus Notes*—This item, under Messaging and Collaboration Services, installs support software for Lotus Notes.

- *Microsoft Exchange Connector for Novell GroupWise*—This item, under Messaging and Collaboration Services, installs support for Novell GroupWise.

- *Microsoft Exchange Key Management Service*—This item, under Messaging and Collaboration Services, installs the optional Exchange-specific security add-on that complements management of Certificate Services, also optionally provided by the NOS.

- *Microsoft Exchange System Management Tools*—This item installs the Exchange System snap-in, necessary to manage the Exchange components. You can also install this item separately for remote administration.

- *Microsoft Exchange Chat Service*—This item installs the Internet Relay Chat Server software. This selection also requires the installation of the System Management Tools and Exchange Messaging and Collaboration Services.

- *Microsoft Exchange Instant Messaging Service*—This item installs software that supports the IM feature. This selection also requires the installation of the System Management Tools and Exchange Messaging and Collaboration Services.

After you have chosen the appropriate component services, the next step involves choosing the type of installation. Because of the versatility and stability of the legacy Exchange 5.5 product, you can add new Exchange 2000 Server installations to existing legacy Exchange organizations. Many corporate environments may not convert to a native Windows 2000 environment for some time in the future and thus will most likely run their messaging services in a mixed-mode environment. The Installation Wizard allows you to either add Exchange 2000 Server to an existing legacy Exchange 5.5 organization or create a new Exchange organization (the default choice). When you select the default choice, a new screen prompts you for a name for the new organization. You are then asked to agree to a Per Seat licensing agreement. As with previous versions of Microsoft server software, Per Seat licensing of services requires any client computer requesting services to have a Client Access License for those requested services. Unlike older versions of server software, Exchange 2000 does not offer a Per Server license by default.

After you have responded to these screen prompts and selected a service account, the Installation Wizard provides a read-only version of the Component Selection screen that shows the selected components. You can now choose to go back through the previous screens to modify your selections or begin the actual installation by selecting Next. The Installation Wizard then copies system files and begins the installation process.

As mentioned in the "Preparing a Working Environment" section earlier in this chapter, if you, or an administrator with greater access privileges (such as access to the AD schema), took the preparatory step of extending the AD schema before deployment, your Exchange installation will now, at this point, proceed without interruption. If, however, you do not modify the AD schema before installation, the Installation Wizard periodically stops the installation process and prompts you to request confirmation to perform this task. If you began the installation process with a login user account that has appropriate access permissions to the DC and AD schema, this installation process continues to completion. If the installation is run by an administrator without proper security access, the installation displays a message explaining that conditions have not been met to continue the installation, and the installation session ends. Separate groups of people with varying scopes of authority can thus handle the process of extending the AD schema and independently install the application software. This separation in scopes of authority reminds us that Windows 2000 and the future .NET framework are running truly distributed services in what will eventually be a loosely coupled, enterprise-wide, operating environment.

Other Installation Features

The installation steps for adding messaging servers in existing Exchange 2000 organizations are similar to those of a new installation. AD already supports an existing organization, so no preparatory steps are necessary to extend the AD schema. You can run the setup from a CD-ROM or network distribution server. The organization name, because it already exists, is read only and cannot be modified. You are, however, prompted to choose Administrative and Routing Groups to communicate with other Exchange servers in the existing organization. Make certain you select a service account that is common to all other Exchange servers in the organization. There are no other differences in the installation procedure.

You can also automate the deployment of Exchange servers by scripting the installation process. The Installation Wizard writes the answers to all screen prompts in an ASCII initialization file named setup.ini. The Exchange Installation CD-ROM has sample files stored in the Batsetup subdirectory under the Support folder. You can create a batch script that will run the setup program with the customized information stored in this initialization file.

Step 3: Verification

Post-installation tasks are critical when you install Exchange 2000 or other application software of this complexity. Best practices recommend that you clear all event logs and reboot your physical server. Depending on events recorded in your system and application logs, you can verify that all Exchange system components are running in, for example, the Services node under Services and Applications in the Computer Management console. It is, of course, critical that you start Microsoft Exchange System Attendant because all other Exchange component services depend on its operation. You can verify that services are running on a remote Exchange server by using the Connect To Another Computer feature in the Computer Management snap-in. You can track the details of every operation performed during the installation of Exchange 2000 in an ASCII text log file called Exchange Server Setup Progress.log, located in the system root directory.

Other post-installation tasks that you need to perform include:

➤ Delegating administrative responsibility to other administrators, especially through the Exchange Administration Delegation Wizard

➤ Creating server policies that define email address generation

➤ Creating mailbox stores, connectors, Storage Groups, and indices for public stores

➤ Confirming client access to mailboxes

➤ Configuring realtime collaboration services

➤ Performing both a full system backup and a refresh of the Emergency Repair Disk

Step 4: Installing Supporting Software

After you have verified the integrity of the core messaging and collaborative services, there is a large independent software vendor (ISV) community from which you can acquire a wide range of support software. These add-on products and supporting software include:

➤ Backup software

➤ Virus checkers

➤ Content or document management software

- System monitoring and performance management software
- Facsimile (fax), Wireless Application Protocol (WAP), and Systems Management Services (SMS) connectors
- Directory synchronization
- Unified messaging

Although many products such as fax servers and WAP are not for most organizations, backup software and virus checkers are important additions to any organization. When sampling these different packages, it is important to follow the same procedure as that for installing server application software. The information-gathering stage may need to be just as comprehensive as it was for the initial Exchange installation. Similarly, the verification stage is important especially because you purchase these support packages to enhance services that the system already provides. It is imperative that you recheck all the core services for any conflict or disruption.

Steps 3 and 4 actually work together, and in most cases, are repeated several times during the installation process. After you install core services, it is important to apply quality assurance tests to verify that the messaging platform functions properly. Once you verify core services, it is typical to install additional service packages to extend services. In turn, you need to systematically test these services for core service levels, as well as their integrative tendencies (where appropriate) with other services that the platform already provides. You will find that many installations now typically follow these four steps because distributed services are, in fact, coexisting and communicating through other layers in the network structure.

Chapter Summary

This chapter addressed issues involved in installing an Exchange 2000 server. Here are some particularly significant points to remember:

- Managing an installation begins with proper instrumentation and careful planning. Instrumentation can be categorized as user oriented (functional) and server oriented (physical or structural). Tools need to measure a variety of services, including directory services, transportation/protocol services, storage services, and administrative services.
- The Windows 2000 management model leverages the MMC in its ability to provide a common framework, supporting a wide range of snap-in tools. These tools extend from simple tasks on a local machine to enterprise-wide services.
- TS proves to be an important tool in remote maintenance and control.

- Installation prerequisites include installing properly functioning network protocols such as Dynamic DNS and the nondefault NNTP running under IIS.

- Extending the AD schema before and separate from the actual installation of Exchange provides a convenient separation of tasks that requires high-level, forest-wide access rights from more basic administrative tasks. It also offers a way to ensure replication of schema changes before the actual installation process begins. Two utilities, ForestPrep and DomainPrep, which run as part of the setup.exe program, can be run separately or, in a single domain environment with sufficient access rights, as part of the installation process.

- An Exchange administrator account must have membership in the EnterpriseAdmin and SchemaAdmin groups to run ForestPrep and DomainPrep.

- You should always consider the recommended physical requirements of an application server as the minimal (least desirable) configuration and evaluate them in terms of the planned workload characterization of the target physical server.

- Exchange 2000 Server must be installed on a Windows 2000 server product, in a domain with a DC acting as a GC Server. The server must have access to the DC and Dynamic DNS as well as have IIS and NNTP running locally.

- It's best to write transaction logs to small disks with FAT file structures. For reliability purposes, RAID 1– (mirroring and duplexing) is a recommended best practice. To maximize both performance and fault tolerance, you should store data stores as well as other mission-critical data on NTFS-formatted disks that run as RAID 5 disk subsystems.

- Exchange installations include three modes: Typical, the default selection that installs all available Exchange components; Minimum, which installs main messaging and collaborative services but not System Management tools; and Custom, which provides a choice of combinations.

Review Questions

1. Which of the following tools is particularly useful in the area of storage management?
    a. AD Users and Computers
    b. Exchange System Manager
    c. DNS console
    d. ADSI

2. What are the major advantages of TS over Exchange System Manager? [Check all correct answers]

    a. You can use TS to run any software.

    b. TS can manage an Exchange server over slow dial-up connections.

    c. TS runs better than an Exchange 5.5 administrative program over a dial-up connection.

    d. TS client runs without configuration.

3. Which of the following protocols is an installation prerequisite for Exchange 2000 Server?

    a. Dynamic DNS

    b. NetBEUI

    c. DHCP

    d. SNMP

4. What new service has Exchange 2000 added to Exchange Server's range of features?

    a. SMTP services

    b. Mailbox services

    c. Chat service

    d. Conferencing

5. Which Exchange 2000 products require a good deployment plan? [Check all correct answers]

    a. Exchange 2000 Enterprise Server for the SOHO environment

    b. Exchange 2000 Server for the SOHO environment

    c. Exchange 2000 Enterprise Server for all environments

    d. All of the above

6. In a typical installation procedure that involves gathering information and resources, installation, and verification of installed services, and applying additional support software, when is a backup recommended?

    a. After installation

    b. Before installation and after verification

    c. After application of additional software

    d. Answers a and c

7. What task is necessary when you are preparing an environment for an Exchange installation?

   a. Confirm the NetBIOS name of the server targeted for Exchange installation.
   b. Create service accounts for future use.
   c. Log on using the service account that the ForestPrep utility especially designated to install Exchange Server.
   d. Answers a and c.

8. Which of the following statements is true?

   a. You must use the ForestPrep and DomainPrep utilities before you run the Exchange Installation Wizard.
   b. ForestPrep and DomainPrep were designed for security reasons.
   c. Any user with administrator permissions can run DomainPrep.
   d. It is not necessary to run either ForestPrep or DomainPrep before installing Exchange 2000 Server in a single-domain environment.

9. What group memberships need to be assigned to an Exchange administrator user account to run the ForestPrep utility in a mixed-mode environment and install Exchange 2000 Server? [Check all correct answers]

   a. EnterpriseAdmin.
   b. SchemaAdmin.
   c. DomainAdmin.
   d. None of the above; you don't run ForestPrep in a mixed-mode environment.

10. What is the minimum memory requirement for Exchange 2000 according to Microsoft?

    a. 64MB
    b. 128MB
    c. 256MB
    d. 512MB

11. Which of the following statements is true?

    a. You should stay current with service packs.
    b. You should stay current with hot fixes.
    c. All of the above.
    d. None of the above.

12. What conditions support a successful Exchange 2000 Server installation? [Check all correct answers]
    a. The Exchange server can be installed on a Windows 2000 DC with access to an AD GC Server.
    b. The server must be installed on any standard Windows 2000 server product running IIS with HTTP, SMTP, and FTP.
    c. The Exchange server must be able to access other servers using Dynamic DNS.
    d. All of the above.

13. When you install the first Exchange server in a domain, what is created?
    a. An organization
    b. An Administrative Group
    c. A Routing Group
    d. All of the above

14. Which of the following statements is true?
    a. Transaction logs are best written to stripe sets.
    b. Transaction logs are best written to duplexed drives.
    c. Transaction logs are best written to NTFS file systems.
    d. None of the above.

15. Which of the following statements is true?
    a. Message information stores are best written to RAID 0 disk subsystems.
    b. Message information stores are best written to RAID 1 disk subsystems.
    c. Message information stores are best written to RAID 3 disk subsystems.
    d. Message information stores are best written to RAID 5 disk subsystems.

16. What is missing from a Minimum Mode installation?
    a. Collaborative Services
    b. System Management Tools and Chat Service
    c. System Management Tools
    d. Answers a and c

17. What ASCII file is used to automate the installation of Exchange 2000 Server?
    a. batsetup.ini
    b. setup.ini
    c. batinstall.ini
    d. install.ini

18. What file records the details of every operation during installation?

    a. Exchange Server Setup Progress.log

    b. setup.ini

    c. install.ini

    d. bootlog.ini

19. Which of the following are considered post-installation tasks that are part of the verification process? [Check all correct answers]

    a. Checking client access to mailboxes

    b. Creating mailboxes

    c. Installing fax connectors

    d. Creating server policy regarding default address generation

20. What tools allow you to verify services running on a remote Exchange Server?

    a. TS client

    b. Computer Management snap-in

    c. All of the above

    d. None of the above

Real-World Projects

Wilhelm Sichs knows that two of the most important administrative tasks are monitoring and queue tracking. Having come from another consulting job, he is anxious to build a baseline of performance against which he can evaluate the health of the Exchange system he has inherited. When message tracking is enabled, Exchange Server maintains daily logs that contain a running history of all messages transferred within the organization. Wilhelm doesn't have any previous data or experience with this system, so he wants to begin tracking messages to monitor the message flow into and within his organization. He will then consider diagnostic logging to build his baseline records.

Project 6.1

To configure message logging:

1. Start System Manager.

2. Select a particular server by expanding the Server node. If necessary, expand any Administrative Groups to expose any one particular server.

3. Right-click on the particular server and select Properties.

4. On the General Properties sheet, select Enable Message Tracking. This selection tracks messages for all messaging components on this particular server. By

enabling the option directly above this one, Enable Subject Logging And Display, you can store message subjects in the message-tracking log file.

5. If you want to maintain these log files, notice that the text box on the right side of the panel is enabled. By default, Exchange removes log files older than seven days. If you want to increase this period, enter a different value in the text box adjacent to Remove Files Older Than (Days): on the right side of the panel. If you want to maintain all log files, deselect the Remove Log Files option button in the Log File Maintenance section.

Exchange Server creates message-tracking logs daily. They are stored in the Exchsrvr*ServerName*.log directory, where *ServerName* is the name of the particular Exchange server. Each tab-delimited ASCII text log file is named by creation date according to yyyymmdd.log. You can use a text editor, database, or spreadsheet to import and read these files.

Project 6.2

Wilhelm wants to log diagnostic messages to detect performance problems among the Exchange servers he manages. Unlike the message-tracking logs, though, diagnostic log entries are written to event logs and require the Event Viewer to view them. Wilhelm knows that diagnostic logging can significantly impact system performance. He wants to balance his need for information to prevent future problems with daily performance. He also knows that there are four levels of logging: None, the default level; Minimum, creating summary entries; Medium, creating summary and detail; and Maximum, a complete audit trail. Wilhelm compromises by choosing Minimum. He decides to follow the best practices recommendation of increasing the level of logging detail only when a distinct issue needs to be tracked.

To enable diagnostic tracking:

1. Start System Manager.

2. Select a particular server by expanding the Server node. If necessary, expand any Administrative Groups to expose any one particular server.

3. Right-click on the particular server and select Properties.

4. On the Diagnostic Logging Properties sheet, notice the Services list. Click on a service in this window to see the category and logging level appear in the detail window on the right.

5. Select a category in the right detail window. Notice how the logging levels are enabled below the panel.

6. Choose a logging level for a particular category.

7. Click on OK.

Events generated by these choices are recorded in the Application log of the Windows 2000 Event Viewer. You can access the Event Viewer in a variety of ways; for example, under Administrative Tools in the Programs menu, select Computer Management. Upon choosing a computer to connect to, choose the server whose logs you wish to view. Under System Tools, access Event Viewer and select Application Log.

CHAPTER SEVEN

Client Configuration

After completing this chapter, you will be able to:

✓ Understand the different categories and flavors of software clients used to request messaging and collaborative services

✓ Distinguish differences among Outlook, Outlook Express, and Outlook Web Access (OWA)

✓ Describe the range of properties available to customize client software

✓ Outline the steps involved for installing Outlook as a client

✓ Configure Outlook profiles for varying work conditions

✓ Understand the implication of OWA and the Web Store as it relates to networked client software

As an administrator, you have a responsibility to your end-user to choose best-of-breed tools with a feature set that will not only satisfy the user's immediate needs, but will also accommodate future changes in the environment within which that user works. Best practices recommend acquiring skills in the configuration of several different messaging clients when you first begin learning about Exchange 2000. This chapter provides an overview of both the common network-based clients, as well as the Web-based browser client.

The Range of Exchange Clients

It is important to understand the nature of Exchange clients and what features they provide in an organization. As an administrator, you may quickly discover that one large company can use several different clients, because each client offers particular features and benefits that meet specific messaging objectives for specific segments of the user population. Without standardized policies and practices, a patchwork quilt of client software grows, adding greater complexity to both support and maintenance. Workers become accustomed to specific program features throughout their careers and, when they move on to other jobs, they typically carry their preferences with them. Similarly, corporate culture can rule the decision-making process; determining workplace tools based more on popularity, majority, and comfort than on performance and features. A favorite tool quickly spreads and immediately generates a protective layer of dedicated end users who will resist any change. The "favorite tool syndrome" is common in most organizations and becomes part of the corporate culture. It can be both a blessing and a curse for some administrators. If you grow accustomed to configuring one mail client at one site, you gain expertise, but you become one-sided in terms of technical experience. You need to be prepared to learn and configure other mail clients at other sites because, at some point in your professional career, you will encounter them. In fact, although most organizations use Microsoft Outlook as the main client, it is not the only client that will work with Exchange Server.

Exchange 2000 administrators provide messaging and collaborative services to a vast array of clients to fulfill Microsoft's objective of information from anywhere, at any time, through any device. In the distributed services world of Windows 2000 enterprise, a server will not provide services unless there is some client requesting those services in a client/server architecture. Administrators must know how to configure and troubleshoot these many Exchange clients to support their end-user population. Different clients utilize different mail protocols, like Post Office Protocol 3 (POP3) and Internet Mail Access Protocol 4 (IMAP4), in different ways, depending on what segment of the user population a person happens to come from. Two categories of client/consumers have emerged, however, and signal a shift toward a wider distribution of services across public networks like the Internet. The example of the multiprotocol Web browser client using Microsoft Outlook Web Access will be discussed in its own separate section later in this chapter. The other category is older than Web-based clients and more conventional. Many flavors of networked clients that access information stores across private local and wide area networks. Examples of some of the more common networked client applications clients used to request Exchange 2000 services are:

➤ Microsoft Outlook clients, including Windows 97, 98, and 2000

➤ Microsoft Outlook Express

➤ Microsoft Exchange

➤ Microsoft Schedule+

➤ Unix mail

➤ Macintosh mail

Even from among this abbreviated list of mail clients, your choice depends on what features are needed by your end users. Best practices recommend the consideration of additional factors that will significantly contribute to the variable cost components of total cost of ownership (TCO), such as, for example, support, training, and maintenance. You also need to evaluate ease of installation, extensibility in client software design, scalability, upgradability, and interoperability with different mail standards, as well as changing end-user needs as your organization matures over time.

Microsoft Outlook 2000

The Microsoft Outlook client was officially introduced with Exchange Server 5 as a desktop information manager and fundamental replacement for Schedule+, discussed later in this chapter. Outlook 2000 is Microsoft's latest version of what is now commonly regarded as the premier messaging client. Unlike Lotus Notes, one of its closest software competitors, it is fundamentally a messaging tool. Though successful in providing this one core service, Outlook provides many additional features that prove it can consolidate desktop information within the confines of one software interface. From a design perspective, it is a mixture of several field-tested components such as Exchange Client, Schedule+, and Microsoft Project. It also provides a customizable user interface that allows you to generate electronic forms.

The Outlook client is a complete messaging, scheduling, and content-management solution that is positioned, like a capstone, on the most popular PC-based pyramid of office application products—Microsoft Office. The Outlook feature set, however, extends beyond the leverage of the collection of Office products. Outlook can directly access many Exchange features, including public folders, so users can collaborate on projects and automate their workflows. Another design feature is support for application add-ins, which are third-party modules that extend the product's core functionality. In fact, Microsoft encourages third-party developers to use Outlook to develop applications. For example, you can now use a third-party add-in for encryption and digital signatures to make users' mail more secure.

The Outlook client, and especially the Windows 2000 one, has one predominant feature: It is an integral part of Microsoft's Office application package. In fact, the current Office 2000 itself comes in a variety of "flavors," including Small Business Edition, Standard Edition, Professional Edition, Premium Edition, and Developer Edition. No matter what edition of Office 2000 you purchase, the Outlook 2000 client integrates all other Office components within one common interface. Similarly, all editions of Exchange 2000 you buy (such as Enterprise Edition and Standard Edition) also seamlessly interface with the Outlook 2000 client.

Outlook Features

Part of any deployment plan includes "marketing" the feature set of the software to the user population. This technique not only prepares your users for changes in their daily working environment, but also can generate a positive, collective corporate consciousness that helps complete what is often a very painful process. Outlook as a tool provides features that significantly improve productivity. Presenting many of these features, both in demonstrations and hands-on training shortly before deployment, can dramatically improve morale and in fact speed up deployment. Outlook is a powerful and robust application that leverages many Office features with centralized access. Its default Outlook Today screen presents key bits of personal information—such as a calendar, a list of tasks to be performed, an inbox, drafts, and outbox mail—to the user on a single, graphical user interface. This personal management tool in the context of time management very often excites people because office workers immediately recognize already-familiar Office toolbars and work methods. They can leverage these software skills with new functionality, such as:

➤ *Views*—Customized views of email and calendars in a single location for daily event planning.

➤ *Protocol support*—Support for multiple Internet protocols, including POP3, Simple Mail Transfer Protocol (SMTP), IMAP4, Lightweight Directory Access Protocol (LDAP), Network News Transfer Protocol (NNTP), vCard (the Internet standard for virtual business cards), and iCalendar (a feature used to schedule users across the Internet through group scheduling).

➤ *Contact management*—Mass mailings for email and fax distribution to all address book and personal contacts.

➤ *Web publishing*—Publishing of group or personal calendars as a Hypertext Markup Language (HTML) Web page.

➤ *Mailbox support*—A single universal Inbox for all email messages.

- *Integration with Office tools*—A simple or Microsoft Word–based editor to create messages in plain text, rich text, or HTML.

- *Auditing*—A journal tracking system of tasks, phone calls, email, or other messaging objects.

In fact, there are so many possible features that some business concerns choose to limit some of the software's functionality, even in a standard installation of Outlook 2000. As an administrator, you need to follow your corporate objectives, your support resources, and your personal experience in providing those functions most beneficial to your corporate needs. Make sure your client machine has personal folders set up in the form of PST files because it will be holding information that the schedule, task, and contact-management features use. You can create these files by accessing the Properties sheet of the Outlook client and selecting Personal Folders under the Services tab. You can create these PST files on the local hard drive.

Outlook Service Options

Microsoft, in fact, provides a selection of service options during installation of the Outlook client. *Service options* refer to distinct sets of common messaging features appropriate for different circumstances. For example, a fundamental selection is email accessible; Outlook performs many desktop-management features on a standalone, non-networked workstation. Alternatively, when Outlook is networked, it provides messaging services through some private mail system or corporate workgroup, as well as through the Internet and public mail systems. These options are categorized as separate features that include:

- *Corporate Or Workgroup Client*—This provides the most comprehensive feature set in Outlook 2000. Outlook can function as a mail client on a corporate messaging system. For instance, you can decide to use Outlook over your local area network (LAN) with Exchange Server, Microsoft Mail, or even Lotus Notes. Corporate policy typically determines the use and location of PST files because the client workstation more likely than not has a data store on a central corporate server. PST files stored locally on a user's machine divides the responsibility of support and maintenance between administrator and end user. In some work environments, this division is actively discouraged because of additional overhead involved in the end user doing his or her own backups, as well as the greater risk of data loss.

- *Internet Mail Client Only*—This is equivalent to the non–mail-aware mode described above, except that it functions as an Internet mail client. You can use task-, contact-, and schedule-management features, as well as Internet-based messaging. In the absence of some corporate messaging system, you can connect to any POP3-, SMTP-, or IMAP4-compliant mail server across some public network like the Internet. You must also make certain that PST files for personal folders are available to hold messages created by the other features.

> *No E-Mail*—This uses limited features of Outlook 2000 in a nonmessaging mode. Though not part of the core services, these robust personal management features include personal time-management and scheduling-management features, task-management features, and contact-management features. Microsoft has marketed these non-networked, standalone features of Outlook as a personal information manager (PIM). The disadvantage of using this mode of operation is that it is not mail aware by default.

Exchange 2000 stores mail messages on the server, eliminating the need for personal folders or PST files. Some legacy "store and forward" systems, such as Microsoft Mail, require these personal folders to store messages. Depending on user requirements, these data stores may be located on local workstations rather than on a shared server. These folders are subject to corruption and data loss, as well as present a security risk through outside access. The best ways to protect these PST files are to password protect them and to make certain they are backed up regularly.

Microsoft Outlook Express

Outlook Express is a totally different version of application software from Microsoft Outlook and thus has fewer features. Outlook Express is available when you install Microsoft Internet Explorer (IE); it is also the default mail client for Microsoft Windows 98. This product focuses on three different functionalities: email messaging, newsgroups, and directory service lookups.

Outlook Express Email Messaging

Outlook Express supports basic messaging using the POP3, IMAP4, and SMTP protocols. You should be able to use Outlook Express with Exchange 2000 to retrieve messages. However, Outlook Express is not a "native" Exchange Server client like its Messaging API (MAPI) sibling standard Outlook. If you need access to public folders or Outlook forms, Outlook Express is not recommended. You can use Outlook Express for multiple email accounts so users can retrieve messages from multiple mail servers. You can also set client-side rules for certain incoming mail, but you cannot set server-side rules. You need to use the Rules Wizard in Outlook 2000 to perform this task.

Outlook Express Newsgroups

Most mail clients, including Outlook Express, can read content from Internet newsgroups using the standard NNTP protocol, which operates over port 119. Mail clients are usually referred to as *newsreaders*, which require access to "news servers." This is one example where Exchange 2000 is useful. Outlook Express can access an Exchange 2000 public folder as a newsgroup using NNTP. However, when accessing a public folder in Exchange, you have to consider which client created the entry in the public folder itself. If you use any NNTP-compliant reader like Microsoft Outlook to create the entry, you can access all contents using a POP3-compliant mail retriever like Microsoft Outlook Express.

Outlook Express Directory Service Lookups

Outlook Express can actually query many companies' directory services by using LDAP. For example, Windows 2000 uses Active Directory (AD) to store similar information regarding users, groups, and computers. So, in essence, Outlook Express makes an LDAP query to AD over Transmission Control Protocol (TCP) port 389 to get information about a user or group. You can configure Outlook Express to make all LDAP queries directly to a domain controller (DC) that resides in a Windows 2000 AD.

Exchange Client

Exchange Client was the default mail client for all versions of Exchange Server through Exchange Server 5. This default client changed when Microsoft released Exchange Server version 5.5. The client came in both a 16-bit and a 32-bit form for Windows, as well as a 16-bit form for MS-DOS and Macintosh.

You are probably already using Exchange Client if you have older versions of Exchange Server in your current environment. It's interesting to note that Exchange 2000 fully supports Exchange Client, but Microsoft will probably not improve upon this client in future releases of Exchange Server. Even if you use Exchange Client in an Exchange 2000 environment, you do not have access to some of the advanced features provided by the other mail clients discussed above.

With Exchange Client, you can perform basic messaging and even access public folders. You cannot perform scheduling unless you also incorporate Schedule+. You might question the functionality of the 16-bit version of Exchange Client (which is similar to the Macintosh version), but remember that it does provide basic functionality such as email, personal calendaring, and task lists. Best practices recommend standardizing all users on the 32-bit version of Exchange Client.

Schedule+

Schedule+ was the default client for scheduling and contact management for all versions of Exchange Server up to and including version 5. When Exchange Server 5.5 came along, Schedule+ was rapidly replaced by the scheduling, contact, and collaboration features that the Outlook client provided.

Most existing Exchange environments use either the original Schedule+ or the most current version, 7.x. These versions are used on 32-bit and 16-bit Windows systems, as well as Macintosh systems. You can always migrate existing data from a Schedule+ client to an Outlook client. It is important to remember that you can integrate Schedule+ with an Exchange 2000 server, yet Schedule+ won't be improved upon in future versions of Exchange Server. You can even have a mixture of Schedule+ users and Outlook users in the same Exchange environment because they access the same information.

Note: Outlook clients have more functionality than legacy Schedule+ clients. In fact, Outlook provides messaging features such as Journal and Notes not found in the now rarely used Schedule+ clients. Outlook also provides custom views and advanced printing options not found on Schedule+ clients. Best practices recommend that you migrate users off Schedule+ clients as a matter of standardizing software clients.

Unix Clients

You can use Exchange 2000 with standard Internet mail clients. This means the clients themselves support standard Internet email protocols like POP3, IMAP4, and SMTP. You have to remember that there is no Outlook client for the Unix operating system, so for Unix users to connect to an Exchange 2000 server, they have to use either a third-party Internet mail client or OWA.

Macintosh Clients

Macintosh users have almost the same options to access an Exchange 2000 server as Unix clients—that is, they can access Exchange Server with their own third-party POP3 or IMAP4 email client, or they can use a Macintosh-based Web browser to retrieve mail. There is, however, yet another way for Macintosh clients to use Exchange Server. Microsoft provides the Outlook Client for Macintosh, which has many features in common with the 32-bit version of Outlook for Windows. This version of Outlook is known as version 8.2.2. Keep in mind that Macintosh has both a 16-bit version and a 32-bit version you can work with. Microsoft will most likely develop a new version of Outlook so that Macintosh users can enjoy even more advanced features of Exchange 2000 Server.

Installing Outlook Client

You can install Outlook Client in multiple ways: local installation from a CD-ROM, network installation using a network shared directory, or even automated and customized installations using installation wizards. Microsoft prefers using setup wizards for most of its programs. Outlook is no exception. Outlook 2000 installs with a setup wizard using what is called the Windows Installer, a new utility that lets administrators customize portions of an installation or add/remove components long after an installation has been done.

Figure 7.1 shows the Office 2000 Installer when you first install Outlook 2000. We have expanded the Converter and Filters option to show what installation options are available. This window shows all the available components when first installing the Outlook product. You can install the components from the local hard disk if you have ample disk space, install the components to run over the network from a shared folder, install the components to install the first time a user tries to use them, or choose not to install the components at all.

Client Configuration   209

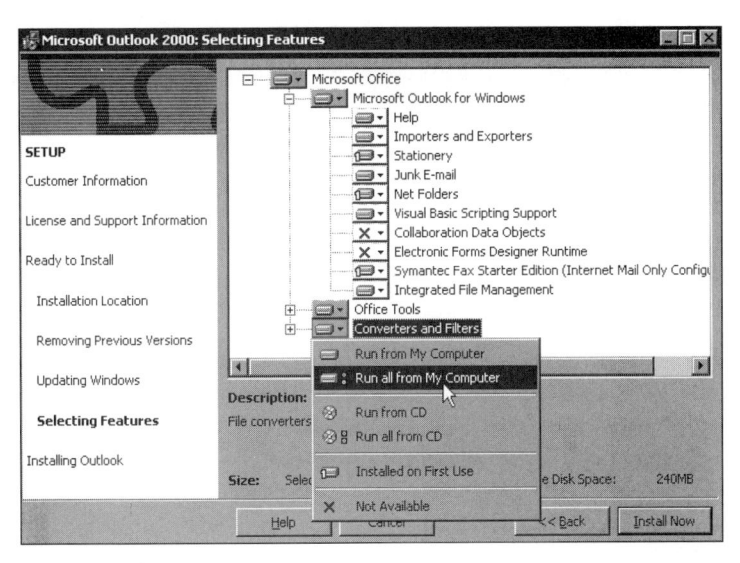

Figure 7.1   The Windows Installer window lets you pick what components to install.

After you select your components, the Installer takes over and finishes all steps required, with very little involvement from the administrator. When the installation is complete, you need to determine the appropriate Outlook 2000 mode to run; these three mode choices determine the method by which mail is accessed. The three choices, as shown in Figure 7.2, are:

➤ *Internet Only*—This mode means that Outlook 2000 will act as an Internet mail client with any mail server that supports Internet mail protocols such as POP3 or IMAP4.

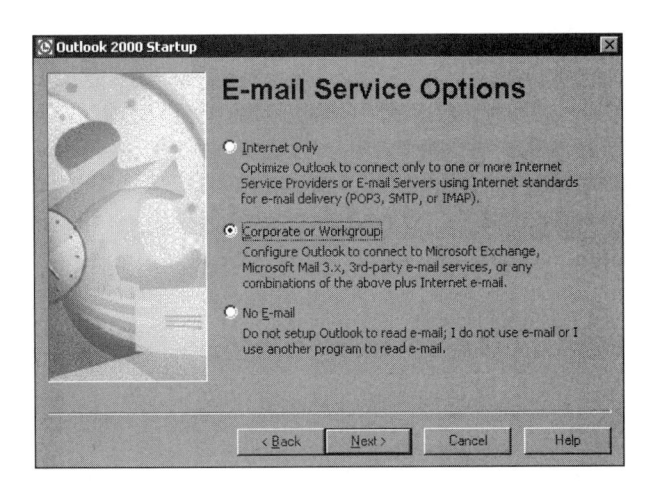

Figure 7.2   The three Outlook 2000 service options.

> *Corporate Or Workgroup*—This mode was designed specifically for use in a LAN that contains at least one Exchange server. However, other mail servers, such as Lotus Notes or Microsoft Mail, will suffice.

> *No E-Mail*—This mode means that Outlook will be configured to act as a PIM, giving you contact-, scheduling-, and task-management features only.

Best practices recommend some version of IE running on your client machines rather than another browser client. Microsoft recommends that you install IE 4.02 or later. After you select your service option or mode from the choices, the setup routine prompts you for the name of the Exchange server you are connecting to, as well as the username of the mailbox you are configuring. Figure 7.3 shows the choices of available information services. You need to have Corporate Or Workgroup services enabled to see these selections and configure your Outlook client to use Exchange Server.

Custom Installations

Installing Outlook 2000 is a relatively easy process, but even so, you may not look forward to installing Outlook on hundreds of machines at once. An administrator's life is tough enough, and fortunately, there are solutions to address this. Microsoft provides three methods to use if you decide to rapidly deploy the Outlook client on multiple machines in a relatively short timeframe.

Technique #1: Command-Line Switches

Although most features of the Outlook client are accessible through a graphical user interface (GUI), there remain system features that you can access only from the command-line interface (CLI). You need to learn the command-line syntax of many executable programs as an alternative method to execute applications and special options that are sometimes associated with them. CLI switches are special instructions added at the end of the command-line text that activate alternative

Figure 7.3 Configuring a user mailbox to connect to an Exchange server.

modes of operation. You can typically display a list of these CLI arguments if you type the executable program name followed by a space and "/?". This almost universal argument displays a usage menu showing CLI switches and modifying arguments associated with that executable program. For example, you can use switches with special options that use a *package file* called the Microsoft Installer package file (a file that ends with an .msi extension). Table 7.1 shows the most common command-line switches used to perform a customized installation of Outlook 2000.

Technique #2: A Setup Information File

To modify the behavior of the setup process, ask yourself the following two questions:

- Is there a file named setup.ini in the same directory as setup.exe?
- Are you using the command-line switch **/settings *INI file path*** to specify an INI file with a different name?

If the answer to either question is yes, use setup.ini or the INI file you specified to modify the normal behavior of the setup process. A setup information file can actually specify all parameters that you normally type at a command prompt. By setting this up in advance, you can precheck your file for errors, as well as enforce your own special settings. You can create this type of file using a simple text editor, such as Microsoft Notepad or WordPad.

Initialization, or INI, files are text-based listings of configuration information in which every line you type represents one portion or segment of the installation process. To include your own annotations in an INI file, type a semicolon at the beginning of a line and then type your comments. (The semicolon is the cue for the computer to ignore that line when it reads the file.) Microsoft provides an actual setup file in its *Microsoft Office 2000 Resource Kit*.

Table 7.1 Command-line switches used to install Outlook 2000.

Switch Name	Purpose
/a *MSI file path*	Used to create an administrative install point using an MSI file.
/f [*reinstall modes*] *MSI file path*	Used to repair an installation using different repair methods.
/g *language ID*	Used to specify which language you want to use. English is the default language and has an ID of 1033.
/I *MSI file path*	Used to specify the name of the MSI file you will use during installation. Do *not* use this switch with the /a option.
/l [*option*] *logfile path*	Used to specify what log file to use during installation.
/q [*options*]	Used to specify the amount of information that should be presented on a screen during installation.
/settings *INI file path*	Used to specify the path and settings file you are using for an automated installation.
/x *MSI file path*	Used to uninstall Outlook.

Technique #3: The Custom Installation Wizard

Use the Custom Installation Wizard that is part of the *Microsoft Office 2000 Resource Kit*. You can download this from **www.microsoft.com/office/ork/2000/appndx/toolbox.htm**.

The wizard works with the Windows Installer and allows you to manipulate certain steps of the actual installation. You can choose a path to install Outlook 2000, define a list of servers for Windows Installer to use, hide certain options from users during setup, or even add custom files to the installation. There is even a feature to allow you to customize desktop shortcuts for Outlook 2000. To work with the Custom Installation Wizard, it helps to understand a little about the kinds of files the Windows Installer uses. These files are categorized as:

- *Package (or MSI) files*—The Microsoft Office Custom Installation Wizard uses these files to run Office setup from an administrative installation point. If you are using Microsoft Systems Management Server, the wizard defines the files that make up the software application to be distributed and includes package configuration and identification information.

- *Transform (or MST) files*—These files temporarily modify the behavior of the package files so that you can customize an Office 2000 installation. You create them to modify or restrict Office 2000 setup from an administrative installation point.

Remember that package files never change. They are really huge databases that describe all your configuration information. Transform files contain the modifications you want to make as Windows Installer is installing Outlook. In a typical GUI-based installation of Outlook 2000 that is locally installed and does not use any customized settings or wizards, you start the wizard and complete the options as displayed.

Outlook 2000 Profiles

A typical corporate configuration is designed so that Outlook interacts with Exchange 2000 Server mailboxes. In Windows 2000, this means that Exchange Server ultimately interacts with Windows 2000 directory services and user accounts. If you can set up one user to interact with Exchange Server, implementing multiple users with Outlook also becomes an easy task. There is, however, a difference between an Outlook profile and an Exchange mailbox. You need to understand how both these entities interact with Windows 2000 accounts. A *profile* is a collection of settings you configure on the client side. It is fundamentally a set of "information services" stored on your local machine and accessible on demand or through default when the Outlook client is launched. You want to make reference to your Exchange server and some previously entered mailbox recipient when you

Figure 7.4 Entering a specific Exchange server and mailbox when creating a profile.

configure a profile (see Figure 7.4). This profile can then be used to alter services and configurations, such as for network use or downloading files from the Internet. Figure 7.5 shows two profiles and the drop-down list from which one profile can be selected as the default configuration. Figure 7.5 shows the original MS Exchange Settings profile and a newly added A New Exchange Profile. Note that the lower drop-down menu provides a choice of which profile to use upon starting Microsoft Outlook.

Usually, a machine already has a default profile set up. When a user clicks on the Outlook icon, information in the default profile is used to determine which mailbox to use on the Exchange server. You can easily see a list of all current profiles on your machine by starting Outlook and choosing Tools|Services. You should see something similar to Figure 7.6.

Figure 7.5 Selecting a possible default profile with which to start the Outlook client.

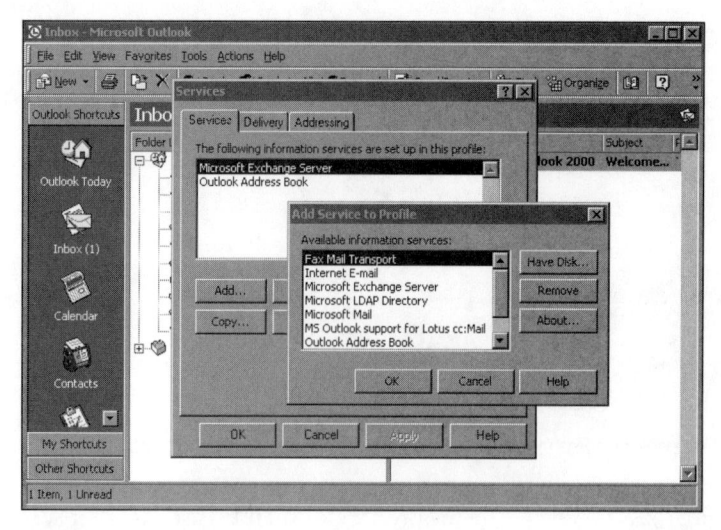

Figure 7.6 Setting up profiles for a mail client in the Outlook 2000 Tools menu.

Multiple Profiles in Outlook 2000

The support of multiple profiles is particularly advantageous if you share your machine with other users and don't want multiple people using the same configuration information. You might even be using the same machine for different purposes (for example, a laptop machine used at work and at home). Multiple profiles help you manage these customized settings depending on your work environment.

To view a profile in Outlook 2000, choose Tools|Services (refer to Figure 7.6 for the resulting dialog box). Alternatively, if you right-click on the Outlook icon and choose Properties, you will see the MS Exchange Settings Properties dialog box. You have the option of adding, removing, reconfiguring, or copying profiles from this dialog box. Choosing the Add button allows you to configure additional services to a profile. To add a profile, click on the Add button and it will start the Inbox Setup Wizard. If you highlight Microsoft Exchange Server and click on the Properties button, you will see something similar to Figure 7.7.

Multiple Mailbox Access

This section covers situations where you may have to provide access to more than one mailbox to the same user or to multiple users. On any given machine, you can configure multiple Outlook 2000 profiles. You can assign each profile to a different user, which means that different users can access different Exchange Server mailboxes.

A more common scenario is to allow one user to access different Exchange Server mailboxes using the same alias or mailbox name associated with a Windows 2000 user account. For example, your administrative assistant can open your mailbox when you are away on business. Ultimately, Exchange 2000 Server security and

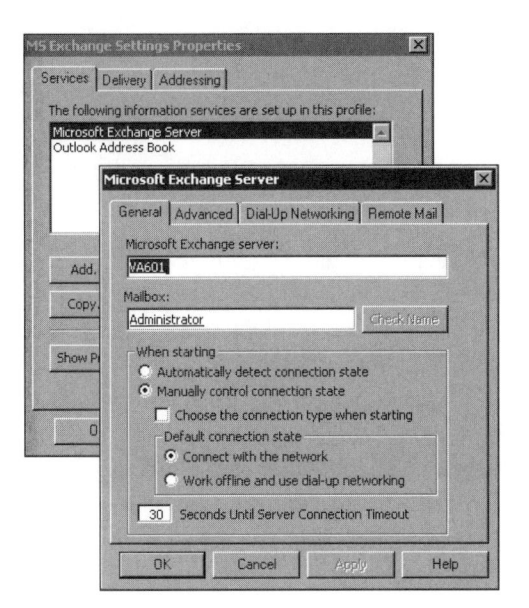

Figure 7.7 Selecting the General tab under Exchange Settings Properties.

access control are intimately tied to the Windows 2000 security model. For example, when you log on to a domain as a client and request access to the network, a Windows 2000 DC provides you with an access token. You can use this access token to request and receive services from, for example, an Exchange 2000 server. The Exchange server or any other service provider queries an Access Control List (ACL) consisting of two subcomponents: a Discretionary Access Control List (DACL) and a System Access Control List (SACL) on which user permissions are stored. These internally maintained system lists determine whether you will be granted or denied access to messaging or collaborative services.

You would need to perform several operational steps to give someone access to your mailbox in Exchange Server in Windows 2000:

1. Select Active Directory Users and Computers under Administrative Tools in the Start menu, or access it through the Microsoft Exchange cascading menu under Programs in the Start menu.

2. Enable Advanced Features under the View menu in the Microsoft Management Console (MMC).

3. Select the user account listed on the detail side of the Console screen when you expand the Users node on the left.

4. Right-click the user object and select Properties.

5. Select the Exchange Advanced tab on the page of specific user's properties.

6. On the Exchange Advanced tab, choose the Mailbox Rights button to open the Permissions dialog box. The Mailbox Rights dialog box has an Add button for selecting users or groups from the Active Directory.

7. Click the Add button and add additional users or groups that will have permission to access the mailbox.

Even though administrators traditionally are needed to grant access to a user's mailbox, in a collaborative environment, users can delegate access to certain mailboxes or Outlook. In Outlook, you can access the Delegates panel through the Options Properties sheet under Tools. Alternatively, right-click on any specific object such as Calendar or Task, and select Properties. Figure 7.8 shows the Calendar Properties sheet and its own Add screen (which appears when the Add button is selected). The Add panel opens under the Permissions dialog box for the selected object, which, in the figure, is the Calendar. In the Add box, you can assign users a variety of permissions, such as creating, deleting, and editing items.

Outlook Web Access (OWA)

Outlook Web Access, called the Web Client in legacy Exchange 5.5, describes a client environment in which users can access mailbox data and public folder data using standard Internet browsers. Figure 7.9 shows the basic architecture where service requests are mediated across a network. These requests using HTTP are interpreted by a Web server by davex.dll, a software layer that communicates with the Exchange Store through EPOXY, the Exchange interprocess communication

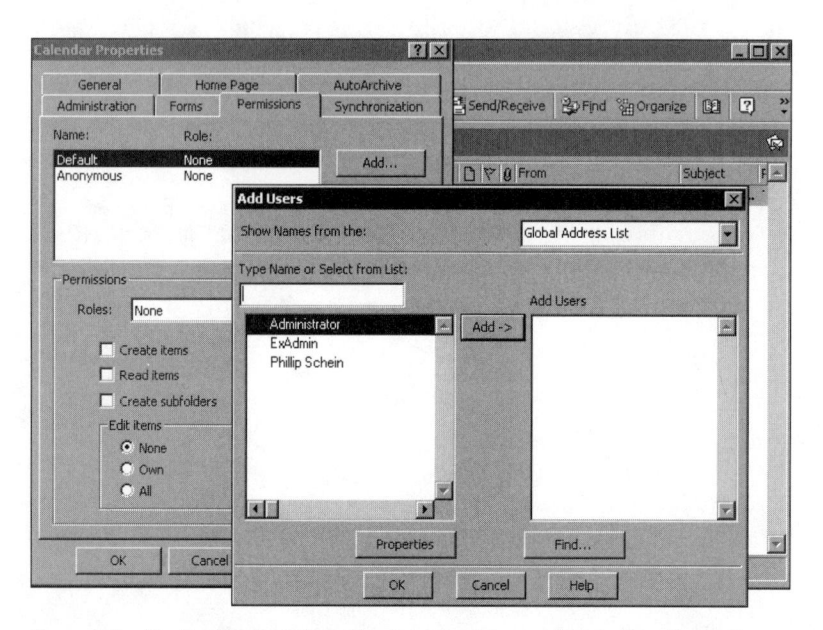

Figure 7.8 The Permissions dialog box from the Advanced tab in User Properties.

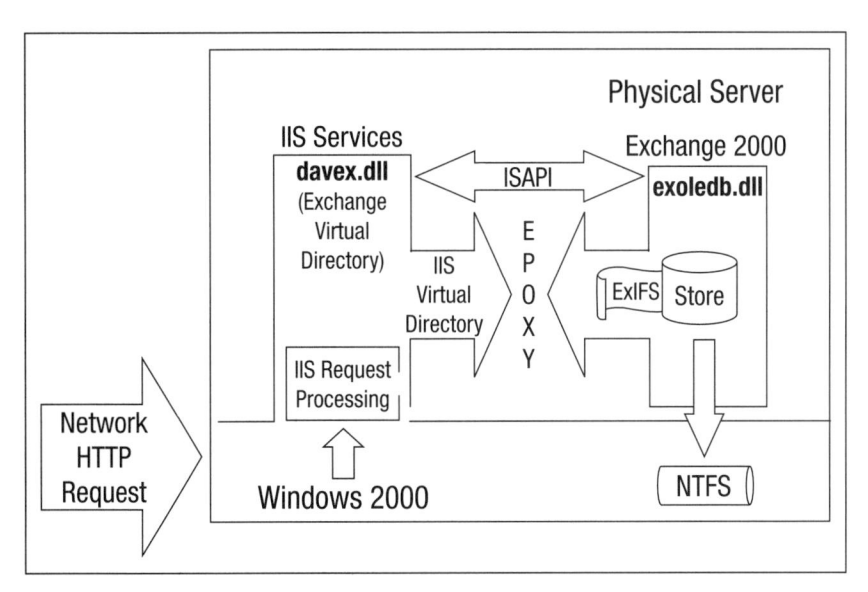

Figure 7.9 The block diagram showing OWA architecture.

channel. OWA is an important feature to incorporate in mixed-client environments such as Windows, Unix, and Macintosh. In fact, for most Unix clients, OWA is the only solution for email access, calendar management, and public folder access using Exchange 2000 for the back end. You can install OWA as a standard component of Exchange 2000. There are differences, however, between the OWA client in Exchange 2000 Server and the OWA client in Exchange Server 5.5, the main difference being a new file system called the Web Store and the protocols that access it.

Web Distributed Authoring and Versioning (WebDAV) Protocol

WebDAV is a distributed authoring protocol used to access OWA. It has a set of headers and methods that extend HTTP to provide capabilities for overwrite protection, properties, and namespace management. Known as simply DAV, WebDAV is both a network file system suitable for the Internet and a protocol for manipulating the contents of a document management system via the Web. It allows a network protocol to create interoperable and collaborative applications. Some major features of this protocol include:

- *Concurrency control*—This prevents the "overwrite problem," where two or more collaborators write to the same resource without first merging their changes.

- *Properties*—Extensible Markup Language (XML) properties provide storage for data, such as a list of authors on Web resources. A new protocol—the DAV Searching and Locating (DASL) protocol—provides searches based on property values to locate a Web resource.

- *Namespace manipulation*—DAV supports copy and move operations because resources are often copied or moved as a Web site grows.

- *Advanced collections*—There is now support for ordered collections, where a server maintains a single persistent ordering of Uniform Resource Locators (URLs) in a collection. Clients can now remotely create a redirect to other resources.

- *Versioning support*—These support operations, such as retrieval of history lists and previous versions of a resource, facilitate project management, and enhance the development life cycle of a resource. Version controls provide multiple authoring supports for the development of a single resource.

- *Access control*—This feature allows users to set and clear Access Control Lists (ACLs) to Web resources, allowing collaborators to remotely add and remove people from a list of collaborators for any resource.

DAV is a protocol and not an application programming interface (API) because it extends HTTP. It adds new HTTP methods and headers, and specifies how to use new extensions, as well as how to format request and response bodies. Additional information about this protocol and the use of its extensions is available at **www.webdav.org**.

OWA

OWA provides a way for users to access their mail or calendar information through a standard Web browser like Microsoft IE or Netscape Navigator. Minimum requirements for browser clients are Microsoft IE version 3 or later and Netscape Navigator version 3 or later. Software that is version 3 or later ensures that HTML 3.x features such as frames, scripting, and Java are supported. You can install OWA when you install your Exchange server. It provides most of the features available in the fully installed Outlook 2000 client.

Using OWA as your mail offers several advantages. Because a standard browser can be used for mail retrieval, you can avoid installing different clients. The browser client, a common tool found on most computers, can function as a mail client on many different platforms, such as Macintosh or Unix clients. The browser provides a "universal interface" for people who have to log on from different machines. Users access the same information without having to create different mail profiles for specific mail clients on different machines. In fact, users have access to public folders on your Exchange server using OWA. Your users have the ability to query AD on a DC for user or group information, as well as to access most of the functionality provided through a regular Outlook 2000 client, including email, calendaring, public folders, and collaboration. Figure 7.10 shows the view of a user's mailbox from OWA through an Outlook client.

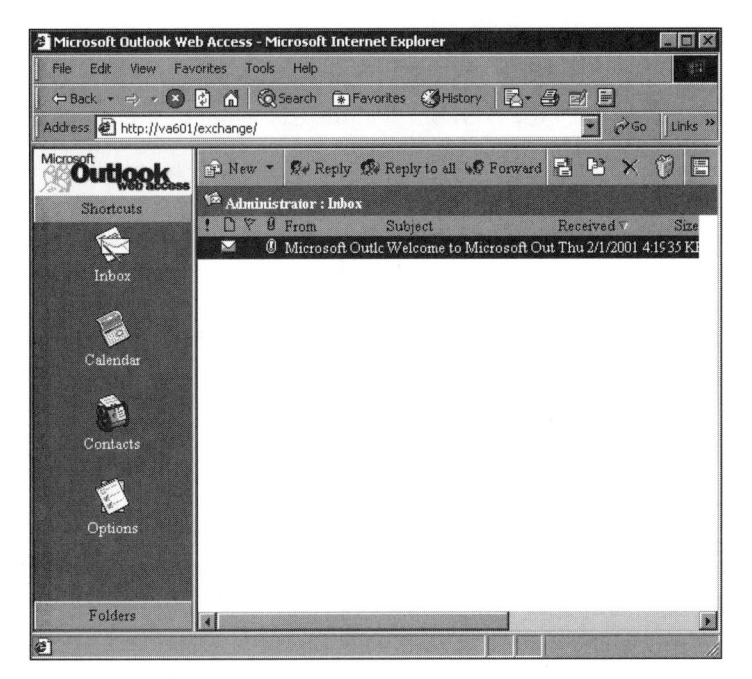

Figure 7.10 A user's mailbox from OWA through an Outlook client.

Unfortunately, even feature-rich browser clients such as OWA have a few missing features. For example, you cannot use OWA to replace the full-featured Outlook client for 16-bit Windows systems or Macintosh systems, nor do you have access to the Personal Address Books (PAB files) or any PST files or personal folders; they are "local" to some physical machine. Features such as spell checking, message flags, and Inbox rules are also not supported when using OWA. You cannot search for messages or view free/busy information nor recall a message or deleted item. In addition, neither the use of Outlook forms nor the ability to work offline is available through an OWA client. Tasks and the Journal feature are not implemented. (The Journal feature automatically records activities by item [email, meetings, tasks] and by Microsoft document type [Word, Excel, Access, PowerPoint] for specific contacts. These objects are arranged on a Gant Chart timeline.) Finally, as an administrator, you cannot create a public folder or manage its permissions.

The Web Store

The Web Store provides a repository for managing everything from email messages and Web pages to other documents. It integrates many types of services into a single structure, so it's easy for users to find and share information with one another. The Web Store supports many protocols, including Hypertext Transfer Protocol (HTTP). It includes support for Web Distributed Authoring and Versioning

(WebDAV) and even Extensible Markup Language (XML). Every object in the Web Store has a Uniform Resource Locator (URL) associated with it. You can see the versatility and usefulness of the Web Store in the following example.

If you create a folder called Secret Documents, you can, in a networked environment, create a network share to this folder from your workstation. An OWA client across the Internet can also access this folder because of the Web Store. Different users can thus access the same information in different ways, including by using any standard Web browser. It's easy to share information if you create a Web folder in advance. In fact, these folders are already built into Microsoft Office 2000. You can always create a new Web folder if you add a network place into My Network Places in Windows 2000. Even Windows 98 lets you do this if you go to My Computer | Web Folders.

It is important for an administrator to understand the advantages and disadvantages of OWA before fully deploying this means of accessing messaging services. As discussed earlier in this chapter, some of the advantages of OWA include access using any standard Internet browser and support for embedded items, ActiveX objects, and multimedia objects embedded directly into a message. The browser of choice is, of course, Microsoft IE version 5 or higher. As mentioned earlier, disadvantages include a lack of support for offline storage. Users must connect to an Exchange server to actually view any information. OWA does not support any type of digital encryption or digital signatures. It has very limited view options for scheduling meetings or managing a list of tasks compared to the other versions of Outlook discussed previously. Finally, there is no support for Outlook 97 forms.

OWA Administration

You should administer and manage OWA by using Microsoft's Internet Information Services snap-in the MMC. If you open the MMC and expand the containers pertaining to Internet Information Server (IIS), you will see three virtual roots created during installation. The Exchange virtual root (http://*server*/exchange) will point to a mailbox folder (MBX) that, for example, resides on some mailbox server in your domain. The OWA server is installed by default during the Exchange 2000 installation. The Exchange virtual root (http://*server*/exadmin) and the public virtual root (http://*server*/public) are both added directly to the IIS directory tree structure and point back to the actual Exchange directories in the MBX folder, as shown in the tree diagram of the M: drive in Figure 7.11. In addition, other virtual servers, each with separate configuration, including bound IP addresses and port numbers, as well as authentication, can be created on the same physical server. Virtual instances are useful in a variety of special situations that require support from multiple domains, such as different DNS configurations requiring reverse lookup, or the need to communicate to separate domains with different authentication schemes.

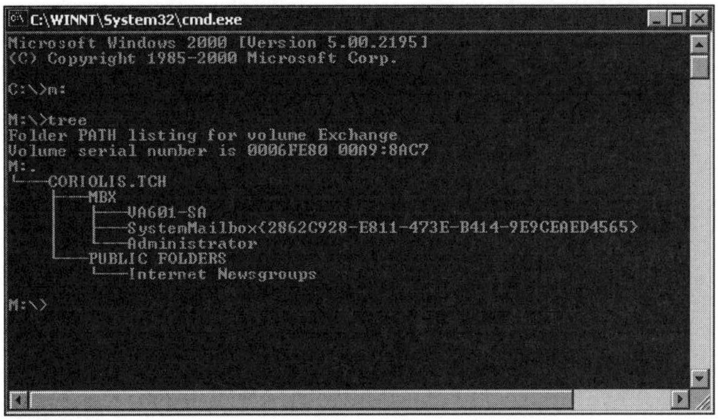

Figure 7.11 A tree diagram of directories in the mailbox folder on the Exchange Server.

You must consider several important factors when deploying OWA. In addition to determining baseline service levels, you need to actively monitor your servers using performance monitoring tools found, for example, in the Performance console. Establish performance baselines for key components like memory, disk, network, and processor. OWA has changed considerably in design. Exchange 5.x OWA uses Active Server Pages (ASP) to communicate with the messaging platform through both Collaboration Data Objects (CDO) and MAPI. This affects performance; for example, it limits the number of concurrent users using OWA. In Exchange 2000, however, OWA does not use MAPI or ASP technology. Instead, Exchange OWA is a part of the Web Store. It only uses IIS for protocol services. Thus, the architecture and the servicing of requests are different. In Exchange 2000, performance bottlenecks usually originate from poorly maintained physical components and resources, such as insufficient memory or hard drive storage space rather than from badly scripted Web pages.

Another important consideration is IIS authentication methods used to properly configure OWA. You need to know which ports are being used to access Internet email (usually TCP port 80). You also need to consider the impact of access in relation to using firewalls, proxy servers, or secure channels like Secure Sockets Layer (SSL), which uses port 443 for communication, and Kerberos authentication (a security protocol used by Windows 2000 Server). Finally, you must have a basic understanding of the Internet protocols that OWA uses.

Authentication of Accounts

Verification of a user's identity can be achieved through a variety of authentication protocols in Windows 2000. Microsoft's implementation of Kerberos v5 (RFC 1510) is the preferred method and the default protocol in a native mode environment. The versatility of Windows 2000 lies in its ability for DCs to negotiate an authentication method with a client. If the default Kerberos authentication method fails, a domain controller will revert to a downlevel protocol, such as NT LAN Manager (NTLM challenge/response) authentication method, and query the client for security credentials in the form of username, password, and domain before allowing access to network resources such as a mailbox. A critical Microsoft operating system theme of Single Sign-On (SSO) significantly affects this process. Any user accessing network resources should not have to enter their security credentials more than once to access a system resource or service. Thus, a separate Security Attention Sequence (SAS), commonly known as a logon dialog box requesting username, password, and domain, is shown only if an initial userid fails to satisfy security criteria during the logon process to a mailbox.

Requesting Exchange Services through OWA

By default, all users can access OWA, without special configuration, by typing the server's uniform resource locator (URL), which specifies the server name and the *userid*. When this request for service is made from within the boundaries of an enterprise, *hostname* and *userid* are sufficient. From outside the boundaries of an enterprise, it is necessary to use a fully qualified domain name such as **hostname.domainname.tld** (where *.tld* is the top-level domain, like .com or .edu), the name of the virtual mail directory, and the name of the user mailbox. Thus, by default, OWA does not present users with the typical SAS before access to Exchange services unless the provided security credentials fail some security criterion. The URL is used to pass security credentials to the Web server. Figure 7.12 shows steps that you should follow to see whether an OWA server is functioning as intended. You perform these steps at the client using browser software:

1. A user logs onto an OWA server using a URL address such as **http://servername/exchange/userid** from an intranet through an HTML form. When that same user accesses the same server from a public network like the Internet, she uses **http://hostname.domain.tld/maildirectory/userid**.

2. The user is authenticated by the Web server, and the Web server passes the userid information to Active Directory (AD) directory services, which resolves the *userid* to some mailbox location and redirects the service request.

3. The location of the mailbox is returned to the Web server, which can then be used to access the data stores.

4. OWA returns an HTML page to the user's client browser, through which the user can access her mailbox and other messaging services.

Internet Mail Protocols Supporting OWA

The major Internet protocols used with OWA include POP3, IMAP4, SMTP, and NNTP. SMTP is, in fact, the de facto standard server-side mail protocol on the

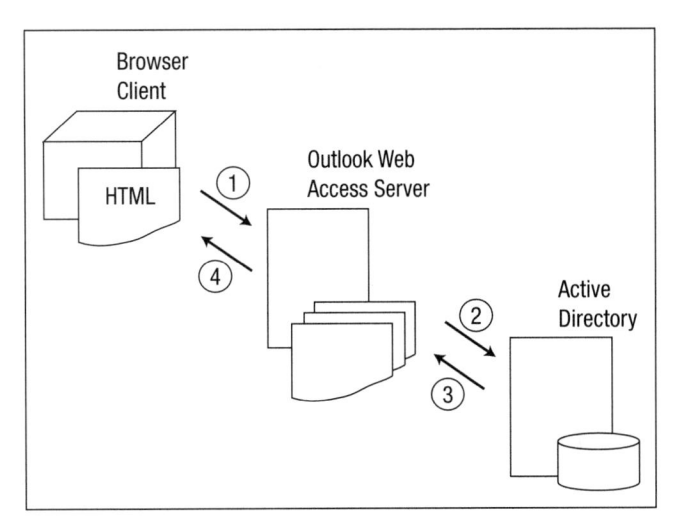

Figure 7.12 Accessing services through OWA.

Internet. The most common—but unfortunately weakest—client protocol in terms of features is POP3. Both SMTP and POP3 offer the broadest accessibility to messaging systems.

POP3

The POP3 protocol allows any computer to access a server that is holding mail for that computer. The computer itself cannot manipulate that data; it can merely download that mail from the server. Once it's downloaded, the server tries to delete any copy of that mail from its memory unless you have physically configured your client to keep a copy of that mail on the server. This protocol is a small but fast one designed for simple mail retrieval. If you want to send mail, you need the SMTP protocol or a connection to a remote mail server.

Many people don't realize that POP3 has a client side and a server side. The server starts the POP3 process by listening on port 110. If you, as a client, want to use this service, you need to establish a connection with your server, which then sends you an opening message. Any POP3 commands sent between you and the server are not case sensitive.

The three basic states for a POP3 session are:

➤ *Authorization*—When a server connection is opened, the POP3 server sends you a greeting; the client must authenticate itself to the POP3 server.

➤ *Transaction*—The session enters this state after authorization when the server exchanges mail with the client. The client's mailbox is "locked" so messages are not modified or deleted until the transaction is updated.

▶ *Update*—During this phase, the client issues a **quit** command, and the POP3 server releases all resources allocated to the client. The server sends a final "goodbye" message, deletes all messages, and terminates the TCP connection to the client.

IMAP4

The IMAP4 protocol is actually an enhancement or improvement to POP3. Recall that once a message is downloaded from a server, it is deleted from that server. This can be quite frustrating to a user who needs to work from several different machines. Once mail has been downloaded onto one machine, he or she cannot download it to another machine.

IMAP4 was developed to allow users to leave their mail on a server and to allow remote access to mail messages. So, you can say that IMAP4 extends the POP3 protocol to allow online and offline storage and retrieval of mail. IMAP4 also allows users to manage their own mail configurations and to share mailboxes. You can actually manipulate mail on the server instead of just downloading a copy of it from the server. Remember that clients use TCP port 143 to connect to a server running IMAP. The server itself is said to be in a certain state at any given time. The client has to know which state the server is in so it can issue the proper commands. Configure the IMAP4 server to show public folders to all clients. Also, best practices recommend fast message retrieval, in which messages are retrieved without prior knowledge of their exact sizes.

SMTP

SMTP originated from File Transfer Protocol (FTP). It is actually the native transport protocol used for Exchange 2000. When you install Windows 2000, you will notice a "base SMTP" service that is installed as part of IIS 5. The essence of SMTP is that you can pass information between two computers and create message headers that will automatically specify all sources and destinations involved.

All Internet protocols are defined in documents called Requests for Comments (RFCs), which are published on the Internet at a variety of sites (such as **www.faqs.org/rfcs**) for viewing by the general public. The SMTP standard is documented in RFC 822. A basic SMTP connection can be conceptualized, where Harry accesses a SMTP service using the Telnet client from the command prompt of his workstation:

1. Harry types "telnet mailhost 25". If the system cannot open a Telnet session, a message is returned stating that the connection failed; otherwise, a confirmatory heading appears.

2. Harry wants to contact Sarah. He uses a console command to enable local echo so that his display shows the characters he types at his keyboard.

3. Harry types "mail from: harrys@mycompany.com", which indicates the sender of his message, and presses the Enter key.

4. The server responds with an OK acknowledgment.

5. Harry types "rcpt to: sarahn@hercompany.com", which identifies the recipient of his message, and presses the Enter key.

6. The server responds with an OK reply.

7. Harry types "data" and presses the Enter key.

8. The server responds with a message telling Harry to begin his text input.

9. Harry enters the entire message, including headings, that he wishes to send to Sarah. To terminate his message, he presses the Enter key (commonly referred to as a default carriage return/line feed, CRLF), types a period, and presses his Enter key again.

10. The server responds with a "mail received OK" response and terminates the connection.

Each SMTP command is sent in American Standard Code for Information Interchange (ASCII) form as a 7-bit character set, and they are always sent one command at a time. You'll notice from this interchange that one reply is sent for every command sent. SMTP protocol is a simple transfer specification; it does not support multiple commands sent from one host to another simultaneously, nor does it support the use of an eighth bit in its packet stream. UUEncode (Unix to Unix Encode), a Unix copy utility that is used to transmit data among various domains, is a tool that extends the functionality of SMTP. This copy tool converts a file containing 8 bits of data into a file containing 7 bits of data. A recipient who receives UUEncoded mail via SMTP has to use UUDecode to convert this message back to an 8-bit standard.

Multipurpose Internet Mail Extensions (MIME) is another standard you may be familiar with. It allows you to send different types of messages across different mail servers. This standard has extended the functionality of SMTP by allowing the simpler SMTP to carry binary information in the form of an attachment along with the mail message. Thus, several files of varying content can be wrapped up into one single message. The body of each message specifies a "content type" that tells you what kind of file you are dealing with. For example, you will see some messages with the label "image/jpeg". This means the file probably has a .jpg extension and can be opened with Microsoft Paint or some similar graphics package. You can make the associations between the file types and the programs that open them by using either the Exchange System Manager or Windows Explorer (choose Tools | Folder Options | File Types).

SMTP is known as an *open message transfer system*. This means that any computer running the SMTP service can accept connections from any other computer running the SMTP service. Certain message transfer systems, such as the X.400 messaging protocol, are closed. Exchange 2000 Server enjoys greater interoperability with many more email systems than Exchange Server 5.5 ever did because of the functionality of SMTP.

This chapter deals mainly with client issues. There are other important aspects of SMTP that occur on the server side as well. You will learn in Chapter 9 that Exchange 2000 Server allows you to create multiple SMTP virtual servers on the same physical server so that you can have different configurations set up for different services. Troubleshooting SMTP means knowing about the various virtual server settings and making sure that all servers have unique Internet Protocol (IP) addresses and port numbers.

NNTP

NNTP allows you to distribute, retrieve, and post news articles on the Internet. You have to subscribe to a newsgroup to retrieve content from that newsgroup. The nice thing about subscribing is that you don't have to retrieve every single item contained within the newsgroup. Without NNTP, users would have to resort to the older methods of distributing or retrieving news items: Internet mailing lists and Usenet.

A server that provides mailing lists is also known as a *list server*. This machine, sometimes referred to by its service program name ListServ or Majordomo, distributes news using distribution lists (DLs). The distribution process involves a user/subscriber sending a message to a DL and the DL sending a copy of this message to all subscriber/members in the list. This usually requires large amounts of disk space and CPU resources. The length of time required for a message to be fully propagated across all members of even a lengthy DL is relatively short, and therefore it is an extremely effective way to distribute information.

Usenet is a variation on this idea; it stores and retrieves messages from a central location instead of sending emails to each subscriber on the list. Usenet allows subscribers to select only the messages they want to read. NNTP is actually modeled after the Usenet specification in RFC 850. It runs as a service on a server and accepts connections from other hosts on a LAN or the Internet. NNTP uses TCP port 119 to make a connection. A command consists of a command word followed by some parameter; commands are not case sensitive. As with SMTP, each command line can contain only one command, and commands cannot be continued on the next line.

Exchange 2000 uses NNTP to create asynchronous group discussions arranged in a hierarchical structure. This functionality was provided in legacy Exchange 5.5 through the Internet News Service. In fact, you can configure your Exchange

Server to talk to external NNTP servers so that certain Usenet groups are made available to users inside your LAN. Exchange 2000 also allows you to create multiple NNTP servers inside your organization so users can connect to a collection of servers. This is known as a *master-subordinate layout* and provides fault tolerance if a main news server goes offline for any reason. As previously mentioned, an NNTP server normally communicates over TCP port 119; secure channels use the Secure Socket Layer (SSL) protocol over TCP port 563.

Legacy Features

Microsoft has always provided backward compatibility in its software products. Two hold-over features in Exchange 2000—remote mail and scheduled connections—provided functionality when systems were less efficient and considerably less robust than more modern platforms like Exchange 2000 or its older sibling, Exchange 5.5. The ability to stay online in the early years of network connectivity was expensive and far more difficult to manage as compared to the communication systems we have today. Remote mail and the automatic scheduling of connections, though clearly antiquated in relation to today's methods of online accessibility, were, at the time, critical. They could transfer data across physically separate systems during, for example, nonpeak, early morning hours when bandwidth was available and long distance telephone tariff charges were relatively low (compared to the daytime rates). The greatest disadvantage of these techniques is the required maintenance involved in monitoring the synchronization process.

One solution to monitoring these specialized transfers of data is to schedule connections for the exchange of information on some predetermined basis. Scheduled connections ensure that synchronization occurs regularly but still often requires user intervention to set the timing of these synchronization events. Figure 7.13 shows a remote connection scheduled on an hourly basis for the transfer of mail. As you can see from the figure, this screen was accessed through the Tools|Services|Exchange Server Properties|Remote Mail menu features and tabs. Remote connection features are still available and provide a very easy solution to what might prove to have been a difficult problem. For example, a virtual server's root directory provides mailbox accessibility within a local domain. Providing that scheduled mail access to similarly remote mailbox servers can still be a practical solution to transferring mail inexpensively. SMTP transports deliver those messages according to specifications outlined in RFCs 821 and 822. The links between a message queue on one server and a targeted destination server can thus be active, ready to be activated, in a retry condition, scheduled to attempt a connection, waiting for some remote command (to, for example, dequeue or release its contents [TURN/ETRN]), or malfunctioning and frozen.

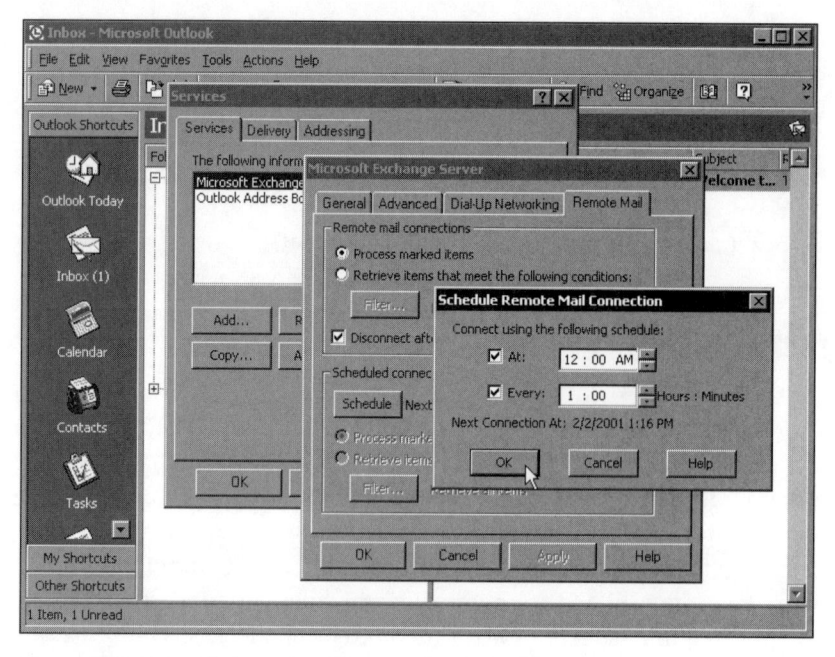

Figure 7.13 Scheduled remote mail connection through Exchange Server Properties.

Remote Mail

Though most users access messaging services across a LAN or a wide area network (WAN), a messaging system must still support remote access. Outlook 2000 provides this service in three distinguishable "flavors":

➤ *Dial-up connectivity*—Remote access is provided via a dial-up network (DUN) connection that results in full online connectivity.

➤ *Offline synchronization*—Offline replicas are synchronized via an asynchronous connection.

➤ *Filtered or selective synchronization*—Message headers are downloaded for review, and subsequent synchronization is based on selecting specific messaging objects.

DUN has been the mainstay of the road warrior since the time of the Matrix, the messaging-based Internetwork of remotely accessible computers that predates the Internet by about 10 years. DUN has improved significantly on both the client and server sides and now supports messaging as well as all forms of non-network-based connectivity solutions. It is the "from anywhere" component of Microsoft's messaging and collaboration goal of "access at any time, with any device, from anywhere." DUN raises the issue of what to do with messages once you receive them from the server. Thus, offline storage is also an important part of an end user's experience. Offline synchronization has, in fact, been available since the introduction of Windows 95 in the form of that special file object called the Briefcase. This specialized desktop container epitomized the synchronization process early in software development by simplifying offline storage mechanisms. The container object itself manages the synchronization of only those target components that differ in some way from their source. Filtered synchronization allows greater control of using resources for transferring data. In situations where resources are limited, the ability to select what is updated can save both time and money.

Scheduled Connections

Fundamental to automating remote mail, scheduled connections is still a relevant concept even in the world of Microsoft.NET servers. Exchange 2000 enables you to schedule regular maintenance tasks such as cleaning up deleted items and synchronizing Information Stores (ISs) with other servers in the Exchange organization. You use the IS Maintenance Properties sheet to schedule these events. Similarly, the Outlook client provides up to 16 scheduled sessions for transferring messaging between client and server.

Configuring Remote Mail and Scheduled Connections

You can configure Outlook 2000 to connect to an Exchange server through a dial-up connection and process mail using very specific criteria. For instance, you can configure Outlook 2000 to establish a dial-up connection to Exchange Server every 30 minutes and retrieve only messages with attachments that were sent yesterday. The key is using dial-up connections to connect to an Exchange server. If you don't see the Services option, you need to reconfigure the client for Corporate Or Workgroup use rather than Internet Mail, and then rebuild the Outlook client.

To begin configuring remote mail, open Outlook 2000 and click on the Tools menu. You have to view the properties for your current Microsoft Exchange Server profile. In Outlook 2000 under Tools|Services, open the Microsoft Exchange Server Profile. Select the Manually Control Connection State radio button and the Work Offline And Use Dial-Up Networking radio button. Under the Dial-Up Networking tab, choose a connection to use for remote mail. If you don't have an existing connection to use, you can configure a new connection by selecting New and completing several additional Properties sheets.

On the Dial-Up Networking tab, choose the Use The Following Settings At Logon radio button so the user is not prompted for connection settings. Select the Remote Mail tab, and then click on the Process Marked Items radio button. Select the Disconnect After Connection Is Finished checkbox to have Outlook automatically disconnect after sending and receiving mail. Click on the Schedule button under Scheduled Connections and choose the At Schedule option. Specify a time to send and receive mail, such as 12 P.M. every day. After making all the appropriate selections, click on OK and close Outlook 2000. Choosing Process Marked Items means you'd like to remotely send and receive all mail with Exchange Server. You could have chosen criteria such as Only Transfer Mail That Is From My Manager. In that case, you would click on the Retrieve Items That Meet The Following Conditions radio button.

Chapter Summary

This chapter addressed many client-configuration issues, including:

► Mail clients support standard mail protocols such as POP3, IMAP4, SMTP, and NNTP. POP3, for example, allows users to retrieve copies of messages from any mail server. IMAP4 extends the functionality of POP3 by allowing users to manipulate mail on a server instead of merely downloading a copy of it. SMTP, the native Exchange transport protocol, allows you to identify source and destination hosts in the process of sending mail. Finally, NNTP allows users to query for and distribute news from Internet newsgroups.

► Use Outlook 2000 for full messaging and collaboration. You can install it as a standalone product or as part of Office 2000 in three different configurations: Internet only, for users who connect through the Internet from home using standard Internet mail protocols; Corporate Or Workgroup, for users who connect directly to your LAN, containing at least one Exchange 2000; or No E-Mail, for users who don't need email connections because they are using a different mail client.

► Choose Outlook Express if you have many mobile users or you do not want the full functionality of the Outlook client. This product is installed automatically with Microsoft IE. Though good for basic email and much easier to configure than Outlook, Outlook Express does not support calendar management, scheduling, or many collaboration features.

► OWA came with Exchange Server 5.5 and was formerly called the Web Client. Use this client for secure access to email using a standard Web browser. IE version 5 or later supports the same features that Outlook 2000 does, such as calendars and scheduling. There is no need to configure the client side. The opening screen can be customized with a corporate logo, and email can be accessed from anywhere.

► Other Exchange Server clients include the 16-bit or 32-bit Exchange Client, which runs on older versions of Exchange Server. However, enhancements for this client will not be made in future versions of Exchange Server. Exchange Client used Schedule+ for scheduling and contact management. This client will similarly not be improved upon in future versions. Finally, Unix clients can connect to an Exchange server using standard Internet mail clients or the OWA client.

➤ You can install mail clients on multiple machines in many ways, including command-line switches and setup information files in package, or MSI, files. Setup information files let you modify the behavior of the setup process by making changes to the setup.ini file.

➤ Office Custom Installation Wizard works with the Windows Installer, allowing you to manipulate certain steps of the installation process. The actual file that modifies the behavior of the MSI file is called the transform file or MST file.

➤ Remote mail and scheduled connections for an individual user require a dial-up connection and are good for mobile users or people who need to access information from any remote site. Mail can be processed using very specific criteria.

Review Questions

1. Which of the following describes an add-in component?
    a. Calendar Plus
    b. Schedule+
    c. Outlook+
    d. Schedule+Calendar

2. Which of the following is not a typical Office 2000 package?
    a. Office 2000 Advanced Server Edition
    b. Office 2000 Small Business Edition
    c. Office 2000 Standard Edition
    d. Office 2000 Premium Edition

3. Outlook 97 can do everything that Outlook 2000 can do except which of the following?
    a. Support POP3 and IMAP4.
    b. Publish a team calendar as a Web page.
    c. Send mail to DLs.
    d. Allow you to send mail on behalf of another user.

4. Which service option lets you use only the contact-, task-, and schedule-management features of Outlook 2000?
    a. Corporate
    b. Workgroup
    c. No E-Mail
    d. Internet Only

5. Which service option allows you to use messaging in addition to Outlook's contact-, task-, and schedule-management features?

    a. No E-Mail

    b. E-Mail Only

    c. Internet Only

    d. Corporate Or Workgroup

6. By default, what page is the first page when you initially start Outlook 2000 on your desktop?

    a. Internet Only View

    b. Corporate Or Workgroup

    c. All Tasks View

    d. Outlook Today

7. E-mail Support for email within Outlook Express is similar to what service option or mode in Outlook 2000?

    a. Internet Mail Only

    b. No E-Mail

    c. Internet Service Mode

    d. Workgroup

8. What protocol can you use to retrieve mail messages from Exchange 2000 using the Outlook Express client?

    a. POP2

    b. POP3

    c. IMAP3

    d. SNMP

9. Why do you need IE version 3 or later to support OWA features?

    a. You need this to support HTTP version 1.1.

    b. You need this to support the features of HTML version 3.

    c. You need this to support the features of HTML version 3.2.

    d. You need this to support the features of HTML version 4.

10. OWA was not intended to replace the features of Outlook 2000 for which of the following systems? [Check all correct answers]

    a. 16-bit Windows systems

    b. 32-bit Windows systems

    c. 16-bit Linux systems

    d. 32-bit Macintosh system 7.5 machines

11. Which feature is not supported in OWA?

    a. Basic calendar functions

    b. Personal Address Books

    c. Group scheduling

    d. Basic public folders

12. What is the Outlook client for a Unix system known as?

    a. Korn shell

    b. Internet mail client

    c. Outlook Express

    d. Exchange Web Client

13. What package file is normally used to customize the setup of Outlook 2000 when you are using command-line switches?

    a. INI files

    b. MSF files

    c. MST files

    d. MSI files

14. What switch should never be used with the **/a** command-line switch when you are customizing the setup of Outlook 2000?

    a. **/I** *MSI file path*

    b. **/f** *MSI file path*

    c. **/j** *MSI file path*

    d. **/settings**

15. How can you check for the current profile that your Outlook client is using?

    a. By choosing Tools|Profiles when you first log in

    b. By choosing Tools|Services when you first log in

    c. By opening the Properties sheet of the Outlook icon on your desktop

    d. By opening up the Properties sheet of your Inbox when you first log in

16. What software is sufficient to send mail via SMTP? [Check all correct answers]

    a. Outlook Express

    b. Outlook

    c. Telnet

    d. FTP

17. What software protocol or specification provided SMTP with the ability to manage binary file attachments?

   a. None; SMTP, as originally specified, can handle binary attachments
   b. ESMTP
   c. MIME
   d. FTP

18. By default, how does OWA handle user authentication?

   a. It relies on AD to authenticate users.
   b. It does not manage the authentication of users.
   c. It passes security credentials to the Web server for authentication of users.
   d. It uses HTML to authenticate the user.

19. What do you do if your Outlook client is configured only for Internet mail?

   a. Remove the software package and install Outlook Express.
   b. Remove and then reinstall the Outlook software package.
   c. Go to the Mail Delivery page under Tools | Options and reconfigure mail support.
   d. Go to the Mail page under Tools | Accounts and add the Exchange Service to your profile.

20. Which statement is false?

   a. OWA provides users with access to mailbox data.
   b. OWA passes service requests through IIS.
   c. HTTP service requests are passed to Exchange across EPOXY.
   d. DAV is an OWA application programming interface.

Real-World Projects

Henry has been promoted to email administrator at his local college. His school consists of local email users and remote email users, including faculty, staff, and students. Students are constantly connecting to their email accounts from off-campus locations, and Henry's job is to configure the new Exchange server to make this work.

Henry has been reading about remote mail in Exchange 2000. He realizes that the following facts make this situation ideal for remote mail:

➤ Users at another campus want to connect to Exchange Server using dial-up connections.

▶ Laptop users want to retrieve their email while studying at home using a dial-up connection to the school's Exchange server.

He can't wait to test remote mail on his new IBM ThinkPad 600 laptop, left behind by his predecessor.

Project 7.1
To configure remote mail for Outlook 2000:

1. Start Outlook 2000 and then choose Tools|Services.

Tip: If you don't see the Services option, don't panic. You have to configure the client for Corporate Or Workgroup use and then reconfigure the Outlook client.

---

2. Look for the Services tab and then double-click on Microsoft Exchange Server Profile.
3. Select the Manually Control Connection State radio button.
4. Select the Work Offline And Use Dial-Up Networking radio button.
5. Select the Dial-Up Networking tab and then choose a connection to use for remote mail. (If you don't see an existing connection, choose New.)
6. On the Dial-Up Networking tab, choose the Use The Following Settings At Logon radio button so the user is not prompted for connection settings.
7. Select the Remote Mail tab and then click on the Process Marked Items radio button.

Tip: Choosing Process Marked Items means you'd like to remotely send and receive all mail with Exchange Server. You could have chosen criteria such as Only Transfer Mail That Is From My Manager. In that case, you would click on the Retrieve Items That Meet The Following Conditions radio button.

---

8. Select the Disconnect After Connection Is Finished checkbox to have Outlook automatically disconnect after sending and receiving mail.
9. Click on the Schedule button under Scheduled Connections and choose the At Schedule option. Specify a time to send and receive mail, such as 12 P.M. every day.
10. After making all the appropriate selections, click on OK and close Outlook 2000.

Henry has finished configuring remote mail on his laptop and makes sure he had a proper Dial-Up Networking object set up for his next dial-up connection. After launching Dial-Up Networking in his Windows 98 Control Panel, he is able to retrieve the mail he wants. He is now an official road warrior.

Project 7.2

Henry wants to change the configuration of the client from Internet Only to Corporate Or Workgroup after the initial installation on some of the student machines.

To switch from Corporate Or Workgroup to Internet Only:

1. Start Outlook 2000 and then choose Tools|Options.
2. Select the Mail Services tab and click on the Reconfigure Mail Support button at the bottom of the dialog box.
3. Select Internet Only and click on Next.
4. Click on Yes to complete the change in configuration.

To switch from Internet Only to Corporate Or Workgroup:

1. Start Outlook 2000 and then choose Tools|Options.
2. Select the Mail Services tab and click on the Reconfigure Mail Support button at the bottom of the dialog box.
3. Select Corporate Or Workgroup and click on Next.
4. Click on Yes to complete the change in configuration.

CHAPTER EIGHT

Recipient Management

After completing this chapter, you will be able to:

✓ Understand recipient types in Exchange 2000 and how they have changed from legacy versions of this product

✓ Recognize how the paradigm shift in Exchange 2000 recipient management has changed functional boundaries between an Exchange administrator and a system administrator

✓ Analyze the change in administrative models and roles needed to support recipients in an Exchange 2000 organization

✓ Perform basic mailbox management administrative procedures

✓ Control a recipient object's range of functions through configuration of key property settings

✓ Describe various Active Directory (AD) components that Exchange 2000 uses

✓ Understand how user attributes in the AD control the features of, for example, mailbox-enabled recipients

✓ Recognize the range of options available on a recipient's Properties sheets

✓ Use address lists to distribute messages in an Exchange 2000 environment

✓ Distinguish the differences between system and recipient policies

✓ List the various AD management tools that are particularly useful in Exchange 2000 administration

Exchange 2000 is an architecture designed to deliver a wide range of messaging and collaborative services. Recipient management has changed from the legacy concept of listing destinations of message flows to providing services to a universe of named objects. This chapter uses this change in the basis of management to define categories of recipients to whom services are provided and to explain how these recipients are defined, maintained, restricted, and managed in real-world workflow situations. You can group together collections of these recipients for more efficient servicing. Managing identity and permission issues of groups and address lists is an important concept because mastering the topic lends itself to greater efficiency when you are performing messaging tasks. Finally, we cover authentication, authorization, and permission management in general under a discussion of policy.

Recipient Types

Microsoft has stated that future versions of Windows 2000 will focus on greater distribution of services, greater accessibility from "any device, anywhere, at anytime," and an increased emphasis on content and knowledge management (KM). This change in perspective is in contrast to the monolithic approach to software design that characterized legacy versions of Exchange, SQL Server, and other older network operating systems (NOSs). In each of these closed software operating environments, a registered application user logged into a controlled environment that typically operated "above" and separate from the NOS.

Windows 2000 has shifted the paradigm from application server to service provider accessible on a public network. Server providers like Exchange 2000 respond to requests made by users who are managed through the NOS. As with the monolithic designs that have preceded this new paradigm, both monolithic application servers and the more contemporary service providers deliver access to datastores specifically allocated to authorized users. The nature of these datastores and the range of clients that can access them, however, have been enhanced significantly. One important design theme in both Exchange 2000 and Windows 2000 features that distinguishes Exchange 2000 from the older legacy architecture is the emphasis on both extensibility and scalability. For effective deployment, Exchange 2000 requires companies to invest significant resources. Once Exchange is in place, however, the messaging and collaborative platform provide a layer of software over Windows 2000 that is designed to accommodate a greater range of modification than all previous Microsoft NOSs. Examples of these modifications to the NOS can be found in the upgrades of both the feature set of SMTP and Collaborative Data Objects.

Exchange 2000 coordinates a recipient's messaging destinations through specific attributes associated with the Active Directory (AD) record of a named user account, often called a *principal*. This record enables authenticated and authorized clients to log on to computers and domains. Remember that a principal account can also be associated with a service-providing application rather than a person. Destinations for messages sent to these principals are "known" throughout the enterprise because they are written directly to the NOS. Exchange 2000 is responsible for providing service to these principals, which use a software client to access a wide, and extensible, variety of recipient types from both internal and external network locations. These recipient types include:

- *Mailbox-enabled AD principal (user) account*—This most common recipient is also referred to as a *mailbox*; you need a named AD object for Exchange to allocate space for messages. You can assign a single datastore to several principals. In addition, one user can delegate its access to another. User accounts are not only added to groups but can appear in the Global Address List (GAL). There is a difference between mail-enabled users like contacts and the more common, mailbox-enabled users. Only AD objects can be mailbox enabled and have space allocated to them.

- *Mail-enabled AD group*—This recipient type, historically known as a *distribution list (DL)*, is a collection of principals treated as a single administrative unit. A single message, sent to the group object, is automatically distributed to all members of the group. This recipient is a container for users, contacts, other groups, and public folders. It is divided into two subtypes: security groups, used to collect objects that have a common access level to resources, and distribution groups, which are used only for distributing email. Groups can have universal, global, and domain local scopes.

- *Contact*—This recipient type, formerly called a *custom recipient*, is more a placeholder than an actual object whose address redirects messages to other messaging systems. A contact is a mail-enabled user account that does not have authorization to access domain resources. Although contacts do not have mailboxes, you can add contacts to groups. Contacts are a recipient type, so you can add them to the GAL.

- *Public folder*—This recipient type is actually a specialized type of datastore. A wide range of authenticated users can access messages in these containers. This recipient type provides a hierarchical organization to its contents, as well as the ability to synchronize its stores with similar public folders throughout an enterprise. In fact, these contiguous collections of public folders—which appear only in the AD and GAL if they are mail enabled—can form trees. Subfolders in these trees are not mail enabled by default. Exchange 2000 allows you to create an unlimited amount of general-purpose folder trees.

The best way to manage these recipient types is by directly manipulating AD objects. You manage servers primarily by using the System Manager Microsoft Management Console (MMC) snap-in. Recipients are arranged by site in a Recipient container accessible through the AD Users and Computers snap-in. You can rearrange mailboxes, groups, and contacts within organizational units (OUs) without the difficulties you encounter when arranging recipients in legacy Exchange containers due to tight coupling with the physical structure of the organization. The functional and logical arrangement of people has been uncoupled from the boundary constraints found within the physical topologies of the network sites. This newfound flexibility in arranging objects in organizational containers provides better mapping of recipients to the logical setup of a corporate environment than that found in legacy Exchange 5.5. Because members of these units can be changed with associated physical changes, the OUs also provide more expeditious servicing of changing needs within your user population.

Account Management

The paradigm shift mentioned throughout this and other chapters in this book impacts directly on you as an Exchange 2000 administrator in the way you perceive the relationship between you and your user population. Managing users in a messaging and collaborative system is now more a part of administering the NOS than administering Exchange Server. Drawing boundaries between different domains and OUs within them may not be within an Exchange administrator's purview. Nevertheless, these administrative boundaries affect how you can effectively offer Exchange 2000 messaging and collaborative services within an organization. Although the logical, administrative organization does not have to be constrained by the physical network, centralized as opposed to decentralized administrative models will affect how the user population is serviced.

Administrative Models

A *centralized model* manages accounts that typically populate small to medium-sized organizations that are well connected through high-speed network links. This model is based on a legacy single domain model and is, in fact, recommended by Microsoft as the best implementation plan for Windows 2000. A *decentralized model* more likely accommodates large or geographically separated business entities dispersed over wide areas and using connections with a variety of throughput speeds. You can no longer deploy an Exchange messaging system without carefully considering the topology and effectiveness of the underlying NOS. Native Exchange 2000 design amplifies the efficiencies, as well as the dysfunction, of a deployed Windows 2000 installation. Mixed-mode environments provide few advantages when compared with the cost of installation and only encourage migration to a fully enabled native-mode installation.

Administrative Roles

Installing Exchange 2000 extends the structure of objects in native-mode AD to accommodate the additional properties and methods necessary to function in a messaging and collaboration environment. Thus, AD Users and Computers displays additional tabs on each Properties sheet such as Exchange General and Exchange

Features, as well as new methods listed in the context menu you see when you right-click on an object. Figure 8.1 shows the various Properties sheets including advanced features available following the installation of Exchange 2000. The close integration of AD with Exchange has a significant impact on how you manage accounts in the messaging organization. As an administrator, you need to have a sound understanding of how AD is organized and how administrative roles and boundaries are scoped within the enterprise space of your organization.

Administrative roles and boundaries in Exchange 2000 are, thus, just as much a function of native-mode Windows 2000 as the Exchange application itself. Although you can manage recipient objects using legacy Exchange servers in a mixed environment, best practices suggest using AD Users and Computers to administer all aspects of servicing your user population. You will have the greatest success in running an enterprise-wide system if you can use both nested OUs and properly scoped groups to simplify administrative tasks. For example, a user can exercise administrative control over all OUs or a single designated OU. Similarly, domains may have one controller or many controllers that replicate changes made to AD objects. Your organization can have many domain trees that form a forest, introducing new issues of synchronizing information. Special domain controllers called Global Catalog Servers contain full replicas of objects in their own domain but only partial replicas of remote objects that populate other parts of the forest. We have mentioned that the physical placement of servers as well as the hierarchical design of datastores and domain controllers can have subtle but significant effects on the successful and rapid exchange of messages across the enterprise.

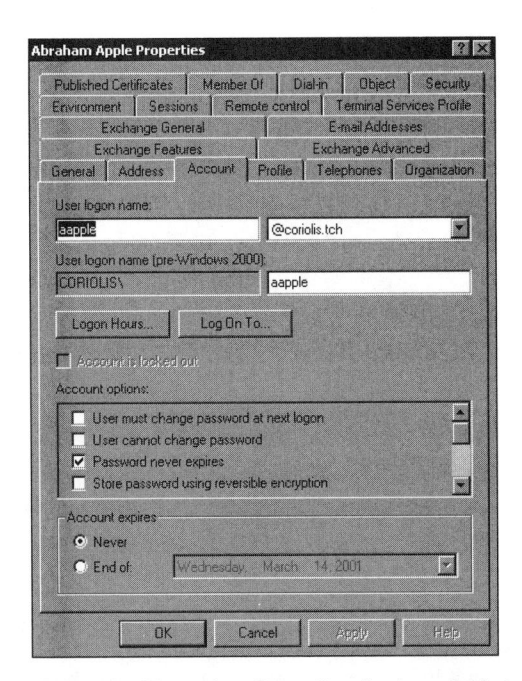

Figure 8.1 The various Properties sheets available to a recipient object.

Access to objects and resources in the form of permissions and the granting of rights to principals also impact the administrative role. Recipient managers can in fact function in a dual capacity as system administrator and Exchange administrator or just as the manager of Exchange objects. Similarly, their responsibilities may extend to the physical side of the installation, where server-side optimization and performance are bound by the clarity in the assignment of Routing Groups and the site topology. These administrators must have appropriate permissions to various aspects of not just the Exchange server but also the AD so that valid AD principals can access their mailbox stores to retrieve messages. You should place Exchange administrators in descriptively named security groups that have adequate permissions to access both AD and Exchange. Best practices suggest that you assign permissions to security groups and not to individuals. This is so that anytime in the future, you can change group memberships quickly and efficiently without introducing possible permission conflicts or errors associated with the broader group designations themselves. Each principal assigned to a group receives the rights and permissions of that group; although individuals may change, group categories are typically a persistent part of the organizational structure.

Mailbox Management

The most common task when you are administering an Exchange system is performed in the right-hand detail pane of the AD Users and Computers MMC snap-in. Right-click on a recipient to display a context menu and select Exchange Tasks. This action launches a wizard that performs most Exchange-related tasks (such as Create Mailbox). In fact, when you install Exchange 2000, several MMC extensions are installed for AD Users and Computers that support, for example, different protocol connectors. When you create a new user in AD Users and Computers, the New User Wizard presents two dialog boxes; a first requesting full name and logon information and a second requesting a password. Exchange 2000 adds a third screen, shown in Figure 8.2, that requests information needed to automatically create a mailbox. The Recipient Update Service (RUS)—which Exchange Server provides at customized intervals—actually creates the objects. Mailboxes are created upon the initial user logon and, in fact, require you to build various destination addresses that support, for example, the Simple Mail Transfer Protocol (SMTP) and X.400 address spaces. RUS processes these addresses and creates a proxy for each address before mailbox-enabled users can successfully gain access to their workspace.

The Exchange Task Wizard performs functions like moving and deleting mailboxes. You can move mailboxes from one location to another when, for example, you replace a server. When you delete a mailbox, all messages contained inside it are permanently destroyed. If, alternatively, you delete a user account, the mailbox itself is marked for deletion and remains on the system until you enable cleanup systems. You can also use the Exchange Task Wizard to assign external email addresses to recipients. Recipients and some descriptive properties are listed in the GAL and are

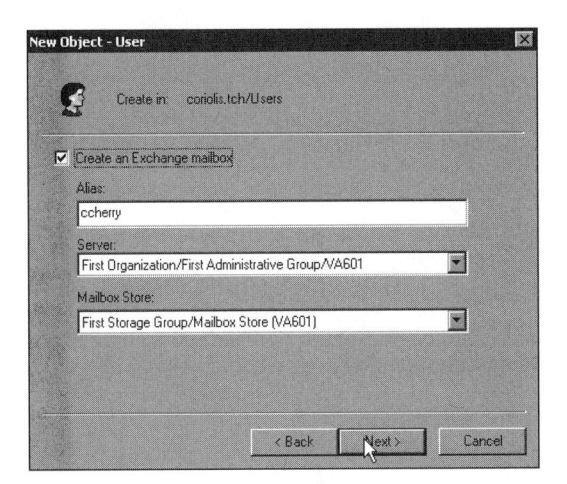

Figure 8.2 How Exchange 2000 modifies the New User Wizard dialog box.

thus readily accessible to other users. Recipients that are only mail enabled rather than mailbox enabled cannot store messages on an Exchange server.

Contact Management

Contacts appear just like mailboxes in the GAL but point to resources outside the Exchange organization. These mail-enabled aliases contain both addresses and rules for handling the exchange of messages. When messages are sent to them, they redirect the message to a foreign messaging system. You can create a contact by selecting New Contact in the Action menu of the AD Users and Computers console. You enter a full name and display name in the available fields just as you would when creating a new user, followed by address options. Figure 8.3 shows the various address options when you click the Modify button that appears on the New Object dialog box for contacts. Contacts are thus mail-enabled users who do not have access to domain resources.

Group Management

Groups have served as an administrative tool for several generations of Microsoft operating systems. They hold users and other groups so that you can assign rights and permissions easily. Just as in legacy NT 4, best practices recommend assigning rights and permissions to groups rather than users. All members of a group typically inherit the attributes of that group. Thus, it is easier to configure a group one time than to configure every person within that group individually. A group can be mail enabled and serve as a DL borrowed from earlier Exchange versions. Groups are also visible in the GAL.

Create groups as you would other recipient objects. One way is to go to the Action menu and select New Group. Enter a group name and select the scope and whether the group type is Security or Distribution, as shown in Figure 8.4. Although you

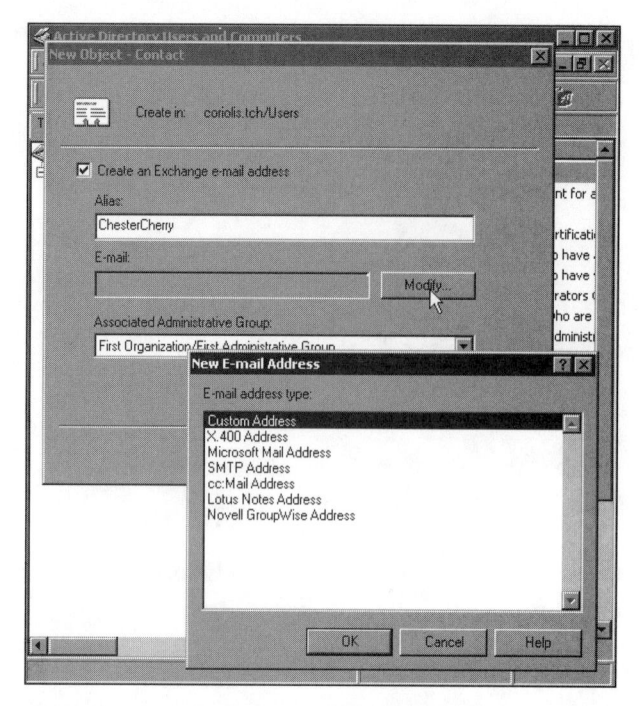

Figure 8.3 The address options available when you are creating a new contact.

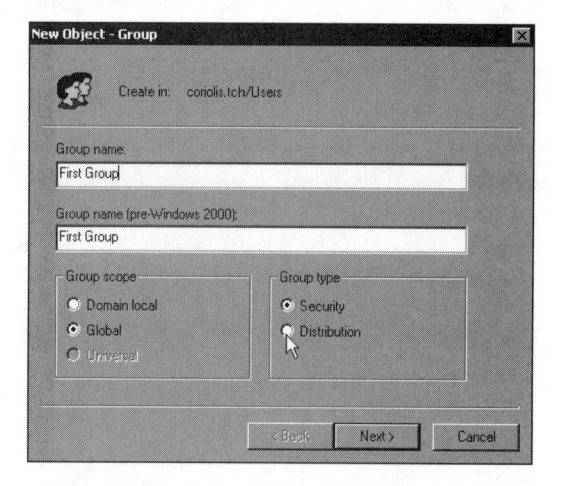

Figure 8.4 Creating a new Exchange 2000 group.

can use a security group to distribute messages, a distribution group does not serve any purpose other than distributing messages. The wizard then prompts for Exchange email address information on a separate screen. Here you can specify the mail address and alias. Distribution groups by definition require an email address. Once the group is created, you add other recipient objects to it.

Recipient Settings

A fundamental design change in Exchange 2000 is the differentiation and specialization of directory services outside the Exchange application. Directory services is a fundamental part of the authentication and authorization security function, so it exists within the NOS whether or not a messaging system is installed. Windows 2000 implements its directory services through AD. When you install Exchange 2000 for the first time, the design or schema of AD is extended. Some of these changes are apparent when you select any recipient object in AD Users and Computers and then choose Properties from the Action menu or right-click on the particular object in the Details window pane on the right side of the dialog box and similarly select Properties from the context menu. By default, recipient properties are displayed on the Exchange General, Exchange Features, and E-Mail Address dialog boxes. In Advanced mode, the Exchange Advanced dialog box is also a selectable Properties sheet. You can also edit many of these attribute settings on a global scale using System Manager.

The next section elaborates on each Properties sheet found under each recipient object's Properties. You typically configure the following recipient settings through System Manager globally. You can, of course, override a system-wide setting by reconfiguring specific options in the specific tabs at the object level. Key settings you need to configure are:

➤ *Email addresses*—Proxy addresses are defined through recipient policies and constructed by RUS for recipients to receive mail. By default, each recipient has one SMTP and one X.400 address. Each recipient has one address, marked in bold, that is considered the primary messaging path that will appear in the From field of all outgoing messages. You cannot delete a primary address. If there is more than one proxy address of the same type, you are prompted to select the intended one.

➤ *Content format*—Any particular SMTP format is configured at the organization-wide level of a messaging system in Internet Message Formats, located in the Global Settings node of System Manager. Depending on corporate objectives, you can configure different formats for specific domains. This is especially useful when your organization has legacy sites that do not necessarily support current protocols like Multipurpose Internet Mail Extensions (MIME). You might, for example, consider changing the order of the display name from its default pattern of <*first name*> <*last name*> using Active Directory Services Interface (ADSI) Edit. Another consideration is the email SMTP format of **alias@mycompany.com**. You can, for example, create an organization-level recipient policy that uses %g (first name),%s (last name), and %i (middle initial) for an email address.

- *Delivery restrictions and options*—Delivery settings define outgoing and incoming message size limitations and universal or restricted access of users to each other. You can also block incoming messages from external sources in Message Delivery under Global Settings in System Manager. Other options allow you to delegate authority to send messages on behalf of a recipient and to automatically forward mail to another recipient in the organization.

- *Storage limits*—A common tool in resource allocation is the administrative ability to manage storage quotas. The administrator can set limits on datastores that will trigger warning messages or block the composition or receipt of messages. Nondelivery Reports (NDRs) are generated and directed to sender, recipient owner, or both. The administrator can set datastore limits and then override these levels for special recipient objects.

- *Protocol settings*—Depending on the network topology, the administrator can enable or specially configure various recipient protocols like Hypertext Transfer Protocol (HTTP), Internet Mail Access Protocol 4 (IMAP4), and Post Office Protocol 3 (POP3).

- *Published information*—The administrator must determine levels of visibility of various recipients in the GAL. It is sometimes expedient to hide recipients so that the general user population does not know the identity or property of that object. Similarly, best practices recommend especially hiding the list of group members so that any one user in the group cannot view the membership when mail is distributed. Members of the Exchange Administrators accounts and Exchange Server accounts do, however, have access to these hidden objects.

User Attributes

Exchange-related attributes are added when the AD schema is extended. Just as in legacy Exchange versions, new user creation automatically triggers creation of a mailbox recipient object. This is because it is assumed that every named object in directory services needs to have access and be accessible to other users in the domain or enterprise through the messaging system. Best practices recommend that one group of administrators handles all user-related activities because the primary way to manage users is through access to the AD. This automatic configuration and control extends across both mailbox- and mail-enabled user objects—users and contacts. Mailbox-enabled users are valid AD objects with server-based storage allocated to them; contacts are mail enabled but do not have access to domain resources. The attributes associated with each show this primary difference. We will discuss the attributes of mailbox-enabled users, the most common recipient object, first. Three tabs are used to enable features for mailbox-enabled recipients like users: General, Organization, and Exchange General.

General Tab

The General tab, shown in Figure 8.5, contains basic user information. The tabs shown in Figure 8.5 and arranged at the top of the Properties sheet provide access to mailbox attributes that you can configure or customize. The first, middle, and last names are automatically concatenated to create a display name that appears in the AD Users and Computers console. Other descriptive information on this panel is published in the GAL.

Organization Tab

The Organization tab, shown in Figure 8.6, provides information that relates to the principal's title, department, company name, an immediate superior, and a list of people who report directly to the specific user. This information is published in the GAL and can be used to create customized address lists.

Exchange General Tab

The Exchange General Tab provides configuration information that affects the user's mailbox. The panel in Figure 8.7 shows a read-only mailbox store name. You can enter an alias or alternative name for the user that systems unable to resolve the full display name can use.

The following three buttons are also available on the Exchange General tab:

➤ *Delivery Restrictions*—You use this dialog box, shown in Figure 8.8, to configure default or maximum outgoing and incoming message sizes in kilobytes.

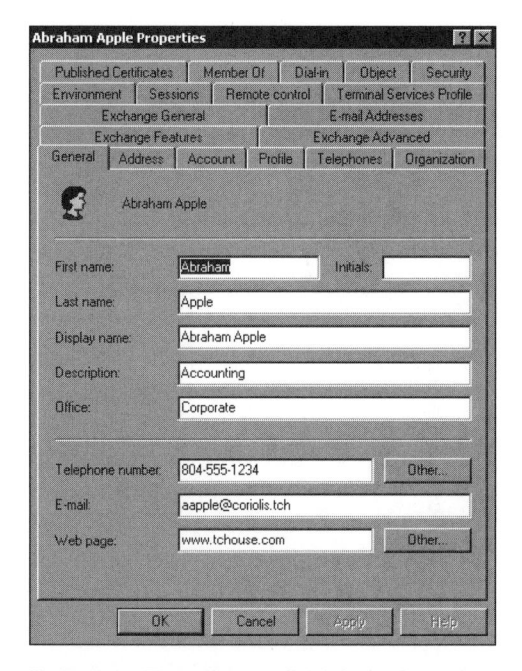

Figure 8.5 The options available in the General tab.

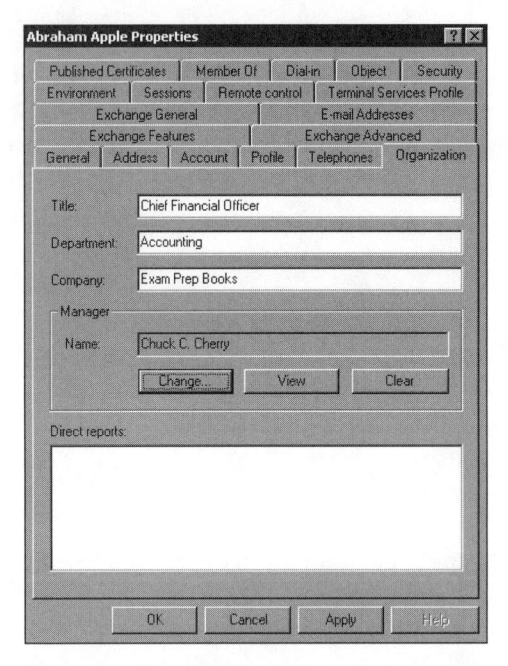

Figure 8.6 The options available in the Organization tab.

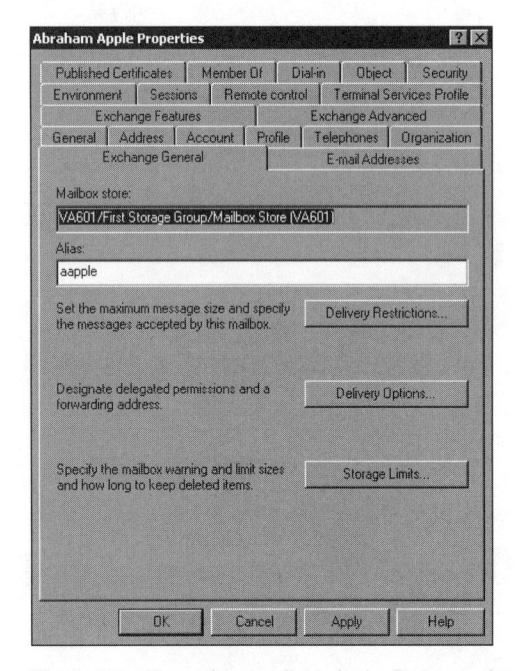

Figure 8.7 The options available in the Exchange General tab.

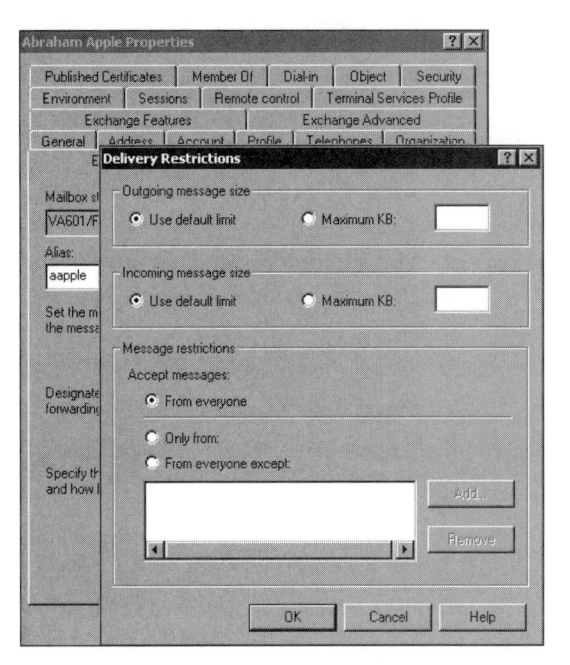

Figure 8.8 The options available in the Delivery Restrictions panel, accessed through the Exchange General tab.

Messages that exceed these limits are dropped by the system and replaced with an NDR message. The lower panel, Message Restrictions, controls incoming messages from everyone, the default condition, from everyone except designated senders, or exclusively from designated senders. You can populate the designated sender list only with recipients listed in the AD.

> *Delivery Options*—This dialog box, shown in Figure 8.9, allows the primary user to delegate access to this mailbox in the form of Send On Behalf permission. You grant this ability to any recipient listed in the AD. Messages sent using this permission appear as though they come from this mailbox but include names of both the primary user and delegated proxy. The middle panel in this dialog box provides space for you to assign a forwarding address for messages sent to this mailbox. Messages can be routed to both the primary and forwarded addresses or directly to the alternative recipient. Finally, you can configure recipient limits such that, by default, a single message can be sent to an unlimited number or some maximum number of recipients.

> *Storage Limits*—This dialog box, shown in Figure 8.10, configures parameters for both storage limits and deleted item retention time. There are three storage limit conditions aside from the mailbox store defaults: Issue Warning At, where you can configure a maximum datastore size in kilobytes; Prohibit Send At, where outgoing messages are rejected at a datastore size in kilobytes; and finally,

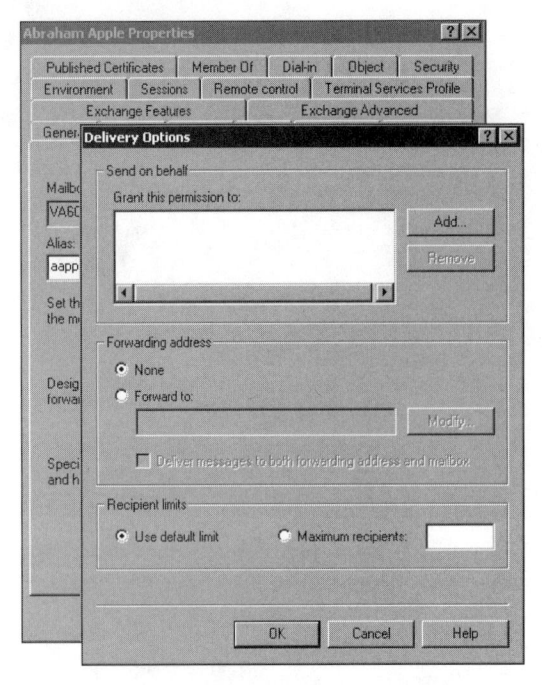

Figure 8.9 The options available in the Delivery Options panel, accessed through the Exchange General tab.

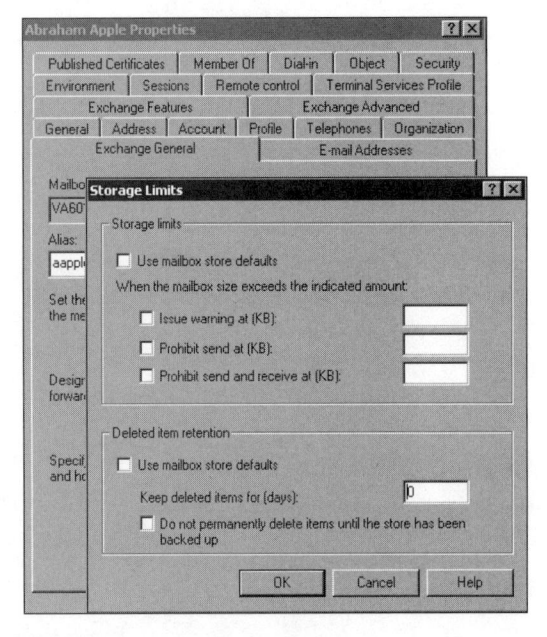

Figure 8.10 The options available in the Storage Limits panel, accessed through the Exchange General tab.

Prohibit Send And Receive At, where both outgoing and incoming messages are rejected at a datastore size in kilobytes. Prohibitions are removed as soon as datastore sizes fall below the defined limits. The calculated size of the datastore includes messages in the Deleted Items folder. NDR messages are generated for all rejected messages. In the lower panel, you can define the maximum retention time for deleted items. You can choose the default value for the entire datastore, specify a limit, or select not to delete items until the store is backed up.

Note: *If you want to remove items from the user's personal datastore, you must delete them from the Deleted Items folder. In Exchange 2000 and in Outlook version 8.03 or later, you can recover these items within the configured limits of the Deleted Item Retention time.*

E-Mail Addresses Tab

The E-Mail Addresses tab, shown in Figure 8.11, provides alternative addressing for other message systems that the administrator can customize. When you click the New button, you see the dialog box shown in Figure 8.11 from which you can add email address types. Four types of alternative address schemes are configured by default: cc:Mail, Microsoft Mail, SMTP, and X.400. A recipient, for example, can have multiple addresses, such as different SMTP addresses like **support@mysite.com** and **webmaster@mysite.com**. Both addresses are routed to the same recipient.

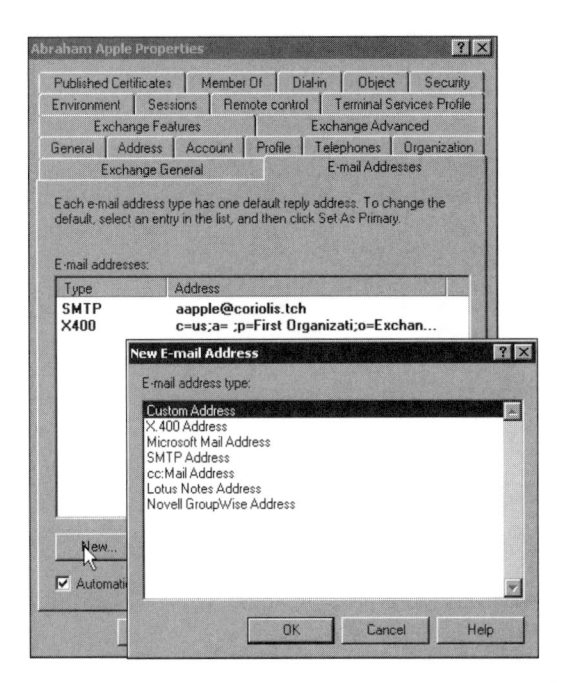

Figure 8.11 The options available when you select New in the E-Mail Addresses tab.

Note: *As with many options, you can configure addressing at the object level in the E-Mail Address tab of the Properties dialog box, as well as globally for the entire site by making configuration changes in the AD using ADSI Edit. Be careful because this is a change in the configuration naming context; it will be replicated to all domain controllers (DCs) in the forest.*

Exchange Features Tab

The Exchange Features tab, shown in Figure 8.12, allows you to activate collaboration features like Instant Messaging (IM) and voice messaging (VM) for the specific recipient. Figure 8.12 shows the properties of a selected feature, IM. As you can see this feature is disabled. You must enable these features before the recipient can use them.

Exchange Advanced Tab

The Exchange Advanced tab, shown in Figure 8.13, shows the simple display name that you use as an alternative to the full display name when you cannot use that name because of, for example, differences in character sets of multiple language versions of the Exchange Server product. You can hide the recipient from Exchange address lists. The recipient performs normal functions but does not appear in the GAL or other customized lists.

Note: *All recipients except public folders are displayed in the GAL.*

Also in the Exchange Advanced tab, you can downgrade high-priority mail bound for X.400 message systems to normal priority. This option ensures that outgoing

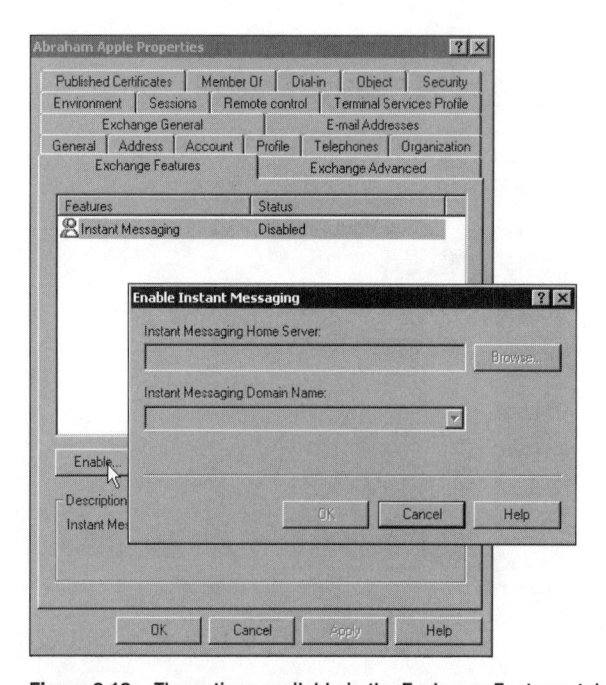

Figure 8.12 The options available in the Exchange Features tab.

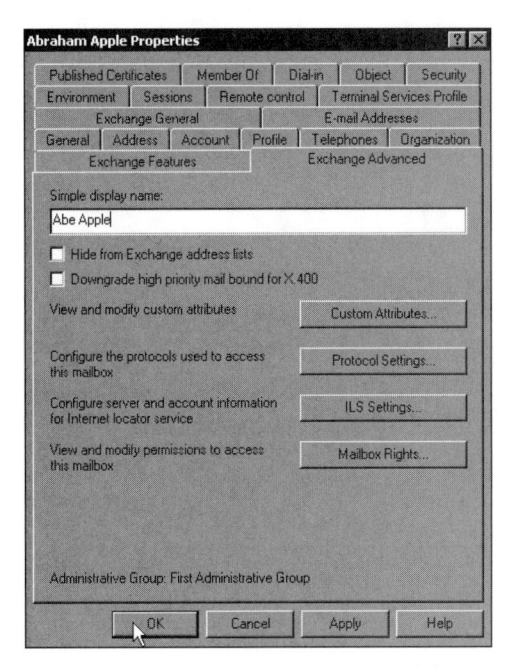

Figure 8.13 The options available in the Exchange Advanced tab.

messages through X.400 connections, which are typically slower than Routing Group or SMTP links since they usually interface with foreign legacy mail systems, do not significantly affect the Exchange system's throughput. Finally, you can access four other subpanels in the Exchange Advanced tab:

➤ *Exchange Custom Attributes*—This dialog box, shown in Figure 8.14, provides 15 user-defined data fields. These fields are published in the GAL and can be used to create customized lists. Figure 8.14 shows how you can define a customized value.

➤ *Protocols*—You can use this dialog box, shown in Figure 8.15, to configure individual Internet protocols such as HTTP, IMAP4, Network News Transfer Protocol (NNTP), and POP3 for the specific recipient if those protocols are installed and functioning. Figure 8.15 shows the Protocol Details for IMAP4 when you click the Settings button on the Protocols dialog box.

➤ *Exchange Internet Locator Service*—You use this dialog box, shown in Figure 8.16, to configure your Internet Locator Service (ILS) account so that other users can contact you through Microsoft NetMeeting, a standalone peer-to-peer service application. This service, which runs outside Exchange 2000, allows group collaboration on documents and audio and video connections, and a shared whiteboard.

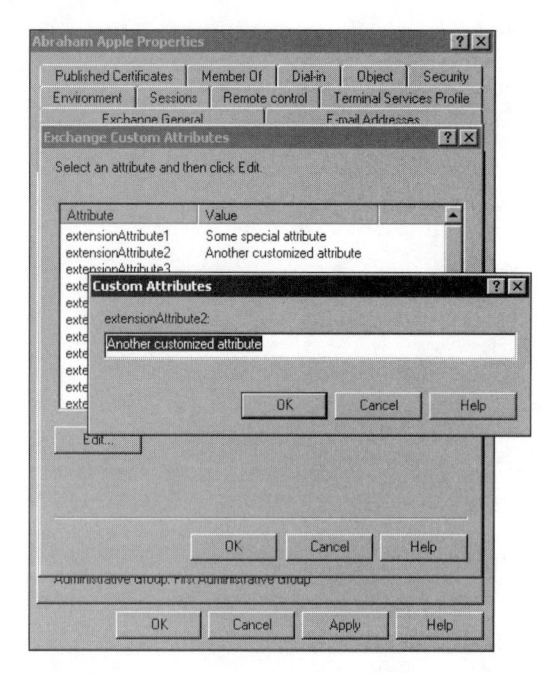

Figure 8.14 The Exchange Custom Attributes dialog box, available from the Exchange Advanced tab.

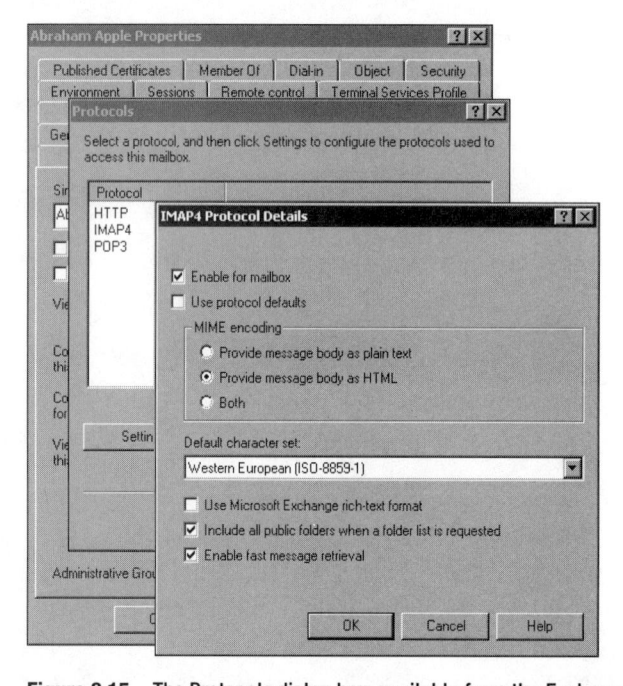

Figure 8.15 The Protocols dialog box, available from the Exchange Advanced tab.

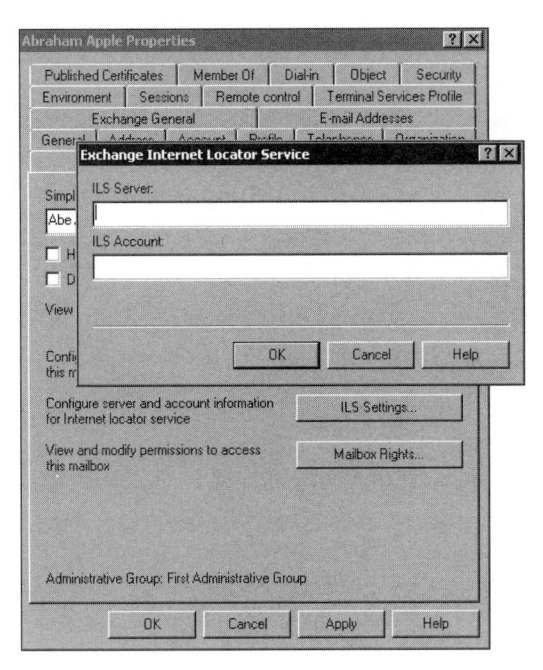

Figure 8.16 The Exchange Internet Locator Service dialog box, available from the Exchange Advanced tab.

➤ *Permissions*—This dialog box, shown in Figure 8.17, provides an access control interface to a specific recipient. Both the Exchange Admins and Exchange Domain Servers groups, in addition to the assigned user, have rights to the recipient object. You can add, allow, or deny various permissions to other users listed in the AD. Some of these access rights include deletion of mailbox storage (assigned to administrators by default), read permissions, change permissions, Take ownership (assigned to administrators by default), mailbox ownership, and Send As (where, unlike with delegation, the sender's real identity is hidden). There is also a primary mailbox owner, which differs from mailbox ownership in its ability to exclude access to the recipient object to all but one owner.

Member Of Tab
The Member Of tab, shown in Figure 8.18, provides the listing of groups to which the user belongs. You can add these groups from AD.

Contact Attributes
Fewer tabs are available on a contact's Properties sheet than on a user's Properties sheet. The General tab allows you to modify aliases, addresses, and delivery restrictions. Since storage resources are not allocated to contact recipient objects, there are no options to configure storage limits or delivery of messages as there are similarly

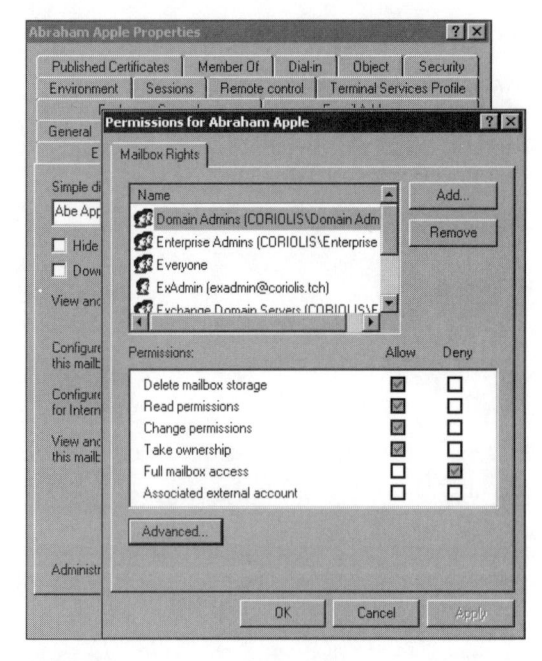

Figure 8.17 The Permissions dialog box, available from the Exchange Advanced tab.

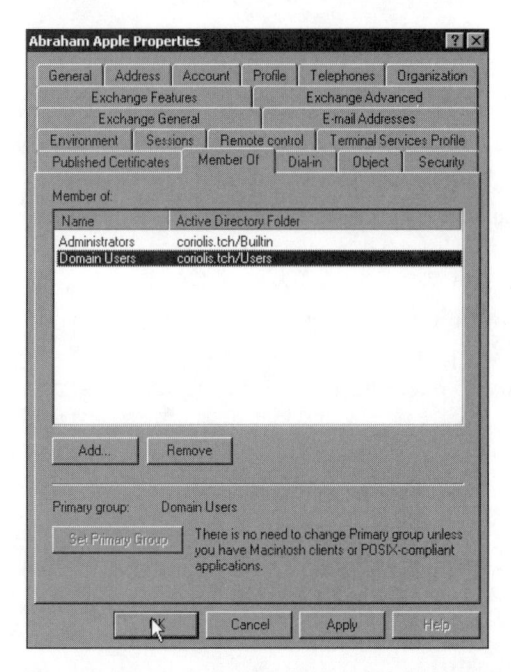

Figure 8.18 The options available in the Member Of tab.

available to mailbox-enabled recipient objects. For the same reason, the Exchange Advanced tab does not allow you to configure protocol settings or mailbox rights.

Group Attributes

You can configure a group the same way you change properties of user mailboxes and contacts. In general, all recipient objects have Properties sheets with similar tabs. Some tabs—such as Profile and Remote Control—however, don't exist on a group object. Three tabs in particular distinguish a group recipient object from other recipient objects: Members, Managed By, and Exchange Advanced.

Members Tab

The Members tab, displayed in Figure 8.19, lists members of a group. The Add button allows an administrator to select additional members from the AD listing. In contrast, the Remove button deletes selected members from the group list.

Managed By Tab

You use the Managed By tab, displayed in Figure 8.20, to assign an owner to the group object. A group owner, by default, is the administrator who creates the object and manages the group's membership. Owners can designate any valid AD user, contact, or group in the GAL. An Exchange client or the Outlook application can modify group membership; AD Users and Computers is not a necessary tool to perform this task. Best practices recommend delegating group ownership and its associated administrative roles to a user or group with immediate concerns for properly managing the specific recipient object.

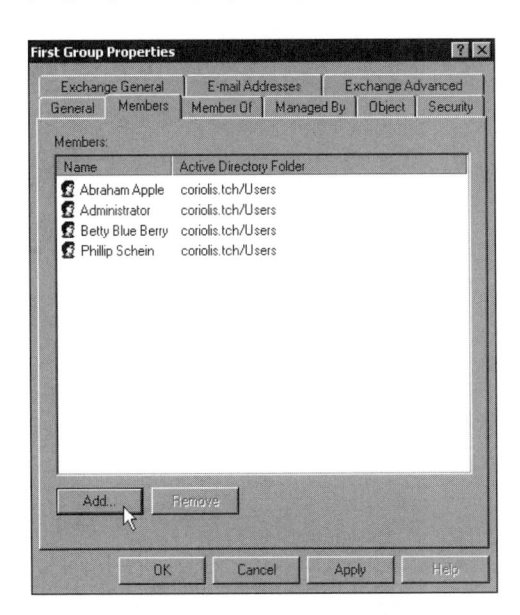

Figure 8.19 The options available in the Members tab of the First Group object.

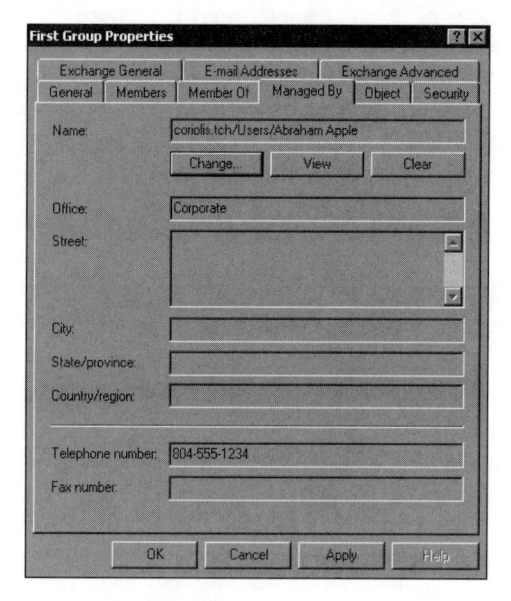

Figure 8.20 The options available in the Managed By tab.

Exchange Advanced Tab

The Exchange Advanced tab, shown in Figure 8.21, as usual, contains several options in addition to a simple display name and Custom Attributes button. Options specific to DLs are:

➤ *Expansion Server*—A single message sent to a group must be expanded so that each member in the group receives a copy of the message. The Message Transfer Agent (MTA) on a single Exchange server provides this expansion service. By default, any server in a site can provide this service, so, typically, the home server of the message sender expands that message for the group. You can, however, designate a specific server with especially large memory resources and high processor speed to perform this function without significantly affecting the machine's overall performance.

➤ *Hide Group From Exchange Address Lists*—This option hides the group from the GAL and all other address lists.

➤ *Send Out-Of-Office Messages To Originator*—Users can configure their Exchange client to automatically reply to incoming messages while they are away from the office. The sender receives automatic responses to messages sent to the specific group object. This option, when set, consumes large amounts of bandwidth by generating unnecessary network traffic in a large organization.

➤ *Send Delivery Reports To Group Owner*—If an owner has been assigned to a group, this option forces a notification message to be sent to that user whenever an error is generated due to nondelivery of a message to a group member.

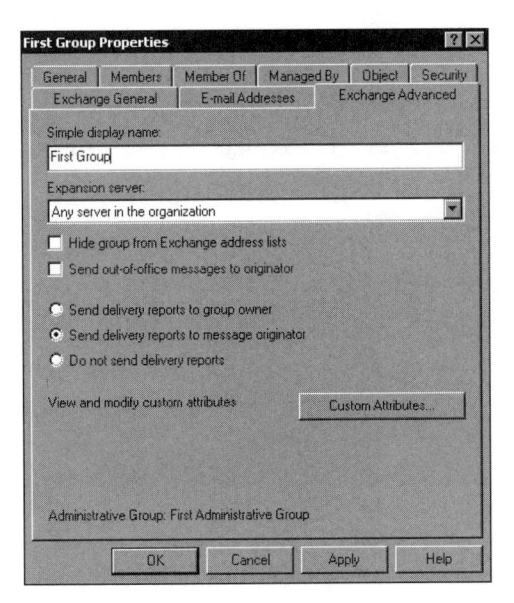

Figure 8.21 The options available in the Exchange Advanced tab.

➤ *Send Delivery Reports To Message Originator*—If an error in delivery occurs, a notification message is sent to the message sender regarding nondelivery.

Address Lists

Address lists transform data, amorphous collections of recipient objects and their attributes, into information that fosters efficient messaging and builds effective collaborative platforms. Messaging clients such as Outlook are especially designed to use these lists of recipients, which simplify sharing common information. The more attributes are used to distinguish one recipient from another, the greater the information value of those attributes and the more easily the search engine can distinguish one object from another during a retrieval process. The organization of common, customized attributes provides a foundation for associative relationships among recipients that might prove useful in advanced Boolean searches for content rather than the legacy matching of similar data objects.

You use address lists to distribute email messages in a relatively simple way; that is, a single message sent to a DL. The ability to send a single message to a recipient object composed of many members saves both administrative overhead and network bandwidth. Another advantage to an address list is the uncoupling of publishing content from managing the subscription listings. RUS maintains list membership based on defined attributes of principal objects located in the AD. The shift from handling lists of recipients to building recipient objects with common attributes is limited only by the extension and use of AD object attributes. Users can access complete directories of recipients or specific subsets based on customized lists.

Customized lists are also useful when you must download offline address lists to resources of modest storage size, such as laptop computers, especially compared to the storage capacity of network servers. The address list makes the download as well as the offline storage a practical alternative to remote connectivity. Exchange 2000 provides greater flexibility in GAL customization and offline address lists than legacy Exchange products, achieving the broadest possible range of connectivity scenarios.

During its initial setup, Exchange 2000 installs several address lists that are available by default to all Exchange users—All Contacts, All Groups, All Users, All Conferencing Resources, Public Folders, and GAL. The list of conferencing resources is part of other address lists features previously available in legacy clients such as Schedule+. Exchange 2000 provides address lists to support functions related to scheduling, lookup locations, and time management. Other software applications, such as Microsoft Project and Teamwork, use the ability to send messages to objects such as printers, rooms, and expensive equipment to automate workflows and simplify the administration of scheduling. However, you cannot change the criteria used to create these default address lists, nor can you rename or delete the lists themselves.

Administrators can create customized lists based on system-defined or user-customized attributes. You can create an address list by right-clicking on, for example, All Address Lists in System Manager and selecting New Address List. From the Create Exchange Address List dialog box, you can select Filter Rules, shown in Figure 8.22. Named attributes, such as Department in a recipient's General tab under Properties, can provide important selection criteria for organizing thousands of recipients into meaningful collections of information. The address lists are actually Lightweight Directory Access Protocol (LDAP) queries that are applied as a filter to current listings of AD recipient objects. Name these address lists in ways that reflect their filter criteria just as you would label stored queries applied to a relational database. Best practices recommend leveraging the hierarchical structure of these lists. You can create a top-level empty address list and assign related lists beneath it. This practice will help you organize lists in a clearly defined manner for both remote administrators in your Enterprise organization and local general users who are accessing these many lists through client software. For example, you can create empty, top-level lists that are organized by region. Within each of these containers, you can create department address lists such as Accounting, Sales, Marketing, and Human Resources. The GAL will now have a clearly defined structure.

Exchange 2000 depends upon two specific management functional areas (SMFAs) in its recipient management services to maintain recipient information. The first is concerned with system objects located in the Configuration container that is published across the forest. Its Properties sheet is shown in Figure 8.23. The second, which physically runs on an Exchange Server, is the RUS, which maintains address lists within each domain. There are multiple instances of RUS, by definition, within a forest of multiple domains because each domain must have at least one RUS.

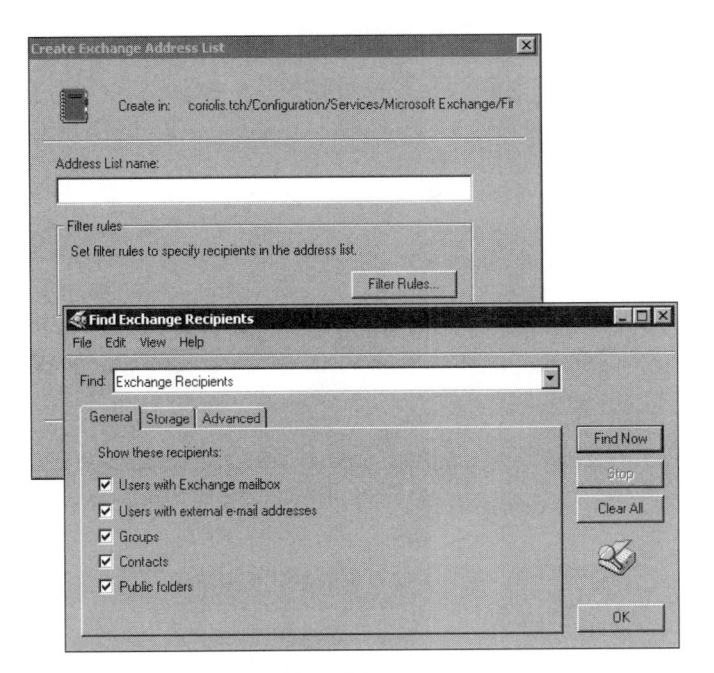

Figure 8.22 Creating an address list.

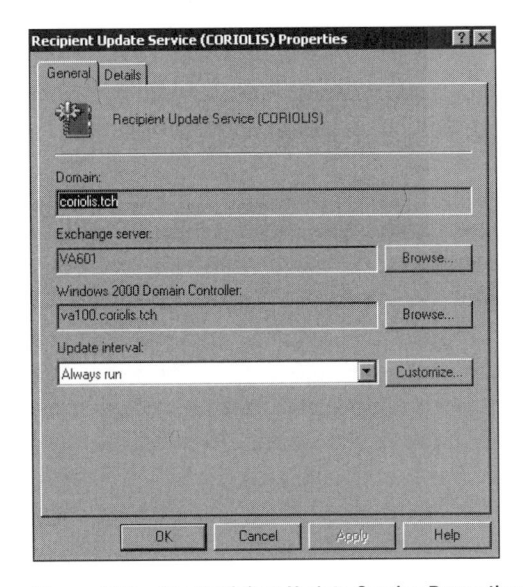

Figure 8.23 The Recipient Update Service Properties dialog box.

However, you can also have multiple instances of RUS within a single domain to administer different recipient policies. You can use a RUS located on a remote Exchange server if you don't have an Exchange server physically located in your domain. A RUS must have Read/Write access to one specific DC. Similarly, multiple instances of RUS within a domain, like other directory-related services such as the Global Catalog (GC) server, can overcome network connectivity issues such as response latencies due to low-speed network connections. As an administrator, you can configure when this service updates changes made in the AD recipient stores since the last service run. If you right-click on the RUS node in System Manager, you can manually force RUS to run an update or actually rebuild all recipient lists and policies. If you want to apply a single policy on demand, you can similarly right-click on Recipient Policies under the Recipients node and select the Apply This Policy Now feature. Best practices recommend avoiding completely processing or rebuilding lists because such operations, depending on the characteristics of the messaging system, can take a significantly longer time and consume far more resources than updating.

Policies

Policies are a major theme when you are administering a Windows 2000 enterprise. With the potential scalability of the platform, it was essential that Microsoft provide an administrative tool that delivered central administration, simplified administration, and granular control of all AD objects without increasing total cost of ownership (TCO). Group Policy is a key component in the implementation of Windows 2000 security services. System and recipient policies play a similar role in an Exchange 2000 organization. We do not discuss system policies in this chapter because we are dealing with the functional side of the Exchange design paradigm.

Policy, the collection of configuration settings applied across a namespace of objects, is the primary method of controlling NOS and application services in an enterprise environment. This tool simplifies administration by globally applying configuration settings. Best practices applied to all levels of an enterprise recommend that you systematically configure the largest administrative unit possible in NOS or application services. As an administrator, you can exercise the option to override global configurations at the object level. Following the pattern in the Exchange 2000 design of uncoupling function from structure, there are two policy categories: system polices that are applied to server objects, and recipient policies that affect the AD objects we have discussed in this chapter. Remember that at the policy level, especially in a native Windows 2000 and Exchange 2000 environment, one subtle change can replicate through an entire forest and dramatically affect service performance.

Default Recipient Policies

Default recipient policies differ in implementation depending on whether an Exchange organization is in a mixed-mode or native-mode environment. In a legacy Exchange 5.5 site, only one default policy can be compatible with legacy site addressing schemes and mailboxes physically located on site servers. In a native Exchange environment, default policy automatically generates, for example, SMTP or X.400 address proxies for all recipients with the domain name. By modifying this policy, which applies to all mail-enabled recipient objects, you can update attributes such as email addressing throughout the entire organization. You can delete or modify alternative address proxies at the object level. You can create additional recipient policies, and through filtering, apply settings to specific object types and individual objects that match a parameter value. Additional policies can either overwrite or be appended to attribute settings as primary values. For example, a policy that sets an addressing scheme would be written to each object as a primary address; current default addresses would be reset as secondary addresses. In the absence of a default policy, the first recipient policy you create is set as the default. Determining a primary policy is based on priority in an environment with multiple policies; default recipient policy has the lowest priority and is applied only in the absence of other policies that affect an object.

New Recipient Policies

To define new policy, you must define the object to which the policy will apply. Best practices recommend testing queries using the **find** command. This common menu-driven tool is actually an LDAP query interface that creates a filter based on AD attributes according to Request for Comments (RFC) 2254. You can create a policy that generates email addresses for users, groups, and other mail-enabled recipient objects like contacts based on specific filter rules. Using the **find** command helps you troubleshoot the range of objects to which a recipient policy will be applied. Once created, the actual LDAP query is displayed in the General tab of the specific recipient policy. Use this policy to, for example, modify an SMTP addressing scheme so that messages using different addressing schemes (such as **sales.mysite.com** and **mysite.com**) will be directed to the same mailbox-enabled recipient. Similarly, you can modify the object addressing scheme so that, for example, it appears as **<first name>.<last name>@support.mysite.com** by providing a template such as **%g.%s@support.mysite.com**. You can make these changes in the E-Mail Address tab under a recipient object's Properties sheet. The address panel from which you can choose alternate E-mail address types is shown in Figure 8.11.

If a recipient object is affected by two or more policies, the highest prioritized policy applies. If you need to create or modify a recipient policy, you can force the changes to be applied immediately rather than wait for RUS to update all valid objects. A new policy is typically applied to all subsequently created objects. When creating such a custom policy in an established organization, remember to manually apply changes to existing objects and select that option to apply the change to existing users when the policy is created.

When you wish to remove a policy, you typically modify specific attributes in existing objects manually. On a global level, there are three ways to remove policies or proxy addressing schemes in an existing organization so that they are no longer applied to recipients:

- *Proxy is disabled*—Clear the option box on an existing proxy object. Any new objects under this particular policy will not receive this proxy address. As noted earlier, you must manually change attributes in existing objects.

- *Proxy is removed*—Deleting the proxy prevents new objects from receiving the addressing scheme. Existing objects will still have the proxy address. Note that you cannot delete an object's primary addressing scheme.

- *Policy is removed*—Deleting a policy object prevents new objects from receiving the addressing scheme but has no effect on existing records. You must manually remove each addressing scheme at the object level. Furthermore, you may need to manually apply a new policy to each orphaned object. This is not a recommended procedure, especially because any one policy may have more widespread effects on a domain or organization than you may have anticipated.

Sometimes it is necessary to perform additional configuration changes to accommodate Web clients. It is recommended that you create a corresponding HTTP virtual directory for each SMTP addressing domain and map the directory to the mailbox datastores for that domain. Mapping this virtual directory provides Exchange 2000 the ability to locate a recipient object's specific datastore. Another recommendation is to add the default SMTP domain as a secondary addressing proxy for all recipients so that this proxy address provides an alternative method for Exchange 2000 to deliver messages.

Maintenance and Support

Unless there is a high security need, best practices suggest using OU naming conventions that have relevance to both local and remote administrators, especially in a multinational enterprise. OUs provide flexibility in mapping logical workflows, administrative scope, and security boundaries. Consider a hierarchical design where top-level nodes relate to the enterprise structure of your business enterprise. You have the additional flexibility of creating more specific subgroups within the larger regional or national OUs as the corporate organization grows.

Basic Management Tools

Exchange 2000 uncouples SMFAs such as managing recipients from structural details and constraints. Thus, unlike legacy Exchange 5.5, which approached management from a single-system viewpoint, Exchange 2000 can be easily divided into server and user management areas. The former, more structural, role of server management is more readily implemented through the MMC snap-in System Manager. You handle users, and other recipients like contacts and groups, by directly manipulating the AD; specifically, the AD Users and Computers console. The Exchange 2000 installation includes both the System Manager and AD Users and Computers .msc console files. Such files are automatically installed only on DCs;

their inclusion in the Exchange installation ensures that an administrator will have access to the AD from any Windows server platform. Other AD management tools that administrators should know how to use include:

➤ *NTDSUTIL*—This utility performs maintenance by managing the operations master roles (formerly FSMO roles) within a forest; it acts directly on the AD datastore ntds.dit. You can also use this tool to manage LDAP policies that control the way the protocol delivers its directory services within the enterprise. For example, the configuration of the memory page size controls how many entries are returned upon submission of an LDAP query. You can set this maxpagesize property through the NTDSUTIL interface.

➤ *ADSI Edit*—This utility performs low-level AD object manipulation. A similar, low-level AD editor is LDP.

➤ *NTBACKUP*—This utility is the standard file-level backup utility that works locally, as well as online, to create copies of AD and other datastores. Always consider using this utility before using any of the others listed here.

➤ *ESENTUTIL*—This utility performs low-level operations on Extensible Storage Engine (ESE) datastores. Both AD and the Exchange Information Store (IS) are ESE databases. This utility can not only compress the stores but also perform minor repairs.

➤ *LDIFDE*—This utility is an LDAP bulk import/export utility that also performs operations based on a text-based script. Conversely, this utility can analyze and export information about AD entries to an output text file. Data is stored in proprietary LDAP Data Interchange Format (LDIF). This utility processes updates that extend the AD schema to accommodate new and enhanced object attribution when the first Exchange 2000 server is installed in the forest.

Although ADSI Edit and LDIFDE are part of the *Windows 2000 Server Resource Kit* and specifically installed in a user-defined directory, the other utilities are standard operating system tools located in the System32 subdirectory under <*systemroot*>.

Chapter Summary

This chapter addressed many of the issues involved in managing the recipients in an Exchange 2000 organization. Here are some particularly significant points to remember:

➤ Mailbox-enabled recipients are equivalent to Exchange 5.5 users; mail-enabled recipients are equivalent to Exchange 5.5 custom recipients.

➤ An administrator must have at least view-only permissions to create mailbox-enabled and mail-enabled recipients. An Exchange View Only Administrator does not have to be a local machine administrator; he or she just needs sufficient permissions to open and view System Manager on a local machine.

➤ RUS processes requests for the creation of mailboxes and creates proxies for each address space associated with a recipient's destination addresses. A newly created user cannot log on to the system and create a physical mailbox until this process is completed.

➤ It is recommended that you configure recipient objects at as global a level as possible, under, for example, Global Settings in System Manager or through system policies rather than at the recipient object level. Minimize wherever possible configuring specific recipient objects.

➤ Both Exchange Server and Exchange Administrator group accounts have access to all hidden objects in the GAL and groups.

➤ Exchange 2000 recipient policy selects objects based on LDAP queries and configures multiple email addresses for them; mixed-mode legacy sites do not support this method of administration.

➤ Every domain must have at least one RUS running on an Exchange 2000 server with a unique connection to a DC.

➤ RUS is used to generate and modify recipient objects by updating recipient policies. The service processes incremental changes on a scheduled basis rather than rebuilding all recipient policies, which would require significantly greater time for all objects to be reconstructed.

➤ New policies, especially applied to existing systems, are not, by default, applied to existing objects under another policy. Most changes to existing objects require a manual reconfiguration. Similarly, deleting a recipient policy or disabling or deleting an addressing proxy does not remove the addressing scheme of existing objects.

➤ It is a good practice to map a virtual directory for each additional SMTP domain defined in a recipient policy.

Review Questions

1. Which of the following objects are valid Exchange 2000 recipient types? [Check all correct answers]

    a. Mailbox-enabled users

    b. Mail-enabled users

    c. Groups

    d. Contacts

    e. Public folders

2. Which Exchange 2000 recipient types correspond to an Exchange 5.5 custom recipient? [Check all correct answers]
   a. Contacts
   b. Mail-enabled users
   c. Groups
   d. Mailbox-enabled users
   e. Public folders

3. Which administrative model is best to use when network connections between sites are slow?
   a. Single master model
   b. Decentralized model
   c. Centralized model
   d. Master domain model

4. What service creates the address proxies just before mailbox creation?
   a. Recipient Upgrade Service, provided by Exchange Server
   b. Recipient User Service, provided by Exchange Server
   c. Recipient Update Service, provided by Exchange Server
   d. Recipient User Service, provided by Active Directory

5. If you delete a user account before deleting the mailbox, what happens to the mailbox?
   a. It is deleted immediately after the user account is deleted and is not recoverable.
   b. It is marked for deletion and can be recovered on the system until a cleanup is performed.
   c. It is marked for deletion and remains on the system but is not recoverable.
   d. None of the above.

6. Mail-enabled users perform what function?
   a. They hold addresses to redirect messages.
   b. They apply rules to determine whether or not to redirect messages.
   c. Answers a and b are correct.
   d. They can store or forward messages based on their configuration.

7. What happens when attributes are applied to a group?
    a. The contents of the group inherit all the attribute changes.
    b. The contents of the group may or may not inherit attribute changes.
    c. The contents of the group inherit the attribute changes, but these changes may be overridden at the object level.
    d. None of the above.

8. Which statement is true?
    a. Security groups can distribute a message but do not act like distribution groups.
    b. Distribution groups can act like security groups and have permissions assigned to them.
    c. Distribution groups can have rules but not rights applied to them.
    d. Distribution groups can have rules applied to them.

9. What information in the General tab of a user's Properties sheet is published in the GAL?
    a. Only the display name appears in the GAL.
    b. All the information in the General tab, including the Web page URL, appears in the GAL.
    c. The first name, initial, last name, display name, description, office, telephone number, and email address appear in the GAL.
    d. None of the above.

10. What information in the Exchange General tab of a user's Properties can be changed? [Check all correct answers]
    a. Mailbox store
    b. Alias
    c. Delivery restrictions
    d. All of the above

11. When outgoing message sizes exceed delivery restrictions in the E-Mail tab, what happens to the messages?
    a. The messages are not sent.
    b. The messages are sent but at a low priority.
    c. A message flashes on the user's console.
    d. None of the above.

12. NDR is a special message generated under what conditions?
    a. When Exchange Server fails to start.
    b. When an incoming or outgoing message triggers a predetermined threshold or condition.
    c. When the network generates a diagnostic report.
    d. Never; the special message is called an NDM.

13. The E-Mail Address tab provides which alternative addresses by default? [Check all correct answers]
    a. Novell GroupWise
    b. Lotus Notes
    c. cc:Mail
    d. Microsoft Mail

14. The option to hide a recipient from the GAL is available in which tab under Properties?
    a. General
    b. Advanced
    c. Exchange Features
    d. None of the above

15. Which Properties tab provides the option to use up to 15 customizable data fields?
    a. Custom Fields
    b. Exchange Advanced
    c. Exchange Features
    d. Profile

16. Which properties would not be accessible from the Properties sheet for a contact? [Check all correct answers]
    a. Storage Limits
    b. Managed By
    c. Exchange General
    d. Exchange Advanced

17. Which properties would not be accessible from the Properties page for a mailbox-enabled group? [Check all correct answers]
    a. Managed By
    b. Object
    c. Profile
    d. None of the above

18. Once created, the LDAP query is accessible through which Properties tab?

    a. It is not displayed in Properties; it must be accessed in other ways.

    b. Exchange Advanced.

    c. Exchange Features.

    d. None of the above.

19. Which is the least preferred way to remove an addressing proxy?

    a. Proxy is disabled.

    b. Proxy is deleted.

    c. Policy is removed.

    d. None of the above; all methods are equal in outcome.

20. What utility specifically performs compression and minor repairs on both the AD and Exchange Information Stores?

    a. LDIFDE

    b. ADSI Edit

    c. ESENTUTIL

    d. NTDSUTIL

Real-World Projects

Nate Ocho is responsible for a 1,250-user messaging system that covers 6 sites over 3 states in the northeast part of the United States. He wants to create a customized recipient policy for three sites in New Jersey. Although system policies affect server-side configuration objects, recipient policies control users, contacts, and groups. Exchange 2000 controls the generation of default email addresses through recipient policy. Nate can perform an administrative task for all users through a simple policy-driven setting. Recipient policies update the object properties stored in the domain-naming context in the AD. The AD replicates these changes as part of directory services.

Project 8.1

To create a recipient policy:

1. In System Manager, right-click on Recipient Policies under the Recipients node.

2. In the context menu, Select New|Recipient Policy.

3. Type a descriptive name in the Name field in the General tab.

4. Click on Modify to display the Find Exchange Recipient dialog box. In the Advanced panel of the Exchange Recipients tab, you can select a recipient

object to which this policy will apply by searching on a field. The various conditions you can use to identify valid recipient objects include matching (Starts With, Ends With, and so on) field values.

5. Create a filter for this particular policy by selecting Add. Select the OK button when you have finished defining all the filter rules.

6. Select the OK button to create the recipient policy.

This policy will be applied the next time RUS is run.

Project 8.2

Nate now wants to confirm when RUS is scheduled to run.

To determine or modify address list update intervals:

1. Start System Manager and select Recipient Update Service after expanding the Recipients node in the Console tree. You should see at least two recipient update service nodes in the right pane of the console window. There will be one enterprise configuration service and one domain service for each domain in the organization.

2. Right-click on the RUS you want to review and select Properties. Note that there is also an option in the context menu to Update Now And Delete.

3. In the Properties sheet, note the service's configuration settings. You can modify the Update Interval by selecting from several options in the drop-down list, including Always Run, Run Every Hour, Run Every 2 Hours, Run Every 4 Hours, Never Run, and Use Custom Schedule.

In addition, you can set folder, message, and AD rights. You can also designate a public folder administrator.

Nate confirms that the service runs every four hours. He decides to leave the settings alone.

CHAPTER NINE

Routing Management

After completing this chapter, you will be able to:

- ✓ Explain from a historical perspective the relationship between X.400 and the development of the Exchange architecture

- ✓ Describe the advantages of remote procedure calls (RPCs) over Simple Mail Transfer Protocol (SMTP)

- ✓ Discuss the benefits of using SMTP rather than the X.400 protocol

- ✓ Compare legacy SMTP services in Exchange 5.5 with those in Exchange 2000

- ✓ Discuss how the legacy SMTP virtual server has changed in Exchange 2000

- ✓ Understand why Multipurpose Internet Mail Extensions (MIME) has enhanced SMTP

- ✓ List some of the features available in Extended SMTP (ESMTP)

- ✓ List the components in the Transport Core

- ✓ Learn how incoming messages are processed

- ✓ Change the status of the Routing Group Master (RGM)

- ✓ Describe characteristics of link state routing

The purpose of this chapter is for you to learn how Exchange routes messages between two Exchange servers and from Exchange Server through a specialized software layer, called a connector, to foreign messaging systems. We begin with a historical perspective that explains the role of X.400 in the design of the legacy Message Transfer Agent (MTA) and the messaging platform in general. We then explain why Simple Mail Transfer Protocol (SMTP) has now become the de facto messaging protocol standard. We next compare the legacy Internet Mail Service (IMS) with the SMTP service now available in Exchange 2000. We describe how Multipurpose Internet Mail Extensions (MIME) and Secure MIME (S/MIME) have broadened the protocol's appeal and how the enhanced features in Extended SMTP (ESMTP) have provided the services necessary for the protocol to assume a dominant position in an enterprise environment. After a brief discussion about collaborative data objects, we discuss the changes in the routing mechanism that Exchange 2000 uses to process messages. we discuss how messages are processed within the Transport Core. We then describe the organizational aspects of Routing Groups and conclude with a detailed discussion of the link state algorithm (LSA) and how you determine routing information for the various connectors.

Historical Perspective

Microsoft has rebuilt message routing in Exchange 2000. The legacy MTA efficiently routed messages through a wide selection of connectors, discussed in greater detail in Chapters 10 and 11. However, Exchange 2000 has significantly increased the speed of the Exchange 5.5 IMS by changing the design of the message model based on remote procedure calls (RPCs) to one based on SMTP. Another change has been the shift away from the internal Directory Service (DS) to standards-based Lightweight Directory Access Protocol (LDAP) and Domain Name System (DNS). The role of the MTA is steadily decreasing in significance as an SMTP-based Transport Core assumes greater responsibility for moving messages across network connections.

Along with this change in routing engine came a change in how messaging routes are determined. The legacy Gateway Address Routing Table (GWART), used to determine message flows in Exchange 5.5, has been replaced by a dynamic routing algorithm in Exchange 2000. This algorithm is based on updated data about the state of network links throughout the messaging organization. Factors that have driven these changes are important to understand because they help predict where the software design will change in future versions.

RPCs and SMTP

Legacy Exchange Server was a messaging platform designed to run in an NT 4 domain model. This architecture was efficient but based on a proprietary design that used Microsoft API (MAPI) and RPCs over what was by necessity a collection of servers that communicated across local area network (LAN) links. RPCs ran efficiently but did not scale well as networks increased in size. The success of RPCs rested on a tight network mesh that supported the overhead traffic that the RPCs generated in acknowledgements. Although a high-capacity bandwidth greater than, for example, 64Kbps existed, the legacy RPC-based site connector, discussed in Chapter 2, was the connectivity method of choice. However, as the service load increases, performance of either X.400 or SMTP provides a more reliable alternative to the site connector. The concept of domains has shifted to the concept of the enterprise, and the dominance of the Internet has seized a chokehold on the design of network architecture. This problem of bandwidth, compounded by the loose connectivity between systems, has forced messaging systems away from RPCs and toward more efficient messaging protocols like SMTP. SMTP is superior to RPCs over low-bandwidth or low-quality connections.

X.400 and SMTP

SMTP, originally defined in Request for Comments (RFC) 821 in 1982, is the primary messaging protocol for both Windows 2000 and Exchange 2000. It has become the de facto messaging protocol on the Internet as well. When Exchange Server 4 was marketed in 1992, however, it was not the messaging protocol of choice. In fact, at the time, members of the networking industry, especially in Europe, championed X.400 as a well-defined messaging specification. SMTP at the time did not accommodate binary attachments, the nontext extensions to any mission-critical operation. Thus, the early designs of the Exchange Server MTA were based on X.400 specifications by default and used RPCs to transmit information. Microsoft has taken the original MTA code acquired from an outside company, based the transport core on this X.400 model, and reworked the engine. This is why the now-legacy X.400 address is still an intimate part of the software and necessary to route messages to Exchange 5.5 mailboxes.

The MTA has been the source of the robust speed with which messages were routed through servers to mailbox destinations. Messages have been quickly accepted from the Store, addresses have been routed, and the messages have been sent to their destinations in a highly efficient fashion. X.400 connectors are better integrated into the MTA than other connectors. They have less overhead in the form of utilized bandwidth when messages are sent between locations. However, this efficiency in design actually limits X.400 outside the defined boundaries of, for example, the NT 4 domain model. Legacy Exchange 5.5 is considered a closed backbone message transfer system because of these very efficient X.400-based connections. All peer MTAs are explicitly defined. In an enterprise or on the Internet, explicit connections are problematic because one server typically doesn't know where to route messages before they are received. Each SMTP server, alternatively, functions as its own MTA, routing messages based on information supplied through outside directory services like DNS.

The expansion in scope of delivery and the need for greater network efficiency has brought about the change in protocol from RPC to SMTP as well as the deployment of more Exchange 2000 servers. Thus, the role of the MTA will be relegated to a support position for legacy X.400 systems. For now, though, the MTA is still responsible for RPC-based communications among Exchange 5.5 servers in mixed-mode organizations. It also supports legacy workflow connections fashioned from the Exchange Development Kit (EDK) and add-on components like fax connectors.

Legacy SMTP Services Compared with Those in Exchange 2000

When you compare legacy Exchange 5.5 SMTP features as provided by the IMS connector with those now available in Exchange 2000, the most significant difference is how SMTP is deployed. Table 9.1 lists some major differences.

SMTP Virtual Servers

A major difference between legacy Exchange 5.5 and Exchange 2000 is the support of SMTP virtual servers, service providers composed of an assortment of physical hardware and software resources that are, in reality, a logical representation rather than a physical server. You can create on the same physical server multiple SMTP virtual servers that can provide separately configured services to different messaging systems. Virtual servers on the same physical server must belong to the same Routing Group. In most cases, however, there is little reason to have more than one. Multiple virtual servers do not improve messaging system throughput because these servers are multithreaded. This means that the server process runs different subfunctions simultaneously and can thus optimize delivery of the protocol services. If, however, you have, for example, different domain names, you can configure a virtual server to support each one. Multiple virtual servers could also accommodate different user groups with specific authentication requirements.

In the legacy product, the SMTP protocol is bound to a specific port and remains associated with it as a single instance or process. For example, TCP port 25 is the

Table 9.1 Comparison of SMTP services in Exchange 5.5 and Exchange 2000.

Exchange 5.5 IMS	Exchange 2000 SMTP Service
Service provided as a separate software layer, IMS connector	Service provided as a layer in both the network operating system (NOS) and Exchange
Partial support for ESMTP	Full support for ESMTP
A single SMTP connection	Multiple SMTP connections as virtual servers (described later in this chapter)
A single SMTP namespace	Each SMTP virtual server supports a separate namespace
Connector dependent on DNS	Virtual servers use either Active Directory (AD) via the Routing Group connector (RGC) or DNS for the SMTP connector
A single set of configurations	Each virtual server has a separate set of configurations
No specific features for event handling	Special event handlers through event sinks

only network port that handles SMTP traffic in an Exchange 5.5 server. Alternatively, Exchange 2000 defines a virtual server as a socket; that is, the combination of both protocol and port. If the SMTP protocol is configured or bound to a range of Internet Protocol (IP) addresses, the virtual server can process messages directed to any of those ports. The default configuration, however, is to have an SMTP virtual server listen for incoming messages on port 25. Thus, each virtual server has a unique configuration and IP address. Each Exchange 2000 server has at least one virtual server with a defined namespace that runs on port 25 and listens to all addresses. This SMTP virtual server is the foundation for both SMTP connectors and RGCs. A way to verify the feature list of an SMTP server is to use the Telnet service to query an SMTP server on port 25 with the **ehlo** command. A list of keywords will be returned.

MIME and S/MIME

The basis of support in X.400 rested in its comprehensive and well-defined specifications. Compared to X.400, SMTP was a limited protocol that transferred only 7-bit ASCII text from server to server. Unfortunately, systems needed greater flexibility than just the transfer of text-based documents. A new protocol, MIME, supported additional binary extensions or attachments to this simple transfer protocol. MIME (RFCs 1341 and 1342) did not replace SMTP; it extended SMTP's functionality and, in fact, gave it the flexibility to eventually dominate all other messaging protocols like X.400.

MIME defines different parts of the message—header, body, and attachment—and includes various header fields to specify content. MIME-encoded messages use a Base64 encoding scheme, which translates the binary data of an attachment into a form that is transferable as a simpler 7-bit transmission. The original specification has been modified to handle secure transmissions of data. S/MIME manages security by using encrypted messages that can be reliably transmitted between SMTP connectors. The encryption process, supported since Exchange 5.5, requires keys to both encode and decode the messages.

ESMTP

In 1995, the command structure of SMTP was extended to accommodate greater interaction between servers. In addition to handling more complex forms of data through MIME and S/MIME, SMTP expanded its functionality with new commands in Extended SMTP (ESMTP) as defined in RFC 1869. In fact, these extensions were formalized with an Internet governing body, the Internet Assigned Number Authority (IANA), to ensure that a target or receiver SMTP server could communicate the extended support features it supported to a source or sender SMTP server. The ability of servers to communicate their protocol feature set to other servers will facilitate future extensions to SMTP or any other messaging protocol.

Exchange 2000 uses new features to provide support for the changes in, for example, the routing algorithm. These new features are part of the ESMTP feature set and include:

- *Pipelining*—This feature (RFC 2197) allows servers to issue instructions without suffering delays due to slow command acknowledgements. The original SMTP specification (RFC 821) monitored transmission flows by passing control acknowledgments from receiver back to sender before issuing subsequent "send" instructions to correct for unreliable systems. Pipelining minimizes the number of acknowledgements exchanged during a transmission, thus reducing excess data transmissions and decreasing network overhead. This overall reduction in network utilization, as well as increased speeds in command transmission, improves client/server communications.

- *8-bit clean*—The SMTP transport must comply with a Transmission Control Protocol (TCP) 8-bit-per-byte transmission channel. It must also comply with the 8-bit MIME specification and new media types as specified in, for example, RFC 1652. As mentioned earlier in this chapter, MIME provides for binary attachments and supports international alphabets, which demand a 128-character set. This feature complies with these specifications so that protocol packets are exchanged across servers without translation or conversion.

- *Delivery Status Notification (DSN)*—This feature provides notification when messages are successfully delivered. Exchange 2000 supports this notification specification as defined in RFCs 1891, 1892, and 1894. This feature is important because it standardizes the forms of notification received through different interfaces like Outlook Express and Outlook 2000. The DSN that is received through the Outlook 2000 interface comes from a system administrator rather than the postmaster and provides an opportunity for the sender to resend the original text of the message.

- *Binary Data Transfer (BDAT) or chunking*—Chunking is the way SMTP message content is divided up and sent as one or more data statements. Each of these statements is terminated with a special control character string that communicates the termination of the unit or chunk of data to the receiving server. When you are dealing with large encoded attachments commonly used in messaging systems, BDAT, a part of chunking, replaces the method of simply chunking data into data units with definable termination strings. BDAT passes an argument that specifies the length of the data stream so that the receiver of the message knows when the transmission is complete without having to interpret the terminating control string when it reaches the receiving server. BDAT is always used between Exchange 2000 servers and is the default when you are directing outbound messages. This ESMTP-provided data chunking is a significant improvement over X.400 transmissions, which use both acknowledgments and other control features.

Basic Windows 2000 SMTP also supports the extended feature set. Some of the enhanced features that are available in both Windows 2000 and Exchange 2000 are:

➤ *VRFY and EXPN*—VRFY as defined in RFC 821 confirms that a message can be delivered to a local recipient. EXPN, another feature defined in RFC 821, expands distribution lists (DLs) into their separate listings of recipients.

➤ *ETRN*—This feature, defined in RFC 1985, extends the **turn** command, which reverses sender and receiver roles. The **turn** command enables a client to download a message without any validation of the sender. ETRN offers a way for a client to request a download for a specific message queue. The host of the message queue can determine whether or not to honor the request.

Other commands available with ESMTP include:

➤ **auth** *(RFC 2554)*—Provides support for the negotiation of some authentication methods between a client and a server from which the client requests services.

➤ **size** *(RFC 1870)*—Measures message size and a server's maximum size limit.

➤ **tls** *(RFC 2487)*—Provides Transport Layer Security (TLS) for secure transmissions necessary when using smart cards as part of a user authentication protocol.

The ESMTP feature set can be accessed from the command line using a Telnet client. Typing "EHLO" will confirm availability of the ESMTP features and return the list of commands shown in Figure 9.1.

SMTP Services

The Exchange 2000 platform, as well as Windows 2000, uses SMTP for its fundamental messaging services rather than remote procedure calls. Both the NOS and Exchange 2000 depend on SMTP for server-to-server communications. It is a basic

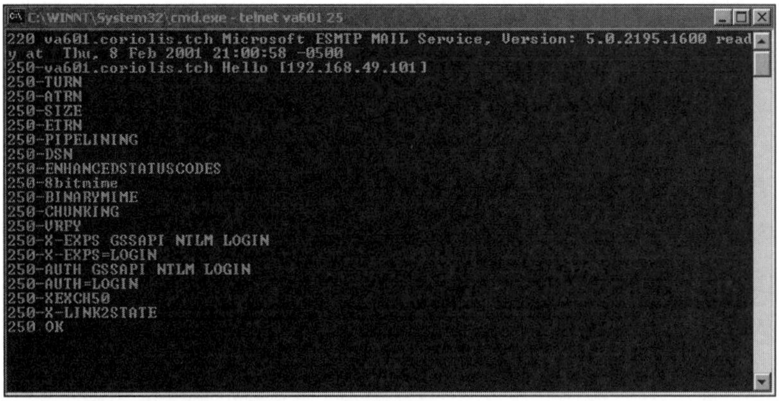

Figure 9.1 The ESMTP feature set.

server-to-server messaging system without support for recipient objects or mailboxes. Though the mail protocol is found in all Windows 2000 software products, many features of SMTP are disabled in the Professional version. The importance of the protocol's relationship with IIS, which manages Internet protocols in the NOS layer, explains why the Exchange 2000 System Attendant must regularly synchronize the AD with the IIS metabase, even though Exchange interfaces directly with both the RGC and SMTP connectors.

Exchange 2000 has partitioned its supporting services; its configuration information is stored in the AD and its protocol services are provided by IIS in the NOS. You therefore need to regularly update the IIS metabase with regard to any changes in configuration located in the AD. The installation of Exchange upgrades CDO 2 to CDO for Exchange 3 (CDOEX) and provides the base SMTP with the additional features mentioned in the "ESMTP" section earlier in this chapter. The significant difference between CDO 2 and CDOEX is that the latter includes management of mailboxes. It is significant that the base SMTP service layer is upgraded rather than replaced when you install Exchange. This upgrade means that the NOS and Exchange depend upon the SMTP service layer but through different (though complementary) mechanisms. Much like the application of old service packages on legacy operating systems, the reinstallation of the base Windows 2000 SMTP service layer—and, for example, CDO 2—requires you to reinstall dependent application software like Exchange Server and its upgraded CDOEX.

When you install Windows 2000, an SMTP service is installed as a part of the now-integrated IIS 5. The mail transport protocol forms the communication foundation for the NOS. The base SMTP service supports the ESMTP command set. The installation of Exchange 2000 upgrades this base SMTP service layer. The installation adds functionality to the NOS, including the advanced queuing (AQ) engine, the message categorization agent, the Installable File System (IFS) Store driver, and commands that support the LSA (**x-link2state**). These components are all part of the Exchange Transport Core.

Transport Core

The Transport Core is the center of message routing in Exchange 2000. It is composed of four major components:

- *Advanced Queuing (AQ)*—This component handles inbound and outbound messages. It supports the grouping of messages according to final destination in what are called *domain-level queues*. Alternatively, messages can be grouped according to the next drop point or hop through which they will travel on their way to a final destination. The latter grouping is called a *link queue*. The AQ component also generates delivery service notifications.

- *Categorizer*—This component reads message headers and analyzes properties to correctly process messages. Although a limited version of this component is built into Windows 2000 for the expansion of mail-enabled security and distribution groups, the Exchange version has additional features such as monitoring or managing mailbox quotas, mailbox restrictions, connector restrictions, and mailbox storage locations. This topic is covered in more detail later in this chapter.

➤ *Exchange Store Driver*—This driver is the interface between the AQ component and NT File System (NTFS). Windows 2000 ships with a basic Store driver that processes inbound SMTP messages. The Exchange version includes Exchange Installable File System (EXIFS) support, which provides the AQ with direct access to messages in Store.exe.

➤ *Routing Engine (RE)*—This component replaces the Relative ID (RID) master and GWART, which determined routing paths in a legacy Exchange 5.5 organization. The RE makes adjustments in the routing of messages based on updated reports on the state of the network. The eventual route of any one message is based on size, sender, and message priority in combination with assigned costs of links and the current state of those links. Exchange 2000 uses a modified version of Dijkstra's algorithm that Microsoft calls an LSA to provide the link state updates between SMTP servers. This particular algorithm is a commonly used method to determine the shortest distance between two points. This protocol has been proposed as a formal RFC to the Internet Engineering Task Force (IETF).

Transport events extend the function of the Transport Core, whereas protocol events extend the SMTP protocol itself. Base SMTP services are upgraded rather than replaced when you install Exchange Server on a Windows 2000 platform. New features added or enhanced during the installation of Exchange include AQ, enhanced routing, and new command verbs that enable link state routing updates. The upgrade of CDO 2—built into IIS in all Windows 2000 platforms (though, as mentioned earlier in this chapter, simplified in Windows Professional)—to CDO 3 for Exchange (CDOEX) provides the operating system with knowledge of mailboxes. With the addition of Exchange 2000, the relationship of SMTP to Windows 2000 changes; now, the protocol depends more on the messaging platform. Thus, at least for now, you must accompany a reinstallation of SMTP from the Windows 2000 system side for whatever reason with a reinstallation of the Exchange Server software, too.

How Components Work Together

The Transport Core is the portal through which both inbound and outbound pass during message system exchanges. The following steps describe the traffic flow:

1. Messages enter the Transport Core and in all cases are placed in the Inbound Queue. Message sources are numerous. For example:

- Messages from other Exchange servers travel on SMTP services and are processed through the EXIFS often as NTFS files.
- Exchange 5.5 messages are transferred by the MTA through RPCs.
- MAPI messages originating from mailboxes are processed through the Store.
- Internet-based clients, using Internet Message Access Protocol 4 (IMAP4) or Post Office Protocol 3 (POP3), pass messages via SMTP through IIS and then through EXIFS into a streaming file.
- Web Distributed Authoring and Versioning (WebDAV) clients access EXIFS directly and thus, like MAPI, use a direct connection to the Store to generate WebDAV messages.

2. From the Inbound Queue, the Advanced Queuing engine uses the Categorizer to process these inbound messages, checking for various properties like mailbox quotas and routing permissions. Distributions lists are expanded here too.

3. Once processed, messages are placed in the Categorized Message Queue while the Transport Core process checks for triggered routing events such as filtering words. Here, the body and any attachments can be scanned and, if necessary, returned to the sender. A query against the Domain Mapping and Configuration Table tells the Transport Core process to route the message for local delivery or to an SMTP virtual server.

4. Messages intended for local delivery and not for an SMTP virtual server are placed in a local delivery queue.

5. From there, the message is either passed to the Exchange Store driver or to the MTA. Messages allocated for SMTP virtual servers are redirected to destination queues that handle different domains.

6. The Connector Manager handles SMTP server links from these destination queues. If the routing engine determines that a hub server is unavailable, the Connector Manager reroutes the message via another hub. All outbound mail is dispatched using SMTP.

Two queues handle routed messages. Domain queues are maintained on a per-domain basis. Notice the queue for messages to ny.coriolis.tch in Figure 9.2. Alternatively, messages are stored in link queues and maintained for routes mapped on a hop-by-hop basis. Queuing by destination is a departure from how legacy IMS connectors worked, where all messages were held in a single outbound queue. Problems in the delivery to any one domain blocked deliver to all other destinations. Multiple available routes between Routing Groups (discussed later in this chapter) are an important enhancement in reliability of delivery. Furthermore, the new routing engine attempts to find alternative paths among the other available routes, further reducing the possibility of downtime.

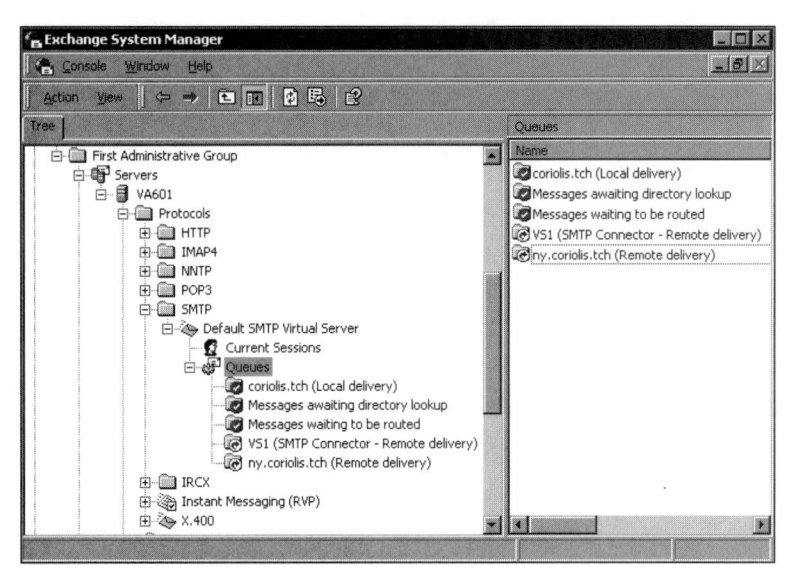

Figure 9.2 The queues that handle routed messages.

Processing Incoming Messages

A major design achievement is the growing number of ways messages can arrive at an Exchange 2000 server. In summary, however, they all come together at the message Categorizer in the Transport Core. This is the path in which messages flow:

1. The most common way messages can arrive at an Exchange 2000 server is probably across TCP port 25 from other SMTP servers acting as clients. This port is monitored by IIS, and, when the new message arrives, the SMTP process generates a process thread to handle it.

2. At some point here, a protocol event may fire even before the message is fully received to confirm its acceptability or it may reject it before the message transaction is done.

3. A Store driver event is fired when the transaction is completed.

4. The Windows NTFS Store driver is used here (rather than EXIFS) to increase overall consistency within the system because the Exchange executable files are located on the same drive as the mail drop directory. If the drive fails, the Exchange server, as well as delivery of mail to the mail drop directory, fails. Messages are redirected or returned rather than partially processed. Furthermore, directing messages into an NTFS folder rather than the Store uncouples the initial receipt of the mail from messaging processing and delivery.

5. The new message is placed in an OnSubmission queue, which also fires an event. If an error in delivery of the package is detected at this point, a nondelivery notification message can be sent back to the sender, or the message can

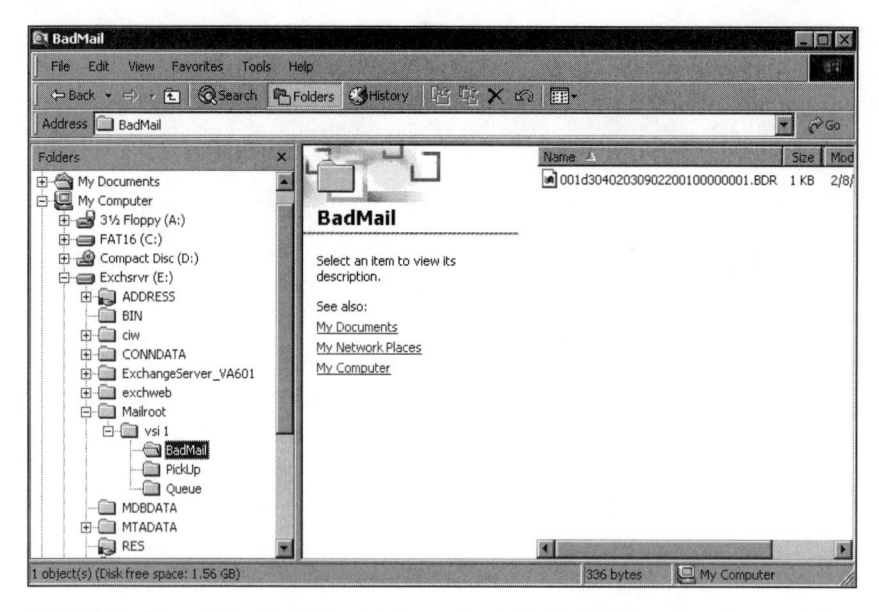

Figure 9.3 An example of a message being redirected to BadMail because of a processing error.

be redirected to the BadMail directory, shown in Figure 9.3. In fact, any error encountered while the incoming SMTP message is being processed forces the message to be removed from the queue and placed in the BadMail directory.

6. Messages destined for local delivery are inserted into the Store.

By the way, outgoing messages are handled the same way, except that IIS-provided protocol services read them out from the Store via EXIFS. Figure 9.4 shows a nondelivery notification message sent back to an OWA client. Notice how the cursor has turned into a hand, indicating that the actual message can be read through a hyperlink to the file itself.

MAPI Messages

MAPI clients do not use IIS to connect to the Store. Once a message is accepted, through, for example, the MTA, the Store notifies the Transport Core Store driver that the message is waiting in a special SendQ folder. The Transport Core Store driver processes the content of the message and submits it to the AQ. MAPI messages sent between Exchange 2000 servers using SMTP are translated into Transport Neutral Encapsulated Format (TNEF), which can rapidly be returned to MAPI properties and content. Messages are formed from RFC 822-compliant headers and an application-specific body. Exchange 2000 servers use SMTP, so you need to convert TNEF to MIME before TNEF is transported across a network (unless it's transported as binary content). Messages directed outside an organization using the MIME can thus end up 25 to 30 percent larger than TNEF encoded messages. This is a general criticism of SMTP as compared to X.400. However,

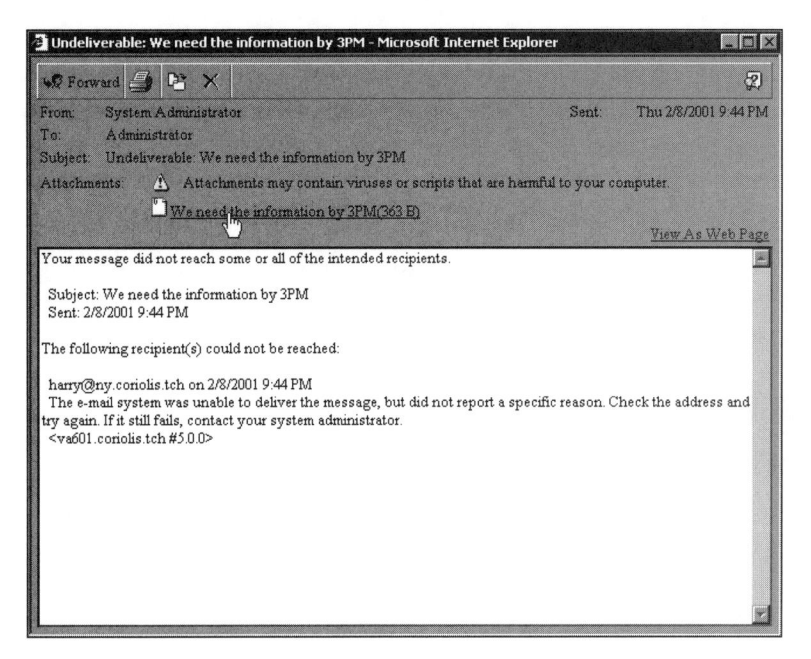

Figure 9.4 An example of a nondeliverable report returned to an OWA client.

even though the X.400 protocol adds less overhead to packets than SMTP, the actual method of SMTP communication is simpler and thus compensates for these rather complicated conversions of data.

Just like in the legacy Exchange 5.5 process, the MTA handles X.400 messages in Exchange 2000. After a message is accepted, the MTA places it into an MTA-Out folder located within the Store. The Store driver moves it eventually to the AQ and the pre-Categorizer queue. Foreign connectors maintain their own MTA-Out folder. The incoming message, once accepted, is processed the same way as X.400 messages.

Categorization

The AQ component processes all inbound messages and places them in the pre-Categorizer queue. The Categorizer then performs several tests on each message, including:

➤ *Address resolution*—The sender and receiver addresses are applied to AD stores for name resolution. Upon resolution of the receiver address, Categorizer determines restrictions such as a recipient mailbox quota or other limitations on either sender or receiver. If the recipient is a DL, the list is expanded. If the receiver cannot be resolved, the recipient is marked as unknown.

➤ *Message format*—The message format and properties are checked to ensure the message can be rendered properly.

▶ *Request for multiple copies*—Some messages might require special handling because different recipients require different versions of the same message (such as when one receiver in a list of recipients can be found but another is not listed in an address book). In some cases, one recipient may have a local mailbox whereas another in the same organization must receive the message through delivery across other MTAs in the organization.

After categorization, messages are directed to a prerouting queue where AQ determines how to redirect the messages for the final phase of routing through this particular Exchange server.

Outbound Mail

Recipients with mailboxes are identified in the AD of an Exchange 2000 server. If an attribute in their AD entry includes the distinguished name of the mailbox store, the message for the recipient is delivered at the location to which that path points. Thus, an examination of a routing table on a neighboring server immediately determines if a mailbox destination exists on that contiguously linked server, or in other words, within one *hop*. This kind of information is stored in a next-hop identifier. A mailbox stored on the same server is made locally; the message is placed on the local delivery queue. Messages stored in queues remain in the Store or NTFS directory until they are actually transmitted, typically in a subdirectory named queue under mailroot. Delivery to other Exchange 2000 servers in the same Routing Group or over an RGC are placed in an appropriate outbound queue—either link or domain—until actually dispatched.

Exchange 2000 maintains accurate information about link states by replicating configuration information along with link state information under the control of the AD. If a domain is unreachable, the SMTP service registers a warning in the system event log. Link queues are transient and appear only when in use, whereas the messages waiting directory lookup queue and the messages waiting to be routed queue are visible. When messages are found in the first queue, the Categorizer has not yet processed them. Messages in the second queue, however, may indicate that the Categorizer cannot retrieve routing information from the routing tables in memory. In addition to confirming that a Global Catalog (GC) server is available to the Exchange server, review the application event log to confirm that the system is running properly.

Routing Information in the AD and DNS

The RE needs to know the IP address of a mail server to route mail. The advantage of SMTP is that it relies on the mail exchange (MX) DNS record in the DNS server to locate mail servers for handling domain mail traffic. If MX records are unavailable, a mail server uses an address (A) DNS record, which specifies a host address, to locate mail servers in the domain. The AD can also look up a mail server if it is located inside an organization. The AD can provide the RE with the target mail server's Globally Unique Identifier (GUID), which is a 128-bit number assigned to every object in the AD. The RE can determine a host name by using the GUID. The host name, in turn, is resolved to an IP address just as it would be if you used an MX record. Given the importance of mail service, these redundant methods of identifying and routing messages add a layer of fault tolerance to the process of locating a mail server if routing information is somehow incorrect or missing.

Routing Groups

A Routing Group is nothing more than an administrative container. Unlike Exchange Server 5.5 sites, a Routing Group can be created before a server joins them in both native and mixed modes. It provides an organization structure separate from the actual deployment of physical servers. When deciding to create a new Routing Group, consider the following factors:

- Availability of stable links
- Availability of bandwidth
- Need to schedule transmissions between servers
- Transmission of large messages
- Need to restrict connectivity among users

The issues of availability of stable links and bandwidth, rather than issues of user policy, will typically have the greater influence as you decide whether a new Routing Group will benefit your organization. Routing Groups are very similar to the legacy Exchange 5.5 concept of a site. Within a site, peer machines link to each other across high-speed connections, forming a topological mesh across which messages are transferred with significant delay. These messages are transferred via SMTP except when legacy servers are also part of the Routing Group in a mixed-mode configuration. As explained earlier in this chapter, when legacy servers are part of an Exchange organization, the MTA transfers messages using the RPC protocol.

Topologies

You can use one of several strategies to link Routing Groups in a supportable and flexible message routing topology. Some routing configurations, shown in Figure 9.5, include:

- Hub and spoke
- Full mesh
- Backbone layered

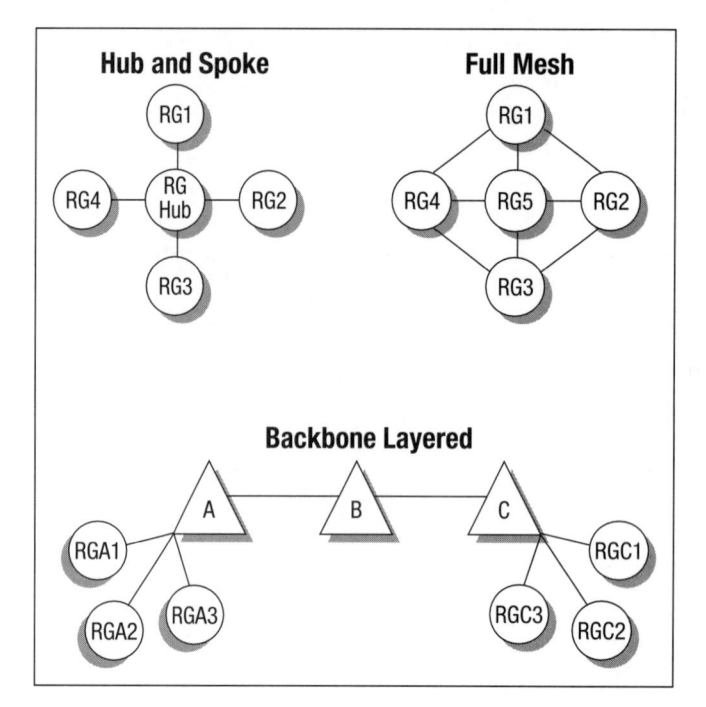

Figure 9.5 Examples of routing topologies.

The hub and spoke configuration is the most common of these three routing topologies. Traffic from the wide area network (WAN) and the Internet passes through the hub and thus facilitates monitoring and troubleshooting. The hub as a central point through which all traffic flows can be used to more rapidly triangulate a fault in the network as compared with, for example, a full mesh scheme. The primary disadvantages of this configuration include inability to communicate in the event of a hub failure (because there is only one central passage of traffic), and the necessity for packets to add additional "hops" through the hub on the way to other Routing Groups.

The full mesh scheme, an example of which is the Internet, provides the greatest fault tolerance of all three routing topologies because connections are built between all Routing Groups. Messages are routed according to the least number of hops from their source to their final destination. Unfortunately, the number of connections in a full mesh topology grows rapidly as compared to the other two topologies according to the following formula:

number of connectors required = total number of Routing Groups less 1

The main advantage of the mesh topology is the minimum number of hops between Routing Groups as compared, for example, to the additional hop always required through the hub in a hub and spoke configuration. Exchange 2000 uses the link state table (LST) to great advantage, especially in this topology, because the

LST is designed to track and adjust traffic in response to dynamic changes in flow conditions across all linkages as a whole rather than through a minimal number of avenues, such as through a hub or backbone. Thus, in configurations with few Routing Groups, full mesh may be the most effective topology to deploy.

In larger, more geographically separate Exchange organizations stretching across regions of limited bandwidth connections, the backbone layered topology is the most advantageous of the three topologies. Although several hops are required due to the overhead of the backbone itself, this configuration is the only efficient way for islands of high bandwidth to connect across long distances. Several disadvantages include the longer latencies involved in passing through the backbone, the vulnerability of the backbone itself to failure, and the need to support many more connections than either the hub-and-spoke or the mesh configuration would require. Nevertheless, the backbone can offer an economy of scale in terms of the speed and efficiency of the backbone traffic itself, which can compensate for latencies experienced at the local source and the remote destination.

Creating a Routing Group

To create a Routing Group, in the Routing Groups container, select New | Routing Group in the context menu, as shown in Figure 9.6. The Routing Groups container is basically another container within the Configuration container for the organization of various Exchange objects. After you create a group, you can add servers by, for example, clicking on and dragging the icon in System Manager to the Members folder in the new Routing Group.

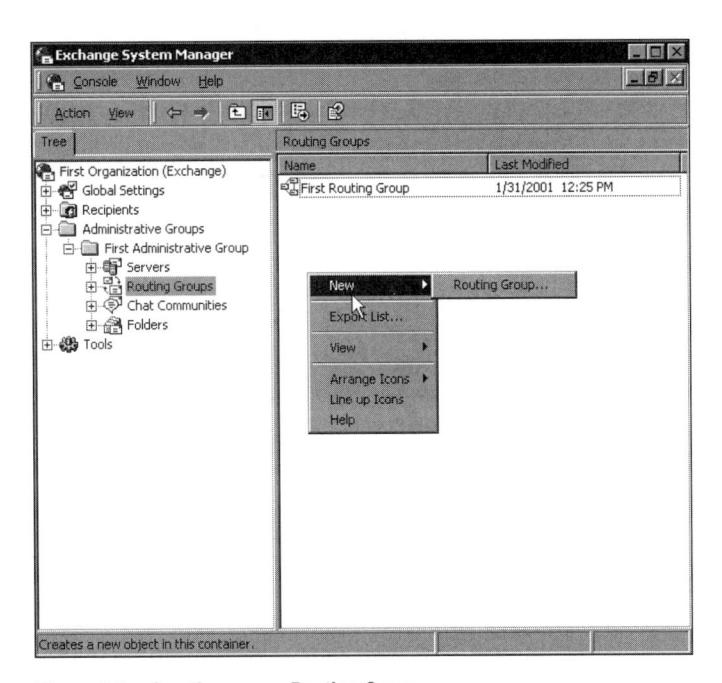

Figure 9.6 Creating a new Routing Group.

Assigning Servers

Although assigning servers is generally easier to use than the legacy site concept, doing so has several restrictions. For example, if a server is a bridgehead for a connector, its position within the organization is fixed; you cannot move this machine to a different Routing Group. Connectors and Routing Groups provide an organizational structure to routing tables; major changes in their relationship to other servers within this structure can have disastrous effects. To move such a server, it is necessary to first delete connectors and thus release the candidate machine from any relationship with other machines in the organization.

The Role of the Routing Group Master (RGM)

The first server (or person for that matter) that creates some kind of administrative unit in Windows 2000 tends to inherit some special roles with respect to that unit. In the most fundamental way, the first person who installs the operating system is the administrator or super user. Similarly, the first server in each Routing Group is defined as the Routing Group Master (RGM). This server assumes this role by default. An administrator, of course, can change it. The most important task this role performs is maintaining the link state table (LST). This important information is automatically shared among all servers in a Routing Group. Updates of linkages between servers are relayed to this RGM, which, in turn, broadcasts information to all members of the Routing Group. All members of the group in fact keep their own copy of this LST in memory. The RGM acts as a contact point for the entire group. As shown in Figure 9.7, changing the RGM role is as simple as selecting in

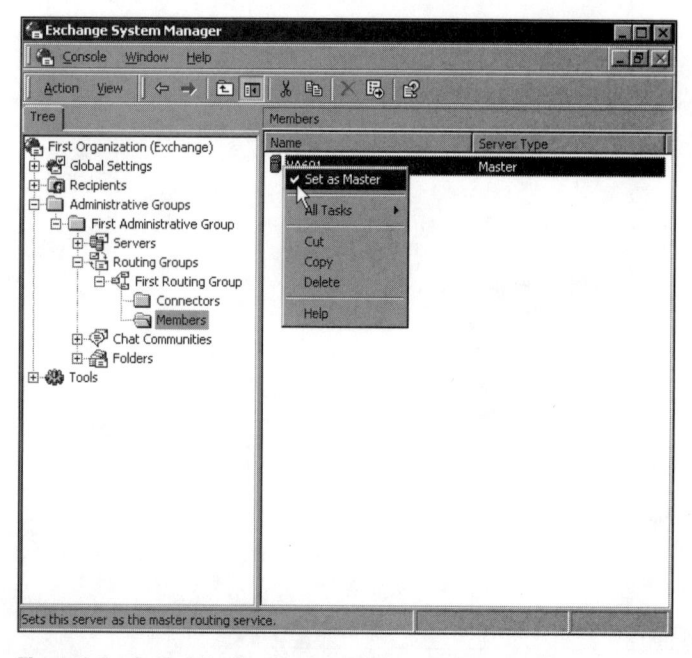

Figure 9.7 Setting the Routing Group Master feature.

System Manager, in the Routing Group of choice, under the Members node, the specific server to which you want to assign this role and, in its context menu, selecting the Set As Master feature. If, for whatever reason, an RGM is unavailable, all routing is performed based on the more recent copy of the LST replicated to all members of the Routing Group.

All updates for the Routing Group are recorded in the RGM. It is important to consider this when moving or migrating servers. The most important aspect in your planning when adding a Routing Group or moving a server between groups is allowing sufficient time for changes to replicate through the enterprise and among RGMs. If that Master server fails, the remaining servers in the Routing Group may use routing information that is no longer current. Best practices recommend that you track which servers are Masters among your Routing Groups. In the event you are unable to set this role in the server's own context menu, you can use ADSIEDIT to manually assign the RGM role. The Master server updates all the other servers in the Routing Group across TCP port 691.

Link State Routing

The major difference between legacy Exchange 5.5 and Exchange 2000 is that the legacy version used GWART to manage routes that messages can take to reach a final destination. GWART, however, did not track moment-by-moment changes in these routes; it recorded cumulative costs and next-hop information. Exchange 2000 uses LSA instead of GWART. In fact, Exchange 2000 sends updated routing information between servers in two ways:

➤ *Between Routing Groups*—The LST is passed between bridgehead servers to the RGM. SMTP over TCP port 25 is used instead of the LSA protocol over port 691 if either the RGC or the SMTP connector is used. The **ehlo** command is sent to confirm that the server is using ESMTP as soon as a connection is started.

➤ *Within a Routing Group*—The LST sends updates between bridgehead servers using the routing server across the assigned TCP port 691. The information is passed using a proprietary Microsoft protocol, LSA. Based on these updates, the RGM broadcasts changes to all the servers in the Routing Group.

The link state protocol greatly improves upon the more static mapping used in the legacy product. As mentioned earlier in this chapter, it operates over TCP port 691 within the Routing Group. The RGM is the primary beneficiary of this information and, as mentioned in the "The Role of the Routing Group Master (RGM)" section earlier in this chapter, acts as a central administrative focus for the group. Alternatively, bridgehead servers exchange the information over TCP port 25.

The LSA itself forms the foundation for the Open Shortest Path First (OSPF) protocol, which routers today use. The LSA propagates the routing conditions almost in realtime. Thus:

- Exchange servers make the best routing decisions because they determine the route before the message is directed downstream.

- Message loss is eliminated because alternative route information is propagated to each server.

- Message looping is eliminated.

Networks that combine link state information and build collaborative tables for routing are called *directory-enabled networks*.

Link state information is especially important when an organization has multiple Routing Groups with multiple paths among groups. The RGM maintains the link state information and shares it with other RGMs in other Routing Groups. The link state information includes only information in a binary form; that is, whether the link is up or down. This information is held in memory instead of being written to disk. If the RGM fails or needs to reboot, this information needs to be replicated from other RGMs in the organization. Routing information, connector information, and costs are actually stored in the AD naming partition, and as mentioned during the discussion of DNS records, the link state protocol references each connector by its GUID.

Finally, if an RGM goes offline, a new master is not automatically determined through an election or promotion process. A new RGM must be manually configured to refresh the link state information that each server in the group is referencing.

Chapter Summary

This chapter addressed issues involved in message flow and routing in an Exchange 2000 server. Here are some particularly significant points to remember:

- Exchange 2000 has improved performance by shifting from RPCs to SMTP. The role of the MTA is being gradually diminished with migration of servers to native mode. At this point, the MTA supports legacy X.400 connections and expands DLs.

- Performance of either X.400 or SMTP has always delivered better performance over low-bandwidth or low-quality connections than RPC-based message exchanges. With the increasing looseness of connectivity, SMTP, with its flexibility in targeting servers, has gained a dominant position among messaging protocols.

- The most significant difference between legacy IMS and Exchange SMTP is the use of the SMTP virtual server configured as a socket; that is, the combination of protocol bound to a specific TCP port. The system can now support multiple servers at any one time.

- MIME extends the support for data types to include additional binary extensions or attachments. S/MIME manages security by using encrypted messages that can be readily communicated across SMTP connections.

- The ESMTP feature set includes features such as pipelining and BDAT, which decreases overhead and increases the transmission of data across the SMTP connection.

- Exchange 2000 has partitioned its supporting services such that configuration information is stored in the AD, and the management of protocol services has been delegated to Internet Information Services, which is now part of the NOS.

- Parts of SMTP, a fundamental network protocol for Windows 2000, are actually upgraded during the installation of Exchange 2000. For example, Exchange upgrades CDO v2 to CDOEX (version 3) and enhances the base SMTP feature set, such as adding support for advanced queuing, message categorization, the installation file system Store driver, and feature support for the link state algorithm.

- Transport events extend the function of the Transport Core, whereas protocol events extend the SMTP protocol itself. The protocol events include a greater dependency on Exchange once it is installed in a system rather than on the NOS.

- The queuing messages for routing according to destination is a significant change from legacy Exchange 5.5, where all messages were held in a common queue. This change in design minimizes loss of services due to some problem with delivery of a single message.

- MAPI clients do not use IIS to connect to the Exchange Store. MAPI messages sent between Exchange servers are translated into Transport Neutral Encapsulated Format (TNEF), which is designed to rapidly render property and content information. The message sent via SMTP must be translated into MIME from the TNEF and adds significant overhead, especially when messages are transported across a network. Despite the addition to overhead when using SMTP rather than X.400, SMTP is simpler to deploy and thus compensates for more complicated conversions of data.

- The Advanced Queue component of the Transport Core processes all inbound messages and places them in the pre-Categorizer queue. The Categorizer then performs several functions, including address resolution, confirmation of properly rendered message formats, and special handling requirements. After categorization, messages are directed to final routing.

- Mailbox-enabled recipients are identified in the AD; the distinguished name of their mailbox store is used for delivery.

➤ Link queues are transient and appear only when in use while the Message Waiting Directory Lookup queue and the Message Waiting To Be Routed queue are always present.

➤ Exchange 2000 maintains information about link states by replicating configuration information, along with link state information, through the AD.

➤ SMTP has an advantage over other connectors like X.400 because it relies on the mail exchange (MX) DNS record to locate other mail servers.

➤ The first server in each Routing Group is defined as the Routing Group Master (RGM) responsible for maintaining the link state table. Updates of linkage conditions are thus relayed to this RGM.

➤ A major difference between Exchange 5.5 and Exchange 2000 is that whereas the legacy version used Gateway Address Routing Table (GWART), which was managed by the MTA to determine routes, Exchange 2000 uses a link state algorithm (LSA) instead. LSA improves on the static mapping of the GWART; it propagates routing conditions almost in realtime and eliminates message loss because alternative routes are immediately propagated to the mail server. Networks that combine this link-state information are called directory-enabled networks.

Review Questions

1. Which statement is false?

    a. MAPI and RPCs work efficiently in a single-domain model.

    b. X.400 and SMTP work efficiently under native-mode Exchange 2000.

    c. RPC and SMTP work efficiently under native-mode Exchange 2000.

    d. SMTP works efficiently under both legacy and Exchange 2000.

2. Which factors significantly limit the use of RPCs in an enterprise environment? [Check all correct answers]

    a. Low-speed connectivity

    b. Loosely defined connections

    c. High-capacity bandwidth

    d. Low-quality connections

3. Which factor significantly limits the usefulness of X.400 in an enterprise environment?

    a. Low-speed connectivity

    b. Loosely defined connections

    c. High-capacity bandwidth

    d. Low-quality connections

4. What is the most significant feature MIME provides when combined with SMTP?
   a. Security
   b. Increased throughput
   c. More complex data types
   d. Extended feature set

5. What effect do pipelining and BDAT have on throughput of X.400 communications?
   a. Network overhead is reduced.
   b. Because of chunking, X.400 is as fast as SMTP in mixed mode but not native mode.
   c. In native mode, X.400 connectors are faster than SMTP connectors.
   d. None of the above.

6. Which statement is true?
   a. Windows 2000 supports the extended SMTP feature set.
   b. ETRN reverses the message flow between sender and receiver.
   c. VRFY checks the integrity of an SMTP message.
   d. Answers a and c.

7. What is a major difference between IMS in Exchange 5.5 and SMTP in Exchange 2000?
   a. The use of sockets
   b. The use of a virtual server
   c. ESMTP
   d. Answers b and c

8. What is an important practice when you are working with Exchange 2000 and SMTP?
   a. Configure IIS properly.
   b. Reload Exchange 2000 after reinstalling SMTP services.
   c. There is none; SMTP is automatically installed with Exchange 2000 Server.
   d. There is none; SMTP is automatically installed with Windows 2000.

9. What components are part of the Transport Core? [Check all correct answers]
   a. AD
   b. AQ
   c. Categorizer
   d. RE

10. What two queues handle outbound messages? [Check all correct answers]
    a. Domain queue
    b. Link queue
    c. Outbound queue
    d. Message queue

11. How is performance affected by the addition of a second SMTP virtual server?
    a. There is a decrease in throughput.
    b. There is an increase in capacity.
    c. There is an increase in throughput.
    d. There is no change in throughput.

12. What happens to a MAPI message when it is sent over SMTP connections? [Check all correct answers]
    a. Nothing.
    b. It is converted to SMTP.
    c. It is converted to TNEF.
    d. It may be converted to MIME.

13. In Exchange 2000 native mode, what is the MTA used for?
    a. The expansion of DLLs
    b. Processing of RPCs from Exchange 5.5 servers in the organization
    c. X.400 connectors
    d. Answers a and c

14. What functions does the Categorizer perform? [Check all correct answers]
    a. Address resolution
    b. Verification of message formats
    c. Handling of multiple message copies
    d. Word indexing

15. Where is information about mailbox recipients stored?
    a. In the Exchange data stores
    b. In AD directory services
    c. In routing tables
    d. In EXIFS

16. Which of the following handles replication of Exchange link states?
    a. System Attendant Services
    b. Directory Services
    c. Link State Table Services
    d. AD Sites and Services

17. Where can an Exchange server find information that will help locate other nearby mail servers? [Check all correct answers]
    a. AD
    b. M DNS record
    c. A DNS record
    d. C DNS record

18. What is the most important role for an RGM?
    a. Routing messages in a Routing Group
    b. Broadcasting the LST to members of the Routing Group
    c. Running the LSA for members of the Routing Group
    d. Coordinating information with bridgehead servers

19. What is the procedure to change an RGM in a Routing Group?
    a. Select the Set As Master feature in the context menu of the specific computer under the Member node.
    b. Change an attribute in the Routing Group Properties sheet.
    c. You cannot change this role.
    d. You must change a property in AD Users and Computers.

20. How does Exchange 2000 send link state information among servers?
    a. Within a Routing Group, via IIS on the RGM.
    b. If an SMTP connector is used, SMTP is used.
    c. Answers a and b are correct.
    d. None of the above.

Real-World Projects

Jessie Nein is having problems with an Exchange server. On one server, he wants to queue the mail for remote triggered delivery. Jessie suspects that ESMTP is not configured correctly. He first wants to test the feature set on the server and if necessary turn on the ESMTP features. The name of the server he wants to check is SS1.

Project 9.1
To create a Telnet session to determine whether ESMTP is supported:

1. Open the Start menu and select Run. In the the Run dialog box, type "CMD".
2. At the command prompt, type "TELNET SS1 25". The server responds with a text line that reads "READY" and the system date.
3. At the command prompt, type "EHLO" and wait for a response. If the server supports the **ehlo** command, it returns a list of keywords.
4. At the command prompt, type "HELO". The server SS1 returns a list of keywords.

Jessie does not get an ESMTP list of keywords when he types "EHLO". He concludes that this server is running the basic SMTP protocol rather than the Extended SMTP. He must now enable ESMTP.

Project 9.2
To enable ESMTP support:

1. Start System Manager.
2. In Connectors, right-click on the specific SMTP connector and select Properties.
3. Click on the Advanced tab.
4. To enable ESMTP, check the top option box that says Send HELO Instead Of EHLO. (To disable ESMTP, simply uncheck that option.)
5. Click on OK.

Jessie has turned ESMTP on. He repeats the Telnet session and ESMTP test, and confirms that the extended features are now enabled. He now wants to configure remote triggering of mail delivery.

Project 9.3
To request ETRN/turn from a different server:

1. Start System Manager.
2. In Connectors, right-click on the specific SMTP connector and select Properties.
3. Click on the Advanced tab.
4. To configure remote triggered message delivery, select the middle option on the Properties sheet labeled Request ETRN/TURN When Sending Messages.
5. Click on OK.

Jessie has confirmed that the server is using ESMTP and has now configured a feature that will allow the triggered delivery of queued messages.

CHAPTER TEN

Interoperability

After completing this chapter, you will be able to:

✓ Explain general concepts that relate to both legacy and Exchange 2000 connectors

✓ Outline steps for the installation of any Exchange 2000 mail connector

✓ Compare legacy Exchange connectors to their current-version counterparts

✓ Define the major characteristics and properties of Routing Group connectors (RGCs), Simple Mail Transfer Protocol (SMTP) connectors, and X.400 connectors

✓ Use legacy connector models to explain current and future connector features

✓ Compare Exchange 5.5 and Exchange 2000 transport protocols

✓ Understand the differences and similarities of various connectors

✓ Understand issues involved in connecting to third-party mail systems like cc:Mail, Lotus Notes, and GroupWise

✓ List the components of the Microsoft (MS) Mail for PC connector

✓ Use MS Mail as a model for many third-party shared-file messaging systems

✓ Outline steps involved in directory synchronization

The purpose of this chapter is for you to learn how Exchange can coexist peacefully with other systems, such as Lotus cc:Mail, Lotus Notes, Novell GroupWise, and Microsoft (MS) Mail. With respect to Exchange 2000, these systems are considered "foreign systems."

Although best practices and common sense would suggest using one messaging system, it is not unusual to see some corporate environments using three or four such systems. By "messaging system," we mean an electronic mail system, as well as other complementary services such as faxing, voice over Internet Protocol (IP), chat capabilities, and Instant Messaging (IM). Some of these services, such as IM, have been imported into the work environment because of user awareness made possible through access to services such as America Online and its Instant Messenger feature. Alternatively, companies deploy different systems because they want to upgrade to a new messaging platform in stages. Whether you are upgrading from a legacy system or are simply trying to establish communications with another company, you need to make two different mail systems communicate or interoperate with each other. You need software components called *connectors* to communicate with separate systems.

Exchange 2000 Connectors

The message routing architecture of Exchange 5.5 was based on the concept of sites. All servers in a given site required a type of permanent, high-bandwidth connection. In Exchange 2000 Server, we now talk about different but related concepts—Routing Groups, Administrative Groups, and domains. Servers are now placed in Routing Groups, which are collections of "well-connected" Exchange servers that have permanent, full-time connections. Routing Groups typically match a physical network topology, whereas Administrative Groups are based on the logical or administrative design of a corporation in terms of, for example, Marketing, Accounting, and Human Resource groupings. Domains are an operating system concept. Whether dealing with legacy NT 4 or Windows 2000, a domain remains the basic unit of administration and the key boundary within which security policies are applied. The other important point to remember is that connectivity in a Routing Group is based on Simple Mail Transfer Protocol (SMTP).

By default, Routing Groups are hidden from Exchange System Manager because small organizations typically do not require more than the one Routing Group created during installation. It would be necessary to create additional Routing Groups if reliable connectivity to new servers added to an existing organization were unavailable, if workflows of an organization were divided among locations and divisions, or if delegation of authority required you to partition business units. Communication among Routing Groups is accomplished through a software component called a *connector*. *Intersite communication* describes two Exchange sites exchanging messaging information with each other. A connector is installed on each server to allow information to pass between the sites.

The biggest difference among connectors in Exchange 2000 is in the definition of *sites*. In legacy Exchange, a site was a physical unit; in Exchange 2000, it is uncoupled from any physical definition or limitation and is applied as a logical construct. The Message Transfer Agent (MTA) in legacy systems is responsible for transferring all information in multiple-site environments. This is also the basic design structure of Exchange 2000. Messaging connectors have existed primarily to allow communications between an Exchange site and, for example, a foreign mail system like Novell GroupWise. Since the introduction of Windows for Workgroups, Microsoft has always designed its software products to provide built-in network interoperability; Exchange Server has been similarly designed to provide not just reliability, scalability, and extensibility, but also service interoperability. Two examples of software providing network interoperability included the Internet Mail connector and the X.400 connector, discussed later in this chapter. Both connectors translate Exchange messages into common messaging formats that a wide range of foreign mail systems can then route to their own messaging clients.

SMTP does not replace MTA. An enhanced MTA works with both Exchange Server 5.5 and Exchange Server 2000. SMTP is used to connect to most mail systems, however, so you use the MTA to typically connect to legacy external X.400 mail systems. SMTP is the native protocol for Exchange Server 2000. It has really replaced the remote procedure call (RPC) protocol used in previous versions of Exchange, and it has distinct advantages over RPC. For example, SMTP is more tolerant of low-bandwidth situations than RPC; it requires less bandwidth. In other words, you can deploy servers to Routing Groups, which, in the past, could not support an Exchange 5.5 site because of connectivity issues. Another advantage is that you can now more easily manage Routing Groups independent of Administrative Groups. You do not need to keep servers within site boundaries, as was necessary in Exchange 5.5.

Installing Connectors

Many connectors are not a necessary part of the default Exchange installation. Often, deployment plans schedule installation and testing of core services before adding the complexity of software that will interoperate with other site locations or organizations. To install a connector, perform the following steps:

1. Using your Exchange CD-ROM, launch the Setup Wizard and enter the preliminary data information regarding licensing.

2. In the Action column for Microsoft Exchange 2000, select Custom. If the product has already been installed, select Change.

3. Select Microsoft Exchange Messaging And Collaboration Services and click on the Install button.

4. Select the respective connector and click on Install.

5. Click on the Next button to confirm your selection, and complete the wizard operation by clicking on OK.

Basic Connector Properties

Every connector historically has basic properties needed for proper configuration; examples of these are address space and cost. A specially designated server, the bridgehead server, uses this cost information to transfer messages.

Connector Address Space

An *address space* is a specification associated with a connector or gateway that identifies a message protocol class. Often, it is a subset of a complete address. This is nothing more than a logical path you defined so that an MTA could determine how messages could be delivered to their final destination using a specific connector. Each connector is basically a path through which messages flow among Routing Groups. An address space has to have at least one address space definition to operate correctly. The format of this address space depends on whatever format is native to the foreign mail system. For example, if you send a message to an X.400 network, you reference an X.400 address space to guarantee proper delivery of the message. Every X.400 address takes the form g=Bill;s=Smith;p=acme;c=uk, and so on (these parameters and others are discussed later in this chapter). It is important that one connector include multiple address space entries, with each address space targeted to a different foreign messaging system. You configure an X.400 connector to send messages to a remote Internet Mail system, as well as a remote X.400 mail system. You need to define a separate address space in the connector for each mail system you want to reach with that connector.

Connector Cost

The purpose of assigning costs to connectors in both legacy Exchange and Exchange 2000 is to determine which path to use across various connectors among different sites. The MTA chose a connector to use in delivering incoming messages or relaying outgoing messages. Multiple connectors were used for load balancing as well as fault tolerance among sites. *Load balancing* refers to two or more active connectors sharing a load; *fault tolerance* refers to design redundancy where one connector operates as a standby in case another connector fails. Different cost measures apply to each connector on a scale of 1 through 100. The lower the cost, the more frequently the MTA used that connector. For example, a connector with a cost of 1 was used more frequently than another connector with a cost of 50, and so forth. For true load balancing to occur, all connectors must have the same cost. For fault-tolerance purposes, one connector is preferred and therefore has a higher cost than another connector.

Bridgehead Servers

Specially designated Exchange 2000 servers that host Routing Group connectors (RGCs)—discussed later in this chapter—are called *bridgehead servers*, a term we introduced earlier in this chapter that you will be familiar with if you've worked a lot with Exchange Server 5.x. This type of server acts as a gateway through which messages flow in and out of your Routing Groups. When a bridgehead server receives a message that requires an intersite delivery, the server attempts to determine the target server's IP address using standard resolution methods based on Domain Name System (DNS). If more than one server has an RGC configured to transfer messages among locations, it can provide fault tolerance by acting as a redundant bridgehead server that allows for message fail-over in case of a system failure. A lower-cost value can be associated with the redundant connector controlling the message flow.

Like site connectors in Exchange Server 5.5 you can tell your RGC, in Exchange 2000, to go through a bridgehead server in a remote site, or you can tell it to go directly to target servers. However, there is one major difference that stands out between Exchange 2000 and Exchange 5.5. Although you use costs associated with each connector to optimize message routing, costs do not cause, for example, nondelivery of mail. The route of any one message is based on a least-cost algorithm. Each Exchange server has a copy of a regularly updated compilation of current server and network conditions that cover the entire messaging topology of which it is a part. In fact, Exchange 2000, unlike legacy Exchange, uses this link-state table to make a routing decision. Link states and routing are discussed in Chapter 9.

Exchange Connector Types

Exchange 2000 provides several choices of connectors, including:

- *RGCs*—This connector class is the easiest to configure and can accommodate multiple target bridgehead servers, any designated server acting as a gateway or source server for outbound connections, and a target server for inbound connections. These connectors also support older versions of Exchange, although you need to configure the legacy software with its own site connector to communicate with the RGC.

- *SMTP connectors*—These connectors connect Routing Groups or vintage versions of Exchange running Internet Mail Service (IMS). These connectors also support a pull relationship, where a server triggers delivery from another message queue in another server, as well as a secure exchange of messages using Secure Sockets Layer (SSL). The connectors include authentication of remote domains before mail transmission, delivery scheduling, and multiple permission levels for users.

> *X.400 connectors*—These connectors can establish a messaging route between Routing Groups or a Routing Group and an X.400 system. You can configure them using different protocol stacks, such as Transmission Control Protocol (TCP), X.25, or Remote Access Services (RAS). X.400 connectors are unidirectional; you must configure them in both directions.

Note: *Windows 2000 currently does not provide Active Directory (AD) replication over a dial-up connection. TCP X.400 connectors over a dial-up Routing and Remote Access Service (RRAS) connection are of limited use except in emergencies.*

Exchange 2000 RGCs

RGCs are the most common connector in an Exchange 2000 organization. To use this connector, you need at least two Routing Groups on different physical servers, and at least one server must be the Routing Group master. From Exchange System Manager, you need to see these groups and configure the RGC for both directions because RGCs are one-way connectors. Best practices also recommend that you configure one or more servers with RGCs in both the local and remote Routing Groups as fault-tolerant bridgeheads.

RGCs use SMTP and are more tolerant of low bandwidth than, for example, legacy connectors that rely on RPCs (discussed in the "Legacy Exchange 5.5 Site Connectors" section later in this chapter). Unfortunately, the major disadvantage of RGCs is that they are unidirectional. This connecting software layer establishes a one-way connection from one server in one Routing Group to another server in another Routing Group. If you want to establish a two-way connection, you have to create two connectors. After you create one end of your connector, you are automatically asked if you want Exchange Server to create a connector for your remote Routing Group. If you accept, the newly created connector has the same settings as those you chose for your local RGC. Be careful working with both Exchange 2000 servers and Exchange 5.x servers at the same time. An RGC functions like a *site connector* in Exchange 5.x servers. If your Exchange 5.x servers are in a separate Windows NT domain, the RGC can connect as an account in that NT 4 domain.

Legacy Exchange 5.5 Site Connectors

You used site connectors in Exchange Server 5.x to configure two or more sites to communicate with each other. These connectors worked through the MTA to transfer messages to a remote site, and they kept a list of target servers at the remote site. Any messages delivered to a target server would then be delivered to their final destination within the remote site (unless the target server *was* the final destination for such messages).

Site connectors sometimes delivered messages to a *messaging bridgehead server* within a remote site using RPCs. Legacy Exchange required a permanent, high-speed connection between the sites themselves to support these legacy connectors, considered the most efficient and fastest connectors that came with Exchange Server 5.x. No message translation was needed between sites, but you had to configure a service account that the local MTA used to authenticate itself on the remote site's server. You could use the same service account in different sites only if both sites belonged to the same Windows NT domain. Configuration got complicated if multiple NT domains were involved. An understanding of the domain model and of one-way and two-way trust relationships was very important.

Another issue with site connectors relates to costs. Site connectors themselves were assigned a cost factor in the General tab of the Properties sheet for the site connector in the Exchange Administrator graphical user interface (GUI) tool. However, each target server in the remote site could be assigned a cost for load-balancing or fault-tolerance purposes. When you transferred information between two sites, Exchange always used the lowest-cost connector first. After choosing the lowest-cost connector, Exchange chose the lowest-cost target server in the remote site. Costs for target servers ranged from 0 through 100. A cost of 0 was assigned to servers that were used 100 percent of the time, whereas a cost of 100 was assigned to servers that were used only if no other server was available.

RGCs and Legacy Exchange 5.x Site Connectors Compared

For Exchange 2000, RGCs are not the same as legacy site connectors used in Exchange 5.x. An RGC contacts target servers in a sequential order that you specify, not according to costs. Best practices recommend specifying multiple bridgehead servers to provide a fault-tolerant connection. RGCs are more efficient than site connectors because they use SMTP as a native transport protocol. SMTP is more tolerant of lower-bandwidth situations and requires less overhead compared to the RPCs made by site connectors. Furthermore, configuration is simplified when you upgrade. An Exchange 5.5 bridgehead server that is already configured with a site connector converts to an RGC. It can communicate with Exchange 5.x servers using RPCs, as well as Exchange 2000 servers running SMTP. You can also schedule when messages pass between your RGCs based on time as well as size. For example, you can schedule the exchange of messages that are more than 1MB when your bandwidth requirements are not so high (such as in the early morning). Neither of these options was available using legacy Exchange Server 5.x site connectors.

SMTP Connectors

You can use SMTP connectors to connect a local bridgehead server to remote servers like other Exchange 2000 servers, legacy Exchange servers, non-native SMTP-compatible messaging systems, or Internet SMTP mail hosts. With these connectors, you can encrypt messages and use stricter authentication methods than you can with, for example, RGCs. In fact, the SMTP connector counterpart in

Exchange Server 5.x was the Internet Mail connector. Both connectors were designed for communication with the Internet or a foreign environment that did not include any Exchange servers. As already described, the major difference between legacy Exchange and Exchange 2000, however, is that the legacy server bound the protocol access to a specific port. Exchange 2000 does not restrict, for example, SMTP mail exclusively to a single port like TCP port 25; instead, it defines a socket, or combination protocol and port number, to a virtualized SMTP server. Thus, a virtual server can provide messaging services to any range of IP addresses. When you upgrade from a legacy Exchange system, the default virtual server (SMTP over TCP port 25) assumes IMS. The connector uses DNS Mail Exchange (MX) records, or a smart host, to route a path to a destination mail host. A *smart host* is a designated host that acts as an intermediary in routing messages to a predefined destination. If the destination mail system supports Extended SMTP (ESMTP), this extended feature set is available as well.

Thus, this connector differs from an RGC in, for example, how you configure both encryption and authentication. In some cases, you may need to encrypt some or all of your mail, and in some cases, you may need to authenticate users in a remote domain or site before you can send a message to them. Figure 10.1 shows the General Properties sheet for the SMTP connector in Exchange Server 2000. Here, you name the connector and DNS options. Other available tabs include:

> ► *Delivery Options*—Unlike RGCs, SMTP connectors can queue mail for remote triggered delivery to manage the message flow. By default, SMTP connectors don't force delivery of queued messages. Forcing delivery is necessary, however, if you choose remote triggered delivery. Not forcing delivery causes delays

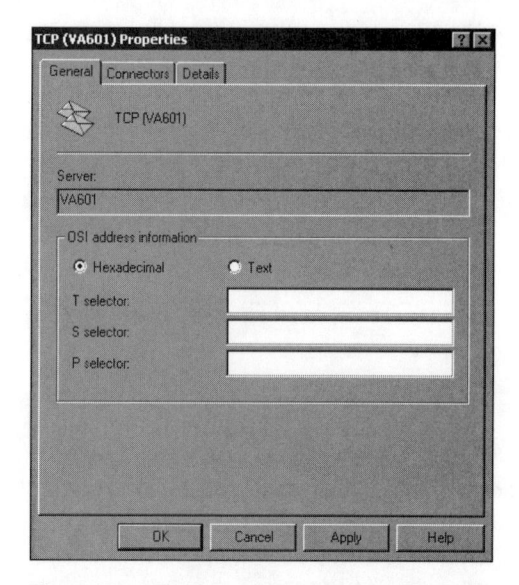

Figure 10.1 The General Properties sheet for SMTP connectors.

because clients wait for connection timeouts and then retry connections. The **turn** (for SMTP) and **eturn** (for ESMTP) protocol commands allow a mail client to request a server to start processing queued mail.

▶ *Advanced*—Send SMTP commands such as **ehlo** or **helo**. By default, the **ehlo** command is a start command signifying that Exchange 2000 Server can use the ESMTP command set.

▶ *Address Space*—Specify an address space that the connector will use as a destination domain. You can specify address spaces for most mail systems, including SMTP, X.400, Lotus cc:Mail, and Novell's GroupWise messaging system.

▶ *Connected Routing Groups*—As an alternative to specifying an address space in the Address Space Properties sheet, you must use this Properties sheet to specify which Routing Groups will be connected to the local Routing Group. The connector requires a listing of Routing Groups close to it.

When you install the SMTP connector, you define a local bridgehead server through which all messages are transmitted, as well as a connector scope. You can create a *connector scope* that allows certain servers to use the connector. Use a *bandwidth rule* to decide whether to deploy the SMTP connector where you need a bandwidth within, for example, a specific range (such as 16Kbps and 64Kbps). Don't use the SMTP connector just because you want to transport SMTP-based mail. RGCs are suitable for normal SMTP operations and for when you have at least 64Kbps of available bandwidth. RGCs use SMTP as their native transport protocol. SMTP connectors, alternatively, are best when you have available bandwidth of between 16Kbps and 64Kbps or when you require security measures such as encryption and authentication in exchanging messages with a remote domain. Both connectors let you schedule messages for transmission at certain times to better balance service loads or when bandwidth utilization is high.

X.400 Connectors

X.400 connectors, based on the Comité Consultatif International Téléphonique et Telegraphique (CCITT) (now known as the International Telecommunication Union [ITU]) X.400 standard, are very similar to legacy Exchange Site connectors in that they use bridgehead servers to route messages. The only difference is that X.400 connectors cannot use target servers. X.400 makes a clear distinction between bridgehead servers and target servers. All messages must go through a bridgehead server in a local domain, which then talks to a partner bridgehead server in the remote domain. X.400 connectors are the most generic of all connectors and can help you link to a host of foreign mail systems, including any X.400-based mail system. They allow you to control operation times as well as who sends mail to a remote site. They also require less bandwidth compared to legacy site connectors.

The X.400 standard uses an addressing method that reflects a hierarchical structure. It displays your position in a messaging environment. For instance, the X.400

address for Santa Claus, who works at NorthPole Industries, would look something like this:

```
c=US;a=Logistics;p=NorthPole;o=Alaska;s=Claus;g=Santa
```

Each parameter represents a certain X.400 value:

- **c**—Means your country.
- **a**—Equals your administrative management domain.
- **p**—Means your private management domain (this is really your Exchange organization).
- **o**—Means your X.400 organization (or your Exchange Server Administrative Group).
- **s**—Means your last name (surname).
- **g**—Means your first name (given name).

These naming requirements for X.400 connectors are similar for both legacy Exchange and Exchange 2000. In both cases, you first must install an MTA *transport stack* and then the connector itself. You configure this transport stack for a particular Exchange server. A transport stack is a record of information about the underlying hardware and software components that make up your messaging infrastructure. Transport stacks exist at the server level for any given server; connectors exist at the Routing Group level and use transport stacks.

In Exchange Server 5.x, you could configure three network transports for the X.400 connection: TCP, X.25, and RAS. Exchange Server 2000 also has three MTA transport stacks, depending on which hardware or software you have running on your network. Table 10.1 compares these transport protocols.

There are some disadvantages to using X.400 connectors. Reasons for not using them include:

- All information passing through these connectors must be converted to a message, which reduces transmission speeds. Site connectors, which do not perform this translation, are almost 20 percent faster than X.400 connectors.
- These connectors require more configuration steps compared to site connectors. Unlike site connectors, X.400 connectors have to be configured for each site separately. Site connectors automatically prompt you for information about your remote site, whereas X.400 connectors require you to manually configure each side of a connection.
- With these connectors, more bottlenecks occur in your system because any mail going through these connectors must pass through a single messaging bridgehead server (as compared with site connectors, which can target a

designated server in a remote domain without going through a messaging bridgehead server).

- If you change settings on one side of an X.400 connector, you may get occasional messages reminding you to configure the other side of the X.400 connector. You have to properly configure both sides of this connector before the connector will work.

Microsoft likes to concentrate exam scenarios around two main connectors: the X.400 connector (because it is based on a widely accepted international standard) and the MS Mail connector. In this chapter, we will concentrate on message flows using these two connectors as examples. Understanding these two connectors will help you relate to similar processes used to configure other connectors used in Exchange Server.

Working with X.400 connectors in Exchange 2000 requires you to create one of three transport stacks, as well as create the actual connector.

Table 10.1 Comparison of Exchange transport protocols among versions.

Protocol	Exchange Version	Description
TCP/IP	Legacy 5.x	The MTA used port 102 to communicate messages.
Open Systems Interconnection (OSI) Transport service definition class 4 (RFC 1006) TP4/Connectionless Networking Protocol (CLNP)	Legacy 5.x	This was a transport provider on top of the TCP/IP protocol suite that used the Windows NT TP4 driver and communicated with remote systems that used the OSI TP4 protocol for message transport. CLNP, when used on top of the TP4 driver, allows you to transfer data without requiring a separate connection request.
TP0/X.25	Legacy 5.x	This provided dial-up communications using special X.25 software and adapters installed on each server. A separate MTA transport stack is required for each X.25 port.
TCP/IP	Exchange 2000	Uses Windows 2000 TCP/IP services to run X.400 messaging systems over a TCP/IP-based network.
TP0/X.25	Exchange 2000	This stack uses a special type of port adapter for dial-up communications that conform to the OSI X.25 specifications.
RAS	Exchange 2000	This stack provides RAS over standard communication devices. You must install RAS on the host server for this to work properly, but it is not a protocol of choice. Windows 2000 does not allow you to replicate AD information over a dial-up line. Thus, Exchange 2000 loses much of the dial-up networking advantages over legacy messaging products like Exchange 5.5. It replaces this technology, however, with far more sophisticated tools, such as Terminal Services, which provides for remote control of resources but through a different technology.

Creating the Transport Stack

Use the Exchange System snap-in to create an MTA transport stack. Transport stacks exist at the server level, so each stack is associated with a particular Exchange server. However, each connector you create that uses this transport stack exists at the Routing Group level. This means that you can configure multiple MTA transport stacks within one Routing Group.

To create a transport stack, follow these steps:

1. Select the X.400 folder in the Protocols container of the server where you want to install the stack.

2. Right-click on the MTA object and click on New on the shortcut menu.

3. Choose TCP/IP X.400 Service Transport Stack. You will see a Properties sheet for the transport stack that you can use to configure the stack.

The available Properties sheets under the transport stack node are:

- *General*—Shows the server name and OSI Address Information. It allows you to change the display name for the MTA transport stack, as well as to configure OSI addressing information. Only Exchange Server 2000 uses this transport stack, so OSI addressing values are an available option that defines the connector address in a generic manner for use by other services and applications compliant with OSI standards.

- *Connectors*—Indicates which connectors use this stack. It shows all the connectors in your Routing Group that can use this MTA transport stack. When you first create a transport stack, this list is blank.

- *Details*—Provides space for an administrative note for this object.

You need to configure transport stacks before you actually configure an actual X.400 connector, a very common "foreign mail system" that works with most Exchange Server mail systems.

Creating the X.400 Connector

To create the X.400 connector, you first create an MTA transport stack. Use the Exchange System Manager snap-in tool used with the Microsoft Management Console (MMC) to do this. Select the Connectors container of the Routing Group in which you want to create your connector. Then, create a connector based on a specific protocol stack such as TCP, as shown in Figure 10.2.

You can create a new connector by using one of two methods. Either right-click on the Connectors container and choose New, or select the Action bar and choose New. Using either method produces the screen shown in Figure 10.3. The accompanying tabs are explained later in this chapter.

Interoperability 311

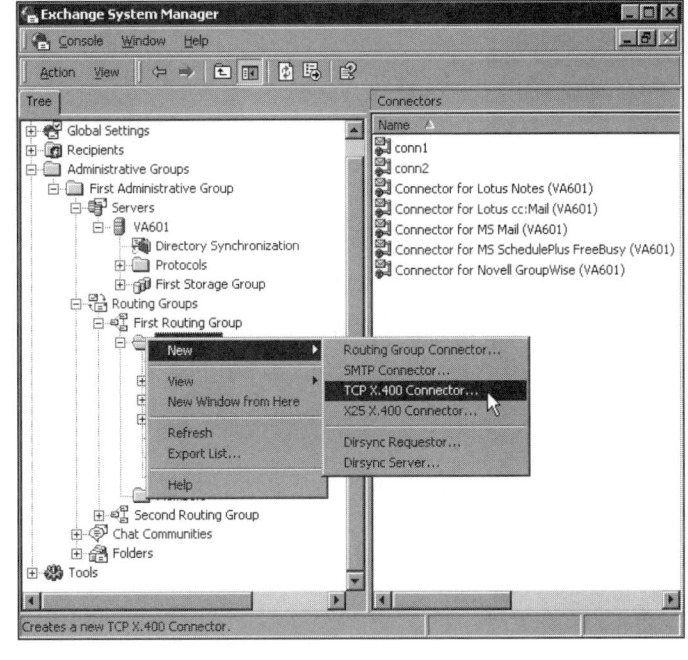

Figure 10.2 Creating an X.400 connector in the Connectors folder in System Manager.

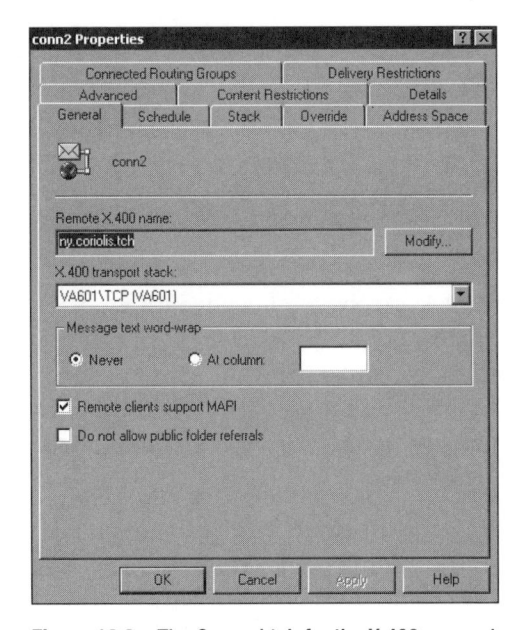

Figure 10.3 The General tab for the X.400 connector.

The General Tab

This General tab, as shown in Figure 10.3, defines basic naming and connection information. The options here are:

- *Name*—This is the connector name as it appears in the scope window of the System Manager listing of connectors.

- *Remote X.400 Name*—This option defines remote server connections.

- *X.400 Transport Stack*—This option defines your transport stack.

- *Message Text Word-Wrap*—This option specifies whether the system allows messages to use the word-wrap feature. This field defaults to Never; word-wrap is disabled on all outgoing messages.

- *Remote Clients Support MAPI*—This option indicates whether clients support Messaging Application Programming Interface (MAPI) and transmit rich-text format with every message.

- *Do Not Allow Public Folder Referrals*—This option prevents remote system users from accessing public folders that may be configured in your local Routing Group.

The Schedule Tab

The Schedule tab, shown in Figure 10.4, provides the scheduling information for when your connector can be used. The shaded area represents the selected times. The four scheduling values for this tab are:

- *Never*—Permanently turns off the connector to, for example, perform maintenance.

- *Always*—Allows connections to and from your server at any time. This is the default.

- *Selected Times*—Allows you to control availability of bandwidth, especially when, for example, users do not require immediate messaging capacity. You use this schedule if you have a very busy network or if you need to perform repairs on your network. You can also choose 1 Hour or 15 Minute resolution of the scheduling grid when the radio button in the Detail View section on the right is enabled.

- *Remote Initiated*—Allows remote servers to connect to your server, but the local server cannot initiate the connection. Use this feature to exclusively receive messages.

The Stack Tab

You use the Stack tab of the X.400 connector, shown in Figure 10.5, to specify address information regarding a foreign X.400 system. In other words, you specify the IP address of the foreign system, and maybe additional OSI addressing information for the foreign system. You can enter OSI information to distinguish Exchange

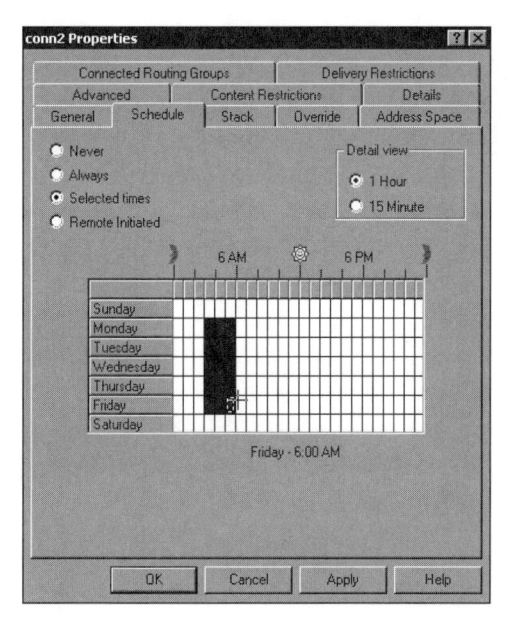

Figure 10.4 The Schedule tab for the X.400 connector.

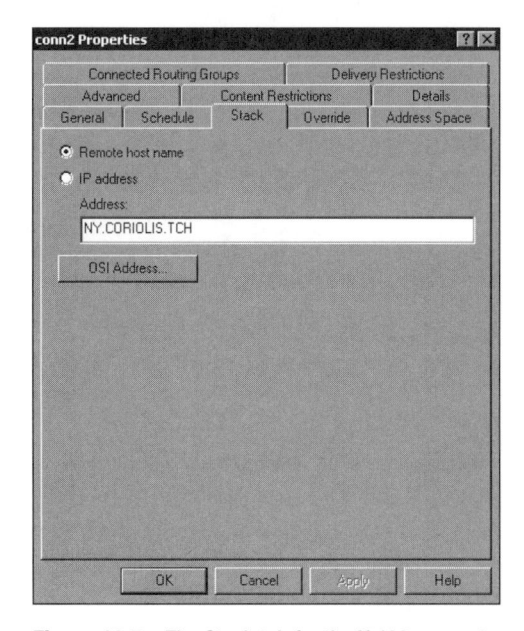

Figure 10.5 The Stack tab for the X.400 connector.

from other services using the protocol stack. Figure 10.6 shows the OSI Address panel, which is accessible through the Stack tab. You can also enter information (as either text or hexadecimal values) pertaining to the Transport Service Access Point (TSAP) in the T selector, Session Service Access Point (SSAP) in the S selector, or Presentation Service Access Point (PSAP) in the P selector.

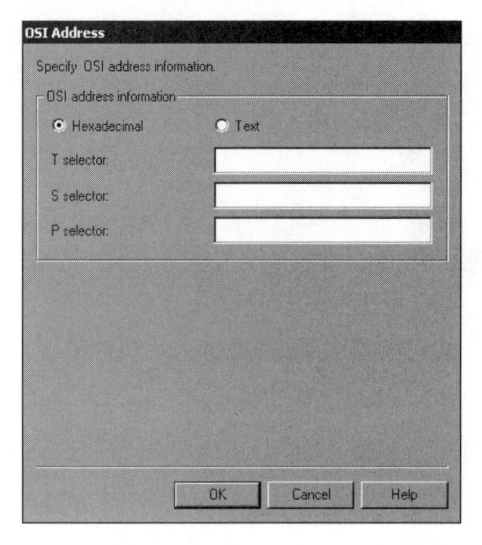

Figure 10.6 The OSI Address panel under the Stack tab for the X.400 connector.

The Override Tab

The Override tab, shown in Figure 10.7, lets you configure settings that will override or preempt local MTA settings when messages are sent over the X.400 connector. The only time you should adjust these settings is if you are connecting to a foreign X.400 system. If you are connecting to another Exchange Routing Group, it's best to leave most of these settings as they are. If you want, you can override the name or password of your local MTA using this tab. Sometimes, you

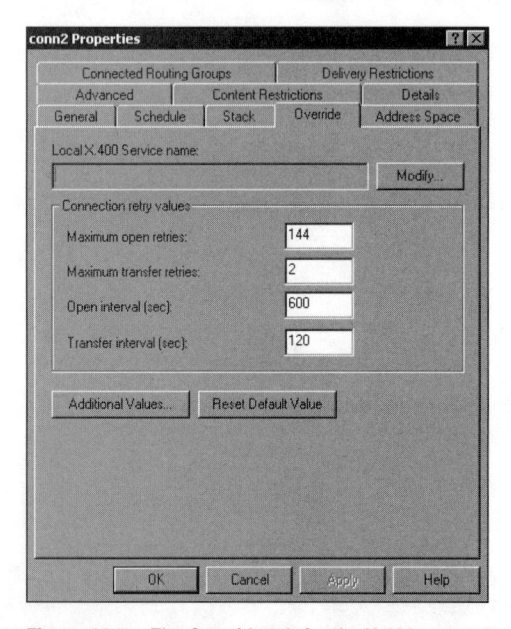

Figure 10.7 The Override tab for the X.400 connector.

have a conflict because the MTAs on foreign systems cannot accept characters you are using on your local MTA. You can use override values only for an X.400 connection (not other types of connections!).

The Address Space Tab

The Address Space tab, as shown in Figure 10.8, is important for foreign systems that do not use the same addressing scheme as Exchange Server. In the email address **pschein@tchouse.com**, characters to the right of the @ symbol are referred to as the *address space*, or where the message is to be received. This configuration tells the MTA that all messages are to be sent using SMTP. It is necessary to configure an address space for a foreign X.400 system to which you intend to exchange messages. The MTA decides if all messages will be sent over the X.400 connector. You can add an address space by clicking on Add. This feature allows you to specify the kind of address space you want to use (e.g., X.400, SMTP, cc:Mail, and so on). All X.400 addresses are case sensitive.

The Advanced Tab

The Advanced tab of the X.400 connector, shown in Figure 10.9, is concerned with links and message attributes. You should be aware of these three checkboxes:

- *Allow BP-15 (In Addition To BP-14)*—A standard known as Body Part 15 (or BP-15) is part of the X.400 recommendation and supports advanced messaging features like encoding attachments. BP-14 refers to a 1984 standard, whereas

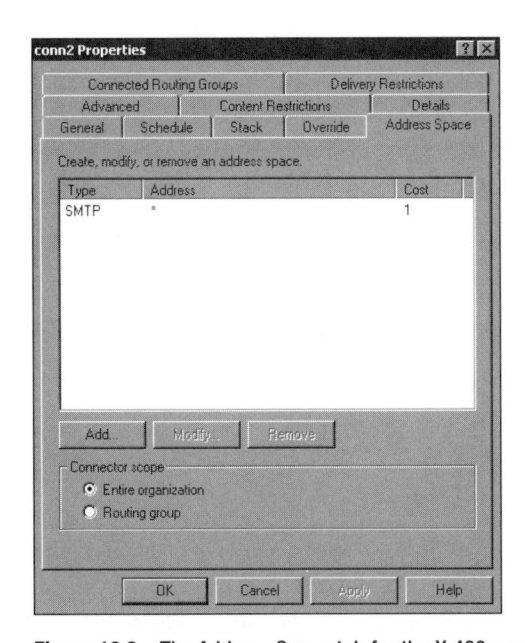

Figure 10.8 The Address Space tab for the X.400 connector.

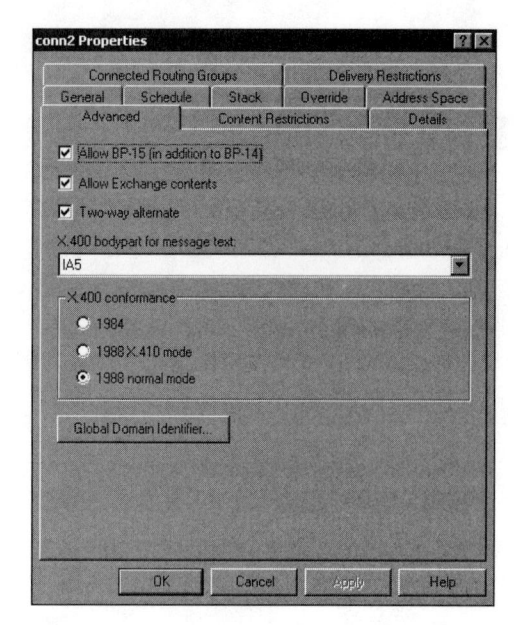

Figure 10.9 The Advanced tab for the X.400 connector.

BP-15 refers to a more recent 1988 X.400 standard. Of course, BP-14 supports far fewer features compared to BP-15. If you don't choose BP-15, you are forced to use the BP-14 standard.

➤ *Allow Exchange Contents*—Checking this box ensures that a remote X.400 system you are connecting to will support features like rich-text format. Many Exchange clients already support these features.

➤ *Two-Way Alternate*—Checking this option helps improve transmission speed to a remote X.400 system that you want to connect to. The two-way alternate standard means that two X.400 systems connected to each other take turns or alternate between sending and receiving information.

In addition, the Advanced tab provides other choices, such as:

➤ *X.400 Bodypart For Message Text*—This area helps you specify how you want the message text to be formatted. You should accept the default value of IA5, which means International Alphabet 5. You should change the default value if you are communicating with a foreign system that is using a type of foreign-language application.

➤ *X.400 Conformance*—Here you will see three radio buttons: 1984, 1988 X.410 Mode, and 1988 Normal Mode. Exchange 2000 supports two primary recommendations of the X.400 standard: one issued in 1984, and the other issued in 1988. The 1988 X.400 recommendation has two versions: X.410 Mode and Normal Mode. Best practices recommend using the default setting of 1988 Normal Mode.

➤ *Global Domain Identifier (GDI)*—Select this button to prevent message loops that may occur with outgoing messages. By default, the GDI information should remain unchanged.

The Content Restrictions Tab

You use the Content Restrictions tab, shown in Figure 10.10, to restrict message types using criteria defined according to the following terms:

➤ *Priorities*—Determine the value range (High, Normal, or Low).

➤ *Types*—Specify the content (either System Messages or Non-System Messages).

➤ *Size*—Restrict a message size in K.

The Details Tab

The Details tab is standard across all objects and provides space for an administrative note. It also provides creation and last modification date information.

The Connected Routing Groups Tab

You use the Connected Routing Groups tab, shown in Figure 10.11, only when you are trying to connect an Exchange Server 2000 Routing Group with an Exchange Server 5.5 site using the X.400 connector. Although messaging works even if you don't configure this Properties sheet, if you omit information here, Exchange 2000 may not "know" it is connected to another Exchange site. This could cause problems when you share public folder data between the two servers.

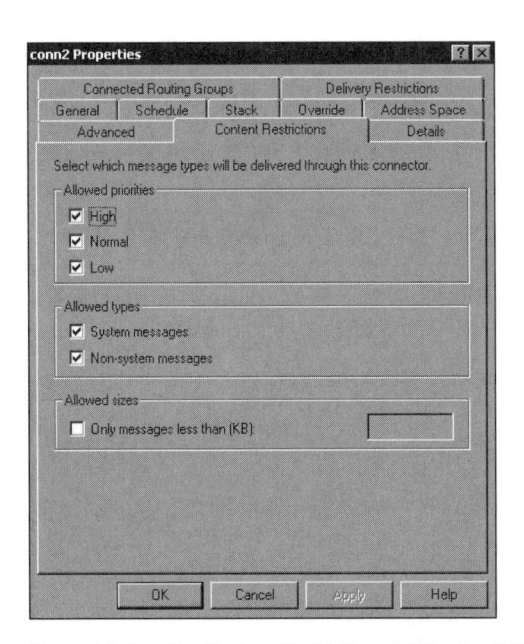

Figure 10.10 The Content Restrictions tab for the X.400 connector.

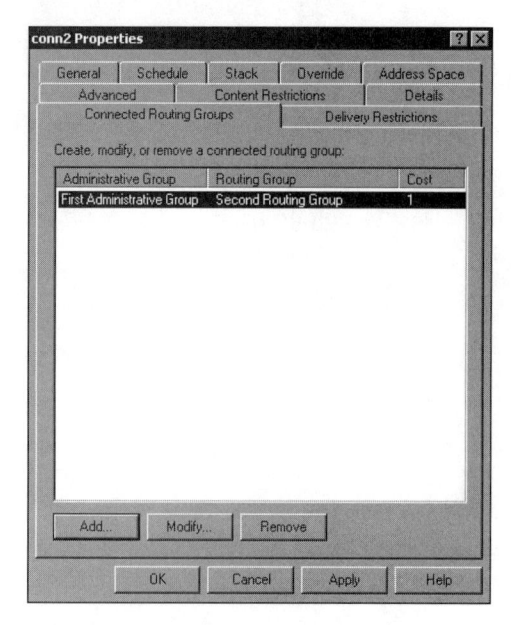

Figure 10.11 The Connected Routing Groups tab for the X.400 connector.

The Delivery Restrictions Tab

The Delivery Restrictions tab is where you can control who can send messages using the X.400 connector. You have two available choices:

➤ Allow all users to transfer messages over the X.400 connector except for those users you expressly deny. By default, all users are allowed to send messages over the X.400 connector. If you want to expressly disallow someone, just click on Add, and then select a user from your address book.

➤ Deny all users from sending messages over the X.400 connector except for those people that you expressly allow to send messages. This is the exact reverse of your other choice. Remember that, by default, all users are allowed to send messages over the X.400 connector. You can always decide to limit the people who can use this connector.

Other Mail Systems

You have just seen how you could configure Exchange 2000 to work with a foreign X.400 mail system. However, Exchange Server 2000, like Exchange Server 5.5, works well with many other foreign mail systems that exist today. We discuss the issues of connecting to foreign mail systems in more detail in Chapter 11. For example, Exchange Server works with Lotus cc:Mail, Lotus Notes, and even Novell's GroupWise solutions for mail delivery. In addition, MS Mail, a relatively simple shared-file messaging system consisting of shared folders on a network server, was used for quite some time before Exchange Server became popular. Understanding this coexistence leads to a greater appreciation of the power and extent of today's Exchange Server.

Lotus cc:Mail

Some of you may be working in an existing Lotus cc:Mail environment. This mail system uses a Post Office Database for mail storage. Most cc:Mail users have become used to Database version 6 or 8. You can still use an Exchange connector called the *Lotus cc:Mail connector* to exchange messages with a foreign cc:Mail environment. You can even synchronize directories between the two systems.

You need to remember several important facts when working with this type of connector on an Exchange server:

- An Exchange server can run only one instance of this connector.
- This connector can service only one cc:Mail Post Office.
- An Exchange shadow Post Office and the cc:Mail systems have to be on the same local area network (LAN).

You also need to understand the components involved with the cc:Mail connector for Exchange. The connector is a Windows NT Server or Windows 2000 Server service. It has three distinct components:

- *cc:Mail import/export programs*—These executables either import Exchange Server messages into a cc:Mail Post Office or export a cc:Mail message into an Exchange server. If you install any type of cc:Mail connector on your Exchange server, you need these programs on your Exchange server.
- *Connector for cc:Mail Service*—This is a Windows service that transfers messages between the Exchange server and the cc:Mail Post Office.
- *Connector for cc:Mail Store*—This is a group of directories on Exchange Server used for messages in transit.

Message Flows between Exchange and cc:Mail

When Exchange Server sends a message to someone on a cc:Mail network using Exchange Server 2000, Exchange Server submits this message to the MTA, which then transfers the message to the connector for cc:Mail. This service converts your message into ASCII format (along with any attachments you have) and puts the message into the connector for cc:Mail Store. Finally, the cc:Mail import program delivers the message or produces a Nondelivery Report (NDR) if the message cannot be delivered.

Microsoft Exchange and Novell NetWare

Although Exchange Server has to run on a Windows NT or Windows 2000 platform, other machines you have on your network can run on any other operating system, including the one belonging to Novell, called NetWare. Novell's latest version of NetWare is 5.1, released in early 2000. Many companies use various versions of NetWare and its mail product, called Novell GroupWise.

Any Novell client on any LAN segment (or remote wide area network [WAN] segment, for that matter) can access an Exchange server if the following conditions are present:

➤ *Gateway Service for NetWare and Client Service for NetWare are running on the system.* You need to install these services directly onto your Exchange server so that you can utilize protocols such as Internetwork Packet Exchange/Sequenced Packet Exchange (IPX/SPX), the proprietary network protocol on legacy Novell networks.

➤ *Service Advertising Protocol (SAP) must be installed correctly on your Exchange server so that all NetWare clients can access it.* This protocol is essential if your Exchange server and Novell servers exist on different subnets or different LANs altogether.

➤ *The NetBIOS protocol must be supported on your Exchange Server.* If it is not, clients cannot communicate.

➤ *All NetWare frame types for Ethernet packets must be configured correctly.* In a mixed NetWare environment, it is not uncommon to use mixed frame types such as 802.2 and 802.3. You can even configure mixed frame types on a single Exchange server if you're using the Microsoft-developed NWLink protocol.

Configuring Novell Clients

When problems occur between Novell NetWare and Microsoft Exchange Server, it is important to verify that the NetWare client can properly access the Exchange server. Similarly, the Microsoft client must be able to access the NetWare server. Any workstation that needs to access both a NetWare server *and* an Exchange Server requires:

➤ NetWare client software (either the Microsoft Client for NetWare or Novell's Client32 software) loaded on the workstation

➤ Microsoft client software (usually Client for Microsoft Networks for Windows 95 or Windows 98 machines, or the Workstation Service for a Windows NT/2000 machine)

You cannot load the Microsoft Client for NetWare and Novell's Client32 software at the same time. You have to pick one of these; Novell recommends its true Client32 for full NetWare Directory Service functionality.

MS Mail for PC Networks

Exchange 2000 Server includes a connector for MS Mail, which allows messaging connectivity and directory synchronization between Exchange 2000 and MS Mail for PC networks. Use this connector over a LAN or an X.25 connection. Microsoft created this connector not only for transparent messaging between these two networks, but also to help migrate legacy MS Mail networks to newer Exchange Server–based messaging platforms.

Mail systems such as MS Mail use a shared-file messaging architecture, where a centralized Post Office is composed of shared folders located on a network server. Mail recipients are given access to one of these shared folders. If you send mail to a user, the client on your machine intercepts the message and saves it in the other user's shared folder. The other user's client software checks this folder regularly for new messages. Using the MS Mail connector on your Exchange Server creates a shadow MS Mail Post Office. The term *shadow* is used because no actual mailboxes are created in this functional Post Office. The hosting Exchange server appears to the MS Mail messaging system as an MS Mail Post Office. When an Exchange server "talks" to an MS Mail Post Office through the connector for MS Mail, it uses a service that moves messages between the shadow Post Office on the Exchange server and the MS Mail Post Office.

The connector for MS Mail has three components. Each component mimics a function that is performed by the actual components of an MS Mail system. These components are:

- *Mail connector Post Office*—This is the shadow Post Office and is equivalent to a Post Office in MS Mail. It is a temporary holding place for any message transferred between an Exchange server and a real MS Mail Post Office.

- *Mail connector Interchange*—This service assists with routing messages between the Exchange server and the shadow Post Office.

- *Mail connector (PC) MTA*—This service helps route messages between the shadow Post Office and the actual MS Mail Post Office. The Interchange never deals with the actual MS Mail Post Office, but the MTA does.

The Mail connector (PC) MTA is important because you can configure only one MS Mail connector on an Exchange server. Each connector provides support to multiple actual Post Offices. Thus, one connector can use several Mail connector (PC) MTAs to connect to several actual Post Offices. This Mail connector (PC) MTA has an equivalent MTA in MS Mail. When an MS Mail system user sends a message to an Exchange recipient, all three components—the connector Post Office, the Interchange, and the MTA—are used to send the message.

The following steps occur when an MS Mail user sends a message to a Microsoft Exchange user:

1. The Mail connector (PC) MTA receives the message from an MS Mail Post Office and puts this message in a queue.

2. The Mail connector Interchange checks the Mail connector Post Office regularly for new messages.

3. If a new message is found, the Mail connector Interchange retrieves it and converts the message to an Exchange-readable format.

4. The Mail connector Interchange puts the message into a queue for the Exchange Server MTA.

5. The Exchange Server MTA routes the message to the intended recipient.

If a Microsoft Exchange user sends a message to an MS Mail recipient, Steps 1 through 5 are executed in reverse order.

Configuring MS Mail

It is not surprising to find MS Mail material on an Exchange Server exam. Although this shared-file messaging system is no longer in common use, its architecture is generic. If you know how to migrate an MS Mail system to Exchange Server, you understand how to handle any other shared-file messaging systems. You must configure the MS Mail connector to work over a synchronous LAN connection or over an asynchronous RAS dial-up connection. Remember that you can configure only one connector for MS Mail on any *one* Exchange server, although each connector can reach multiple Post Offices on the MS Mail system.

Use Exchange System Manager to configure an MS Mail connector in Exchange Server 2000. Verify the installation by checking the Connectors container. The connector for MS Mail has a configuration object in the Connections container in the Exchange System Manager management tool. The Properties sheets that you use to configure this connector include:

➤ *Interchange*—Most properties sheets open to a General tab in Exchange; however, the MS Mail Connector Properties sheet opens immediately to the Interchange tab. The Interchange tab, as shown in Figure 10.12, is where you specify an administrator's mailbox and how the MS Mail connector will move information between Exchange Server and the MS Mail Post Office. The Interchange tab has two important settings:

➤ *Maximize MS Mail 3.x Compatibility*—This option provides for the Microsoft standard called Object Linking and Embedding (OLE). OLE allows you, for example, to embed or link a single PowerPoint slide into an Excel worksheet by using cut-and-paste or click-on-and-drag techniques

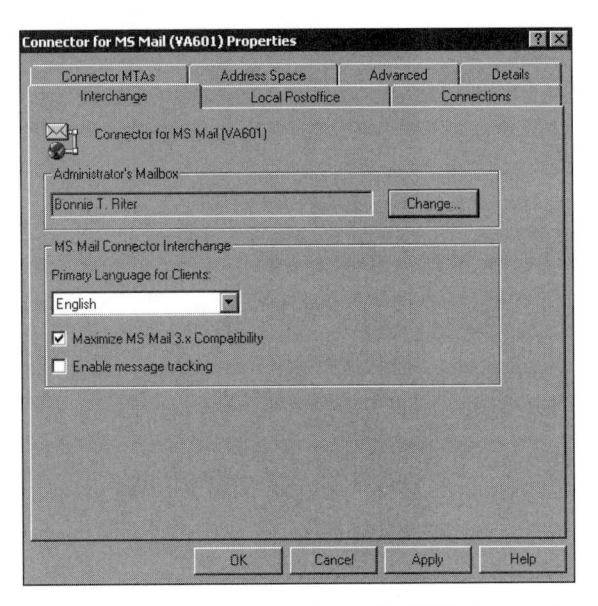

Figure 10.12 The Interchange tab for the MS Mail connector.

available through the Windows architecture. When you enable this option, you allow MS Mail 3.x clients to view any OLE type objects.

- *Enable Message Tracking*—This option allows you to track messages sent from an Exchange server to an MS Mail Post Office for diagnostic purposes. The feature is enabled at the server level. Once Enable Message Tracking is enabled, Exchange Server keeps a log of messages transferred to and from the local messaging platform.

- *Local Postoffice*—You use this tab to configure your shadow Post Office. Here, you want to define your network name, the name of the Post Office, and possibly a password used for authentication purposes for dial-up users.

- *Connector MTAs*—You use this Properties sheet to create a connector MTA to transfer messages between your shadow Post Office and your MS Mail Post Office. Create one connector MTA for every MS Mail Post Office to which you will establish a connection. When you create a new connector MTA, you have the following options:

    - *Logging*—Notice that Logging options include both messages sent and received. Consider what you specifically want to track when you first set up a connector MTA and want to test it.

    - *Polling Frequency*—The two options allow you to change how often the MTA checks for new messages in the shadow Post Office. To pick between the two options, click on the Options button. The first option asks MTA to check for these changes every 60 minutes. The second option asks the MTA to check for new messages every five minutes.

➤ *MS Mail Connector (PC) MTA Options Box*—The options you can select here include a maximum size for messages that can be transferred over the MTA. You can also cause the shadow Post Office to shut down if no disk space is left in your MS Mail Post Office, as well as specify whether the MTA will start up automatically when the system boots or whether it has to be manually started.

➤ *Connection Parameters*—There are two radio buttons for you to choose from here. You can select either LAN, or Async and LAN. Your choice will override any setting you make on the Connections tab (discussed next).

➤ *Connections*—Use this Properties sheet to build a list of MS Mail Post Offices that your connector for MS Mail will service. Upon an initial setup, the shadow Post Office is listed by default. Remember that the shadow Post Office is located on your Exchange server. By default, the only Post Office listed on this Properties sheet is the shadow Post Office. Create a new Post Office by clicking on the Create button on the right side of the panel. No matter how many Post Offices are created, however, the connector for MS Mail always tries to deliver a message to a Post Office three times before sending out an NDR. You can change this number of attempted deliveries at any time.

Directory Synchronization

Without synchronization, Exchange Server would be unable to maintain address information with foreign messaging systems. You must enable synchronization so that your Exchange server exchanges address information with other messaging systems compatible with the MS Mail directory synchronization protocol. Both Exchange and MS Mail use similar processes to support directory synchronization. MS Mail, too, has a directory synchronization protocol that synchronizes directories on every Post Office in the MS Mail environment. If you change the address of one Post Office, that change will be replicated automatically to every other Post Office in the same system. The actual synchronization protocol uses two Post Office components:

➤ *Directory Server Post Office*—You can have only one of these Post Offices, and it is the main database of all directory changes.

➤ *Directory Requestor Post Office*—A requestor submits a change to the Directory Server Post Office. It also asks for updates made by other Directory Requestor Post Offices.

The following steps are executed to maintain changes and updates:

1. Every Directory Requestor Post Office has a *directory synchronization agent*, which regularly sends changes to a Directory Server Post Office.

2. The Directory Server Post Office combines all changes and sends all updates to *each* Directory Requestor Post Office.

3. The MS Mail program called dispatch.exe takes these changes, processes them, and merges them into the address list of every Directory Requestor Post Office.

Exchange Server uses a similar protocol for directory synchronization to the one MS Mail uses. You have to configure directory synchronization on both sides. The only difference for Exchange Server is that you can configure it as either a Directory Synchronization Requestor or a Directory Synchronization Server. If you already have an MS Mail Post Office configured as a Directory Server Post Office, you have to configure Exchange as a Directory Synchronization Requestor.

Directory synchronization is normally a complex process, especially for MS Mail systems. Steps 1 through 3 seem to indicate a relatively painless process of updating and processing changes. In fact, however, if you "look under the hood," you see a complex process. For example, dispatch.exe runs on a machine by itself along with another program called external.exe. The dispatch.exe program starts another program called nsda, which starts yet another program called reqmain, and so on. We recommend you at least remember dispatch.exe as the loader program used to initialize the process.

Two more items are noteworthy regarding MS Mail. You need to understand a process called *Dirsync synchronization* for an MS Mail network. Generally speaking, every Post Office in an MS Mail network keeps a directory of all the recipients in that Post Office. If you have many Post Offices on your network, you use the Dirsync process to synchronize directory information among all these Post Offices.

The Dirsync process involves two steps:

1. A Post Office is designated as a Dirsync server.
2. All remaining Post Offices are then called Dirsync requestors.

The dispatch.exe program uses three timed events that control the synchronization of information between a Dirsync requestor and a Dirsync server. These events are:

➤ *T1 event*—Means that all Dirsync requestors send any changes to their directory to the Dirsync server. This event affects all Post Offices in the MS Mail network.

➤ *T2 event*—Means the Dirsync server starts dispatch.exe, which combines all directory information from all Dirsync requestors and the Dirsync server into one Global Address List (GAL). The Dirsync server sends this list back to all Dirsync requestors.

➤ *T3 event*—Means that each Dirsync requestor rebuilds its own GAL based on information retrieved from the Dirsync server. This event occurs on all Post Offices in the network.

After T1, T2, and T3 occur, every Post Office on the network uses a common GAL. Exchange Server is normally set up as a Dirsync requestor. You can, however, use Exchange as a Dirsync server.

Chapter Summary

This chapter briefly reviewed the issues that are involved in interoperability between spatially separate Exchange sites in an organization. Key issues covered include:

➤ Exchange 2000 has broadened the concept of sites to include Routing Groups and Administrative Groups in keeping with changes in the approach to managing a Windows 2000 enterprise.

➤ There are three basic routing connectors: Routing Group connectors, SMTP connectors, and X.400 connectors.

➤ Each connector acts as a gateway used to exchange messages that have an address space. This address space defines the format or structure of the message, as well as properties that affect its contents.

➤ Routing Group connectors replace legacy site connectors as the easiest connectors to configure in an organization. One major difference is in the replacement of RPCs with a more efficient protocol, SMTP. This substitution has several advantages, including lower overhead. It is also a native Windows 2000 transport protocol.

➤ SMTP connectors add features to a connection, including authentication and encryption security features.

➤ X.400 connectors remain the legacy connectors of choice because many non-Exchange products have used X.400 standardized architecture for many years. Their addressing method is also standardized based, using the hierarchical structure of an older X.500 ISO specification.

➤ All connectors support common delivery-restriction features that can restrict system-related and non–system-related content, control messaging from specific recipients, and set limits on the maximum size of messages.

Review Questions

1. What components does the Exchange 2000 concept of site include? [Check all correct answers]

    a. Administrative Groups

    b. Routing Groups

    c. Physical sites

    d. Domain Controller

2. What connector type does Exchange 2000 provide?
    a. Group connector
    b. Site connector
    c. TCP connector
    d. None of the above

3. Which protocol or service must be installed before you can build an X.400 connector?
    a. RAS
    b. NetBEUI
    c. IP
    d. SNMP

4. Which connector supports SSL?
    a. RGC
    b. SMTP connector
    c. X.25 X.400 connector
    d. SNMP connector

5. Which connector provides a variety of authentication methods?
    a. RGC
    b. SMTP
    c. X.400
    d. All of the above

6. The format of a connector address space depends on which factor?
    a. The format of the foreign mail system
    b. The format of the local and foreign mail systems
    c. The connector type and format of the local and foreign mail systems
    d. The connector type and local mail system

7. What assignment of cost would balance a service load across two servers?
    a. Assigning any cost measure over 50 to both machines.
    b. Assigning a cost measure under 50 to one machine; the other cost does not matter.
    c. The cost measure is overridden if you enable Load Balancing on the General Properties sheet of each Exchange server.
    d. Answers a and c.

8. What assignment of cost would create a fail-over relationship between two servers?

   a. Fail-over relationships can be implemented only with hardware.

   b. Assigning a cost measure under 50 to one server and over 50 on the another server would create a fail-over relationship between two servers.

   c. Assigning a 0 cost measure to both servers would create a fail-over relationship between two servers.

   d. As long as the costs are identical, it does not matter what cost you assign to both servers.

9. Which of the following statements is true?

   a. Bridgehead servers are no longer used in Exchange 2000.

   b. If more than one server has an RGC, it can act as a fail-over bridgehead server.

   c. Bridgehead servers support only one connector type: SMTP.

   d. Bridgehead servers use Dynamic Host Configuration Protocol (DHCP) to route intersite messages.

10. When you are using Routing Groups, which guidelines do you need to apply? [Check all correct answers]

    a. To install a connector, you need to have one Administrative Group and one Routing Group.

    b. To install a connector, you need to have at least two Routing Groups.

    c. Unlike with the constraints you have when using Exchange 5.5, with Exchange 2000, Routing Groups typically match the administrative workflow.

    d. Deploy servers to different Routing Groups that have similar connectivity characteristics.

11. What protocol do Exchange 2000 Routing Group connectors use to exchange messages?

    a. Remote Procedure Calls.

    b. Simple Transfer Mail Protocol.

    c. Although Routing Group connectors use Simple Transfer Mail Protocol by default, they can also use Remote Procedure Calls.

    d. None of the above.

12. Which of the following statements is false?
    a. Cost values can be arbitrarily assigned to target servers.
    b. A cost value of 0 is used to indicate the server should be used 100 percent of the time.
    c. A cost value of 100 is useful when you are creating a redundant server.
    d. Cost values are no longer used.

13. What is the difference between IMS and SMTP connectors? [Check all correct answers]
    a. IMS connectors are no longer supported in Exchange 2000.
    b. IMS connectors were bound to a specific TCP port.
    c. SMTP has replaced IMS and defaults to TCP port 25.
    d. SMTP is bound to a specific socket.

14. An SMTP virtual server refers to which DNS record first to determine message routing?
    a. A record
    b. Mail Exchange record
    c. C record
    d. M record

15. What bandwidth rule is most applicable when you are deciding between RGC and SMTP connectors?
    a. SMTP is best when bandwidth is not specified.
    b. SMTP is best when bandwidth is specified between 16Kbps and 64Kbps.
    c. SMTP is best when bandwidth is specified less than 64Kbps.
    d. None of the above.

16. Which is the best connector to use when corporate security objectives include the use of smart cards?
    a. RGC or SMTP.
    b. SMTP or X.400.
    c. SMTP.
    d. Any protocol; the NOS provides security services.

17. Which connectors provide for the scheduling of mail flows? [Check all correct answers]
    a. RGC
    b. TCP - X.400
    c. X.25 - X.400
    d. SMTP

18. Which connectors provide for the restriction of System versus Non-System message types? [Check all correct answers]

   a. RGC

   b. TCP - X.400

   c. X.25 - X.400

   d. SMTP

   e. All of the above

19. What conditions are required for a Novell client to access an Exchange 2000 server? [Check all correct answers]

   a. Gateway Service for NetWare and Client Service for NetWare must be properly configured on the Exchange server.

   b. NetBIOS and SAP must be supported.

   c. NetWare frame types or the NWLink protocol must be properly configured and running.

   d. IIS must be running for Exchange 2000 to function correctly.

20. The connector for MS Mail includes which components? [Check all correct answers]

   a. Mail connector Post Office

   b. Mail connector Exchange

   c. Mail connector (PC) MTA

   d. Mail connector shadow Post Office

Real-World Projects

Robin Langenfilter knows that bridgehead servers act as local and remote communication relays for Routing Groups and that each connector handles this hardware component in a different way. With RGC, you have multiple bridgehead servers but only a single remote target server. With SMTP, you also have one or more bridgehead servers in the form of local virtual servers. There is no "hardwired" target server; you use an intermediary smart host or directly reference an MX record through a DNS query. These resolved servers become the remote targets. Finally, with X.400, you configure one local bridgehead server and one remote bridgehead server through local and remote names. Robin wants to examine what levels of security are configurable for each connector. Robin examines the levels of security control she has over messages flowing through an RGC connector.

Project 10.1
To configure RGC access:

1. Start System Manager.

2. In the Connectors node, right-click on the RGC you want to configure and select Properties in the context menu.

3. Click on the Add button on the General Properties sheet to configure the list of servers able to send messages over this connector.

4. Click on the Add button on the Delivery Restrictions Properties sheet to exclusively accept or reject messages from users listed in AD.

5. Click on the Add button on the Remote Bridgehead Properties sheet to select target servers.

6. Select the appropriate level of allowed priorities on the Content Restrictions Properties sheet—High, Normal, or Low.

7. Select the allowed type of message—System Messages or Non-System Messages.

8. Select a maximum size for messages.

Robin now switches her attention to SMTP connectors. She knows that these connectors anonymously access remote domains to send messages; they don't authenticate connections by default. Robin wants to configure an SMTP connector to pass authentication credentials. She also knows Exchange 2000 supports three different authentication methods in addition to anonymous access: basic authentication, where the credentials are passed as clear text to the target server; integrated Windows authentication, where credentials are securely passed over the connection; and transport layer security (TLS) encryption, where a smart card or X.509 certificate is exchanged. Robin wants security with as little maintenance overhead or chance of technical complications as possible. She selects Basic authentication because it is the most compatible method with remote server security systems.

Project 10.2
To configure SMTP connector access:

1. Start System Manager.

2. In the Connectors node, right-click on the SMTP connector you want to configure and select Properties in the context menu.

3. Select the Outbound Security button in the Advanced panel.

4. Enable Basic authentication for the widest possible compatibility and select Modify.

5. Complete the Account, Password, and Confirm Password fields in the Outbound Connection Credentials dialog box and confirm the entry by clicking on OK.

Finally, she directs her attention to X.400 connectors.

Project 10.3
To configure X.400 access:

1. Start System Manager.

2. In the Connectors node, right-click on the X.400 connector you want to configure and select Properties in the context menu.

Note: A remote X.400 name and security credentials has to be included in Setup to configure this connector.

3. Click on the Modify button on the General Properties sheet to confirm the remote X.400 name and password.

4. Click on the Do Not Allow Public Referrals option box at the bottom of the General Properties sheet. This option prevents public folder referrals through this connector to other servers in the connected Routing Groups.

5. Select the appropriate level of allowed priorities on the Content Restrictions Properties sheet—High, Normal, and/or Low.

6. Select the allowed type of message—System Messages and/or Non-System Messages.

7. Select a maximum size for messages.

8. Click on the Add button on the Delivery Restrictions Properties sheet to exclusively accept or reject messages from users listed in AD.

9. Define Selected Times For Transmission and Remote Initiated Transmissions on the Schedule Properties sheet. Shaded areas represent the selected time periods.

Robin, having previewed the range of access control features in the selection of connectors, decides that SMTP is probably the most flexible connector to use when configuring the majority of the servers in her Exchange organization. It provides a range of authentication methods and the least amount of maintenance in targeting remote servers.

CHAPTER ELEVEN

External Connectivity

After completing this chapter, you will be able to:

✓ Outline the steps involved in planning the connection to foreign systems

✓ Know what components are critical parts of a functional and structural audit

✓ Explain how to best configure Recipient Update Service (RUS)

✓ Outline the configuration options for a Microsoft (MS) Mail connector

✓ Outline the configuration options for a Lotus cc:Mail connector

✓ Outline the configuration options for a Lotus Notes connector

✓ Outline the configuration options for a Novell GroupWise connector

✓ Discuss the role of Active Directory Connector (ADC) in a mixed-mode environment

✓ Describe how to configure System Network Architecture Distribution System (SNADS) and Professional Office System (PROFS) in a mixed-mode environment

✓ Discuss the role of Microsoft Metadirectory Services in multisystem environments

The chapter continues the discussion that we started in Chapter 10, where we described the various messaging connectors that you use to exchange messaging and collaborative data with foreign systems. Email systems were one of the primary online services provided through network systems even before the popularity of the Transmission Control Protocol/Internet Protocol (TCP/IP)-based Internet and World Wide Web. Bitnet, Fidonet, and other mail systems ran on standalone machines that were programmed mostly during early morning hours to pass electronic mailbags across telephone dial-up connections all over the world. Companies similarly provided whatever support was necessary to maintain a reliable exchange of messaging. In this book, any non-Microsoft system with respect to Exchange 2000 is considered a foreign system.

In this chapter, we begin with the critical planning that must be performed to successfully connect mail systems. Unlike an installation, which usually grows outward from a single source, projects requiring external connectivity are rigidly constrained within well-known, established mail systems. A review of the existing topologies and current loads, as well as projections about future workloads, is critical. Especially when interfacing with legacy systems, many solutions come only from experience. Although it might not be possible to anticipate the need for some contingency plan, thorough strategic planning may decrease the likelihood of some unexpected event or condition. Following our discussion of planning, we review the connectors, which are also covered in Chapter 10. We describe how to collect information and plan the establishment of messaging flows that extend Exchange 2000 and Exchange 5.5 to foreign systems like Lotus Notes, Novell GroupWare, IBM System Network Architecture Distribution System (SNADS), and IBM Professional Office System (PROFS). We thoroughly cover the many properties each connector has to help differentiate one interface from another. We conclude with a discussion of the need for directory synchronization and Microsoft's Metadirectory Services software, which provides a scalable framework within which information can be integrated and synchronized across heterogeneous systems.

Strategic Planning

Strategic planning is necessary before you establish an external connection from an Exchange 2000 system to some other system. You must first identify and understand the foreign messaging system to which you plan to establish a connection. You need to conduct extensive audits that expose both physical and functional areas. Your focus must include not just the software configuration of these links, but also how Active Directory (AD) directory services or some comparable service provider manages the system, as well as any changes you will introduce to build connectivity. We will discuss AD objects as examples of the principal recipients in a messaging system. You would similarly identify and define objects in the foreign system that are likely candidates for the receipt of messages and other collaborative-type objects.

Identifying a Foreign System

You need to identify the mail systems on both sides of the connecting linkage (your own system and the foreign system with which you intend to exchange messages). As we discussed in Chapter 10, Exchange 2000 provides software interfaces or connectors to a wide variety of systems, including legacy Microsoft (MS) Mail, Lotus Notes, and Novell GroupWise. We will discuss more common legacy systems like and IBM SNADS and PROFS later in this chapter. You use Simple Mail Transfer Protocol (SMTP) connectors to connect to Internet mail systems like Netscape and OpenMail. X.400 connectors usually connect to legacy proprietary systems that typically predate Internet-based systems.

During your planning stages, you need to determine how many users are on each foreign system, as well as the amount of information that will flow across your connectors. When you design your connector architecture, you also need to determine the workload characteristics (such as the composition of the mail in terms of package sizes and flow patterns) of messages exchanged with the foreign user population. In this way, you can deploy the proper number of connectors in the most strategic locations to maintain the fastest, most reliable message transfers.

Performing a Structural and Functional Audit

You perform an audit by methodically listing all information that relates to your subject. Your tracking of information will fully define your subject matter and establish boundary conditions. The subject matter can be either structural, functional, or a combination of both. With respect to messaging systems, you need to document the kind of message transfer, the topology, and the capacity of the target foreign mail system to which you intend to connect. A physical audit of these foreign systems—including physical resources, network connectivity and protocols, geographic distribution of servers, and proximity to mail servers—is a critical step you must take when you are planning your deployment. An audit includes both the structural and functional architecture of the foreign mail systems, as well as the operating system (OS) it runs on. Verify the functional organization of the system behind the message infrastructure to determine how users exchange messages among themselves and through the connector with your local messaging system. The foreign system's functional organization may require you to, for example, construct bridgeheads to control message flow from both a maintenance and security perspective that were not essential before you established connectivity. Best practices recommend not running connectors, for example, on mailbox-hosting servers.

Your physical audit will help you determine the number of foreign servers and the data stores they hold. Depending on the number of connectors you need and the distribution of data stores, you can consolidate connectors on one dedicated server. Often, an Internet email connector handles a larger proportion of mail traffic than, for example, X.400. Similarly, SMTP connectors typically run on dedicated servers.

Depending on user data store configuration and available hardware, you may need to reorganize the topology of computers to balance the load of messaging traffic.

From information collected during audits, you can assess from a holistic perspective what design issues and constraints will shape your deployment. Best practices recommend setting size limitations on documents. You need to know the range of document sizes flowing through various parts of the messaging system and across potential connections. Each connector can control the size of transferred documents. From your audit, you can identify a connector's current bandwidth utilization and the overall capacity of local resources like CPU processing time. Strategically placed bridgehead servers will be vulnerable to attack through modalities such as a denial of service (DOS) attack caused by a mail storm, which rapidly consumes local resources and interferes with normal message exchange. You need to identify these areas of weakness. You can then consider or actually proactively purchase a second processor for a dedicated server that hosts a connector, additional hard drive space that accommodates messaging queues, and a second bridgehead that adds fault tolerance to the system. Identify any automated mail applications that can create heavy mail traffic during short periods of time during daily peak hours of operation. Project that usage over time in terms of increased growth resulting from that new connectivity. Unlike establishing a new deployment, which will at least during a startup phase grow at a linear rate, establishing external connections can result in explosive exponential growth shortly after they are established due to previously unseen levels of demand for service. You also need to anticipate the replication of services like data stores in Public Folder trees; what information is regularly accessed, and what referrals are made to these folders from across the organization. It is also necessary to confirm the proper configuration of the client-side office applications, such as mail clients, that are using these connectors.

A strategic plan regarding how you will implement directory synchronization with the foreign system—although not essential before you join the two mail systems—may now suggest potential consumption of critical bandwidth provided by poorly located connections. To facilitate access to the user population, it is essential for you to judiciously place Global Catalog (GC) servers on the near side of slow links. Finally, the physical and functional merge in the area of policy-based management of resources. When connecting to foreign systems, you must understand remote policies and standards. The naming conventions used in the foreign systems might, for example, use a different combination of first and last names. Translation of information exchanged between two systems may require time and additional resources. If you don't properly anticipate this, it can lead to considerable confusion among users, duplicate record assignments, and communication bottlenecks when the two systems interoperate.

Identifying Named Objects

The audit information you collect should expose both the hardware and software issues that support the deployment and configuration of connectors. From an organizational perspective, you must determine how the added email systems will affect the AD structure, which authenticates and categorizes objects within the directory namespace. This includes issues like directory schema, naming conventions, synchronization, and replication. On the remote side, your structural and functional audits will help you identify what connectors are necessary to support the foreign system. AD uses Lightweight Directory Access Protocol (LDAP) rather than Directory application programming interface (API). Connecting older systems with proprietary directory synchronization scripts may not work as expected in an Exchange 2000 AD environment.

It is important to understand recipient objects and how they are stored in Exchange 2000 because these object entities are mapped to users and services in the real world. The topic of recipient object management was discussed in Chapter 8. Exchange 2000 defines several categories of named objects in its messaging infrastructure—users, contacts, mail-enabled users, and organizational units (OUs). You need to identify common objects across messaging systems to build information flows and to anticipate problems that the transforming of data between similar objects will have on performance.

Users

Similar to an *object* in legacy Exchange 5.5, the *user object* in Exchange 2000 is a named principal in Windows 2000 AD. Its primary role in the directory is to provide security credentials that are accessed to authenticate the actual user logging on to the network and requesting some network resources. The named object is associated with a username and a logon password; authentication of these two object attributes entitles the bearer to enterprise resources within the scope of some predefined set of permissions. A user object can have an email address and an Exchange 2000 mailbox. When a user is created in AD for authenticated access to the enterprise, you have the option, if Exchange Server is installed, to simultaneously create an Exchange 2000 mailbox for that user.

Contacts

A user object that has an email address on a remote mail system is called a *contact object* in Exchange 2000; the equivalent object in legacy Exchange 5.5 was called a *custom recipient*. Contacts cannot access Windows 2000 resources because they are known but not authenticated by the network operating system (NOS) through AD. For example, if foreign users access a foreign host system to send or receive messages within your local Exchange system, they don't need to access the forest resources of your Windows 2000 enterprise. They simply have an object record in the local Exchange system and a target email address on the foreign system. Thus, when local Exchange users want to send messages to foreign users, Exchange users access the Global Access List (GAL) and consequently complete their exchange of information just as they would if the recipient were another local Exchange user.

Mail-Enabled Users

A user with a mailbox container on a foreign system is called a *mail-enabled user* in AD for authentication purposes but has a foreign email address. Unlike contacts, these recipient objects have access to enterprise resources because they log on to the Windows 2000 enterprise. These mail-enabled users can be found in the GAL.

Organizational Units (OUs)

OUs are administrative containers composed of objects, such as user and group accounts, administratively managed as one unit. When you establish external connectivity to other mail systems, best practices recommend that you separate named objects in other systems from your local user population by storing the foreign users in a separate OU. Thus, foreign users from Lotus Notes or Novell GroupWise are separated from your local users in their own OU.

Global Catalog (GC)

Two fundamental operations in any mail system are the search for and retrieval of addressing information. Email addresses identify recipient objects to various connectors. These operations conform to specific formats so that they can properly address messages destined for both the local Exchange system and a host of foreign systems. The General Catalog server generates the Global Address List (GAL) in Exchange 2000 and retrieves addressing information by mail client software. Mail clients like Outlook 2000 directly query the GC server for this information to direct their mail to a proper location. Other mail clients request addressing information from the Exchange 2000 server, which, in turn, forwards the request to the GC server. The GC maintains a copy or replica of specific components or attributes of named objects found in the AD. Thus, to run an enterprise efficiently, you must carefully deploy GC servers throughout an enterprise, especially on the near end side of slow links.

Recipient Policy

Email addressing formats are defined in recipient policies. A *recipient policy* is the collection of configuration settings that define how local systems behave across your entire enterprise. This policy-driven form of managing systems provides a major cost savings over the configuration of specific objects because it is performed in one operation rather than at the object layer, when you must change the configuration of multiple objects in an organization. Email addresses are an example of a recipient policy. They define the valid format for the exchange of inbound information across mixed messaging systems. A recipient policy automatically generates email addresses for the recipients defined by the recipient policy you apply to the messaging system. Thus, once connectors are installed in Exchange 2000, the recipient policies can create valid addresses for foreign systems like Lotus cc:Mail, Novell GroupWise, MS Mail, Lotus Notes, Internet SMTP, and legacy X.400 namespaces. Unlike the more general protocol specifications of SMTP and X.400 that target other servers, however, you must enable the address in the Email Address tab under Recipient Policy | Properties. Note the individual checkboxes on the left adjacent to each address type. These address types correspond to connectors installed in the system. In Exchange 5.5, these user email proxy addresses were created on the Site Addressing tab in the Exchange Administrator program.

Recipient Update Service (RUS)

A domain using AD objects with Exchange attributes requires a specially designated domain controller that runs RUS and generates the email proxy addresses specified in the recipient policies for each user on the mail system. You need to carefully plan which domain controller will host RUS and how often RUS will run in the domain. If your users do not use proxy addresses, best practices recommend that you set the RUS schedule to Never Run. Alternatively, when you make frequent changes (such as during a migration), it is advised to run RUS daily or as needed, and always shortly after any updates have been applied to the AD.

Connector Review

Exchange 2000 provides many of the same connectors previously available in legacy Exchange 5.5, which we discussed in Chapter 10. You select these connectors during the installation, through the Installation Wizard. The Component Selection screen, shown in Figure 11.1, shows the selection of connectors. We will cover these connectors in greater detail later in this chapter. For now, here is a brief overview of them:

➤ *Exchange MS Mail connector*—Though a Microsoft product, MS Mail uses a store-and-forward architecture that is significantly different from the Exchange client-host architecture. Directory synchronization is performed through the MS Mail directory synchronization protocol, discussed in Chapter 10. Special messaging objects (such as meeting requests) and the use of the free/busy calendar objects are synchronized with the Schedule+ Free/Busy connector.

➤ *Exchange Lotus cc:Mail connector*—This software provides connectivity to another mail system with significant (though steadily decreasing) market share, cc:Mail. The connector provides built-in directory synchronization between cc:Mail and AD in both the DB6 and DB8 versions of this mail product. cc:Mail has undergone significant revisions that directly impact on the importing and exporting of data, so the mail connector must interface with the proper cc:Mail version to work properly.

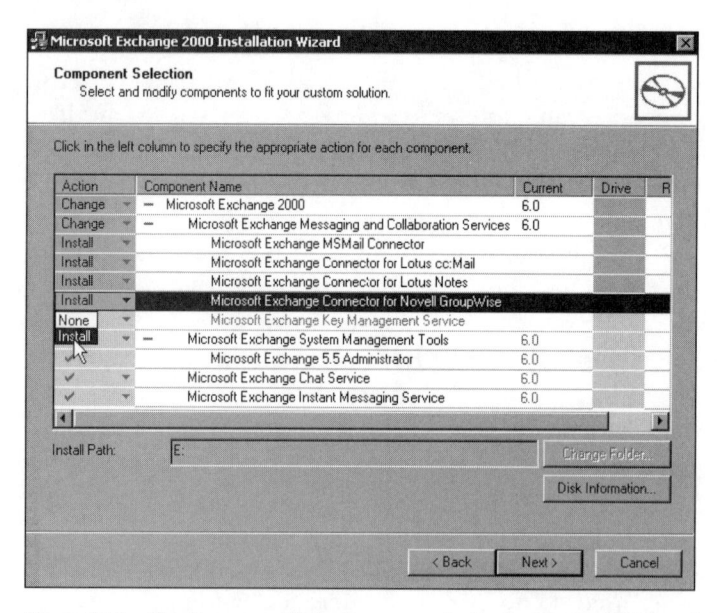

Figure 11.1 The Component Selection screen in the Exchange 2000 Installation Wizard.

> *Exchange Lotus Notes connector*—This connector provides both connectivity and directory synchronization with Lotus Notes Server. It enables you to exchange messages, including mail and meeting notifications.

> *Exchange Novell GroupWise connector*—This connector provides connectivity and directory synchronization between Novell GroupWise and AD. The Exchange system supports the Novell calendar and meeting request objects.

As shown in Figure 11.2, System Manager shows all the installed connectors under the Connectors folder. These connectors have the same function—the connection of some foreign mail system to Exchange Server. The connectors often share common properties. We will explain the full feature set in the discussion of Lotus cc:Mail. We will then refer back to those common connector features and figures when they appear in other connector descriptions further along in the chapter. In a similar way, we will also reference back to relevant figures displayed in the first discussion that follows.

Exchange MS Mail Connectors

In Chapter 10, we discussed Exchange MS Mail connectors in great detail. Although the mail system is architecturally different than Exchange, and the connector reflects this legacy structure, MS Mail is a member of the Microsoft family of products and not a competitive, foreign mail system, unlike other connectors listed in this chapter. We discuss it at great length because, even though it is a legacy product, it is representative, from an architectural perspective, of many older store-and-forward mail systems based on the X.400 specification.

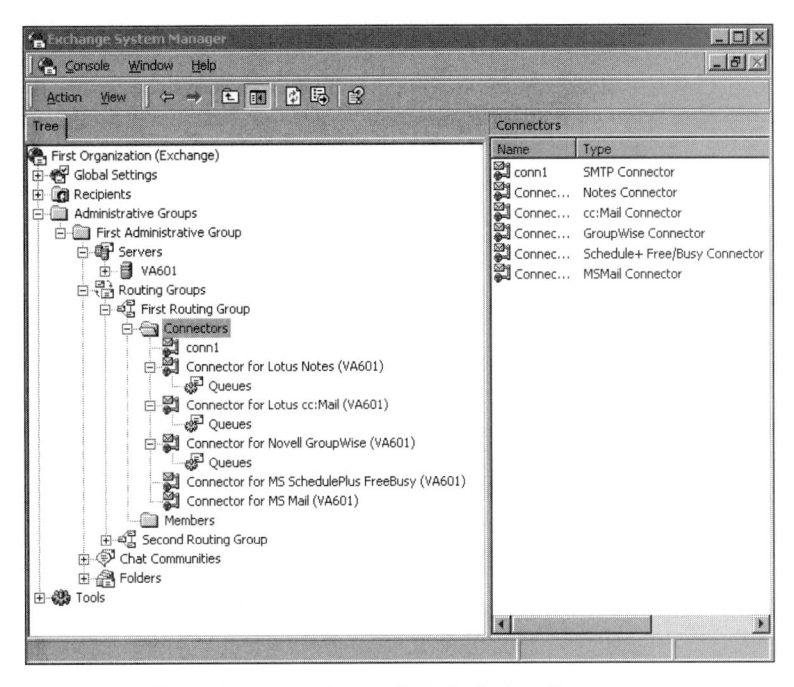

Figure 11.2 The various connectors available in System Manager.

Exchange Lotus cc:Mail Connectors

The cc:Mail connector, like the other connectors discussed in this chapter, has a large choice of tabs that you can configure from the Properties option in the context menu when you right-click on the Connectors node in System Manager. Several tabs that are found in cc:Mail are common among all Exchange 2000 connectors. Such common tabs include Address Space, Delivery Restrictions, Import Container, Export Containers, and Details.

cc:Mail Directory Synchronization and the Post Office Tab

Users of cc:Mail are added to the AD as contacts, mail-enabled users, and mail-enabled users with disabled accounts, whereas the synchronization of directory stores is built into cc:Mail connectors. The mail-enabled user with a disabled account is exactly like the mail-enabled user except that, for security reasons, the administrator must manually re-enable the account rather than have the synchronization process perform the action in an unattended manner. All connector configuration information is accessible through System Manager. Directory synchronization is version specific. You must verify that the cc:Mail routing (or shadow) Post Office has the latest versions of import.exe and export.exe installed. The Lotus cc:Mail connector works best if you connect to a DB8 version Lotus cc:Mail post office.

The synchronization mechanism in cc:Mail is Automatic Directory Exchange (ADE), which you enable in the lower left corner of the Post Office tab; see Figure 11.3.

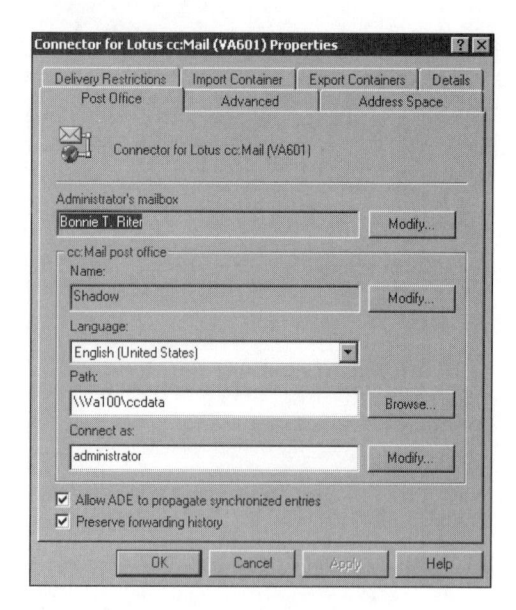

Figure 11.3 The Post Office tab for the Lotus cc:Mail connector.

(You can also use this tab to configure key information like the Administrator's Mailbox, and to select the cc:Mail Post Office location.) Remember that the cc:Mail Post Office name is limited to 256 characters. As with other synchronization processes, the ADE update must occur regularly to keep the cc:Mail user directory current in all the post offices in the cc:Mail system. Most large installations follow a hub-and-spoke or backbone design. In addition, it is common to have customized mail synchronization procedures running in different parts of the system to adjust for changes in time zones and irregular traffic flows. The Exchange administrator needs to remember that there can be only one connector with both message and directory synchronization. You can install connectors that synchronize only strategically positioned message hubs, whereas ADE synchronizes post offices on the cc:Mail side of the system.

One design approach is to have a layered backbone topology where several layers of cc:Mail hubs are hierarchically arranged across several regions. Tier 1 hubs form the trans-region backbone. User Post Offices connect through Tier 2 hubs for message flow; Tier 1 hubs connect only to other mail hubs, providing cross-region transfers. In this approach, the Exchange architecture would have a topology similar to the physical structure of the cc:Mail system. Local messages flow through one shadow post office located on the Exchange server to a remote hub from which the Lotus cc:Mail router program redirects the mail. Figure 11.4 shows this configuration. Notice that each Exchange 2000 Routing Group has one connector attached to a cc:Mail hub, but only the leftmost connector performs directory synchronization with AD. This configuration is based on the assumption that cc:Mail's ADE is working properly and that all directory objects in the foreign mail systems are current and stable. Notice other Exchange/cc:Mail links that do not perform

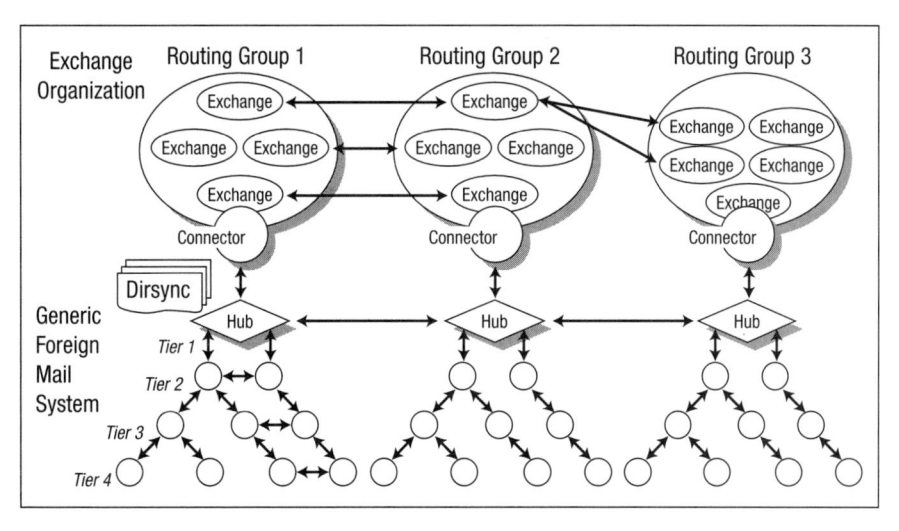

Figure 11.4 A generic deployment showing external connectivity.

directory synchronization. Best practices recommend using a shadow post office that does not have cc:Mail mailboxes as the target hub to route messages to other post offices.

As shown in Figure 11.3, you configure the message size and directory update schedule of a linked Exchange/cc:Mail mail system on the Exchange Server Post Office tab. Best practices recommend performing directory synchronization before and after ADE finishes its replication process, especially during periods of normally low network utilization. The cc:Mail user directory is imported from a remote Post Office into a specially designated, dedicated container on the local Exchange side of the connected mail systems.

Advanced Tab

The Advanced tab, shown in Figure 11.5, is common to cc:Mail, Novell Group-Wise, and Lotus Notes connectors. It allows you to specify the maximum Message Size (in K); the default is No Limit. You can also use preconfigured values or a customized calendar to schedule directory synchronization. You can use the Synchronize Now button to force directory synchronization on demand. Best practices recommend scheduling the synchronization during periods of low network volume. cc:Mail synchronization propagates the entire GC to the cc:Mail directory; similarly, all directory entries in the connected cc:Mail post office are propagated to the AD.

Address Space Tab

You use the Address Space tab, shown in Figure 11.6, to determine the address type for which the connector is responsible. This tab is common to all the connectors cited in this chapter, you can separate cc:Mail traffic by setting a mailbox and post office that will determine which connector is responsible for which post office messages.

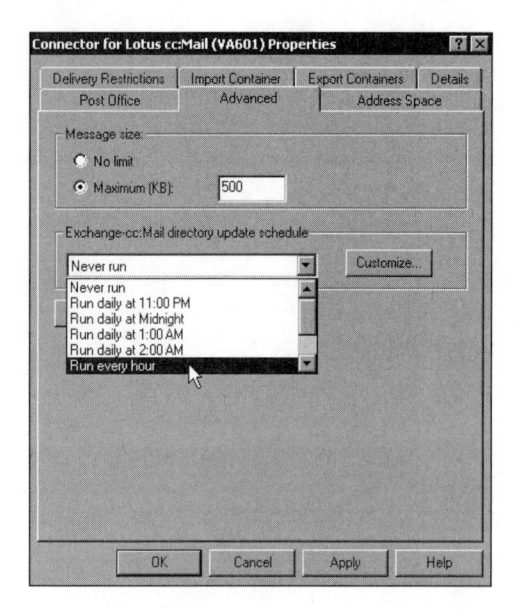

Figure 11.5 The Advanced tab for the Lotus cc:Mail connector.

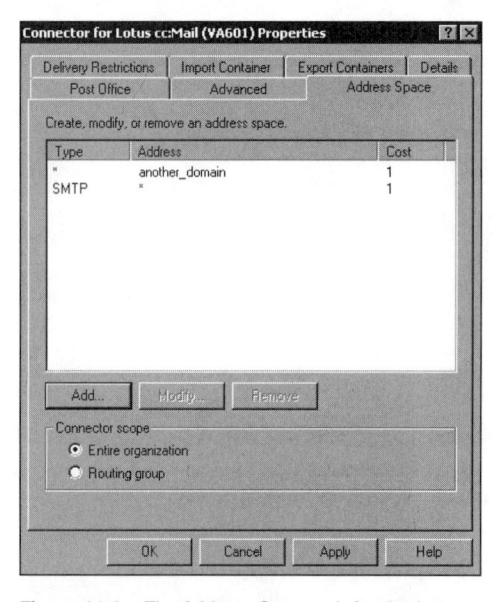

Figure 11.6 The Address Space tab for the Lotus cc:Mail connector.

Delivery Restrictions Tab

You use the Delivery Restrictions tab, shown in Figure 11.7, to restrict access to or to receive messages from specific recipients listed in AD. Across all connectors, it is identical and provides the same functionality.

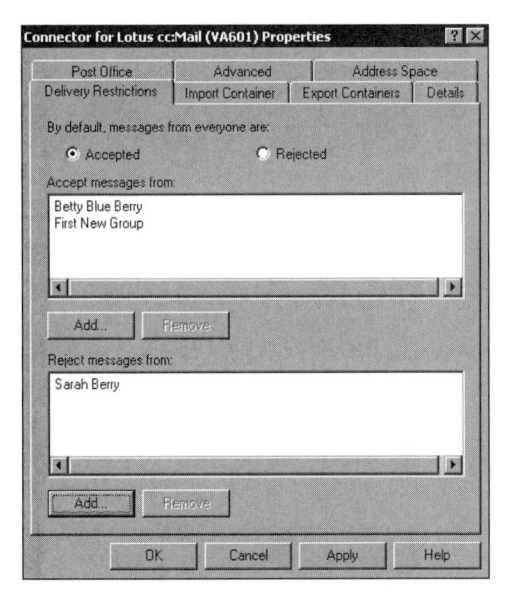

Figure 11.7 The Delivery Restrictions tab for the Lotus cc:Mail connector.

Import Container Tab

Import Container and Export Containers are tabs that are common to the three main connectors. You use the important Import Container tab, shown in Figure 11.8, to separate users from a foreign mail system by directing them into their own container. Create this OU before changing settings on this page. Use this tab to point these foreign users to the dedicated container in which to import foreign

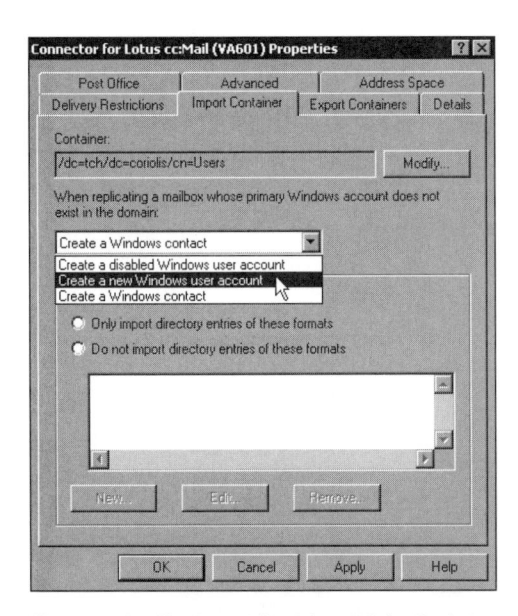

Figure 11.8 The Import Container tab for the Lotus cc:Mail connector.

mail system recipient objects. You can divide cc:Mail users into three groups: contacts, mail-enabled users, and disabled Windows accounts. Another best practice is the creation of a deleted account container as well that can store deleted but not destroyed account objects. Because most account objects have access control lists and credentials associated with them and the resources they have created like folders and documents, the actual deletion of a user account is rarely performed. Such an action would create orphaned objects in most secure NOS environments. Redirecting user accounts to a deleted account container isolates the objects but preserves the credentials that can be used by an administrator to assume ownership of some resource and access to it. You can also use filters to control the propagation of addresses in Exchange. The import options include Import All Directory Entries, Only Import Directory Entries Of These Formats, and Do Not Import Directory Entries Of These Formats.

Export Containers Tab

The Export Containers tab, shown in Figure 11.9, is yet another common feature among the connectors cited in this chapter. It controls the extraction of AD objects transferred to cc:Mail. It is common among all the connectors listed in this chapter because is specifies a container from which Active Directory objects, such as users and groups, are exported to the foreign mail system directory services. Use this tab to synchronize contacts and groups back to cc:Mail.

Details Tab

The Details tab, shown in Figure 11.10, is found in all connectors used by Exchange 2000 Server. The Details tab shows the creation date of the specific Exchange

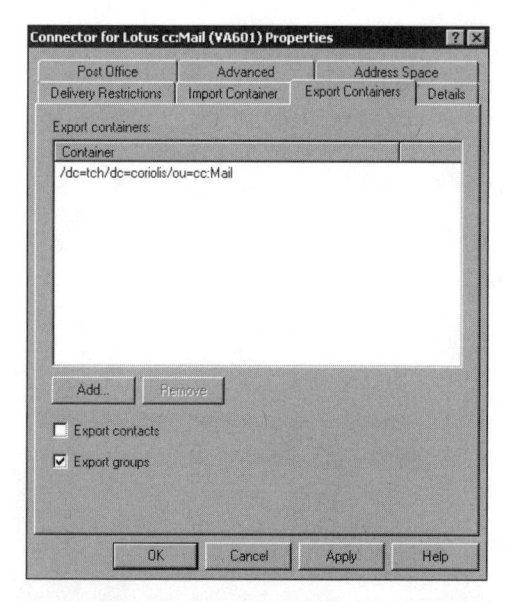

Figure 11.9 The Export Containers tab for the Lotus cc:Mail connector.

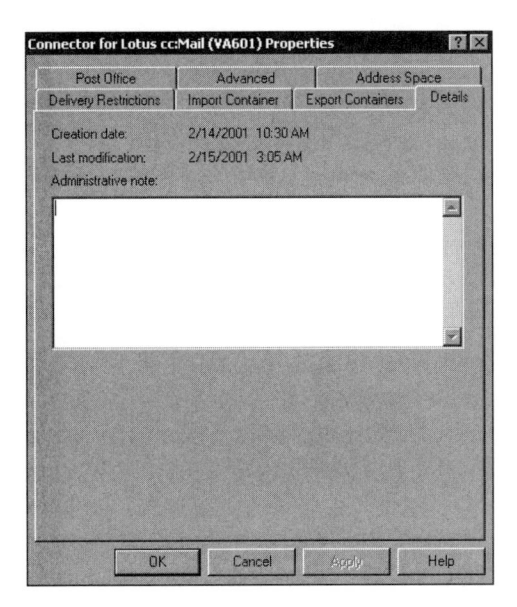

Figure 11.10 The Details tab.

object and the date it was last modified. There is also space for you to leave an administrative note.

Exchange Lotus Notes Connectors

Exchange Lotus Notes connectors connect Exchange 2000 with Lotus Notes servers. They provide built-in messaging and directory synchronization as well as handle meeting request objects. Aside from synchronization between AD and the Notes address book, these connectors provide the same functionality in Exchange 2000 as they did in legacy Exchange 5.5. As in previous versions of this software, these connectors provide delivery status information such as read receipts, delivery receipts, and Nondelivery Reports (NDRs). Messages are transferred with options such as levels of importance (High, Normal, and Low) as well as types such as Private and Confidential.

The Notes connector uses \exchsrvr\conndata\dxamex and \exchsrvr\conndata\dxanotes directories during the synchronization process as the location for permanently storing field information and mapping files. These mapping files are used to translate entries between the two connected mail systems. You can edit mapping files like mapnotes.tbl and mapmex.tbl using any text-based editor; the files contain single-line instructions that you use to create simple mapping associations. Figure 11.11 shows an example of a mapnotes.tbl text file. Mapping files help in both translating entries and in the transformation of proprietary file format features. Rich-text format (RTF) file type supports a linking feature that is similar to hypertext, called DocLinks. Messaging objects that use this proprietary feature can

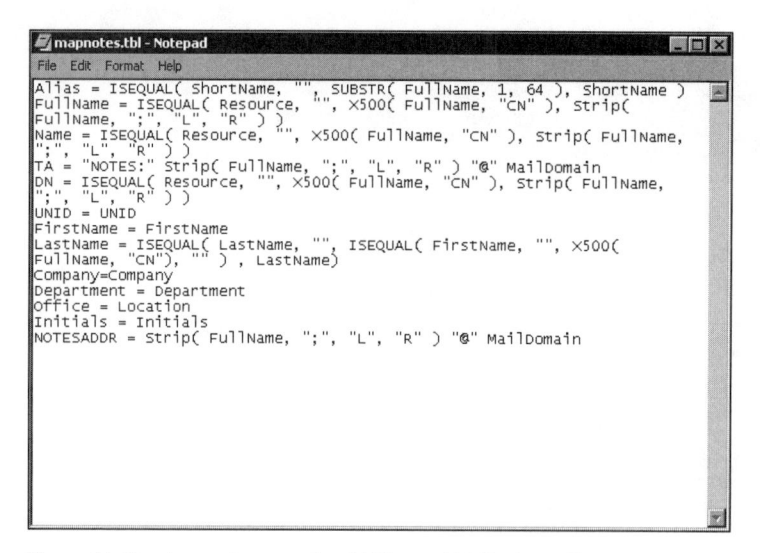

```
mapnotes.tbl - Notepad
File Edit Format Help
Alias = ISEQUAL( ShortName, "", SUBSTR( FullName, 1, 64 ), ShortName )
FullName = ISEQUAL( Resource, "", x500( FullName, "CN" ), Strip(
FullName, ";", "L", "R" ) )
Name = ISEQUAL( Resource, "", x500( FullName, "CN" ), Strip( FullName,
";", "L", "R" ) )
TA = "NOTES:" Strip( FullName, ";", "L", "R" ) "@" MailDomain
DN = ISEQUAL( Resource, "", x500( FullName, "CN" ), Strip( FullName,
";", "L", "R" ) )
UNID = UNID
FirstName = FirstName
LastName = ISEQUAL( LastName, "", ISEQUAL( FirstName, "", x500(
FullName, "CN"), "" ) , LastName)
Company=Company
Department = Department
Office = Location
Initials = Initials
NOTESADDR = Strip( FullName, ";", "L", "R" ) "@" MailDomain
```

Figure 11.11 A sample mapnotes.tbl file used by the Lotus Notes connector.

be converted to be more compatible with the document features used in the Exchange and Microsoft environment through file format conversions specified, for example, in the Lotus Notes Connector General tab, where a drop-down list provides alternative Windows-compatible file formats.

To install the Notes connector, you need to create a security ID file for the connector in the foreign Notes environment that is password protected and has appropriate rights to Notes databases. The Exchange connector ID in Notes requires Manager rights with delete permissions on the mail router database specifically associated with the Exchange 2000 domain configured in Notes. Install a Notes client version 4.6 or higher on the server that hosts your local Exchange messaging system. The connector uses the same DLL files that are installed with the Notes client. Just as with other connectors, System Manager can configure this connector for directory synchronization and messaging.

The tabs available for the Notes connector are General, Address Space, Delivery Restrictions, Dirsync Options, Import Container, Export Containers, Advanced, and Details.

General Tab

The General tab, shown in Figure 11.12, provides space for the fully qualified domain name (FQDN) of the Notes server. It also specifies:

➤ *Notes INI File Location on the local host*—By default, this is %system%\notes.ini.

➤ *Connector Mailbox*—This is the mail router database where the Notes connector targets all the messages sent to the Exchange mail system.

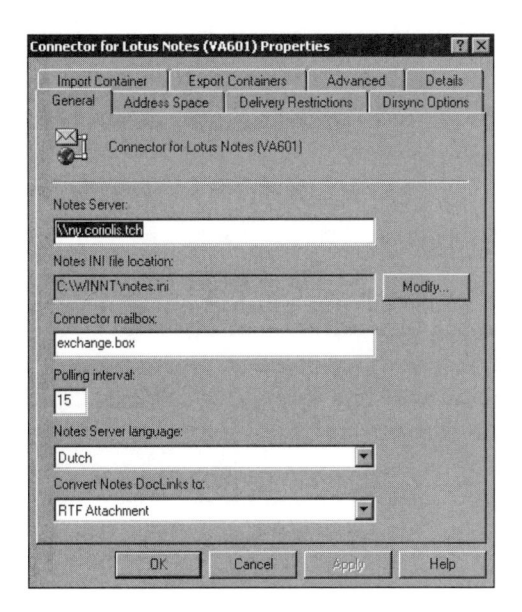

Figure 11.12 The General tab for the Lotus Notes connector.

- *Polling Interval*—This defaults to 15 seconds. It is how often the connector checks the mailbox for messages queued for delivery to the Exchange system. Best practices recommend keeping this value at this relatively short interval unless bandwidth utilization is very high.

- *Notes Server Language*—This option determines the operating country or national language (human) of the connected Notes/Domino Server.

- *Convert Notes DocLinks To*—This gives you a choice of three ways to convert DocLinks to a comparable feature in the Exchange environment: an RTF attachment, a Uniform Resource Locator (URL) shortcut, or an Object Linking and Embedding (OLE) document link.

Address Space Tab

The Address Space tab is common to all connectors (refer back to Figure 11.6). Most mail systems use general regular expressions like asterisk (*) and the question mark (?) for routing messages. During your structural and functional audit, you should have determined whether you plan to deploy several servers. You use the Address Space tab to configure which connector handles messages with specific destinations. For example, **NOTES: *@ coriolis.tch** would direct messages addressed to **coriolis.tch** to the connector with this specific address space. Refer back to the discussion of this tab in the "Exchange Lotus cc:Mail Connectors" section earlier in this chapter.

Delivery Restrictions Tab

The Delivery Restrictions tab, which allows you to accept or reject messages from specific recipients listed in AD, is common to all connectors. Across all connectors, it is identical and provides the same functionality.

Dirsync Options Tab

The Dirsync Options tab, shown in Figure 11.13, determines the behavior of the Notes address book. You can customize the Exchange-Notes directory update schedule, change characteristics of the address book (like the default name), choose to which Windows 2000 domain controllers (DCs) it is propagated, and add address books. For example, you can record all Notes users who also use Exchange mailboxes in a separate address book and control how that segregated group is propagated among domain servers in the Exchange environment. The default address book name is names.nsf, so you can remap the address book name as source=names.nsf and target=coriolis.nsf. Doing so separates the user population and the way lookups are performed in the local Exchange environment. If you change address book names, you must also modify the notes.ini file. The propagation of group options enables Exchange users to address messages to groups of Lotus Notes users by specifying a group name as a recipient. As with a DL, when the message arrives at the targeted Notes/Domino server, Notes expands the message and delivers it to each member of the group.

Import Container Tab

You use the Import Container tab, shown in Figure 11.14, to create contacts or users in AD from the Notes directory entries when you are replicating a mailbox

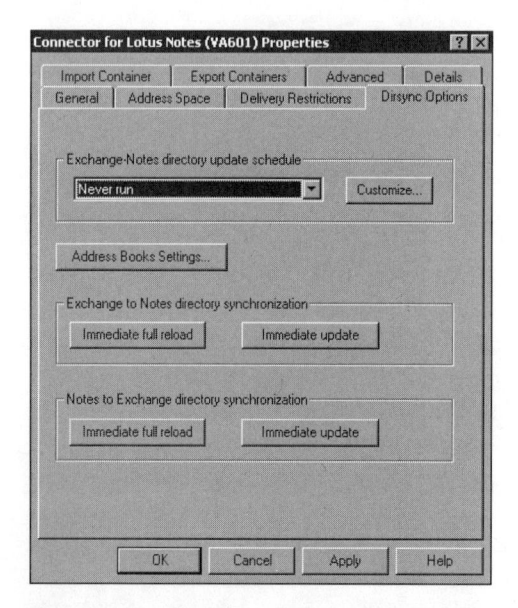

Figure 11.13 The Dirsync Options tab for the Lotus Notes connector.

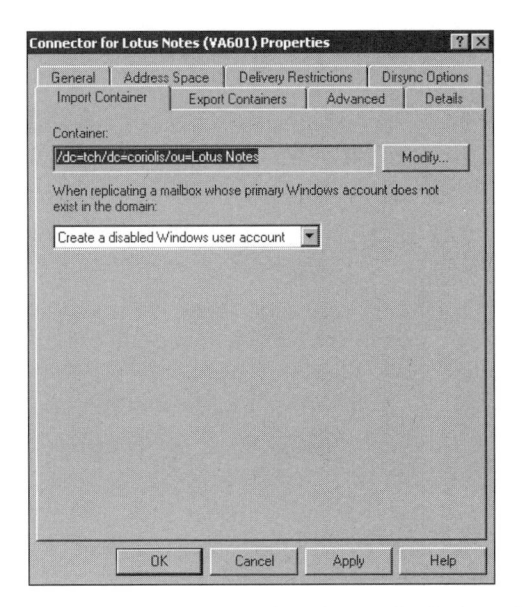

Figure 11.14 The Import Container tab for the Lotus Notes connector.

for which a primary AD account does not exist. This tab provides three alternatives: to create a Windows contact, Windows user account, or a disabled user account. The distinction between contact and user account involves access to enterprise resources. The disabled user account allows the importation process to proceed but forces an administrator to take additional action as a way to authorize use of the newly created account and logon privileges. Refer back to the discussion of this tab in the "Exchange Lotus cc:Mail Connectors" section earlier in this chapter.

Best practices recommend that if you decide to change the import container or modify imported objects, you first delete all Notes objects in the current container and then resynchronize the directory information between the two messaging systems. The recommended procedure is to perform a full reload of all object information from the Notes environment.

*Note: When you import a directory list from a customized Notes environment, the exchsrvr\conndata\dxamex\amap.tbl file has a **NOTESADDR** attribute set to 128 bytes. This is the maximum size of imported Notes address book records. Records exceeding this length are truncated upon importation and the information is lost to AD. Changing this attribute corrects the situation and saves you from having to spend tremendous amounts of time reentering user data when user accounts coexist with or migrate from a Notes environment.*

Export Containers Tab

The Export Containers tab, shown in Figure 11.15, specifies a container, which includes users, contacts, and groups, from which you wish to export AD objects. Refer back to the discussion of this tab in the "Exchange Lotus cc:Mail Connectors" section earlier in this chapter.

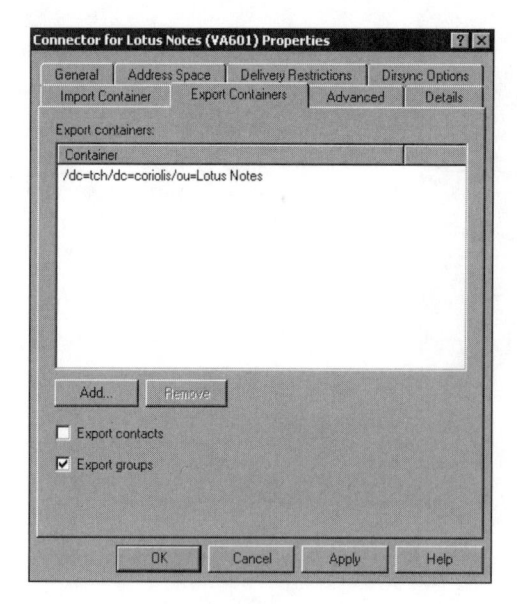

Figure 11.15 The Export Containers tab for the Lotus Notes connector.

Best practices suggest that the objects are transferred to a specially designated Notes name and address book. You can add as many specially designated containers as you want, as well as specify whether or not to include contacts and groups with the user objects. This tab is also where you can specify the synchronization of DLs.

Advanced Tab

The Advanced tab, shown in Figure 11.16, lets you perform various tasks:

- ➤ It provides options for a Notes Letterhead, which appears on the Notes message when an Exchange user sends mail to the foreign system.

- ➤ You can specify a Notes Router Mailbox. By default, it is called mail.box. The Notes router mailbox database is a connector ID that requires depositor rights on this database or Exchange mail will not be delivered to the foreign mail system.

- ➤ This sheet also has an option that describes how to order delivery of the messages: by priority; first in, first out (FIFO); or by size.

- ➤ There is a Notes Database Maintenance Schedule option that defaults to Never Run. This schedule allows you to compact the database, which prevents fragmentation and keeps files from becoming too large. You can use pre-configured times or customize your own schedule.

- ➤ Another feature on this tab is Routable Domains, which identifies specific Lotus Notes domains as destinations to which the connector can direct downstream

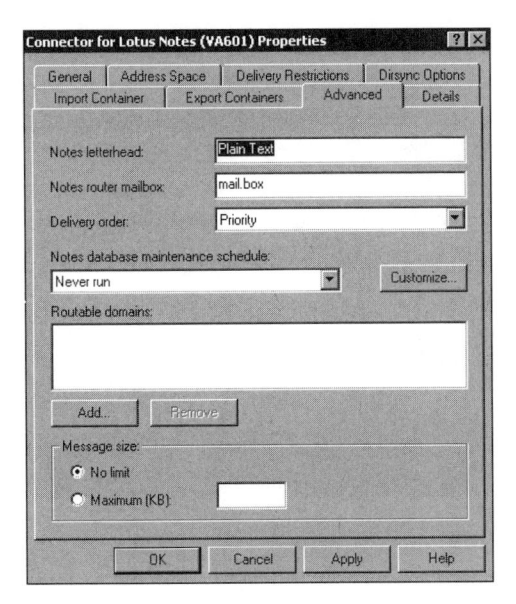

Figure 11.16 The Advanced tab for the Lotus Notes connector.

Exchange messages. The Notes domain names that are listed on this tab are not directly connected to the Exchange server running the connector.

➤ Finally, there is an option to specify the maximum Message Size in K.

Details Tab

The Details tab is common to all the connectors listed in this chapter. It shows the creation date of the specific Exchange object and the date it was last modified. Refer back to the discussion of this tab in the "Exchange Lotus cc:Mail Connectors" section earlier in this chapter.

Exchange Novell GroupWise Connectors

Exchange Novell GroupWise connectors allow you to synchronize mail and directories between the GroupWise server and NT. When a message is sent from Exchange to GroupWise, the address of either the contact or mail-enabled user is referenced in AD. GroupWise users have a target address in AD that points to its mailbox on the Novell GroupWise server. The connector translates the message into a format that the Novell system (called GroupWise API format) can read. Once the message is translated, the Novell mail server manages it. Messages sent from Novell to Exchange are first checked against a link configuration table (called a GroupWise API gateway) that interfaces GroupWise with Exchange. From this software interface, the Exchange connector for Novell GroupWise handles the messages. The connector passes messages to the Exchange Message Transfer Agent (MTA), which then routes them to their intended recipient.

The configuration file directory, \exchsrvr\conndata\dxagwise, is where Exchange stores the directory synchronization portion of the connector, which includes files that define fields to be synchronized and mapping rules of entries going from local Exchange to remote GroupWise systems and vice versa. You configure the Exchange GroupWise connector by selecting options from among the seven available tabs: General, Address Space, Delivery Restrictions, Dirsync Schedule, Import Container, Export Containers, and Details, described as follows:

General Tab

The General tab, shown in Figure 11.17, contains the API gateway path; the NetWare account name, which is typically a member of the Novell Directory Services (NDS) group called NTGateway; restrictions on message size; and the order of message delivery.

Address Space Tab

The Address Space tab, shown back in Figure 11.6, is common to all connectors and provides a monitored space that defines the type and format of messaging addresses the connector will use to determine where messages are routed, such as to another Routing Group or foreign mail system. Refer back to the discussion of this tab in the "Exchange Lotus cc:Mail Connectors" section earlier in this chapter.

Delivery Restrictions Tab

The Delivery Restrictions tab, shown back in Figure 11.7, is common to all connectors. It is used to determine what messages will be accepted or rejected from a

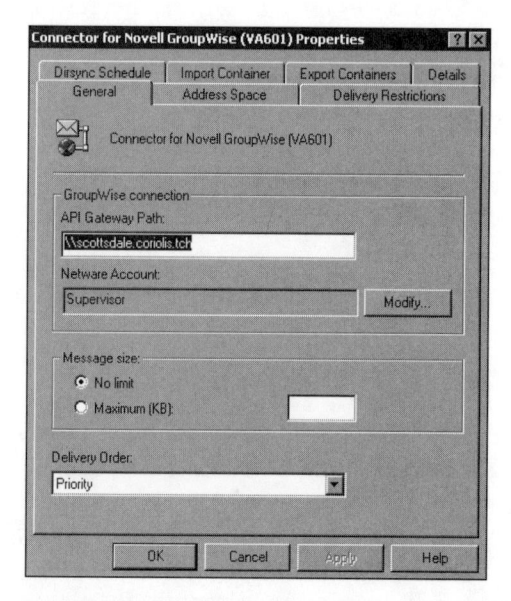

Figure 11.17 The General tab for the Novell GroupWise connector.

sender listed in the directory that is passing messages across the connector. Rejected messages are returned to the sender.

Dirsync Schedule Tab

The Dirsync Schedule tab, shown in Figure 11.18, provides the configuration options for directory synchronization. The various options include Exchange-GroupWise Directory Update Schedule, which defines when the synchronization will occur. Best practices recommend limiting the frequency of synchronization; run this process when you make changes to the address book in GroupWise or AD in Exchange. Other options that modify the synchronization process are Immediate Full Reload and Immediate Update.

Import Container Tab

The Import Container tab, shown in Figure 11.19, is the place that you can configure where GroupWise entries are stored. You need to plan your storage area before you configure this tab. You also use this tab to set options to filter any GroupWise directory entries during the import process. In the lower panel, you can specify domains as well as other recipient objects that are imported into a specific container. When you select the Only Import Directory Entries Of These Formats option, you can click on the New button, which brings up the Import Filer dialog box, in which you can write the filter criterion. You can use an import filter that uses either a general regular expression like the asterisk (*) and the single-position question mark (?) or one that uses the same format as a GroupWise address (GroupWise_domain.Post_office.object_ID) to filter these objects. Refer

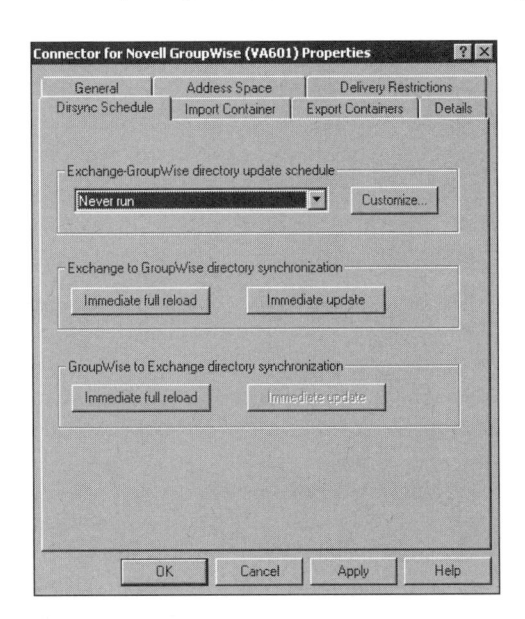

Figure 11.18 The Dirsync Schedule tab for the Novell GroupWise connector.

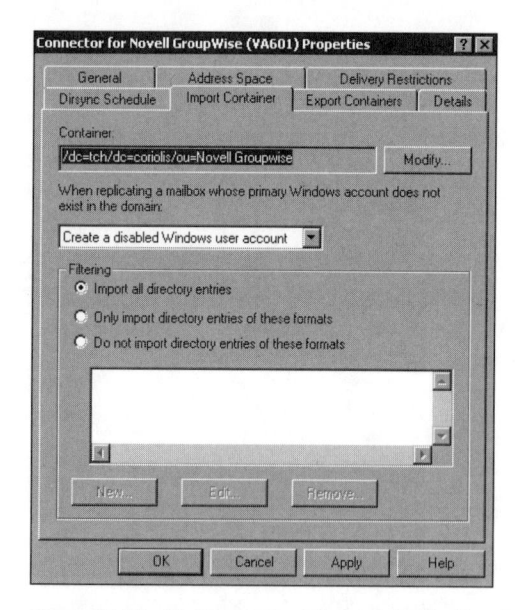

Figure 11.19 The Import Container tab for the Novell GroupWise connector.

back to the discussion of this tab in the "Exchange Lotus cc:Mail Connectors" section earlier in this chapter.

Best practices recommend separating each foreign mail system into different OUs. This tab uses the same contacts, mail-enabled users, and disabled Windows accounts options available with the other connectors.

Export Containers Tab

You use the Export Containers tab, shown in Figure 11.20, to configure the extraction of AD objects from Exchange for transfer to GroupWise. You can also synchronize contacts and groups. Refer back to the discussion of this tab in the "Exchange Lotus cc:Mail Connectors" section earlier in this chapter.

Details Tab

The Details tab contains administrative information. Refer back to the discussion of this tab in the "Exchange Lotus cc:Mail Connectors" section earlier in this chapter.

Mixed-Mode Environments

Exchange 2000, of course, coexists with Exchange 5.5. If you have upgraded from an Exchange 5.5 environment, you have the option of leaving connectors intact and building a mixed-mode environment rather than replacing all software with Exchange 2000 components (which is called native mode). When you add Exchange 2000 to a mixed-mode environment, you need to bring Active Directory Connector (ADC) into the environment.

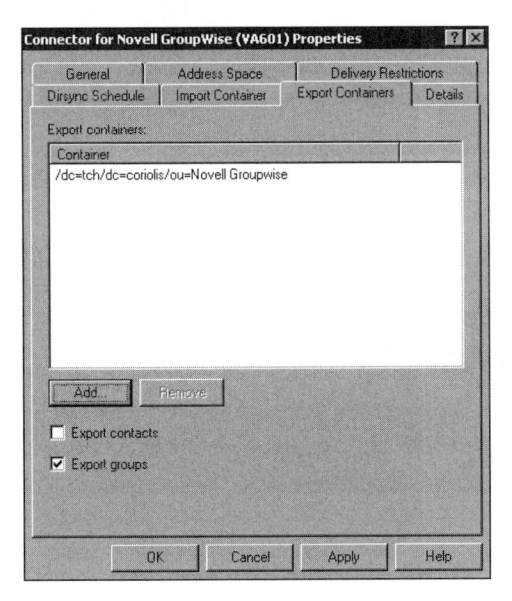

Figure 11.20 The Export Containers tab for the Novell GroupWise connector.

ADC

ADC is a specialized software component that allows Exchange 5.5 mailbox-enabled users to synchronize with AD. This synchronization is necessary because legacy Exchange software is monolithic in structure and maintains its own internal directory stores. Requests and lookups in a mixed-mode environment are sent to the AD. There is reciprocity between the two systems such that Exchange 2000 mailboxes appear on the legacy side in the Exchange 5.5 GAL. Similarly, any proxy addresses are also propagated between the two systems. RUS, discussed earlier in this chapter, plays a critical role in updating any recipient proxy addresses and thus ensures that the legacy side has the proper proxies for its AD entries. The ADC updates several objects by converting them into their AD counterparts; custom recipients become Exchange 2000 contacts, and legacy mailboxes become mailbox-enabled users with a Windows 2000 account or disabled Windows 2000 account. The use of ADC and related matters are discussed in more detail in Chapter 16.

Routing in a Mixed-Mode Environment

Most discussions of Exchange Server include references to other environments. Though not common, there are businesses that mix personal computers with mainframe computers. In our experience, Microsoft certification exams will have at least one question that mentions Exchange Server interoperability with the legacy distributed services software running System Network Architecture Distributed Services (SNADS) and Professional Office (PROFS) on a mainframe. Often, you need to keep at least one legacy Exchange server running on a network to provide support for calendar connectors with the legacy applications. Neither SNADS nor PROFS is available on Exchange 2000. To improve network throughput, best practices recommend keeping the connectors on a separate server in the same site rather than distributing them across Routing Groups, which will significantly slow down the connectivity. The configuration of connectors, however, has not changed significantly from the way it was done in Exchange 5.5. Follow these steps to introduce a new connector in Exchange 2000 and to remove it from Exchange 5.5:

1. Install the connector to a foreign system running an Exchange client.
2. Create an SMTP connector on the local Exchange server.
3. Create an Internet Mail Service (IMS) or add an address space to the legacy Exchange 5.5 server.
4. Confirm that the ADC is synchronized between Exchange 2000 and the legacy site by confirming that directory registers have been updated on both sides of the mail system.
5. Remove the connector from the Exchange 5.5 site.

SNADS and PROFS connectors are not included in Exchange 2000, so integrating these legacy mail systems requires Exchange 5.5 running typically in a mixed-mode environment. The basic configuration of these legacy mail and application services is shown in Figure 11.21. Notice that the IMS and SMTP connectors are linked to each other and that the Exchange 5.5 server is actually interfacing the SNADS connector on one side and the Exchange server on the other. Thus, the legacy Exchange server is acting here like a high-level gateway between the legacy equipment and Exchange 2000.

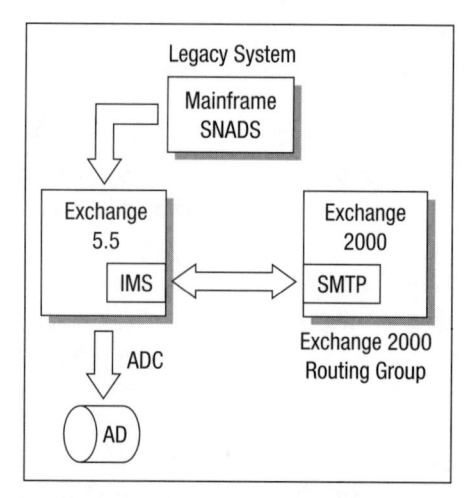

Figure 11.21 Exchange 5.5 as a gateway.

Directory Synchronization with Mainframe Environments

As with the deployment of any connector, the planning stage is critical. With SNADS and PROFS, software specifically designed for the mainframe environment, the connector has to remain on the Exchange 5.5 server that is acting as a gateway. The directory synchronization process remains functional on the legacy Exchange machine because the Exchange 2000 side of the gateway interface does not affect the legacy host's systems. Similarly, ADC keeps the AD synchronized with the legacy Exchange gateway.

Microsoft Metadirectory Services

If you have multiple directories, however, you need to consider another service, Metadirectory Services, which provides an infrastructure within which you can integrate directories, messaging systems, NOSs, databases, and other applications. Multiple directory systems share updated file information that is fully synchronized with AD. In fact, Metadirectory Services can synchronize data with other mail systems. You can install it on a server in a target forest.

Metadirectory Services uses a generic LDAP management agent. It works with AD to provide a scalable, distributed framework for integrating and synchronizing information shared between AD and other heterogeneous namespaces and data sources like Microsoft Exchange, Lotus Notes, NDS, Microsoft SQL Server, Extensible Markup Language (XML), and other OSs. In fact, Metadirectory Services combines the mailbox-enabled users and groups in each Exchange organization and recombines them into a single compound directory Microsoft calls a *metaverse* while still tracking the origin of each directory entry back to its source organization.

The Management Agent tool works well with legacy Exchange 5.5 Directory API but not with ADC. The tool does, however, mirror the contents of a Windows 2000 forest or some other namespace. Agents, mirroring multiple forests, or namespaces create a virtual metaverse or common namespace. The metaverse or namespace is replicated by Metadirectory Services, which distributes the directory-based information yet maintains internal integrity of each separate universe or namespace.

Chapter Summary

This chapter briefly discussed the issues involved in secure communications. The main points to remember are the following:

> ➤ Strategic planning is critical before you establish an external connection to a foreign mail system. Part of the planning stage is identifying all aspects of the foreign system, including the number of users involved, the functional organization of the company, the flow of traffic between the foreign system and the local system, and the physical architecture on which the foreign mail system is

running. You need to plan how to implement directory synchronization on the foreign system when it has interfaced with the local Exchange mail system. Care must be taken not to synchronize directories frequently; rather, you should do so only when you have changed directory and user information in order not to raise network utilization. In a multiple-directory environment, Microsoft Metadirectory Services provides a way to synchronize data across all applications by creating a directory structure called a metaverse, without compromising the integrity of any namespace.

- The GC is important when you are searching for and retrieving addressing information. Outlook 2000 can access the GAL directly, but older clients must first query the Exchange server, which in turn proxies the information to the GC server where a replica of specific components or attributes of AD are maintained. The email addressing formats are defined in a recipient policy, which is a collection of configuration settings that define how a local system behaves across your entire enterprise. RUS generates the email proxy addresses specified in the recipient policy for each user on the mail system. If your users do not use email proxies, you should set RUS to Never Run.

- The connectors included with Exchange 2000 are Exchange MS Mail, Exchange Lotus cc:Mail, Exchange Lotus Notes, and Exchange Novell GroupWise. When replicating directory records and importing them into an Exchange environment across these connectors, you can divide cc:Mail users into three categories: contacts, mail-enabled users, and disabled Windows accounts. You can use filters to control the propagation of addresses into the Exchange namespace. The Exchange administrator must remember that only one connector should handle directory synchronization.

- ADE, enabled in the Post Office tab of the cc:Mail connector, is the synchronization mechanism in cc:Mail. It must run regularly to keep directory information stored in each cc:Mail post office current. You configure restrictions on message size and directory update scheduling between some local Exchange system and the cc:Mail system through the Post Office tab of the cc:Mail connector.

- Aside from AD synchronization, the Notes connector provides the same functionality it did in legacy Exchange 5.5. This functionality includes delivery status information such as read and delivery receipts, and NDRs. Messages are transferred with options (such as priority) and types (such as private and confidential). In addition to RTF, the file type supports DocLinks, which is like hypertext. The connector converts this proprietary feature into an RTF attachment, a URL shortcut, or an OLE link.

- To install the Notes connector, you need to install the Notes client on the local Exchange machine and a Notes ID with sufficient rights on the foreign mail system. System Manager can perform all necessary configuration adjustments on the local mail system. You use the Address Space tab to determine to which connector Lotus Notes messages will be directed. You use the Dirsync Options tab to determine the behavior of the Notes address book, which is called names.nsf by default. The Advanced tab describes how often the database is compacted and identifies which Notes domains downstream from the connector you can target for Exchange mail.

▶ If you change an import container or modify imported objects, it is recommended that you delete all existing objects on the local Exchange mail system and resynchronize the systems by performing a full reload of all foreign system objects.

▶ The Export Containers tab specifies the local container from which AD recipient objects are exported to the foreign directory service object, such as the Notes address book.

▶ The Novell GroupWise connector translates an Exchange message into a proprietary format that the Novell mail system (called the GroupWise API format) can read. All mail exchanged between linked systems is passed across the GroupWise API gateway.

▶ For GroupWise connectors, you use the filtering feature in the Import Container tab to set options that pertain to importing directory entries. You can apply regular expressions like the asterisk and question mark to the filter mask.

▶ You use ADC to synchronize legacy Exchange 5.5 directory objects with AD objects in Windows 2000. The ADC converts legacy objects such as custom recipients and mailboxes into Exchange 2000 objects like contacts and mailbox-enabled users.

▶ Legacy mail systems like SNADS and PROFS do not have dedicated connectors in Exchange 2000. You must build a mixed-mode environment in which Exchange 5.5 acts as a gateway and interfaces the legacy mail systems with AD.

Review Questions

1. What is the recommended setting for RUS when users do not use email address proxies?
    a. Run Every Hour.
    b. Run Once A Day.
    c. Run Whenever AD Has Been Modified.
    d. Never Run.

2. What directory objects does the ADE synchronize?
    a. Directory data between Exchange 5.5 and Exchange 2000
    b. Directory objects between cc:Mail Post Offices and Exchange
    c. Directory objects between Notes and Exchange
    d. None of the above

3. When you replicate foreign mailboxes whose primary Windows accounts do not exist, what object categories can you create? [Check all correct answers]
    a. New Windows accounts
    b. New Windows accounts that are disabled
    c. New Windows accounts that are deactivated
    d. Windows group accounts

4. What components on the foreign mail system are critical when you install the cc:Mail connector? [Check all correct answers]
    a. import.exe
    b. export.exe
    c. A security ID
    d. Dispatch

5. What additional component is required on the local Exchange server for the Notes connector to function correctly?
    a. The dynamic link library installed with the Notes client
    b. A Notes security ID
    c. Mapping files
    d. All of the above

6. What connectors are included with Exchange 2000? [Check all correct answers]
    a. cc:Mail
    b. GroupWare
    c. Notes
    d. SNADS

7. What tab allows you to filter objects before they are added to directory listings?
    a. Address Space
    b. Import Container
    c. Filter
    d. Address

8. What tab is common among cc:Mail, Notes, and GroupWise connectors?

    a. Import Container

    b. Export Containers

    c. Advanced

    d. Delivery Restrictions

9. What tab in the Novell GroupWise connector controls message sizes and delivery order?

    a. Delivery Restrictions

    b. Import Container

    c. Post Office

    d. General

10. What is the recommended best practice when you are configuring an Exchange cc:Mail connector?

    a. Link a single connector to the largest post office to facilitate synchronization of directory information.

    b. Link a single connector from a Routing Group to a post office without mailboxes to synchronize directory objects.

    c. Link as many connectors as are necessary to different post offices to improve the propagation of directory information.

    d. Link as many Routing Groups as are necessary (a single connection from each Routing Group) to different backbone hubs to synchronize directory objects.

11. Which feature in the cc:Mail connector enables you to synchronize directory objects?

    a. The ADE option box on the General tab

    b. The Directory Synchronization button on the Post Office tab

    c. The Synchronize button on the Dirsync Options tab

    d. Another feature on the Post Office tab

12. What tab in the Notes connector can reduce the size of the Notes database?

    a. Address Space

    b. Advanced

    c. Import Container

    d. Export Containers

13. To what file types does the Notes connector convert Notes DocLinks? [Check all correct answers]

    a. DOC attachment
    b. URL shortcut
    c. ASCII text
    d. OLE link

14. In which subdirectory are the text-based mapping files for Exchange connectors?

    a. conndata
    b. notes
    c. exch_data
    d. table_data

15. What address space expressions in, for example, the Notes connector, would configure that connector to receive all mail for mydomain.tch? [Check all correct answers]

    a. **MAIL @ mydomain.tch**
    b. *** @ mydomain.tch**
    c. *** IN mydomain.tch**
    d. Add the name of the domain in the text box on the Address Space tab

16. What feature specifically handles the directory synchronization of the Notes address book?

    a. ADE
    b. Dirsync
    c. Import
    d. Domino

17. What is the default name of the Notes address book?

    a. notes.ini
    b. mail.box
    c. names.nsf
    d. users.dat

18. When you configure the Novell GroupWise connector, the NetWare account name is typically a member of what NDS group?

    a. Administrators
    b. Domain Administrators
    c. Notes Administrators
    d. None of the above

19. In what Novell GroupWise connector tab can you filter imported directory entries?

   a. Filter
   b. Filtering
   c. Import Container
   d. Address Space

20. Which statement is false?

   a. SNADS and PROFS require a mixed-mode environment.
   b. SNADS can connect to any Exchange server in a mixed-mode environment.
   c. When you use AD, ADC must be installed along with PROFS.
   d. You can use SMTP and IMS to connect Exchange servers in a mixed-mode environment.

Real-World Projects

Bonnie is in charge of an Exchange server that runs several connectors, including one that links to a cc:Mail system in Cincinnati. She just received a call that although directory synchronization is running, new users don't appear on the Exchange side of the connection. She needs to troubleshoot the problem or at least verify that her side of the messaging system is properly configured and running. She begins by listing possible points of failure in the system. Assuming all the systems are running properly on the cc:Mail side, the following areas could be causing the problem:

➤ The connector is not running.

➤ Directory paths may be incorrect.

➤ The Export Containers tab may be mapped to the wrong container on the system.

She now takes this punch list and begins to check the various configuration settings.

Project 11.1

To check if the connector started:

1. Start System Manager.
2. Select the appropriate Routing Group.
3. Expand the Connectors folder.
4. Click on the Connector icon.
5. The details window on the right should show the queue and its current state of operations. Bonnie sees that the queue is active.

Project 11.2
To check if the directory paths are correct:

1. Start System Manager.
2. Select the appropriate Routing Group.
3. Expand the Connectors folder.
4. Click on the Connector icon.
5. Right-click on the particular connector node.
6. Trace down and select Properties.
7. On the Post Office tab, confirm that the Administrator's Mailbox is properly configured to ensure that any connector-related administrative messages are being received.
8. On the Post Office tab, confirm that the name of the post office and the logon name are correct. Remember that the cc:Mail Post Office name is limited to 256 characters. Also remember that in international systems, there may be a language-specific conversion problem. Confirm that the language specified in Language above the Path box is the same as that in the Windows 2000 Server Regional Settings in the NOS.
9. Confirm that the directory path for the cc:Mail post office follows DOS naming conventions.
10. Confirm that the user named in the Connect As textbox has sufficient security permissions to access various file services.
11. Confirm that the Allow ADE To Propagate Synchronized Entries box is checked so that entries are allowed to synchronize from AD to cc:Mail directory stores.

Project 11.3
To check if export container properties are correct:

1. Start System Manager.
2. Select the appropriate Routing Group.
3. Expand the Connectors folder.
4. Click on the Connector icon.
5. Right-click on the particular connector node.
6. Trace down and select Properties.
7. In the Properties sheet, select the Export Containers tab.

8. In the open dialog box, confirm that the box specifies a container that holds Exchange recipient addresses that you want to export to the foreign mail system. If the container is located in a different domain, confirm that the domains have properly configured trust relationships and that permissions are properly configured.

Bonnie has confirmed that the configuration of the connector is correct, so she directs her attention to other possibilities that may be outside the Exchange server configuration. One very important issue is the versions of import.exe and export.exe. She reinstalls the two cc:Mail executable programs from a fresh copy of cc:Mail and solves her problem.

CHAPTER TWELVE

Secure Communications

After completing this chapter, you will be able to:

✓ Define security policy and identify resources that are vulnerable to security attacks

✓ Identify different kinds of resources and the security they require

✓ List security-attack categories and give examples of each

✓ Discuss various auditing techniques to expose system risks and security threats

✓ Describe ways to minimize exposure of resources listed in Domain Name System (DNS)

✓ Categorize firewall technology by rule-based policy

✓ Compare different firewall topologies

✓ Discuss symmetric and asymmetric encryption techniques

✓ List key Certificate Services components

✓ Describe how to create an enterprise Certificate Authority (CA)

✓ Outline the steps to install Key Management Service (KMS)

This chapter includes topics that relate to communication issues surrounding Exchange 2000. Your responsibility as an administrator includes safeguarding the integrity of the public and private data stores. Exchange Server as a server product makes data resources and information accessible to authorized users. Exchange 2000 is especially vulnerable to breaches in security because it exposes a broader range of data to a wider audience than any prior versions of the messaging product. The promise of access to data anytime, anywhere, from any device extends far beyond the range of legitimate use by authorized individuals; it also exposes corporate resources to parties with questionable intentions. We first briefly define the scope of security issues, including definitions of security, ways to categorize resources, security vulnerabilities, and security controls. Having identified what is at risk and who poses these threats to you, we then consider the roles that Domain Name System (DNS) and both hardware and software firewall technologies play in these issues. We then discuss Exchange Server services that strengthen security through authentication, confidentiality, and integrity. We conclude our discussion with the steps necessary to install Key Management Service (KMS) and Certificate Services.

Exchange 2000 Security

Protecting the integrity of a messaging platform includes managing risks to both physical and digitized or computerized corporate resources. In fact, an Exchange 2000 theme is providing collaborative information from both messaging and other sources, like the unstructured data from Office 2000 products. Information is built on this greater accessibility to unstructured, sometimes unrelated, data stores. Knowledge management (KM), whether as content management through software portals such as SharePoint Portal Server—product codename, Tahoe—or automated document integration through BizTalk Server 2000, increases asset valuation, as well as the probability of external or internal security attacks. It is important to remember that very often, the intention of any single or distributed attack is not only to destroy a network, but also to adversely impact the business enterprise that hosts it. Once integrity and goodwill are undermined, they are sometimes impossible to repair.

Security Policy

Though the concept of security vulnerabilities is constantly changing, Exchange 2000 is built upon several services—such as Key Management Service (KMS) and Certificate Services, discussed later in this chapter—that both protect and provide targets from attack. A general definition of security thus involves physical, as well as logical, or digital property and security controls like authentication, authorization, and confidentiality. In terms of scope of authority, security issues relating to the creator/operator of systems are often complicated by political and emotional factors. Notions of appropriateness and subordination are arbitrary but must be addressed in terms of corporate security objectives.

Exchange administrators in large corporations most likely are subordinate to others charged with security for an entire corporate structure. We use the term "appropriateness" to describe what are often arbitrary decisions made by managers about who has access to what object to perform an action at a particular time. A corporate culture dictates the appropriateness of this access and these actions. Determining appropriate actions in the context of an organization leads to a hierarchical structure made up of those who can do and those who ask others to do. Any company with a computer network must determine appropriateness of actions and, thus, a security policy. That security policy formalizes appropriateness, subordination, and formalized procedures called *security protocols*. The International Organization for Standardization (ISO) defines security (in ISO 7498) as one or more methodologies that minimize the vulnerabilities of assets, which include both digital data and physical resources. *Vulnerability* is defined here as access to a business asset (either through overt or covert means) that is not intended by design or implementation. *Attack* and *threat* are synonymous with vulnerability.

Defining Assets

We use a layered model to classify network assets. From a physical perspective, the lowest layer in that model is the local machine itself. A networked computer can be a workstation or what we will call a server defined as a computer designated to perform a specialized function. Exchange 2000 is an application server installed on a specially designated machine dedicated to providing messaging and collaborative services. Other application servers provide dedicated services as well. We call any single machine, whether workstation or server, a *local resource*. Protecting this local resource can range from user training to actually securing equipment in a physical cage or secured enclosure.

Network resources include actual cable jacks, cable bundles, and main (or intermediary) distribution frames (MDFs or IDFs). Cabling connects local resources to network concentrators (hubs), routers, and telecommunication interfaces. Network resources are often harder to physically secure than standalone machines, software libraries, or data because, by definition, they support (or "network") many local resources. It is common for only authorized personnel to have access to collections of these network resources, usually located in what is called a wire closet, wire center, or wire house, depending on the installation size.

You also see different security roles among local resources; for example, an individual assigned as a local system administrator may not have responsibilities that cover Exchange administration and vice versa. Organizations usually assign different scopes of authority to teams of personnel with regard to these network and local resources.

The scoping of authority for physical assets that include both network and local resources clearly follows a layered model such as the Open Systems Interconnection (OSI) Reference Model. This seven-layer model, shown in Figure 12.1, places

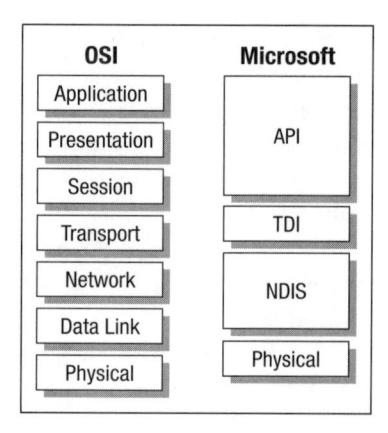

```
         OSI              Microsoft
   ┌──────────────┐   ┌──────────────┐
   │ Application  │   │              │
   ├──────────────┤   │     API      │
   │ Presentation │   │              │
   ├──────────────┤   │              │
   │   Session    │   │              │
   ├──────────────┤   ├──────────────┤
   │  Transport   │   │     TDI      │
   ├──────────────┤   ├──────────────┤
   │   Network    │   │              │
   ├──────────────┤   │    NDIS      │
   │  Data Link   │   │              │
   ├──────────────┤   ├──────────────┤
   │   Physical   │   │   Physical   │
   └──────────────┘   └──────────────┘
```

Figure 12.1 The OSI Reference Model and the Microsoft Model.

physical connectivity on the bottom; various transport protocol layers (the Data Link layer, Network layer, and Transport layer) all run on top of this physical substrate. Above these more functional transport layers is an application layer that provides actual services the user can see and use. We also show you the Microsoft four-layer version of this same reference model, where emphasis is placed on the boundaries or interfaces rather than on the actual layers themselves. At the top there is an Application Programming Interface or API. Below that layer is the Transport Device Interface layer, which corresponds, in general, to protocol services. Below that layer are the more structurally oriented Network Device Interface Specification and Physical layers. The application interface layers (Session, Presentation, and Application) in the OSI Reference Model and the API layer in the Microsoft Model are still part of the network operating system (NOS). Exchange Server and other Microsoft.NET application servers like it rest on top of this seventh layer of the NOS. In legacy products like Exchange 5.5 and SQL Server 7, these layers remained distinct and separate. With .NET servers like Exchange 2000, services in both the NOS and application server are integrated, and the distinct layers have blurred. Extension of the Active Directory (AD) scheme to accommodate Exchange 2000 objects and attributes demonstrates how NOS services integrate with an application server.

Information resources, digital rather than physical or logical resources, are all about specific objects. These named objects or principals are the users, machines, and services that make up an enterprise. Thus, they are distributed in directory services that are replicated throughout the enterprise. The concept of Single Sign On (SSO), where any user can log on from anywhere in the enterprise, requires this wide distribution of directory data. From a security perspective, it is advantageous to decentralize information repositories because there is no longer one clearly defined target. This same decentralization in storage also provides a significant disadvantage because the now decentralized data is harder to protect than data in one central repository. Multiple locations provide greater accessibility to a single isolated or distributed attack. You see another example of distributed information in the multitier design of many e-commerce and World Wide Web–based applications. The presentation (or client) software is separate from the business logic software and databases commonly used in software application development. The information or database resources, which most likely have the greatest asset value, are separate from programming code and are distributed apart from other components in the enterprise structure.

Security Threats: Defining Vulnerabilities

Security protocols recognize that the primary communication medium for the system—and therefore the organization—is the network infrastructure under the purview of, for example, a network administrator. Access to these network pipelines, with, for example, a hardware device that can "sniff" the information passing within the pipe, provides an opportunity for the unauthorized interception and perhaps manipulation of "privileged" data that travels between local resources. We can classify these kinds of security attacks as one of three modalities:

- *Interference*—A security attack that renders the target unavailable or unusable

- *Interception*—A security attack that covertly captures a data stream through either direct monitoring or redirection of the stream

- *Impersonation*—A security attack that permits a third party to intercede on behalf of one of the principals in the information exchange without the other principal's knowledge

Vulnerability to attack has both increased and decreased with the wide dissemination of information resources. Table 12.1 describes the various assets and their security vulnerabilities.

Security threats are typically either accidental or intentional. Although the popular press publicizes the exploits of those who intentionally exploit security vulnerabilities in computer systems, most security breaches within a corporate environment are accidental and caused by innocent or uneducated users who perform an action that exposes a security weakness in an organization. These breaches do not have to

Table 12.1 Corporate resources and examples of security vulnerabilities.

Resources	Examples of Security Vulnerabilities
Local	Malicious software code such as Trojans, viruses, bacteria, and worms
Network	Network address interception, interference, and impersonation
Application server	Unauthorized or unauthenticated physical access
Business logic	Unauthorized or unauthenticated logical access; focus on service integrity
Databases	Unauthorized or unauthenticated logical access; focus on data integrity

be network related. Disclosure of a password is as much a security breach as reading Transmission Control Protocol (TCP) packets passing through network cabling. These accidental exposures may remain undiscovered or unexploited. They nevertheless pose as serious a threat to the system as vulnerabilities that are used to compromise a system's integrity. Just because you learn what the Exchange administrator's password is doesn't necessarily mean you will use that password. Intentional attacks, however, are exploited in typically a methodical way.

The accidental or intentional exposure of security vulnerability can present a tantalizing opportunity to an unauthorized individual or outside agent. Distinguishing a youngster with sophisticated knowledge (a *script kiddie*) as a casual hacker from an employee with little to do or a paid individual engaged in corporate espionage is of little consequence here. The hacking process begins when the individual, to gain additional information about the compromised system, subsequently uses that accidental or intentionally exposed vulnerability to "see how things work." If, for example, you notice the password an Exchange administrator enters at his console, and return to your own desk to see if the password works on your machine, you are performing an intentional act and have begun the hacking process! The three stages in hacking a system are as follows:

1. *Discovery*—During this stage, the individual performs reconnaissance, gathering information complementary to the exposed vulnerability. In fact, a hacker may leave and return after a period of time, so as not to attract attention. Discovery includes the process of mapping system services and often involves the simplest of social-engineering attacks: asking someone for privileged information. At the level of the local resource, gathering information about hardware configuration—including, for example, the manufacturer and model of a network interface card (NIC)—is a critical part of the process. Component identification can lead to exploitation of known security problems specific to those components. These vulnerabilities would have remained present but unknown without this detailed information. Using the same NIC for workstations and mission-critical servers simplifies deployment and support; it also simplifies the discovery process. Additional areas of interest are services that are concurrently running on an application server, TCP ports used to support those running services, and physical characteristics of the system, such as network topology. Knowledge of system defaults and commonly used configurations rapidly accelerates this phase of the attack.

2. *Penetration*—The discovery process maps the terrain and provides choices for a specific target. Once the operating environment exposed by the vulnerability is identified, the attack becomes relatively simple in that the system responses can be anticipated and therefore either exploited or avoided. As with the deployment of any system, a thorough discovery phase, knowledge of the specific system based on discovery, and careful planning make this phase of the hacking process relatively trivial.

3. *Control*—Depending on the objectives of the hacking episode, typical goals in this phase include destroying evidence of a security breach; securing legitimate passwords; creating new, hidden vulnerabilities for later exploitation; creating legitimate user or service accounts; or leaving a robot program that will self-initiate some logic or respond to a remote control, or move to another system or other services within the network.

From the corporate perspective, the act of discovery is just as punishable as gaining active control over a system or service. A more sophisticated security attack may exploit some vulnerability to stage another attack. This tactic is used to distribute the sources from which a future attack is launched, as well as to confuse or destroy evidence that would incriminate the perpetrator.

Security Measures

The Microsoft certification for Exchange 2000 administrators stresses competency in daily operational procedures, as well as troubleshooting techniques. It also tests your knowledge regarding installation and configuration of an Exchange server in real-world scenarios. Microsoft insists that candidates have hands-on experience with their server products for at least a year prior to certification. This hands-on experience exposes a candidate to concepts and methods that, though seemingly only distantly related to Exchange administration, are in fact, best practices and critical methods. This section covers various forms of auditing as a proactive problem-solving methodology, security controls as definable corporate objectives, and structural topologies that provide security. Test scenarios use these themes and topics as starting points for describing situations that test the problem-solving abilities of candidates.

Auditing

One method of determining whether any network has security vulnerabilities or can withstand the discovery, penetration, and control phases of a hack is to perform a regular and thorough audit of every aspect of the information-processing system. This auditing process can include both the automated and manual collection of information about the systems and the personnel who run them. You can perform three key steps in determining the security needs of your corporation:

1. *Baseline analysis*—One of the least expensive and probably most descriptive tools available to an administrator is the collection of baseline information through the regular and systematic study of log files. This provides you with a baseline of activity against which you can compare a new or unusual occurrence. Along with baseline information, an audit of physical security that includes personnel entrusted with keys is appropriate. Determine whether environmental controls are in place and backup equipment is available. One

security control is accessibility; not having spare replacement parts can seriously undermine a recovery effort. An audit of services running on a network is also important. If some services are not needed nor have dependencies on, for example, a local machine, stopping them frees local system resources, possibly lowers network utilization, and eliminates service interactions that expose system vulnerabilities.

2. *Risk analysis*—This audit process determines which resources are exposed and therefore at risk. The audit would include an inventory of software configurations that show the use of well known system default settings. Standard naming of key folders, user names, directory structures, scripted business logic, and default passwords all pose a risk because they are either known or highly predictable during the discovery phase of a security attack.

3. *Threat analysis*—This process determines paths of possible penetration. Through this analysis, you can identify and block several probable attacks from both external and internal staging areas, including an employee's workstation. The primary difference between a risk and a threat analysis is that the risk analysis examines internal resources and assets, whereas a threat analysis determines security targets and system vulnerabilities as perceived by an individual with undesirable or misguided intentions.

You need to perform both risk and threat analysis in the context of a corporate culture and corporate security objectives. Probable attacks must be plausible and realistic in view of the type of industry and the perceived value of assets your corporation holds. However, you should never underestimate the intentions of a vengeful, disgruntled employee.

Security Controls

Several key security control concepts are used to thwart most security attacks and are a fundamental part of any suite of security services. Upon identifying areas of high risk, you can use these control concepts to reduce the probability of an attack. These controls include:

➤ *Authentication*—A process or protocol that verifies the identity of a user or principal by comparing a logon username and password to an independent set of security credentials. Exchange 2000 Server relies on the NOS and directory services to authenticate users. It also relies on connectors like Simple Mail Transfer Protocol (SMTP) to provide additional support through protocols like Secure Sockets Layer (SSL) and transport layer security (TLS).

➤ *Authorization*—Granting or assigning rights or permissions to perform an action or use a network resource, respectively. Permissions and rights are delegated to AD directory services in the NOS.

► *Confidentiality*—A method that protects data from unauthorized access, usually through encrypting/decrypting the original clear text into/from unreadable cipher text. Exchange Server relies, for example, on a connector like SMTP to provide additional support by using asymmetric encryption methods (discussed later in this chapter).

► *Integrity*—A method that guarantees the original form of a message is unaltered from the time it is created until the intended recipient opens it. Public Key Infrastructure (PKI) provides methods that guarantee information is not altered between the time it is sent and the time it is received. PKI is discussed later in this chapter.

► *Nonrepudiation*—A method that proves that a condition or transaction has undeniably occurred. Use of asymmetric encryption can also prove that a particular party was involved in an event or transaction.

Many of these controls, such as authentication and authorization, overlap because named users (commonly called *security principals*) typically need or want to access resources once their identity is verified. Others, like encryption and integrity, work together to prove a message was not only received intact but also was confidential. Thus, these controls provide an operational benchmark to secure most, if not all, network operations.

DNS Considerations

Among information and resource assets are the address lists of your network and local resources. Whereas an Exchange administrator associates users and contacts with address lists, a hacker is more concerned with the address list of local resources. Application servers like Exchange Server, SQL Server, and domain controllers (DCs) are assigned static Internet Protocol (IP) addresses so that client service requests and dependent network services can locate them on the network. The address list used to locate the name of, for example, the closest SMTP server and resolve it to its IP address is found in DNS. Windows 2000 Dynamic DNS holds a list of all strategic resources available within the enterprise.

Most corporations keep an internal DNS server within the secured boundaries of their enterprise because a list of internal system addresses is a very probable security target to an outside agent. DNS entries tend to be limited to the most necessary resource-specific servers. For example, an external DNS server, exposed to outside networks like the Internet, is configured with Mail Exchange (MX) records that specify only SMTP servers responsible for the processing of outbound mail. Thus, only the servers listed on these records are known outside your corporate enterprise. When you use the **nslookup** command with the parameter **set type= mx**, you see the published list of MXs available through DNS. (Nslookup is a command-line utility that is part of the TCP/IP suite.)

The information available in MX records is useful for those who want to impersonate or spoof an SMTP server. If outside agents know the email address of a recipient within your organization, they can, using online services such as Telnet, launch an email attack. One way to reduce such a threat is to enable your SMTP virtual server to perform reverse DNS lookups, where IP addresses are resolved back to a valid host and domain. This would complicate the impersonation attack and force the use of valid IP addresses. However, although the reverse lookup significantly reduces this particular threat, it also severely impacts server performance. A more practical alternative is configuring servers to accept connections from a specified, and therefore known, host. Some companies that rely on an Internet Service Provider (ISP) can forward their SMTP traffic to the ISP servers, although doing so is not practical in larger corporations.

Bridgehead Servers

Using a single, designated server to connect to the Internet reduces risks of attack. Use bridgehead servers to limit the number of resources published, for example, in the MX records. As we discussed in Chapter 10, you can configure Routing Groups to pass outbound SMTP traffic through a bridgehead server. In smaller organizations, you would configure the bridgehead server to send and receive packets from a specifiable—and therefore known—host, such as an ISP mail server.

A single bridgehead server is not only easier to manage but, in the event of attack, easier to contain than several Exchange servers with their own independent connectors. Unfortunately, the price of containment to protect your enterprise if you were to suffer a sustained security attack is termination of services provided by that particular bridgehead server.

Firewall Technology

A firewall is a combination of hardware or software technology that can control the passage of network packets between a trusted network and an untrusted network. This filtering process usually controls inbound and outbound data flows from a private network. The technology works like a fireproof wall used in buildings; it partitions and manages the passage of packets from one network namespace to another. Malicious activity that might occur on one side of this barrier will have little if any effect on the network activities occurring on the other side of the barrier. Firewall technology controls access to or from a private network, as well as traffic within internally secured intranets inside already known and trusted domains. The technology provides a safe and easily managed namespace because you can enforce the logging of network activity, alarm features, and an authentication process at the transport protocol level. When combined with other security features, this technology thwarts the efforts of potential attackers because it is time consuming to subvert. In real-world terms, the best strategy in building defenses against a cyberattack is to force attackers to waste their time and resources surmounting many separate barriers rather than seeking one single, allegedly impenetrable technology.

A variety of firewall configurations monitor the passage of network packets between networks. Network packets are identified by source or destination IP addresses, source or destination TCP/User Datagram Protocol (UDP) port numbers, or network services. They are examined and, depending on defined rules, allowed or denied passage through the barrier that separates the two networks. Firewall technologies are categorized as those that:

➤ Allow network traffic to pass unless specifically denied.

➤ Deny network traffic to pass unless specifically allowed.

Although the technology is effective and, with the advent of DSL and cable modem connectivity for home computers, as commonplace as an uninterrupted power supply, it has limitations, including:

➤ All network traffic must pass through the firewall; any alternative or rogue pathways totally compromise security.

➤ Integrity and authenticity cannot be verified at the transport level, so firewall technology is vulnerable to forged packets, spoofing, and malicious code.

➤ The best technology works only as effectively as the personnel who run it. In fact, firewall technologies can conversely cause catastrophic security failures because overconfident information technology (IT) professionals usually underestimate the consequences of a firewall's misuse or misconfiguration.

Kinds of Firewalls

The most basic firewall technology filters each network packet that passes through it. A *packet filter* inspects the packet contents according to a predefined set of rules. Packet filtering is the first line of defense in protecting a private network from unauthorized ingress or egress. Packet filtering is relatively inexpensive because some network routers, which typically read a packet's contents to determine its destination address regardless of any possible security role, usually perform this filtering function. This technique can be performed at the Data Link, Network, or Transport layers of the OSI Reference Model and in the TDI and NDIS layers of the Microsoft Model.

Another device that can monitor the passage of network packets is a *proxy server*. This application server can replace one network address of, for example, a private network, with another address that is available for use on a public network. Thus, although outside parties can direct messages to this published IP address, the actual IP address of internal network resources remains hidden from outside sources. Proxy servers can work as circuit-level gateways, where packets are filtered according to predefined rules and reassigned an IP address to pass to the alternative network. Circuit-level gateways actually separate the private networks from the public ones by using different IP addresses while reading source and destination information like a packet filter.

Alternatively, the packets can pass between two separate networks at a higher, more application-oriented level in the OSI Reference Model rather than at lower levels in the form of datagrams. *Application-level gateways*, when compared with circuit-level gateways, perform a function similar to packet filtering, but at the Application layer. At the Transport and Network layers, the system understands only source and destination addressing. Though assigning a TCP/UDP port number as a source or destination suggests the use of a specific network service, the firewall device does not understand the actual packet contents. An application-level gateway, alternatively, not only understands addressing information, but can also read the packet contents. In addition, it can, for example, scan for the presence of viral code signatures in a mail attachment. Application-level gateways are more sophisticated than circuit-layer gateways and require you to configure each client to function with it. Firewall technologies incorporate a combination of packet filtering, circuit-level gateways, and application-level gateways in controlling network traffic passing through the monitored zone.

Firewall Topologies

Firewall technologies provide a barrier behind which private networks can safely provide local and network resources. They perform some level of packet analysis on each packet as it passes across this barrier. Medieval castles protected villagers from marauding bands of barbarians in exactly the same way. The castle drawbridge provided the only entrance into the inner courtyard area and safe zone. A variation in this castle design forced outsiders to travel through a long narrow passage before finally gaining access to a safe zone and village area beyond. This long passageway allowed the outside parties to be inspected for weapons, albeit from the top of high walls. If weapons were spotted as the parties passed through the corridor, the passageway would be blocked at both ends, and the invading party would be trapped and rained upon with stones and hot lead. Thus, the narrow passageway or demilitarized zone (DMZ) provided a choke point through which all outsiders traveled to gain admittance; if need be, they could be stopped and quickly dealt with appropriately at this point.

Firewall technologies, designed in a similar fashion, have adopted terms that parallel those used in medieval castle architecture. Most technologies use packet filtering as a first line of defense, so network traffic passes through a specially designated server. This host, called a *bastion* because it represents the most fortified part of the castle, typically handles nothing except these packet streams passing in and out of the private network. Sometimes, the bastion host is configured with more than one NIC. Under these conditions, it has multiple IP addresses and is called *multihomed* rather than single homed. Multihomed servers act as a circuit-level or application-level gateway because packets pass from one NIC and IP address range to another. If a packet-filtering device, such as a router, is placed in front of the bastion, it acts like a screen in the same way a castle drawbridge funneled traffic across a moat. Some common firewall architectures, sometimes called *topologies*, include the following:

➤ *Packet-filtering router*—A packet filter analyzes the network packet header fields for IP addresses and port numbers. Advantages include ease of installation and low overhead. Disadvantages include the skill required to configure it, the fact that it is a single device, and its lack of additional features, such as logging and alarms.

➤ *Screened-host (single homed or multihomed) firewall*—The bastion host adds an additional level of security to packet filtering. The packet filter sends its stream of inbound packets directly to the bastion host. When built with one NIC, a screened host, also called a single-homed bastion, processes inbound packet streams and can function as a circuit-level or application-level gateway. Both internal and external packet flows must pass through the bastion. The screened host has an advantage over just packet filtering because it adds a second level of defense. The disadvantages of this method are the cost of the bastion as well as the reduction in performance as packets pass through a second gateway. A multihomed bastion, which is actually a screened host with two NIC cards, adds significantly greater protection than a screened host with one NIC card because the host must pass the IP packets from one of the multiple NICs to the other as the stream passes through the firewall; the IP (packet) forwarding feature is disabled. Thus, when you use a screened multihomed host, an intruder would have to subvert the router and both NICs to bypass the monitoring effects of the firewall technology.

➤ *Screened-subnet firewall (formerly DMZ)*—This configuration resembles the narrow passage that creates a choke point for the packet streams. A subnet adds significant strength to this kind of topology and hence is the most secure. It is an entirely separated range of IP addresses that interrupts the passage of packet streams. The packet filter screens the traffic as usual. The bastion, however, transfers traffic to an entirely separate network on which other local resources like an Exchange server, modem pools, or dedicated Web server are installed. This subnet is a virtual intranet between two packet filters; the filters control traffic moving between the private and public networks.

➤ *Three-pronged screened subnet*—This topology consists of a firewall that interfaces the public network, the private network, and the screened subnet. Packet streams are controlled at all three interfaces through multiple zone definitions. Thus, in this topological arrangement as opposed to, for example, the simpler DMZ, more firewalls are interposed between the external public and internal private networks and the isolated subnet. The midground screened subnet, like a castle keep, lies between two or more firewalls. One firewall is interposed between the public network and the screened subnet, whereas the second firewall is a barrier between the screened subnet and the internal network. Best practices recommend that you use different firewall technologies when you deploy these two barriers to further thwart efforts to subvert the security system.

Integration of Firewalls with Exchange 2000

If you plan to provide services such as Outlook Web Access (OWA), you are by definition increasing risk of exposure. You must use a firewall topology that incorporates a screened subnet area. You could, for example, install an Exchange front-end server stripped of any references to internal resources, such as a local copy of AD or other databases that could provide clues about the internal structure of your enterprise. You must configure the external packet filter to allow HTTP traffic to pass through TCP port 80 or the more secure SSL port 443. The front-end server, functioning just like a bastion host or bridgehead server, would make directory requests on behalf of external clients. An internal packet filter or screen would be configured to allow Lightweight Directory Access Protocol (LDAP) access over port 3268 to the nearest Global Catalog (GC) server. Access to a client mailbox would run on SSL and pass through port 443. Kerberos authentication support would function in a similar way, except that it would use port 88. The Exchange front-end server would impersonate the client once a Kerberos ticket was presented to the external packet-filtering device. Multilayer firewalls, like midground screened subnets, maximize the network security. In addition, the growing use of smart application filters recognizes content and applies complex rules dealing with, for example, both protocols and IP addressing, in the form of policies. Risks are reduced because group rather than individual security policies are easier to enforce or modify through their broader scope.

Exchange Server Security

Messages sent over the Internet use an SMTP connector, which does not provide any form of security. Thus, SMTP packets are easily intercepted. Addressing information is then used to spoof or impersonate a bogus server that sends email to an internal corporate messaging system. To provide message security, you need to implement some form of advanced security features. Exchange provides these features through its relationship with the NOS and optional software component that you can install through Exchange 2000, the Key Management System.

We begin with the concept of keys. We can share the same secret key and encrypt and decrypt messages in a symmetrical fashion, or we can use different keys to pass our messages securely between us. We then proceed to the key-holding services and a chief authority that validates a key and the credentials for use. Finally, we conclude our discussion with the management system that handles the keys we have in circulation.

The Key to Security

Exchange 2000 protects and verifies messages by using all the encryption services provided by native mode Windows 2000, including public key encryption and the Kerberos protocol. Both legacy and Exchange 2000 support advanced security features that use a variety of clients, ranging from Microsoft Windows 3.x–based clients to Macintosh clients. Advanced security features include signing and sealing messages generated by a client such as Microsoft Outlook. Message signing allows a user to place a digital signature on a message so a recipient can verify that the message originated from that user. Message sealing encrypts a message with its related attachments so that it can be unsealed using only a special key. Whereas Exchange 5.5 used NTLM to authenticate users, Exchange 2000 uses Kerberos when Windows 2000 runs in native mode. Outlook Web Access is especially affected by this change in authentication protocols. Kerberos protocol is designed to work in a distributed services environment where a server running OWA can request services of another server using a user's security access or session ticket. Legacy Exchange, which can use only NTLM authentication protocol, will not support the impersonation of a user. Other methods that increase the system overhead, such as using Secure Socket Layer (SSL) protocol, are necessary to encrypt the logon session.

Public Key Encryption in Exchange Server 5.5 and 2000

With asymmetric encryption in Exchange Server 5.5, every mailbox was assigned a key pair, with one key being publicly advertised and another being a private, secret key known only to the user. You use the terms *public key* and *private key* or *secret key* when talking about asymmetric keys. The specifications for these keys are decided when the cryptographic service provider or CSP is selected during the installation of Certificate Services in Windows 2000, as shown in Figure 12.2. The public key was a fixed-length string that was made available to all users. Exchange Server 5.5 actually used two public keys—one to seal or encrypt a message, and the other to verify a message—and two private keys, with each private key complementing a public-key operation. One private key was used to sign a message, and one was

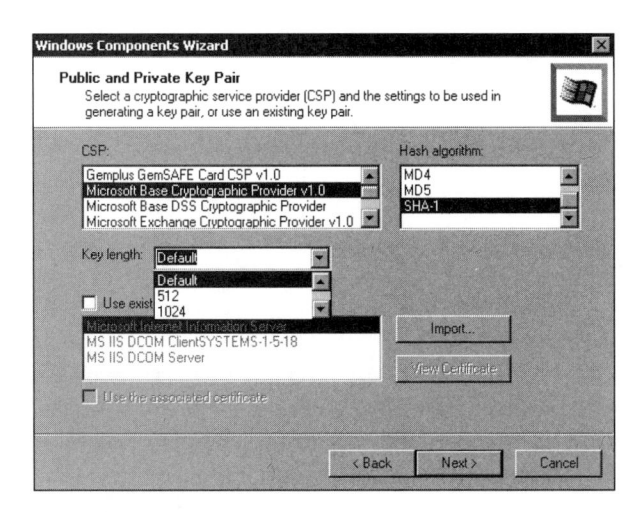

Figure 12.2 Public and private key pairs.

used to decrypt a message that was encrypted. Private-key encryption meant that users would keep on their computer an encrypted security file that contained a fixed-length string. Asymmetric keys are not identical, because one key is used to encrypt the data, and a different one is used to decrypt data. Exchange 2000 also uses symmetric encryption, which incorporates a shared, secret key that both encrypts and decrypts messages. Both the sender and the recipient of a message share the same secret key. Although this method encrypts large amounts of data quickly, it requires a secure method for the sender and receiver to exchange key data.

You distribute public keys by providing access to them in a centralized location such as public folders or in AD. Private keys are not distributed; only the owner of the private key has access to it. A *key pair* consists of complementary public and private asymmetric keys. With key pairs, either the public or the private key can encrypt or decrypt data because each complements the other. However, both Windows 2000 and Exchange 2000 Server use public keys to perform data encryption and private keys to decrypt coded cipher text. It is therefore critical to keep the private key secure. This public-key technology is the basis for Windows 2000 Certificate Services, discussed later in this chapter.

The Authority behind the Key

A certificate authority (CA) is some trusted source of security credentials for members of some defined namespace, organization, or group. The authority assumes the role of guarantor of the binding of security credentials with a public key bundled in a digital certificate. CAs not only issue digital certificates through which parties can trust each other implicitly, but also create the public and private key pairs. A CA's private key "signs the certificate," and this certificate is used to verify a party's signature. Both clients and CAs maintain a list of trusted certificates. However, you can also place certificates on a certificate revocation list (CRL). This listing includes all certificates that are explicitly distrusted. You can set trusted certificates to expire after a random time period has elapsed.

You can install different kinds of CAs. As shown in Figure 12.3, the Installation Wizard for Certificate Services offers several choices as follows:

▶ *Enterprise root CA*—This is the default selection when installing a CA and is the top level CA in a certification hierarchy. It signs its own certificates and publishes them to other CAs in the enterprise. A root CA cannot be designated by another entity as a root; it must be self-signed. Self-signing means the public key in the certificate and the key used to verify the certificate are the same; the issuer and the certificate's subject are the same. It is the most trusted CA in an enterprise. This is a CA that is unconditionally trusted by a client. You must install it before you install any other CA. It requires that AD be properly installed and running because it uses directory services to distribute the published certificates.

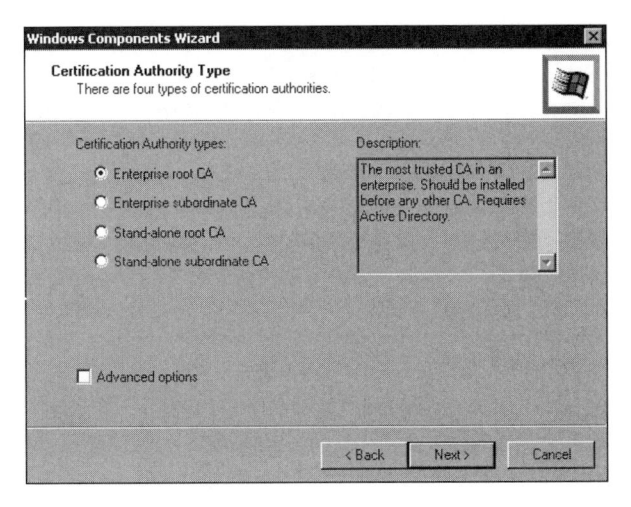

Figure 12.3 Types of CAs.

- *Enterprise subordinate CA*—This is a CA where the public key in the certificate and the key used to verify the certificates are different; the certificates are signed by the enterprise root CA. All certificate chains lead to this single source, the root CA. Thus, a CA issues certificates to another CA in order to build a hierarchy of trusted entities or, in this case, enterprise subordinate CAs. It also requires AD.

- *Standalone root CA*—The feature that distinguishes an enterprise root CA from a standalone root CA is that the enterprise root CA requires AD and a standalone root CA does not. Thus, a standalone root CA is also the most trusted CA in a CA hierarchy. It doesn't have to be a member of a domain. If, however, the CA is installed on a domain controller, it will use AD especially to replicate information.

- *Standalone subordinate CA*—This is a standard CA service that can issue certificates to any user or computer. Because it is a subordinate CA, it must obtain a CA certificate from another CA. It performs the same role as an enterprise subordinate CA but, because it is standalone, does not require AD.

KMS

Exchange 2000 Server relies on Windows 2000 for security services, including Certificate Services. An optional component called KMS is available during the Exchange 2000 installation; it provides additional support in maintaining data integrity through message encryption and digital signatures. KMS works with Windows 2000 Certificate Services (discussed later in this chapter) to provide a centralized public key infrastructure that works together with the NOS to provide a secure messaging authentication system. The Windows 2000 PKI consists of Certificate Services, digital certificates, cryptographic service providers (CSPs), and certificate stores for storing certificates. AD services complement PKI in providing a way to distribute public keys used in encrypting email messages. Exchange administrators now incorporate Certificate Services and PKI to design and maintain public-key security systems. KMS also adds an administrative tool to this feature set; it performs the vital function of key recovery. The *client* does most of the administrative work involved in messaging security, including generating the keys, storing the keys, and encrypting and decrypting messages. Clients such as earlier versions of Outlook store all users' keys and certificates in an encrypted EPF file in a specially designated area called the *IE protected store*, whereas Outlook 2000 stores all this information in the local machine system Registry. Keys are discussed later in this chapter.

Legacy KMS

Windows 2000 provides security using a variety of authentication techniques and protocols, including:

- *Kerberos 5*—This is the default protocol used for authentication purposes in Windows 2000.

- *SSL/TLS*—These protocols are used for connection-oriented security, such as that used on the Internet.

- *NT LAN Manager (NTLM) authentication protocol*—This is the Challenge/Response protocol that is given for backward compatibility with Windows NT 4.

- *Digital certificates*—These are used with the PKI design and are mostly for authenticating users who are external to your organization.

The KMS server as early as legacy Exchange 5.5 used three additional server-based components:

- *Windows NT Key Manager Service*—The main component of advanced security in Exchange 5.5. This service allowed the KMS server to function as the Certificate Authority (CA).

- *KM Security Dynamic Link Library (DLL)*—This component supported secure communication between a client and a server. All key requests were passed on to KMS through this DLL (also known as seckm.dll).

- *KM Database*—This component kept information regarding users' key pairs.

If you wanted to use asymmetric encryption in Exchange 5.x, you installed KMS as a separate add-on component, especially because NT 4 did not provide this functionality as native services. Some organizations already have KMS running using an older version of Exchange Server, such as version 5.5. This should not cause any concern because you can upgrade these servers to Exchange 2000 KMS (you can have only one KMS server per Exchange organization). Exchange 2000 KMS is compatible with KMS servers running Exchange Server 5.5 and Service Pack 1 (SP1). Best practices recommend that you run the most current Service Pack for legacy Exchange Server, which, at this writing, is SP3.

Management of the Key

With all that has been said about public and private keys, they are, however, not enough to secure your most sensitive data. Both the public and private keys used in an asymmetric encryption algorithm are stored in a specially designated server called a certificate authority (CA) that provides certificate services. Certificate Services offer many security features, including authenticating the key holder with a digital certificate through the Enrollment Agent. A *digital certificate* verifies a user's identity. Windows 2000 *certificates* are a fundamental part of Windows 2000 PKI. Digital certificates generally follow the X.509 standard and typically contain:

- The public key
- Name of user or service
- A unique serial number of the certificate
- A validity date or expiration date of the certificate
- Issuer's unique ID
- Subject's unique ID

The CA verifies the validity of the digital certificates that identify two parties exchanging information. The X.509 standard normally describes different levels of authentication, such as *simple authentication*, which means a password is used as the only verification of someone's identity. Another type of authentication is known as *strong authentication*, which requires PKI technology. For two users to communicate using strong authentication, they must use the same authentication algorithm during the specific exchange of information. Certificates are created and managed in Windows 2000 using Certificate Services. Installing Certificate Services provides you with a way to issue and manage digital certificates on behalf of your corporation. You can trust a digital certificate if you trust the source of the digital certificate, which is the CA. (CAs are discussed in more detail later in this chapter.)

Certificate Services components include:

- *Entry module*—You enter certificate requests here.
- *Certificate Services module*—This service module contains certificate templates, which define certificate attributes; the Policy module, which determines the approval or rejection of a certificate request; and the certificate database, where all certificate transactions and requests are stored.
- *Exit module*—This component sends certificates to the location specified in the original request.

KMS installs its own cryptographic service provider (CSP), which holds users' private keys so only the KMS server has access to them. Certificate Services generates a user's certificate based on requests from KMS. KMS also uses the concept of a trusted third party (TTP). Certificate Services can also generate a user's certificate based on a request from a TTP server acting on behalf of a KMS server. A CA's certificate is embedded within the client software when it enrolls through a KMS and the CA. All clients can thus trust each other's certificates because the same CA issued them. The root CA certificate has a default lifetime of two years.

Installing Certificate Services

Normally, Certificate Services is installed during the installation of Windows 2000, but you can install it at any time by using the Add/Remove Programs applet in the Control Panel. Selecting this applet should open the Windows Components Wizard dialog box. If you select the Certificate Services checkbox and click on Next, you are told that this server cannot be renamed or moved from your current domain once it's installed.

The installation of Certificate Services requests the name of your CA. The CA on the local machine, va601.coriolis.tch, running Exchange 2000 will run subordinate to the enterprise root CA (va100.coriolis.tch, as shown in Figure 12.4). Figure 12.5 shows the final certification path. Windows 2000 uses this CA name to identify all CAs and requires that each CA name be unique. When you are finished installing Certificate Services, you restart Internet Information Server (IIS). You also see a shortcut to the Certification Authority snap-in in the Administrative Tools menu under Start|Programs.

You also configure options for public and private keys when you install Certificate Services, which was shown earlier in Figure 12.2. This includes choosing the CSP,

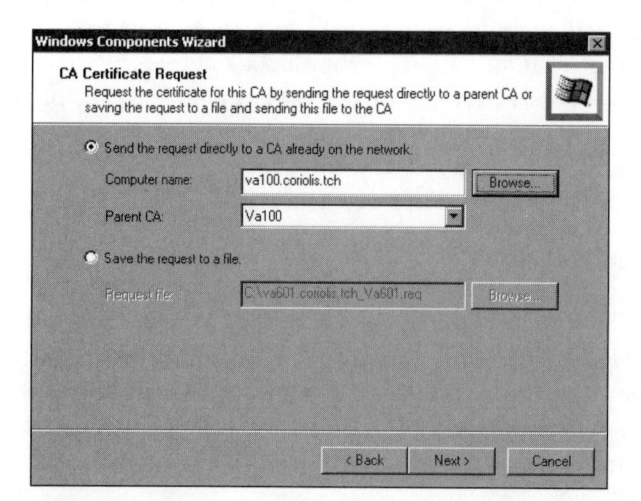

Figure 12.4 The CA certificate request, performed during installation of a subordinate CA.

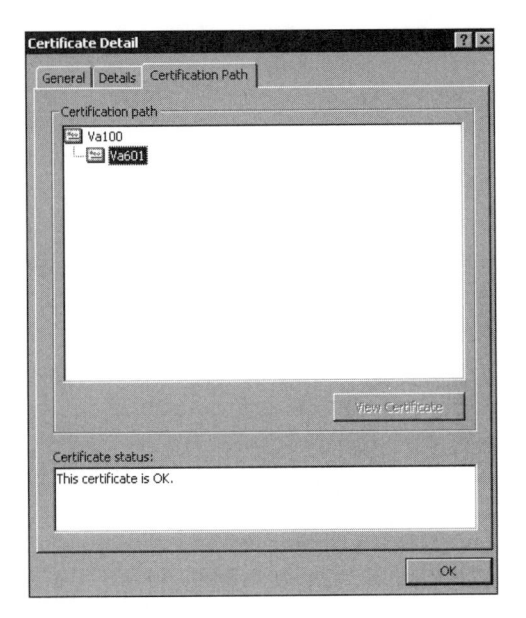

Figure 12.5 The certification path.

which you use to generate your public and private keys, and choosing your hash algorithm. The default algorithm is Secure Hash Algorithm-1 (SHA-1), which produces a 160-bit hash value and is similar to Message Digest 5. SHA-1 provides the strongest cryptographic security among the hash algorithms given. The default key length shown is 512 or 1,024 bits, depending on whether you are using a Base Cryptographic Provider or Enhanced Cryptographic Provider. The longer the key value, the longer the life of a private key.

Certificate Services provides services for Web enrollment and viewing certificate information. When Windows 2000 finishes installing Certificate Services, it automatically installs a service called Web enrollment support, by default, on that same machine. You can, however, install this Web enrollment form on another Windows 2000 machine. When users access this HTML form using the Uniform Resource Locator (URL) **http://server_name/certsrv**, they can select Retrieve The CA Certificate Or Certificate Revocation List to retrieve the CA's certificate or the current CRL. Users can frequent this Web page using a browser if they want to obtain a new user certificate.

Creating an Enterprise Root CA

To use certificate services, you must have a root CA functioning somewhere in your enterprise. Because Windows 2000 is designed to run in native mode with AD functioning, the creation of an Enterprise Root CA is the recommended practice. The first installed CA is the root CA. To create an enterprise CA, follow these steps:

1. Open the Certification Authority MMC snap-in and locate the Policy folder.
2. Right-click on this folder and select New | Certificate To Issue.
3. Choose your Exchange Certificate Template to install.

As shown in Figure 12.6, Exchange 2000 uses three templates to issue certificates to users:

➤ *Enrollment Agent (Computer)*—This allows KMS to issue certificates on behalf of Exchange advanced security users.

➤ *Exchange Signature Only*—This is used for digital signatures only.

➤ *Exchange User*—This encrypts mail and digital signatures.

KMS and AD

KMS, like Exchange 2000, is deeply integrated with Active Directory directory services. The Windows 2000 AD maintains information—such as user accounts and group memberships—for your CA. AD holds trust lists and CRLs as well as your user certificates. KMS communicates with Certificate Services through the Policy module of the CA. The Policy module inside the CA actually defines your certificates and templates used by the KMS. The KMS has its own encrypted database that stores users' key pairs. Currently, there is no way to view this database because it is strongly encrypted. Use the Exchange System Manager snap-in to administer KMS. Because of the integration between KMS and AD, you see a Security tab on the Properties sheet of every user account following installation of Certificate Services and the KMS add-on component for Exchange Server 2000.

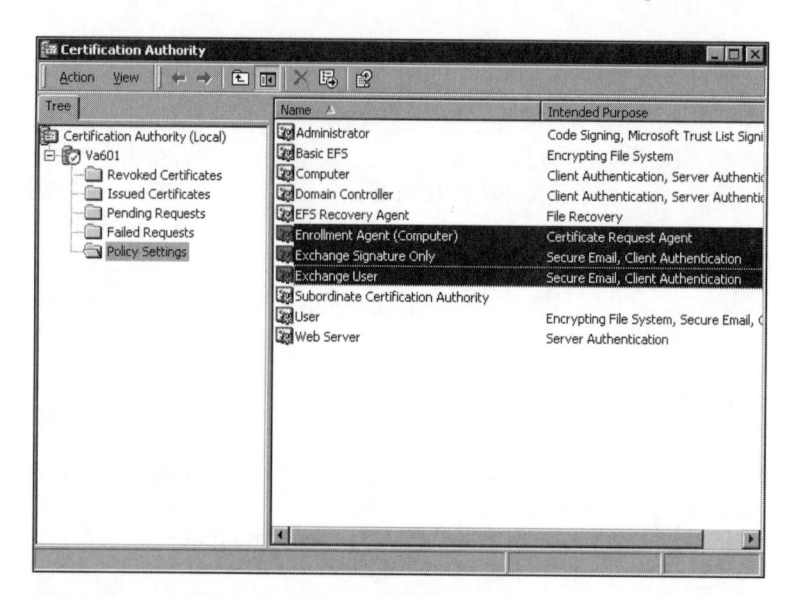

Figure 12.6 Three template choices for KMS.

KMS uses AD to enroll users. KMS requests certificates for users from Certificate Services. These certificates are used to create two key pairs for every user—not two keys, but two key pairs. One pair is created on the client for digital signatures. This key pair is private and stored on the client's machine. The other pair is for encryption and is created on the KMS server. Use the Exchange System Manager snap-in to enroll a user through the dialog box shown in Figure 12.7. Each enrollee will receive and process a digital ID certificate through Outlook, as shown in Figure 12.8. This process requires the following steps:

1. Click on the Advanced Security container and right-click on the Key Manager object in the right-hand windowpane.

2. Select Enroll Users. If you want individual users, select the Display An Alphabetic List Of User Names from the Global Address Book section and click on OK.

3. Select users you wish to enroll through KMS. Clients receive a token or notification via email advising them of their advanced security temporary key. They will be instructed to open their Outlook client software, choose Security under the Tools|Options menu, and select the Get A Digital ID button located at the bottom of the page. Security will then be set up for them on the Exchange server.

4. If you want to enroll a group of users, select the Display Mailbox Stores, Exchange Servers, And Administrative Groups Of Eligible Users option. When you are selecting users, choose the containers that contain users you want to enroll. Each user receives an email message that confirms enrollment.

Figure 12.7 The temporary digital ID providing Advanced Security privileges.

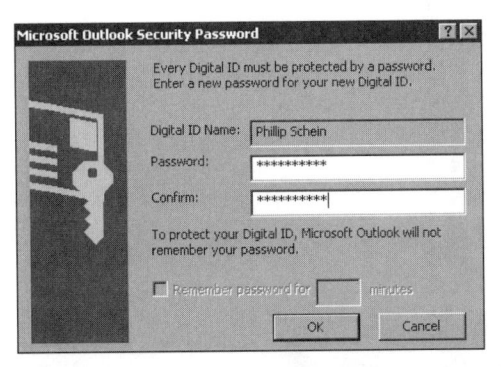

Figure 12.8 Get A Digital ID (Certificate) accessed from Tools|Option in Outlook.

Alternatively, you can configure users to receive certificates in Advanced Security through AD Users and Computers instead of through KMS. In fact, an administrator can use a user's Properties sheet in AD Users and Computers to recover the user's certificate and lost encryption key or revoke advanced security privileges. In some cases, you may prefer to use AD Users and Computers because of the additional detail given for each user in the other Properties sheets. At the top of the Exchange Security Properties sheet, you can view details such as users' current security status, their current KMS server, and even when their certificates were activated. Unlike using Exchange System Manager, where you select tasks from a cascading menu, AD Users and Computers provides a single dialog box which you access as follows:

1. Open AD Users and Computers.
2. Highlight the Users node in the scope window on the left side.
3. Right-click on a specific user account in the Details pane and choose Properties.
4. Go to the Exchange Features tab and find the Features column.
5. Click on E-Mail Security and then click on the Properties button.
6. Enter the appropriate password in the Key Management Service Login dialog box.
7. The Exchange Security Properties sheet, as shown in Figure 12.9, appears. Select one of the three buttons to enroll the user in Advanced Security features, recover the user's certificates and encryption keys, or revoke the advance security privileges.

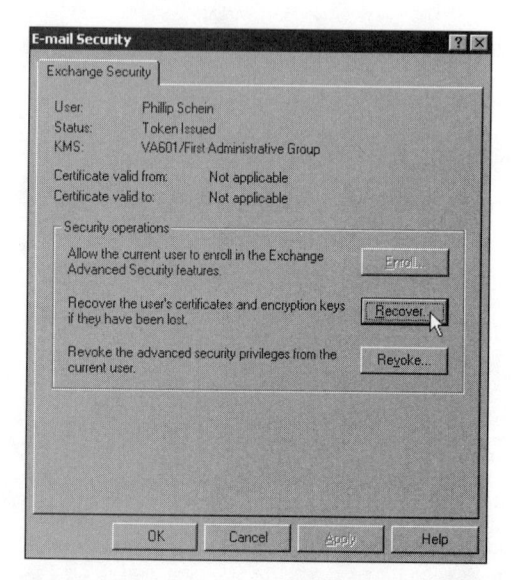

Figure 12.9 A user's Exchange Security Properties sheet.

Installing KMS and Using KMS Passwords

To install the Key Management Services, you must perform the following steps:

1. Start the Exchange 2000 Installation Wizard from the CD-ROM to install KMS. Remember that Exchange defaults to Typical Installation Mode.

2. Change the installation mode to Custom to select the KMS component from the Component Selection screen.

3. You must enable the appropriate action for each component before you can access the Action drop-down list adjust to Key Management Service. Select Change for Microsoft Exchange 2000, for Microsoft Exchange Messaging and Collaboration Services, and finally Install next to Key Management Service. Click on the Next button at the bottom of the screen. Make certain you install the System Management Tools along with your KMS server; choosing a Custom installation does not automatically include installation of the System Management Tools.

4. You need to install KMS into an Administrative Group. There can be only one instance of KMS in an Administrative Group.

5. Select a startup password. Either type a startup password manually every time you open your KMS management console, or store this password on a floppy disk in a file named kmserver.pwd. Copying the certificate to diskette and hard drive is shown in Figure 12.10. In either case, make sure you write down the password in a separate location. Unauthorized access to this password grants the user complete access and control to your KMS database.

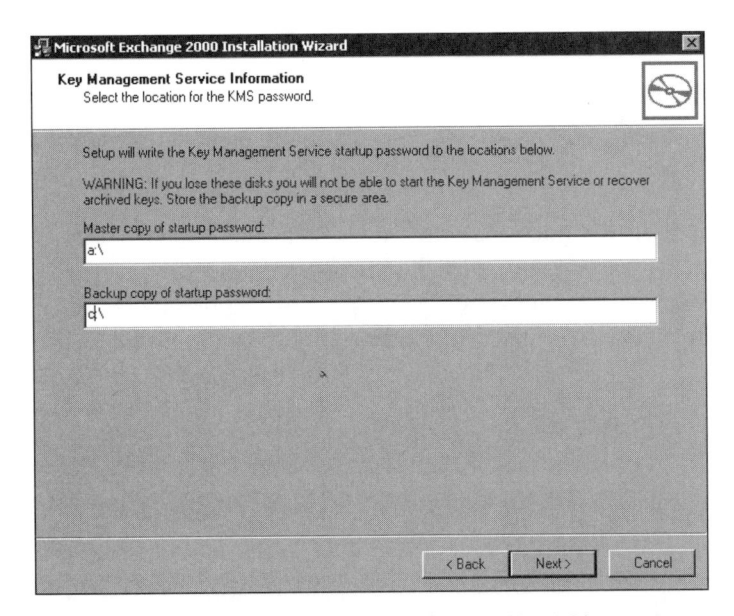

Figure 12.10 Copying the certificate to diskette and hard drive.

6. Next, grant management permissions to KMS. Add the KMS computer account to every Certificate Services server that issues certificates to KMS. The KMS server must have Manage permissions on the Certificate Services server.

7. Open the Certification Authority snap-in and right-click on the specific CA you are using.

8. Select the Security Properties sheet under Properties.

9. Select Add and choose the computer name for every KMS server in your company.

10. Make certain the Allow column for Manage Permissions is checked. Your Permissions box should show three permissions: Manage, Enroll, and Read. Permissions are either Allowed or Denied.

During the installation process, you are prompted to specify where you wish to store the KMS startup password. You can either manually enter this password or store it on a microdiskette. Security policy prevents the KMS service from automatically starting. Best practices recommend that you save the password to diskette and a backup copy of the password to the local hard drive. It is not a good idea to manually enter the password during startup. If you use a diskette to store the certificate password, it must be in the drive on startup. Because the file when saved to diskette or hard drive is not encrypted, it can be viewed with the appropriate security access. Best practices recommend reconfiguring the BIOS so that it is password protected and does not boot from the A: drive. In addition, the backup copy of the file should be written to a hard drive using EFS or is somehow secured by means other than NTFS permissions. It is also important to secure the microdiskette in a safe location separate from the location of the KMS server.

To install KMS successfully, regardless of which version you are using, perform the following steps:

1. Install Windows 2000 Certificate Services on the local machine.

2. From the Policy Settings node in the MMC Certificate Authority snap-in, install at least three Exchange certificate templates—namely, Exchange User, Exchange Signature Only, and Enrollment Agent (Computer). Notice there is also an Enrollment Agent; this is not the correct certificate template.

3. Install Exchange 2000 KMS using the Exchange Installation Wizard.

4. Determine the location of the startup password for KMS.

5. When KMS is installed, modify (if necessary) the algorithms in the Encryption Configuration Properties sheet.

6. Configure the KMS settings by right-clicking on the KMS node and starting the service.

7. Once the service has started, choose from a variety of actions, such as enroll users, revoke certificates, recover keys, export/import users, save KMS certificates, and change password. Or double-click on the Key Manager icon, enter the administrator password, and access the Key Manager Properties divided into General, Administrators, Passwords, and Enrollment Properties sheets.

Start the KMS service with the Exchange System Manager snap-in. After you have installed the KMS server, there is a new container called Advanced Security. This container appears in the Administrative Group into which you installed KMS. If you select this node, you see two objects: Encryption Configuration and Key Manager in the right pane, as shown in Figure 12.11. Right-click on the Key Manager object in the right pane, select the Start option, and enter the KMS password. You can enter the KMS password either in the popup dialog box or from the floppy disk where you saved the kmserver.pwd file created in previous steps.

You can use the Key Manager object to add other KMS administrators in order to delegate administrative functions and responsibilities. By default, the person who installs KMS is allowed to administer the key services. You can add additional administrators by right-clicking on the Key Manager object and selecting Properties. Enter your administrator password and select the Administrators tab; this tab is shown in Figure 12.12. On that tab, select Add and choose one or more users who are allowed to administer your KMS server. Similarly, you enroll users in security by generating a token sent by email to the user. From the Properties page of the Key Manager, you access the Enrollment tab, as shown in Figure 12.13. You have the option of sending a customized Welcome Message, which includes a temporary key

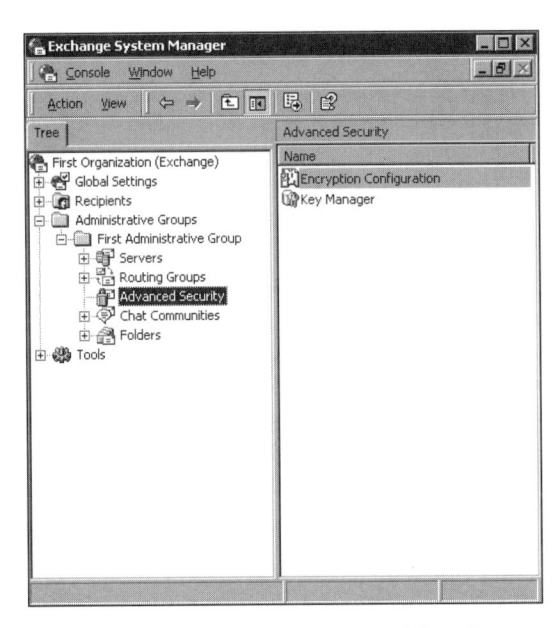

Figure 12.11 The two nodes in Advanced Security.

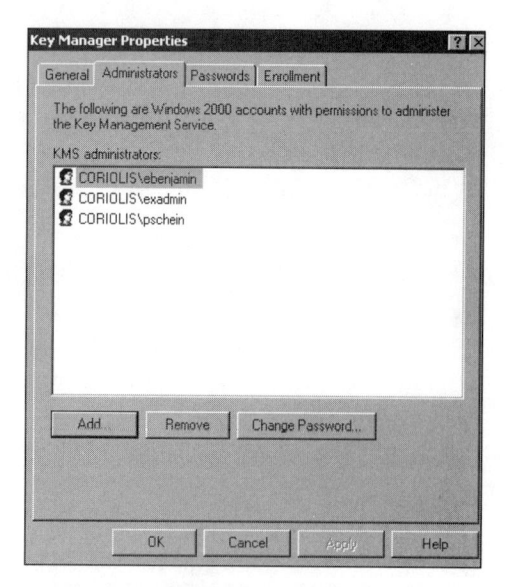

Figure 12.12 Adding CA administrators through Key Manager Properties.

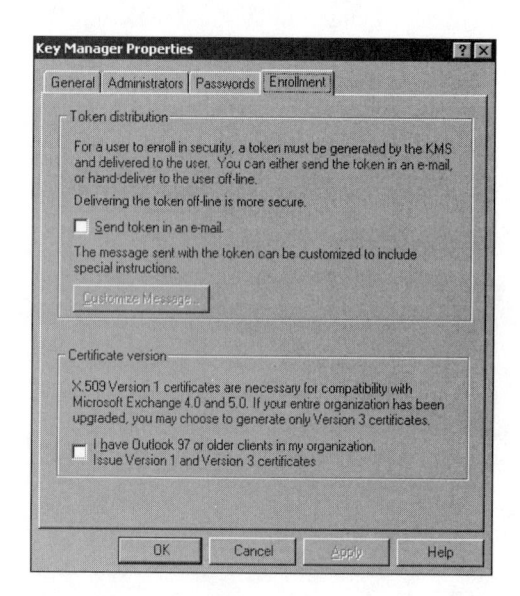

Figure 12.13 The tab for selecting token distribution during the enrollment process.

that can be used to access the permanent key you will generate for the user. You select users from the Enroll Users screen shown in Figure 12.14. You access this screen through Advanced Security in System Manager. One way is to double-click Key Manager and enter the Key Management Service Login. Select the Enrollment tab in the Key Manager Properties sheet. An enrollee uses the temporary key enclosed in their Welcome message to accept the actual Digital ID.

Figure 12.14 The selection of users during the enrollment process.

When you initially installed the KMS server, you created a password that this server used to start KMS and access the KMS database. The default KMS password is "password". Best practices recommend changing this password the very first time you run the KMS server. If you add additional administrators later, you can give them their own administrative password. They can change their passwords at any time. To change an administrative password, follow these steps:

1. Open Exchange System Manager and select the Advanced Security container.
2. Right-click on the Key Manager object in the right-hand pane and choose Properties. You see the dialog box shown in Figure 12.15.

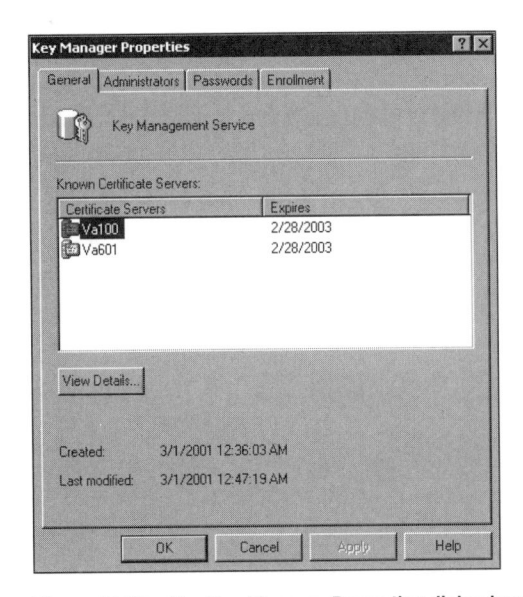

Figure 12.15 The Key Manager Properties dialog box.

3. Select the Administrators tab and click on Change Password after selecting the administrator whose password you want changed.

Any KMS password must contain six characters at a minimum. You use Passwords Properties under the Key Manager Properties sheet to configure multiple password policies. KMS operations need only one administrator password. However, you can configure specific functions to require authentication from multiple administrators. If, for example, you had three different administrators, you could require several different passwords.

Chapter Summary

This chapter briefly reviews the issues that are involved in secure communications:

- We discussed PKI in Windows 2000 and showed how Windows 2000 provides authentication security control using Kerberos 5, NTLM Challenge/Response, digital certificates, or SSL/TLS. PKI is a collection of resources that work together to provide secure messaging authentication systems, including Certificate Services, digital certificates, policies to manage the certificates, and certificate stores for storing certificates.

- Exchange Server uses encryption technology that incorporates both symmetric and asymmetric keys. Symmetric keys are identical private keys shared between the sender and the recipient of a message. Asymmetric keys are not identical; one key is used to encrypt data and a different key is used to decrypt data.

- KMS is an optional add-on component to Exchange Server. It is an advanced security tool that protects your data integrity through two mechanisms: digital signatures and message encryption. One of the main functions performed by this service is key recovery. The KMS database archives a copy of any user's encryption key pair. KMS communicates with both AD and Microsoft Certificate Services.

- Windows 2000 certificates form the core of the Windows 2000 PKI systems. We described how to install Windows 2000 Certificate Services to create a CA that would issue digital certificates, which verify a user's identity as corroborated by a third party. Information about these certificates is maintained in AD, including user account names and group memberships.

Review Questions

1. Which general security attack classes could compromise system vulnerabilities in a DNS server? [Check all correct answers]

    a. Interference

    b. Interception

    c. Impersonation

    d. Interaction

2. Which phase(s) in a hacking episode is/are facilitated when system defaults are used during an installation?

    a. Discovery

    b. Penetration

    c. Control

    d. All of the above

3. Which phase(s) of hacking is/are considered a serious breach in corporate rules of conduct?

    a. Discovery

    b. Penetration

    c. Control

    d. All of the above

4. Which security control addresses the discovery phase in hacking?

    a. Authentication

    b. Authorization

    c. Accessibility

    d. Accountability

5. A security audit includes what kinds of analyses? [Check all correct answers]

    a. Risk analysis

    b. Baseline analysis

    c. Problem analysis

    d. Physical analysis

6. What utility provides you with a listing of your enterprise MXs?

    a. DNS

    b. DNSlookup

    c. DSlookup

    d. NSlookup

7. What online utility can be used to impersonate or spoof an SMTP server?
    a. Tnet
    b. Telnet
    c. Telenet
    d. Testnet

8. Which of the following could be considered a firewall? [Check all correct answers]
    a. A hardware device that routes packets
    b. A software technology that monitors a packet stream
    c. A combination of various technologies that separate public from private networks
    d. A packet filter

9. What basic features distinguish a firewall from other devices? [Check all correct answers]
    a. Logging capabilities
    b. Packet filtering
    c. Caching
    d. Name resolution

10. Firewall technologies can be categorized by what rules? [Check all correct answers]
    a. Allow traffic to pass unless specifically denied.
    b. Deny traffic to pass unless specifically allowed.
    c. Specify what traffic can pass.
    d. Specify what traffic cannot pass.

11. What does a proxy server specifically do to reduce security risks?
    a. It acts like a caching server.
    b. It replaces one service with another.
    c. It acts like a bridgehead.
    d. It maps a publicly known IP address to a private, internal IP address.

12. What are the differences between a circuit-level gateway and an application-level gateway? [Check all correct answers]

    a. A circuit-level gateway transfers a packet from one IP address to another at the network level.

    b. An application-level gateway can read the contents of a packet.

    c. An application-level gateway transfers a packet from one IP address to another at the network level.

    d. An application-level gateway is slower than a circuit-level gateway.

13. What firewall configurations can use physically separated IP ranges? [Check all correct answers]

    a. Packet-filtering router

    b. Screened host (single homed)

    c. Screened host (multihomed)

    d. Screened subnet

14. Which firewalls provide multiple zone definitions? [Check all correct answers]

    a. A screened subnet

    b. A three-pronged screened subnet

    c. A midground screened subnet

    d. All of the above

15. What port must be allowed to pass packets when you are running OWA over an unsecured channel?

    a. Port 80

    b. Port 25

    c. Port 443

    d. Port 434

16. What port must be allowed to pass packets when you are running OWA over a secured channel?

    a. Port 80

    b. Port 25

    c. Port 443

    d. Port 434

17. KMS provides what type of security controls?

    a. Integrity

    b. Confidentiality

    c. Authentication

    d. All the above

18. Which statements are true? [Check all correct answers]

    a. Digital certificates follow the X.508 guidelines.

    b. Digital certificates should always be trusted.

    c. Digital certificates include the issuer's unique ID.

    d. Digital certificates are issued by a CA.

19. What is the default lifetime of a root CA certificate?

    a. There is no set lifetime.

    b. There is no default lifetime; the user determines the time during installation.

    c. Two years.

    d. Ten years.

20. What is the one vital function that KMS performs?

    a. Key generation

    b. Key tracking

    c. Key recovery

    d. Key authentication

Real-World Projects

Steven Keller needs to arrange for the sales staff of his company to communicate with the home office across the Internet. He has decided to recommend the use of standard browser software to simplify administration from the end user's perspective because all the salespeople know how to access the Internet, and they use browsers daily. He decides to first establish secure communications using the SSL protocol because this protocol offers the broadest range of secure communication services, including smart cards and other security methods. Alternatively, he uses basic authentication to control incoming connections and, in combination with SSL, to encrypt the clear text that is passed during the basic authentication logon procedure.

Steve first secures his SMTP virtual server by installing a server certificate. To configure secure SSL communications, Steve creates a certificate request for the Exchange server he wants to use for secure communications, submits the certificate request to the CA, installs the certificate on the Exchange server, and configures secure communications on a per virtual server basis.

Steve now completes the security setup for his virtual server.

Project 12.1
To create and enable a certificate for use on a virtual server:

1. Start System Manager.
2. Expand the appropriate Administrative Group in which your selected server is located.
3. Expand the Protocol node and the server you have selected.
4. In the SMTP node, select the virtual server that will use secure communications.
5. Right-click on this virtual server, go to Properties, and select Access.
6. Select Certificate in the Access Properties sheet.
7. Use the Web Certificate Wizard to create a new certificate.
8. Send the certificate request to the CA.
9. Upon receipt of the returned certificate, use the Web Certificate Wizard to process the request and install the certificate.
10. On the Access Properties sheet, select Communication.
11. In the Security dialog box, select Require Secure Channel.
12. Confirm these selections by clicking on OK; click on OK again to exit the page.

Steve decides to enable an authentication method that is widely accepted yet secure. Basic authentication in combination with SSL will encrypt the clear-text password so that logons to his system are secure.

Project 12.2
To enable support for an authentication method:

1. Start System Manager.
2. Select Properties for the SMTP virtual server on your physical server in the Protocol container.
3. Select Authentication on the Access Properties sheet.
4. Select Basic Authentication to enable this authentication method.
5. Enter your domain in the Default Domain text box to ensure proper authentication.

6. Confirm the entry and click on OK to exit the page.

Steve has now installed a secure method of communication across the Internet using a standard browser and SSL. The basic authentication process, which he uses to log on to his corporate messaging system, is easily accessible yet encrypted for security purposes.

CHAPTER THIRTEEN

Collaboration

After completing this chapter, you will be able to:

✓ Understand the role of collaboration technologies in business applications

✓ Install Chat Service and channels in an Exchange 2000 messaging environment

✓ Configure a chat community

✓ Describe Conferencing Server components

✓ Discuss Instant Messaging (IM) functionality in Exchange 2000

✓ Install the IM Service

✓ Describe various configuration options for IM

Communication, collaboration, and control are the distinguishing characteristics of GroupWare, software applications designed for collective use by a large population over a distributed area. The biggest GroupWare application is, in fact, the World Wide Web on the Internet. It is not surprising that these characteristic features categorize the many services Exchange 2000 delivers as the Windows 2000 messaging and collaboration service provider. This chapter explores Exchange 2000 collaboration features, otherwise known as Real-Time Collaboration (RTC) services, which include Chat Service, Conferencing Server, and the Instant Messaging (IM) Service.

With the growing popularity of Internet chat rooms and Usenet newsgroups, forms of networked collaboration are emerging as a highly productive business tool. In fact, in relation to the three Cs (communication, collaboration, and control), collaboration is at the heart of knowledge management (KM). Features such as instant messaging or video/data conferencing, because of demand by both individuals and business, are now becoming formalized as networking standards. Exchange Server is one of the first business servers to provide many of these popular and useful features. However, some, such as video and data conferencing, are shipped as separate products. Microsoft has made collaboration a key component in some of its products, notably the Office application suite, which includes Excel, Word, Access, and PowerPoint, and the personal information manager, Outlook.

Exchange Server, together with Microsoft Office 2000, provides improved collaboration functionality such as workgroup scheduling, discussions, and document tracking. Other Microsoft.NET servers (like the soon-to-be-released SharePoint Portal Server—product codename, Tahoe) will leverage this user information with content management. SharePoint, like Exchange 2000, uses Microsoft's Web Storage System repository technology. It provides collaborative features such as document management, search, subscription management, and inline discussions through both the Web Store and Microsoft Office data stores. Some highly sophisticated features like digital dashboards embellish on, for example, simpler collaborative tools like public folders available in legacy versions of Exchange Server. The use of public folders for company-wide collaboration and workflow management was featured in both legacy Exchange Server 5.5 and Outlook 97; these services have been enhanced in Exchange Server 2000, Office 2000, and specifically, Outlook 2000.

This chapter begins with a background discussion of general collaboration features and protocols. We then discuss Chat Service features that were introduced with Exchange 5.5. We will also introduce Conferencing Server and the Instant Messaging Service as other complementary Exchange collaboration services. You can always find additional information on any of these topics online at the Microsoft online Exchange Server Developer Center, at **www.microsoft.com/exchange/**.

Collaboration Concepts

Microsoft.NET is built on service-providing software that is multitier in structure and service oriented in function. As mentioned in Chapter 1, the Knowledge-Management Paradigm introduces functional roles called consumers, brokers, and service providers within this multitier, distributed services environment.

The Knowledge-Management Paradigm

Generic Architecture for Information Availability (GAIA) describes the roles and operations involved in locating, requesting, and receiving digital resources and services (collectively called *products*) in a globally brokered distributed information environment. In addition to the three main GAIA roles of consumer, broker, and service provider as supplier, there is also a complementary helper role, described as an application software layer that assists in mediating the "service" transaction. In GAIA terms, *helpers* provide to the information broker functional support that delivers services in discrete transactions called *actions*. In the Knowledge-Management Paradigm, you need to consider the complex, distributed-services environment where one consumer contacts one or more brokers for an online service that requires the contribution of many component services from many independent and physically distributed service providers. The broker mediates this transaction for the consumer. GAIA transactions are composed of one or more specific actions defined in generic terms, such as search, locate, order, and deliver. The broker performs as a single front-end object for the consumer; it transparently coordinates all the back-end transactions, no matter how they are physically distributed. This front-end/back-end (FE/BE), distributed-services structure is a major architectural feature of Exchange 2000. Knowledge management models, such as the Common Management Information Services (CMIS) and GAIA, were discussed in Chapter 1.

Collaboration with Exchange Server

Exchange 5.5 allowed users to work with Outlook 98 forms for collaborative purposes. These forms were designed using the Outlook email client. It is helpful to review a little of what these forms did so you can better understand how collaboration has been enhanced in Exchange Server 2000.

A *form* represented a method of posting and gathering information using email, and was a great replacement for regular types of paperwork. An example of a form developed with Outlook was a help desk trouble ticket. Using Exchange Server 5.5, you could develop different types of forms for collaboration, including report forms for sending reports to users, and request forms such as a purchase requisition form. Other types of forms included survey forms, organization forms, and personal forms. When forms were used to communicate information to a group of people, they became known as *collaboration tools*. Microsoft itself used the term *collaboration development* to describe the task of designing forms.

Outlook forms were one example of a product that supported true collaboration. But collaboration among a group of co-workers extends beyond simple forms. Many organizations now desire more realtime interaction, or what's known as *synchronous communication*. You could use Microsoft's NetMeeting for this purpose, or you could use asynchronous communication for group collaboration in the form of email messages being sent among the groups.

In this chapter, we discuss synchronous technologies. These include the Exchange Chat Service and IM. Such technologies actually help companies lower total cost of ownership (TCO) because these special forms of synchronous communication reduce overhead caused by traditional paper trails and telecommunication costs. Realtime collaboration also helps reduce travel costs and product development cycles.

Microsoft Exchange Chat Service

Microsoft has designed several different collaboration services to fit different commercial scenarios. The Microsoft Chat Service is based on Internet Relay Chat (IRC), an extremely reliable Internet communication protocol. Chat services, for example, provide users with one-to-many or many-to-many group communication methods in realtime using the same network protocol as that used for Internet discussion groups. The chat feature, added to the existing Exchange messaging infrastructure, provides a virtual meeting place for scheduled or on-demand meetings among your colleagues or with your distant clients.

Microsoft Chat Service provides the greatest advantages to open forums or private or public discussion groups, organized meetings, and business clients using standards-based browser and client software. Using this type of technology also depends on the deployed hardware, but it typically supports thousands of concurrent users in one chat room on any given chat server. The Internet communication protocol, IRC, has, for many years, reliably supported tens of thousands of concurrent users around the world. IM—covered later in this chapter—like IRC, is best for one-to-one communication across the same ubiquitous and relatively inexpensive Internet Protocol (IP)-based network connections.

IRC supports realtime dialogue between two or more people. It is based on the concept of a *channel*, a virtual (online) communication space shared by many people, more commonly referred to as a *chat room*. Upon "joining" a chat room, you share information with other chat room members for the purpose of discussion and collaboration. IRC is in widespread use on the Internet today. In fact, Microsoft has extended this protocol as extended IRC (IRCX) with new commands for management purposes. IRC is based on Request for Comments (RFC) 1459. Users connect to a chat server using Transmission Control Protocol (TCP) port 6667 or 7000. Port 6667 is usually the first port number assigned to the first chat community you establish by default, although you can use any port that is not in use by another service.

People meet on designated channels, categorized as dynamic or registered, for group discussions. A *dynamic* channel is a temporary channel your client software creates using special commands such as IRC **join**. One or more people, serving as a channel host or operator, manage the channel or chat room from an external client. A host is defined as the first person that "joins a channel." A *registered* channel is one that a system administrator permanently creates. Registered channels typically run automatically whenever Chat Service starts on a chat server. You can see all the nonhidden channels that are launched from your client using the IRC command **list**.

The main difference between dynamic channels and registered channels is the relative permanency of the virtual meeting space. Another key difference is that only dynamic channels have channel hosts or channel operators (also known as *system operators* or the contraction *sysops*, borrowed from earlier managed online facilities like bulletin board services). Sysops control a chat community's dynamic channels from the chat client and can control registered channels for which they have been given permission. They can also close a chat room using the IRC command **kill**.

Administrative Controls for Chat Service

As channel host, you can control certain features of the chat server. You can, for example, control who can or cannot connect to your chat room and whether or not chat rooms are *secure* or *cloneable*. A secure channel or chat room means that access has somehow been restricted. A cloneable channel is a registered channel that duplicates itself when a member limit is reached. You restrict access if you are using some form of authentication, or if you want to control who can "talk" in a chat room at any given time. Just as with any other named resource, you can allow only certain groups of users to access a channel using the security that is built into Active Directory (AD). You can design a cloneable chat room that creates a copy of itself when a predetermined member limit has been reached. Only registered, permanent channels can clone themselves; all settings are copied over to the duplicate channel.

In addition, you can allow access to chat rooms using the concept of *user classes* and *user bans* (bans are discussed later in this chapter). A user class, to which you assign users and permissions like any other group, is created outside the scope of AD. Membership in a "class" can be based on network user logon, domain name, client IP address, and even login. Class membership determines your ability to join other dynamic, temporary channels, and it can even prevent someone from becoming a channel owner or operator.

Creating a user class is not difficult; you do so using the Exchange System Microsoft Management Console (MMC) snap-in. You need to find the Classes folder under Chat Communities in System Manager, as shown in Figure 13.1. Right-click on

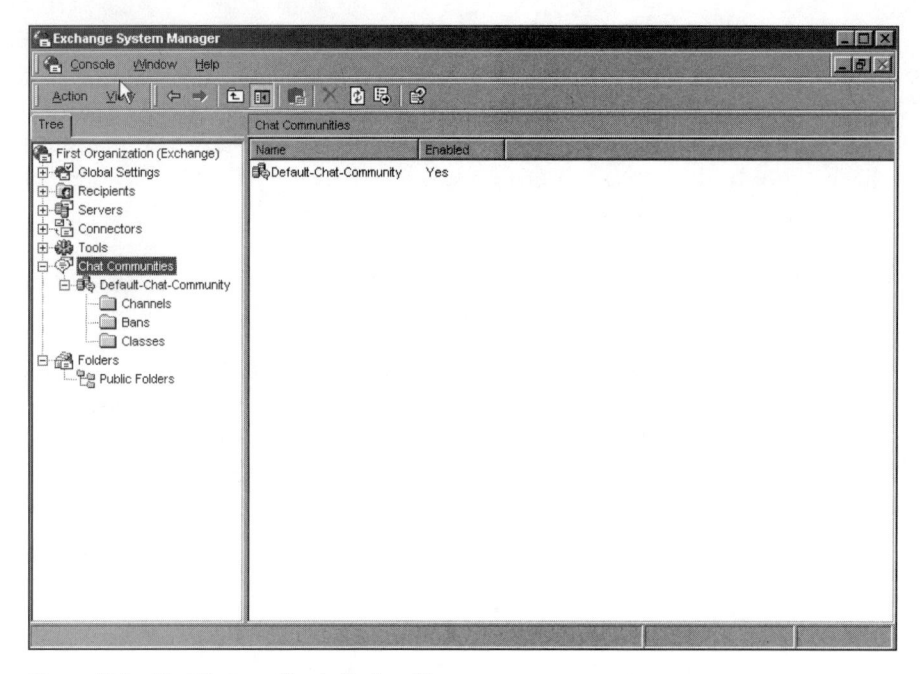

Figure 13.1 Chat Communities in System Manager.

Classes and choose New | Class. Enter a class name and then configure a Member Scope in the first Properties sheet, General. You can configure the Member Scope in two ways: using an identity mask or using an IP address with a subnet mask. Identity masks, as shown in Figure 13.2, can use wildcard characters such as an asterisk (★) or question mark (?). Each identity mask uses three distinct fields: Nickname, User

Figure 13.2 The Member Scope of the class.

Name, and Domain Or IP Address. For example, the three fields for a user class containing all users who use the nickname "Santa" from anywhere would be:

- Nickname: Santa
- User Name: *
- Domain Or IP Address: *

The second Properties sheet available when you are creating a user class is Access, as shown in Figure 13.3. It allows you to define a class based on a user's logon state and what users are not permitted to do. Select the Hide Class Members' IP Addresses And DNS Names option so that one chat member cannot misuse the network address of another chat member. The third available Properties sheet is Settings. You use it to secure your chat server from any security breaches. There are four Attack Protection Levels (ranging from none to High), as shown in Figure 13.4. Each Attack Protection Level corresponds to a delay time in seconds. Using a protection level of Low for a chat invitation, for example, corresponds to a delay time of two seconds. These delay times are added to other delay times that occur in your chat community. The Settings Properties sheet allows you to configure Limits and Delays. The Limits properties are:

- *Maximum IP Connections*—This controls the number of connections per IP address for this user class. It does not apply to a system operator.
- *Maximum Channels User Can Join*—This controls the number of simultaneous channels or chat rooms a user can join. This information is controlled based on a user's nickname.

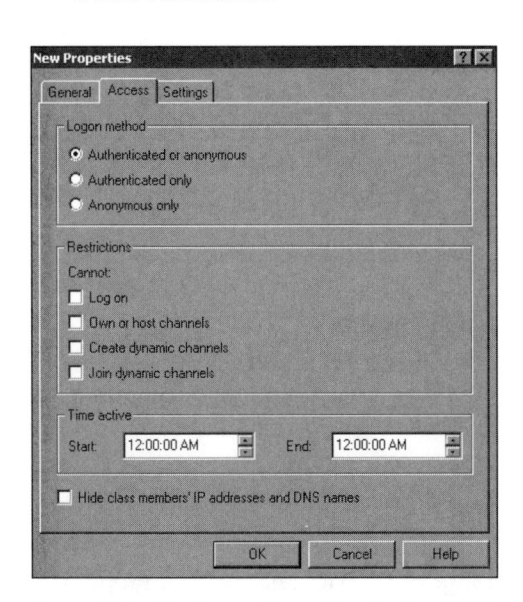

Figure 13.3 The Access Properties sheet under Chat Classes.

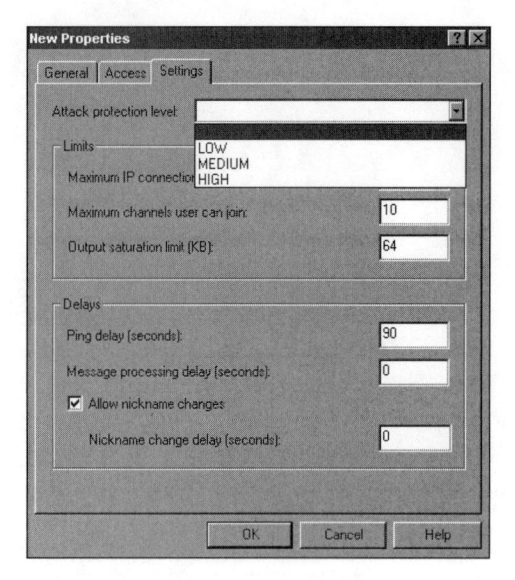

Figure 13.4 Attack protection levels.

- *Output Saturation Limit (KB)*—This number shows how much data your chat server will buffer or queue for a client before the connection is terminated.

The Delays properties on the Settings tab are:

- *Ping Delay (Seconds)*—This is the number of seconds used to ping an active client to see if it is present on the other side of an active connection. A client responds to a ping message from a server by sending a pong message in return. The timeout value for this delay can range between 15 and approximately 3,600 seconds.

- *Message Processing Delay (Seconds)*—This is the number of seconds the server waits before processing the next message from any client. Notice the default value of 0 seconds here (you can go as high as 10 seconds if you wish).

- *Nickname Change Delay (Seconds)*—This setting, again in seconds, controls how often users can change their nickname.

Another important parameter is user bans. Use this parameter to restrict individual users from accessing a specific chat community. Any attempts at accessing a banned chat room will fail. You can ban chat communities by either their domain name or their IP address. However, community-specific rules imply that users banned from one chat room may be able to access other chat rooms.

The procedure for banning users is similar to that for creating user classes. You find the Bans container within Chat Communities in the Exchange System Manager. Right-click on this container and choose New|Ban. The General Properties sheet will appear, as shown in Figure 13.5. You can ban users based on their nickname, username, domain name, or IP address.

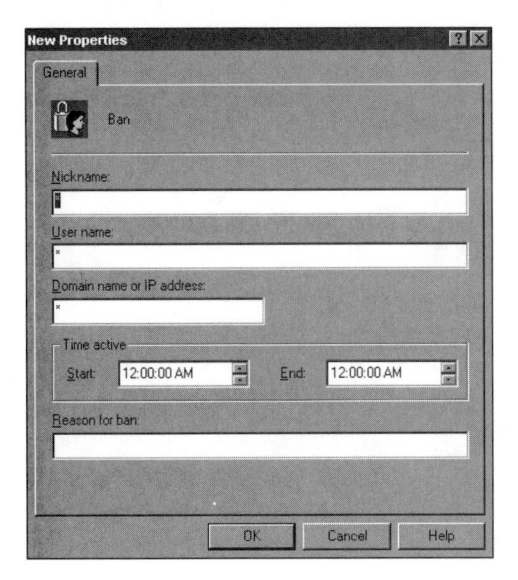

Figure 13.5 The General Properties sheet for the Bans container in Exchange System Manager.

Creating a Chat Community

Once you have created user classes, you must create chat communities. These chat communities are associated with administrative groups in Exchange 2000. When you install Chat Service for the first time, a special chat community is created in the First Administrative Group. This default chat community is called Default-Chat-Community. As with most other default values, you may want to change this name for political, functional, or security reasons.

Use the Exchange System Manager snap-in tool to create your chat communities. Right-click on Chat Communities and choose New | Chat Community. Default-Chat-Community Properties, shown in Figure 13.6, appears. It contains five tabs: General, Channels, Messages, Security, and Authentication:

➤ *General*—Use this Properties sheet to name new communities and provide descriptive titles. Community names, limited to 63 characters, cannot contain spaces and must end with a letter. Set your Connection Limits here. Make certain the value of Maximum Anonymous Connections is less than that of Maximum Total Connections (both default to 10,000). Finally, specify whether you want client DNS names resolved by choosing Disable, Attempt, or Require.

➤ *Channels*—Use this Properties sheet to select channel defaults, such as the default language for your chat room. Configure users who create dynamic channels to become the host for a channel here. You can enable dynamic channels for your community as well as the maximum number of users allowed on any dynamic channel in your community (between 0 and 99,999). A 0 value means you are allowing unlimited membership. Check Chat Sysop Joins As Owner to grant owner status to chat users with sysop permissions when

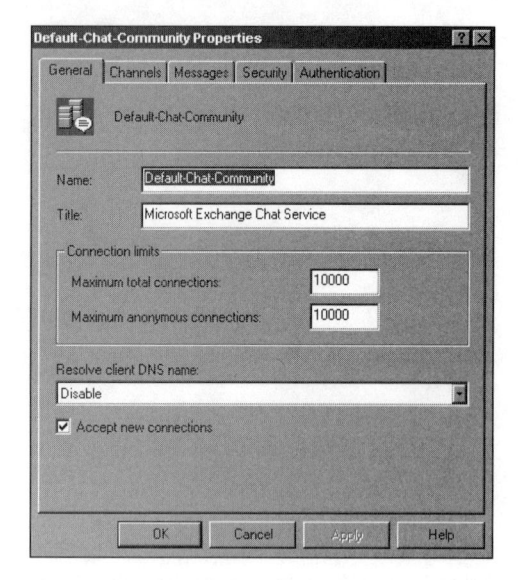

Figure 13.6 Default-Chat-Community Properties in Exchange System Manager.

they join a dynamic channel. A registered channel is not affected by this particular option.

▶ *Messages*—Use this Properties sheet to specify a message of the day (MOTD), What's New, a system message, or a general liability message that you want displayed to users who use the IRC **admin** command.

▶ *Security*—Use this Properties sheet to list the users and groups to whom permissions have been assigned.

▶ *Authentication*—Use this Properties sheet to set authentication properties for your chat communities. It is associated with Active Directory security.

Use the General Properties sheet to name your channel following specific naming conventions. For example, a channel name can contain a maximum of 200 characters. Every channel name must begin with a valid prefix like #, &, %#, or %&. This prefix identifies the type of channel in use. For example, a pound sign (#) or ampersand (&) identifies an IRC channel. A prefix containing two characters (e.g., %#) denotes an extended channel using the IRCX protocol. An extended channel uses the Universal Character Set (UCS) UTF-8, which provides an extended character set so that users can participate in a discussion in any language. Select the Create This Channel When The Service Starts checkbox on the General Properties sheet so that your channel is always available when Chat Service is running.

Sometimes, it is necessary to disable but not delete a certain community. Alternatively, you can permanently remove a chat community. To disable a chat community without removing it, clear the Accept New Connections checkbox on the General tab. If you recheck this box, the specific community is re-enabled and back in service. You do not have to restart the Chat Service when you enable or disable this feature.

After you have created a chat community, you must connect this community to your chat server. Use Exchange System Manager to find the server object that is hosting your chat community. Underneath this object, you will see a container labeled IRCX. Right-click on this container and select Properties. Select the Add button on the General Properties sheet to add a new community. Every community you add has to be identified by a unique IP address.

Every chat community needs at least one channel to support chat dialogues. Use the Exchange System snap-in tool to create different types of channels. In Exchange System, right-click on the Channels container under Chat Communities and select New|Channel. The New Properties dialog box will appear. Six tabs—General, Access, Security, Modes, Messages, and Extensions—are available.

To remove a chat community, disassociate it from the server that is hosting it. You can delete it in three ways:

- In Exchange System Manager under Properties for the IRCX container, you can see all communities associated with a given server. If you select Remove, the community is no longer associated with the chat server.

- Clear the Enable Server To Host This Chat Community checkbox in the Properties sheet for the specific chat community. Doing this maintains the server association and does not delete the community's configuration.

- Delete the chat community from the chat community's container in the Exchange System Manager snap-in tool.

The Access tab of a channel's Properties sheet allows you to configure channel modes, which control the channel's visibility to a user. Visibility settings, as shown in Figure 13.7, are:

- *Public*—Nonmember users can obtain information about a channel from any chat client using the IRC **list** command.

- *Private*—Nonmember users can obtain the name and number of members of a channel from a chat client by using the IRC **list** command.

- *Hidden*—This mode is equivalent to a public channel except that you can't find it using the IRC **list** command. Channel properties are visible only if you know the exact name of the channel.

- *Secret*—Nonmember users of the channel cannot locate this channel using queries.

You can configure additional modes for your channel on the Modes tab. For example, you can configure host notification when a user cannot join. You can also allow channels to be cloned and channels to be moderated. When you check Allow This Channel To Be Cloned, you are allowing all registered channels to duplicate themselves when your member limit is reached, whatever limit that may be. If you create a cloneable channel called ChannelA with a member limit of five, the sixth

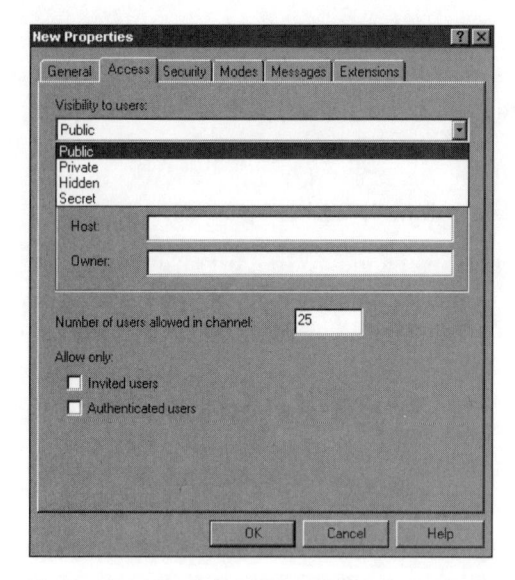

Figure 13.7 The Access Properties sheet for configuring channels.

user who attempts to join ChannelA is assigned to a new channel called ChannelA1. There is a 99-clone limit for all systems; each clone is a new channel.

On the Modes panel, you can also choose speaking restrictions based on the size of your channel. For smaller channels, check the Moderated box, which limits users from posting any messages to a moderated conversation unless they have permission. Alternatively, select Auditorium for larger channels where users cannot send messages to each other but speakers can both see and send messages to all channel participants. Limit the accessibility of users to channels based on invitation or authentication according to a predefined security scheme.

On the Messages panel of the Community Properties sheet, you can specify a message of the day (MOTD) that will be seen by all users when they join the chat community or, alternatively, when they type "motd" at the command line.

On the Extensions Properties sheet, you can configure filters on your channel if you want to block any kind of socially objectionable language. Some chat communities now filter sensitive communications, including invitations on all channels, both registered and dynamic. To use this feature effectively, create a list of restricted words. If a message contains a filtered word, the entire message is blocked. The user who initially sent the offensive message is notified.

To create a restricted list, use the Exchange System snap-in to locate the IRCX folder underneath the specific server node. Right-click on this container and select Properties. Then, right-click on the chat community you want to filter and select Extensions under Properties. Next, right-click on IRCX, choose Properties, and choose the chat community you want to filter. Click on Extensions and verify that your Profanity Filter extension has been selected. You can apply filters on many different levels as well as set multiple filters for different groups. Each filter has a different word list. If you want to apply a different word list to different messages, you need to create a new filter.

The Chat Client

The chat server was introduced with legacy Exchange 5.5; it runs on Exchange 2000 Server products. Legacy versions of Exchange used a client called Microsoft Chat 2. However, Exchange 2000 does not support Chat 2; you must install the Chat 2.1 client, available in a variety of locations, including the Exchange Server 5.5 Service Pack 3 (SP3) CD-ROM. When you install this product, you see two tabs used for configuration: Connect and Personal Info. The Connect tab prompts you for which server and community you want to connect to. The Personal Info tab allows you to update or modify your personal information such as your name, nickname, and email address.

A user can log on to Chat Service with dynamic channels either enabled or disabled. If dynamic channels are enabled, the user specifies a name of a chat room that is already running and "joins" the room. If dynamic channels have been disabled, a user must manually join a room. All users are initially placed in a common room named Room1. A user can jump from this room to any other room. To display a listing of available rooms, choose Room|Room List. If dynamic channels are enabled for a given chat community, users can create a chat room from the Chat Room List Properties sheet.

The client view of Chat Service is divided up into three windowpanes: a small lower pane, where users communicate by typing messages to other room members; a large middle pane, where messages are displayed; and a small right-hand windowpane, where the other users in the same room are listed. The large middle pane displays messages in either a cartoon-like form or as plain text. If you toggle between these two views, you lose the message history accumulated in the windowpane. If you right-click on a member's name listed on the right windowpane, you obtain character information (such as an email address) about that selected member.

Right-clicking on a member's name in the member list on the right windowpane displays a context menu. Chat room hosts can use this shortcut menu to eject a user from a room for whatever reason. They can inform other room members that this person has been ejected. Ejecting people from a room does not prevent them from returning. Hosts can use the Ban/Unban selection on the shortcut menu to permanently keep users out of a particular room. Users can also inform other members if they are temporarily unavailable. Similarly, you can customize the chat client by selecting View|Options from the chat client. Six Properties sheets control the configurable aspects of the client software: Character, Background, Automation, Personal Info, Settings, and Comics View. With these tabs, users can choose what communications they see (e.g., whispers or invitations), what avatar or character they would like to have represent them in the room (under the Character Properties sheet), and an automatic greeting that is displayed whenever those users are the hosts of the room.

Intranet Technologies

Many businesses use collaborative-type technology to communicate either internally with members of their organization or externally with clients and prospective customers. This emerging technology provides a competitive edge to many e-commerce businesses by increasing person-to-person (P2P) interaction without significant increases in overhead. Collaboration, even within a subsection of an organization's enterprise (such as a local intranet within the larger corporate enterprise), can significantly improve workflow and document management. The Marketing, Sales, or Training departments can thus function in a relatively secure communication "sandbox." Firewalls and other technologies typically protect the enterprise from a public network such as the Internet. Configuration across these important protective devices can, at times, be complicated. Nevertheless, it is more commonplace than in the past. An Exchange administrator typically provides the solutions to have these collaborative tools accessible to external parties such as vendors or suppliers.

One alternative for many companies who have neither resources nor time to provide full-feature collaborative services is to outsource an intranet. It functions as a private Web site and provides a quick and relatively secure solution for company communications. Users post whatever information they want to the intranet for access by other staff members, selected users, remote clients, or prospective customers. Many firms "rent" a full intranet that provides complete virtual services (such as shared scheduling calendars, messaging, and document sharing) without the responsibilities of onsite technical support and management.

Consider outsourcing an intranet for collaborative purposes if your organization cannot or does not have a "heavy" technology investment. Some outsourced intranet services are nominally priced and provide secure access from anywhere, facilitating the sharing of documents with staff or clients using common browser software. It is a good idea to test the feasibility of these services almost immediately and without risk of major capital investments. Another way to check it is to use a prototype, which allows your organization to more carefully plan the sizing and deployment of an actual collaborative infrastructure.

Using the Exchange Conferencing Server for Collaboration

Another special add-on tool that complements the Exchange 2000 messaging infrastructure is called Conferencing Server. This product is similar to Microsoft's NetMeeting software except that Conferencing Server offers server-side capabilities. Both products have useful features, although Conferencing Server is not a replacement for the NetMeeting package. Conferencing Server adds the capability of multiparty videoconferences through integration with Microsoft Outlook. You can use Outlook directory lists when you schedule a meeting. Conferencing Server uses some NetMeeting features such as a common whiteboard, application sharing, and file transfer. Microsoft created this product to solve many issues related to multiparty videoconferencing, conference scheduling, and bandwidth management. If you decide to deploy this technology, you get access to online meetings with videoconferencing, application sharing, and text chat.

Online meetings are delivered through a standards-based browser client. A live video view of each participant depends on the client interface. The type of meeting, ranging from Public to Public with Password to Private, depends on the level of security you provide. A Public meeting allows authenticated users access to your meeting. Public with Password restricts participants to any user with the appropriate password. Private restricts participants to specific users allowed to participate in the conference.

Online meetings consume two network resources: network bandwidth and a Multipoint Control Unit (MCU). The Exchange T.120 MCU service runs as a Conferencing Server component and is used to interconnect participants of a data conference. This service is installed on Conferencing Server during installation. The Exchange H.323 Videoconferencing Bridge runs as a component of the T.120 MCU. A network can support multiple MCUs, each with separate configurations. As already mentioned, with the addition of the video component, multiparty videoconferencing allows you to see all conference participants at the same time.

The Exchange T.120 MCU service consumes a large percentage of available network bandwidth. Users who participate in multipoint videoconferencing must use the Windows 2000 product on their desktop. The number of users you can see at one time in your browser windows is, however, limited by the physical constraints of both the hardware platform on which the software runs and the network connection. A host operator can impose a limit on the total bandwidth consumed by any single online meeting. Conference Server manages bandwidth consumption by using multicast protocols, which reduce the amount of network traffic generated by these multiparty videoconferencing products. Multicast protocols are broadcast across your network simultaneously to all group members. Thus, many users benefit from one data stream, rather than the same data stream repeating to multiple users. For more information on Microsoft Exchange 2000 Conferencing Server, go to **www.microsoft.com/Exchange/prodinfo/2000/ecs_datasheet.htm**.

Instant Messaging

Chat Service provides a many-to-many or one-to-many synchronous or realtime communication channel for text-based group discussions. It is sometimes called an RTC service. Exchange 2000 Server comes pre-equipped with another RTC component, called Microsoft Exchange Instant Messaging (IM). This service offers similar synchronous service but is exclusively for one-to-one communication among users. IM transfers text among users in realtime. The only difference between IM and email is that email messages are saved in a private Message Store (MS). Message exchanges during an IM session cannot be recovered once the session is terminated. IM is similar to the legacy **net send** feature except that the messaging is bidirectional. IM offers the following benefits:

➤ IM provides a more immediate communication channel than the telephone. Telephone costs, especially involving remote locations, are either reduced or totally eliminated. IM exchanges are much faster than phone calls.

➤ The IM Service runs as a background process, allowing you to work on other projects while communication channels are fully operational.

➤ IM can transfer limited size attachments just like email.

IM, integrated through Exchange 2000 with Windows 2000, uses a scalable architecture that provides security and privacy. An IM client, called a *watcher*, receives presence information about other users or *presentities* (Microsoft's term for a user with available presence information). A watcher can send messages to an "instant message inbox" in any domain that will accept it. Compatible with most firewall technologies, it uses Rendezvous Protocol (RVP), which operates with HTTP 1.1 and Lightweight Directory Access Protocol (LDAP) 3. RVP, based on the concept of presence, is an extension of the WebDAV protocol, which, in turn, is an extension of HTTP 1.1. RVP allows notifications both within and across different Exchange organizations.

IM uses a client/server model. However, although an IM client talks directly to an IM host server, an IM server does not communicate directly with other IM servers. The IM home server maintains presence information for all its assigned subscribers. It also notifies a subscriber of changes in status. Any message sent to a subscriber first passes through the subscriber's home server. Home servers "see" their users as the IM client and function as an "inbox" for them. RVP sends all information through HTTP, and, by default, port 80. This feature allows presence information and instant messages to be transferred among different domains or across, for example, public networks. RVP, like HTTP, is an *asynchronous* protocol and therefore requires less bandwidth than other protocols. When environments are subject to exceptionally heavy message usage, best practices recommend locating IM servers in close proximity to their subscribers.

IM and Domain Name System (DNS)

Every client that sends a message needs to do a DNS service record lookup for the domain that holds the IM server. This lookup requires a DNS record called the service location (SRV) record. DNS uses an SRV record to locate a service such as LDAP or FTP on a network. The record maps the fully qualified domain name (FQDN) of a computer to the service and TCP port through which the service is provided. The domain that holds the IM server can be either a local domain or a remote domain, and it must support the SRV record type. The SRV record lookup returns the host name of the IM server responsible for a domain. If no SRV records are available, the DNS service retrieves an address record (called an *A record*) for that IM server. The SRV record makes it possible for a user's email address and IM address to be the same. Without it, the user's email address would contain the IM domain that typically begins with the "im" host prefix. The process for configuring your DNS server to accept IM is not difficult and includes the following steps:

1. *Create a DNS record.* You need an A record in the DNS database for every IM server you will use.

2. *Configure a routing server.* Clients connect to an IM home server and request a service. If the connected server is not the user's home server, it is acting as a routing server that will proxy or redirect service requests via HTTP. Best practices recommend that your routing servers have a host name of "im". A routing server thus has an FQDN of "im.mydomain.com".

3. *Create an SRV resource record.* This record is for the RVP protocol, which maps directly to the routing server. When an IM client logs on, it queries DNS for the SRV resource record. If the record exists, the IM client contacts the server, who then refers the client to its home server. An SRV record is used so that users' email addresses are equivalent to their IM addresses.

Creating a canonical or CNAME record to provide an alias name is not as effective as using IM. CNAME records are used for aliases in "single-server" environments, where one machine hosts multiple services such as HTTP, Post Office Protocol (POP), and DNS. IM specifically provides a simple, low-bandwidth communication solution with little ongoing administrative overhead and therefore low TCO. For example, IM users do not automatically authenticate themselves before sending an IM message. RVP, in fact, does not require a user to authenticate to his IM home server. The Windows NT LAN Manager (NTLM) security access protocol or the digest authentication method provides any necessary authentication. NTLM is referred to as the Windows Integrated Authentication method or WIA Challenge/Response. The digest authentication method verifies that both parties are sharing a symmetric key or, in other words, a type of *secret* or password, without this shared secret key communicated publicly between them. IM uses the WIA method by default. The Kerberos authentication method, the default Windows 2000 authentication protocol, is not used.

Installing IM

An IM server requires Exchange 2000 Server running on a Windows 2000 Server product and Internet Information Server (IIS) 5. You can configure the Windows 2000 machine as either a domain controller (DC) or member server, though the latter is preferable given the workload characterization of a DC. Virtual servers come in two flavors: a home server and a routing server. A *home server* hosts all IM user accounts; thus, it sends and receives instant messages as well as is responsible for communicating presence information. A *routing server* is not necessary in a single-server type environment because, in fact, a home server can route instant messages just like a routing server. Best practices recommend installing a routing server if you have at least two home servers. Before you attempt to create a virtual server, ensure you have appropriate group permissions in AD. To manage multiple IM users, you must be a member of the Domain Admins group of that hosting domain. Similarly, you must have group membership in the Exchange Admin group to administer IM settings in the Exchange System Manager snap-in.

To install the IM Service, depending on what method of authentication you are using, perform the following steps:

1. *Create the home server.* In the Exchange System Manager snap-in, find the server object that will serve as your home server, and right-click on the RVP container under the Protocols container. Choose New | Instant Messaging Virtual Server and the wizard will start.

2. *Create a routing server.* If you create more than one home server, you have to create at least one routing server. In addition, before you create your routing server, you need an IIS Web site to host it. Steps 3 through 5 will help you with this step.

3. *Configure digest authentication (optional).* This step is optional because, by default, IM uses the WIA method, not the digest authentication method. The WIA method means that users don't have to enter additional usernames or passwords to send instant messages. Unlike with WIA, digest authentication prompts a user for security credentials to authenticate with the IM server. It cannot re-use pre-existing security information. Use the digest method if you're going through a proxy server, or if you're running a non-Windows IM client such as Unix.

4. *Provide access to the service.* To provide IM services, assign the user to your IM home server on the user's Properties sheet in the Active Directory Users and Computers snap-in tool.

5. *Distribute the IM client to your users.* The IM client that comes with Exchange 2000 Server is known as MSN Messenger. Locate this client software on the Exchange 2000 Server CD-ROM under \Instmsg\i386\Client\Usr\mmssetup.exe. You can install this to a network share and install it on users' workstations.

When entering a display name during the creation of a user, specify either a home server or a routing server. You have to associate a Web site with any IM server. Check your Web site for a virtual directory called INSTMSG through which all messages are routed. You have to enable the server to host user accounts using the Instant Messaging Virtual Servers Wizard. Identify your IM routing server with the server_name.domain_name.com naming convention, where you specify the DNS domain name. Accept all other wizard defaults and configure DNS using the appropriate resource records for your IM routing server. Every IM routing server has to have an A record in the DNS database.

Right-click on the user account under the appropriate server node in the Exchange System Manager snap-in and choose Exchange Tasks from the pop-up menu. Using the Exchange Tasks Wizard, you can enable IM and select the IM home server for the user. You can enable IM for multiple users (or all users in your domain) by selecting all users in Active Directory Users and Computers, right-clicking on the group selection, and then choosing the Exchange Tasks Wizard. Enabling IM for multiple users should only be performed one time. Thereafter, you should enable users on an individual basis.

If you need to authenticate users through a proxy server or run IM over foreign operating systems like Unix, it's best to use digest authentication. Based on the HTTP standard, the digest authentication method requires IM to retrieve unencrypted passwords from AD. You have to change the password policy on your DC so that passwords are stored in a reversible, encrypted format. If you use digest authentication and you did not set password policy before creating user accounts, you must reset user passwords following the policy change. To change your password policy using Active Directory Users and Computers, follow these steps:

1. Right-click on your domain organizational unit (OU), choose Properties, open the Group Policy tab, and select Default Domain Policy.

2. Open Computer Configuration, then Windows Settings, and then Security Settings.

3. Open Account Policies, and then select Password Policy. Double-click on Store Password Using Reversible Encryption For All Users In The Domain.

4. Select the Define This Policy Setting checkbox and the Enable radio button, and then click on OK.

Managing IM Servers

Administrative functions regarding IM servers involve moving IM data files to alternate locations on your IM server, or removing an IM server altogether. You can physically remove the IM virtual server from the Exchange System Manager snap-in by right-clicking on the IM virtual server and selecting Delete. Specify where you want your IM users moved. This operation removes the IM virtual server. To remove the IM service entirely, use the Add/Remove applet in the Control Panel.

To take your IM server offline, you must first stop the corresponding virtual server that's defined in the Internet Service Manager snap-in. Right-click on your virtual IIS site and select Stop. At this point, all IM services on your Web site will stop and users will not be able to send messages. You can use the context menu to restart your virtual server when you are ready. In addition to deleting IM servers or taking them offline, you may want to move data files to other locations on a server. Use the Exchange System Manager snap-in to locate the RVP Instant Messaging Protocol container under Protocols. Right-click on this container and change the location for your data and log files on the General Properties sheet.

IM and Clients

We will finish our discussion of IM by talking about client management, sending and receiving messages, and troubleshooting issues. As mentioned earlier in this chapter, the primary client used for IM is the MSN Messenger client software. The product comes free with Exchange Server 2000, which means you don't have to deal with licensing issues (as you would with Exchange Server). Once the client is installed, you can configure special options by choosing Tools | Options. The following five screens offer special configuration options:

- *General*—This tab allows you to customize visual prompts that notify users when an instant message has arrived. You can also allow users to change their display names when they are dealing with a remote domain.

- *Privacy*—This important tab shows you the results of any actions you may have taken with AD or the MSN Messenger client. If you know someone has subscribed to your presence information, you can block that user from subscribing to it, and you can block that user from sending you messages. (Note that you *cannot* block a user from email services or chat services, only IM services!)

- *Exchange*—This tab allows you to configure the IM user logon name. You can also select which service the MSN Messenger client will connect to: either the Microsoft Exchange IM service or the MSN Messenger Service. The latter option requires Internet access.

- *Accounts*—This tab is where you configure MSN Messenger Service account information.

- *Connection*—This tab allows you to configure proxy services for users who dial into your network. The IM client automatically looks for the profile of Microsoft Internet Explorer (IE), and dial-up users need to be directed via proxy to obtain this profile.

Chapter Summary

This chapter discussed collaboration services. Here are some particularly significant points to remember:

- RTC helps reduce overhead for many organizations.

- Chat services are available for users who want to communicate as a group in realtime. Data conferencing services allow electronic conferences where users can share multimedia information. IM is for users who want realtime, but one-to-one, communication with other users.

➤ The Exchange Chat Service provides online group discussions for a range of users. This range covers a few users all the way up to approximately 20,000 concurrent users in one chat room. Chat services are based on the IRC protocol, which supports realtime conversations among multiple users. You learned about the concept of channels, or chat rooms, where people can converse with each other. You also looked at two types of channels: registered and dynamic. Recall that registered channels are permanent, whereas dynamic channels are temporary channels created from a client by using the IRC **join** command. Also, channel hosts manage a channel from the client; only dynamic channels have channel hosts.

➤ Most channels have a sysop who monitors or controls a chat community's registered channels or dynamic channels to which they have permission. You can configure channels to be secure, cloneable, or both. A secure channel is one to which access has been restricted. Channels can also be moderated so only those who are given a chance to speak will do so. A cloneable channel is a registered channel that automatically duplicates itself when a member limit is reached.

➤ User classes let you control connections by groups of users without having to create formal groups in AD. User bans allow you to control access on a per-user basis. When you install Chat Service, a chat community called Default-Chat-Community is automatically created for the First Administrative group. Every chat community is connected to at least one server and needs at least one channel through which chat communications can occur.

➤ Exchange 2000 does not support Microsoft Chat 2 or earlier versions, so you have to install Microsoft Chat 2.1. You can find this on the Exchange 5.5 SP3 CD-ROM.

➤ You have seen the benefits of using Chat Service in your organization and how it can make everyone more productive. You have also seen how IM offers instant, one-to-one communication among users.

➤ IM uses RVP, an extended subset of WebDAV. This, in turn, is an extension of the HTTP 1.1 protocol.

➤ IM clients always communicate with an IM server, even though IM servers don't necessarily have to talk to each other. RVP allows watchers to get presence information about other users. IM uses a home server to maintain presence information for all users assigned to it as well as to issue notification of changes in a user's status. If a client connects to an IM routing server, the server will proxy the user's request or use HTTP redirects to send the client's messages to a specific home server. Clients cache the location of the destination home server for some definable period of time.

- RVP is an asynchronous protocol that uses the standard HTTP port 80; it therefore requires very little bandwidth to operate. Most clients have to perform a DNS service SRV resource record lookup for the domain containing their IM home server using port 80. If no SRV record exists, DNS searches for an A resource record type for the IM home server.

- Most IM clients run under Windows 95 or later, Windows NT 4, or Windows 2000. To use IM, you need IE 5 or later and the Exchange IM Service, found on the Exchange 2000 Server CD-ROM in the \Instmsg\I386\Client directory.

Review Questions

1. What protocol is Exchange 2000's Chat Service based on?

    a. FTP

    b. HTTP 1.1

    c. IRC

    d. XRC

2. Which collaboration technology allows prearranged electronic conferences where users can share multimedia information?

    a. Data conferencing

    b. Chat Service

    c. Instant Messaging

    d. Channel conferencing

3. What type of channel is created by a system administrator and is considered permanent?

    a. System channel

    b. Sysop channel

    c. Dynamic channel

    d. Registered channel

4. Which user can monitor and control a chat community's dynamic channels and registered channels? [Check all correct answers]

    a. Channel host

    b. Chanop

    c. Sysop

    d. Systemop

5. What types of channels, or chat rooms, have channel hosts? [Check all correct answers]
   a. System channels
   b. Dynamic channels
   c. Registered channels
   d. User class channels

6. You have just created a registered channel that automatically duplicates itself when a member limit has been reached. What type of channel is this?
   a. A cloneable channel
   b. A secure channel
   c. A registered system channel
   d. A registered dynamic channel

7. You want to create a user class called Sales and want to control this group's access to a chat community on your network. Where can you configure the member scope for this user class?
   a. Right-click on the Bans container in the Exchange System snap-in and choose Member Scope.
   b. Right-click on Chat Communities in the Exchange System snap-in and select Member Scope.
   c. Right-click on the Classes folder under Chat Communities in the Exchange System snap-in and choose New | Class.
   d. Right-click on the Channels container in the Exchange System snap-in and select New | Class.

8. All IM communication occurs over what protocol in Exchange 2000?
   a. WebRVP protocol
   b. IRC protocol
   c. SRV resource protocol
   d. RVP protocol

9. What type of information can a watcher obtain using the rendezvous protocol? [Check all correct answers]
   a. Presence information
   b. Watcher information
   c. RVP notifications
   d. WebDAV command information

10. You have just created a user class called Sales for your chat server. In the Member Scope configuration screen for this class, you have used the following information:

    - Nickname: "?"
    - User Name: *
    - Domain Or IP Address: *.net

    What does this information imply?

    a. You have left out vital information in your configuration of this user class.
    b. This user class is composed of all users who originate from a ".net" domain.
    c. The user class has incorrect information, which could restrict more users than originally planned.
    d. You have to specify an IP address so that proper restrictions can be applied.

11. Which IM server is responsible for maintaining presence information for any user assigned to it?

    a. WebDAV server
    b. IM routing server
    c. IM home server
    d. IM RVP server

12. What is the first step that occurs when users log onto their IM client?

    a. The IM router queries Active Directory for the home server.
    b. The user's computer queries DNS for an SRV record.
    c. The user connects to the IM routing server.
    d. The IM home server validates the user's Active Directory name.

13. What is the first thing you have to do when configuring DNS for Instant Messaging?

    a. Enter an address record for every IM server into DNS.
    b. Enter a CNAME record for every IM server into DNS.
    c. Configure routing servers that begin with the prefix "im".
    d. Create an SRV resource record for the RVP protocol.

14. What fields does an identity mask for configuring member scope include? [Check all correct answers]

    a. Username
    b. Domain
    c. Nickname
    d. IP address

15. Which is considered the default protocol for authentication in Windows 2000?
    a. NTLM Challenge/Response
    b. Digital certificates in a Public Key Infrastructure (PKI) environment
    c. Kerberos protocol version 5
    d. Secure Sockets Layer (SSL) 3

16. If you authenticate users with digest authentication, what change must you make to password policy?
    a. Passwords must be stored in a reversible encrypted format.
    b. Passwords must be stored in a nonreversible encrypted format.
    c. Passwords must be stored in a reversible nonencrypted format.
    d. Passwords must be stored in a nonreversible nonencrypted format.

17. Which symbols are valid IRC channel prefixes? [Check all correct answers]
    a. #
    b. &
    c. %#
    d. %%

18. What network resource measure is used to describe Conferencing Server?
    a. MTU
    b. MCU
    c. MTA
    d. MCA

19. Which statement is false?
    a. RVP is an extension of HTTP.
    b. IM clients talk to IM servers.
    c. IM servers talk to IM servers.
    d. RVP is an extension of WebDAV.

20. What is one method used by Instant Messaging clients to authenticate to their home servers?
    a. Digest authentication method
    b. Kerberos protocol authentication method
    c. Digital certificate authentication method
    d. Secure Sockets Layer authentication method

Real-World Projects

Thomas Elf has been considering implementing realtime collaboration for his company, VideoDozen Inc. He wants his production team to be involved in group discussions on upcoming projects. He has installed the Exchange Chat Service and has noticed the default chat community installed on his system. This default community has been named Default-Chat-Community.

He now wants to create a new chat community called Production. He knows he can rename the default community but he wants to create additional chat communities under different administrative groups in his Windows 2000 system.

Warning: If you are unsure about an option, cancel the installation and consult, for example, www.microsoft.com/technet/ or www.microsoft.com/exchange/, about the option to be installed.

Project 13.1

To create a new chat community:

1. Start the Exchange System snap-in.

2. Right-click on Chat Communities.

3. Select New|Chat Community.

4. On the General tab, name the new community Production. (The name cannot contain spaces and must be under 63 characters.)

5. Keep the default connection limits, but always remember that the Maximum Anonymous Connections should be less than your Maximum Total Connections.

6. In the Resolve Client DNS Name section, choose Attempt. This directs the server to try hostname-to-IP resolution.

Thomas was pleased with the results so far, but he was concerned about something his manager told him. His manager wanted to configure unlimited membership in this channel and wanted to set dynamic channels with no more than 1,000 users allowed in these channels. He had one more property to configure.

Project 13.2

To configure channel defaults and language options:

1. Keep the Properties sheet open from Project 13.1 and click on the Channels tab.

2. Notice the default number of users allowed on this channel (25). Change this number to 0 to signify unlimited membership in your channel or chat room.

3. Check the Allow An Owner Or Host For Channel box so any user who creates a dynamic channel can become the channel owner.

4. Now check the Allow Dynamic Channels box and type "1,000" in the Number Of Users Allowed In Channel box.

5. Finally, check the last box, labeled Chat Sysop Joins As Owner, to grant owner status to chat users with sysop permissions when they join a dynamic channel. Notice that registered channels are not affected by this setting.

Thomas looked over his work. He wanted to make certain all discussions were conducted with appropriate decorum. He decided to filter out any possible abusive or socially inappropriate language.

Project 13.3

To set up a profanity filter for the channel:

1. Create a filter.

2. Select Chat Server, and then select Extensions in the left pane.

3. Verify that the Profanity Filter extension is displayed in the right pane. If it is not, from the Action menu, choose New|Add Extension. Select the Profanity Filter extension, and then choose OK.

4. Select the Profanity Filter extension in the right pane, and then from the Action menu, choose Properties|Edit Filters.

5. Choose Add Filter.

6. Type a name in the Filter Name box, and then choose OK.

7. Add words to the filter.

8. In the Edit Filters dialog box, select the filter you just created, and then choose Add.

9. Type a word in the Word box.

10. Type a message in the Response To User Of Filtered Word box, and then choose OK. This is a private message sent to the channel member who uses the word.

11. Repeat Steps 1 through 10 to add additional words.

Project 13.4

To apply the filter to the channel:

1. Select the channel in the right pane.

2. From the Action menu, choose Properties.

3. In the Extensions Properties sheet, select the Profanity Filter extension, and then choose Properties.

4. Select Filter Messages To Enable Filtering, and then from the Select Filter box, select the filter you just created.

5. Under Apply To, choose All Messages.

6. Choose Apply, and then OK.

Thomas looked over his work and tested everything to his satisfaction. This was the entire configuration that had to be completed for his new chat community known as Production.

CHAPTER FOURTEEN

Troubleshooting and Monitoring

After completing this chapter, you will be able to:

✓ Use your knowledge of Exchange 2000 to troubleshoot complex configuration issues

✓ Appreciate the subtle differences between server-side problems and client-side problems

✓ Identify trends in network usage so that as an administrator you can better optimize your usage of Exchange Server

✓ Know how to utilize tools inherent in both Windows 2000 and Exchange 2000 so you can more easily spot and correct problems

✓ Learn the significance of a regular and routine backup program as part of your daily arsenal to protect your vital organizational data

In previous chapters, you have seen how you can build Exchange 2000 Server from the ground up to become a highly functioning messaging powerhouse. The final product is nothing more than a collection of finely tuned components. From a practical perspective, we have to wonder what keeps these components continually functioning. The more you ponder this situation, the more you arrive at the realization that you need to intervene somewhat to keep the many components of a typical Exchange server coexisting peacefully and optimally. More simply, we are referring to a regimen of monitoring a system composed of many detailed components, each working together to form a coherent messaging architecture. We are also alluding to actively tuning or tweaking various subsystems to make things run more efficiently. Most systems require some form of monitoring, optimization, and performance tuning, not just to increase the economic life of the system—a goal related to increasing an organization's return on investment (ROI)—but also to optimize the users' experience of a well-designed messaging infrastructure. We want to keep this latter goal in mind because it helps us focus on the very prevalent issue of lowering total cost of ownership (TCO).

This concept of actively monitoring or customizing a system such as Exchange Server cannot be interpreted as an automatic process. Administrators cannot apply one set of changes on one server and hope that they can apply this in a cookie-cutter fashion across all servers within their company. We are taught that no two individuals are exactly alike in terms of genetic makeup; in the same way, you have to start thinking that no two servers or workstations are exactly alike in terms of hardware or software components. Every server that you consider critical to your business processes must be individually evaluated and customized for optimal performance. In addition, each change made to a server's configuration must be both applied sequentially and documented. If you make multiple changes to a given server and problems occur as a result of these changes, it becomes hard to pinpoint which setting has caused the disruption in service. This is why you must emphasize to all personnel within the organization how important it is to document even the smallest changes to a system. In many cases, one administrator is even appointed to sign off on or authorize any change that any other member of the network team makes. Violations of this procedure should be dealt with appropriately to ensure the integrity of established authority.

Before we delve into the fine details of optimizing and monitoring a well-designed Exchange Server organization, we must introduce a caveat: Every coin has two sides; likewise, there are two sides regarding monitoring or troubleshooting an Exchange server. However, be careful not to imply a right or wrong scenario here. Most administrators regularly wrestle with these issues; that is why we bring it up now. The first yellow flag we are raising here points to the flaw of not performing a regular monitoring and maintenance routine within your organization. People in this camp assume that a company's assets cannot be extended past their normal useful life; therefore, only a minimal or extremely irregular maintenance effort is produced just because it's supposed to be done, not because it will help prolong the useful life of the asset. The other side of this coin involves administrators who overdo a good thing—that is, they constantly and forcefully make adjustments even when servers do not need such adjustments. You may find yourself somewhere between these two camps, but our recommendation is best stated as follows: To ignore adjustments to your servers when they are most needed is just as dangerous as making adjustments when there is no need to do so. This adage will serve you well through all your maintenance endeavors.

The concept of maintenance extends beyond merely paying attention to or observing what is happening. Maintaining and monitoring an Exchange organization really involves a sixth sense, or increased sensitivity to what is occurring behind the scenes. There are no rules as far as what service you should monitor or how often you should monitor something. Judgment plays a big role in determining what baseline to establish, what constitutes a deviation from this baseline, and what action to take in cases of abnormal system behavior.

Looking for Trouble in All the Right Places

Do not be alarmed by the title of this section. Good administrators learn to look for problems before problems find them. There is a big difference between being *proactive* and *reactive* within an organization. Troubleshooting any problem involves several skills that all operate simultaneously:

- The skill to recognize that a system is not operating in equilibrium (the ideal state)
- The skill to look up appropriate resources to deal with the issue at hand
- The skill to apply the relevant information discovered so that you can bring a system back to its equilibrium or ideal state

We borrow a simple concept from the field of architecture to illustrate these concepts. When architects design a structure, they must be cognizant of many factors, including the strength of the materials they will be using, as well as how these materials will coexist with the surrounding environment. Both intrinsic and extrinsic factors work together to answer one basic question: What will it take to keep our building standing, no matter what conditions prevail? Astute architects also think, "Why do buildings fall, and how can I prevent our building from falling?" In any scenario, knowing your system inside and out will help you keep that system running; it also helps you discover why problems creep up in the first place and what to do about them if they arise.

Troubleshooting Tools Used with Exchange 2000 Server

Troubleshooting, by itself, is really the art of waiting for something to happen, then resolving whatever happened and acting like it never happened. This sounds too strange to be true, but it is a far-too-often occurrence within an administrator's normal day. This concept of reacting to unknown forces is more defined and subtle than what we make of it here. Like any skill, it involves planning and execution to minimize the impact it may have on your organization.

Having said this, we begin with the premise that most events are either internal or external to an organization. For example, if internal employees cannot access a Web site, the first suspect may be an incorrectly functioning Domain Name System (DNS) server. If those same employees can get past an internal firewall and internal router but still have problems accessing a certain Web site, we can start blaming external routers and gateways. This illustrates a basic dichotomy between internal and external conflicts. Exchange Server, however, has a different definition for "internal" and "external." It is best to see life from the perspective of a *server* or a *client*. Problems occur either directly on the server or directly on the client, and you need to identify where the problem lies. You will be able to come up with solutions for your system if you know your system in detail.

We will now look at a few key tools—eseutil.exe, the Inbox Repair Tool, and the Information Store Integrity Checker (ISINTEG)—you can use to troubleshoot both server-side as well as client-side issues involving Exchange 2000 Server. We will discuss when to use each tool, as well as how to use it in its proper context. Knowing when and how to use a given tool helps to explain why you should use that particular tool in the first place. However, due to space and time restrictions, we are forced to leave out many other useful utilities that all administrators should add to their arsenal of weapons in the fight against server downtime and lost profitability. Tools such as remote procedure call (RPC) Ping Server and RPC Ping Client are essential only because so much of Exchange Server depends on maintaining RPCs between an Exchange client and the Exchange server, or between Exchange servers within a Routing Group.

Without these troubleshooting tools in place, organizations are subject to increased downtime and lost opportunities. For that reason, all new and seasoned Exchange users should familiarize themselves with as many tools as possible and know where they can be found. This information is not just useful for exam purposes; it actually represents the difference between an organization that is fully functioning and one that isn't.

Tip: Two useful utilities found on the Exchange 2000 Server CD-ROM that you may want to use include error.exe and filever.exe. error.exe helps to convert database error codes into readable error message strings. filever.exe displays versions of any EXE or DLL file on your system so that you can keep up to date with the latest files.

The utilities discussed here can be found either on the original Exchange Server CD-ROM or on the Outlook 2000 installation CD-ROM. For example, both eseutil.exe and ISINTEG.exe are found on the Exchange 2000 Server CD-ROM in the \setup\i386\Exchange\Bin directory. The Inbox Repair Tool (scanpst.exe) is found on the Outlook 2000 installation CD-ROM in the \Pfiles\Common\System\MAPI\1033\NT directory.

The Microsoft Exchange eseutil.exe Utility

Knowing when to use eseutil.exe involves understanding important concepts used in Exchange 2000, including both online and offline *defragmentation*. This concept involves rearranging data so that database pages can be filled more efficiently. The goal is to eliminate unused storage. Recall that mailbox stores within a Storage Group really start out as empty database files, which naturally grow as messages accumulate within them. Exchange uses an Extensible Storage Engine (ESE) structure to store data, where every page in a database file is nothing more than a node in a balanced-tree type of structure. Storage Groups are also part of this ESE. The only problem with this scenario involves the size of these databases, which themselves keep growing even when messages are being deleted. New messages are unfortunately written in noncontiguous spaces before the database has a chance to grow in proportion. This phenomenon of random storage is known as *fragmentation*, and the utility you use to effectively deal with it is eseutil.exe.

Warning: Exchange Server provides online defragmentation of databases using the Information Store (IS) service. Every time you start or shut down a server, the IS checks for inconsistencies. However, this type of defragmentation does not reduce the size of databases on the server; this is why you need an *offline tool* like eseutil.exe to actually compact all databases while the IS service *is not running*. You should use this tool with caution and only with assistance from Microsoft Technical Support.

The eseutil.exe utility extracts header information from most log files, including database logs, checkpoint logs, and transaction logs. This provides relevant diagnostic information and helps you ascertain why a certain database is not starting or which transaction logs may need to be replayed. You can run this tool from a command prompt with various switches or options applied to it. The three main options revolve around defragmenting a database, repairing a damaged database, or checking database integrity. Table 14.1 shows examples of common syntax used for this tool. Figure 14.1 shows an example of the proper command-line syntax for an offline defragmentation.

Table 14.1 The eseutil.exe utility used with three main functions.

Switch	Explanation
/D	This option defragments a database by moving any used pages in the database to contiguous areas within a brand-new database. Old contents are written to a temporary database that ultimately becomes the new database.
/R	This is the repair function, which tries to examine your database structure and record any broken link. Attempts to restore these broken links are very slow and could result in data loss. Microsoft recommends using this as a last-resort effort. Sometimes, you may see physical damage to a database in the form of a –1018 or –1019 type error; running **eseutil /p** in these situations may restore the damaged database.
/G	This option checks database integrity; however, it is mostly a read-only utility that does not make any changes to the database itself. It actually checks the database tables and rebuilds indexes on a temporary database named tempedb.edb.

```
D:\WINNT2K\System32\cmd.exe
D:\Exchsrvr\BIN>ESEUTIL /D
```

Figure 14.1 Typing "ESEUTIL /D" from the command prompt within the proper directory path.

The Microsoft Exchange Inbox Repair Tool

Exchange Server supports asynchronous communication. This means that users do not have to be fully connected to Exchange to perform normal work functions. Normally, users establish at least one connection to an Exchange server within an organization. However, these same users terminate or temporarily lose these connections while performing other work-related duties. These facts become important only because users need some way of synchronizing work performed while offline and not connected to the Exchange server. Working offline implies creating folders within the Exchange client with default extensions of .ost (for offline folder stores) or .pst (for personal folder stores). When these files become corrupt (for any reason), you should invoke the Inbox Repair Tool, also known as scanpst.exe, for corrective action.

Imagine a user called Steve who wants to use a personal laptop both at home and at his place of employment. While at work, Steve could connect to an Exchange server using a client such as Microsoft Outlook 2000 or Outlook Express. While at home, Steve has no direct access to the Exchange server unless he maintains a dial-up connection using Windows Remote Access Services (RAS) or a similar service. However, without a definite dial-up connection configured, Steve can still create messages and access public folder information because this data is now stored in either an OST or a PST file that was created while Steve was connected to the Exchange server at work. In fact, Steve can maintain multiple sets of personal folders as a single file with the same .pst extension. Now imagine that some or all of Steve's personal or offline folders have become subject to corruption (as evidenced by inaccessibility or other apparent error messages). What action can he take to recover data stored in offline or personal folders that have not yet synchronized to the Exchange server at work? The answer lies in the Inbox Repair Tool.

You normally install the Inbox Repair Tool during a typical installation of the Microsoft Outlook client (look in the \Program Files\Common Files\System\MAPI\1033\NT directory on the installation CD-ROM for the location of this tool if you are working with an Outlook 2000 client). This tool allows users to enter an exact file name of an OST or PST file that is considered corrupt. However, messages that cannot be repaired are often discarded, and it is highly recommended that you back up the original file before executing the utility. Figure 14.2 shows the Inbox Repair Tool dialog box.

The scanpst.exe utility examines all contents of a corrupted OST or PST file. However, only messages that can be successfully repaired are moved to a folder called Lost and Found that scanpst.exe creates. You can access this special folder from within the Outlook client. All other messages not successfully repaired by scanpst.exe are deleted—they are not placed into the Lost and Found folder. It is recommended that you move or copy the contents of Lost and Found into newly created personal folders to avoid future corruption.

The Microsoft Exchange ISINTEG Utility

Exchange Server is primarily composed of databases housed within larger structures called Storage Groups. You should be especially concerned with caring for and maintaining these databases. It becomes difficult to maintain some databases because they become easily subjected to inconsistencies and corruption. Because they were aware of these potential problems, the designers of Exchange Server have included built-in tools such as ISINTEG, which checks all databases for inconsistencies. ISINTEG is a suite of tests that uses a reference database to check reference counts.

This tool comes with a caveat not applicable to other tools discussed previously. ISINTEG has to create a temporary database to run successfully. This implies that if a Storage Group has more than five databases—remember the limit is six per Storage Group—then running this utility results in failure because it cannot create a temporary database. ISINTEG requires that a database be dismounted and that no

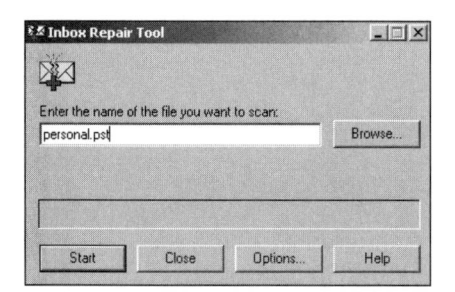

Figure 14.2 The opening Inbox Repair Tool dialog box.

more than five databases exist within any Storage Group. Following these procedures ensures that you can successfully create a temporary reference database.

You can invoke the ISINTEG utility using the following syntax at a command prompt:

```
ISINTEG -s [-fix] [-l logfilename] -test testname
```

The **-s** option refers to a server name, and **-fix** tells ISINTEG to fix any problems it detects. Not using **-fix** results in problems being reported but not fixed. The **[-l** *logfilename*] merely specifies an output log file. If no file name is specified, all **-fix** results are exported to a default file named isinteg.pri or isinteg.pub. Finally, the **-test** *testname* option performs whatever test is selected.

Additional Sources of Help

What should an administrator do if he or she cannot resolve problems with one of the tools discussed earlier in this chapter? We have encountered errors that were so unique that they were beyond both comprehension and resolution. In these cases, smart administrators know exactly where to turn for assistance. In general, you need to formulate a checklist or plan of actions to take in case prescribed procedures do not work as planned. Here is a suggested list of sources that you can—and should—consult when the tools provided do not seem to work:

➤ *Microsoft Exchange 2000 Server Resource Kit by Microsoft Press*—This excellent guide not only provides comprehensive technical information regarding Exchange Server architecture, but also provides a comprehensive set of tools to help administrators troubleshoot multiple problem scenarios.

➤ *Microsoft TechNet*—This subscription service is another invaluable tool that helps administrators evaluate and deploy almost any Microsoft product, including Exchange Server. The information is updated monthly and is comprehensive enough to include not only all Microsoft Resource Kits but also the entire Microsoft Knowledge Base.

➤ *Exchange 2000 Server documentation*—This valuable resource, found on the Exchange Server CD-ROM, contains help files and original documentation in a rich-text format. Many administrators assume that CD-ROM documentation is lacking in many regards, but Microsoft has proved otherwise with what we consider to be a tremendous resource.

Monitoring Trends in Exchange Server

An important but often unattainable goal in any organization is to know the intricate details of every network-management tool or utility and actually implement these tools in depth on production servers. However, this goal is unattainable due to constraints imposed by the quality and quantity of actual problems encountered every day. It is hard to assume that every problem that arises in a given environment can or will be dealt with right then and there. It is also impossible to gauge how much time is needed to analyze the output of whatever utility is being used in a given situation. This is why documentation is stressed so heavily in most organizations that work with products such as Exchange. Documentation is not only done when things go awry, but it is also a continuing process of discovery when administrators regularly monitor trends in network usage.

We would like to expose a subtle yet distinct difference between monitoring a computer system and actually troubleshooting that system. Administrators of computer systems are not taught to monitor their network; they are usually taught to troubleshoot or maintain these systems. Our interpretation of best practices involves a combination of maintaining, monitoring, and troubleshooting production servers. However, this implies a steady and gradually increasing sensitivity to even the slightest variation from normal network activity. You have to know what is considered normal activity before you can begin to worry about deviations from this definition. The practice of establishing normal levels of activity and tracking deviations from these levels is known as *baselining a system*, and this represents the core of the best practice known as monitoring.

Tip: Administrators often wonder how often they should monitor their Exchange servers. This obviously depends on many factors, including the number of mailboxes serviced by each server and the total number of connections being made to each server. To determine optimal levels of monitoring for a given organizational structure, you should thoroughly investigate the product documentation or the Microsoft Knowledge Base at **www.microsoft.com/exchange**. It is assumed that you are adhering to prescribed standards whenever you contact Microsoft Technical Support for advanced assistance.

Although Exchange uses built-in tools and utilities and can be considered a self-preserving system to some extent, individual administrators need to rely on their skill levels and judgments to assess the overall health of a production network. Someone in the organization has to take responsibility for obtaining physical data that can be used to diagnose system problems or even plan for future growth. In the next few sections, we take a look at utilities you can use in both Windows 2000 and Exchange 2000 to help achieve these objectives.

Windows 2000 Monitoring Utilities

Exchange 2000 is very closely linked to the Windows 2000 operating system (OS), so you will find yourself monitoring Exchange 2000 Server with tools that have been built into the Windows 2000 OS. This is by design, yet many organizations do not take full advantage of this integration. You should regularly use the tools discussed here—the Performance Console, Task Manager, Network Monitor, Windows 2000 Event Viewer, and Disk Defragmenter—to obtain pertinent information regarding a production Exchange server-based network.

Performance Console

Windows 2000 Server and Advanced Server offer a tool known as the Performance Console. This tool is an MMC console that contains two snap-ins: System Monitor and Performance Logs and Alerts. The former allows the tracking of network throughput and resource usage, whereas the latter allows for the collection of performance data from either a local or remote computer. Both snap-ins chart the performance of dozens of system parameters in both Windows 2000 and Exchange 2000. You can find this tool by clicking Start | Programs | Administrative Tools | Performance.

The System Monitor snap-in, shown in Figure 14.3, is designed for short-term viewing of data and includes workload balancing tools. You can display a graph or a histogram of system data. You can even integrate some of the functionality of System Monitor into a Microsoft Office application or create an HTML page from a particular performance view.

Note: Previous versions of the Windows NT operating system included the perfmon.exe tool, also known as Performance Monitor. This tool monitored counters associated with objects that were associated with resources or services. For example, you could monitor the time a hard disk takes to fulfill system requests by charting the Avg. Disk sec/Transfer counter for the PhysicalDisk object for the hard drive resources within your existing server.

The goal of using System Monitor is to capture performance data that various components in a computer system generate. This performance data becomes a performance object, which in turn is associated with a given resource. For example, you may want to monitor the Processor object, which contains performance data regarding one or more processors in your system.

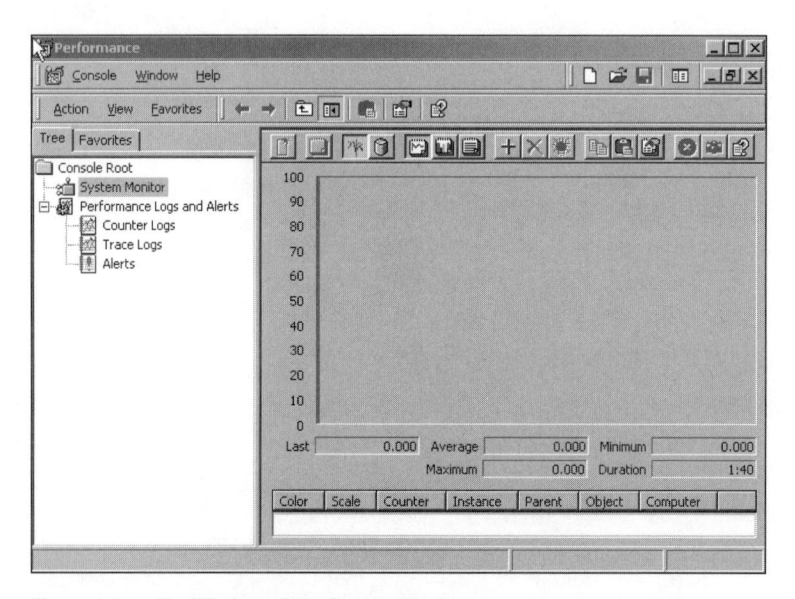

Figure 14.3 The Windows 2000 System Monitor.

The four major components of any computer system are the processor, memory, hard disks, and network. However, some applications, including Exchange Server, may install their own performance objects and performance data. The important facts to remember are that all performance objects contain at least one performance counter and that you can individually view these counters for monitoring or troubleshooting purposes. To add a counter in the System Monitor interface, simply hit the "+" sign on the toolbar. Figure 14.4 shows the Add Counters dialog box.

Warning: Exercise caution when monitoring huge numbers of performance objects with their related counters. Each object can contain multiple counters and generate excessive monitoring; in some cases, this can lead to overhead and performance problems on a production network. A recommended adage to live by is "all things in moderation," and this includes network monitoring.

If you have trouble understanding what a certain counter does, hit the Explain button; Windows 2000 provides a lengthy and detailed explanation of every counter displayed. Figure 14.5 shows a view of the explanation dialog box for the Processor\%Processor Time counter.

The Performance Console together with the System Monitor enables you to balance the workload among multiple servers. It is important to regularly monitor both physical hard disk counters and logical hard disk counters (storage volumes, for example). Table 14.2 lists the physical hard disk counters that System Monitor provides for both troubleshooting and future planning purposes.

Using System Monitor on the same machine as Windows 2000 and Exchange 2000 Server causes a definite increase in hard drive activity and access times. It is recommended that you use dedicated machines for monitoring, if at all possible. Because physical disk performance counters are enabled by default in Windows 2000, you have to manually enable counters for logical drives using a command prompt. These counters are enabled using the **diskperf -yv** command and rebooting your

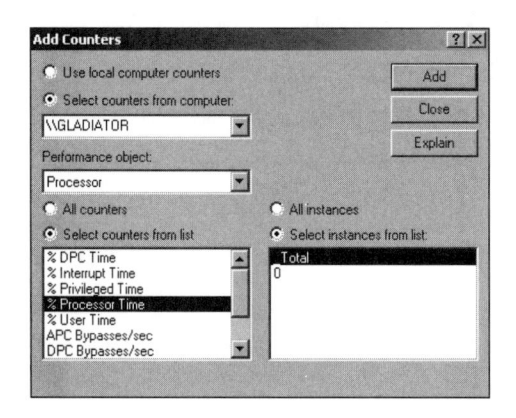

Figure 14.4 The Add Counters dialog box within the System Monitor snap-in.

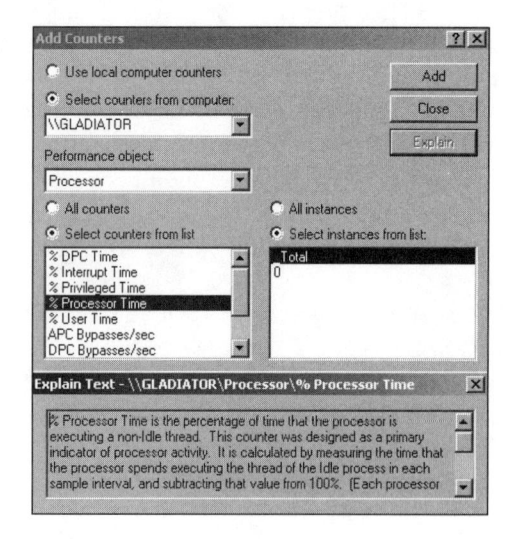

Figure 14.5 The Processor\%Processor Time counter explained within System Monitor.

Table 14.2 Important counters used to monitor a physical hard drive.

Name of Counter	Explanation or Purpose
PhysicalDisk\Avg. Disk Bytes/Transfer	A low value here (under 20K) indicates problems with applications accessing a hard drive efficiently because they require higher seek times than other applications.
PhysicalDisk\Avg. Disk sec/Transfer	This measures how much time a hard drive will take to fulfill a user request. A high rate (more than .2 seconds on average) may indicate potential hard disk access failures.
PhysicalDisk\Current Disk Queue Length	This is the number of requests outstanding on the disk at the time you collect your performance data. This is an instantaneous length, not an average over a time interval. Disk requests are experiencing delays proportional to the length of this queue less the number of spindles on the disks. This difference should average less than 2 for good performance.
PhysicalDisk\Disk Bytes/sec	This counter indicates the overall throughput of your hard drive mechanism.
PhysicalDisk\Disk Reads/sec	This shows the rate of read operations on the disk.
PhysicalDisk\%Disk Time	This is the percentage of elapsed time that the selected disk drive is busy servicing read or write requests.

computer. Typing "diskperf -?" at a command prompt yields helpful information on this command.

Note: Running these disk counters may result in performance degradations, so it may be helpful to use the diskperf -n command at a command prompt to disable these counters when you are not actively monitoring the performance of your disks.

When you are working with Redundant Array of Independent Disks (RAID) devices, note that a RAID device may appear as one physical hard disk in System

Monitor, whereas software RAID devices may appear as multiple drives in the same utility. Monitoring RAID devices using counters such as PhysicalDisk\%Disk Time or PhysicalDisk\Avg. Disk Queue Length can help determine how many system requests are waiting for hard disk access.

System Monitor would not be useful without the added functionality of the Performance Logs and Alerts snap-in, which Windows 2000 Server provides. Using this tool, you configure logs to record relevant performance data. You can also configure notifications when a specific counter goes above or below a predefined threshold level. When an error (for example, a disk input/output—I/O—error) occurs, the monitoring service alerts the log service, which records data in a trace log. You can view logged data directly in System Monitor, or you can export this data to an outside spreadsheet or database of your choice for further analysis. The whole objective of collecting performance data is to determine what is acceptable activity for your particular system. You must collect data that reflects both normal activity and peak activity over varying periods of time.

The objects of most interest include throughput and response time. *Throughput* describes how much work can be done in a given unit of time. Often, the weakest link or slowest point in a network establishes the baseline throughput for an entire system. *Response time* describes how much time is required to complete a given task from start to finish. A good rule to remember is that throughput is often measured from a server perspective, whereas response time is often measured from a client perspective. Figure 14.6 shows the three available log views that you can configure using Performance Logs and Alerts. Right-clicking on Counter Logs and choosing New Log Settings displays the dialog box shown in Figure 14.7 after you give your

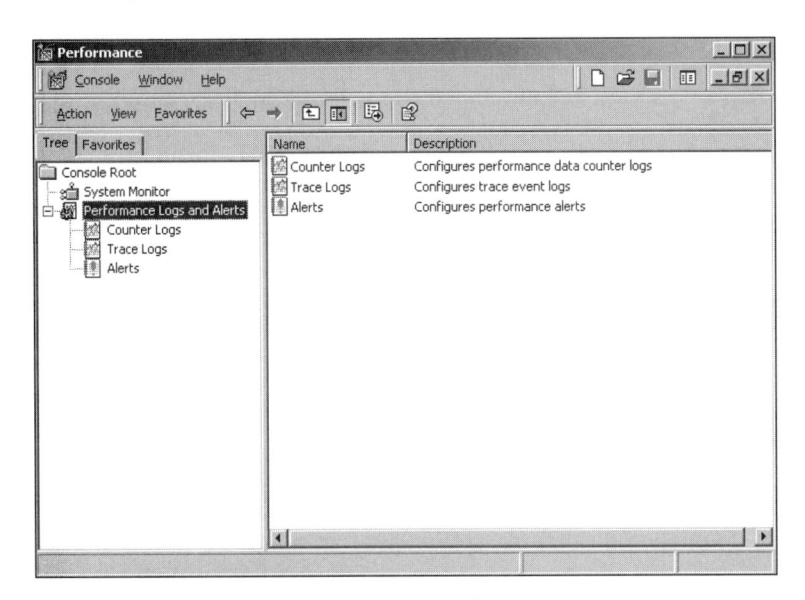

Figure 14.6 The Performance Logs and Alert window.

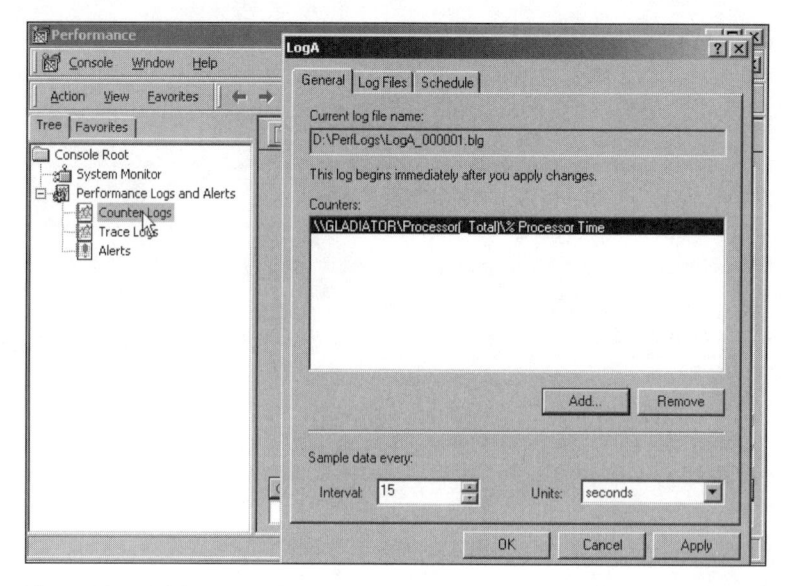

Figure 14.7 Adding a new Counter Log using the Performance Logs and Alerts snap-in.

log a new name. Notice that a file is generated using your new log name and the extension .blg. This log is configured to begin after you apply your changes. The Add button lets you add counters. Finally, notice the default time interval of sampling data every 15 seconds. You can change this after you have added at least one counter.

Here are some suggestions for using the Performance Console:

➤ Use caution when monitoring multithreaded applications, because if one thread is abnormally stopped, the performance data collected for that thread may be reported as another instance or thread for that application.

➤ Do not be alarmed by random spikes or dips in your performance charts. You need to observe counters over varying periods of time and should be more interested in averages than individual instances. Examples of spikes include startup processes that may skew your overall picture.

➤ Performance Console displays data in graph, histogram, or report format. Reports and histograms show only the *last value* of a counter, so using graphs may portray a more accurate picture of performance data.

Task Manager

Task Manager is a popular tool used in Windows 2000 to monitor information regarding memory usage or processor performance. Although it is easy to use and easy to access, it was not designed to supplant or even enhance other tools mentioned so far in this chapter. Task Manager's advantages include monitoring processes (including Exchange 2000 processes) and viewing system performance dynamically. However, it lacks features included with the Performance Console, as well as the information you can obtain using System Monitor counters.

Figure 14.8 shows the Task Manager's Processes tab, which displays a list of running processes along with information regarding their performance. You can invoke Task Manager by right-clicking on an empty space on the status bar of your desktop and choosing Task Manager, or by pressing Ctrl+Alt+Delete and selecting Task Manager. You can see all processes, including applications; relevant Exchange applications you can monitor include the IS (store.exe) and the Web Storage System (inetinfo.exe). The Performance tab of Task Manager, shown in Figure 14.9, displays graphs of processor and memory usage. If desired, you can view processor times in privileged or kernel mode for individual processors in a multiprocessor configuration.

Network Monitor

You use Network Monitor to view and detect problems on the network. Unlike System Monitor, which focuses on activity not related to the network, you use Network Monitor to view and detect problems on the network. If multiple computers have trouble communicating with each other, this tool can help diagnose both hardware and software issues that may be contributing to the problem. The focus of this utility is on capturing network traffic and analyzing network throughput. However, the version that comes with Windows 2000 can do this only on a local network segment.

The Network Monitor utility is in your *%systemroot%*\system32 directory. When first calling this application, you are asked to select a network to monitor. If no distinct choice is made, your local network segment is selected (see Figure 14.10).

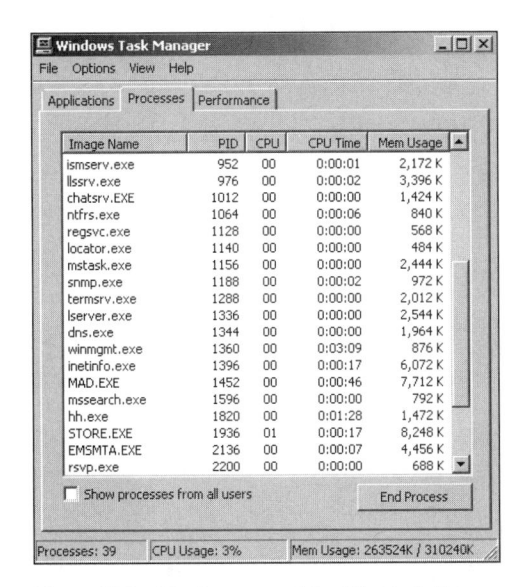

Figure 14.8 The Processes tab of the Task Manager application.

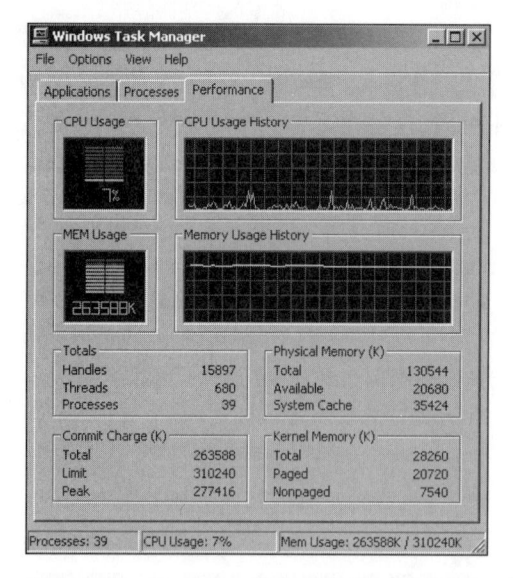

Figure 14.9 The Performance tab of the Task Manager application.

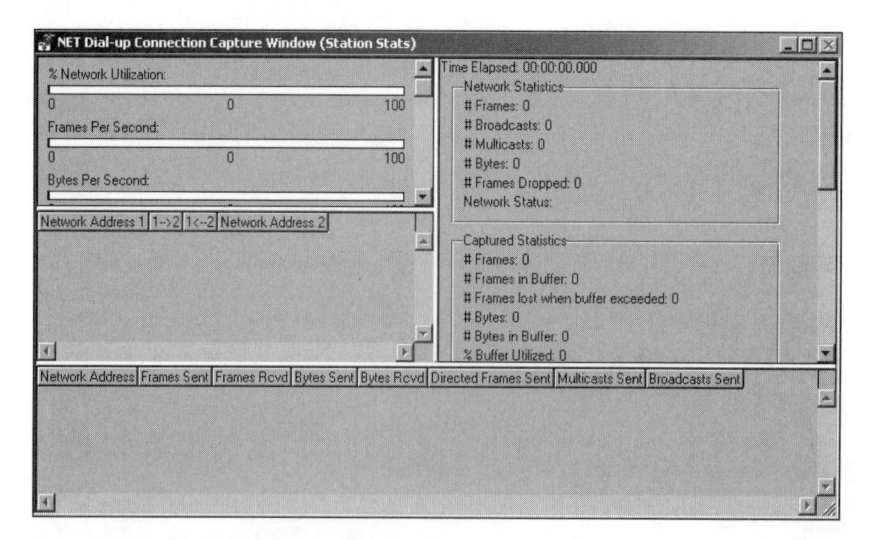

Figure 14.10 The Network Monitor dialog box.

Tip: To monitor traffic on remote network segments, you have to use the fully functional version that ships with Microsoft SMS Server 1.2 or 2. The version that comes with Windows 2000 is considered a "lite" version, though it's fully functional for local segments.

Network analysis in general involves looking at each frame or packet that traverses the network from a source computer to a destination computer. A packet of data sent from a source contains some or all of the following information:

➤ The source and destination address for the frame

- The actual data or message body being sent
- A checksum bit that verifies the integrity of the data

Network Monitor can both capture and display frames being sent to or from your local computer. It also displays network statistics, such as network use or total bytes received per second for broadcast frames. All frames or packets captured are copied into a capture buffer, which is a storage area in memory. Frames are captured using a network driver interface specification driver.

To run this tool, make sure that you have correctly installed the Network Monitor Tools, which installs the Network Monitor console in addition to the Network Monitor driver. Many administrators wrongly assume that these Tools are built into the Windows 2000 network operating system (NOS); however, you must manually install them using the Control Panel Add/Remove Programs applet. The procedure is as follows:

1. Choose Start | Settings | Control Panel.
2. Select Add/Remove Programs.
3. Choose Add/Remove Windows Components.
4. Select Management And Monitoring Tools. This contains the Network Monitor Tools.

A successful installation shows the Network Monitor console in the Administrative Tools program group. The actual Network Monitor driver is located in the Properties for your Local Area Connections. The driver is actually known as the *Network Monitor agent* and is responsible for allowing Network Monitor to collect frames or packets from a network adapter card.

Note: There is one other important use for the Network Monitor agent, but it applies only to the SMS version of Network Monitor. The agent allows the Network Monitor tool that comes with SMS Server to capture and display frames from a remote computer. SMS Server includes Network Monitor drivers or agents for other Windows OSs besides Windows 2000.

Figure 14.11 shows a sample screen of the Network Monitor interface. To actually capture data, you select Capture | Start, as shown in Figure 14.12, and watch as frames are displayed in the Capture window. Only approximately 100 network sessions can be displayed at one time, but you can always reset statistics and display another set of 100 using the Capture menu. Also, you can think of Network Monitor as a giant database of network information, so you can perform database-related actions such as queries or filters to specify only certain types of information that will be monitored. These *capture filters* or *display filters* can filter by protocols—such as Internet Protocol (IP) or Internetwork Packet Exchange (IPX)—or by media access control (MAC) addresses. You can even limit a capture to frames that contain a certain pattern of data.

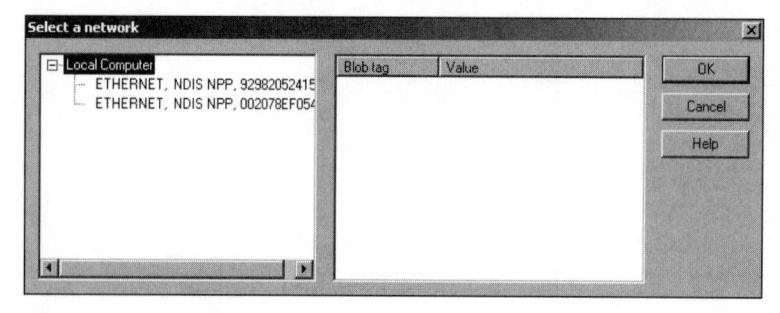

Figure 14.11 The Network Monitor interface screen for a local network segment.

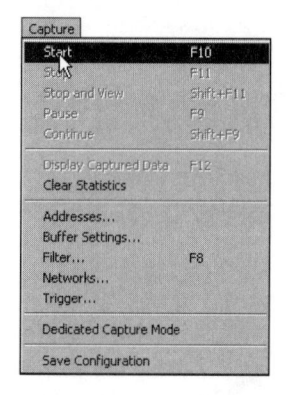

Figure 14.12 Starting a data capture in Network Monitor.

Network Monitor does have some performance issues, however. As with the Performance Console, you may experience increased system overhead or resource usage if your capture buffers are not large enough to handle all the traffic you want to analyze. This is because Network Monitor uses a file that is mapped to system memory to create a capture buffer to copy its data. A recommended procedure is to run Network Monitor in the background to reduce the total system resources this utility uses. To do so, go to the Capture menu and select Dedicated Capture Mode.

Windows 2000 Event Viewer

This tool is unfortunately a very overlooked utility. It should, however, be the first tool you use when systems do strange things. The unfortunate criticism this utility has been subject to is its cryptic interpretation of system events. Currently, no third-party tools remedy this situation, but Event Viewer does distinguish the seasoned professionals from the rookies.

Event Viewer can perform a variety of functions. For example, if you have auditing enabled on a Windows 2000 network, you can view the audit logs that are generated as a result of these audit policies. Any service or program that is integrated with Windows 2000 becomes subject to scrutiny within the Event Viewer application. Exchange 2000 Server is one example of this, as are other third-party programs, such as Checkpoint Firewall-1 or Norton AntiVirus 2000. You should regularly investigate the following three logs:

- *System log*—Contains error events, information events, or warning events (represented by a red stop sign, a blue circle, and a yellow triangle with an exclamation point, respectively). The NOS itself generates these events.

- *Security log*—Mostly contains information regarding audited events described in an organization's audit policy.

- *Application log*—Contains errors, warnings, and information alerts generated by specific applications, such as firewall programs or email programs.

> **Tip:** Each log can range from around 64K to almost 4GB in size, but the default is 512K. You definitely don't want these logs to approach anywhere near 4GB in size for several reasons. One reason is that valid errors and warnings will not be recorded for analysis if the log files are near capacity. Also, overextended log files may sometimes cause background processes to hang and even affect logon behavior. Although there is no recommended maximum size before log files have to be deleted, we recommend monitoring log files on a weekly basis to ensure that system resources are not being wasted.

It is important to keep in mind that these logs are dynamic, and someone or something is recording events at all times. Take care that these logs do not get full. It is actually quite easy to configure replacement of logs older than a week, for example. Use the Properties of each log to control how often the logs will be overwritten or deleted. Not all logs should be deleted; if you archive or back up security logs, they will assist you in auditing any security-related issue you face in the future.

We have to emphasize that not too many administrators train themselves on the importance of checking or reviewing this valuable diagnostic tool. Reviewing this regularly yields detailed system information that can help you avert disaster at a later stage.

Hard Disk Monitoring within Windows 2000 Using Disk Defragmenter

It is often the case with PC systems that critical components are neglected or unattended to until catastrophe hits. Of all the major components in a computer system, the physical hard drive is the one most vulnerable to wear and tear, and it fails all too often. The other major components include memory, processors, and network components. However, memory does not usually become "bad" and is not subject to the same wear-and-tear conditions imposed upon a hard drive. Even an inexpensive processor will outlast a hard drive that is not properly attended to.

Whether you are running Windows 95, Windows 98, or Macintosh OS X, your critical data and applications all depend on a stable hard drive. To guarantee long-lasting reliability, Windows 2000 has given us multiple tools, including the Disk Defragmenter snap-in, to ensure optimal performance of this most valuable asset.

Files become defragmented because Windows 2000 saves files in the first slot it can find. It does not care about using contiguous space, and the result is fragmentation. The ultimate outcome is that it takes longer to access files that are frequently needed. It also takes longer to create new files because precious free space is not contiguous; rather, it is scattered across the drive. Use the Disk Defragmenter snap-in tool to locate any fragmented file and defragment it. After a file is defragmented, it will occupy a single area of contiguous space on the drive. You can defragment a drive or volume regardless of file system, so it will work with FAT16, FAT32, or NT File System (NTFS) formatted partitions. There are two ways to access this useful tool:

1. Using Windows Explorer, right-click on the specific drive you want to defragment and choose Defragment Now on the Tools tab.

2. Using the Microsoft Management Console (MMC) and the Computer Management snap-in, choose Disk Defragmenter under the Console Root folder.

The three portions of a Disk Defragmenter display are as follows:

➤ One portion lists the volumes available for defragmentation.

➤ Another portion shows just how fragmented the volume actually is.

➤ The final portion dynamically updates the volume as it is being defragmented.

Running Disk Defragmenter when resource usage is high is not recommended, because this tool is CPU intensive and affects access times to other programs. Users should get in the habit of regularly defragmenting any drive because fragmented files accumulate rather quickly. Although daily defragmentation is hardly an option, defragmenting on a biweekly or monthly basis will yield satisfactory results. Hard drives become fragmented not only when users install new files, but also when they delete many files. This is why regular monthly defragmentation is a normal part of the system administration experience.

Exchange 2000 Monitoring Tools

Exchange 2000 by itself uses tools that monitor services, links, and protocols. It also integrates with diagnostic tools that the Windows 2000 OS uses. We now look at three of the most useful tools: the Monitoring and Status Tool, diagnostic logging, and Exchange Server monitors.

Exchange 2000 Monitoring and Status Tool

This tool will probably be the primary tool you use to monitor the status of both your servers and your network in general. You use two user interfaces to analyze information provided by this tool: Status and Notifications. Figure 14.13 shows the System Manager console containing the Monitoring and Status folder. You use the Status interface to view servers or connectors within your network, along with a

Troubleshooting and Monitoring 453

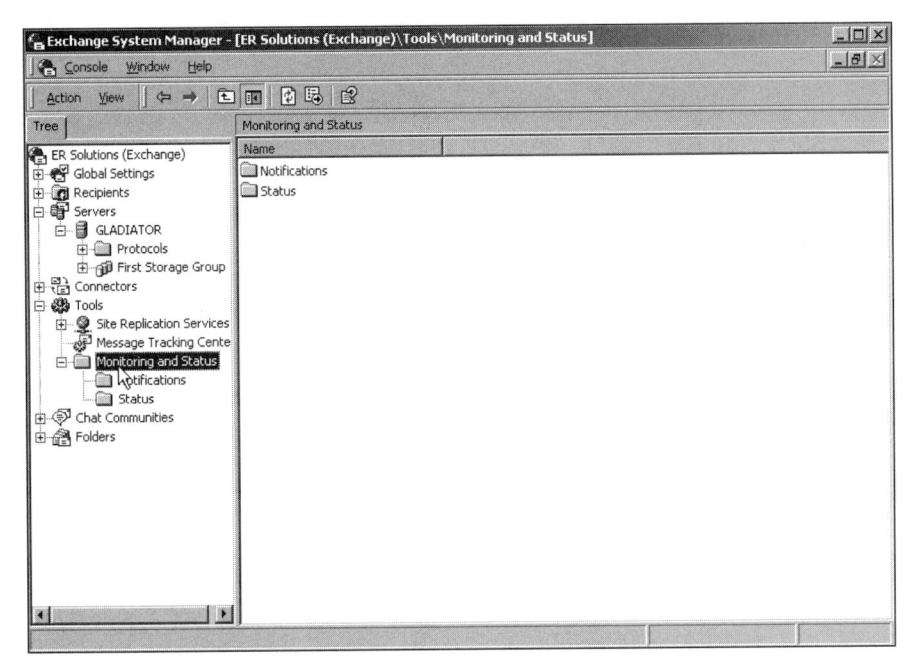

Figure 14.13 The Monitoring and Status folder in System Manager.

status condition. You can even disable monitoring of a given server using the Status interface. Servers and connectors are said to be in certain status states. The following status states apply mainly to servers:

- *Available*—Your server is online and functioning without errors.
- *Unreachable*—A particular service is not functioning.
- *Maintenance Mode*—Monitoring has been disabled for maintenance purposes.
- *Unknown*—The System Attendant (SA) is having problems communicating with your local server.

Status states that apply to connectors include:

- *Available*—The connector is functioning correctly.
- *Unavailable*—A particular service is not functioning on the connector itself.

You can set up Exchange to constantly monitor the performance levels of a wide variety of network services. You can set warning states or even critical states to alert you via email for such components as Simple Mail Transfer Protocol (SMTP) queues, CPU activity, or even hard disk space thresholds. You can find the Monitoring and Status Tool in the Tools folder in the Exchange System Manager snap-in.

It is important to keep in mind that Exchange automatically logs a critical state if any of the following services are stopped for any reason:

- WWW Publishing Service
- Web Storage System (Exchange Installable File System [EXIFS])
- Message Transfer Agent (MTA) stacks
- SMTP service
- System Attendant (SA)

You can add services to these default services for notification purposes. To do so, follow these steps:

1. Choose the Properties sheet of a server within the System Manager snap-in and select the Monitoring tab.

2. Select the Details button and choose a service in the Default Microsoft Exchange Services dialog box.

3. Click on Add and then on OK to finish this process.

Note that you have to configure any notifications through these user interfaces because Exchange Server was not designed to send notifications by default. The Notifications user interface can be used with the Status user interface to set up alerts or trigger a script to alert employees if Exchange has crossed some critical threshold. Figures 14.14 and 14.15 show how to configure an email alert using the Notifications folder.

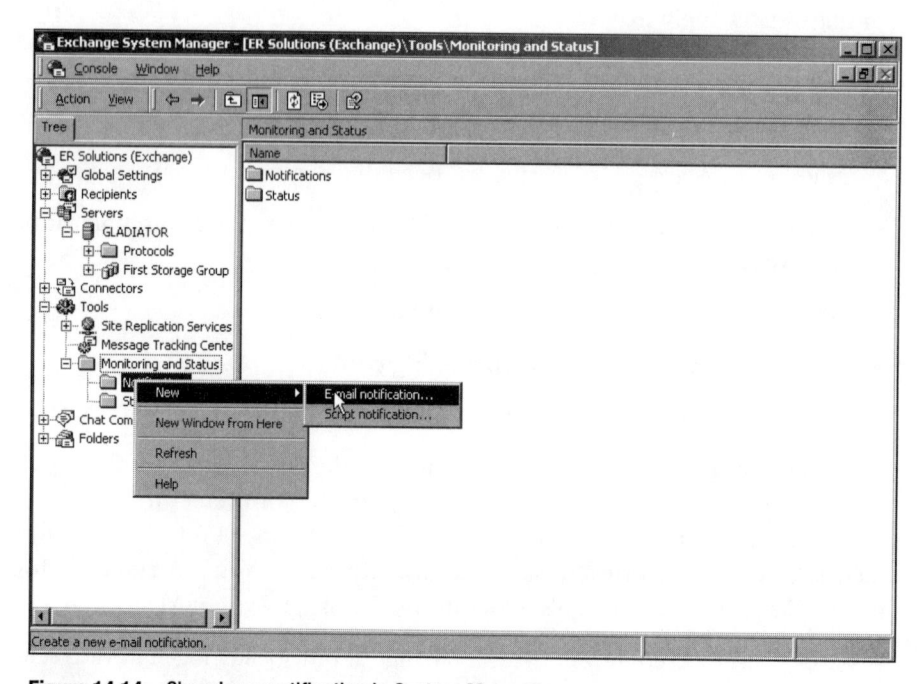

Figure 14.14 Choosing a notification in System Manager.

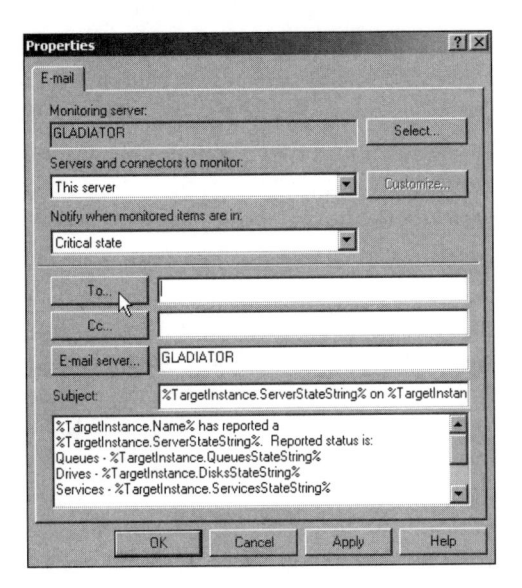

Figure 14.15 Configuring an email notification.

Diagnostic Logging

You use diagnostic logging to monitor Exchange connectors as well as protocol connectors. Most Exchange Server services log certain events to the Windows 2000 application log, which you view using Event Viewer (discussed earlier in this chapter). You will soon discover that diagnostic logging may prove to be one of the most useful troubleshooting tools known to Exchange administrators.

You can log diagnostic data using a server's Properties sheet in the System Manager snap-in. After selecting Diagnostic Logging|Services, you can choose a service to monitor and a related category to monitor. You can monitor many services, including Internet Message Access Protocol 4 (IMAP4), Lotus Notes, the IS system, Public Folders, and Microsoft (MS) Mail. What is important here are the logging levels you choose for the services and the categories you select. You can configure logging levels as follows:

- *None (0)*—Only error messages will be logged.
- *Minimum (1)*—Only warning and error messages will be logged.
- *Medium (3)*—Informational, warning, and error messages will be logged.
- *Maximum (5)*—All messages will be logged.

Tip: Logging levels do not increase sequentially; they are either 0, 1, 3, or 5. A level of 0 implies the recording of basic application and system failures. A level of 5 defines logging for a particular service. A level of 1 or 3 will define intermediate levels of logging. There is technically no level of 2 or 4 defined for logging purposes. Diagnostic logging of Exchange 2000 Server will generate many entries in Event Viewer, especially when set to the Maximum level. Even though the application log file is configured to grow to a maximum size of 512K, you should change this setting to 1MB or higher when using diagnostic logging.

The Maximum logging level obviously generates the most entries in the Windows 2000 Event Viewer application log. Therefore, unless you have a valid reason for configuring Maximum logging (i.e., you have been explicitly told to do so by the Microsoft Technical Support staff to assist in problem resolution), you should refrain from configuring this logging level. In theory, diagnostic logging should be enabled only for strict troubleshooting purposes and should be subsequently disabled.

Exchange Server Monitors

Exchange Server provides tools known as *monitors* that assist you in checking the status of services and connectors that are configured on both Exchange 2000 and legacy Exchange servers. You may recall from Exchange 5.5 that a server monitor checked the condition of one or more servers within a site, and used RPCs to check servers in other sites as well. You could specify actions to take when a particular service or computer had stopped, including restarting a failed server. A link monitor was used to verify efficient routing of messages called PING messages. You had to correctly configure all link monitors in Exchange 5.5 so that you could provide useful information regarding network connectivity.

Exchange 2000 provides similar functionality with respect to server monitors and link monitors. Server monitors still help to check the status of certain services and resources on a specific server. And link monitors still check the status of various connectors configured between two servers. One difference between the legacy Exchange version of these monitors and the current Exchange version is the tool you use to configure them. In legacy Exchange, you used the Exchange Administrator program, whereas in Exchange 2000 Server, you use the Exchange System Manager snap-in tool. Another difference is that in Exchange 5.5, you had to manually create a server monitor for every server in your site. The Exchange Administrator program had to be kept running in the background. Exchange 2000 Server creates a server monitor automatically, and the Exchange System Manager does not have to run continuously.

To view a Server monitor, find the Tools container object using the Exchange System snap-in and expand a folder called Monitoring and Status. There, you find a Status container object. All available monitors are shown in the Contents pane on the left-hand side. You can also right-click on the Status container object and choose to connect to a different server to view a new set of monitored objects on that server. Any server monitor you configure checks resources on your Exchange server, as well as services on your Windows 2000 server.

Server monitors are created by default in a typical installation of Exchange 2000 Server or Exchange 2000 Enterprise Edition. They monitor the following important objects:

➤ SMTP queues

➤ X.400 queues

- Available hard drive space
- CPU usage
- Most Windows 2000 services

Looking at this last item in the list above, you may wonder why you would want to monitor most Windows 2000 services when monitoring your Exchange 2000 Server. You have to realize that some Windows 2000 services significantly affect the performance of an Exchange 2000 server. This should not be surprising in light of the integration between the two products. The default set of Exchange-related services that are monitored include the Exchange IS, the Exchange MTA stacks, the Exchange routing engine, and the SMTP service. In some cases, you may want to add a new group of Windows 2000 services that you want monitored regularly. Examples of new services may include a backup program like Veritas' Backup Exec, which runs as a service in Windows 2000. Some third-party services may affect your Exchange 2000 configuration, and it is wise to monitor the impact they will have. You can even monitor basic Windows 2000 services, such as the NetLogon service or the Workstation service, if you feel they will impact your Exchange organization in any way.

It is not difficult to add a new monitor for a new set of services. Simply open the Properties page for the server in question using the System Manager snap-in and click on the Monitoring tab (shown in Figure 14.16). Double-click on the item

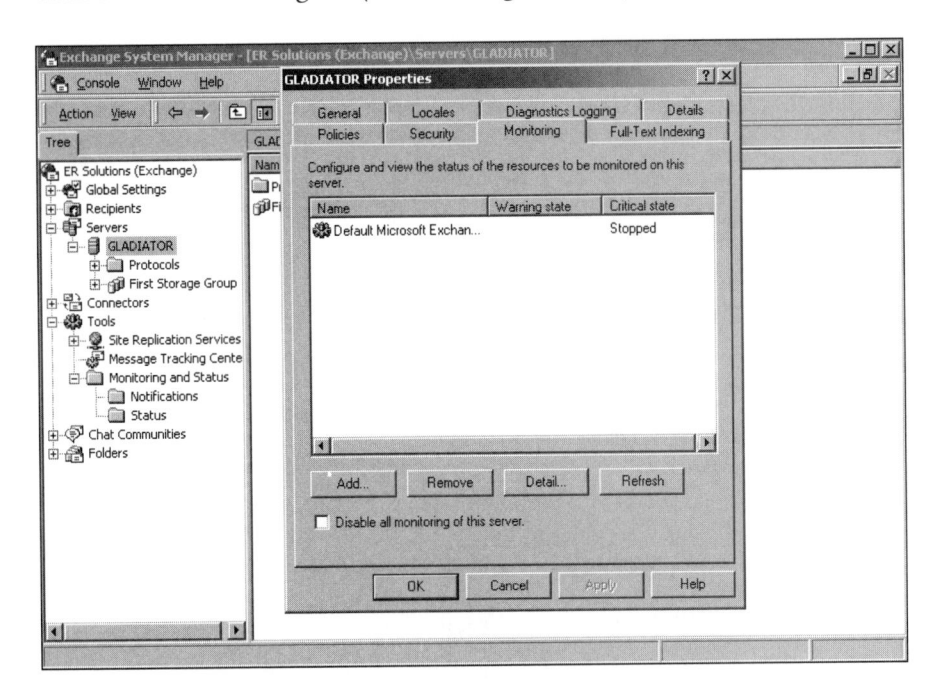

Figure 14.16 The Monitoring tab of a server's Properties page.

marked Default Microsoft Exchange Services and you will see the six default services that are running (see Figure 14.17). Notice the default action of When Service Is Not Running, Change State To Critical. Clicking on the Add button near the bottom of the screen will enable you to monitor other critical Windows 2000 services such as the DHCP Server or the Distributed File System (see Figure 14.18).

Like server monitors, link monitors are created by default for every connector that exists on a server. They are also shown in the same Status container object in the Exchange System Manager snap-in. However, they are not equal to server monitors in all respects. Link monitors show a status of either available or unavailable, and you don't have to contend with any configuration issues. If a link monitor suggests that

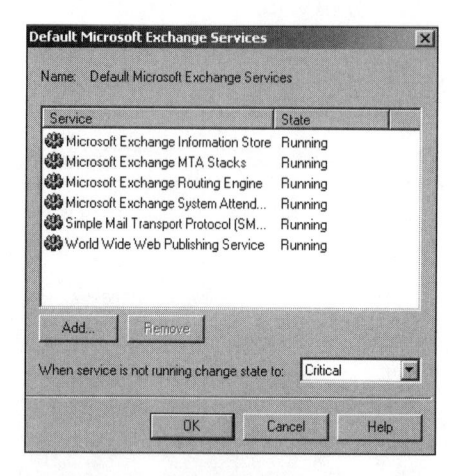

Figure 14.17 The six default services that run under Exchange 2000 Server.

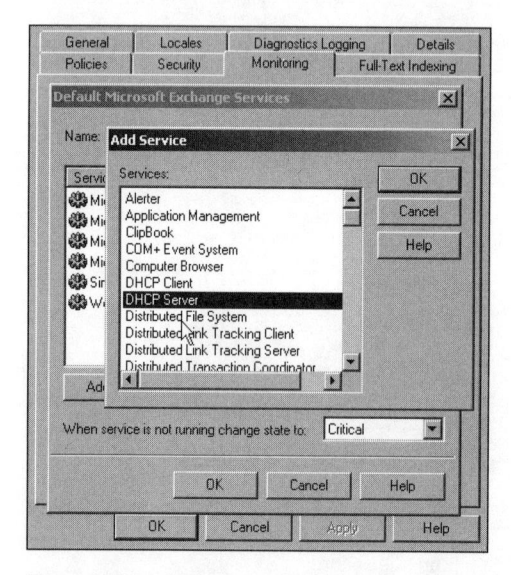

Figure 14.18 Adding other Windows 2000 services to Server Monitor.

one connector is not available, you have other tools at your disposal to help you solve your problem. A related tool, Queue Viewer, helps you view X.400 and SMTP queues, and provides information such as message age or the total number of messages in a queue. Use one of the following methods to access your message queue:

- In Exchange System Manager, go to Servers | Server | Protocols | SMTP | Default SMTP Virtual Server | Queues.

- In Exchange System Manager, go to Servers | Server | Protocols | X.400 | Queues.

- In Exchange System Manager, go to Routing Groups | First Routing Group | Connectors | Third Party Connector | Queues.

Of the many queues, two worth looking at are the Local Delivery queue and the Messages Awaiting Directory Lookup queue. For example, a backlog in the Local Delivery queue may point to a problem with the local Web Storage System.

A key advantage of using monitors is that you can configure notifications in the event of a critical or warning state. Exchange 2000 Server allows you to configure notifications based on email or a script. You do this by using the Exchange System Manager and selecting the Notifications container under Monitoring and Status. Script notifications based on a certain threshold being reached are more useful and interesting than simple email notifications. You could actually configure an automatic shutdown of your Exchange server if an antivirus resource being monitored reaches a critical stage when detecting a malicious virus. The possibilities are endless here, and all administrators should enjoy this added functionality in Exchange 2000.

Disaster Recovery and Planning

In any environment, failing to plan for a disaster is a definite plan to fail. Topics such as disaster planning and regular backups are at the heart of every Exchange server organization. These organizations rely on measures such as off-site tape backups and even redundant backup strategies simply because their entire business structure depends on access to reliable and original data. No organization is too big or too small to consider some type of redundancy in its data. You have to plan for that fateful day when all systems could potentially shut down simultaneously, leaving your organization totally in the dark.

As morbid as the above scenario sounds, too many administrators have assumed that a catastrophic network failure will never happen to them. However, it shouldn't take a complete catastrophe to convince someone that sound backup procedures are necessary. Consider a vice president who has been working on financial projections for more than six months and suddenly loses that information due to a hard drive failing. Those who regularly consider worst-case scenarios will be those who are most prepared to comfortably handle any destructive situation.

We have seen throughout this book the constant integration of Windows 2000 and Exchange 2000 Server. We will see this again in the areas of data backup and data restoration. Here, we will describe how to use the familiar Windows 2000 Backup application to help plan for eventual disaster. Please note, however, that many companies now use third-party software such as Computer Associates' ArcServeIT or Veritas' BackUpExec products instead of Windows 2000 Backup. These third-party products offer similar functionality, but they also bring incredibly enhanced user interfaces and custom configurations that are just not possible with the Windows 2000 utility. The higher prices of the third-party products usually keep them out of the reach of small to medium-sized businesses. Each company has to make its own decision; in any case, we will now focus on the built-in functionality of Windows 2000 Backup.

The Underlying Technology

Understanding backups and restores in Exchange 2000 requires an understanding of the underlying database technology, as well as the various categories of backup available to you. By this time in the book, you know that the Exchange database technology is based on the ESE, part of the Web Storage System. Because Exchange 2000 is now part of Windows 2000, backing up Exchange means also backing up part of Windows 2000, or more specifically, Active Directory (AD).

An Exchange server consists of Storage Groups that are part of the ESE. Every Storage Group consists of a collection of files, including database (EDB) files, streaming database (STM) files, and one set of transaction log files for all databases in the Storage Group. A database may also contain Site Replication Service (SRS) files (which allow compatibility with the Exchange 5.5 directory service) and Key Management Server (KMS) files (for security encryption services). All database files share similar attributes to OS files. Each database in a Storage Group has a Globally Unique Identifier (GUID) assigned to it. A matching GUID is found in the AD of Windows 2000. If the GUIDs do not match, the database cannot be mounted.

All changes to a database are stored in a transaction log file, which stores a list of operations performed on a page in memory. Using these files, you can restore any committed transactions you may lose during a power outage, for example. The log files always maintain a constant size of 5MB (usually, you will see an exact size of 5,242,880 bytes). If they show any other size, the chance is great that they are corrupt. Every Storage Group has exactly one transaction log file assigned to it; it also reserves two log files, res1.log and res2.log. These files are stored in the \log directory and are used only for extra disk space if the service runs out of space. You should never store log files and database files on the same physical drive.

Lastly, become very familiar with the concept of *circular logging*. This was used in previous versions of Exchange, and it has retained its importance in the current version. Circular logging actually reduces the amount of space you need for additional transaction log files because it overwrites these logs after committing them to a database. You should use this type of logging only for data that is not critical or immediately needed. Not surprisingly, it is turned off by default. (The Exchange designers did not want to assume that you wanted your data overwritten by default in case your data was extremely sensitive and needed to be preserved.) If circular logging is enabled, any changes to the EDB file are written to the transaction log files. However, transactions to the STM files are not logged. If you need to restore data, you can "play back" data up to when you performed your last full backup. This is an important concept to keep in mind.

Backing Up Data Using Windows 2000

You use the Windows 2000 Backup tool, called ntbackup.exe, to perform an individual backup for an Exchange server. Microsoft highly recommends that before you use it you download the latest hot fix from their Web site at **www.microsoft.com/exchange/** to obtain the most recent version of this tool.

Backups take planning like any other process and can be more critical than other processes. The normal process of backing up an Exchange Server consists of the following steps:

1. Defining your backup strategy

2. Deciding on the types of data you want backed up

3. Making sure you have the proper resources set up

4. Addressing performance issues

Notice that the process of defining a backup strategy (Step 1) comes before selecting what data will be backed up (Step 2). Even if you consider yourself an implementer rather than a planner, the reality is that if backups are not properly planned and implemented, restoration becomes an elusive goal. For example, some types of backups result in longer restore times; this may not be a desired result for an organization with thousands of users working with time-sensitive information. Also, successful backups should consider adequate hard drive space for both database and transaction log files.

Deciding on the type of data to be backed up is also a nontrivial matter. A lot depends on what the end user views as critical or noncritical data. Administrators often place more importance on such things as configuration data, users' mailboxes, public folder stores, and other databases. A consensus must be reached on exactly what type of data will be chosen for regular backup cycles. It is a good idea to distinguish between data that is constantly changing—*dynamic data*—and data that remains constant over a measurable period of time—*static data*. The data that will be labeled as changing or dynamic will be subject to different backup schemes than data that remains constant or static.

An example of static data is data that does not depend on outside applications or services to run correctly. The Windows 2000 OS and Exchange Server are two good examples of such types of data. Consider most third-party applications as static data. Dynamic data, on the other hand, depends on outside applications and services to generate its own set of subdata. Consider an Exchange Server database or a log file as examples of data subject to constant change. The largest database that we consider to be dynamic is, of course, the AD that resides within the Windows 2000 OS.

Previous versions of Exchange Server backed up the information store as well as the Exchange directory that maintains information about each mailbox. Exchange 2000 will back up configuration information stored in Active Directory, so it is necessary to back up AD using the System State folder within the Windows 2000 Backup utility. This folder allows you to decide whether to back up the following resources:

- Active Directory
- Boot files
- The Registry
- The Sys volume

The SYSVOL is a directory structure within Windows 2000 containing policies and scripts. The default folder structure appears as *%systemroot%*\SYSVOL\Sysvol*domain_name*\Policies or *%systemroot%*\SYSVOL\Sysvol*domain_name*\Scripts. Any changes to the *%systemroot%*\SYSVOL directory on any DC will be automatically replicated to other DCs within your site by default.

You may also want to back up your \Exchsrvr folder in your server's file system, because important information, such as message tracking data, can be found within your file system. If these items cannot be restored, you will have to re-create some of your organizational elements to verify that the contents of your file system match the configuration found within Active Directory.

All backups rely on a combination of software and hardware. The software used can be a built-in tool or a third-party commercial tool. However, the hardware used must be largely compatible with the Windows 2000 OS. Microsoft has designed the Windows 2000 OS so that it automatically checks both hardware and software and reports any issues or conflicts during a typical installation. All hardware used with Windows 2000 should appear on Microsoft's Hardware Compatibility List (HCL), included on the original Windows 2000 Server installation CD-ROM (usually in the \Support\Hcl.txt directory). All hardware on the HCL has supposedly passed a Hardware Compatibility Test (HCT). Windows Hardware Quality Labs (WHQLs) and various hardware vendors perform these tests. If your backup hardware works with Windows 2000 but is not supported by the HCL, it may not be open to technical support via Microsoft Technical Services.

> **Tip:** Always check **www.microsoft.com/hwtest/hcl/** for the most updated version of the HCL. Or visit **www.microsoft.com** and search using the string "HCL".

> **Warning:** Many custom-built computers are running the Windows 2000 OS without any apparent problems. However, Microsoft's support staff may still consider certain hardware used in such models to be unsupported because it is either not listed on the most current HCL or the user is not using a Microsoft-supplied driver to control the hardware. Both conditions must exist for your custom hardware or peripheral to receive adequate technical attention if interoperability problems with Windows 2000 or Exchange 2000 occur.

Once you have met your resource requirements, you will have some idea of how much storage capacity you will need. Backup frequencies range from weekly to monthly, so planning is required to determine the optimal number of tapes you need for all data selected. New backup drives and tape media are appearing on the market almost every week, and astute administrators purchase media that is within budget but also extremely reliable. You should never go by tape capacity alone. (We know of one administrator who mistakenly purchased a tape backup device based solely on advertised claims that its tape media could contain 50GB of data each. What this administrator failed to notice was that this amount referred to compressed data. Most of his backups were not compressed and totaled almost 80GB, so he easily exceeded the capacity of the tape media on every single scheduled backup. Again, let the buyer beware!)

Exchange 2000 depends on AD being installed correctly as well as being available, even during a backup session. We are not suggesting that AD is a crucial component of Exchange 2000; however, AD does store configuration information and user objects on behalf of Exchange Server. Another needed item is the Web Storage System and its corresponding services. If a service happens to shut down unexpectedly, your backup will not proceed. Also, whoever runs the Windows 2000 Backup utility must have Backup Operator rights on the local computer. This is true even if you purchase an off-the-shelf utility like ArcServeIT for Windows 2000. The third-party tool actually behaves as a built-in Windows 2000 service and uses permissions preset in the Local System account.

Performance issues arise when you consider the length of time needed to finish a complete backup and restore cycle. Using fast hardware helps increase performance, but you must sometimes make a corollary decision at this point. In some cases, it may be beneficial to connect the backup unit directly to the machine being backed up; in other cases, it is more beneficial to back up all machines on the network to an offline or near-line jukebox-type unit (or *tape library*, as it is sometimes called). The decision should always depend on which procedure results in fewer network bottlenecks. Performance issues also arise when you are using disk-management schemes such as stripe sets or mirrored sets. A backup routine may actually require twice as much disk space to back up a mirrored Exchange server compared to a server that is not mirrored, because the transaction logs may be placed on a separate drive, which is also mirrored. It becomes necessary at this point to experiment with test backups of various data to establish some type of baseline for future reference.

Before we delve into ntbackup.exe, we must introduce one more area of preparation. This involves choosing a backup category or type, which depends on the importance of the data being backed up. There are five categories, all differing in performance and the time required. One difference among these backup categories is how each one handles the *archive bit* found in every Windows 2000 file. When you create a file, the related archive bit is marked "On." Some backups will set this archive bit to "Off," which implies that the file has been backed up. You can manually set a file's attributes so that it will be archived regardless of which type of backup you perform. In this case, the file will be backed up along with any other files that you have chosen. Table 14.3 shows the types of backups.

When you invoke ntbackup.exe in the \Winnt\system32 folder, you are actually invoking a call to the Web Storage System, which informs the ESE that it is now in backup mode. A *patch file* is generated for every database in the backup, but only if you are doing a full backup. A patch file (PAT) stores transactions for EDB files that have already been backed up. This file is used only during an online backup or restore situation, and there is one such file for every store that is being actively

Table 14.3   The types of backups in Exchange 2000.

Category	Explanation
Full	This backs up all Exchange log files plus the Web Storage System. All transactions already committed are deleted. This type of backup takes the longest to restore but requires only one tape.
Copy	This is equivalent to a full backup but does not delete any log files. This is used in cases where new software is installed. This method is not as prevalent as a full backup.
Incremental	This method backs up all transaction log files and then deletes log files that contain committed transactions. It is the fastest backup process. However, restoring from an incremental backup requires you to have the last full backup performed, as well as all subsequent incremental backups. You cannot use incremental backups if you have circular logging enabled.
Differential	This backup method is similar to a full backup in many ways. It differs from an incremental backup in that it backs up log files prior to a checkpoint file without deleting them. This represents the second fastest restore method. Restoring data requires you to have the latest full backup in addition to the most recent differential backup.
Normal	This method can recognize multiple Storage Groups on any server, as well as multiple databases per Storage Group. This flexibility means you can restore an individual database without having to restore the entire Storage Group. However, every time an individual database is backed up within a Storage Group, the transaction log files are backed up more than once. Therefore, it may be better to back up an entire Storage Group; this way, the transaction log files are backed up only once. We should emphasize that a normal backup is more of a *process* than a *job*.

backed up. There is no patch file if a differential or incremental backup is being used. Whenever the ESE enters backup mode, a new log file is opened.

Exchange 2000 can support both online and offline backups:

> *Online backups*—These are recommended only because the affected databases can continue to run while the data is being backed up. This means that end users do not experience termination of services. Online backups are always preferred to offline backups because users can still perform normal mail operations while files are being backed up. An online backup can be either full or partial; the difference is that full backups copy everything that exists in the database, whereas partial backups copy only log files.

> *Offline backups*—These are performed while the associated Exchange services are not running. They allow you to save copies of database files; however, you must dismount a database before you can perform an offline backup.

Maintaining a Backup Schedule

There are many good ways of scheduling backups within an organization. However, no hard and fast rules exist that work in every single case. Some administrators pay more attention to effective backup schedules than they do to all other aspects of system administration. Although we do not condone disregarding other vital areas of administration, such as monitoring, troubleshooting, or customer support, we do respect the importance and pervasiveness of a finely designed backup solution. You have to actively ensure that tapes are being rotated regularly and that data is being backed up without significant errors. Most backup programs allow you to verify a backup after it has been performed. Windows 2000 has realized the importance of this feature and has definitely included it. However, it may not be a best practice to always take advantage of this feature because additional checksums are written and verified along with data.

According to the *Microsoft Exchange 2000 Server Resource Kit*, you should consider using a media rotation schedule based on a month-week-day model. This means you construct a monthly, weekly, and daily backup set. Tape media are reused on the same day every week. Incremental backups are performed daily, with full backups performed weekly. This weekly backup tape is reused for a monthly backup. You also perform a full backup on the last day of every month and repeat this process every three months. You can take advantage of many such configurations in your own organization. A good rule of thumb is to always have at least two weeks of valid data in your possession, with one week of data maintained in an off-site location. We are surprised at the number of administrators who do not take advantage of off-site tape storage. A number of companies now even offer specialized tape maintenance services at secure off-site facilities for a monthly fee. Best practices suggest that you fully document any backup rotation schedule and make it available to all participants involved in system planning and administration.

The Restore Process

When you need to restore a database or Storage Group, you must dismount it so that users cannot access it. When Exchange enters restore mode, the store.exe process informs the database engine and the ESE enters restore mode. This means that any log or patch files that are being restored are copied to the server in a temporary file so that they will not overwrite current production files. You want to avoid overwriting any transaction log files. After your selected files are restored, a new Storage Group is created solely for the purpose of restoring a database. Sometimes, the status of the Exchange server to which you are restoring files affects the overall restoration process. For example, if the Exchange server to which you are restoring files is acting as a domain controller (DC), you may have to restore AD on that computer first. You cannot successfully restore Exchange 2000 unless you have successfully restored AD.

You will encounter many types of restore in your daily life as an administrator, including restoring online backups, offline backups, log files, an individual mailbox, or an individual database. You may even find yourself restoring an entire server. One of the most common occurrences of a restore involves restoring a single mailbox that has been accidentally deleted. If you happen to remove a single mailbox, you may have to resort to third-party software to restore it. However, one preventative measure you can take to avoid doing this is to set a retention time for a mailbox. This allows Exchange Server to keep deleted items for a certain number of days so that they can be restored. You accomplish this by using the Mailbox Store Properties sheet in the Exchange System Manager. Then, if you accidentally remove a user account, only the user account will be gone. The user's mailbox is kept for approximately 30 days. This feature brings relief to some novice administrators; they can attempt to reconnect the user to his mailbox within those 30 days. You can instantly observe any user whose account has been deleted by looking for a red x in the System Manager snap-in.

You can find the actual ntbackup.exe program in two ways:

▶ Use Windows Explorer to find the path C:*%system%*\system32\ntbackup.exe (usually *%system%* corresponds to the Winnt directory).

▶ The alternative method is through Start | Programs | Accessories | System Tools. You will see the program labeled simply Backup.

Choosing either method displays what you see in Figure 14.19.

When the program opens, you can choose to run the Backup Wizard (recommended for people new to this program), or you can select the Backup tab and configure a custom backup job. If you select the Backup tab, you will notice that you are able to perform full online backups of part or all of your Exchange server services and data files. Figure 14.20 shows the hierarchy of your system using the Backup tab.

Figure 14.19 The opening screen of the ntbackup.exe application.

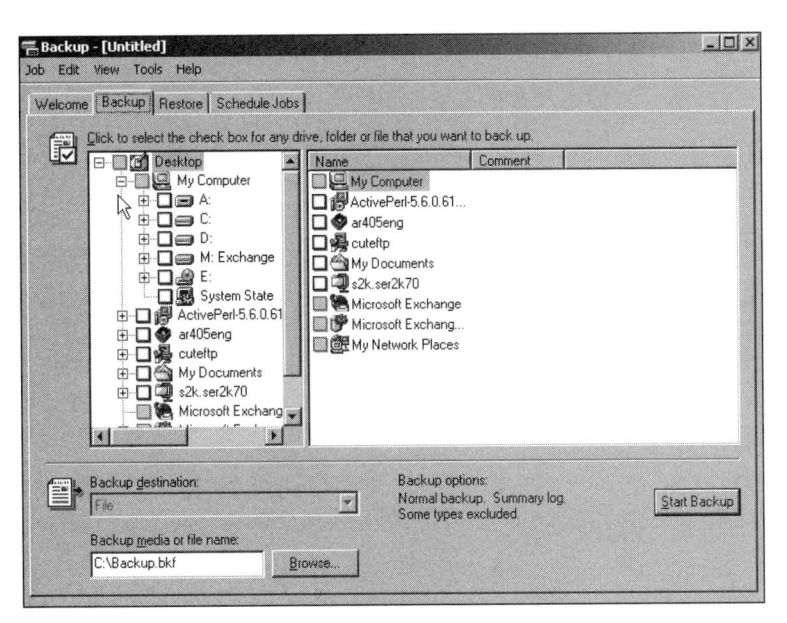

Figure 14.20 The Backup tab of ntbackup.exe, which allows you to choose all or part of an Exchange server to be backed up.

After choosing the source of your backup, you must choose the destination for this backup in the form of tape media or file name. After successfully specifying a destination, you then select the Start Backup button. This brings up a Backup Job Information dialog box, where you can configure the name of your backup set.

Our investigation of ntbackup.exe is not meant to be an exhaustive one; you can find further information about it using the Exchange 2000 Resource Kit or the product documentation that accompanied your Windows 2000 installation. Further investigation will show you how to automate backups in Exchange, or even how to call this application from a command prompt.

Chapter Summary

This chapter demonstrates important facts regarding maintaining Exchange servers. The relevant points to remember include:

➤ You can use tools provided by Windows 2000 to monitor and manage an Exchange 2000 server because of the tight integration between these two products. Actively monitoring an Exchange server is an ongoing process that requires different tools that act coherently to produce a reliable picture of system behavior. You use various tools on the server side and the client side to help you effectively troubleshoot any major problem that may occur in a typical production environment.

➤ The eseutil.exe Exchange Server tool allows you to perform offline database defragmentation while the IS service is not running. The IS by itself can defragment databases while your server is online; however, it does nothing to reduce the size of databases. This is why you must depend on *offline* tools such as eseutil.exe.

➤ A typical installation of Microsoft Outlook provides a tool known as the Inbox Repair Tool, or scanpst.exe. You use this to repair corrupt personal or offline folder files. You can change the default path during client installation.

➤ ISINTEG is a built-in component of Exchange 2000 that you use to check databases for inconsistencies. You have to dismount a mail or public store before running ISINTEG against it. Recall that this utility fails if a Storage Group has more than five databases, because ISINTEG has to create a temporary database to run successfully.

➤ There is a subtle yet important distinction between monitoring a server and troubleshooting a server as problems arise. Monitoring is a proactive term; troubleshooting is a reactive term. Monitoring a system implies establishing baseline levels of performance for various components of the system, including hard disks, memory, and processors.

➤ You can use the Performance Console to chart or graph the performance of dozens of system parameters in both Windows 2000 and Exchange 2000. The set of tools used with the console includes System Monitor and Performance Logs and Alerts. All performance objects have at least one associated counter that you can configure to check instances of any number of server actions.

- Network Monitor is a useful tool that comes installed with Windows 2000, but only as a "lite" version. The full version is found in the SMS installation of Windows 2000. Network Monitor's focuses are on capturing network traffic and analyzing network throughput. The version that comes with Windows 2000 can do these activities on a local network segment only.

- Use the Windows 2000 Event Viewer to view audit logs generated by audit policies, or to view warnings, informational events, or alerts associated with specific system services or applications. The logs generated in Event Viewer are dynamic because events are being recorded by a service at any given moment. Take care so that log files do not become full too often.

- It is important to monitor hard drive activity when you are working with Windows 2000 or Exchange 2000 because of all the system components you can work with. The hard disk is probably the component most susceptible to excessive wear and tear. Performing periodic defragmentation and surface-scan checks of physical disks extends their useful life and results in less corruption of data.

- The primary tool you use to monitor the status of your servers and your network in Exchange 2000 is the Monitoring and Status Tool. It allows you to analyze information using either the Status user interface (to view servers or connectors on your network with their respective status condition) or the Notifications interface (to set email alerts or triggers when a critical state is reached on any server).

- You use diagnostic logging to monitor Exchange connectors and protocol connectors. You can choose between four logging levels: None (0), Minimum (1), Medium (3), and Maximum (5). The Maximum level generates the most entries in the Windows 2000 Event Viewer application log.

- Exchange Server can use monitors to check the status of services and connectors configured on Exchange 2000 servers and legacy Exchange servers. Server monitors are created by default in Exchange 2000 and monitor items such as SMTP queues or CPU usage. Link monitors verify routing of messages using PING messages.

- Accomplished administrators understand the necessity of disaster recovery and disaster planning. These concepts involve selecting a tape backup strategy and fully knowing the underlying database technology used in Exchange 2000.

- You can use ntbackup.exe to back up all or part of an Exchange server. The Exchange version of ntbackup.exe allows for full online backups of any database, Storage Group, or file while certain services are kept running.

Review Questions

1. Which of the following is a valid log used in Event Viewer?

    a. Application log

    b. System configuration log

    c. Event log

    d. Security tracking log

2. By default, how much bigger is an application log file compared to a system log file?

    a. 512 bytes bigger.

    b. 512K bigger.

    c. They are both equal in size.

    d. 512MB bigger.

3. Diagnostic logging allows you to enable four levels of logging. Which logging level corresponds to level 1?

    a. None

    b. Minimum

    c. Medium

    d. Maximum

4. Harry would like to check the status of a group of Windows 2000 services running on a server named Orion so that he can detect critical situations when they arise. What tool will help him do this most effectively?

    a. Link monitor

    b. Server monitor

    c. Diagnostic logging

    d. Event Viewer

5. Which of the following can be used to chart the performance of system parameters running on a Windows 2000 machine?

    a. Event Viewer

    b. netdiag.exe

    c. Network Analyzer

    d. System Monitor

6. What does the System State folder in the Windows 2000 Backup program allow you to do?

    a. Enable or disable circular logging
    b. Enable online disk defragmentation
    c. Specify whether to back up AD and the Sys volume
    d. Specify whether to back up mailbox stores or public stores

7. Why should you back up the Exchsrvr folder in the server's file system as part of a regular backup routine?

    a. Due to defragmentation, this folder may have to be restored at a later date.
    b. Critical information that should always match the information stored in AD exists within the file system.
    c. Circular logging will overwrite this system folder if it is not backed up regularly.
    d. Exchange requires you to archive all files and data contained inside this system folder.

8. If an archive bit on a file is set to OFF, what does that indicate?

    a. It indicates the file has been backed up.
    b. It indicates the file has been restored.
    c. It indicates the file has been defragmented.
    d. It indicates the file has been deleted.

9. Peter has manually set the archive bit for 10 files in the C:\Exchsrvr\Mdbdata directory to OFF. The other 20 files in this directory have their archive bit set to ON. He then schedules a normal backup for this directory. How many files will be backed up in this directory?

    a. All files are backed up, regardless of the archive bit setting.
    b. Only 10 files will be backed up.
    c. All files except the 10 files marked OFF will be backed up.
    d. No files will be backed up unless they all have the same archive bit setting.

10. You want to check if circular logging has been turned on for your First Storage Group on your Exchange server named Pontius. How can you check this using System Manager?

    a. Look on the Details tab for the Storage Group's Properties sheet.
    b. Look on the General tab for the Storage Group's Properties sheet.
    c. You will find this information in the Contents pane of System Manager.
    d. You will find this information in the Details pane of System Manager.

11. What type of file has a .pst extension?

    a. A set of public folders

    b. A set of personal folders

    c. A set of private mailbox stores

    d. A set of private information stores

12. Sue is using Outlook 98 on her machine. She is looking in her Start menu for the shortcut that points to the scanpst.exe utility. Where can she find this?

    a. In the \Program Files\System\Mapi\NT directory

    b. In the \Program Files\Common Files\Mapi directory

    c. In the \Program Files\Common Files directory

    d. In the \Program Files\System directory

13. You type "eseutil /r" at a command prompt in Windows 2000. What are you trying to do?

    a. Examine the structure of your databases and restore broken links.

    b. Defragment your databases by moving used pages.

    c. Check the integrity of your databases.

    d. Restore executable files and system settings.

14. Which of the following displays versions of EXE or DLL files on your Exchange 2000 server?

    a. error.exe

    b. isinteg.exe

    c. filever.exe

    d. checkdisk.exe

15. How does the System Monitor utility relate to performance monitoring in Exchange 2000?

    a. System Monitor is found in Exchange 2000; performance monitoring is found in Windows 2000.

    b. System Monitor is a snap-in tool; performance monitoring describes an actual activity.

    c. System Monitor describes an actual activity; Performance Monitoring is a snap-in tool.

    d. System Monitor is found in Windows 2000; performance monitoring is found in Exchange 2000.

16. What term used in Exchange 2000 describes how much work can be performed within a given amount of time?
    a. Throughput
    b. Queue response
    c. Response time
    d. Bottleneck

17. Which performance monitoring counter will help you chart statistics on the rate at which pages are read from disk to resolve a hard page fault?
    a. Memory\Available Bytes
    b. PhysicalDisk Faults/sec
    c. PhysicalDisk Pages/sec
    d. Memory\Pages/sec

18. Janice has just installed a new database application on her Exchange 2000 Server and has noticed a huge increase in the Processor\Interrupts/sec counter. What could be causing this sudden spike?
    a. Insufficient network throughput for the new application
    b. Insufficient memory to handle the new application
    c. Excessive nonpaged memory given to the new application
    d. Insufficient queue response time for the new application

19. How does Windows 2000 enable PhysicalDisk performance counters to monitor the activity of a physical disk?
    a. You manually enable them by typing "diskperf -yv" at a command prompt.
    b. The Windows 2000 OS activates these counters by default.
    c. You manually enable them by typing "diskperf -ye" at a command prompt.
    d. You enable them using the Computer Management Administrative Tool.

20. You have configured a Minimum logging level for the Information Store Mailbox service. Which statement is true?
    a. Both warning and informational messages are logged.
    b. Only warning messages are logged.
    c. Both warning and error messages are logged.
    d. Only error messages are logged.

Real-World Projects

Bob has been concerned about backing up his new Exchange server. His friends have told him to purchase BackIT Express, a commercial product that guarantees to back up any database or folder in Exchange 2000. However, Bob believes that Windows 2000 provides all the functionality he will need with its built-in Backup tool, ntbackup.exe. He has never really tried ntbackup.exe with his NT 4 server, but he is more than willing to try it now to back up his Exchange server (named Patriot).

Bob knows how to access this tool, but he must select which folders or components will actually be backed up. He also has to decide the type of backup that will be adequate for this job. He will test this utility for two weeks before deciding whether to make it a long-term commitment for his company, SuperPets.

Project 14.1

To access the Windows 2000 Backup utility:

1. Go to the Start menu and choose Programs|Accessories|System Tools|Backup.

2. Click on the Backup Wizard on the Welcome tab.

3. Click on Next and select the Back Up Selected Files, Drives, Or Network Data radio button.

4. Click on Next.

5. Click on the + next to Microsoft Exchange Server.

6. Click on the + next to your individual server name.

7. Put a checkmark inside the box for the Microsoft Information Store

8. Click on Next and then choose File as your Backup Media Type.

9. Under Backup Media or File Name, type "C:\Backup.bkf" and then click on Next.

At Step 9, Bob was staring at a window telling him to complete the Backup Wizard. However, one of the options told him that the Verify option was OFF. Instead of clicking on Finish to end the Backup Wizard, he decided he wanted to change settings to include an incremental backup, not a normal backup. After checking the Resource Kit, he decided to configure advanced settings for ntbackup.exe.

Project 14.2

To configure advanced settings for ntbackup.exe:

1. Click on the Advanced button.

2. Choose Incremental from the drop-down box and click on Next.

3. Click on the Verify Data After Backup checkbox and choose Next.

4. Keep the default setting to Append Data and choose Next.

5. Accept all default backup labels and media labels and then choose Next.

6. You will be asked to schedule your backup; click on the Later button and then type your administrator password when prompted.

7. Complete the Schedule entry by typing a Job name of Job1 and then clicking on the Set Schedule button.

8. Under Schedule Task, choose Weekly. Under Start Time, choose 5:00 A.M.

9. Under Schedule Task Weekly, choose Every 1 Week On and then click on the Monday and Friday checkboxes. Click on OK and then click on Next.

10. Verify your settings on the Completing The Backup Wizard page and then click on Finish to schedule the backup.

Bob was happy with the settings. He decided to schedule another backup job named Job2 using procedures similar to the ones he already did. Once he was confident with his new skills, he documented all the steps and informed his staff of the relevant tasks. He also made sure that his entire staff had appropriate rights and permissions to back up all files and folders on his Windows 2000/Exchange 2000 server by making everyone members of the Backup Operators built-in group.

CHAPTER FIFTEEN

Other Design and Support Issues

After completing this chapter, you will be able to:

✓ Effectively manage and plan for growth in public and private Message Store (MS) databases

✓ Monitor the growth of your user population and message traffic

✓ Benefit from both horizontal and vertical scalability of your Exchange servers

✓ Comprehend the design and implementation of a front-end/back-end (FE/BE) architecture for Exchange 2000

✓ Understand the importance of planning using a best-practice methodology to reduce inherent risks in any Exchange 2000 deployment

✓ Know what questions to ask to correctly assess your current user environment

Chapters 15 and 16 attempt to provide both a telescopic and microscopic view of Exchange 2000 as it relates to scalability issues. We will look beyond mere technical skills and start to consider how to evaluate an existing deployment of Exchange 2000. You have to look beyond written details and checklists to actually view the bigger picture of system administration. We recommend performing an ongoing analysis of your original design scenarios so that you can make corrections or enhancements. The concepts you have learned thus far—including installation, configuration, managing, monitoring, and troubleshooting—are all valuable skills in and of themselves. However, we now want to present a different way of looking at these skills. If the previous chapters have tried to answer "How do you configure x?" (where x represents a component or service of Exchange), then this chapter will try to ask "How is x doing?" or "Will y work better than x?" The old adage "If it isn't broken, don't fix it" still holds true for many Exchange administrators. But a few administrators are starting to ask themselves, "What would happen if we introduced y into our organization?" (where y represents a new way of looking at your existing design and trying to determine the impact of changes in that design).

Previous chapters have touched on differences between Exchange Server 5.5 and Exchange 2000 Server; Chapters 15 and 16 highlight these differences in a more radical way. Understanding the design goals of the original Microsoft design team will help you appreciate these differences even more. The ultimate goal of discussing these original design issues is to help us orchestrate a flawless upgrade from Exchange 5.5 to Exchange 2000. That is the sole focus of Chapter 16. For now, let us concentrate on understanding the theory that forms the stages of a perfectly planned Exchange Server deployment for a typical ongoing business system. We can use what we learn to develop models that will help us manage user traffic and message flows more effectively. This is not a troubleshooting chapter per se, although the concepts we discuss will help you to acquire critical thinking skills. If you learn to "think in Exchange," as the original designers did, you will become more adept at solving problems as they arise because you will know what component or service is directly or indirectly affected.

First, we examine and review the proper stages of planning an Exchange deployment that conforms to the framework of best practices known as the Microsoft Solutions Framework (MSF). (See Chapter 1 for introductory thoughts on the MSF model.) Then, we turn our attention to hardware design issues and planning an effective front-end/back-end (FE/BE) configuration. Finally, we discuss how to evaluate your original planning efforts by focusing on assessing user needs and current resources. At that point, we should be able to offer a full analysis of legacy issues when attempting a migration to Exchange 2000 in Chapter 16.

The Design of Exchange 2000 Server

Every sentence you read from this point on should help answer a basic question for your organization: "Is Exchange Server doing what it is supposed to be doing for my company?" Some administrators purchase this product hoping it will offer all-in-one functionality, whereas others desire simple messaging services and abandon the true functionality that Exchange Server offers. A proper first step in working with Exchange Server is to define from the outset what it should be doing for your organization. You should write a mission statement that describes what you expect and do not expect from deploying Exchange. There is nothing worse than going over budget on a product that does not perform as expected. Properly planning and adhering to design goals often prevent this catastrophe.

The Four Phases of the MSF Infrastructure Deployment Process Model

Remember that any deployment of Exchange Server, whether it concerns an upgrade or a new installation, revolves around a formal plan and a formal project team, according to the strict definition of the MSF. MSF was conceived as a series of models and best practices that help lay the foundation for successfully planning and deploying projects such as Microsoft Exchange 2000 Server. The MSF Infrastructure Deployment Process Model is the basis for an Exchange Server project plan and is based on a team function that adheres to milestone-driven events and schedules. Microsoft recommends taking a somewhat phased approach to project planning. Reviewing these phases will help you better understand the more formal design scenarios presented later in the chapter.

It is insufficient to simply follow formal planning procedures without appreciating the reason behind them. All planning efforts attempt to reduce risk. All projects have a measurable amount of risk inherent in them, and planning reduces risk. Expecting and managing risk involve a team effort. The MSF model's four phases are designed to alleviate damaging exposure to project risk. These phases are:

1. Envisioning
2. Planning (engineering)
3. Developing
4. Deploying

Envisioning

Envisioning refers to defining the scope of your project as well as the limitations of your project. It also involves defining the initial project team and identifying what you believe to be relevant project risks. During this phase, you will also probably define the exact services you intend to offer your users or clients. The key to this stage lies in building a project team and creating a project structure. You want to include peers who will share ultimate responsibility for the overall project. Examples of key personnel to include on this team are:

- *Product manager*—Sets objectives as well as the overall budget.
- *Program manager*—Is responsible for the overall design and implementation.
- *Executive sponsor*—Assists with high-level organizational management.
- *Staff engineer*—Determines all technical configurations and specifications.
- *Trainer/customer liaison*—Supervises end-user training.

This first stage also requires you to create a well-developed mission statement that describes what the design team envisions as the final outcome for the overall project. It states such things as the financial resources needed for the project and the time allowed for the project. It also defines assumptions that the team makes—for example, which person is responsible for Active Directory (AD) configurations, or what will happen with user mail that is older than a certain time period.

Planning (Engineering)

The second stage, the actual planning phase, involves creating detailed functional specifications, gathering information about current services, and drafting master project schedules. We refer to this stage as the engineering stage because it addresses three main areas of concern:

- *What* final solution the project team will deliver
- *How* the system will be designed and tested
- Exactly *when* the project will reach completion, and how the team will recognize that the project is coming to a close

The planning phase consists of both general and specific planning tasks. General tasks include gathering information and identifying the resources at hand. Specific tasks include documenting and understanding the underlying Windows infrastructure, and planning and understanding AD. The latter is very important because Exchange 2000 is tightly integrated with AD and cannot function successfully without it. The planning phase is officially complete when the design team understands and agrees to all functional specifications.

Developing

The developing stage consists of testing or building a prototype system or simulating a production system. You must somehow validate the designs you formulated in earlier stages using hardware similar to what you may be using in a production environment. Your goal here is to slowly introduce a system that has undergone rigorous testing with a control group of users. Testing usually occurs at two distinct levels:

- *Hardware or component level*—Refers to testing individual components to verify that these components meet specified requirements.

- *Systems level*—Involves testing multiple components to guarantee compatibility and performance. Initial problems or imperfections are dealt with in this stage.

Deploying

The final stage, deploying, involves making all services available to all users and evaluating the full performance of a production system. All users are fully trained in the functionality of the product, and systems are closely monitored so that optimization can take place.

Assessing Project Risk

Risks are inherent in every system—even if you follow the four-step process to the letter. You should devise a separate but related risk-management scheme so that you can make a smooth transition from the envisioning stage to the deploying phase without significant downtime. Here are the steps to assess project risk when you are designing or deploying Exchange 2000 Server:

1. *Identify the risk*. Make sure all team members are aware of the significance of the risk at hand.

2. *Analyze the risk*. Once you acknowledge that a risk is present, analyze its importance. Make it meaningful to all team members so that they can assess the probability of project failure.

3. *Plan for risks*. Let team members know that risks usually recur and are unpredictable. You should expect risks and must deal with them as they occur. If multiple risks hamper a project, the team should learn how to prioritize them.

4. *Track risks*. You should eliminate all risks completely or they will come back in a stronger form. Actively track and monitor these risks to prevent recurrence.

5. *Control risks*. Develop warning signs or triggers for future risks, and train team members on appropriate actions to take if they notice any form of these risks in future projects or plans.

Note: Consult the Microsoft Exchange 2000 Server Resource Kit for additional material on project planning and control. The Resource Kit contains a CD-ROM with valuable templates and tools that can assist you in project planning and risk management.

Hardware Design Considerations

As part of understanding the framework for using Exchange Server within an organization, you have to begin to appreciate Exchange Server's many uses. Going back to our original mission-statement concept, you have to decide if Exchange is going to primarily operate as a messaging server or a GroupWare product. Some organizations are now exclusively using Exchange Server for development and collaborative purposes not found in previous versions of this product. How your organization plans to use Exchange will help you decide on what hardware to use, and how you can effectively use Exchange in an FE/BE configuration design. You should make a list of every possible use that Exchange Server will fulfill in your organization. The following list should provide some guidance in this area:

➤ Mailbox server dedicated for user mailboxes

➤ Public folder servers dedicated to holding public folders

➤ FE servers that interact directly with Messaging API (MAPI) clients and proxies' requests to a BE server

➤ BE server, which actually maintains the mailbox and public folder stores for the FE servers

➤ Chat servers dedicated to running the Exchange 2000 Chat Service, so users can share ideas in moderated realtime conversations

➤ Instant Messaging (IM) servers dedicated to running the IM service so that groups of users can exchange basic messages using client-side components in cooperation with Internet Information Services API (ISAPI) server extensions running on an Internet Information Server (IIS) server

We cannot talk about configuring hardware for Exchange without bringing up AD. Deciding how to deploy AD is one major decision you will confront in your quest to design Exchange Server; removal of the directory service from previous versions of Exchange represents the biggest change in Exchange 2000. As you learned in previous chapters, all Exchange objects are now stored in AD. AD includes a brand-new domain model and namespace, which is heavily influenced by Domain Name System (DNS). Remember that AD forms a namespace where the name of any object in the directory is resolved to the object itself. When you design a namespace architecture, the following criteria become very important:

➤ The need to replicate traffic within this namespace

➤ The need to incorporate future namespace restructuring

➤ The need to evaluate the original design of this namespace and to totally change it, if necessary, in the near future

We stress the importance of AD especially for companies that are using legacy versions of Exchange Server. AD actually defines a company's underlying infrastructure. Improperly planning and designing AD results in its unavailability, especially as it relates to Exchange. It also negatively impacts network usage. AD has a logical structure that you must properly plan and control in a production environment. Such things as your domain structure, your forest structure, your organizational unit (OU) structure, and your Windows 2000 site topology influence this logical structure heavily.

Domain design is very important to a successful Exchange project because every forest you create will most likely consist of multiple domains. You must determine the number of domains in each forest, as well as choose a root domain within the forest. Improperly designing domains affects the availability of AD within your network. It also affects such things as client traffic and domain controller (DC) replication. Consider the overhead you will incur by creating additional domains within your Windows 2000 forest. The Domain Administrators group becomes ultimately responsible for every additional domain that is created. The overall domain design has a direct bearing on the hardware that you will use to host Exchange because Windows 2000 requires that every DC host only one domain. Therefore, each additional domain you create requires one additional piece of hardware.

In terms of hardware, it is always best to provide relatively fast drive access together with fault-tolerant hardware configurations. For example, you should provide multiple drive arrays or Redundant Array of Independent Disks (RAID) technology to ensure optimal performance (RAID is covered in more detail later in this chapter). The hardware you choose should be modular and scalable to accommodate future enhancements. You may want to provide separate partitions for paging processes required by your Information Store (IS), or even separate drives for transaction logs to provide increased reliability and recovery if a disaster occurs.

We want to remind you of the importance of AD domain design and Exchange 2000. There is no analogy between the current Windows 2000/Exchange 2000 relationship and the previous Windows NT 4/Exchange 5.5 relationship. In fact, Microsoft has designed the Windows 2000 AD domain structure to have a significantly heavier impact on Exchange 2000 than Windows NT 4 had on Exchange 5.5. You have to consider your domain tree structure very carefully and justify that Exchange 2000 will comply with all necessary requirements of this structure. It becomes very difficult to restructure a domain hierarchy after the fact. Lastly, OU design becomes important because OUs define the location of objects within AD and how they are administered. It is usually best to create OUs to delegate administration and to hide certain objects from administrators. A newer feature of OUs involves associating Group Policies with each other, which enables you to define desktop configurations for both users and their computers.

FE/BE Servers

Now that you have some idea of the interconnections between AD and the hardware that will run Exchange 2000, we can start to focus on more specialized Exchange design configurations—for example, an FE/BE design scenario.

Although it is possible to run every component of Exchange Server on a single machine, it is sometimes best to separate these different components for optimization purposes so that they run on dedicated machines. Doing this makes it easier to configure the servers from a software perspective, and this can only result in machines that are more reliable over time.

Because Exchange 2000 is so highly scalable, it can expand as your company grows. Microsoft has introduced two dimensions to the scalable architecture of Exchange. One dimension is *horizontal scalability*, which involves adding to your existing organization several servers that all perform the same task. The other is *vertical scalability*, which involves enhancing one server to handle multiple tasks. We will introduce basic examples of these issues in the next sections, although an exhaustive examination of scalability in Exchange 2000 is outside the scope of this book.

FE/BE Design Issues

An FE/BE design is a new feature of Exchange 2000 and was never conceived of or implemented in any prior version of Exchange. The design team at Microsoft wanted to introduce a new configuration for Exchange 2000 that allows you to distribute server tasks among multiple computers, or FE/BE systems. An FE server does not host an Exchange 2000 IS. Rather, clients connect to an FE server, which then transmits commands to a specific BE server.

In most FE/BE configurations, the FE ("outward-facing") network provides communication and connectivity to the Internet. All clients in the organization direct their requests and receive a response from the FE server. It even becomes possible to daisy-chain FE servers with a clustering type of solution that involves using Network Load Balancing Service (NLBS). NLBS is included with Windows 2000 Advanced Server Edition. The main point to remember about all FE servers is that they use remote procedure calls (RPCs) to "talk" to a BE server and they help reduce server load in an organization because they are able to directly query the Windows 2000 AD service (using the Lightweight Directory Access Protocol [LDAP]) to determine which BE server holds requested resources for mailbox-enabled users.

In reality, your network is divided into a public interface and a private interface. Microsoft has posted some important recommendations regarding FE server configurations on its Web site (**www.microsoft.com/exchange/**, Article ID Q274219). Among the most important suggestions are:

➤ If the FE server is accepting Simple Mail Transfer Protocol (SMTP) mail from the Internet, store.exe has to be running and at least one private IS must be mounted. If the store is not mounted properly, messages that need to be converted may be stuck in the local delivery queue.

➤ For security purposes, Microsoft recommends that no user mailbox be homed on an FE server Information Store.

► If there are both Exchange 5.5 and Exchange 2000 servers running in the same Routing Group, then the Message Transfer Agent (MTA) Stacks service has to run on the FE server so that the MTAs will bind and transfer mail through RPCs.

A BE server runs AD and handles such activities as name resolution using DNS. It also runs Exchange 2000 Server and holds mailbox stores and directory schemas. By necessity, BE systems require higher capacity and faster hardware than their FE counterparts. They may also need a secondary Internet Protocol (IP) addressing scheme bound to additional network interface cards (NICs), as well as clustering software provided by Microsoft Cluster Services.

BE servers come in two varieties:

► *Standard server*—Hosts an Exchange 2000 IS. A MAPI client can connect to a standard server directly, or it can connect to a standard server using an FE proxy.

► *Combination server*—Acts as *both* an FE server and a standard server. This means that a MAPI client can connect to a combination server and obtain user information from a mailbox store hosted on that computer.

Figure 15.1 shows how a client tries to access information from a BE server.

Be careful when using the term "FE" or "BE." You can configure a server to be an FE server, but you cannot configure a server to be a BE server. This can be confusing at times, but it is important to remember for both testing purposes and real-life scenarios. A BE server is nothing more than a normal Exchange 2000 server that has not been configured to become an FE server. In fact, if an organization does not have *any* FE servers, these terms become meaningless. Just remember that once you introduce an FE server and configure it as such, all *remaining* servers become known as BE servers.

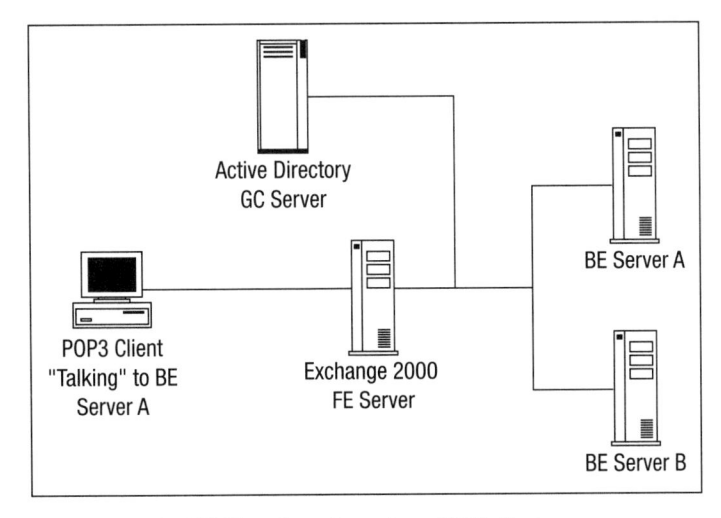

Figure 15.1 An FE/BE configuration using a MAPI client.

FE/BE Deployments

FE/BE deployments have several important benefits, including the following:

➤ *Single namespace*—The primary advantage of an FE/BE server architecture is that it exposes a single namespace. You can define a single namespace for users to access their mailboxes for Outlook Web Access (OWA). Without an FE server, users must know the name of the server that is storing their mailbox. This complicates administration because every time your organization changes and you move some mailboxes to another server, you must inform the users. With a single namespace, users can use the same Uniform Resource Locator (URL) or Post Office Protocol 3 (POP3) client configuration, even if mailboxes are moved from server to server. In addition, creating a single namespace ensures that OWA scales as your company grows. Figure 15.2 shows how FE servers retain their original configurations even with the addition of a new BE home server.

➤ *Firewalls*—You can position the FE server as the single point of access behind or inside an Internet firewall, which is configured to allow traffic from the Internet to only the FE. The BE and therefore the internal network is secured because you have effectively limited the number of access points to the internal network. Because the FE server has no user information on it, it provides a layer of security for your company. In addition, because you can configure the FE server to authenticate requests before proxying them, the BE servers are protected from potential denial of service (DoS) attacks.

➤ *Increased Internet Message Access Protocol 4 (IMAP4) access to public folders*—The IMAP4 protocol allows a server to refer a client to another server. Exchange

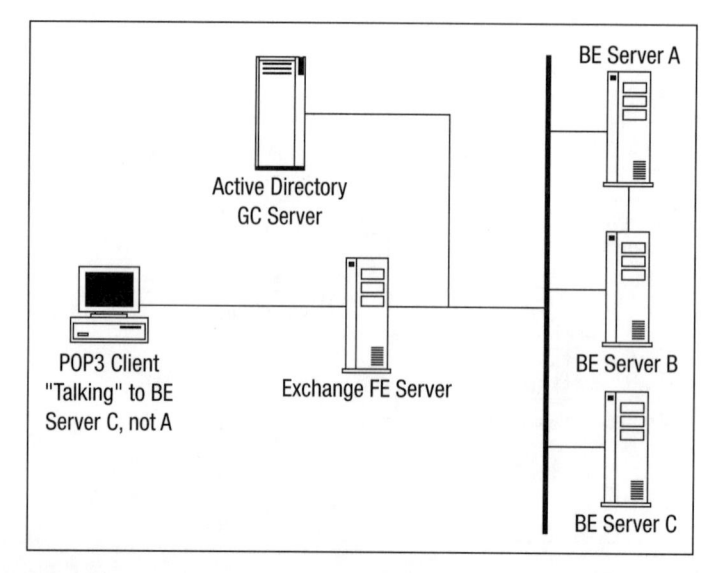

Figure 15.2 Users connecting to a new BE server.

2000 servers support this functionality in cases where a public folder store on one server does not contain the content that the client requested. However, this requires a client that supports IMAP referrals. Most existing clients do not support them. When an FE server proxies a command to a BE server, it automatically handles any referral response that is passed back when a user attempts to access a public folder that does not exist on the primary public server. This makes referrals transparent to clients.

Warning: An FE/BE architecture currently supports only the Hypertext Transport Protocol (HTTP), POP3, and IMAP4 protocols. You can also install SMTP and Network News Transfer Protocol (NNTP) on an FE server. The FE/BE architecture does not currently support the MAPI protocol used by Outlook 2000 clients. This type of topology is not important to MAPI clients because MAPI is not a true Internet protocol like HTTP or POP3.

When to Consider Using an FE/BE Design

An imaginary scenario will help illustrate the significant issues that arise with FE/BE design. A fictitious company, BookEnds, is headquartered in New York. This company has 3 branch offices, in Atlanta, Berlin, and Miami, and 500 retail outlets throughout the United States. A situation like this would seem ideal for an FE/BE-type implementation if all employees required access to all messaging and collaboration functions from all company locations. You certainly don't want all 500 locations accessing the same BE server, especially if you want to have realtime collaboration. FE/BE configurations are very desirable when a large number of users desire multiple services from Exchange. They are even more desirable when this usage occurs over random time periods and when it becomes impossible to predict optimal load levels on any single server. Microsoft suggests an FE/BE design for multiserver companies that want to provide POP3 or HTTP access to their employees over the Internet.

Consider FE/BE designs when the following criteria become important for an organization:

➤ You want to provide reliable messaging services over existing wide area network (WAN) connections, especially slow WAN links.

➤ You want to utilize realtime collaborative-type applications that encourage communication between various staff members in diverse parts of the world.

➤ You want to maintain a single directory of user and group information.

➤ You want to incorporate messaging servers that will not disproportionately increase WAN bandwidth.

➤ You want to provide easy access to corporate email across unreliable WAN connections, even when Internet access is not available.

Notice that WAN bandwidth becomes a critical issue when you incorporate an FE/BE Exchange implementation.

Most applications adversely affect bandwidth, and Exchange Server is no exception to this rule. If our imaginary company was deciding on the best Exchange Server design scenario, it could either place single Exchange servers in each of its retail locations, or it could access remote servers housed in New York, Atlanta, Berlin, or Miami. The deciding factor revolves around WAN connectivity to all four locations. If a store has WAN connectivity, simply put mailboxes belonging to that store on a server that has direct connectivity to that store. If a retail outlet does not have WAN connectivity, make sure it has connectivity to the Internet (using perhaps a dial-up connection), and connect the company to an FE server using OWA or some other POP3-enabled client.

FE Server Security Concerns

An FE design raises some security concerns, however. For example, many organizations are concerned about various forms of user authentication for their network. This becomes an issue with an FE/BE design. The front-end server can do one of two things in this case: It can authenticate users itself, or it can proxy this authentication through to the BE server. This means the BE server also performs authentication. Microsoft recommends that the FE server be configured to authenticate users, particularly when the network is exposed to the Internet.

Only HTTP 1.1 Basic authentication is supported in an FE/BE scenario. This is a fairly simple authentication mechanism defined by the HTTP specification that lightly encrypts all user names and passwords before sending them to the server. To achieve "real" password security in an FE/BE topology, you should consider using SSL encryption in conjunction with Basic authentication. A side effect of using Basic authentication is the lack of support for single logon capabilities. Users normally authenticate once in a Windows domain and are able to access all resources without having to re-authenticate. Using Basic authentication to access HTTP applications, however, implies that users will always be prompted for authentication and will have to re-enter their logon credentials even after logging into their domain.

Warning: An FE server is incapable of supporting NTLM or Kerberos authentication. It also cannot support any type of digest authentication methods.

As mentioned previously, an FE/BE design effectively turns a network into a public interface and a private interface because of the possibility of using multiple NICs on a single machine. Administrators are increasingly placing mail and Web servers behind a firewall in the hopes of blocking Internet attacks. If a client is trying to connect to an FE server using a client like OWA, we recommend using FE servers on a perimeter network segment, also called a demilitarized zone (DMZ). Any location that does not connect directly to the Internet will not have an FE server.

> **Tip:** Make sure you open ports on both your DMZ and your internal firewall, if this is how your network is configured. Doing so enables all Internet mail protocols, such as POP3, to function correctly on the FE server. Some common protocols and their ports are: HTTP—port 80; Secure Sockets Layer (SSL)—port 443; POP3—port 110; and SMTP—port 25.

FE/BE Design Limitations

A company must consider some serious issues if it wants a normal FE/BE configuration, given that it wants to maintain a single namespace for its Exchange servers while not being able to accommodate all users on a single machine. For example, normal network connections for a given environment may allow remote clients to connect directly to a BE server and bypass all FE servers, although the FE servers will be configured to accept HTTP connections from these clients. You may have to spend extra administrative effort in some cases to ensure that remote clients cannot access a BE server directly. A possible solution in this case would be to set up a normal Exchange FE/BE environment and then configure a firewall between the front-end server and the Internet. IP address filtering and port filtering can then be used to limit requests through the firewall to only the FE server and block requests through the firewall to other servers in your organization.

Another issue arises when a company wants to add servers purely for load balancing purposes, without requiring a change in how users access their original mailbox. There is a significant difference between configuring a server to be an FE server that will proxy a request to a BE server, and adding a second Exchange server to distribute the load between mailbox stores and public folder stores. The latter case is not a strict FE/BE-type scenario. Exchange 2000 *redirects* HTTP requests to both public and private folders if they are not located on the server the request was sent to. This does not represent the concept of a single namespace, which is necessary for a true FE/BE architecture.

A final issue arises with a company that wants to roll out OWA to hundreds of users at a time. The goal is to have a single namespace in which users can reach their mailboxes. However, this company is also trying to avoid having a bottleneck at the FE server or a single point of failure. A good suggestion in this case would be to spread the load over multiple FE servers by using Network Load Balancing (NLB). Other load-balancing options would include using DNS round robin or a hardware-based load-balancing solution. It would be best to set up a group of servers as BE servers in the same domain with users distributed over these servers. Another group of servers would function as FE servers, and you would configure NLB on these servers. The only concern would be to ensure that each user is always sent to the same FE server for the duration of a session. This would make use of caching and connection state information already maintained on the FE server. You can set up NLB (and other hardware-based solutions) to do this.

FE/BE Issues to Monitor

An FE/BE design is an example of horizontal scalability, as mentioned earlier in this chapter. We also mentioned that you should perform server sizing if you expect a single server to host additional users or traffic. Before we discuss vertical scalability, here is a list of important issues to monitor regarding the design and support of an FE/BE architecture:

- An FE server must be part of the same Exchange 2000 organization as your BE servers. An Exchange server has to be configured as an FE server.

- An FE server cannot and should not host any users or public folders.

- Before you can use a server as an FE server, you have to restart it, or you must stop and then restart the HTTP, POP3, and IMAP4 services.

- If you do not dismount and delete the mailbox and public stores on an FE server, the public store is not accessible from the FE server.

- Not all services are required on an FE server; this depends on what Internet protocol is being used. Table 15.1 lists some protocols that are commonly used in an FE configuration.

- You do not need to configure SSL on the BE servers when you use an FE server. This is because an FE server does not support using SSL to communicate to a BE server. However, you can configure SSL on the BE servers for clients that can directly access them.

Server Sizing Issues

When configuring or designing Exchange Server to handle additional traffic or user loads, you have to consider the four main components that make up most servers: the disk, the processor, the memory, and the network components. In this section, we discuss RAID and give an example of FE component design issues.

RAID Design Configurations Used for Exchange Server

It is a given fact that disk input/output (I/O) is a valuable measure of performance for any Exchange 2000 server. Examining a disk includes total capacity, room for

Table 15.1 A list of services by protocols used in an FE configuration.

Protocol	Services Needed
HTTP	No Exchange-specific services are required. However, the Windows HTTP service (W3Svc) must be running. The Exchange System Attendant (SA) Service (MSExchangeSA) must also be running if the administrator needs to make changes to the HTTP configuration on the server.
POP3	The Exchange POP3 Service (POP3Svc), the Exchange IS Service (MSExchangeIS), and the Exchange SA (MSExchangeSA) must be running.
IMAP4	The Exchange IMAP4 Service (IMAP4Svc), and MSExchangeIS and MSExchangeSA must be running.

paging files and virtual memory, and disk controller settings. One of the first lessons you learn when administering Exchange is to separate storage for such things as transaction logs and message databases. You should reject any solution that is not fault tolerant. This means you should be using RAID controllers in an active-active mode. Exchange uses different types of RAID technologies. We discuss each in more detail later in this section.

Although there are various implementations of RAID technologies, all share two common aspects. First, they all utilize multiple physical disks to distribute data; second, they all store data according to logic independent of the application for which they are storing data. There are four main implementations of RAID and one related implementation. RAID 0, RAID 1, RAID 3, and RAID 5 represent the overall scope of redundant solutions, whereas RAID 0+1 is a subtype of RAID 1. Understanding the differences in these technologies will help you pick the best solution for a given situation. Here is a rundown of each type:

- **RAID 0**—This is a *striped disk array*, where each disk in the array is logically partitioned so that a stripe runs across all disks. Users see a single logical partition with a defined drive letter. For example, if you save a block of data containing four values to a RAID 0 disk array that contains four physical drives with a logical name of drive D:, the file is distributed in a stripe across all four drives (see Figure 15.3). This is not the best solution, but it is less expensive than RAID 5.

- **RAID 1**—This is a *mirrored* type of disk array, in which two disks are mirrored. For transaction logs, a RAID 1 technology is recommended due to higher performance and reliability concerns compared to other RAID solutions mentioned here. This is a high-availability solution; it costs more than RAID 0.

- **RAID 0+1**—The subtype of RAID 1 known as RAID 0+1 arises when you are using more than two physical disks, so that the disks are striped in addition to being mirrored. Using a six-disk array example, a RAID 0+1 configuration would imply that three physical disks are available for actual data storage. Every time you save your file, for instance, that file will be written to a mirrored disk. This offers the highest performance and availability, but it is not the cheapest.

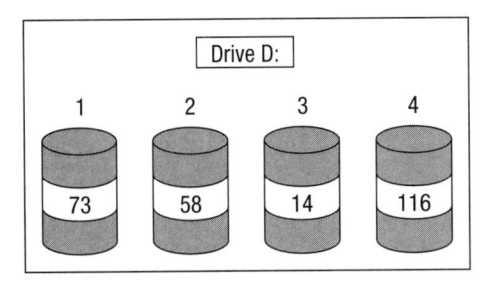

Figure 15.3 A four-drive RAID 0 configuration known as drive D:.

- *RAID 3*—This is the same as RAID 0, but it achieves a higher level of data integrity and fault tolerance by reserving one disk for error correction data. This drive stores parity information that maintains data integrity across all other drives in the disk subsystem. This is low cost but also low performance compared to other RAID solutions.

- *RAID 5*—This is a fully striped array of physical disks similar to RAID 0. The difference is that RAID 5 includes *parity*, which allows you to maintain the integrity of your data on the disk array. Figure 15.4 shows the effect of the parity drive. If one disk in the array fails, it is easy to recover the data from the remaining disks in the array. RAID 5 is usually less expensive to implement than similar RAID solutions, but the disadvantages outnumber the advantages in many situations. For example, it is very slow for reading and writing files, and rebuilding a RAID 5 volume takes longer than rebuilding a RAID 0+1 volume. When using RAID 5, be sure to enable write-back caching to provide sufficient write performance. Exchange 2000 is very write-intensive, so all cache memory should be write-back cache. You configure most cache settings on disk controllers directly. This is less expensive than RAID 1 but not the highest performance.

Given these details, it is not always easy to select the best RAID implementation for a given situation. You have to look at these factors:

- *Cost*—You can evaluate this by calculating the number of disks you need to support your array. The RAID 0+1 implementation is the most expensive because you must have twice as much disk space as you actually need.

- *Performance*—From purely this perspective, RAID 0 is probably the most efficient RAID technology because it writes to all physical disks at once. However, if you place your mailbox stores across a RAID 0 array and one of your physical disk fails, you have to restore these mailbox databases to another working disk array and then restore your transaction log files. Even more problems will result if you store the transaction log files on this same array. RAID 1 is more reliable than RAID 0 or RAID 5 simply because all your data is mirrored after it is saved; however, you are using only half of your total storage space on the disks. RAID 5 is also very reliable and uses total disk space

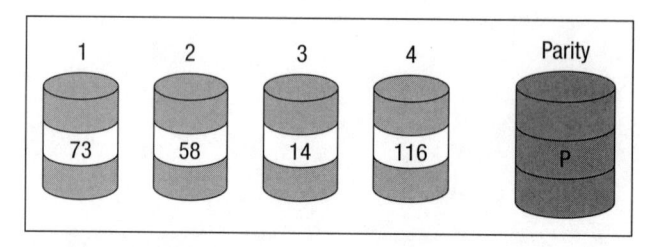

Figure 15.4 A RAID configuration using a parity drive.

more efficiently than RAID 1. A RAID 0+1 implementation produces a much higher performance index compared to a RAID 5 solution based on the maximum number of disk reads and writes.

> *Reliability*—You assess overall reliability by considering the impact a disk failure would have on your data integrity. RAID 0 does not use any form of redundancy; therefore, a single disk failure would require a full restore of data. RAID 0+1 is more reliable because, in this situation, more than one disk would suffer failure before your data is considered lost.

Designing the ideal disk configuration to support existing and future users involves allocating disk space so Exchange can access what it needs in the shortest time possible. It also requires selecting appropriate RAID levels so that cost, performance, and reliability issues are fairly balanced and in proportion to the type of data being stored. For example, most servers contain a system partition that should utilize RAID 1 technology. This partition usually holds operating system (OS) files as well as Exchange 2000 system files. Microsoft recommends placing databases and transaction log files on separate volumes, where one volume represents two or more physical disks that are put into one group using either RAID 5 or RAID 0+1 technology.

For best results, Microsoft recommends either RAID 5 or RAID 0+1, which should result in less support time for your end users. Keep in mind that we are concentrating our discussion on the data that resides within mailbox stores and public folder stores.

Component Design Issues Applied to an FE Server: Example

We conclude our discussion on server sizing by mentioning a few key recommendations regarding processor and memory design for organizations that wish to handle increasing message traffic. We then provide an example of using ideal design guidelines for an FE server running OWA so that you can apply the Microsoft best practices to similar situations. Material covering design scenarios for FE/BE configurations are favorites for testing purposes, so you should be very familiar with these concepts.

Regarding processors, the recommended CPU for Exchange is a 500MHz Pentium II processor. Although Exchange may run on slower hardware, the "more is better" rule applies here. You should also make sure your processor has at least 2MB of L2 cache. The requirement for maximum processing power really depends on how many users you will be servicing. You want to consider multiple processors if your user community consists of more than 500 users. In fact, more than 1,000 users justifies the need for a four-way Symmetric Multi-Processor (SMP) configuration.

Memory for mailbox and public folder servers also depends on the number of users being serviced and is often the first recommended upgrade to a system that is experiencing slow response times. 256MB of RAM can adequately service up to

500 users, whereas 1GB of RAM is recommended for environments containing more than 1,000 users. Memory requirements differ depending on what Exchange server is being used for (for example, a connector server, an FE server, or a video-conferencing server). In most cases, 256MB of RAM is sufficient for small to medium-sized enterprises. FE servers by nature require less memory than these other configurations, especially a POP3 FE server. The memory subsystem in Exchange 2000 does not require as much monitoring as other subsystems because Exchange Server manages this component very well. It knows when applications need memory and is ready to provide it. There are few memory optimization techniques you have to perform, but one that Microsoft recommends highly is to place multiple paging files on multiple physical disks to increase the overall performance of your servers.

Processor, disk, memory, and network scalability are important when you are determining hardware needs for an FE server that will be running OWA for geographically dispersed clients. There are also concerns arising from the use of secure authentication for remote clients. An ideal FE design would be as follows:

- A Pentium III 400MHz processor
- An FE server with at least 1GB of RAM
- Two 100Mbps network cards

Each BE server would be configured with two to four 500MHz processors and 1GB of RAM. Typical environments would achieve 50 percent CPU usage on each BE server with about five SMTP messages being delivered to local mailboxes every second and about two messages being sent to other servers every second.

OWA scales very well on four-processor FE servers. As the number of HTTP connections increases (corresponding to an increase in simultaneous OWA users), the increase in processor usage can be described in a more or less linear fashion. An OWA FE server generally uses approximately 30K of memory for each active OWA connection, assuming that the traffic is not encrypted using the SSL protocol. This means that OWA is responsible for a significant amount of memory consumption on the FE server. As connections increase, the memory required by the InetInfo.exe process increases linearly.

You need to consider the amount of network traffic to your OWA FE server when you are determining your hardware requirements. The minimum network configuration for an OWA FE server is a single 100Mbps full duplex network connection. *Full duplex network connections* can transmit and receive data simultaneously. FE servers that host more than 5,000 connections may either need an additional 100Mbps full duplex connection or be upgraded to a Gigabit Ethernet-based network. To balance the client load across multiple OWA FE servers, you can use NLB. SSL encryption of HTTP sessions between clients and an OWA FE server requires increased CPU and memory resources. If you use SSL to encrypt all sessions between clients and the FE server, CPU requirements can increase by up to three times, based on the number of ISAPI extension requests per second that the FE server handles. You can monitor the number of ISAPI extension requests per second using the Performance Monitor application; they are a reliable indicator of how many OWA transactions occur per second on the FE server. If you deploy SSL encryption on an OWA FE server, you should plan carefully to ensure adequate CPU and memory resources.

Here is a list of points to remember as you design an optimal FE/BE scenario for ongoing business systems that require minimal downtime; you can use this section as a quick reference for determining your hardware needs for an OWA FE server:

- OWA scales well to four-processor servers.
- Use a ratio of one FE server to four BE servers.
- A typical FE server may require 30K of RAM per active connection.
- OWA uses virtually no disk resources, unless the FE server is paging or HTTP-DAV—Distributed Authoring and Versioning (WebDAV)—logging is turned on.
- OWA requires a second 100Mbps NIC if it is servicing more than 5,000 connections.
- You can load balance an OWA FE server using NLB.
- OWA SSL connections require up to three times more processing power and 60 percent more memory on their FE server compared to a FE server that is not using SSL encryption.

Capacity Planning and Assessment

With the release of Exchange 2000 Server, Microsoft is taking a somewhat different approach to server sizing and capacity planning than it used with previous versions of Exchange. With previous releases, benchmark testing was the primary method used for capacity planning, and this often used boilerplate user profiles, so that users were easily labeled as light, medium, or heavy with respect to their mail use. With Exchange 2000, an organization can customize its planning by asking the following questions:

- How many users can I fit on one Exchange server?
- How many Exchange servers can I fit given my AD constraints and limitations?

The key concept of scalability or sizing does not depend only on the number of users per server; the structure of your deployment affects scalability as well. Before making an accurate prediction of the scalability of an Exchange deployment, you need to also consider such elements as the software that clients will use to access mail, the hardware used in the deployment, and the physical deployment itself. You have to look at what actions your users are performing against your servers. Your goals are to compose a combination of regular actions performed by users and to try to predict what resource utilization these actions will produce for your organization as a whole. Properly assessing your environment encompasses all elements of your network, including your hardware, topology, domain models employed, and user base.

Hardware and Topology Issues that Affect Capacity

Hardware is a key component of a total capacity planning and scalability equation. It is a primary factor in the initial stages of an Exchange deployment, and it continues to be a primary factor as the organization evolves and adds more servers later on. You are concerned with supporting as many transactions as possible, and it is obvious that a server with four 600MHz processors can handle more transactions than a server with one 500MHz processor, for example. The topology consists of the hardware, its configuration, the site and domain model that is used, and the overall messaging infrastructure or transport mechanism being used.

To scale for future growth in our messaging environment, we have to consider disk usage and the CPU capacity of various types of servers. For example, disk usage is paramount for a BE server. It is important to assume that all servers of a given type are equivalent to one another, although a production environment may prove otherwise. This means that, ideally, all BE servers should be architecturally and functionally equivalent.

Be careful not to confuse hardware with hardware configurations. It is not enough to argue that so many MB of RAM will support so many transactions without any problems. There are no official hardware configuration standards or scenarios because different servers will provide different services at different times. For example, configuring a BE server with multiple Storage Groups and databases requires more physical memory than a BE server with only one Storage Group or one database. RAID technology, discussed earlier in this chapter, is a similar issue because you have to determine which RAID array will produce fewer bottlenecks for a given user load. For instance, a RAID 5 configuration experiences more disk reads and writes—and hence higher I/O rates—and reaches a bottleneck at lower capacities than a similar RAID 0 configuration.

Exchange Server load balances among Global Catalog (GC) servers and DCs. This is why domain models are important when you are planning and assessing capacity. You should be concerned with the total number of domains and the total number of Windows 2000 sites used in your topology. It is normally assumed that a single site does not span two or more domains. Exchange load balances depending on the type of directory that a particular machine has available to it. For example, Exchange load balances user requests among any GCs that reside in the same Windows 2000 site as the Exchange server itself. However, a DC that resides within the same domain as the Exchange server is chosen at random.

Along with sites and domains, you should also consider the number and arrangement of your Routing Groups because this has a bearing on the number of hops a message takes as it traverses through your system. Evaluate the total number of Routing Groups in your environment and see how many Routing Groups span more than two sites. Also consider how many bridgehead servers you are using in each Routing Group. Keep in mind that message hopping among Routing Groups is a very resource-intensive process.

We recommend developing some sort of capacity-planning model that uses the guidelines and recommendations prescribed in the preceding paragraphs. This model processes and generates output that should prove useful when you scale your existing infrastructure. Many capacity planners use certain guidelines and criteria in developing their results. For instance, capacity planners often target server CPUs with less than 50 percent of their potential capacity. This allows room for peak loads and prevents latencies in message transport to some degree. This number may appear conservative, but it is very important that you approach deployments conservatively. You also have to allow for server-side processing and server-side maintenance routines, which also contribute to latency. Consider using fast disks that support around 100 random I/Os per second or 300 sequential I/Os per second. Excessive load on the disk subsystem can cause serious performance problems, including increased latency and contention. To avoid such problems, we recommend taking a conservative approach when it comes to selecting the number of disk spindles for your subsystem.

Other Factors that Affect Capacity

The total capacity equation factors in the user population as well as topology. The user population consists of the user base, as well as the overall user profile and mail usage scenarios. In any original design scenario, you usually ask the following questions to help plan for capacity usage:

➤ To whom will users be sending messages? Messaging on most networks follows a fairly typical pattern. Users tend to send messages primarily to other users in their domain. Users also need to send messages to other domains as well as Internet users. Developing a broad picture of these traffic patterns can help you plan an effective placement of servers.

➤ What kind of messages are users allowed to send? If your users will be transferring large files to one another via email, you have to make some kind of allowance for this type of traffic. Some organizations put limits on the amount of data that can be transmitted in a single message. Others use quotas for the amount of space that one mailbox can consume.

- Who should be allowed to create public folders? By default, top-level public folders in a Public Folder tree are created on the home server of the user who creates them. By restricting which users can create top-level folders, you can control the placement of public folders on servers. These restrictions also help you manage the public folder hierarchy structure more effectively.

- Will any of your users need to access a foreign mail system? The answer to this question can help you place users and foreign messaging connectors. If one group of users tends to use a connector heavily, you might want to place those users on the server on which the connector is installed. This reduces the number of hops that messages have to take from your users to the foreign system.

- What Internet protocols are running, or what other applications are running on the Exchange server that may be consuming additional resources?

The User Profile

It is easy to optimize your environment from a hardware point of view and neglect what is often called the *user profile*, which helps you analyze client network traffic. Companies constantly struggle to meet user requirements, even after they have spent countless thousands of dollars on high-end processor hardware and gigabit memory sticks. You have to establish a baseline of expected actions against your servers. Optimizing a user is far different than optimizing hardware. In fact, you can never fully optimize a user; this is the challenge of scalability. You need more than the total number of users to assess total capacity; you also need a breakdown of the types of mail clients being used, as well as the number of users considered active at any given time of the day. Knowing this can help you segregate traffic devoted to users and traffic devoted to system activity, such as replication. It is useful to determine peak loads in any environment, with respect to both duration and intensity.

You can collect information on the characteristics of your user population to help you with future deployments of Exchange. Pertinent information includes estimates of how many future users you may have, and how much mail they will be sending or receiving. Using tools such as the Performance Console will also prove helpful, although it will not provide you with all the information you need. When using System Monitor, for example, it is hard to determine how much mail a single user received from the Internet, but at least you will have an idea of how busy or backlogged your message queues are. When you are planning estimates for future use, it is always best to combine actual data generated by Exchange Server with information provided directly by your users.

Assessing Client Traffic

Deploying and using Exchange 2000 in any company requires an in-depth analysis of that company's topology and network structure, as well as its usage patterns. It's hard to quantify exactly the total traffic generated between different Exchange 2000 servers and between an Exchange server and its clients. However, an estimate of traffic patterns helps you determine present and future capacity and aids in troubleshooting specific problems as they arise.

Exchange Server consumes different levels of bandwidth under different circumstances. Microsoft and outside vendors have done various tests, and all parties have tried to determine optimal levels of performance for Exchange. You can find a treasure chest of invaluable information regarding this topic in the *Microsoft Exchange 2000 Server Resource Kit*. The tests conducted by Microsoft revealed information applicable to most Exchange environments. For instance, although network bandwidth is not consumed for cached data, message content significantly impacts network traffic, especially an HTML message. The following conclusions are relevant:

➤ The act of logging on represents a major part of network traffic with respect to MAPI clients such as Outlook 2000.

➤ Outlook 2000 is more integrated with Windows 2000 compared to other MAPI clients because an Outlook client can query AD directly using tools such as DSProxy.

➤ An HTML message generates more traffic compared to the same message in rich-text format.

➤ Among all the Internet protocols used by Exchange server, POP3 generates the least network traffic.

➤ Web folders provide an efficient method of accessing mailboxes and public folders, and generate almost the same level of network traffic that common file shares create.

Optimizing Capacity

Based on our discussions up to this point, you should now be concerned primarily with optimizing a given design. Doing so helps you stay within your defined capacity levels, and it may expose areas where more capacity planning is needed. Capacity troubleshooting and capacity planning go hand in hand.

You can do various things to fully optimize an existing Exchange deployment in the hope of preserving existing capacity and solving common configuration mishaps that disrupt and limit existing capacity. We cover the most common optimization techniques that you can do for a wide variety of subsystems (we cannot cover every single technique available).

You are sometimes faced with users within the same organization who need different configurations (for example, security requirements). One optimization technique involves creating multiple protocol virtual servers because Exchange 2000 allows you to create multiple instances of a protocol server on one computer. Remember that during installation, a default protocol server is created for most protocols, such as IMAP4. For each protocol, you can configure authentication methods and message formats. To distinguish one virtual server from another for the same protocol, you have to specify an IP port number and IP address for each server. Creating multiple virtual servers is useful in cases where you want to distinguish between sending messages over the Internet and sending messages within your local domain. You can even configure external messages (but not internal ones) to be encrypted with transport layer security (TLS).

Because AD is so integrated with Exchange 2000, you can take various actions to optimize how Exchange clients or servers access AD data. Any Outlook 2000 client is known to have the most efficient access to the AD compared to both MAPI and non-MAPI clients. When an Outlook 2000 client connects to an Exchange server, it looks for any directory services on the home server. The client contacts the DSProxy service and receives a referral informing the client that a GC server will handle all future requests to access the directory. This referral mechanism helps reduce the load on the Exchange server. You can optimize this process so that all Outlook clients are forced to go through the DSProxy process without being referred. You can do this by following these steps:

1. Go to the HKEY_LOCAL_MACHINE\System\CurrentControlSet\Services\MSExchangeSA\Parameters Registry entry.

2. Choose the No RFR Service entry.

3. Assign a data value of 0X1.

Clients and servers access the AD directory in different ways. One Exchange 2000 server may actually communicate with multiple AD servers at one time. It usually establishes LDAP connections to nearby DCs and GCs. The order of contact is important:

1. Exchange tries to use DNS to find all the DCs in the domain and attempts to use them sequentially.

2. If a DC is not found within a reasonable time, the directory request is sent to a GC server for resolution.

3. If multiple GC servers exist in a site, Exchange employs them in a round-robin fashion.

4. Normally, Exchange tries to connect to the first 10 GC servers in the same site; however, if no attempt is successful, Exchange tries to contact a GC server outside of this site.

You can see the optimization for server connections to AD using the DSAccess API. Part of this API is the directory cache, which is enabled by default when you start Exchange 2000 Server. You may recall that the GC server is an important component that various applications access. Having multiple GCs is important for workload optimization. The DSAccess API cache allows all Exchange services to cache a directory lookup without querying a GC server. Normally, 4MB of directory entries are cached for five minutes. You can always adjust these values, realizing there is a fine line between performance and data access. It is good to reduce network traffic by increasing the Time To Live setting for entries in the cache, but you may be eating up precious system memory if your cache entries stay there too long. The two Registry keys to monitor for controlling the size of the DSAccess cache are MaxEntries and MaxMemory. Microsoft recommends configuring the cache size using MaxMemory over MaxEntries because doing so gives you more control regarding memory usage for your server. Every client action, such as reading or sending mail, usually involves multiple cache entries; most of these actions consume an average of 3.6K of cache memory. You can use the following estimate to figure the maximum cache size of DSAccess:

$$MaxMemory = 3.6 K * (client\ actions/second) * (Time\ To\ Live\ for\ entries) + 2500$$

For example, let's assume your server will handle about 40 actions per second with a Time To Live for cache entries equal to 900 seconds or 15 minutes. The MaxMemory setting would then be equal to 3.6K times 40 actions times 900 TTL plus 2,500, which equals 132,100K or 132.1MB. To actually set this value in the Registry, follow these steps:

1. Find HKEY_LOCAL_MACHINE\System\CurrentControlSet\Services\MSExchangeDSAccess\Instance0.

2. Select the MaxMemory key and enter a value for the number of kilobytes. You may see a default value of 4,096.

Capacity and Design Troubleshooting Scenarios

We now present some common problems that occur in normal Exchange deployments and their solutions. These problems usually fall within the following categories: installation and setup, AD, Web storage, or performance. For more information, use such tools as the *Microsoft Exchange 2000 Server Resource Kit* or visit the Microsoft Exchange home page at **www.microsoft.com/exchange/**.

Scenario One

Problem: When setting up Exchange 2000, you receive notification that the ForestPrep command did not work.

Solution: Make sure the account you used to set up Exchange has the Schema Admins, Enterprise Admins, and Local Administrator rights to the server.

Scenario Two

Problem: You are attempting to install Exchange 2000, and the setup program fails on numerous occasions.

Solution:

1. Check that all network connections are working properly.
2. Turn off all your Exchange services.
3. Restart your server.
4. Run the setup program again and reinstall all components that did not install the first time.

Scenario Three

Problem: You have just added a new server to a site. The interval between AD directory service replication and public folder replication seems too long. Your Web Storage System is trying to replicate all public folders before the new site has been added to the directory.

Solution: Public folder replication does not take place until the AD directory has had a chance to replicate. Wait for the directory to replicate your new site information. You can force directory replication to occur by clicking on the General tab for your server directory and choosing Update Now.

Scenario Four

Problem: You are trying to add a new Exchange 2000 mailbox using the AD Users and Computers snap-in tool but are unsuccessful.

Solution: You are trying to perform user management without having the System Manager snap-in installed correctly; it is best to reinstall the Exchange Server Management components using the installation CD-ROM before performing further user management functions.

Scenario Five

Problem: You stop and restart the Epoxy service and receive the following error message: "System error 2 has occurred".

Solution: The Exchange Installable File System (EXIFS) runs as a hidden service and allows file-level access to items within a private mail store; this means you cannot see this in the Services box under Administrative Tools.

1. From a command line, type "net stop exifs", then "Subst m: /d", and finally "Net start exifs".
2. If that does not work, some users may have files open on drive M:, which is mapped to the EXIFS service in Windows Explorer. To disconnect all users from a server, type "Netses/ed" at the command line.

Chapter Summary

By reading this chapter, you have gained some perspective on advanced design and support issues. We did not want to merely repeat issues from prior chapters; rather, we wanted to raise your awareness level of what is really going on behind the scenes. To understand and appreciate Exchange 2000, you have to think like the original designers of Exchange did. You have to keep in mind what purpose Exchange will serve in your organization. In fact, planning for an Exchange deployment is really an ongoing, never-ending process of exploration. Original design plans are always open to scrutiny and change. In addition, support issues arise whether your initial design plans are perfect or imperfect. This is why we had to review the proper stages of planning a deployment using best-practice methodologies. Risk reduction becomes an important end goal. Effective design and planning means being able to manage growth in your user base as well as growth in network and messaging traffic.

The relevant points to remember from this chapter include the following:

➤ MSF is a series of best practices that help lay the foundation for successfully deploying projects like Exchange 2000.

➤ The four phases of the MSF Infrastructure Deployment Process Model are envisioning, planning, developing, and deploying. Envisioning helps to define the scope and limitations of your project. This stage requires you to write a mission statement that describes what you envision as your final outcome. The planning stage involves making detailed functional specifications and gathering information about current services. The developing stage consists of testing or building a prototype system to validate the designs formulated in previous stages using hardware similar to what you will be using in your production environment. In the deploying stage, you make all services available to all users and evaluate the full performance of a production system.

➤ AD defines your company's underlying messaging infrastructure; AD has a logical structure that you have to properly plan and control in a production environment.

➤ The domain structure, forest structure, OU structure, and Windows 2000 site topology all influence the logical structure of AD.

➤ An FE/BE design allows you to distribute server tasks among multiple computers and provides the benefits of a single namespace and increased IMAP4 access to public folders. An FE server does not host any Exchange 2000 IS services; it can provide some degree of security by being positioned as a single point of access behind a firewall. A BE server can perform as a standard server that hosts an IS, or a combination of both an FE server and a standard server.

- Your network can benefit from both horizontal and vertical scalability. Horizontal scalability refers to adding multiple computers that all perform the same task. Vertical scalability refers to adding additional services to a single computer.

- You have to understand and become familiar with the various implementations of RAID technologies that Exchange 2000 uses. All of these variations use multiple physical disks to distribute data, as well as store data according to logic independent of the application that is storing the data.

- When considering capacity, you have to look at hardware, topology, the messaging infrastructure, the user base, and the overall user profile and mail usage scenarios.

- Deploying and using Exchange 2000 requires an in-depth analysis of an organization's topology and network structure, as well as its usage patterns. This will help you determine present and future capacity needs.

Review Questions

1. Your company, FlightData, is spread geographically across two continents. Your original topology called for establishing a single Routing Group. Should you keep this original design?

    a. Yes, one Routing Group is sufficient for all topologies.

    b. Yes, one Routing Group is scalable to multiple domains.

    c. No, one Routing Group is needed for each Administrative Group.

    d. No, multiple Routing Groups will manage network bandwidth better than a single Routing Group.

2. Why is it important to have one GC server in each Routing Group or Windows 2000 site that you design?

    a. This will help decrease client lookup traffic across your less reliable WAN links.

    b. This will help increase client lookup traffic across less reliable WAN links.

    c. An Exchange 2000 installation will fail without one GC server in every Routing Group.

    d. A GC server will initiate public folder replication within a site.

3. What part of the MSF process is involved in prototype testing and BE implementation?

    a. Envisioning

    b. Developing

    c. Planning

    d. Deploying

4. A company wants to have POP3 and IMAP4 working on an FE server. What ports should it leave open on the internal network firewall?

   a. Port 110 for POP3 and port 143 for IMAP4
   b. Port 3268 for POP3 and port 110 for IMAP4
   c. Port 110 for POP3 and port 3268 for IMAP4
   d. Port 3268 for POP3 and port 143 for IMAP4

5. Which of the following describe benefits of dividing the functionality of Exchange 2000 across different servers? [Check all correct answers]

   a. Increased WAN bandwidth
   b. Higher restore times
   c. Improved response times
   d. Reduced downtimes

6. You are designing a new Exchange 2000 organization using existing hardware running Windows NT Server 4. Which component of Windows 2000 Server should you install so your planned upgrade will be successful?

   a. DNS service
   b. DDNS service
   c. Proxy service
   d. SNMP service

7. Which of the following structural components directly or indirectly affects the logical structure of Active Directory?

   a. Routing Group structure
   b. Organizational unit structure
   c. Internet topology structure
   d. MMC snap-in structure

8. Richard is about to create three new OUs within his Exchange hierarchy. What are the benefits of creating these objects? [Check all correct answers]

   a. They help delegate administration within your organization.
   b. They require all objects to be accessible by all administrators.
   c. They can help hide certain objects from administrators.
   d. They define the location of objects within Routing Groups.

9. Which of the following best describes the concept of horizontal scalability for Exchange 2000?

    a. Adding several tasks to the same server

    b. Adding several servers that all perform the same task

    c. Adding multiple Routing Groups within the same site

    d. Adding multiple physical disks in a RAID array

10. Bob has configured one of his Exchange servers as a combination server. Can this server host a mailbox store?

    a. Yes, but it can contain only one Storage Group for that store.

    b. No, only FE servers can host an IS.

    c. Yes, because all combination servers host an IS.

    d. No, only standard servers can host mailbox stores.

11. In an FE/BE server configuration, what protocol communicates with a BE server that is running AD?

    a. SMTP

    b. SNMP

    c. MAPI

    d. RPC

12. Sue is configuring an FE/BE server configuration for her company. Her FE server is accepting SMTP mail from the Internet. Which of the following has to be true in this case?

    a. The store.exe service has to be stopped until the IS is mounted.

    b. Sue's BE server has to accept SMTP mail from the Internet.

    c. The Store.exe service has to be running and at least one public folder store has to be mounted.

    d. The Store.exe service has to be running and at least one private IS has to be mounted.

13. Which statements regarding RAID are correct? [Check all correct answers]

    a. RAID 0 is less expensive than RAID 5.

    b. RAID 1 is more expensive than RAID 0.

    c. RAID 3 has the highest cost but the lowest performance.

    d. RAID 0+3 is the highest-availability solution.

14. Harry wants to utilize a high-performance RAID solution for his Exchange server. He wants to use five physical disks to store his data. Will a RAID 0+1 strategy help him in this scenario?
    a. No, he doesn't have enough disks to use RAID 0+1 in this case.
    b. No, a RAID 5+1 solution will benefit him more in this case.
    c. Yes, because he has a minimum of three physical disks, which is required for RAID 0+1.
    d. Yes, as long as the disks are equal in size and geometry.

15. Where are top-level public folders in a Public Folder tree created by default?
    a. In the All Public Folders tree of the first Exchange server
    b. In the root console node of the Exchange organization
    c. On the home server of the user who created them
    d. On the FE server of the user who created them

16. Jane is using Outlook 2000 to access her email, whereas John is using Outlook Express. Which client is more integrated with Windows 2000?
    a. They are both equally integrated with Windows 2000.
    b. Outlook Express, because it is a true MAPI client.
    c. Outlook 2000, because it comes preinstalled with Exchange.
    d. Outlook 2000, because it can more directly query AD.

17. How does the DSProxy service help reduce the load placed on an Exchange server by Outlook 2000 clients?
    a. Clients are directed to a GC server for directory requests.
    b. DSProxy works with DSAccess to reduce the load on Exchange.
    c. DSProxy configures the Registry to not accept requests.
    d. DSProxy reduces the number of protocols used by Exchange.

18. What protocol does an Exchange 2000 server use to communicate with a nearby GC server regarding directory requests?
    a. LDAP connections
    b. RPCs
    c. SNMP traps
    d. RIP for IP

19. What component allows all Exchange Server services to cache directory lookups without querying a GC server?

   a. DSLookup cache

   b. DSQuery cache

   c. DSProxy cache

   d. DSAccess cache

20. You are planning to use multiple Public Folder trees for productivity purposes and to collaborate with external users. You want the content in these trees to be separate from your default Public Folder tree. Which client(s) can view these additional Public Folder trees?

   a. IMAP4 and Web clients

   b. Any MAPI client

   c. NNTP or Web clients

   d. All Outlook 2000 clients

Real-World Projects

Henry has been asked to quickly set up a Windows 2000 test network at the college where he works, ExchangeU. He is already administering a Novell NetWare 4.11 network, but his director is interested in migrating completely to a Microsoft-based network consisting of Windows NT 4 servers and workstations, as well as Windows 2000 servers and Exchange 2000 Server. Henry has a long road ahead of him, but he has read all the required documentation and has implemented the methodologies of the MSF Infrastructure Deployment Process Model. He has just finished setting up Windows 2000 and AD on a DC called Orion.

He has chosen a 500MHz Pentium III server with 256MB of RAM for a BE server running Exchange 2000. This machine will hold user mailboxes and all message stores, and will reside on the same segment as Orion. He quickly checks his documentation and performs the following steps.

Project 15.1
To install Exchange 2000 on a BE server:

1. Install Windows 2000 Server on an NT File System (NTFS)-formatted drive partition on the new machine as a standalone server and call it Phantom.

2. Join Phantom to the same domain as Orion, and make sure SMTP and NNTP are installed and running on Phantom.

3. Launch the Exchange 2000 Setup Wizard on Phantom and click on Next.

4. Click on the I Agree That I Have Read And Agree To Be Bound By The License Agreements For This Product radio button and then click on Next.

5. Type in your product ID number and then click on Next.

6. Select Microsoft Exchange 2000 (Custom) on the Component Summary screen, install the Messaging And Collaboration Services and the System Management Tools, and then click on Next.

7. On the next screen, select Create A New Exchange Organization, and then click on Next.

8. Type "ExchangeU" and select I Agree to continue. Then, click on Next.

9. Watch as Exchange extends your AD schema. Select OK and then Finish.

Henry is careful not to rush because this is the first time he will be working with an FE/BE environment. The next step will be to install Exchange 2000 on an FE server, which is very similar to setting up the BE server. He goes to another new 400MHz Pentium III machine with 128MB of RAM and calls it Mars.

Project 15.2
To install Exchange 2000 on an FE server:

1. Begin with a fresh installation of Windows 2000 Server using NTFS-formatted partitions.

2. Install the SMTP and NNTP services during Windows 2000 installation.

3. Join all computers to the same domain as the other machines.

4. Launch the Exchange 2000 Server Setup Wizard on Mars, click on Next, and then click on the I Agree That I Have Read And Agree To Be Bound By The License Agreements For This Product radio button.

5. Enter your product ID number and then click on Next.

6. At the Component Summary screen, follow these steps:
    a. Choose Microsoft Exchange 2000 | Action | Custom.
    b. Choose Microsoft Exchange Messaging And Collaboration Services | Action | Install.
    c. Choose Microsoft Exchange System Management Tools | Action | Install.
    d. Click on Next.

7. Choose I Agree on the Licensing Agreement screen and then click on Next.

8. Select Microsoft Exchange 2000 on the next screen and select Action | Custom. Then, click on Next.

9. Wait for all components to finish installing, click on Next, and then click on Finish.

At this point, Henry feels like stopping, but he remembers there is one final step to complete. He doesn't have a full FE server yet, and he remembers reading about using the System Manager snap-in tool to promote Mars to an FE server.

Project 15.3

To promote Mars to an FE server:

1. Log on to the BE server Phantom.

2. Start System Manager using Start|Programs|Microsoft Exchange|System Manager.

3. Open the Server tree and right-click on Mars.

4. Click on Properties and check the box labeled This Is A Front-End Server, and then click on OK.

5. Log back on to Mars and reboot this machine.

Henry is now satisfied that he has taken all the necessary steps to create an FE server. He informs the director that he will now monitor all connections to Mars, and that by default, all protocols and services are configured to run on his new FE server.

CHAPTER SIXTEEN

Legacy System Issues

After completing this chapter, you will be able to:

✓ Prepare an existing Exchange environment for an Exchange 2000 Server deployment

✓ Diagnose and resolve problems involving an upgrade or migration

✓ Appreciate critical migration issues from legacy messaging systems and describe the types of migration you can perform

✓ Plan mixed-mode environments that coexist with Exchange Server 5.5

✓ Understand the differences and consequences of both mixed-mode and native-mode operations for Exchange 2000 Server environments

Our emphasis up to this point has been on "green-field" deployments, or environments consisting solely of Exchange 2000 servers. The concepts you have learned in previous chapters have certainly helped you understand new design principles and architectural concepts not present in any prior version of Exchange. It is useful to study Exchange 2000 in isolation from previous versions simply to appreciate the power and functionality this messaging system can provide. However, knowing where something came from can help you predict in which direction it may be headed. Notice the trend toward unified messaging and pure collaboration that is present in this latest version of Exchange; these features were nonexistent in legacy versions. We therefore claim that not only must you identify what is new in Exchange 2000, but you must also comprehend and justify the existence of these features. You should be able to explain why companies would even want different versions of Exchange on the same network and how they can benefit from these new features. In some cases, Exchange 5.5 will continue to provide all the services a company needs in terms of messaging and collaboration. For these organizations, there will be no impetus or momentum to upgrade simply because a new version has appeared. In fact, many organizations fall prey to "upgrade fever" without giving much thought to how the newer version will benefit the company or if it will significantly impact the total cost of ownership (TCO).

After reading this chapter, you will understand both the blessings and the pitfalls of performing an upgrade to Exchange 2000, and you may even begin to appreciate the power that is already hidden—but still unrealized—in previous versions of Exchange Server. This chapter is not supposed to present cookbook recipes for upgrading a server to Exchange 2000. It instead focuses on planning and preparing a successful migration. It also helps you diagnose and resolve common migration issues and manage a peaceful coexistence with legacy Exchange servers. The intent is not to say goodbye to the old Exchange environment but to give it more horsepower by introducing the newest member of the family, Exchange 2000.

Deciding to Upgrade

Before you decide to upgrade or migrate an existing Exchange 5.x or earlier server to Exchange 2000, you have to consider the advantages and disadvantages that are inherent in this process. Every action has consequences—some good and some bad. The decision to upgrade an enterprise usually revolves around the following criteria:

- A vendor is no longer supporting the original product or version.
- The industry is rapidly upgrading to the next version of the product.
- The new product or version has features that will vastly increase a company's productivity and return on investment (ROI) while simultaneously lowering the company's TCO.

There may be other criteria by which to justify an upgrade to Exchange 2000, but these are the most commonly asked questions. When you focus these criteria on Exchange Server, you are forced to ask the following:

- Has Microsoft stopped supporting all previous versions of Exchange Server?
- Are all companies rapidly upgrading to Exchange 2000 Server?
- Does Exchange 2000 have features that dramatically raise ROI while drastically lowering TCO for a typical company?

Answering these questions will help you determine whether you should plan and deploy an upgrade to Exchange 2000. Currently, the answers to those questions provide almost no justification to perform an upgrade or migration: The answers to the first two questions would be a strong "No" at the time of this writing, whereas the third answer would be a resounding "Yes."

You may be faced with similar questions in your career as an administrator. So you must carefully think things through and be prepared to justify any planned upgrade or migration. As you will see, both planning and preparation are key to a successful upgrade. Decisions you make at certain stages cannot be undone or reversed. Also, an upgrade strategy used for one part of your system may not be needed or useful for other parts. This may call for different strategies for different sites. Upgrading Exchange servers to Exchange 2000 is especially daunting in view of how dependent its architecture and components are on Windows 2000. A typical discussion regarding a migration to Exchange 2000 is usually preceded by discussions regarding a migration to Windows 2000. However, our focus will not be on the prerequisite steps needed to deploy Windows 2000. Instead, we want to focus on adequately preparing your existing Exchange environment so that Exchange 2000 can be properly introduced into it. We will assume that you already have a working implementation of Windows 2000 before proceeding to the Exchange 2000 migration. Let us now look at some hardware and software requirements in trying to prepare our environment for a planned upgrade to Exchange 2000 Server.

Preparing Your Environment

Currently, almost 20 million Exchange 5.x Server clients are operating throughout the world. However, it is inevitable that many companies will want to formally migrate their servers to Exchange 2000. It may be that they are just testing some new feature of Exchange 2000, such as Instant Messaging (IM). For whatever reason, they would like to upgrade seamlessly from an old version to a new version. This means they have to meet certain requirements for the upgrade. We now turn our attention toward issues relating to the upgrade process, such as site design and hardware requirements, as well as issues concerning coexistence with prior versions of Exchange server.

Site Design and Site Addressing

Exchange 5.5 sites, as you may recall, were based on administrative and network connectivity requirements. All servers within an Exchange 5.x site communicated with each other via remote procedure calls (RPCs), and each site could span multiple geographically dispersed locations, as long as sufficient bandwidth was available. Communication between servers usually relied on permanent, high-speed connections, and there was little tolerance for low-bandwidth connections unless connectors were employed. In addition, sites made it easier to perform common administration tasks such as adding users or groups. The concepts of organizations and sites have changed for Exchange 2000, so it is important to remember that the criteria used for site design in Exchange 5.5 cannot be easily replicated to a site design for Exchange 2000. Site design is therefore an important legacy system issue.

When you worked with Exchange 5.5 sites, it was important to categorize a server by its function (such as mailbox, connector, and so on). It was also important to know how site addressing would be handled and what default Simple Mail Transfer Protocol (SMTP) format you would use to generate addresses for user mailboxes. This information is still important in a planned upgrade; it will help you determine coexistence possibilities for mixed-mode Exchange 2000 organizations. It will also help you determine the correct Routing Group and Administrative Group architecture for native-mode Exchange 2000 environments. Mixed mode and native mode are discussed later in this chapter.

Directory Services

Directory services are another related legacy system issue. Every Exchange 5.5 server relied on a separate directory service that communicated with other Exchange servers and replicated such information as mapped addresses or routing information. This was done using Lightweight Directory Access Protocol (LDAP), which used Transmission Control Protocol/Internet Protocol (TCP/IP) as a transport protocol. Exchange 2000 is now integrated with Active Directory (AD); Administrative and Routing Groups have now replaced the site concept of Exchange 5.5.

Operating System (OS) and Hardware Requirements

When you prepare for an upgrade or migration, you have to consider certain OS and hardware requirements. Exchange 2000 Server does not install on a system that does not belong to a Windows 2000 domain. This means you have to install Exchange 2000 on a Windows 2000-based machine running at least Service Pack 1 (SP1). Notice that not only must Exchange 2000 be installed in a Windows 2000 AD domain, but all Windows 2000 domain controllers (DCs) in the organization must run Windows 2000 SP1.

Tip: For further instructions and details regarding this requirement, consult Knowledge Base Article ID Q272691 at www.microsoft.com/exchange/.

We see that Exchange 2000 has a much greater dependency on the OS compared to legacy Exchange servers. For example, Exchange 2000 uses the Windows 2000 AD Directory Service (DS) to store both schema data and configuration data. Also, you now manage Exchange 2000 using the Windows 2000 Microsoft Management Console (MMC), not the Exchange Administrator of days past. Even the Windows 2000 Internet Information Server (IIS) service now hosts all transport protocols for Exchange 2000, a clear departure from the architecture of legacy Exchange.

The Importance of AD in a Planned Upgrade

When upgrading to Exchange 2000, you must meet both Windows 2000 prerequisites and Exchange Server version prerequisites. The Windows 2000 prerequisites include establishing a proper domain architecture. You will either build an AD plan from scratch if there are no Windows 2000 domains present, or you will be working with the Active Directory Connector (ADC) if multiple domains exist (ADC is discussed in more detail later in this chapter). Exchange 2000 actually requires several distinct components of Windows 2000 Server, including AD, Domain Name System (DNS), the Network News Transfer Protocol (NNTP) service, and the SMTP service (the default messaging protocol used for Exchange 2000). Of these four components, the one deserving some extra attention is AD.

Note: We are not downplaying the importance of DNS, NNTP, or SMTP. However, we cannot stress enough the importance and interrelationship between Exchange 2000 and AD. Pay special attention to this relationship whenever you work with Exchange 2000. With DNS, just remember that at least one server in a domain must provide name-resolution services with the ability to perform dynamic updates.

Exchange 2000 relies heavily on AD to store configuration information. When you first install Windows 2000, AD does not have the correct structure to store data relevant only to Exchange. If you want to successfully install Exchange 2000, you have to extend this structure, known as the *schema*. This is how rights and permissions are assigned to various objects that Exchange 2000 uses. Rights are actually given to administrators and users at various levels. For example, to install Exchange 2000, you have to belong to the Schema Admins and Enterprise Admins security groups. You also have to have Administrator privileges on the local machine where you will be installing Exchange. Some mail administrators may not possess all these requisite privileges.

Using ForestPrep

Tools such as ForestPrep help you separate tasks that belong to the Schema Admins group from tasks that belong to local administrators. Extending the Windows 2000 schema is an important preparation tool used to install Exchange 2000. To extend the AD schema, you need to run ForestPrep once per forest. You also use it to create the actual organization object in the configuration-naming context and to set up the permission structures. You run it as a command-line enhancement to setup.exe as follows:

```
setup.exe /ForestPrep
```

To run the ForestPrep utility, you need Enterprise Admins, Schema Admins, and Local Administrator privileges. When you update the schema using ForestPrep, it's important to remember that you cannot reverse whatever changes are made to AD. ForestPrep prompts you for an account that contains Full Administrator privileges. Whoever is responsible for installing Exchange 2000 uses this account to perform subsequent installations. ForestPrep uses the information you provide to extend the schema to include information specific only to Exchange. This information is in the files found on the installation CD-ROM in the \Setup\i386\Exchange directory.

Note: *ForestPrep is really modifying or adding classes and attributes within AD. You can get details of what is modified or added in the Exchange 2000 software development kit (SDK) at* **http://msdn.microsoft.com/library/**.

The new objects and attributes that ForestPrep adds are replicated throughout the Windows 2000 forest to all DCs in the schema-naming context. Attributes are also added to a partial replica set, which is replicated to Global Catalog (GC) servers. Note that the replication method that Exchange 2000 uses is far more efficient than the one Exchange 5.5 employed; in Exchange 2000, only changes are replicated between GCs, whereas in Exchange 5.5, a complete record was replicated even if only one attribute had changed. So, Exchange 2000 is efficient because you see replication occurring only between DCs, not between every server in your site.

Hardware Dependencies

Servers can adopt different functions and roles (such as Chat, public folder, mailbox, and so on), so you have to adopt the proper hardware configuration for each specific role. The hardware you choose must also appear on the Microsoft Hardware Compatibility List (HCL) and be supported by Windows 2000 itself. We recommend a minimum hardware configuration of a Pentium II 300MHz processor, a RAID 5 hard disk array, 256MB of RAM, and 5GB of free hard disk space. If your current environment includes various legacy versions of Exchange that use different SPs, then an upgrade to Exchange 2000 requires a server that runs Exchange 5.5 with SP3. If you perform an in-place upgrade of a server, you need an extra 30 percent of disk space just to hold your private and public Information Stores (ISs). You also have to consider the time required for an upgrade, especially when upgrading to the new Web Storage System. A fast SCSI hard drive and a fast processor will definitely help you in this area.

Overall, though, an upgrade to Exchange 2000 will prove to be faster than previous upgrades, simply because any data upgrades will be held off until a user actually requests data for the very first time. The upgrade process averages about 30GB per hour, and the conversion of data is extended over a longer period of time compared to the actual time required for the upgrade itself. It does not matter in what order you upgrade your servers to Exchange 2000. This means that some companies plan to upgrade a public folder server first, whereas others upgrade their mailbox servers first. The good news for Exchange 2000 is that the order of upgrading is now a trivial issue.

It's important to have an idea about which components are being upgraded when you want to abandon Exchange 5.5 in favor of Exchange 2000. Some of the fully upgraded components are:

- Lotus Notes connector
- Lotus cc:Mail connector
- Microsoft (MS) Mail connector
- MS Mail directory synchronization
- Custom recipients (need the ADC)
- Distribution lists (DLs) (need the ADC)
- Mailboxes (need the ADC)
- Message Transfer Agent (MTA) stack (using TCP/IP)
- X.400 connector (using TCP/IP)
- Public folders
- Key Management Service (KMS)
- Outlook Web Access (OWA)

Some Exchange 5.5 components, such as the Professional Office System (PROFS) connector and the System Network Architecture Distribution System (SNADS) connector, are not upgraded to Exchange 2000 features.

Note: The PROFS and the SNADS connectors are not supported in Exchange 2000. Therefore, they are not discussed much in this book. If you need to maintain these connectors, we recommend that you keep at least one Exchange 5.5 server running in your organization for coexistence purposes.

In addition, some components—including Internet Message Access Protocol 4 (IMAP4) and Post Office Protocol 3 (POP3)—are only partially upgraded to Exchange 2000 features. For example, IMAP4 upgrades values in the mailbox store but not values in the configuration.

Other Planning Considerations When You Are Upgrading

Here are some final legacy-system issues you should consider when planning a migration to Exchange 2000:

- When dealing with custom recipients in Exchange 5.5, you now have to use the ADC to move custom recipients over to AD where they will become contacts. You don't have to specify an email address for a contact right away; you can do it later.

- Recipient containers no longer exist in Exchange 2000, as they did in Exchange 5.5. This structure has now become the organizational unit (OU) containers of AD.

- The address book views introduced with Exchange Server 5 have become address lists in Exchange 2000. You now have more functionality with address lists because you have more flexibility in specifying how these lists will appear. You can also re-create your current address book views using the new LDAP filter rules in Exchange 2000.

- Any mailboxes on an Exchange 5.5 server are now mail-enabled AD users in Exchange 2000. A mail-enabled user has at least one email address defined for itself. For example, a contact is a mail-enabled user because one email address is defined for it.

Warning: If a user does not exist in AD before you do an in-place upgrade, Exchange places the corresponding mailbox object in the Message Store's (MS's) deleted items location!

- Exchange 5.5 assigned permissions to public folders using the concept of DLs. Exchange 2000 uses the concept of a Windows 2000 universal security group to do the same thing. Your Windows 2000 forest has to contain at least one native-mode domain to benefit from universal security groups.

Tip: If you don't want to use universal security groups (meaning you don't have to switch to a native-mode Windows 2000 domain), you can use a domain local or global group to control public folder access. This method does require extra administrative effort and maintenance, however.

- Exchange 2000 handles public folder administration differently than Exchange 5.5. Administration is now based on permissions set on various objects such as top-level hierarchies, and you can set these permissions for various actions such as adding replicas. Exchange 5.5 allowed an all-or-nothing approach by applying rights for all actions rather than rights on certain objects.

- You will notice differences in public folder affinity and referrals when you upgrade to Exchange 2000. Public folder affinity is now transitive. For example, if you configure an affinity between site A and site B, and another affinity between site B and site C, an affinity automatically exists between site A and site C. Recall that Exchange 5.5 did not allow this transitive behavior.

- An important issue arises in regard to circular logging. Exchange 2000 disables this feature by default. This behavior differs from legacy Exchange servers because transaction logs help you recover a failed Exchange server. Databases in Exchange 2000 can now share one common transaction log, and circular logging can be applied to one set of databases at a time.

- We see issues arising with respect to OWA in Exchange 2000. OWA was first used with Exchange Server 5 and used Active Server Pages (ASP) to render data from the IS. The current version of Exchange Server allows the Web Storage System to render and retrieve data. This means that you can no longer change the user interface by customizing any ASP files. This also implies that you may not be able to use an Exchange 2000 front-end (FE) OWA server with an Exchange 5.5 back-end (BE) server.

- Most of your Internet Protocol (IP) settings and configurations are carried over to Exchange 2000. However, the NNTP protocol connector is not upgraded, so you must manually create a new NNTP connector. Your NNTP content remains intact within the public folder hierarchy, however.

- Link monitors and server monitors remaining from an Exchange 5.5 server may have to be reconfigured after an upgrade. For a newly upgraded Exchange 5.5 server, no notifications exist, nor is there a default warning state. In any case, Microsoft recommends that you use legacy Exchange servers to monitor other legacy Exchange servers and that you use Exchange 2000 servers to monitor only Exchange 2000 servers. Incorrectly using these monitors may result in false alerts on your network.

- Message tracking is affected by an upgrade to Exchange 2000. Remember that Exchange 5.5 enabled message tracking in more than one location. However, Exchange 2000 turns on message tracking once for the entire server. This could lead to mixed results when you perform an upgrade. If message tracking is left on in any location in Exchange 5.5, it remains on for the entire server once you finish the upgrade.

- There are three methods you should consider when upgrading legacy machines to Exchange 2000 Server:

    - *Perform an in-place upgrade of your Exchange 5.5 servers.* This means upgrading the server as well as the databases on one computer.

    - *Install Exchange 2000 on new hardware in an existing Exchange 5.5 site and then migrate mailboxes and public folders to the new server.* This is known as an across-the-wire upgrade, and single-instance message storage is preserved in this scenario.

    - *Perform a leapfrog upgrade.* It's called a leapfrog upgrade because it allows you to reuse original hardware as the migration progresses throughout the organization. You first add one Exchange 2000 server to an existing Exchange 5.5 site and then migrate all 5.x mailboxes to the Exchange 2000 server. The 5.x server is then converted into an Exchange 2000 server and used to migrate mailboxes from another existing Exchange 5.x server. You repeat this process in leapfrog fashion until you have converted all servers in the organization to Exchange 2000 servers.

The Four Phases of Upgrading to Exchange 2000

This section discusses the phases you need to go through to upgrade an Exchange 5.5 server running SP3 to Exchange 2000. We are assuming here that the typical organization has been running Exchange 5.x (or earlier) on some form of Windows NT. Not all organizations have upgraded to Windows 2000, and many of them face a double-edged sword of learning both Windows 2000 and Exchange 2000. Because of the tight relationship between these two products, you cannot avoid this. Therefore, we present a quick overview of preparing a Windows 2000-based organization for the upgrade to Exchange 2000.

Before you can bring up the first Exchange 2000 server, you must prepare the forest, which is a three-step process:

1. Prepare the forest schema (using ForestPrep).
2. Configure the ADC.
3. Prepare all your domains (using DomainPrep).

Phase One: Preparing the Windows 2000 Forest

To prepare the forest, run Setup using the **/ForestPrep** switch. This prepares your AD schema for Exchange 2000. Perform the following steps only once for your Windows 2000 organization, no matter how many domains will exist in your AD forest:

1. Insert your Exchange 2000 Server CD-ROM and close the Autorun window when it appears.
2. Open a command prompt window by choosing Start | Programs | Accessories | Command Prompt.
3. Type "C:\cd E:" (or whatever your CD-ROM drive happens to be).
4. Type "E:\SETUP\I386>setup /Forestprep" (shown in Figure 16.1).
5. Click on Next when you see the Welcome To The Microsoft Exchange 2000 Installation Wizard screen.
6. Accept the End-User License Agreement (shown in Figure 16.2) and click on Next.

Note: When you run the setup.exe file on a normal basis, you use the Component Selection screen to select other installation options. However, when you use ForestPrep, you cannot change this selection.

Figure 16.1 The ForestPrep command-line option.

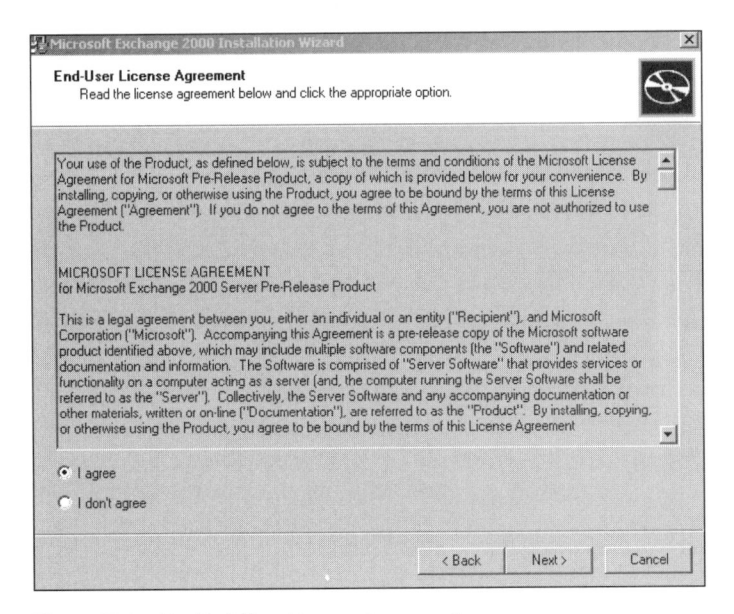

Figure 16.2 The End-User License Agreement screen.

7. The Product Identification screen, shown in Figure 16.3, appears. Here, you can enter your product ID number (found on the back of your installation CD-ROM). Click on Next to see the Component Selection screen, shown in Figure 16.4.

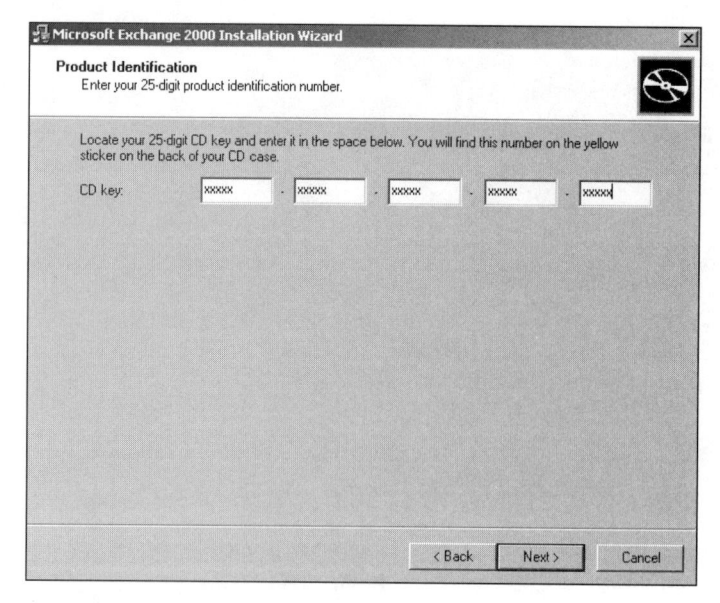

Figure 16.3 The Product Identification screen.

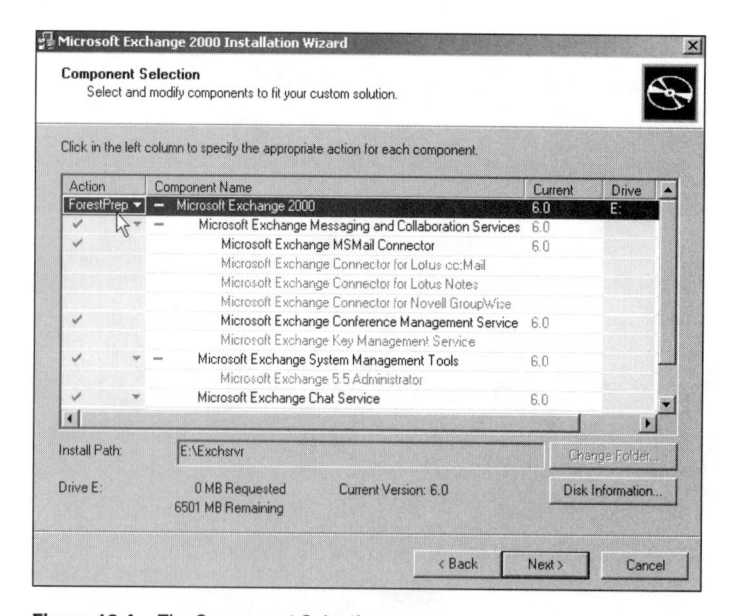

Figure 16.4 The Component Selection screen.

8. If you're satisfied with the default Install Path text box, click on Next.

9. On the Installation Type screen, shown in Figure 16.5, choose Join Or Upgrade An Existing Exchange 5.5 Organization, and then choose Next.

10. On the next screen, Select A Server In An Exchange 5.5 Organization, type the name of any Exchange 5.5 server. The setup program needs this name to get

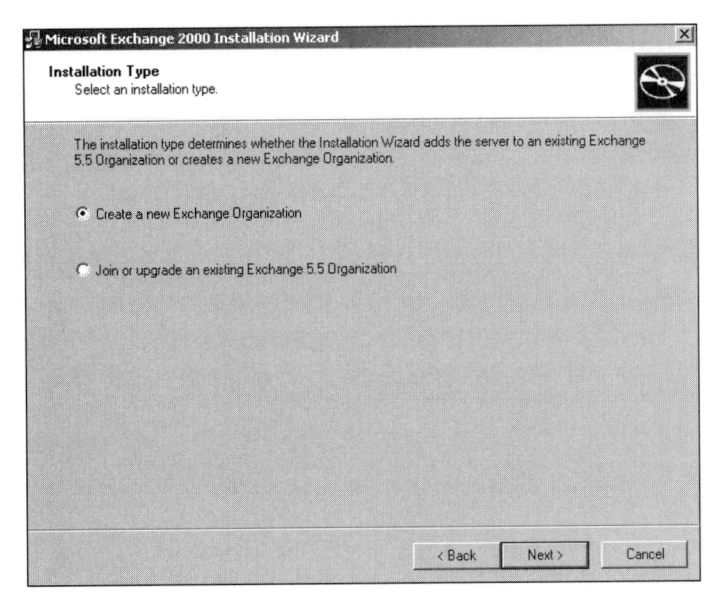

Figure 16.5 The Installation Type screen in ForestPrep.

information about your organization. Enter the name of a local server, and then choose Next.

11. ForestPrep now tries to determine if your logon account meets certain criteria and determines the name of your service account. Just click on OK to accept the information if it is correct.

12. You are now asked for a valid Windows 2000 account, which is either a brand new account or an already existing one. You will use this to administer your Exchange 2000 organization. Select Next when finished.

13. The Service Account screen then prompts you for the password for your Exchange 5.5 service account. Click on Next when finished.

14. Now, you should see the Component Progress screen. It tracks every step in the update process. Here, the schema modifications are completed and setup modifies your Registry.

Warning: The setup.exe program is modifying 10 schema update files in Step 14. If you see a red X where a green checkmark should be, the installation process has failed and you must run the ForestPrep program all over again.

15. The final screen for ForestPrep is Completing The Microsoft Exchange 2000 Wizard. Click on Finish as instructed.

Phase Two: Installing the ADC

Exchange 2000 provides the ADC knowing that organizations will eventually migrate to Exchange 2000 Server over time. The ADC replicates directory information between Exchange 2000 and legacy Exchange 5.5 sites. It consists of a replication engine and is the key to replicating an Exchange 5.5 directory with AD. Always keep in mind the tight integration with AD, which helps you realize high levels of performance by making directory administration easier. You should keep the following points in mind as you go through the steps for this phase:

➤ Installing the ADC requires several Windows 2000 permissions, including Schema Admins, Enterprise Admins, and Domain Administration.

➤ Install the ADC in every domain in your organization.

➤ You can use a separate Windows 2000 account as your service account for an ADC.

Follow these steps to install ADC:

1. Insert your installation CD-ROM for Exchange 2000 into the server on which you want to install the ADC.

2. Browse the CD-ROM and select the ADC directory. Then run setup.exe.

3. You will see the Welcome To The Active Directory Connector Installation Wizard screen. Click on Next.

4. Select Microsoft Active Directory Connector Service Component on the Component Selection screen. You can choose both the ADC and its administrative components here if you desire.

5. Choose the default location for your files on the Install Location screen, shown in Figure 16.6, or click on Browse to select another directory location.

6. On the Service Account screen, shown in Figure 16.7, you can enter the account name and password that you want the ADC to use during normal operations. If your normal logon account is acceptable, choose Next; otherwise, choose Browse and select an alternate account as your ADC service account.

7. The setup.exe program now starts copying files from your installation CD-ROM onto your hard drive. During this step, 10 files of schema updates (which should ideally be run on a DC or GC server that represents your schema master) are installed. Note that these updates are done only the very first time you install the ADC. Registry changes are also made at this time.

8. You have now successfully completed the Active Directory Connector Installation Wizard. The ADC has been installed and is now ready to be configured. Click on Finish as instructed.

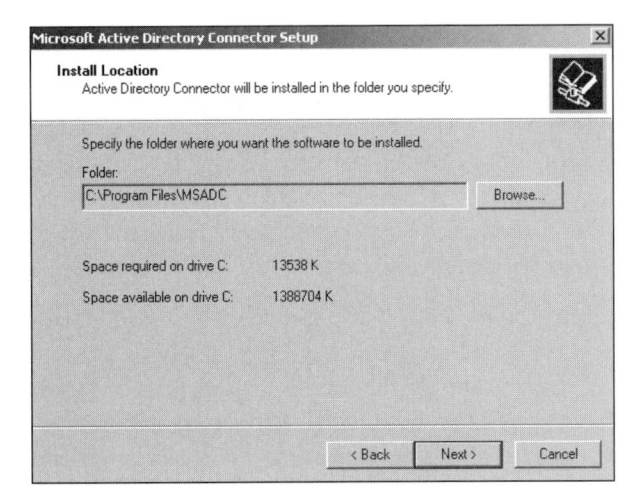

Figure 16.6 The Install Location screen for the ADC.

Figure 16.7 The Service Account screen for the ADC.

Note: *One instance of the ADC can actually be used to define multiple connection agreements, and each separate agreement can go from AD to a different Exchange 5.5 site. The connection agreements can even go to the same Exchange site.*

Configuring Connection Agreements

The steps you just completed to install the ADC defined only a particular service within Windows 2000 and AD. You have not yet defined a relationship between your Exchange sites and AD; therefore, you must configure connection agreements. Here are some relevant facts regarding connection agreements that you must know before configuring them:

- A connection agreement defines items such as the directories being synchronized, the direction of synchronization (one-way or two-way), the method of deleting directory objects, and the authentication of directories.

- You can view two types of connection agreements using ADC: *user agreements*, which replicate recipient objects and their data, and *configuration agreements*, which replicate configuration information specific to Exchange. Only user agreements can be created with the ADC.

- You create a single recipient agreement that populates AD with Exchange 5.5 directory information when ADC is configured for relatively small, single-site organizations. If you are using multiple sites and AD domains, you need multiple agreements between AD and Exchange 5.5 organizations. This happens because an Exchange 5.5 site is responsible only for its own directory information, not that of other sites.

You configure connection agreements using the ADC MMC snap-in tool. Simply right-click on the ADC icon and choose New | Recipient Connection Agreement. This allows recipient information to be transported between Exchange 5.5 and AD.

Figure 16.8 shows the resulting Properties sheets of a new connection agreement ready to be configured:

- *General*—This allows you to select a name for the connection agreement, as well as the direction for replication. Choosing the Two-Way or From Windows To Exchange radio button may result in a warning similar to what is shown in

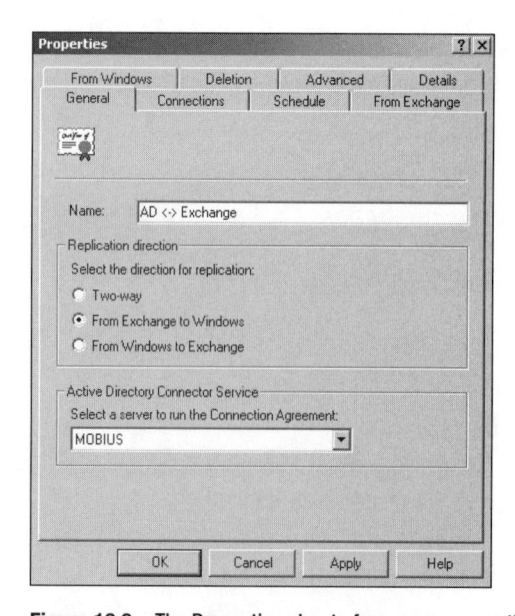

Figure 16.8 The Properties sheets for a new connection agreement.

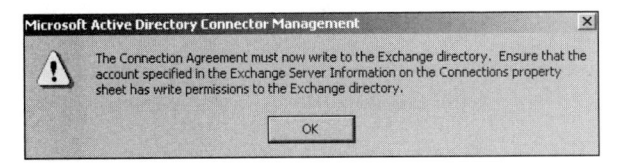

Figure 16.9 The warning displayed when you choose Two-Way or From Windows To Exchange using the ADC MMC snap-in.

Figure 16.9. Notice that From Exchange To Windows is the default choice and does not result in the warning.

- *Connections*—This specifies an account (such as your Exchange 5.5 service account) that has the permission to modify items in the Exchange directory.

- *Schedule*—This allows you to select the time settings for replications. You can even force a replication by selecting the Replicate The Entire Directory The Next Time The Agreement Is Run checkbox.

- *From Exchange*—This allows you to select which Exchange recipient containers will be replicated into AD. You can choose root containers or just subcontainers, but you must make sure that proper permissions have been assigned on the Connections tab.

- *From Windows*—Use this tab only if you are configuring two-way replication, meaning that your connection agreement is capable of both pulling object information from any Exchange 5.5 site and also writing information back to an Exchange 5.5 directory. Using two-way connection agreements in conjunction with directory replication connectors between Exchange 5.5 sites can sometimes produce the undesirable effect of infinite circular replication, known more precisely as *directory triangulation*. To prevent this effect from occurring, most connection agreements interact with resources in only one Exchange 5.5 site at any given time.

- *Deletion*—This allows you to decide if you want your ADC to delete entries in one directory if it finds deletions in the other directory. For example, if you were to delete a user account in Windows 2000, you may also want the Exchange mailbox or custom recipient to be deleted at the same time.

- *Advanced*—This allows you to determine if a connection agreement will be primary. If it is, it will replicate information about Exchange 5.5 objects as well as create new objects if necessary. An agreement that replicates information about objects only is known as a *nonprimary connection agreement*.

- *Details*—This shows administrative details such as the creation date of the connection agreement, the last modification date, and the last synchronization date from both Windows and Exchange.

Phase Three: Preparing Your Windows 2000 Domains

You must establish a Windows 2000 AD domain once for every Windows 2000 domain that will host your user accounts or Exchange server. It is recommended that you perform these steps on all AD domains in your organization. You will be using the DomainPrep tool to prepare your domains. You can access it from the command prompt by typing the following code (where *d* represents your CD-ROM drive letter):

```
C: cd d:
D:>\setup\i386\setup /DomainPrep
```

Warning: Be careful when you type this syntax from your command prompt. Even though **DomainPrep** is not case sensitive, it has to be spelled correctly; otherwise, the setup.exe program will run by itself without invoking the DomainPrep functions.

The steps that you take (and the screens that you see) during the configuration are very similar to those of Phase One, except that the Component Selection screen shows DomainPrep, not ForestPrep (see Figure 16.10). You should not be able to change anything on this screen except the folder where Exchange will be installed. Note that during this process, DomainPrep is creating Windows 2000 groups to host both Exchange administrators and Exchange servers. After this component installation is finished, you will be ready to upgrade your Exchange 5.5 servers.

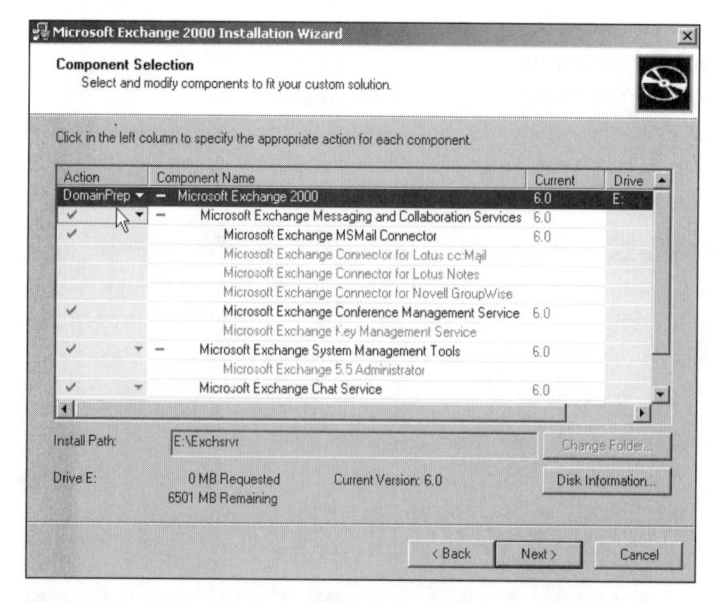

Figure 16.10 The Component Selection screen for DomainPrep.

Phase Four: Performing the In-Place Upgrade of Exchange Server 5.5

The previous phases have dealt with preparing our environment for the actual upgrade to Exchange 2000 Server. We have not really mentioned the concepts of coexistence between Exchange 2000 and Exchange 5.5 in a mixed-mode setting. Our focus remains on upgrading Exchange 5.5 and earlier servers to Exchange 2000 Server. You should also be concerned with diagnosing problems arising from planned upgrades, as well as verifying that all steps in the upgrade process have been completed or dealing with post-upgrade issues. We will cover these issues later in this chapter as well.

One main caveat we can offer here concerning an upgrade to Exchange 2000 is that there is no upgrade path from any version of Exchange *other* than Exchange Server 5.5 running SP3. When performing a basic upgrade to Exchange 2000, recall that you need Exchange 2000 Full Administrator permissions at the Exchange 2000 organizational level as well as Permissions Administrator rights on the site that your server is in. You also need Local Administrator rights to your server. To prepare for this upgrade process, you should probably perform steps that will help you to roll back to your original configuration if you encounter problems after the upgrade.

Rollback Procedures

To prepare for an upgrade, you should perform the following steps so that you can roll back to a working configuration if your planned upgrade does not work for any reason:

1. On your Exchange 5.5 server running SP3 and Windows 2000, open the Computer Management MMC snap-in and expand the Services and Applications directory, shown in Figure 16.11.

2. Select Services, and then select the Microsoft Exchange Message Transfer Agent service in the right-hand pane.

3. Stop the MTA service by right-clicking on the Message Transfer Agent service and selecting Stop. When the service completely stops, you can continue with the next step.

4. Open the Registry Editor by accessing Start|Run and then typing "regedit". Then, click on OK.

5. Look for the HKEY_LOCAL_MACHINE\SYSTEM\CurrentControlSet\Services\MSExchangeMTA\Parameters\MTA database path Registry key. You are trying to confirm the correct path to the \MTADATA directory.

6. Open Windows Explorer and navigate to the \MTADATA directory. You want to back up all your db*.dat files and write down the total original size of this directory. It is important you do not delete these files!

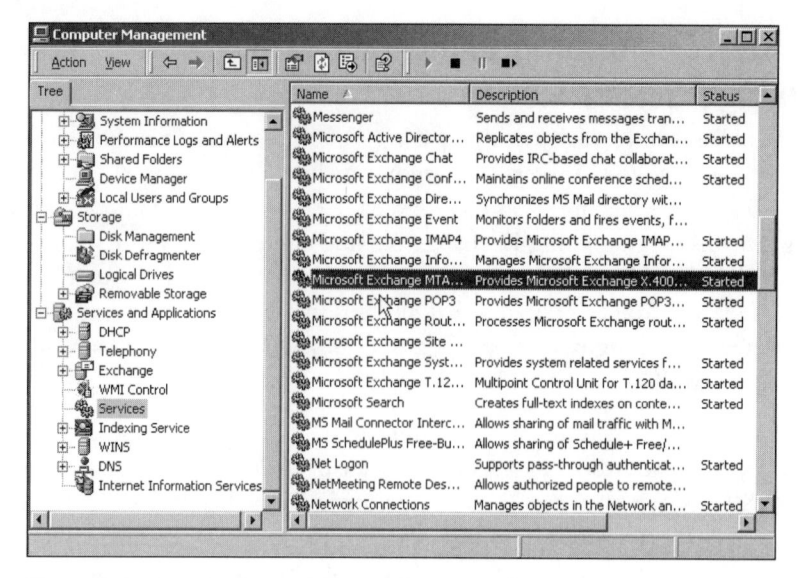

Figure 16.11 The Services And Applications section of the Computer Management MMC snap-in.

7. Go to the \Exchsrvr\Bin directory on your hard drive (usually on the C: partition) and run mtacheck.exe. This program should not detect any errors. If it does, immediately delete *all files* in the \MTADATA\Mtacheck.out directory and run the program again. You will know if the program is successful if you see the "Database clean, no errors detected" message.

8. Now restart the MTA service using the Computer Management snap-in tool.

If the MTA program is successful, you should now perform a knowledge consistency check on your Exchange 5.5 machine running SP3. Follow these steps:

1. Start the Exchange 5.5 Administrator program and find your server object. Under this object, select the Directory Service object.

2. Click on the File menu and choose Properties, or right-click on the Directory Service object and choose Properties.

3. Click on the Check Now button. When the program finishes, click on OK.

If you experience problems running the Knowledge Consistency Checker (KCC), you need to perform a DS/IS consistency adjustment. Follow these steps to do so:

1. Using the Exchange 5.5 Administrator tool, select your server object under the Configuration | Servers folder. Right-click on the object and choose Properties.

2. When the Properties sheets open up, select the Advanced tab and then click on Consistency Adjuster.

3. The DS/IS Consistency Adjustment screen appears. Click on All Inconsistencies and then on OK.

4. If you see a Warning page, simply click on OK. When all the adjustments are completed, click on OK to close the Properties sheet for your server object.

Performing the Upgrade

You are now ready to do the actual upgrade. Remember that the server being upgraded must be running Exchange 5.5 SP3, because there is no other upgrade path from other versions of Exchange. Also, this server must be on a Windows 2000 Server or Advanced Server machine running SP1. You should have access to two different accounts: an Exchange 5.5 Service Account and an Exchange 2000 account with Full Administrator rights and Local Administrator rights on the server being upgraded. Perform the following steps:

1. Place your Exchange 2000 CD-ROM in the CD-ROM tray and let the initial program screen appear.

2. Read the welcome screen, click on Next, read the End-User License Agreement, and then click on Next.

3. Enter your 25-digit CD-ROM key on the Product Identification screen and click on Next.

4. You will now see the Component Selection screen. It shows items that are preselected as Upgrade options if these items were installed on your Exchange 5.5 server. You cannot change the Upgrade states of these items. Simply choose Next to accept the default installation directory.

5. Type your Exchange Server 5.5 service account password on the next screen and then click on Next.

6. View the Component Summary screen to see if all selections have been properly made and click on Next to accept the default installation folder.

7. The Component Progress screen shows three phases during the upgrade process: Preinstallation progress, Installation progress, and Post-Installation progress. This means the upgrade process is performing several different functions on the items that are upgraded. You can view details on these steps by visiting the Exchange_Server_Setup_Progress.log file in the root drive of the machine that is being upgraded.

Note: *You may notice a new connection agreement called ConfigCA created in the ADC MMC snap-in after your upgrade has been completed. This occurs if the server you are using is the first server that has been upgraded. It also occurs if this server has hosted any Exchange 5.5 site directory replication connectors. The purpose of ConfigCA is to replicate Exchange 5.5 configuration information to AD, or Exchange 2000 configuration information from AD to an Exchange 5.5 directory.*

Post-Upgrade Procedures

This section describes actions you can take after a planned upgrade to Exchange 2000 Server. Any upgrade plan can have one of two results: success or failure. You can perform certain procedures to verify if your plan was successful. You will have to perform certain procedures if your planned upgrade fails for any reason. Before undertaking any planned upgrades, we recommend always having a "failover" plan (backup plan) close by, so that you can bring your organization back to working conditions that existed before the upgrade took place. Preparing for a worst-case scenario can save both time and money. This means backing up both your Exchange 2000 and Windows 2000 system data on reliable media and storing that data both on site (for fastest recovery in case of failure) and in a secure off-site location. Most organizations do this before starting their upgrade process. In any case, an upgrade is truly complete only when full backups are present.

Checking If the Upgrade Was Successful

If you want to know that the upgrade process has succeeded, you can verify that the Component Progress screen on the Exchange upgrade program did not display any errors (discussed in Step 7 of the upgrade procedure). You can also view the application or system logs for any error or warning messages related to the Exchange 2000 services. Finally, you can try to mailbox-enable a user account in AD and then connect to the Exchange server using a Messaging Application Programming Interface (MAPI) client to access this user's mailbox. You do this to confirm whether or not you can send or receive mail without errors.

Recovering an Exchange 5.5 Server after a Failed Upgrade

The steps we have outlined for performing an upgrade naturally cannot guarantee a trouble-free upgrade. In real-life environments, problems can—and will—occur. It's important to know how to recover an Exchange 5.5 server after a failed upgrade to Exchange 2000. This is why we recommend superior planning and documentation of all upgrade procedures. You have to know the full consequences of introducing Exchange 2000, especially in an existing Exchange 5.5 site. If part of your design includes moving public folders or mailboxes over to Exchange 2000, you have to know why you want to implement this procedure and what risks you may be subject to. Many companies that implement Exchange 2000 want to move their public folders to this new platform to take advantage of the enhanced features that it offers, such as the Web Storage System, Storage Groups, or multiple public folder databases. Moving public folders from Exchange 5.5 computers to Exchange 2000 computers is one step toward ultimately removing your Exchange 5.5 hierarchy. After you do this, you can convert your organization to native mode (discussed later in this chapter) so that you experience all the advanced features of Exchange 2000 Server. If you are executing a consolidation plan, you can move all mailboxes and public folders from multiple servers running Exchange 5.5 (or earlier) to one Exchange 2000 computer. Or, you can perform a one-to-one mapping of mailboxes and public folder databases, one server at a time.

There are three upgrade failure scenarios you should be aware of:

- You want to recover a server that is not the first Exchange 2000 server on your site.

- You want to recover the first server you tried to upgrade on your Exchange 5.5 site, and you would like to restore it back to an Exchange 5.5 server.

- You want to recover the first server you tried to upgrade on your Exchange 5.5 site, and you would like to upgrade it to Exchange 2000 again.

The first two scenarios require you to use LDAP to delete your configuration connection agreement. You would have to employ an LDAP viewer (such as that provided with Microsoft Windows—known as LDP, or ldp.exe) to modify the following attributes of your server (the new values of these attributes are given in the steps that follow):

- **versionNumber**
- **serialNumber**
- **Administrative mode**

The steps required to use LDP are:

1. Type "ldp" in the Start|Run box and then click on OK to open your LDAP viewer.

2. Find the configuration container labeled CN=Configuration and expand this container.

3. Expand the Services container (CN=Services), the Microsoft Exchange container (CN=Microsoft Exchange), and the Active Directory Connections container (CN=Active Directory Connections).

4. Locate the configuration connection agreement for the server that you want to recover (CN=ConfigCA). Right-click on the container and then on Delete.

5. Find the configuration container (CN=Configuration) once again, and expand it. Then expand the following containers:

    - Services container (CN=Services)
    - Microsoft Exchange container (CN=Microsoft Exchange)
    - Exchange organization container (CN=name)
    - Administrative Groups container (CN=Administrative Groups)

6. Right-click on the Administrative Group to which your server belongs. You will see CN=<Administrative group name>. Click on Modify.

7. In Edit Entry Attribute, type "MSExchangeAdminGroupMode". In the Values field, type "0" to change from native mode to mixed mode, and then click on Replace.

8. Verify this entry in the Entry List, and then click on Enter to confirm your selection.

9. Find the Servers container (CN=Servers) and right-click on the name of your server using CN=<server name>. Then, click on Modify.

10. In Edit Entry Attribute, type "versionnumber". Change the value by typing "2650", and then click on Replace.

11. Confirm this entry in the dialog box that appears, and then click on Enter.

12. In Edit Entry Attribute, type "serialnumber", and then type "version 5.5 (Build 2650.24: Service Pack *x*)" in the Values field, where *x* represents the Exchange Server SP you are currently using.

13. Click on Replace to change the value of your serial number.

14. Confirm these entries in the dialog box that appears, and then click on Enter.

Before running the setup program again to rebuild your Exchange 5.5 server, make sure all references to Exchange 2000 are removed from the Registry. Use either regedit or regedt32 to modify the Registry, but remember that incorrectly using the Windows Registry can lead to disastrous consequences.

Removing Exchange 2000

Warning: The following steps should be undertaken with *extreme* caution. Attempts to restore an existing Exchange 5.5 computer can be prone to failure and is something that should be done only with the assistance of Microsoft Technical Support. It is very easy to miss a step or perform steps out of order. We include this information only to prepare users for a worst-case scenario, and we never urge users to attempt these procedures without having some form of outside assistance available!

In rebuilding an Exchange 5.5 server after a failed upgrade to Exchange 2000 Server, you must remove any references to Exchange 2000 that may reside within your computer's Registry database. Your Exchange product documentation should be able to guide you in the art of restoring your former server; however, the procedures are not always straightforward. You would begin by manually removing Exchange 2000 from your computer. The necessary steps are:

1. Open the Registry Editor by choosing Start|Run and then typing "regedit".

2. Navigate to the HKEY_LOCAL_MACHINE\CurrentControlSet\Services Registry key and remove all keys relating to Exchange 2000 services and drivers from the Registry. These include:

    - DAVEX
    - ESE97
    - ESE98
    - EXIFS
    - EXIPC
    - EXOLEDB
    - IMAP4Svc
    - MSSEARCH
    - POP3Svc
    - RESvc
    - Anything resembling LME or MSExchange

3. Remove the Exchange Setup key from the HKEY_LOCAL_MACHINE\Software\Microsoft\Exchange Registry key and rename the Exchsrvr folders on every drive in your computer.

4. Remove all instances of IIS completely and restart your server. Then, delete the Exchsrvr folders you renamed in Step 3.

5. Using the Exchange Server 5.5 installation CD-ROM, run **setup /r**, and choose the same installation choices that were on the original server. Create a new site with the same organizational name and site name as before.

6. When the setup program completes, run Performance Optimizer and configure the file locations to the same place that your files were located before the failed upgrade.

7. Using the appropriate Exchange Server 5.5 service pack CD-ROM, run **update /r**, and install any post-service pack hot fixes that were previously on the server.

8. Restore all your DS and IS data from a previous backup (you should always back up this data ahead of time for emergency purposes such as this one!) and restart your DS and IS services. You may also want to force directory replication within your original site.

Living in Harmony with Legacy Exchange

Microsoft Exchange 2000 Server is architecturally different from any prior version due to its integration with AD. Many companies want to migrate from Exchange 5.5 Server to Exchange 2000 Server, but this brings up some interoperability concerns. To make the transition process smoother, Microsoft has created a couple of services, such as enhanced connectors, that make coexistence with legacy Exchange servers very reasonable. They provide flexibility that was not really possible in earlier versions of Exchange Server. Knowing how these tools can assist you will help make the migration process as smooth as it can be for your organization.

In this section, the term *coexistence* describes a configuration in which different versions of Exchange Server are installed in the same Exchange organization simultaneously. This setup is more commonly known as a *mixed-mode* configuration. Running Exchange 2000 Server in mixed mode means that it can interoperate with all prior versions of Exchange and tolerate the differences among the various versions. When your system is running in mixed mode, any rules that applied to previous versions of Exchange Server also apply to Exchange 2000 Server. Even after you install Exchange 2000 Server, you can still install additional Exchange 5.x servers into your organization if you desire.

The issue of coexistence between Exchange 5.5 and Exchange 2000 Server has other important implications. For example, it helps an organization slowly *decommission* existing Exchange 5.5 servers while it slowly migrates to a complete Exchange 2000 environment. After a successful installation of Exchange 2000 Server, an organization may want to move mailboxes from servers running Exchange Server 5.5. This allows them to take advantage of new features offered by Exchange 2000, such as the Web Storage System and multiple mailbox stores. Some companies will decide not to move mailboxes onto all of the Exchange 2000 computers in their organization. For example, they may want an Exchange 2000 computer to act as a bridgehead server in a multiserver location, or as a front-end computer in a FE/BE configuration.

Coexistence is not something that should be taken for granted. There are specific tools that will be provided to make coexistence a reality for any organization. The two main tools we discuss in this section include the Site Replication Service and the Active Directory Connector. It is very important that you understand the implications of using these services because they both have very specific functions. Their intent is to help maintain two different directories simultaneously so that directory information seems transparent to end users. For example, the Site Replication Service (SRS) can take the Active Directory version of your Exchange 2000 directory and turn this into an Exchange 5.5 site. Exchange 2000 servers will suddenly resemble Exchange 5.5 servers. This is the essence of coexistence and interoperability. The ADC is used to replicate directory information between

Exchange 5.5 and Exchange 2000. Another tool that proves useful in coexistence strategies is the Move Mailbox utility. We will provide more details on these tools in the subsections that follow.

Using Site Replication Service (SRS)

Installing Exchange 2000 into an existing Exchange 5.5 site means that your existing Exchange 5.5 organizational name is replicated over to AD, and AD uses this as your Exchange 2000 organizational name. If you do not join an existing site when you first install Exchange 2000, you are forced to choose a brand new organizational name. This implies that you could potentially have two different organizational names running for the same company! Even worse, your Exchange 5.5 organization will view your Exchange 2000 organization as a foreign mail system. This means that you must use a connector (discussed later in this chapter) to transfer messages between your two organizations. You will know if you are running a mixed-mode operation if you see two new services being installed (mixed mode is also discussed later in this chapter). When the first Exchange 2000 server is installed into an existing Exchange 5.x organization, the SRS and ADC services are installed automatically. (ADC is covered in the next section.) These two components work together to provide replication between Exchange 5.x servers and Exchange 2000 servers. A connection agreement is automatically established in the ADC service between AD and the SRS database so that directory replication can occur. SRS allows the Exchange 5.5 directory to coexist with the configuration-naming partition of AD, whereas the ADC allows replication between the Exchange 5.5 directory and the domain-naming partition of AD. It is very important to keep these differences in mind.

Note: Remember that AD has three naming partitions: the configuration-naming partition, which defines your organization's connectors and protocols; the domain-naming partition, which contains all objects in AD for a domain; and the schema-naming partition, which contains all object types and their attributes. In this section, we are looking only at the first two naming partitions.

The following are relevant points to remember regarding SRS:

➤ SRS consists of an application known as srsmain.exe and a database known as srs.edb. It also contains transaction logs in Extensible Storage Engine (ESE) format. It installs the same set of databases as a Storage Group, which you can find by default in the \Exchsrvr\srsdata folder. However, unlike a Storage Group, the SRS database cannot be mounted or dismounted. You have to start and stop this service using the Services utility. SRS has its own Consistency Checker that runs as part of the srs.exe executable file.

➤ SRS services are disabled by default when you have more than one Exchange 2000 server installed into an existing Exchange 5.5 site.

- SRS uses port 379 for LDAP so that it can communicate with AD.
- SRS installs its own read-only connection agreement called ConfigCA. This agreement is for two-way communication between SRS and AD, *not between* AD and the Exchange 5.5 directory.

Using the ADC Service

To completely understand how Exchange 2000 can coexist with Exchange 5.x or earlier servers, you have to thoroughly appreciate the purpose and functions of SRS and the ADC. The ADC acts as a complement to SRS. Relevant points to consider about the ADC are:

- The ADC runs on a Windows 2000 DC and synchronizes the Exchange Server 5.5 directory with the Windows 2000 directory. Unlike the SRS, the ADC replicates information between the Exchange 5.x directory and the domain-naming partition in AD.
- The ADC actually comes in two versions: one that comes with Windows 2000 and one that comes with Exchange 2000 Server. The Windows 2000 version allows you to copy directory information in an Exchange 5.5 site over to the Windows 2000 AD. The Exchange 2000 version also lets you synchronize directory information with Windows 2000, but it primarily works with SRS. Installing Exchange 2000 Server automatically updates the Windows 2000 ADC to the Exchange Server version.
- You synchronize directories by defining connection agreements. The ADC manages these connection agreements. At least one of these has to be a *primary* connection agreement, with the rest being *nonprimary* connection agreements. A primary agreement tries to create new objects in a target directory when synchronizing objects from one directory to another. A nonprimary agreement does not create new objects in the Exchange 5.5 directory. Instead, it replicates attributes between an Exchange 5.5 mailbox and its corresponding Windows 2000 object. These connection agreements usually contain information such as server names, objects to be synchronized, and a synchronization time schedule. Remember to define the direction of replication by specifying either one-way or two-way connection agreements.
- If you are working with a single Exchange 5.5 site, you need only one connection agreement to duplicate the same Exchange 5.5 container structure in AD.

The Move Mailbox Utility

As stated before, some administrators introduce an Exchange 2000 Server into an existing Exchange 5.5 site for the sole purpose of decommissioning their Exchange 5.5 servers. With the new server in place, the goal now becomes to move mailboxes or public folders over to the new server. Before the administrators can complete this process, they need to have an Exchange 2000 server installed in the same Exchange site in which their current mailbox servers or public folder servers are installed. When executing this consolidation plan, they can move both mailboxes and public folders from multiple servers running Exchange 5.5 to a single Exchange 2000 computer, or they can perform a straight one-to-one mapping from server to server. Although mailboxes and public folders are similar, they have slightly different prerequisites.

The account you use to perform the migration process for mailbox stores or public folder stores must have Exchange Administrator privileges in the Exchange 2000 Administrative Group in which the Exchange 2000 computer is installed. You would also need Exchange Administrator rights in the Exchange 5.5 site that contains the mailboxes or public folders to be moved. To move mailboxes between Exchange 5.5 and Exchange 2000, you must use a workstation or server on which the Exchange 2000 management tool is installed. The tool you will use is the Windows 2000 Active Directory Users and Computers MMC snap-in, which can be installed from the Exchange 2000 Server installation CD. If you need to reinstall the management tools, simply run Setup from the Exchange 2000 Server installation CD and select a custom installation. On the Component Selection page, you would choose to install only the Exchange 2000 management tools.

Before moving mailboxes or redirecting public folders, you need to perform a full backup of your system. This ensures that if the worst occurs, you are able to recover your data. It is also helpful to disable any antivirus program you have running on your computer before performing the actual backup. Certain antivirus programs can cause errors with the Move Mailbox utility. An antivirus package will scan any attachments in the information store that have not been previously scanned before releasing them to the Move Mailbox utility. Move Mailbox will not recognize this condition of "being scanned" and will respond with an error or will terminate the Move Mailbox operation.

Note: *Although Microsoft has produced a fix for this "being scanned" condition, the best workaround is to disable all antivirus packages before you use the Move Mailbox utility. Please refer to the Knowledge Base article found at* **http://support.microsoft.com/support/kb/articles/q271/5/47.asp** *for further information regarding the Move Mailbox Utility and the Antivirus API.*

Regardless of whether you get an error message, before proceeding with this upgrade process, you should perform backups of both the sending and receiving Exchange computers. This is because of the risk (although it's a very small risk) that there might be a disk failure *after* you have moved the mailboxes, but *before* you have completed the second backup. You move the mailbox between Exchange computers by using the Windows 2000 Active Directory Users and Computers snap-in. When you move mailboxes between servers, the following process takes place:

1. A connection is made to both servers. If the connection attempt fails, the move operation fails.

2. Assuming that the connection is good, messages are then copied from one server to the other. If at any point during this process a problem occurs, the process fails, and any data that has already been copied is deleted.

3. After the messages are copied, the directory service is updated to reflect the new location of the mailbox (in this case, both the Windows 2000 Active Directory and the Exchange 5.5 server directory). If this fails in any way, the new data is deleted and the system reverts to the old location.

4. After the mail has been successfully moved, the mail is deleted from the old server. The chance that the process would get this far and fail is extremely small. If the migration makes it to this point, you can consider the operation to be a success.

Warning: You cannot perform the move mailbox procedure using the **Move Mailbox** command in Exchange 5.5 Administrator. If you try to do so, you will receive a message saying that there has been an internal processing error. Your only remedy would be to restart the Exchange Administrator program or the server (or both).

You want to ensure that users are not logged on during the Move Mailbox operation to prevent any permissions problems when moving mailboxes. You can check the Private Store object in the Exchange 5.5 Administrator program to see if any users are currently logged on. After all users are logged off, close down their clients so that they will be able to log off from Exchange cleanly. An example of using the Move Mailbox utility can be found in Project 16.1 of the "Real-World Projects" section at the end of this chapter.

Mixed Mode vs. Native Mode

Both Windows 2000 and Exchange 2000 use the concepts of mixed mode and native mode. Although they are somewhat similar, you should know the differences. The default operation for Windows 2000 Server is mixed mode. This refers to a domain that has a structure similar to that of a Windows NT 4 domain. Mixed-mode designs can be useful for interoperability purposes, but they can bring some disadvantages as well, including:

➤ As in Windows NT 4, you are limited in the number of objects that can exist in your directory.

➤ You are prevented from adding user objects to a new group you want to create.

➤ You are not allowed to change an existing domain local group to a universal group within Windows 2000.

➤ Any existing Exchange 5.5 site is seen as an Administrative Group in Exchange 2000.

➤ You may be limited by which Routing Group a server can be placed into. This is because the Administrative Group associated with a particular server defines Routing Groups.

A good rule of thumb to follow for mixed-mode operations is to have every Exchange 2000 Administrative Group contain at least one Routing Group with an Exchange 2000 server.

Warning: The concept of mixed mode is further complicated by the concept of mixed management. You implement a mixed management model when your organization consists of *only* Exchange 2000 servers. You then create Administrative Groups to manage different functions. For example, one group can handle routing functions, whereas other groups can manage server and recipient policies. Be careful not to confuse these terms on the exam.

Switching to a native-mode design in Windows 2000 allows you to reap the full benefits of an AD domain but requires you to upgrade all legacy DCs to Windows 2000. The advantage of native-mode Windows 2000 over mixed mode is scalability, meaning you are not constrained by the limitations of the Security Accounts Manager (SAM) database inherent in a Windows NT 4 system and its 40,000-object ceiling.

Note: A native-mode Windows 2000 domain cannot include any Windows NT 4 DCs, but it can contain a Windows NT 4 member server. Native-mode designs actually make the Exchange 2000 installation process a lot easier to manage than mixed-mode designs, because it is easier to work with group creation.

Applying the concepts of mixed or native mode operations to Exchange 2000 Server brings us slightly different results compared to Windows 2000 Server. A mixed-mode Exchange configuration simply means that you have compatibility with previous versions of Exchange server. In fact, a native-mode Windows 2000 domain can contain a mixed-mode Exchange server design! Every Exchange organization object in AD has the **msExchMixedMode** attribute. When you install the first Exchange 2000 server into an existing Exchange 5.5 site, this attribute has a value of **True** and forces Exchange 2000 to operate in mixed mode.

Mixed-mode designs can be useful for interoperability purposes, but they can bring some disadvantages as well. For example, any existing Exchange 5.5 site will be seen as an "Administrative Group" in Exchange 2000. Also, you may be limited by which routing group a server can be placed into. This is because the Administrative Group that is associated with a particular server defines Routing Groups. A good rule of thumb to follow for mixed-mode operations is to have every Exchange 2000 Administrative Group contain at least one Routing Group with an Exchange 2000 server.

The following example may help to clarify these points. You have two Administrative Groups called AG1 and AG2. AG1 has two Routing Groups within it called RG1 and RG2. AG2 has two Routing Groups within it called RG3 and RG4. If you assign a server named Orion to RG1 in AG1, it cannot be a member of RG3 or RG4 because they are associated with a totally different Administrative Group. You cannot assign a server to a Routing Group that is associated with a different Administrative Group than the Administrative Group of which the server is a member. This is a very important concept to grasp regarding mixed-mode configurations.

Issues Regarding Mixed-Mode Environments

Sometimes, you cannot avoid using a mixed-mode environment. Although we recommend that organizations use native mode to obtain flexibility with Routing Groups and Administrative Groups, you may be forced to work with legacy Exchange servers in some situations. For instance, your organization may have acquired another company that continues to work with Exchange 5.x servers and has no need to upgrade to Exchange 2000 Server. Or you may be working with Exchange 5.x directory replication bridgehead servers that will continue to function within your new environment. In any case, you will face some nontrivial issues when working with mixed-mode design implementations. They include:

▶ *Routing masters*—Every Exchange 5.x site has a *routing master*, which is the first Exchange 5.5 server in a site. This server maintains the Gateway Address Routing Table (GWART), a list of all the address space information for all connectors within a site. Introducing an Exchange 2000 server forces an administrator to select which server will function as the routing master. If an existing Exchange 5.5 router server is upgraded to Exchange 2000, the choice becomes easy. However, if there are more Exchange 5.5 servers and connectors than Exchange 2000 servers and connectors, it is best to leave an Exchange 5.5 server as the routing master. The GWART replicates to AD in a mixed-mode Administrative Group, and routing masters monitor this object.

Note: *You can visit the Microsoft Web site at* **http://support.microsoft.com/directory/** *and query Article ID Q235396 for information regarding routing masters used for legacy Exchange servers.*

▶ *Offline address books*—There is now no synchronization of offline address books between legacy Exchange servers and Exchange 2000 servers. Exchange 2000 generates an offline address book from AD. Recall that offline address books contained lists of recipients to whom a remote user could address a message. Remote users would download offline address books and use them to send mail to other recipients in an organization. Exchange 2000 has a default offline address list that is compatible with Exchange 4 and 5 servers, but you have to enable this manually. When this address list is enabled, Exchange 2000 supports a Microsoft Outlook client that connects to an offline address book on the Exchange 2000 server.

- *Public folder replication*—You can replicate individual public folders between Exchange 5.5 and Exchange 2000, and clients can access replicas on either system. There is actually very little difference between public folders in these two systems. You can replicate both the public folder hierarchy and the public folder data between any versions of Exchange. However, remember that Exchange 2000 supports multiple public folder trees, whereas Exchange 5.5 has one tree. Also, Exchange 2000 has a default public folder tree called Public Folders, which MAPI clients such as Microsoft Outlook can see. However, these MAPI clients do not see any other public folder trees you create. Also, you may not duplicate permissions to public folders set in Exchange 2000 within Exchange 5.5.

- *Populating AD before migrating to Windows 2000 Server*—Consider an organization that wants to upgrade an existing Exchange 5.5 installation to Exchange 2000 and synchronize this with a migration from Windows NT 4 to Windows 2000 Server. This company has multiple Exchange 5.5 servers. Its upgrade plans necessitate some type of coexistence between Exchange 5.5 and Exchange 2000. This means that any Exchange 5.5 user has to be configured as a mailbox-enabled user in AD before the company can fully implement Exchange 2000. It must use the ADC so that the proper Exchange 5.x data can be imported into AD. The ADC creates a disabled user account in the root domain of the new Windows 2000 forest for each Exchange 5.5 mailbox. These disabled user accounts contain all the necessary configuration information such as email addresses. When the organization is ready to upgrade to Exchange 2000, the user mailboxes can be moved from the Exchange 5.5 server to the new server, and the old Windows NT 4 domains can be upgraded to Windows 2000 by joining the same forest that Exchange 2000 is using. The problem with this scenario is that two accounts exist in AC for each Exchange user migrated. One account is the disabled user account created by ADC; the other is the newly upgraded account provided when the accounts were moved. You must run the AD Account Cleanup Wizard, adclean.exe, which merges all duplicate accounts found in AD. This tool merges all attributes of the disabled account into the upgraded account and deletes the disabled account. The result is one mailbox-enabled account for every original Exchange 5.x user.

- *Being unable to view Public Folders*—Sometimes, users attempt to access a public folder by expanding the Public Folders item in Microsoft Outlook and they see the "Unable to view Public Folders. Profile not configured." error. Such users may have a mailbox that is homed on an Exchange 2000 server but points to an Exchange 5.x server for public folders. These users cannot connect to the public IS when they log on. You may find some users pointing to an Exchange 2000 public folder server and others pointing to an Exchange 5.x server public folder server. Make sure that all mailbox stores on the same Exchange 2000 server are pointing to the same Exchange 5.x public folder server.

Connectors and Coexistence with Legacy Exchange

Organizations usually have a messaging system in place when they are ready to migrate to Exchange 2000 Server. These companies know in advance that they have to exchange messages or share directory information among different messaging systems. This means identifying the current connectors used on Exchange 5.5. For optimal throughput, Microsoft recommends placing all connectors on a separate server in the same site. It even makes it possible to deploy Exchange 5.5 and Exchange 2000 servers in the same Routing Group without affecting connector efficiency.

To make deployment of Exchange 2000 Server easy, Microsoft has included a set of tools that support coexistence with other mail systems while a company plans its migration strategy. The tools usually include:

- A connector for the specific messaging system being decommissioned
- The Exchange Server Migration Wizard to migrate users to Exchange
- The Windows 2000 AD Account Cleanup Wizard, adclean.exe, which merges contacts, mailboxes, and AD user accounts (discussed earlier in this chapter)

Migration involves moving an existing messaging system to a computer that is running Exchange 2000 Server. It also involves making a copy of your existing mailboxes, messages, and other data, and importing that information into Exchange 2000. It is critical to plan your migration strategy carefully to avoid downtime and minimize the potential effect it could have on your unsuspecting users.

Exchange 2000 Server supports the migration of many connectors used in Exchange 5.5, including the Lotus Notes connector, the MS Mail connector, the Lotus cc:Mail connector, and the Novell GroupWise connector. You usually migrate connectors using the Migration Wizard, a standalone application installed during Exchange setup. This wizard consists of two components: source extractors and a migration file importer. The *source extractors* copy directory information, messages, and collaboration data from existing messaging systems and saves this data in a file using a format that the Migration Wizard can import. The *migration file importer* imports the directory and collaboration information over to Exchange 2000 via Active Directory and adds data to the Information Store. We discuss a sample connector migration later in this chapter.

You can access the Migration Wizard from Start | Programs | Microsoft Exchange. When the Migration Wizard imports directory information from an existing messaging system into Exchange 2000, information is written to AD. The Migration Wizard copies the user information from the source directory and searches AD to find any matches. It then adds the information to the matching object or creates a new object based on the migrated information. In some cases, you may find multiple objects and must merge them back into a single and active account.

Note: *Migration can be either a one-step or a two-step process. A one-step migration extracts files from a foreign messaging system and imports these migration files directly to Exchange 2000 in one operation. A two-step migration extracts migration files from another messaging system and edits or reviews these files if necessary. The files are then imported directly into Exchange 2000.*

Follow these steps to use the Migration Wizard, your primary migration tool:

1. On the Start menu, choose Programs | Microsoft Exchange | Migration Wizard. Read the Welcome screen and then click on Next.

2. The Exchange Server Migration Wizard screen appears, shown in Figure 16.12. Select a migration option and then click on Next.

3. You now see the Import Migration Files screen, shown in Figure 16.13. At this point, you will be ready to extract migration files from your existing messaging system. It is helpful to map a drive letter to the server that will contain your migration files before you begin this step. Click on Next.

4. The Migration Destination screen, shown in Figure 16.14, appears. Here you can migrate private folders to a computer running Exchange Server, or you can migrate private folders to a personal folder (PST file) for each user. After making your selection, click on Next.

5. The File Location screen, shown in Figure 16.15, appears. Here you specify the path to the migration files, which normally consists of a packing list (PKL) file and multiple primary (PRI) and secondary (SEC) files.

The rest of the Migration Wizard (not shown here) uses directory information from your messaging system to create user objects in Active Directory. New users

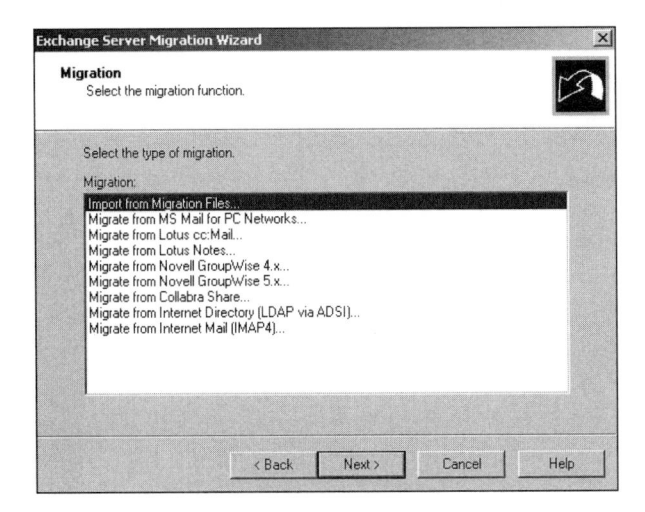

Figure 16.12 The Exchange Server Migration Wizard.

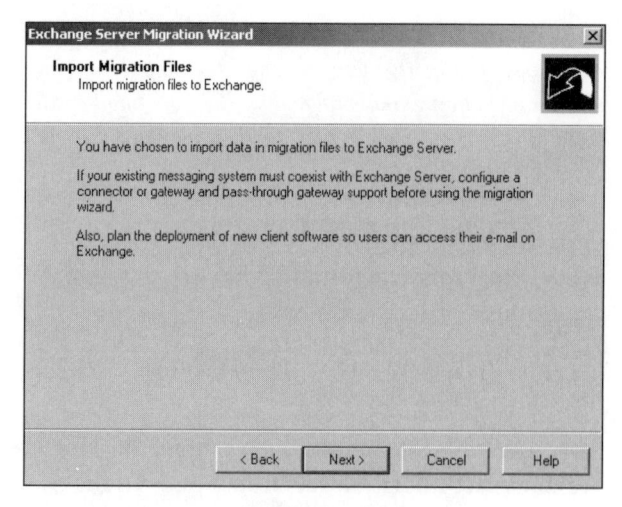

Figure 16.13 The Import Migration Files screen.

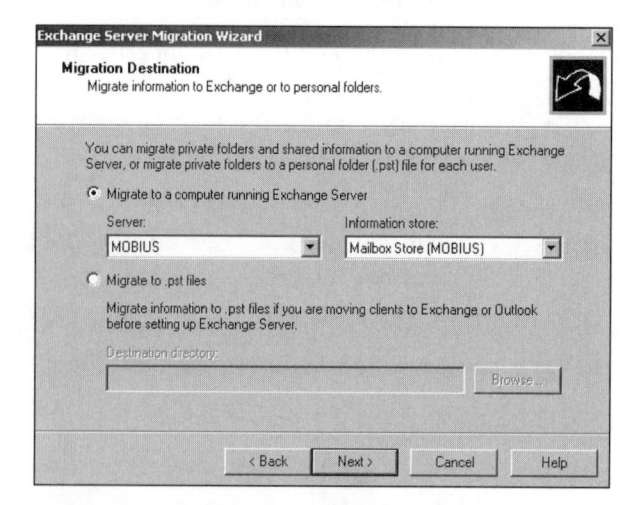

Figure 16.14 The Migration Destination screen.

are created by selecting a checkbox labeled Information To Create Mailboxes on the Migration Information screen. Mailboxes are also created in the mailbox store. The Migration Wizard copies all user information from a source directory and searches AD to find a match. It will either add information to the matching object or create a new object based on migrated information. A problem that sometimes occurs is the creation of duplicate accounts during the migration process.

The process of migrating connectors usually begins with configuring Exchange Server 5.5, which normally has a configured connector to a foreign mail system. Let's suppose that a current connector has a value of 20. Follow these steps to migrate this connector over to Exchange 2000 Server:

Legacy System Issues **547**

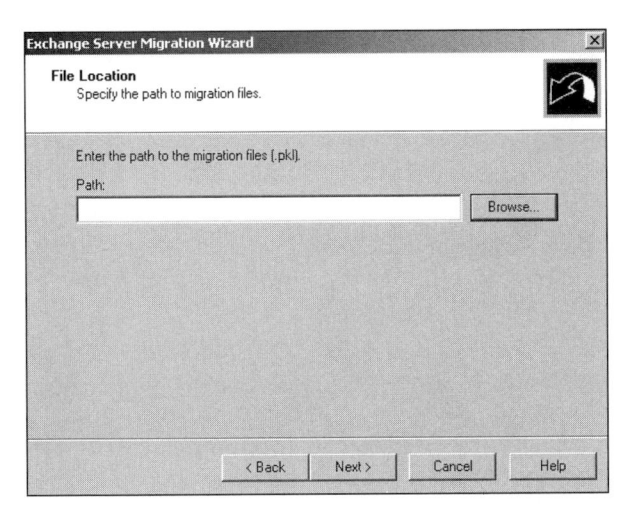

Figure 16.15 The File Location screen.

1. Add a new connector (for example, an SMTP connector) to the Exchange 2000 server and assign it a value less than 100 but greater than the value for the Exchange 5.5 connector. Figure 16.16 shows an example of how to add a connector in Exchange 2000 by selecting Connectors|New|SMTP Connector, and Figure 16.17 shows a view of the Properties sheets for a new SMTP connector.

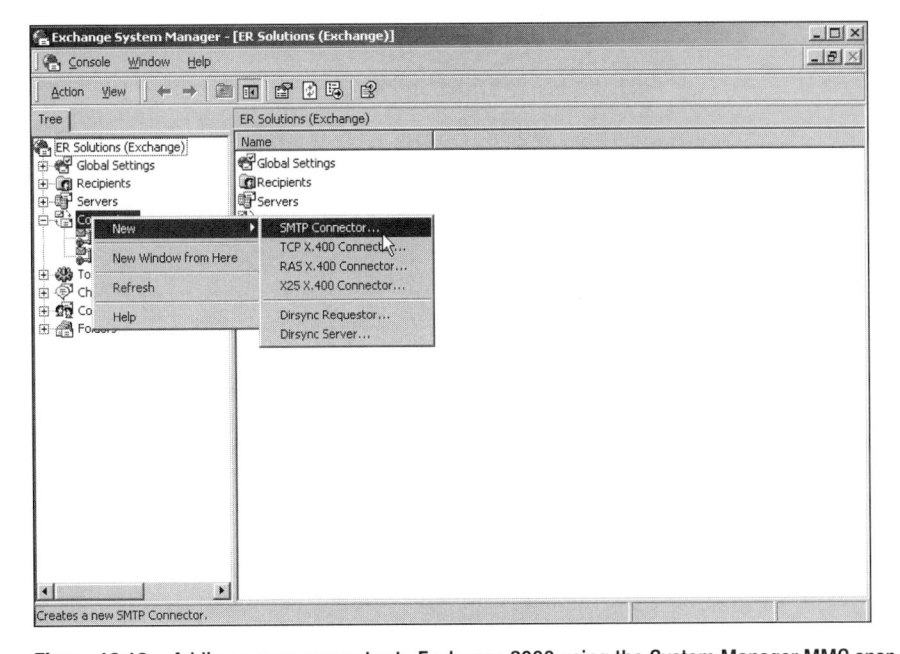

Figure 16.16 Adding a new connector to Exchange 2000 using the System Manager MMC snap-in.

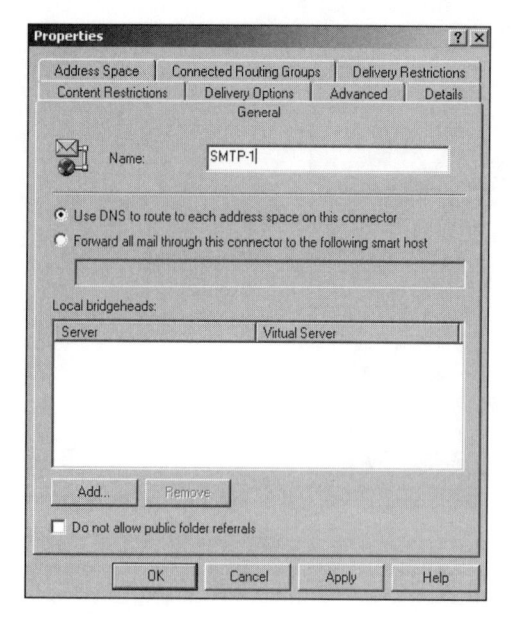

Figure 16.17 The Properties sheets for a new SMTP connector created in System Manager.

Tip: If you assign your new connector a value of 100, it is used only if the Exchange 5.5 connector is offline. You do not want this to happen because you would like to test this new connector while the old connector is still being used.

---

2. Add an address space to the Exchange 5.5 server for testing purposes and verify that the ADC is synchronizing between sites. Then, modify the cost of the new connector so that it equals the cost of the old connector. This ensures that the two connectors will run in parallel for some time.

3. When you are sure that the new connector can process your normal workloads, change the cost of the old connector to 100. Again, this effectively disables the old connector unless the new connector goes offline.

4. As a last resort, you can completely remove the old connector from the legacy Exchange server, or you can upgrade the legacy Exchange system to Exchange 2000.

Chapter Summary

The relevant points to remember from this chapter are:

► Legacy Exchange 5.5 sites were based on administrative and network connectivity requirements because all servers within the site communicated using RPCs.

► Site design made administration tasks (such as adding users) simple in Exchange 5.5. However, the criteria you use for site design in Exchange 2000 are different than those for Exchange 5.5.

- Exchange 2000 has a greater dependency on the Windows 2000 OS than Exchange 5.5 and uses the AD directory service to store both schema and configuration data.

- A planned upgrade to Exchange 2000 Server requires several components of Windows 2000 Server, including AD, DNS, the NNTP service, and the SMTP service.

- Extending the schema of AD allows you to assign rights and permissions to objects that Exchange 2000 Server uses.

- The ForestPrep tool requires that you successfully deploy Enterprise Admins, Schema Admins, and Local Administrator privileges.

- All mailboxes on an Exchange 5.5 server become mail-enabled AD users in Exchange 2000 with at least one email address defined for that object.

- You can do three kinds of upgrades with Exchange 2000 Server: an *in-place upgrade* on one computer, which requires an Exchange 5.5 server running SP3; an *across-the-wire* upgrade, with Exchange 2000 installed on new hardware in the existing site and mailboxes and public folders being migrated to the new server; and a *leapfrog method*, which allows you to reuse original hardware as the migration progresses throughout your organization.

- There are four phases related to the upgrade process. Phase One involves preparing the Windows 2000 forest schema. Phase Two involves installing the ADC, which replicates information between Exchange 2000 and legacy Exchange 5.5 sites. Phase Three requires you to prepare Windows 2000 domains using DomainPrep. Phase four involves the actual in-place upgrade to Exchange 2000 Server.

- Planning an upgrade also involves planning a rollback to an original configuration that existed before the upgrade. This involves running the MTACheck utility as well as the KCC.

- Sometimes, a planned upgrade to Exchange 2000 temporarily coexists with legacy versions of Exchange Server, which results in a mixed-mode environment. Any rules that you can apply to previous versions of Exchange Server are also applicable to Exchange 2000 Server.

- A mixed-mode configuration creates two new services on the Exchange 2000 Server: the SRS, which allows the Exchange 5.5 directory to coexist with the configuration-naming partition of AD; and the ADC, which allows replication between the Exchange 5.5 directory and the domain-naming partition of AD.

- SRS consists of the srsmain.exe application and the srs.edb database. It uses port 379 for LDAP communications with AD.

- ADC helps you synchronize directories by defining connection agreements. It has two versions: a Windows 2000 version and an Exchange 2000 Server version. The Windows 2000 version replicates directory objects in the Exchange 5.5 site; the Exchange version works with SRS and replicates configuration data, allowing Exchange 5.5 and Exchange 2000 servers to coexist peacefully.

- The concepts of mixed mode and native mode apply both to Windows 2000 and Exchange 2000, but not in the same context. Windows 2000 operates in mixed mode by default and contains some of the limitations found in Windows NT 4 domains. Native-mode Windows 2000 allows you to enjoy the full benefits of an AD domain. Mixed-mode Exchange means that Exchange 2000 is coexisting with Exchange 5.x or earlier versions. Native-mode Exchange does not allow interoperability with legacy Exchange servers and achieves maximum flexibility with Routing Groups and Administrative Groups.

- When upgrading, you should consider many legacy system issues, including routing master selection, offline address books, and public folder replication. Exchange 2000 becomes the routing master if an existing Exchange 5.x router server is upgraded to Exchange 2000.

- Upgrading to Exchange 2000 usually involves migrating the connectors that existed with your Exchange 5.x servers. Exchange 2000 supports many legacy connectors, including the Lotus Notes connector, the Lotus cc:Mail connector, the Novell GroupWise connector, and the Microsoft Mail connector.

- When migrating connectors, it is best to add a new connector to the Exchange 2000 server and assign it a cost factor that is greater than the cost of the Exchange 5.5 connector, but less than 100. Assigning a value of 100 effectively disables the connector, making it unavailable for testing and validation purposes. When the new connector can process normal workloads, you can remove the Exchange 5.5 connector from the legacy server or upgrade the legacy server to Exchange 2000.

- The Migration Wizard can help you import directory information from existing messaging systems into Exchange 2000.

Review Questions

1. How did legacy Exchange servers within an Exchange 5.x site communicate with each other?

    a. By using SMTP processing.

    b. By using RPCs.

    c. They replicated directories using ldp.exe.

    d. They used directory-replication connectors.

2. Why are directory services considered an important legacy system issue when they coexist with Exchange 2000 Server?

   a. Exchange 2000 is tightly integrated with the ADC.
   b. Both Exchange 5.x and Exchange 2000 use similar directory service structures.
   c. Every legacy Exchange server communicated with other servers using LDAP.
   d. RPCs relied on the LDAP protocol for intrasite replication.

3. Which Windows 2000 service hosts transport protocols for Exchange 2000?

   a. RPC
   b. IIS
   c. NNTP
   d. SMTP

4. As part of a planned upgrade for his company, Steve is migrating all Windows NT 4 domains to a new AD domain architecture. Besides AD, what components are considered crucial to a successful migration to Exchange 2000? [Check all correct answers]

   a. The Domain Name Service
   b. The Network News Transport Service
   c. The Simple Network Management Protocol Service
   d. The Simple Mail Transfer Protocol Service

5. One server in your Windows 2000 domain provides name-resolution services. What else must this server be able to do so that Exchange 2000 will operate properly?

   a. Perform dynamic updates
   b. Perform random updates
   c. Perform automatic IP addressing
   d. Update routing tables

6. Jane is trying to install the first Exchange 2000 server in her organization. To do this, what groups must she belong to? [Check all correct answers]

   a. Enterprise Admins
   b. Domain Admins
   c. Schema Admins
   d. Exchange Admins

7. What does the command **setup.exe /ForestPrep** accomplish?

    a. It creates the organization object in the schema-naming context.

    b. It creates the actual organization object in the configuration-naming context.

    c. It creates multiple organization objects in the configuration domain.

    d. It creates one organization object in the domain-naming context.

8. What rights are needed to execute the ForestPrep utility? [Check all correct answers]

    a. Enterprise Admins

    b. ForestPrep Admins

    c. Schema Admins

    d. Local Administrator

9. Mike has just finished upgrading a legacy Exchange server to Exchange 2000 Server. He notices that his legacy Lotus cc:Mail connector and MS Mail connector have been upgraded. Which component will not be upgraded?

    a. IBM Office Vision connector

    b. Lotus Notes connector

    c. MS Mail directory synchronization

    d. Custom recipients

10. How are custom recipients in Exchange 5.x represented in Exchange 2000?

    a. As custom recipients

    b. As contacts

    c. As mailbox-enabled custom objects

    d. As custom users

11. Barbara is performing an in-place upgrade of her Exchange 5.x server. She has not yet created the user Harry. Where will Exchange 2000 place the new user object after the upgrade?

    a. The new user object will be created in a special Administrative Group called Temp.

    b. The new user object will be found in the first Storage Group that is created.

    c. The new user object will be found in the message store's deleted items location.

    d. The new user object will be created in the Recipient container of AD.

12. How does Exchange 2000 assign permissions to public folders?
    a. By using Schema Admins permissions
    b. By using local distribution groups
    c. By using universal security groups
    d. By using global and local groups

13. Judy has configured public folder affinities on her Exchange 5.x server. Site A has an affinity for site B, which has an affinity for site D. Will she benefit from transitive affinity in this situation?
    a. No, Exchange 5.5 does not allow any transitive behavior.
    b. Yes, as long as there is a two-way trust between site A and site D.
    c. No, Exchange 5.x allows for one-way replication only.
    d. Yes, public folder affinities are transitive for both Exchange 5.x and Exchange 2000.

14. How does circular logging affect disaster recovery efforts for both Exchange 5.5 and Exchange 2000?
    a. This feature is enabled in Exchange 5.5 and allows older transactions to be archived to an .mdb file.
    b. This feature is disabled in Exchange 5.5 and prevents incremental backups from being performed.
    c. This feature is enabled in Exchange 2000 and prevents corruption of data.
    d. This feature is disabled in Exchange 2000 and aids in recovery of a failed server.

15. Don used Active Server Pages to render data using Outlook Web Access on his Exchange 5 server. He wants to continue using OWA after upgrading this server to Exchange 2000. What component will now render his data?
    a. WWW Publishing Service
    b. NNTP Service
    c. Information Store
    d. Web Storage System

16. You have enabled message tracking on one of your Exchange 5.5 server computers for various protocols and connectors. After upgrading this server to Exchange 2000 Server, what will happen to the message-tracking feature?
    a. Message tracking will be enabled for the entire server.
    b. Message tracking is disabled by default for Exchange 2000.
    c. Message tracking will be enabled for the same protocols and connectors as Exchange 5.5.
    d. Message tracking will now be managed by AD.

17. What is the first phase to overcome when you are upgrading a Windows 2000-based organization to Exchange 2000 Server?

    a. Installing the ADC

    b. Preparing the Windows 2000 domains

    c. Preparing the Windows 2000 forest schema

    d. Performing an in-place upgrade

18. You want to define three connection agreements, with each agreement going from AD to a different Exchange 5.5 site. How many instances of the ADC will you need in this scenario?

    a. Three instances per site.

    b. One instance in total.

    c. One instance per site.

    d. There is not enough information given.

19. Which type of connection agreement, created with the ADC, replicates recipient objects and their data?

    a. User agreements

    b. Recipient agreements

    c. Configuration agreements

    d. Mail-enabled agreements

20. What is the purpose of the connection agreement ConfigCA, installed by SRS?

    a. This allows one-way communication between SRS and AD.

    b. This allows two-way communication between AD and the Exchange 5.x directory.

    c. This allows two-way communication between SRS and AD.

    d. This allows one-way communication between AD and the Exchange 5.x directory.

Real-World Projects

Debbie has been waiting months for her Director to approve an upgrade from Exchange Server 5.5 to Exchange 2000 Server. She has been administering a site with two Exchange 5.5 servers that host 1,000 mailboxes and 20 public folders. She receives approval on the upgrade project and purchases a new 500MHz Pentium III computer with 256MB of RAM. She installs Exchange 2000 on this machine and joins it to her existing site. She ultimately wants all servers upgraded to Exchange 2000 Server. But she now faces a difficult decision. Her company would like to redirect some of its users and public folders over to the new Exchange 2000 server.

She also needs to add some new employees to this new server. Her IT team meets the following morning and discusses the best way of achieving these goals.

Project 16.1

To prepare to move mailboxes to the new server:

1. Perform a full backup of the Exchange 5.5 server in case you experience failures with the Move Mailbox function.

2. Disable all antivirus packages before using the Move Mailbox utility. (For more information, refer to the TechNet Web site at **http://support.microsoft.com/support/kb/articles/q271/5/47.asp**.)

3. Check the Private Information Store object in the Exchange 5.5 Administrator program to see if any users are currently logged on. If they are, contact them to make sure they are not currently working. All clients must be logged off the system while you migrate their data.

4. Use the Windows 2000 administrative utility AD Users and Computers to move mailboxes. You cannot do so using the Move Mailbox utility in the Exchange 5.5 Administrator. If you try to do this, you receive a message saying that there has been an internal processing error. Before you begin, write down the name and password for an account that has Exchange 2000 Administrator privileges and Exchange 5.5 Administrator privileges.

5. Go to Start|Programs|Microsoft Exchange|AD Users And Computers.

6. Expand the domain that contains the user accounts and then expand the OU that contains the user accounts.

7. Select the user accounts with the mailboxes you want to move. On the Action menu, select Exchange Tasks.

8. When you see the Welcome To The Exchange Task Wizard screen, shown in Figure 16.18, click on Next. On the Available Tasks screen, shown in Figure 16.19, click on Move Mailbox, and then click on Next.

9. On the Move Mailbox screen, select the Exchange 2000 server that will host the new mailboxes, and then click on Next.

10. You see the mailboxes being moved. Click on Next.

11. On the Completing The Exchange Task Wizard screen, review all the mailboxes that were moved and then click on Finish.

Debbie now decides to redirect some of her users to the public folder database that has been created on the new Exchange 2000 server. However, one of her users is complaining that her mail is not being redirected to the new server. Debbie grabs

Figure 16.18 The Welcome To The Exchange Task Wizard screen.

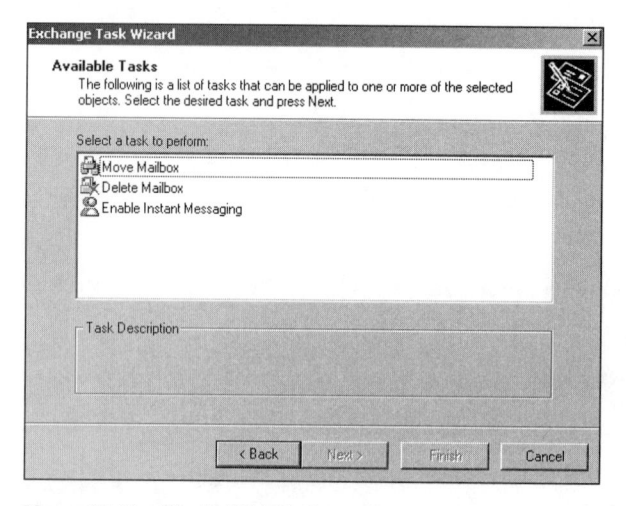

Figure 16.19 The Available Tasks screen.

her Resource Kit and frantically walks over to her concerned user. She decides to try to redirect this client.

Project 16.2

To manually redirect a user connection to the new server:

1. First check to see that Outlook is not currently running on the user's machine and that the user is not logged on anywhere else on the network.

2. Click on Start|Settings|Control Panel, and then double-click on the Mail icon.

3. Select Microsoft Exchange Server and then Properties.

4. Delete the name of the old Exchange 5.5 server in the Microsoft Exchange Server field, and then type in the name of the new Exchange 2000 server.

5. After clicking on the Check Name button, verify that both the user's name and the server's name are now underlined.

6. Close the Properties sheets for the Microsoft Exchange Server, as well as those for the MS Exchange Settings dialog box.

7. Finally, close Control Panel and restart Outlook on the user's machine.

As luck would have it, the mailbox on the new Exchange 2000 server opens without any errors. Debbie is just about to head home when she receives one final request. She needs to deal with redirecting public folders. Before doing so, however, she wants to run the DS/IS Consistency Adjuster against the public ISs on her Exchange 5.5 server.

Project 16.3
To run the DS/IS Consistency Adjuster:

1. Go to the Exchange 5.5 server and click on Start|Programs|Microsoft Exchange|Exchange 5.5 Administrator.

2. Navigate to the server in your site and select the Properties for that server (by right-clicking on the server object).

3. Click on the Advanced tab and then on Consistency Adjuster. The DS/IS Consistency Adjuster dialog box appears.

4. Select the Synchronize With The Directory checkbox, and reset the home server value for public folders homed in unknown sites. See Help for more information. Also select the Remove Unknown User Accounts From Public Folder Permissions box.

5. Click on OK. You will see a progress bar that informs you that the DS/IS adjustment is in progress.

6. Close the server's Properties sheet by choosing OK.

Debbie now checks the Event Viewer (especially the application log) to see if she has to deal with any serious hardware or software errors as a result of what she has done so far. She notices some entries that relate to the **MSExchangeISPublic** component, but this is normal and should not cause any concern. Her final assignment is to move public folder resources using the Exchange 2000 System Manager tool.

Project 16.4

To migrate public folders using Exchange System Manager:

1. Open up the System Manager on the Exchange 2000 server by clicking on Start | Programs | Microsoft Exchange | Microsoft Exchange System Manager.

2. Select the public folder you want to replicate and check its properties by choosing File | Properties.

3. Click on Replication. Then, click on Add to view a list of servers to which you can replicate this public folder. This list shows only servers that have public folders. Select the Exchange 2000 server and click on OK.

4. Choose the urgency of the replication in the Replication Message Priority field as Urgent (you are not satisfied with the default setting of Not Urgent) and click on OK to start the replication.

Debbie knows that there is no way to set a home server for public folders in Exchange 2000. But she is happy with this new arrangement because it is so much easier to create or modify public folders using the Exchange 2000 System Manager than using the Outlook client, as she did with Exchange 5.5. She is not worried about public folders that fail this migration process because they are still on her original server. In fact, a copy of all public folders will remain on her original server even after they have been replicated to the new Exchange 2000 server. Debbie decides to call it a day and informs the team of her success.

CHAPTER SEVENTEEN

Extending the Platform

After completing this chapter, you will be able to:

✓ List the major features of the Web Storage System

✓ Describe Exchange 2000 as a Web service provider

✓ Name the requisite services of any repository-based enterprise application

✓ Describe the process flow of an Outlook Web Access (OWA) service request

✓ List the steps involved in displaying an object through OWA

✓ Discuss how browser versions affect the OWA interface

✓ Describe the process flow in accessing an Outlook Inbox using Web Distributed Authoring and Versioning (WebDAV)

✓ List the advantages of front-end/back-end (FE/BE) configurations

✓ Differentiate between generalized and specific markup languages

✓ Distinguish features of Hypertext Markup Language (HTML) and Extensible Markup Language (XML)

✓ Name the specific components that enhance Internet Explorer 5 (IE5)

✓ Discuss the benefits of using Web Forms

✓ Discuss the Universal Data Access architecture

✓ Outline differences between ActiveX Data Objects (ADOs) and Object Linking and Embedding for Databases (OLE DB)

✓ Describe the Microsoft.NET framework architecture

This chapter concludes a long discussion of Exchange 2000. We began this book by describing a paradigm shift in the field of information technology (IT) from data processing in the late 1960s through information sharing in the 1970s and 1980s to knowledge management (KM). Microsoft has used several catch phrases to describe this theme. The one most relevant to this chapter is information "anytime, any place, from any device." This chapter shows how Exchange 2000 provides the foundation for that KM. We begin our chapter by discussing the Web Storage System. We show throughout the chapter how a .NET Server like Exchange 2000 with inherent multitier features—such as front-end and back-end server topology, partitioned services, and extensible Web Store—has been designed to easily provide Web-based service. We continue with a discussion of Outlook Web Access (OWA), the Web Distributed Authoring and Versioning (WebDAV) and Hypertext Transport Protocol (HTTP) protocols, and front-end/back-end (FE/BE) servers. The combination of standard browser client, OWA, and Web Store meets the Microsoft objectives of "information from anywhere, at any time, using any device." Exchange 2000 is positioned as the information broker in this scenario, much like how Lotus positioned its premier product, Notes/Domino—a field-tested application platform that provides communication, collaboration, and programmatic control—in the 1990s.

Next, we discuss markup languages, including Hypertext Markup Language (HTML) and Extensible Markup Language (XML). Then, we cover Internet Explorer 5 (IE5), which is becoming an alternative client for Exchange Server on the Web. It has undergone substantial enhancements that support Internet protocols, including its XML engine. This browser client will play an increasing role in future Web-based server management, in addition to its data-entry role through application interfaces like Web Forms. We then discuss various Web solutions. Next, we discuss various application programming interfaces (APIs) such as Object Linking and Embedding for Databases (OLE DB) and its more accessible subset, ActiveX Data Objects (ADOs), from the perspective of the Microsoft .NET framework. These programming interfaces have provided access to many objects stored within the messaging and collaborative structure of Exchange. We continue our discussion with these specific Collaborative Data Objects (CDOs) and how Exchange 2000 has enhanced their functionality. We conclude with a discussion of the possible role of Exchange 2000 in a distributed services environment and vision of its role as a .NET framework.

Web Storage System

The Web Storage System is the cornerstone on which Exchange 2000, a messaging and collaboration system, and Windows 2000, a provider of directory services and network operating system (NOS) core services like security and auditing, have come to rest. The Web Storage System schema defines the formats of the objects that are stored in the Web Store and integrates a wide, extensible range of knowledge sources into a central repository. Exchange 2000 provides an interface to its contents through intranet clients like Outlook and Internet clients like a standard browser and OWA. To simplify our discussion, we use the terms Web Store and Web Storage System interchangeably.

As a consumer of information services, you request services from either a broker like Exchange or directly from the Web Store. These service providers are extensible, so you can define a set of properties for a specific item and then control how it is used. The property that defines intention or purpose is called the *content class*. What makes the Web Store significant is a design that provides access to every item within its namespace. The ability to locate those items as resources in a systematic and human-readable way is provided by HTTP through the now common Uniform Resource Locator (URL). The concept of the Web Store is to provide a namespace of all collaborative objects using an HTTP URL and a standard Web browser. Thus, consumers/end users can directly access folders or collaborative objects like calendars by appending a named directory or object to the end of the URL used to access their mailbox. Named URLs also allow users to perform operations on these messaging and collaborative objects through explicit URL addressing.

Microsoft suggests that the Web Store is a scalable infrastructure within which we can consolidate all kinds of information, including messaging, collaborative information, file systems, and Web-related data. The Web Store is one of several supporting legs on which Microsoft is building a platform for its vision of "knowledge workers without limits." The integration of knowledge sources is found in one repository that provides the following key services to any enterprise-based application:

- *File system services*—To integrate structured data (such as databases with unstructured data like streaming data from the Web and information stored in proprietary Microsoft Office documents), a data model must accommodate both hierarchical and heterogeneous collections of data.

- *Database services*—Services must accommodate an extensible assortment of data types. A data query language must be capable of more complex searches than those typically performed within a file system on a Windows platform. Support issues here include the updating process of viewed data, where applications maintain consistent and accurate views of all items.

- *Collaboration services*—These services now extend beyond simple messaging, the collection of contacts, and calendaring objects to realtime collaboration that involves audio and video information.

The file system and database services require an extensible way to identify and manage content. The manners in which these services are used also require tremendous flexibility. Creation, manipulation, and deletion of isolated data, or larger knowledge objects like group calendars and task lists, will occur spontaneously and without previous preparation or planning. Although you do not have to define a property as a file system or database object before you use the Web Store, you can ensure rapid execution of search queries to retrieve it from the data store once it is placed there by creating some definition of its nature or content. All three systems must be able to support such spontaneous activity. This storage system supposedly removes barriers that obstruct the sharing of heterogeneous data by combining the features of these three service areas as they relate to Exchange 2000 and other Microsoft server products, as well as Microsoft Office 2000 products. Microsoft views the Web Store as an enterprise-based application service that provides ubiquitous client access. The benchmarks for its success are improved productivity and a lower total cost of ownership (TCO) through broader access to resources.

Extending Data Access

The Web Store is the focus for many of the technologies discussed in this chapter because it is actually the container for both structured and unstructured data. The Store now has the potential of providing a central repository for messages, their attachments, collaborative objects like calendars and task lists, and the heaps of data stored in the various Microsoft Office application formats like Excel's XLS, Word's DOC, PowerPoint's PPT, and Access's MDB files. To accommodate the greater number of categories, we need to extend the transport protocol to move these objects between the service provider and the consumer requesting the service. This extension must provide support for a variety of document formats, such as rich HTML and other Web-based scripting languages, Win32 file structures, streaming file formats, offline folder objects, and native collaborative objects. Database management plays a major role in the extension of these services.

Rich HTML Support

Especially with the introduction of IE5, but beginning with IE4, Dynamic HTML (DHTML) support of scripting and robust Document Object Models (DOMs) has added richness to the standards-based HTML. A DOM is a standardized API that provides programmatic control over a document's content, structure, formats, and processes. The Web Store leverages these native features in the more current versions of the browser client. Legacy browser versions 3.x are also supported with functionality provided by increased server-side support. HTML, IE5, and DHTML are discussed in more detail later in this chapter.

Scripting Support

Web-based applications are collections of distributed components and services. Like their standalone counterpart, component-based software, distributed applications require rich methods and properties to manage the many transactions and service requests passed to other services providers across the stateless environment of the Internet. Solution providers must compensate as they transition from the client-side richness of DHTML to deficiencies inherent in the simple scripting of HTML/XML pages. Solution providers do not necessarily encounter this change in feature sets when they move Win32 component applications from one hardware platform to another.

The advantages of porting component-based application software, however, do not outweigh the expense involved in scaling services or extending functionality. Applications using distributed services are alternatively easier to scale and deploy than their component-based counterparts. The Web Store supports the development of Web-based applications by hosting technologies like Active Server Pages (ASP), discussed later in this chapter. Scripting support of this technology, however, is not sufficient to deliver the quality of productivity tools available when you use Win32 component architecture. Thus, the Web Store supports the same database interfaces that Microsoft ADO scripts use to deliver the common database-intense software application. The Web Store's OLE DB 2.5 provider is a complex foundation upon which ADO, a subset of OLE DB scripting, runs. Thus, database services—including data query and data manipulation of language components, as well as transaction support—are available. The Web Store also includes full-text content indexing. We discuss ADO and OLE DB in more detail later in this chapter.

Microsoft Win32 Support

The Web Store must support extensible Web-based data types as well as legacy (Win16) file types and document models typically found in the network-based Win32 interface. It leverages resources in existing file systems by supporting an interface that virtualizes the NetBIOS (Win32) share name. You can utilize folder-based resources in the Web Store environment, providing access to unstructured data that heretofore was inaccessible to Web-based manipulations. It is significant especially in terms of TCO that end users accustomed to sharing folders will not notice any differences in handling the data through their browser client across the Internet as compared with Windows Explorer in a LAN environment. There is no need for end-user support or software configuration when you access these resources.

Another important characteristic of the Web Store is its ability to provide property promotion, especially when dealing with Office file types stored in the Win32 file system. The Web Store provides consistent views of the information independent of the client used to access that information, which again minimizes the need for end-user training. Properties from documents are automatically promoted and populate all record fields used in the viewing interface. Thus, for example, the Outlook Inbox displays all file types as common entities in a unified view of information consistent across multiple clients. This universal Inbox integrates information, eliminates concurrent access to multiple applications, and enhances productivity by providing a customizable view of data that can be replicated on demand.

Streaming Store

Just as Exchange 2000 has accommodated new types of multimedia messaging with audio and video components, the Web Store can natively accommodate very large message units with attachments. The important streaming store feature is the file streaming interfaces that provide the retrieval access. When so many storage types are involved, it is especially important to be able to ensure that the intended meaning of data is retained. To maintain the quality of information, the Web Store minimizes the number of file type conversions; the data is natively stored in the Web Store.

Offline Folders

The Web Store allows you to integrate online/offline data stores so that you can support the needs of a user population that is more often remote than on site. Beginning with the Briefcase object in Windows 95, synchronizing online folders and documents with offline stores has become a necessity among users who tend to find themselves accessing network resources from portable platforms. The shift toward Web-based access has freed users from the relatively synchronous connections that a corporate workstation provides. Although the need to explicitly synchronize folders and their contents is critical to version control systems, end users often overlook this. With offline folders available in Windows 2000, the Web Store synchronizes the folder contents regardless of how the data is accessed. This replication model provides support without an increase in TCO because it is transparent to the end user and therefore requires no additional training.

Native Collaboration Objects

The Web Store allows you to automatically integrate what might be more appropriately termed *knowledge objects* with collaborative functions like messaging, contacts, calendaring, and workflow. Thus, a financial report in the form of an Excel workbook can be scheduled for review using a specific interface. This integrative process is achieved through an object model that leverages on-demand and programmatic access to data objects. A knowledge object is not the same as a data object; a knowledge object is truly an entity that the consumer or end user manipulates independent of the Web Store or Exchange. The ability your users have to shape their working environment according to individual needs with personalized knowledge objects like calendars or task lists is an example of the difference between data processing and KM. Data access is standardized using well-known APIs such as ADO and OLE DB, so development time is minimized. In addition, popular authoring systems like Microsoft FrontPage further expand access to the collaborative resources that the collaborative platform provides.

Database Management

To deliver database services, the Web Store must perform very fast searches and lookups. The native database manages index documents for common key fields as well as attachments. The Web Store offers transaction logging at the database level. It uses write-ahead transaction logs like Exchange 2000 to ensure data integrity through redundancy. Data replication is supported at the folder level so that replicas of data can exist on multiple servers in the Exchange organization. Folder replica management also balances application loads, especially when you are dealing with data that is frequently accessed. Using multiple databases is also another way to improve reliability. Finally, at the system level, the Web Store supports Windows 2000 active/active clustering. Web Store services on one machine can assume control over data managed by the Web Store services on another machine if hardware malfunctions. Active/active clustering minimizes downtime and, when actually implemented, is totally transparent to the consumer/end user.

Web Store Events

Exchange 2000 allows you to programmatically respond to store events and build the rules to make decisions. It can respond to events that involve data objects such as adds, moves, and changes, as well as the starting and stopping of services. Developers can create applications or scripts that program the responses to these events. When a specific event occurs in the Web Store, the Exchange system fires an event. You can program the System Services layer to notify other applications or services in response to that event. These applications that respond to a specific event are called *sinks*. In addition to allowing you to define your own event sink, Exchange uses predefined sinks for numerous tasks. Thus, a program that monitors a workflow can initiate specific processes in response to the system's conditions or states and programmatically redirect that workflow without supervision or outside control. Alternatively, event sinks can validate items when they are saved to the Web Store. Other event sinks can be embedded or launched from scripts written for a specific application.

Web Storage System events are the responses the Web Store provides to service requests from other service providers between the Data Services layer and the Application Logic layer; the consumer/end user does not directly interface with this architecture.

With improvements in hardware capacity and response times, enhancements in scripting language, a broader use of APIs (discussed later in this chapter), and the ability to offload more processing to the client side of the transaction, the event architecture in Exchange 2000 has changed from a legacy client-host, component-oriented architecture to multitier, distributed systems. There are three application types:

- *Desktop*—This application model is monolithic; Presentation, Application Logic, and Data Services layers are all located on the computer.

- *Two-tier*—This model is the classic client-server model where a workstation hosts the Presentation layer and data services are located on the host/server. Business or application logic can be located on the client, the host, or both machines.

▶ *Three-tier (or multitier)*—Traditionally, the multitier approach has been conceptualized as three distinct service layers. In a three-tier architecture, presentation, business logic, and data elements are conceptually separated. Presentation elements are what the user manipulates or uses to make service requests. These elements thus handle requests for services developed by the application logic, which out of necessity is located on the server side. The business logic (or rules) provides whatever services are requested, either directly or through the contribution of another service provider. The data layer provides the repository structure.

If, for the purposes of this discussion, we divide multitier architecture into Presentation, Business (Application) Logic, and Data Services layers, we see a design that is Web and service oriented. The fundamental layer in a multitier architecture is the Data Services layer, where resources are stored and retrieved. The technologies now available through Exchange 2000 and other application servers have shifted the IT paradigm from data processing through information services to the management of knowledge objects in highly collaborative environments. Thus, the sophistication of the Presentation layer in terms of specifying extensible types of objects must grow in tandem with the capacities of the Data Services layer, where these objects are stored, catalogued, and retrieved.

Web Services

Microsoft has defined a Web service in technical literature as an application delivered as a service that is integrated with other Web-based services using Internet standards. This means that you can access resources using standard URL addressing. A Web service, running transparently and leveraging other services to minimize its own overhead, should provide some value that theoretically is not available from any other source. In Chapter 1, one model we described—Generic Architecture for Information Availability (GAIA)—is of particular interest because it provides a terminology well suited for a distributed services environment. GAIA describes roles and services involved in brokering information, which changes the administrative role in maintaining Exchange 2000 Server from simply "fixing pipes" to custom tailoring collaborative solutions.

We have slightly reworked the GAIA model so that we refer to consumers, brokers, and service providers to accommodate the distributed services environment found in a multitier, e-commerce architecture. We use these roles at many functional levels of exchanging information and managing knowledge. If you approach Exchange Server as a conceptual "knowledge broker," you will be better prepared to manage the many services it provides, from messaging to realtime collaboration. Our emphasis on providing solutions rather than fixing "broken pipes" echoes Microsoft's test objectives; in the Windows 2000 environment and especially dealing with Exchange 2000, your job description is more "architect" than "plumber." Given the functional role models of broker and service provider, you can, as administrator, successfully leverage the accessibility that OWA provides with the rich feature set of commands available from extensions to the HTTP transport protocol. These extensions have been added through WebDAV. From a structural viewpoint, the careful planning of topology through the use of front-end and back-end servers (FE/BE) adds reliability through redundancy, and optimized performance through service load balancing. The ability to provide solutions of even greater specificity through, for example, Web-based Forms using Web-based scripting languages (discussed later in this chapter), significantly changes the Exchange administrator's potential scope of activities and job description.

OWA Architecture

OWA has shipped with Exchange for quite some time. It uses ASP technology to render the contents of a user's mailbox in HTML. Users log in from anywhere using a standard browser with a well-known interface to read their mail. OWA provides an access method that accommodates Web-based, roving users. The standardized browser client and simplified configuration are critical issues in providing a kind of universal access to messaging and collaborative services, in addition to the Web stores. For many years, Microsoft has considered its Exchange client as a universal Inbox. Now with changes in the API and greater exposure of stored objects through OWA, digital dashboard (providing a ready-made framework within which knowledge workers can customize their selection of displayed data and services) has replaced the Inbox moniker. Web services offered through OWA—provided especially by IE5 with its HTML and XML enhancements—can expose more than just mailboxes.

In general, OWA provides many functional benefits, including support for:

- *Light messaging*—OWA provides an alternative to the full Outlook 2000 client through the well-known and readily accessible standard browser client. Especially over public networks and where control over configuration is not practical, this form of access to messaging services provides a practical solution to communication needs.

- *Roving users*—With OWA, you minimize the need to configure a client, and you don't need Messaging API (MAPI) profiles to configure the appropriate workspace for a workstation. Therefore, you can administer remote or roving users using more general system policies and standard profiles than you can with network users. MAPI is discussed in more detail later in this chapter.

- *Kiosk and Information Sources*—This new service outlet provides access to mailboxes and public information with little maintenance or overhead.

- *Migrations and rapid deployment*—OWA provides continuity of services during interim periods of migration, or loss of services during maintenance periods or deployment.

Requesting and Delivering Services

OWA in Exchange 2000 does not use MAPI to access the mailbox store, nor does it use ASP technology for client access. You access OWA via HTTP. We can conceive of the OWA interface as a brokering service or proxy for all messaging traffic directed toward messaging and collaborative objects. When the OWA client requests services, Internet Information Services (IIS) acts as a proxy for the messaging traffic between the Web client and Exchange Server. IIS acts as an interface by accepting the client requests that use the WebDAV extensions to HTTP (discussed later in this chapter). IIS passes the requests to the OWA Internet Information Services API (ISAPI) layer, which either directly accesses a Database layer or proxies the request to a remote server that provides this service. ISAPI, the API for IIS, then locates the requested object's URL and redirects the client to a script that provides the logic to respond to the service request associated with a target object.

The request and delivery of services are described in the following process flow:

1. A user enters a URL such as **http://servername/exchange/mailbox** in a browser Address box.

2. The Web server authenticates the user and determines the user's Windows 2000 account by displaying a pop-up Secure Attention Sequence (SAS) dialog box that requests the username, password, and domain, just like when a user attempts to access network resources on a local workstation.

3. The location of the mailbox is determined from a query to Active Directory (AD).

4. OWA services return an HTML page composed of navigational bar and mailbox contents similar in appearance to the multidocument interface (MDI) used by Outlook to display a user mailbox and its contents.

When an end user accessed OWA from a legacy Exchange server, OWA used a separate logon page to authenticate users rather than an SAS pop-up dialog box (as described in Step 2). Other distinctions between legacy OWA and Exchange 2000 OWA are that legacy Exchange used cookies to monitor the client session and provided a logout button that terminated the session. Exchange 2000 OWA does not provide a logout button; instead, when ending a session, the user must close all browser windows and thus all running OWA instances.

Displaying Objects

Exchange 2000 OWA displays objects using the following process flow:

1. A consumer/end user, through a standard browser, requests an email message or another collaborative object.

2. The Exchange ISAPI layer in IIS 5 receives and brokers the request.

3. The Web Storage Service determines the type of object, the specific item, and whether the user is authorized to access it. If the authenticated consumer has authorization to access the object, it is returned to the ISAPI application.

4. Exchange ISAPI determines, based on the object's attributes, the appropriate form for this object type from form definitions in the Forms Registry. If a form definition is not found, a default form stored in wmtemplates.dll provides the services. If the browser language is not English, other template libraries are accessed in \Exchsrvr\Res\Directory.

5. Once the form is selected, the ISAPI Application layer parses the form and makes service calls to the Web Storage System to complete the form with the appropriate data objects.

6. Exchange ISAPI renders the form in the appropriate HTML or XML scripting code and returns the form to the browser.

7. The browser renders the scripting code and displays the information in an HTML document.

It is significant that in this process flow, OWA renders a markup language appropriate for the client browser. Depending, for example, on the version of the browser, HTML or a combination of HTML and XML scripting is returned to the browser client for display. Non-Microsoft browsers receive HTML code that conforms to the older HTML 3.2 standard, whereas IE5 and more recent versions receive DHTML code that performs more complex operations within the browser DOM. Various markup languages are discussed later in this chapter.

Server Access

Outlook clients interact directly with Exchange Server services. OWA clients, using any standard browser, interact with IIS Web services. The browser client communicates typically from outside the enterprise namespace by using the HTTP protocol with WebDAV extensions. When IIS receives a request to access an object in the Web Storage System, it passes the request to the Exchange ISAPI application, which, in turn, communicates with the Data Store layer in the Web Storage System. The Web Storage System responds to the service request, the ISAPI layer renders it in HTML, and the browser on the client side presents it to the consumer/end user.

HTTP and WebDAV

Basic HTTP has been extended to accommodate a broader range of data types and service operations. WebDAV—Request for Comments (RFC) 2291, 3023—is a new technique that transforms the entire Web Store into a collaborative writable medium. Since 1999, WebDAV has provided HTTP with an increased feature set for providing services. WebDAV, written by the Internet Engineering Task Force (IETF) with help from Microsoft, extends the versatility of the Web Storage System as well as many other applications, especially because of its integration with XML (discussed later in this chapter). WebDAV enables collaborative publishing to Microsoft Web servers across the Internet, supports Web folders in Microsoft Office 2000, and provides an interface that allows access to the hierarchical database found in the Web Store. WebDAV allows Web-based applications with APIs using HTTP requests to manipulate data objects like their networked application counterparts.

Key features of the WebDAV extensions include:

- *Locking features*—The use of long-duration concurrency or locking controls and shared write locks allows collaborative writing to the same resource without fear of corruption in the integrity of the object. The functioning of this locking mechanism is independent of the specific network connection in use. Thus, this feature provides for wide-scale collaboration without disruption (because public network connections are unreliable) and improved scalability (because open connections consume local resources).

- *Properties*—XML scripting provides properties for metadata that can further refine the definition of an element. WebDAV can read and manipulate the XML syntax. XML is discussed later in this chapter.

- *Namespace manipulation*—WebDAV provides an extensible feature set as the containers that hold data objects change location in Internet space.

In general, browser clients access, for example, their Universal Inbox using WebDAV according to the following process flow, shown in Figure 17.1:

1. The browser client issues an HTTP **get** request.

2. IIS receives this service request and passes it to the Exchange ISAPI layer, davex.dll, for processing.

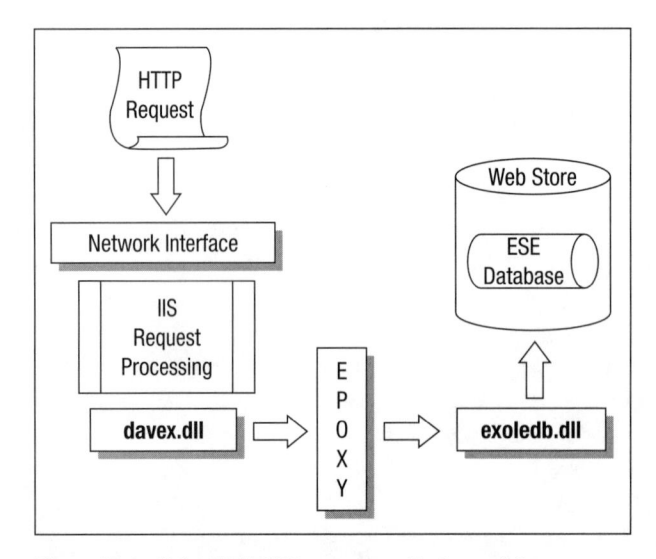

Figure 17.1 Using WebDAV to access an Exchange Inbox.

3. WebDAV forwards this request to the Web Storage System in Exchange Server, exoledb.dll, across the specialized EXchange InterProcess Communication channel (EXIPC)—more commonly called EPOXY, as you can see in Figure 17.1. exoledb.dll renders and processes this service request by accessing the Web Store or Extensible Storage Engine (ESE) database to retrieve the specific object's properties.

4. Once the Inbox properties are retrieved and parsed, Exchange Server routes information back to the client along the same path in reverse order.

Thus, a browser client, using HTTP, can retrieve a document (**get**) or submit or store a document (**put** or **post**) through this process flow into the Web Store. In fact, WebDAV provides commands to search, move, copy, delete, lock, and unlock data objects, as well as make new collections of resources in folders.

FE/BE Architecture

The division of labor in an FE/BE architecture—introduced in Chapter 1—is very similar to that of a multitier architecture, which these days is typically becoming the foundation for Web application development and e-commerce projects. In a distributed services or multitier architectural environment, one or more FE servers broker OWA service requests by redirecting them to BE servers that physically host the mail stores. BE servers form a more efficient database service layer than a single monolithic server because their physical separation from the front end provides less work for the local system and greater opportunity to scale the data stores more easily. Such a distributed environment is also better because it provides simpler options for scalability and the introduction of fault-tolerant architectures. In addition, distributed services help workflow through easier load balancing.

Advantages of FE/BE architecture include:

➤ *Single namespace*—Best practices recommend referring to all servers that provide a common service like mailbox storage with a single name. As you add local storage resources to accommodate increased user demand, the separation of FE and BE equipment makes scaling the Data Services layer a simpler task than if data were stored in a single hardware storage unit. You can add other BE servers without changing the front end because the FE has been freed from the more resource-intensive activities through the partitioning of services. The FE servers provide a single namespace from both the client/consumer viewpoint and from the perspective of the BE data layer to which service requests are directed. Thus, an OWA client uses a nonspecific URL such as **http://owa.coriolis.tch/exchange/username**. Once you redirect server access to the appropriate BE machine, fulfilling the service request for data is the same. You can also apply other features like Network Load Balancing to the FE servers to further expand capacity. Finally, the single namespace provides a subtle security advantage over a monolithic server because the mission-critical data stores are never exposed to public access.

- *Offload Secure Sockets Layer (SSL)*—The argument for separating the more resource-intensive operations of storage and retrieval from brokering service requests also applies to cryptographic services. Encrypting and decrypting messages are processor-intensive operations. Providing these services impacts tremendously on a machine's local resources. If you provide such services on an FE machine rather than on the same server, partitioned service layers greatly enhance the performance of the entire messaging platform.

- *Public folder referrals*—One of the limitations of Internet Message Access Protocol 4 (IMAP4) is its inability to support public folder referrals. FE/BE architecture can accommodate this weakness in the protocol by actually retrieving the public folder information.

- *Server location*—Separation of services simplifies the deployment of, for example, firewall technologies. You can physically separate BE servers from FE servers by placing the BE servers behind firewalls. You can configure the firewalls to pass traffic from only specific FE servers.

- *Security*—Security is enhanced because FE servers exposed more directly to public access can only broker or redirect a service request; they do not provide their own data resources.

Another benefit is a division of labor in the use of FE servers that broker service requests and BE servers that fulfill the requests. If the local Exchange server has a mailbox data store, OWA accesses the mail store directly. We define an FE server in the context of our discussions as an Exchange 2000 server that does not host a public folder or mailbox data store, but instead functions as a proxy or broker. We can call the FE a proxy or broker because it forwards service requests to a remote server able to process the request. A BE server, on the other hand, is an Exchange 2000 server that maintains the data store. Thus, if the local Exchange server is an FE server, OWA uses HTTP to proxy the service request to the appropriate BE server. The FE server uses Lightweight Directory Access Protocol (LDAP) to query a directory services provider (in this case, AD) for the path to the BE data store that hosts the user's mailbox. HTTP/WebDAV, Post Office Protocol 3 (POP3), and IMAP4 browser clients support FE/BE architecture.

Markup Languages

Scripting languages specify the operational flow of events and the manipulation of data structures that contain many different types of Web-based resources. Markup languages, a part of this interpreted rather than compiled family of source codes, use their tags to describe the appearance or meaning of the data structures defined and manipulated by other scripting languages like ECMAScript (formerly Javascript), Personal Home Page (PHP), Active Server Pages (ASP) technology, and Perl. The many changes scripting languages are undergoing, from a static page description language (HTML) through dynamic interactive scripts (DHTML) to extensible metalanguages (XML), are radically altering the scope of control that both developers and end users can programmatically exert on Web-based data objects. The origin of markup languages, which provide portability across different software applications and environments to the underlying content they modify, is rooted in the printing industry, where the phrase *to mark up text* referred to editing a printed document. The term *markup* specifically refers to tagging elements in digitally rendered documents to either modify the appearance of the text or establish a document's structure and meaning for output to a medium like a printer or computer console. Many word processing applications use this technology. Many office workers who used earlier versions of the WordPerfect product could reveal the code or tags by simply toggling screens.

The process of markup consists of inserting tags (or *tokens* or *wickets*) in front of and (usually) behind a string of text to change the appearance or meaning of the enclosed information. Tagged text is often referred to as *source code* or *a document*; the Web browser software renders it. Rich-text format (RTF), a common file type among word processors, is a markup language that is rendered by word processing software. It can produce italicized words, bulleted lists, and block quotes. To view the actual markup in an unrendered RTF document file, use a 16-bit text editor like Notepad. Both Microsoft Word and Corel WordPerfect process RTF file format so that the content is rendered as a fully formatted document on the display monitor. In our example, it does not matter what machine or word processor package we use to view the document; it is still fully formatted.

Specific vs. Generalized Markup Languages

Two types of markup languages are used: specific and generalized. Specific markup languages generate code specific to an application or device. Generalized markup languages describe the structure and meaning of the text, but not how the text should be used. Thus, RTF uses a specific collection of tags to mark up (format) text using popular word processing packages; it does not work with text editors. The problems with specific markup languages are that the set of tags are limited, the document is not universally portable, and the markup language is not standards based (that is, the source code is not easily translated to other markup languages used in other situations or on other media running on other systems).

Generalized markup languages are based on a concept of describing text independent of the Presentation layer—the platform device and/or software application. Thus, the language describes structure rather than format or style. To develop cross-compatibility and extensibility, you need to strictly control the syntax of the language to minimize hybrid and proprietary dialects of the parent code. Beginning in the early 1970s, IBM proposed the Document Composition Facility Generalized Markup Language (DCF GML). This working language led to the development of Standard Generalized Markup Language (SGML), which the International Organization for Standardization (ISO) adopted in 1986 (ISO 8879). The original objective of SGML was to format information for efficient distribution, search, and retrieval. It is actually a *metalanguage*—a language that defines other languages. Because of its intended scope and metalinguistic tendencies, SGML is very complex. For example, it identifies the characters used in the document, uses document type definitions (DTDs) to define structure, provides for identification of logical objects called *entities*, and allows for the incorporation of external data. It also supports a minimization technique that allows for relaxation in some of the syntactical patterns. An important omission is the absence of tags that describe how the data should appear in a chosen medium.

Web Markup Languages

Whereas specific markup languages originated in the printing industry, Web markup languages have roots in the nonlinear medium of the online world. Both HTML and XML are derived from SGML and are thus standards based. Both languages provide a grammar for text-based scripts interpreted by now commonplace browser client software. Whereas the older HTML describes the appearance of elements within the layout of some Web page, XML provides a metalanguage extending this tagged grammar to encompass and define the content of any data structure that can be rendered by some browser client, such as Internet Explorer.

HTML

HTML, a text-based scripting language that describes how data should appear on the Web browser screen, was developed so that document specifications could be separate from appearance. SGML defines HTML at all levels and documents these specifications in a series of DTDs that you can reference at **www.w3.org**. From the beginning, however, HTML suffered from conflicting de facto standards promulgated by both Netscape and Microsoft through the use of proprietary HTML extensions or dialects of the parent code. In addition, there was not a move toward international language support until version 4.01, when a markup tag that specified language was added to the vocabulary. Prior to this version, the HTML Working Group of the IETF (**www.ietf.org**) had not defined language in specifications. Furthermore, URLs are written into the script of the document (commonly referred to as *hard coding*). This limitation in the language forces you to continually maintain any script because of the dynamic nature of referenced Internet resources. HTML does not allow you to associate hyperlinks to specific elements other than specially targeted hypertext references (commonly referred to as *internal links*) or multiple locations using one reference. HTML also follows the minimization technique of SGML in that this coding syntax is not extremely rigid.

Validation of HTML code implies only technical or syntactical integrity, a strict compliance with the DTD. The browser can typically interpret poorly written code and successfully render it. This presents difficulties to application developers, who depend on a consistent interpretation of how programming is written. Another problem when you use HTML is that you can't maintain data in the form of variable names, values, or data structures across separate sessions. HTML was designed to format a table, not store the data in it. With HTML, you cannot define both document format and data structure.

The components of HTML (that is, the elements and attributes) are categorized as physical and logical. Physical elements and attributes define exactly how the content will be displayed. Thus, we can display a horizontal rule as 50 percent of the viewable browser window or 200 *pixels* (picture elements that are the distinguishable clusters of luminescent phosphorous) from the left side of the viewable window. Logical HTML elements or attributes, similar to XML elements (discussed shortly), describe the format of content enclosed within the tags. With logical elements, the browser uses the markup elements and attributes to identify content and then displays it accordingly.

The rebirth of HTML came in its marriage, in January 2000, to XML. The markup language spawned from this union is called Extensible Hypertext Markup Language (XHTML). This more rigid scripting language, in which source code is syntactically well formed and valid, provides a way to define content as well as describe appearance.

XML

In 1996, an XML Working Group began developing a new markup standard that was structurally more capable than HTML but considerably less complex than SGML. The objectives of this new language, XML, included:

➤ Universal usability across software clients and applications

➤ Compatibility with SGML so that legacy applications that comply with the SGML standard can easily interface with this new language

➤ Simplified development, which includes a minimal number of development tools, minimal syntactical options and language dialects, rapid application development through interpretation rather than compilation, and source code that can be easily sight-read

A theme of the working group has been to keep the standard concise rather than adding many options that facilitate authoring but complicate the XML markup language itself. Another important theme is that XML is the perfect medium for creating Web applications rather than designing page layouts. Other characteristics of XML include:

➤ It creates and passes messages to call methods to provide a programming interface.

- It separates content from presentation using XML documents and Extensible Style Language (XSL) pages (we will discuss XSL shortly).

- It uses several other languages (in addition to HTML)—such as Simple Object Access Protocol (SOAP)—to package requests for services provided by another server and thus supports a wide variety of applications, especially those using SGML-compatible message formats.

The basic components of an XML document are elements, attributes, and comments. Development of XML applications requires elements and attributes that are logical in origin and under the user's control. XML documents require a consistent syntax within which authors can define their own tag sets so that these defined elements are reusable according to a stated set of rules. Documents are thus self-describing scripts that contain all the rules for that particular class of document. You typically use Microsoft XML Notepad to work in a document. Elements mark up sections of an XML document, and content is usually contained within the XML tags. You also have elements, called *empty tags* or *singletons*, which do not contain content. Attributes modify the behavior of the markup tag. Comments can be embedded in the code to help orient the reader. You must follow very specific rules when using and placing tags so that all XML documents are well formed and valid. A well-formed XML document:

- *Contains a DTD*—The XML DTD is important because XML is extensible; you define or extend the meaning and structure of the XML tags. Unlike with HTML, which has predefined tagged keywords, you create the language that describes your text. The DTD provides the syntactical rules for the descriptive tags you create. The server-side or client-side processor can verify the integrity of the document according to the author's stated rules. A valid XML document is a subset of valid SGML code, ensuring both portability and extensibility of the content to other platforms, both today and in the future.

- *Has the proper hierarchical structure*—This is where a single container tag or root surrounds all other entities and tags declared and written in a syntactically correct and balanced manner.

- *Has properly declared tags*—A major difference between HTML and XML is in tag symmetry; in a proper hierarchical structure, empty tags do not exist.

When formatting your XML document, you use either a Cascading Style Sheets (CSS) text file or an XSL style sheet. The use of style sheets was popularized with the introduction of DHTML—a marketing term both Netscape and Microsoft use to differentiate their version 4 Web browsers from earlier products. CSS was a key component in this cross-browser technology and an important tool in purifying the HTML code for a rebirth and refocus in functional purpose. The latest version of CSS—level 2 (released in March 1998)—includes commands for object positioning on the display screen without major changes in scripting syntax.

You create a simple XML style sheet using XSL by loading the XML data into the client-side DOM, formatting the contents according to the style sheet specifications, and displaying the information. In fact, XSL is actually two languages in one; it consists of a transformation language that can transform XML into a well-formed HTML document and a language that applies formatting objects to XML code. These two features can work independently of each other so that you can transform XML without applying formatting rules, and vice versa. XSL improves upon CSS because it enables you to format and display both XML elements and attributes; CSS works only with the element. Also, XSL enables you to dynamically manipulate data; CSS, an older technology, displays only static XML data.

XML derives its flexibility from the use of an extensible metalanguage that is basically a grammar describing another grammar. XML allows you to build your own tags that define your own content or data. You write a script that executes a SQL-based query via ADO and obtain a recordset or equivalent data structure. Your XML tags describe various aspects of your data dictionary or field elements of that data structure. If your Presentation layer needs to display the content of the recordset in a particular way, XSL modifies the view of the data. For example, the following code snippet, written at the top of an XML script, transforms XML content into an HTML table based on the view defined by another text file, simple.xsl:

```
<?xml-stylesheet type="text/xsl" href="simple.xsl"?>
```

XSL as a language provides two major benefits. It is a transformation language for XML documents that enables you to transfer the content into other document formats that conform to SGML. It also provides an XML vocabulary for formatting semantics that provides the foundation for more complex formatting rules applied to more complex XML content. No software available supports all aspects of these specifications. The presentation or view of the data is independent of the programmed output through the combination of XSL and XML. Instead of integrating styling instructions with a Visual Basic–based application, current Web browser versions like IE5 can take full advantage of a markup language like XSL and direct browsing capabilities. XSL also provides for document transformation. XSL transforms an XML page into an HTML page or document rendered in another compatible medium, as shown in Figure 17.2.

Internet Explorer 5 (IE5)

Microsoft IE5, the latest version of the browser client, allows users to view and navigate XML documents just as they do HTML documents. IE5 can receive both HTML 4 and XML 1, which provide greater breadth in object selection and manipulation on the client side of the message exchange than earlier browser versions that rendered legacy HTML. The outward appearance of the document in CSS or XSL is identical to how HTML looks. The XSL software processor in IE5

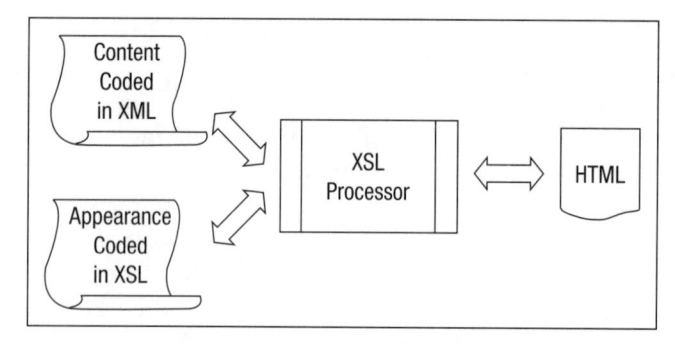

Figure 17.2 XML information transformed by XSL for any display device.

applies style sheets to XML content in a way that uncouples content from appearance. Thus, large amounts of client-side scripting overhead are removed from the content, often referred to as an XML *tree*. This separation allows developers to provide the same content to, for example, devices like a software browser, palm-top device, or wireless phone by simply applying different style sheets. The XSL processor can function on both the server and client sides of the Internet exchange. If it's run on the server side, all XML content is transformed to HTML or another display format before being sent to the client. Alternatively, if the XSL processor is executed in the client browser, both the XML document and XSL style sheet are sent to the browser, where the final display of the material is rendered.

The DHTML enhancements in IE5 provide greater client-side functionality than the features available in earlier scripting languages. DHTML also improves client response times, which is especially important when you are accessing resources across a public network. In addition, these enhancements improve server workload because processing is done within the client-side browser. Older client software reverts back to server-side processing to provide these OWA services. You can access DHTML behaviors more easily using simple CSS syntax than through scripting because CSS can use one external text file that contains format specifications affecting an entire collection of HTML documents; scripting typically affects only the document it is written in. The DHTML behaviors differ from ActiveX controls (discussed later in this chapter) in the way they are built; they use HTML components (HTC files) rather than C++ or Java compiled code. Thus, a more predictable security model is applied with the DHTML behaviors than with regular HTML because the security is a part of the native HTML scripting rather than from the operating system (OS) in which the document is displayed.

IE5 also provides greater programmatic control over other aspects of the document than legacy browser clients. For example, developers have greater control over the printing of documents than they did with earlier versions of the browser. You can access the Print dialog box by using the **window.print()** function, as well as adjust page layout before or after printing is completed.

Web Forms

Legacy Exchange 5.5 used ASP technology and OWA to create a Web-based application that looked and acted, for the most part, like its component-based counterpart, Outlook. The Outlook Forms Converter in Exchange 5.5 created custom HTML forms from the same ASP technology. Exchange 2000 has improved on these scripting approaches by using the Web Store.

Web Forms is a customized Web-based application that uses the Web Store and works within OWA as well as customized applications. The product is fundamentally based on HTML, so it is both browser and platform independent, running on both the newer IE4 and IE5 client through DHTML behaviors and older browsers running HTML 3.x or earlier versions. Thus, in the IE5 browser, Web Forms leverages both HTML and XML elements so that a developer can associate the fields with other objects or information in the Web Store to more rapidly create customized applications. FrontPage 2000 and the legacy FrontPage Web Form Authoring add-in simplify this process.

Exchange 2000 provides a more functional OWA Web Store than the legacy Exchange ASP scripting. It includes a broader range of Exchange objects like Outbox, calendar, and scheduling information to which the fields in Web Forms can link. Thus, the HTML scripting in the form prompts for a value, and, when the Web form is submitted, delivers it directly to a newly created object in the Web Store. All messaging and collaborative information is displayed in either the browser window or frames. You can access forms from a variety of libraries available in a drop-down list within the Choose Form dialog box, as shown in Figure 17.3, accessed from Choose Form in Tools|Forms.

Web Solutions

Collaborative application development has been a major theme in Exchange Server over the years. In earlier versions, Visual Basic Forms Designer was the only tool that developers had. It was robust and useful, but it too was intimidating and not well integrated with Exchange objects. MAPI, though available, was too complex for rapid application development, and coding a quick form required access to one or two data objects. This situation changed, however, with the introduction of technologies like ASP that have simplified the complexity of the coding process through interpretative scripts rather than component coding compiled into some kind of machine-executable code.

With the development of interpreted scripting, a variety of gateway methods have been developed to interface various scripting languages with different Web services. Rather than accessing database information directly, common gateway interface (CGI) scripts translated service requests into coded instructions that Web servers

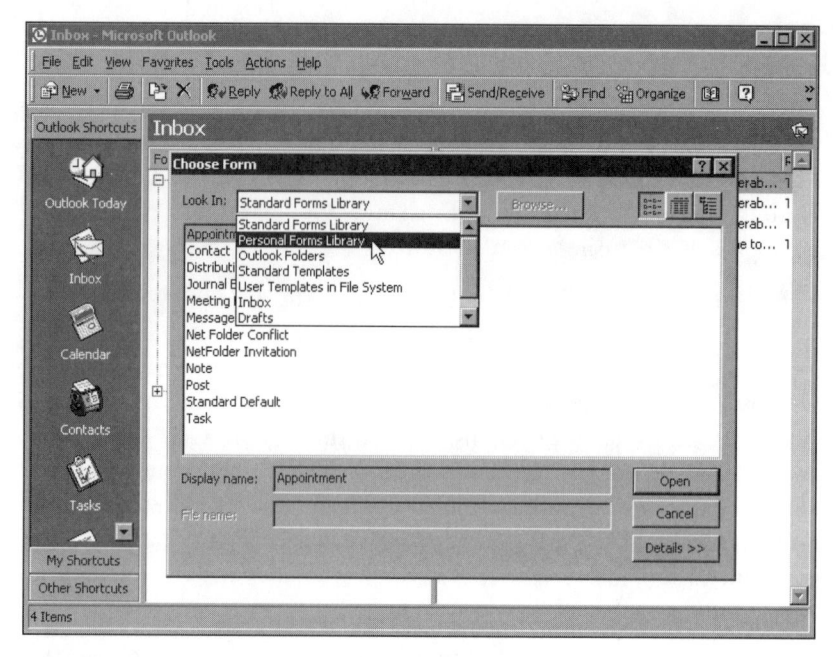

Figure 17.3 Accessing Web Forms through Outlook.

could process. Several methods access system and Registry information to process programmed instruction that provides server-side operations and resources. They include Open Database Connectivity (ODBC), Java Database Connectivity (JDBC), ColdFusion, and Active Platform.

ODBC

This Microsoft interface provides a simple way to access database information without specialized knowledge or even complicated code. The ODBC driver is a layer of software that communicates directly with a database that is assigned a data name called a data source name (DSN). The ODBC driver manager functions as an interface for a script or application that has generated a service request using, for example, SQL. The driver manager directly references the specific database provider using appropriate security credentials and other parameters. The script or application can then communicate through the established connectivity to access the data resources. The ODBC standard, though originally designed as a proprietary interface, is now considered a de facto standard that relational database products like IBM's DB2 and Oracle, as well as desktop applications like Microsoft Access and Excel, use. In NT 4 and Windows 2000, you must register the ODBC-compliant database as a system data source. In addition, for the ODBC-compliant database to be accessible to a user's interface with the resource from a Web-based environment, the system Registry must know that the database is there. This is necessary for service requests to be properly directed in the system.

JDBC

This Sun Microsystems interface provides an alternative interface to ODBC for a server to work with SQL-compliant databases. This, along with ODBC, has become a de facto standard in the server-side manipulation of database information. JDBC, like ODBC, uses system Registry entries to provide database services to Java through the Java API. SQL statements are processed within Java programs as Java objects. Although both ODBC and JDBC require specific drivers to operate, Java-related drivers tend to be compatible with more programming languages and OSs than ODBC-related drivers.

ColdFusion

Originally written as a CGI script, ColdFusion is now a compiled program that is packaged as both a Web authoring system and a separate Cold Fusion server that is necessary to facilitate database access using the Cold Fusion Markup Language (CFML). This solution uses a proprietary markup language, ColdFusion Markup Language, which provides an application-development environment with high-level query and retrieval functions but limited complexity in programming. It interfaces with the Web server through the appropriate API (such as ISAPI or Netscape API) as an add-on or plug-in.

Active Platform

Microsoft Active Platform is the foundation for designing and developing Internet and intranet business applications. It is a three-tier client/server model that has an extensible component-based architecture. Active Platform provides a simple-to-learn and easy-to-implement development environment because you use the same set of tools for both the client-side and server-side components. The platform is divided into three parts: ActiveX, Active Server, and Active Client.

ActiveX

This term connotes not a programming language but a set of technologies for delivering services to the Internet and intranets. ActiveX includes ActiveX controls and ActiveX scripts. ActiveX controls are versions of OLE software controls that have been reduced in size and overhead to optimize their use on the Internet. Both ActiveX and OLE are based on the Component Object Model (COM), which Microsoft uses to build software applications. COM provides specifications that are designed to ensure that two objects can interact and communicate with each other regardless of programming language or OS platform. *ActiveX scripting* is the collective term for JScript (Microsoft's open implementation of JavaScript) and VBScript. JScript 5.5 is the first scripting language that fully conforms to European Computer Manufacturers Association ECMAScript specifications.

Active Server and Active Client

The term Active Server describes IIS or any other Web server that supports Microsoft server-side scripting (more commonly known as ASP technology). An ASP script leverages both server-side processing power and HTML by using reusable software objects built into a DOM. The ASP application is made up of various elements that together form a usable interface that provides a service. Each application is composed of a collection of various text-based files, server objects, and components joined together by ASP scripting coded directly in the HTML document. ASP is easier to use than, for example, CGI scripting, because it is native to the Windows NT and 2000 platforms, often working directly through the ISAPI layer. It thus works more intimately with other software layers in the Microsoft OSs than an interpreted CGI script located "out of process."

Active Client is any browser that can support ActiveX components. The Internet Explorer family has naturally been able to complement Active Server because Microsoft developed both of these software components. Active Client is the primary presentation layer of any Web-based application. It must support the client-side scripting of Dynamic HTML, which mixes static HTML descriptive elements with interactive pieces of script written in interpreted codes like ECMAScript (formerly JavaScript), VBScript, and more recently, XML. Thus, the Active Client provides a robust user interface that leverages server-side functionality.

With Active Server Pages technology, you can create scripts with the same tools as Active Client and embed the specialized code within HTML. In addition, ASP can use Active Server components to keep an HTTP connection with the database server open and functioning in a persistent manner over time through a feature called *keep alive*, which optimizes the scripting performance. A CGI script will, alternatively, create or spawn a new process on its server platform for every new service request.

Active Server comes with the following predefined Active Server components that help build applications within an application:

- *Server-side scripting*—VBScript, ECMAScript, Perl, CGI, REXX, Java, ISAPI
- *Client-side scripting*—VBScript, ECMAScript, ActiveX controls, Java
- *Server-side objects*—Built-ins that control the ASP engine
- *File system objects*—Virtual, physical, and root directories, Access Control Lists (ACLs)
- *Server-side components*—COM-based objects that are scalable, manageable, and distributable
- *Text*—ASCII text that forms both HTML and XML tags

As you can see, there are many components of ASP technology. They are actually part of a larger model called Universal Data Access architecture, shown in Figure 17.4.

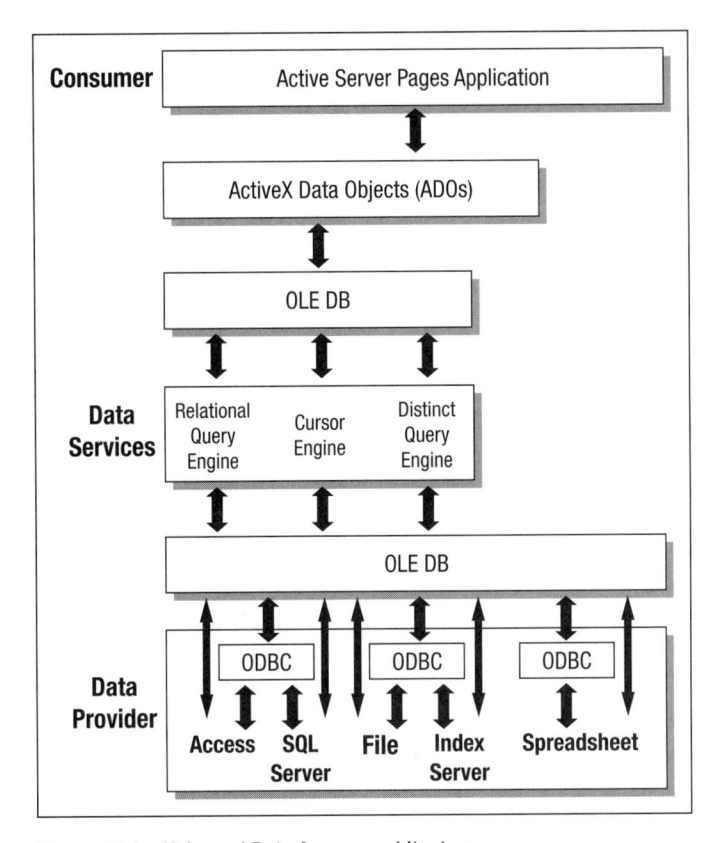

Figure 17.4 Universal Data Access architecture.

Universal Data Access is the Microsoft umbrella strategy that provides access to data in a client/server environment or intranet. It is relational or nonrelational. Diverse data sources are made accessible through the Microsoft Data Access Components (MDAC). This consists of new versions of ADO, OLE DB, and ODBC, which are supported as one release.

Exchange APIs

Exchange offers a large range of technologies that you can use to rapidly develop applications as well as leverage predefined and tested methods to access data objects from the Web Store. Exchange 2000, like Windows 2000, is built as an extensible platform. It provides this feature by using standards-based and well-known APIs. These component interfaces are actually libraries of reusable functions that collectively form dynamic link library (DLL) files. A developer can write source code that requests these functions to perform a service. Aside from the fact that using these functions is simpler than writing new code, the function specifications are well known, the code is reusable, and the performance is guaranteed to work.

OLE DB and ADO

One component that builds data-driven dynamic Web applications is ADO, a subset of a larger, more complex API, the OLE DB model. OLE DB provides a scriptable interface that permits servers to share both structured and unstructured data types, including multimedia. It is a specification for a set of data-access interfaces that enable a multitude of data stores to work as a single unit. Exchange 2000's OLE DB provider allows direct access to the Web Store. OLE DB, unlike ODBC, accesses both structured and unstructured information; databases; and, for example, Word and other Office file types. In highly technical terms and as shown in Figure 17.5, ADO provides an interface, whereas OLE DB, like ODBC, actually accesses the data source. This is why OLE DB, which deals with a broad range of data, is so much more complex than ADO as a programming API.

ASP works with ADO to provide database connectivity. ADO is part of a bigger picture, the COM that Microsoft formulated to support the development of applications through the conceptualization of separate software objects, written in different languages yet working in a complementary and supporting capacity. As mentioned earlier in this chapter, you use the ADO interface to access objects in the Web Store. ADO provides support for all Microsoft database APIs and contains built-in features that provide developers with access to client-side dynamic objects. Thus, for example, you can use the ADO API to query specific records in a relatively easy sequence of programmatic steps.

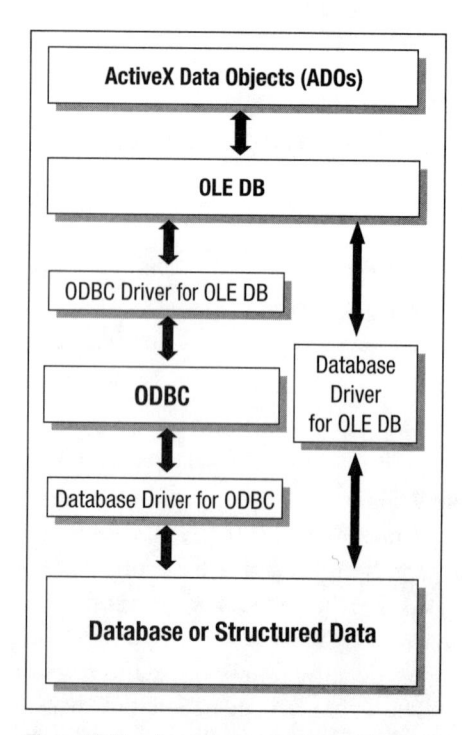

Figure 17.5 Accessing a database using ADO.

ADSI

Active Directory Services Interface (ADSI) is a standardized Windows-based interface for multiple or metadirectory applications. A *metadirectory* is a network-level directory service that organizes and manages resource and permission information from separate network OSs. You use ADSI to access the entire range of objects found in AD directory services—from machines and groups to user attributes. This interface also provides access to user information from a Web-based application. ADSI can leverage capabilities and features from other network OSs and directory services that use well-known or standards-based protocols such as LDAP, Novell Directory Services (NDS), and NT Directory Services (NTDS).

CDO

The CDO library provides an API that simplifies complex operations that specifically involve messaging objects (such as calendars, tasks, and scheduled events) so that they are easily accessible and manageable in the Web Store. CDO is an API specification that defines the objects, interfaces, functions, and properties of each messaging and collaborative object. CDO, along with OWA, was introduced with Exchange 5.5. CDO in Windows 2000 is a Simple Mail Transfer Protocol (SMTP)-based library. Exchange 2000 upgrades Windows CDO during its installation and adds new features and a larger range of functions to the CDO libraries. Exchange 2000 CDO is compatible with all existing libraries and works with ADO and OLE DB.

MAPI

You use this industry-wide standard for writing messages and workflow applications to create and access many of the oldest mail applications and messaging systems. It provides a uniform environment for development and standard use. You can program a simple request from any program to access a messaging service through an entry point in the DLL and pass a record to an externally defined messaging structure. Full MAPI conforms to the Microsoft COM. CDO was designed to simplify much of the coding needed to use the many MAPI features.

.NET Framework

Exchange has been described as the first .NET server. Microsoft's .NET software initiative proposes to simplify the development and deployment of Web applications and services. Even if Microsoft's initiative never achieves full fruition, Exchange 2000 remains an extensible platform for messaging and collaborative services fundamental to any e-commerce undertaking. Exchange 2000 blends transparently into the infrastructure of an enterprise while delivering levels of service appropriate to the 24x7 world of e-commerce on the Internet. This reliability and extensibility have positioned Exchange Server as a fundamental Web service layer in the proposed .NET landscape.

The .NET framework, shown schematically in Figure 17.6, gives you a unified approach when you are developing and deploying Web applications and services. It is a layered infrastructure that rests on core network OS services. This initiative is a necessary step in providing loosely connected distributed services in both a private namespace (like a corporate enterprise) and a public network (like the Internet). The framework provides a common language runtime engine, though "engine" probably does not carry the correct connotation. .NET is a framework within which solutions are assembled or interconnected rather than a platform on which these component parts are run.

It is important to remember that unlike legacy Exchange 5.5 operating on NT 4, Exchange 2000 requires that the network OS it runs on have IIS 5 installed as a properly configured component. This is another example of partitioned services that specifically characterizes .NET servers and Windows 2000 in general. We can discuss the .NET framework or any generic multitier architecture built on top of OS services and still use Figure 17.6.

As we have discussed throughout this book, the theme of partitioning system services so that you can distribute them throughout an enterprise in Exchange has been a significant architectural trend. Although the details are outside the scope of this book, the .NET architecture is significant in that Exchange is considered the first in a family of distributed service providers. Although the concepts in this chapter are more often associated with Web application development, our thesis here is that all these features are built into the Exchange 2000 design and were intended to create a central broker of information services useful in any Internet-based endeavor. Component-based software applications have powered enterprise and commercial interests for many years. As their popularity has grown, constraints concerned with distribution and licensing have increased as well. Web services are evolving into a virtual ocean filled with floating objects and functionality into which you can plug your standard browser software. These Web-based objects and

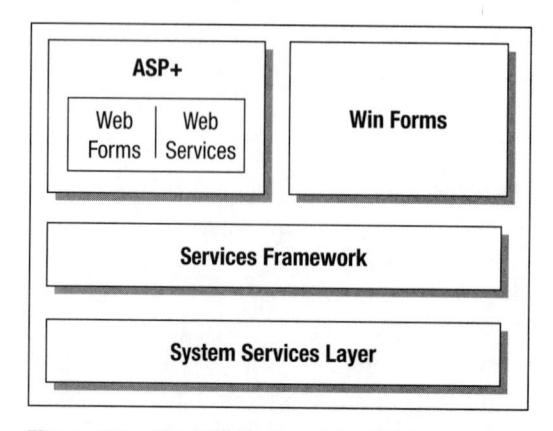

Figure 17.6 The .NET framework architecture.

services, though still problematic especially in the area of security, attract much attention because they clearly provide more value than component-based software in the areas of scalable services.

In the first chapter of this book, Figure 1.1 shows a pyramid composed of the various new service providers Microsoft has released since the beginning of 2000. Commerce Server 2000, providing scalable business-to-consumer (B2C) and business-to-business (B2B) sites with analytic tools, sits at the apex of this family of .NET servers; we have put Exchange 2000 at the base. The development of online services is based on both messaging and process. A component-based software application doesn't require a messaging platform, but it also doesn't scale well across an enterprise, much less the Internet. The World Wide Web has entangled our earth and our information technologies in a digital mesh. In less than 50 years we have evolved from blinking lights, banks of toggle switches, and 128 kilobytes memory to digital dashboards, knowledge objects, and memory measured in gigabytes. As inhabitants of a global village, we have come to expect information wherever we are, at any time, and from any available device. Exchange 2000 provides the messaging and collaborative platform on which document and content management are built. It provides an infrastructure much like Active Directory provides a namespace because communication and collaboration are fundamental to activities, culture, and the social cohesion of humankind. No matter how great the interest in online services, the need for reliable messaging will always overshadow process features because there is no workflow without communication and no progress without collaboration. If an extensible platform combines both messaging and collaborative services, it will, in fact, provide the perfect foundation on which to manage knowledge or engage in forms of public or private activity. Exchange 2000 is positioned as that Web-based application platform; as its administrator, you are positioned to coordinate and direct its services.

Chapter Summary

This chapter reviews the issues that are involved in extending the Exchange platform:

- ▶ The Web Storage System is based on three key service areas: file system (Win32) support services, database services, and collaboration services. The Exchange 2000 structure is partitioned so that the Web Storage System handles all database issues.

- ▶ Web Store support of both the Web-based data types and older unstructured data like Office file types in the Win32 file system extends the range of data objects that can be accessed and managed through programmatic control. It's significant that these data objects are accessible from the same interface and displayed without discernable differences through an interface like a digital dashboard. Features like property promotion, which automatically provides a consistent view of data, support the concept of a universal Inbox as well as the platform and application independence of displaying the data.

- Rich HTML support, specifically in the forms of DHTML and XML, leverages the native features of the Web Store and provides client-side processing performance benefits.

- You can monitor Web Storage events by using event sinks, which are applications to which notifications are sent if a defined system condition is met or occurs. Event sinks form the basis of the programmatic control of dynamic events that occur with Exchange 2000 or another associated service layer.

- Web service clients differ in terms of their DOM. These DOMs render information encoding in scripting languages. Thus, differences in the display of content arise from how the DOM interprets the syntax of the scripting language.

- You can think of server components like OWA as brokering service layers for all messaging traffic. For example, in the case of proxy requests, ISAPI receives service calls to IIS 5 and relays them to the Web Store. This partitioning of services mirrors the Presentation layer, Business Logic layer, and Database layer multitier architecture model.

- OWA in Exchange 2000 is accessed by HTTP and interacts with IIS rather than the legacy approach of using MAPI and ASP technology.

- Significant support for Web Storage Services comes from the HTTP and WebDAV extensions, which provide a way, using URL addresses, to locate and manipulate CDOs. WebDAV provides an extensible way to identify and manipulate content and extends the capability of HTTP with a greater set of commands and features like concurrency controls, namespace manipulations, and enhanced properties.

- FE/BE architecture provides various benefits, including a single namespace and the offload of CPU-intensive processing like encryption, public folder referrals, and isolated server location to simplify security like firewall technology.

- Markup languages use specialized tags to indicate special treatment of text in a text-based script. Specific markup languages generate code that is specific to an application or platform; generalized markup languages describe a structure and meaning of the text but not how the text should be used. Thus, generalized markup languages are based on describing text independent of the Presentation layer.

- HTML and XML are standards-based markup languages derived from SGML. HTML is a page description language, whereas XML primarily defines content. XML is an attempt to create universal usability; compatibility with other SGML-compliant scripting languages; and simplified, rapid development of Web-based applications. XML is well defined and valid. XSL can both format and translate the content defined by the XML script. The transformation of XML to, for example, HTML allows you to easily alter the view of data to accommodate different methods of presentation, such as desktop display and cellular phone display.

➤ Script support helps to extend the Exchange messaging platform because processing can be offloaded to the client side when IE5 and DHTML are used as coding instructions. In addition, the Web Store supports the same ADO interfaces as the older component-based programs use to manipulate data. These scripts can access the same OLE DB provider compiled programming language used to handle data.

➤ Server access is enhanced in Exchange 2000 because Outlook clients make service requests directly to Exchange Server. Browser clients access the message stores through OWA, which interfaces with IIS Web Services. This partitioning of service responsibility on the server side improves response performance. IE5—with native capacity to support HTML, DHTML, and XML—provides a broader range of accessible objects than legacy browsers and offloads services to the client.

➤ Web Forms and the use of OWA provide advantages such as easily deployed light messaging, low-overhead management of roving users, easily deployed kiosk and information source outlets, and backup support during migration.

➤ Two cultural approaches have become de facto standards in the server-side manipulation of database information: Microsoft's ODBC and Sun's JDBC. Other implementations include ColdFusion.

➤ Microsoft's Active Platform is composed of ActiveX, Active Server, and Active Client (IE). ASP technology is a key solution to server-side scripting.

➤ Exchange 2000 provides several different APIs for programmatic control of data objects, including ADO, ADSI, CDO, MAPI, and OLE DB.

➤ Exchange has been described as the first .NET server because of its design and positioning in relation to the Windows NOSs and other servers and service layers that rely on messaging and collaborative support.

Review Questions

1. You can transform XML to HTML using what language?
    a. HTML
    b. XML
    c. XSL
    d. XHTML

2. If you needed to write scripting code that modifies the appearance rather than the content of information, which language(s) would you use?

    a. HTML
    b. XSL
    c. XML
    d. Answers a and b

3. In a three-tier application model, what are the three tiers? [Check all correct answers]

    a. Presentation layer
    b. Data layer
    c. Network layer
    d. Business Logic layer

4. In OWA architecture, what layer or service authenticates the user?

    a. AD
    b. IIS
    c. ISAPI
    d. SAS

5. What service or layer in OWA determines the proper response form to a service request?

    a. IIS
    b. ISAPI
    c. EXIFS
    d. Forms Registry

6. The browser client communicates with what service or layer when requesting data services?

    a. Web Store
    b. EXIFS
    c. IIS
    d. EPOXY

7. When OWA returns a request to an IE5 browser, what scripting languages can it use to render its response? [Check all correct answers]

    a. DHTML
    b. HTML
    c. XML
    d. XSL

8. What protocol(s) does OWA use to proxy service requests to BE servers?
   a. HTTP
   b. LDAP
   c. SMTP
   d. Answers a and b

9. What benefits does an FE/BE architecture provide? [Check all correct answers]
   a. A single namespace
   b. A single sign on
   c. More efficient SSL encryption/decryption services
   d. Easier deployment of security measures

10. What are the key specific management functional areas (SMFAs) built into the Web Store? [Check all correct answers]
    a. Database services
    b. File system services
    c. Security services
    d. Protocol services

11. Which is not a key feature of the Web Store?
    a. Support for rich HTML
    b. Support of Win16 applications
    c. Support for ADOs
    d. Folder replication

12. What benefit does OWA provide with significantly less overhead than the full-featured Outlook application?
    a. Policy-based management
    b. Messaging and collaborative services
    c. Remote user support
    d. Web Forms

13. In what scripting languages are forms rendered for IE5 browser clients? [Check all correct answers]
    a. HTML
    b. The same markup language as IE3
    c. XML
    d. The same markup language as IE4

14. What features are provided with WebDAV extensions that are not found in HTML alone? [Check all correct answers]

    a. Concurrency control

    b. Log tracking

    c. Protocol control

    d. Extensible code

15. What is not an objective of the XML language design?

    a. Universal usability

    b. SGML compatibility

    c. Rapid development

    d. Backward compatibility with HTML

16. Which statement about DTD is false?

    a. DTD defines how elements are displayed.

    b. DTD defines rules that validate a document's syntax.

    c. DTD means that a document is a self-describing script and more portable than a script without DTD.

    d. HTML uses DTD.

17. What are the most significant XML characteristics? [Check all correct answers]

    a. Documents are well formed.

    b. Documents are valid.

    c. Documents are cross compatible.

    d. Documents are standardized.

18. Where is the XSL processor located?

    a. The processor is on the server side.

    b. The processor is on the client side.

    c. It is a separate processor running complementary to a server.

    d. Answers a and b.

19. Which statement about IE5 is false?

    a. It allows you to view both XML and HTML code.

    b. It provides a greater opportunity to perform client-side tasks than legacy browsers like IE3 and IE4.

    c. It provides greater programmatic support for scripting than legacy browsers.

    d. It uses C++ and Java compiled code rather than HTC files.

20. Do you have to change your standard browser configuration to read XML code?
    a. Yes.
    b. No.
    c. You can configure the browser to read XML if you know the browser version.
    d. You can configure IE4 or later browsers using an XML processor plug-in; IE5 reads XML code directly.

Real-World Projects

Harry has noticed that when he opens email using a standard browser and the URL **http://servername/exchange/harrys**, a hyperlink on the right side of his screen says, View As A Web Page. If he clicks on the link, he can see the message just like a Web page. He wants to learn more about how this is done. He knows this message has been rewritten in HTML.

Harry wants to see how the HTML source code is written. He is using IE5 to view the HTML document. In the IE5 menu bar, Harry selects View|Source. A Notepad window showing the HTML source code opens. Harry examines this source code carefully. He notices that the script contains the markup tags that begin with "<" and end with ">". He recognizes the lengthy DTD and notices several **<META>** key words. Finally, enclosed within several tags, he sees his message.

Harry wants to try writing his own simple script.

Project 17.1
To create a simple HTML message:

1. From the desktop, right-click on the display area and select New|Text Document.

2. While the label is highlighted, type "testdoc.htm" and press the Enter key. The three-letter extension is important. You should see an error message that says, "Rename—If you change a filename extension, the file may become unusable. Are you sure you want to change it?" Click on Yes. Your object should reappear with the IE icon.

Note: Hiding an object's file extension as a desktop preference is the default. To avoid problems when writing scripting language code, best practices recommend showing file extensions. To do so, access the View option from any Explorer window and disenable this feature. In Windows 2000, it is located under Tools|Folder Options.

3. Open the newly created document in your IE browser window. It is a blank screen.

4. Select View|Source from the menu bar. You have opened a second window in Notepad.

5. To create a simple HTML script, enter this code exactly as follows:

```
<html>
<head><title> Test Script </title></head>
<body bgcolor="#ff0000">
This is a test message.
</body>
</html>
```

6. Select File | Exit and then click on Yes to save your changes.

7. Either press F5 on your keyboard or select View | Refresh. You will see a red screen with your message in the browser window.

Project 17.2

To create a simple XML script from the HTML script you just created:

1. Reopen the text editor view of testdoc.htm by selecting View | Source.

2. Add the following line of code to the top of the HTML source code above the opening **<HTML>** tag:

```
<?xml version="1.0">.
```

3. Go to the **<body>** tag and change **#ff0000** to **#ffff00**, which replaces the hexadecimal code for the color red with the code for the color yellow.

4. Select File | Exit and then click on Yes to save your changes.

5. Press the F5 key on your keyboard to refresh your browser. The screen will turn yellow.

Harry knows that HTML and XML code are very similar. In fact, XML uses HTML code words except that it applies more rigorous grammatical rules to the code. It is said to be well defined and must be valid. Harry also realizes that one item missing from the XML script is a DTD. Nevertheless, he knows that adding the opening **<?xml version="1.0">** is sufficient to have the code parsed by the XML processor in the IE5 browser. Harry expects the code to work. He realizes that he actually didn't use XML to define any content. He is going to try doing that as soon as he can find a book about XML syntax.

CHAPTER EIGHTEEN

Sample Test

Question 1

What native transport does Exchange 2000 Server use to provide a scalable messaging system?

○ a. Network News Transport Protocol

○ b. Simple Mail Transfer Protocol

○ c. Post Office Protocol

○ d. Internet Message Access Protocol

Question 2

In which type of file does Exchange 2000 Server store native content, such as MIME content?

○ a. In an STM file

○ b. In an IFS file

○ c. In an IMAP file

○ d. In a POP file

Question 3

What activities become possible using the Installable File System in Exchange 2000? [Check all correct answers]

❑ a. It allows you to dedicate servers to specific tasks.

❑ b. It allows you to use Exchange Server as a repository for applications.

❑ c. It allows you to map a mailbox as a shared drive.

❑ d. It allows you to reduce network traffic for certain segments.

Question 4

How many public folder stores are found in a default server installation of Exchange 2000?

○ a. There are multiple stores but only one public folder hierarchy.

○ b. There are multiple hierarchies but only one public folder store.

○ c. There are no public folder stores enabled by default.

○ d. There is one store and one hierarchy by default.

Question 5

What component of Exchange 2000 Server now hosts the SMTP and POP3 protocols?

○ a. The Web Storage System

○ b. The ESE

○ c. The first available process

○ d. The inetinfo process

Question 6

What is the primary function of the EXIPC within Exchange 2000?

○ a. It allows users to connect to virtual front-end servers.

○ b. It allows rapid transfer of data between the IIS process and the Web Storage System process.

○ c. It allows processing of SMTP within IIS rather than the Internet Mail Service.

○ d. It allows the System Manager to configure the SMTP service instead of the System Attendant.

Question 7

How does Exchange 2000 Server fit into Microsoft's new paradigm shift?

○ a. It forces Microsoft to focus on providing superior technical services.

○ b. It forces Microsoft to become the premier messaging service provider.

○ c. It helps Microsoft deliver more encompassing technology through its .NET initiative.

○ d. It helps organizations achieve "five 9" reliabilities.

Question 8

How are Web-based applications represented according to the Windows DNA model?

○ a. As a combination of a user interface, business logic, and data services

○ b. As a combination of loosely coupled distributed services

○ c. As a protocol-independent architecture in which to analyze services

○ d. As a combination of specific management functional areas

Question 9

Which of the following describe critical roles defined by the Generic Architecture for Information Availability (GAIA)? [Check all correct answers]

❏ a. A customer

❏ b. A broker

❏ c. A supplier

❏ d. A helper

Question 10

What is the underlying goal of the Microsoft Operations Framework model?

○ a. To provide guidance on managing enterprise-based technologies

○ b. To manage discrete transactions known as actions on behalf of a consumer

○ c. To perform a single front-end object for a consumer

○ d. To manage physically separate processes to provide a unified service

Question 11

How does a messaging system such as Microsoft Mail differ in concept from a system such as Exchange Server?

○ a. Microsoft Mail resembles a host-centric system, whereas Exchange Server resembles a shared-file system.

○ b. Microsoft Mail resembles a shared-file system, whereas Exchange Server represents client/server technology.

○ c. Microsoft Mail consists of a General Post Office, which manages message flow, whereas Exchange Server utilizes the System Attendant for message flows.

○ d. Microsoft Mail is a synchronous messaging system, whereas Exchange Server is an asynchronous messaging system.

Question 12

Which part of an email message can be described as an external payload that provides a method for transferring documents to a recipient?

○ a. The attachment

○ b. The signature

○ c. The message body

○ d. The message header

Question 13

What component helps an Exchange Server–based messaging system communicate with a foreign email system and actually translate between the two mail formats?

○ a. Administrative Group

○ b. Routing Group

○ c. Connector

○ d. Message Stores

Question 14

How has the X.500 directory services model enhanced the X.400 messaging model?

○ a. It provides multiple namespaces for most systems based on the X.400 standard.

○ b. It helps provide a framework in which to develop a single namespace of resources.

○ c. It establishes a Directory System Agent for the X.400 MTA.

○ d. It allows DUAs to request directory services from a local DIT.

Question 15

Which service included in Exchange 2000 shows an indication that Microsoft is trying to incorporate various nonmail information-sharing services in its new messaging architecture?

○ a. Unix-to-Unix Copy for transferring ASCII text messages

○ b. MIME encoding for transmitting non-ASCII binary files

○ c. LISTSERV for managing distribution lists

○ d. Microsoft Repository for managing programmable data stores

Question 16

What would be the appropriate product to install for a business that required a 15GB database, automatic installation and configuration, and Internet connectivity?

○ a. Microsoft Exchange 2000 Server

○ b. Microsoft Exchange 2000 Enterprise Server

○ c. Microsoft Exchange 2000 Advanced Server

○ d. Microsoft Exchange 2000 Conferencing Server

Question 17

What component of the Exchange 5.x architecture was equivalent to the MS in the X.400 specifications?

- ○ a. System Attendant
- ○ b. Private Information Store
- ○ c. Message Transfer Agent
- ○ d. Directory Service

Question 18

You have a single server running in a legacy Exchange 5.5 site. You have not yet configured any external connectors for messaging transport outside your site. What is the purpose of the MTA component in your current configuration?

- ○ a. It converts messages from its default MAPI format to an X.400 format.
- ○ b. It temporarily resolves names through directory service lookups.
- ○ c. It assists in public folder replication as well as internal message transport.
- ○ d. It assists in the expansion of distribution lists in your system.

Question 19

Which Exchange service now functions as the center of communication among an administrator, Certificate Services, the System Attendant, and the cryptographic service provider?

- ○ a. Key Management Service
- ○ b. Certificate Authority
- ○ c. Microsoft Management Console
- ○ d. Microsoft Directory Synchronization Service

Question 20

Your manager tells you that your new Exchange 2000 Enterprise Server will need to handle mixed-mode connections for both inbound and outbound message flow. You tell her that the SMTP transport will manage this function effectively. What else must you consider for full message functionality in this case?

○ a. The SMTP protocol should handle all communications in this scenario.

○ b. Various connectors will be needed to guarantee message connectivity in this scenario.

○ c. The SMTP transport will handle native communications, whereas an X.400 connector should handle any mixed-mode communications.

○ d. The SMTP transport that works with the MTA will effectively handle all message transports because you're installing the Enterprise edition of Exchange Server.

Question 21

When looking at the workflow of a legacy Exchange server, what would you state as the primary difference between the IS and the MTA?

○ a. The IS monitored servers and connections, whereas the MTA replicated information.

○ b. The MTA managed routing and delivery, whereas the IS handled message storage.

○ c. The IS controlled access to the MS, whereas the MTA replicated remote directory services.

○ d. The MTA performed local delivery functions, whereas the IS referenced store.exe for remote delivery.

Question 22

You have just implemented a new Exchange 2000 Server project for a hospital. You are now concerned with ongoing operational aspects of your new Exchange site and want to conform to the MOF model of operations. What key issues are you most concerned with now? [Check all correct answers]

❑ a. The issue of forming collaborative solutions on a layer distinct from the actual operating system

❑ b. The prospect of enhanced scalability for your new messaging infrastructure

❑ c. Whether your implementation will deliver promised features at agreed-upon service levels

❑ d. How closely you can integrate protocol services with directory services

Question 23

When you consider implementing an installation of a production Exchange 2000 system that will not include any legacy messaging systems, what will be the first phase of your installation plan?

○ a. Creating a deployment scenario that validates and optimizes your enterprise design

○ b. Deploying the structural aspects of your enterprise domains, sites, and schemas

○ c. Implementing the changeover from a solutions framework to an operational framework

○ d. Preparing the Active Directory via modifications in the enterprise schema

Question 24

You would like to work with a new console, using the Windows MMC, to administer a just-released third-party snap-in tool. What command syntax should you use to create a new console root container in Author Mode?

○ a. **mmc /a filename.msc/path**

○ b. **mmc path/filename.msc**

○ c. **mmc path /author filename.msc**

○ d. **mmc path/filename.msc /a**

Question 25

What do standalone snap-in tools have in common with extension snap-in tools with regard to the Windows 2000 MMC and Exchange Server?

○ a. Both instrumentations function without any additional support from other snap-ins.

○ b. Both components conform to the multidocument interface specification.

○ c. Both interfaces may increase an organization's TCO by using nonstandard console frames.

○ d. Both components are opened in Author Mode by default.

Question 26

You have two SMTP email addresses for every user in your organization and would like to control the conditions under which one of these addresses will be used. Would Exchange 2000 Server support your efforts to implement this type of control?

○ a. Yes, because server-side management centralizes control of all SMTP messaging.

○ b. No, only a system policy can adjust SMTP settings in a distributed environment.

○ c. Yes, by using a single recipient policy class that controls email address generation.

○ d. No, the default policy in the Recipients Policies container prohibits multiple SMTP addresses.

Question 27

Which of the following is not a correct statement regarding Administrative Groups in native mode?

○ a. Membership in one Administrative Group precludes membership in a Routing Group that belongs to a second Administrative Group.

○ b. Once membership in an Administrative Group has been assigned, you are prevented from moving a server to another Administrative Group.

○ c. The Exchange Tasks Wizard enables you to move mailbox data stores between servers within an Administrative Group.

○ d. You can create one or more Routing Groups to handle message transfer within Administrative Groups.

Question 28

Your IT director has justified an upgrade to Exchange 2000 Server based on specific user requirements. Users in your company want to easily publish HTML documents that are stored in public folders using Microsoft Word. How can you best satisfy this end-user requirement in a technical fashion?

○ a. Establish Instant Messaging services for the end users.

○ b. Implement Exchange 2000 with its Web Store and the IFS.

○ c. Allow full-text indexing of documents in mailbox stores.

○ d. Define administrative policies for managing mailboxes.

Question 29

Why is it recommended that Exchange 2000 servers be placed in a DNS zone on a Windows 2000 DNS server?

○ a. Even legacy Exchange servers relied on DNS as their preferred naming service.

○ b. Exchange servers use RPCs and DNS to locate other servers.

○ c. Clients query DNS to locate the nearest Global Catalog server.

○ d. This action is recommended only if using DNS bind 4 or later.

Question 30

You are planning your Exchange 2000 environment and have discovered a one-to-one relationship between the number of Active Directory forests and your Exchange organizations. How will this affect your Exchange GAL?

○ a. The GAL can display users from only a single forest.

○ b. The GAL can display users from multiple forests.

○ c. The GAL is not affected in any way unless you exceed minimum thresholds.

○ d. The GAL is part of the configuration partition of Active Directory.

Question 31

Bob wants to install Exchange 2000 for the first time and does not know whether he should run ForestPrep. All his Exchange servers will be in a single domain, and the domain contains the schema master. What two other conditions must be true so Bob does not have to run ForestPrep?

❑ a. All the Exchange users will be in the domain.

❑ b. Domain-level permissions should be delegated to specific Exchange 2000 processes.

❑ c. Bob is using an account with Enterprise Admin and Schema Admin permissions.

❑ d. Bob will first use the Windows 2000 LDP tool to edit data in AD.

Question 32

Bob now wants to help his friend upgrade an existing Exchange 5.5 organization. What should Bob instruct his friend to do before running ForestPrep?

○ a. Run DomainPrep to make changes to the local domain naming context.

○ b. Run Exchange 2000 setup to upgrade an existing Exchange 5.5 server.

○ c. Run user connection agreements to synchronize Exchange 5.5 mailboxes.

○ d. Install the ADC to extend and replicate the current schema to all DCs.

Question 33

You have an Exchange server named Orion and a virtual directory pointing to m:\books.com\MBX. The virtual directory points to your users' private folders. All users share a common SMTP naming convention of *userid*@**books.com**. How will user Frank access his private mailbox using Outlook Web Access?

○ a. By typing "http://Orion/Frank@books.com" in a browser window

○ b. By typing "http://Orion/Frank" in a browser window

○ c. By typing "http://exchange/Orion/" in a browser window

○ d. By typing "http://Orion/exchange/Frank" in a browser window

Question 34

You have a POP3 client that points to one Exchange 5.5 server for incoming and outgoing mail, as well as for LDAP directory services. If you decide to upgrade this server to Exchange 2000, would you need to implement any other changes with regard to your POP3 client?

○ a. Yes, your LDAP server will have to be changed if the Exchange 2000 Server is not configured as a Global Catalog server.

○ b. Yes, you will now need one server for incoming mail and one server for outgoing mail.

○ c. No, the original configurations remain intact even after you upgrade to Exchange 2000 Server.

○ d. No, all server fields remain valid, but you may have to repoint clients to an existing Global Catalog server in a remote administrative domain.

Question 35

Sue is administering a legacy Exchange 5.5 organization and wants to create three recipient containers for her users' mailboxes. Why is this not a recommended practice?

○ a. It becomes difficult to move mailboxes among various containers.

○ b. It is hard to create an OU structure to delegate control over users.

○ c. You can't adjust attributes for messaging groups with multiple containers.

○ d. Using multiple containers limits the use of the Delegation of Control Wizard.

Question 36

What is the relationship in Exchange 2000 between moving a user mailbox and moving a user object in Active Directory?

○ a. Mailboxes can be moved between mailbox stores after you move the user object in AD.

○ b. Mailboxes can be moved between servers only if you move the user object in AD.

○ c. Mailboxes can be moved between mailbox stores regardless of whether user objects are moved.

○ d. Mailboxes can be moved between Routing Groups if the user object is moved in AD.

Question 37

What is true of the Administrative Views area on the General tab of an organization's Properties sheet in Exchange 2000 Server?

○ a. The Administrative Group interface is enabled by default.

○ b. The Administrative Group interface is disabled by default.

○ c. Your organization has to be in native mode to view Administrative Groups.

○ d. Administrative Views are configured using **regedt32** and the MMC.

Question 38

Bill has set up Routing Groups for his Exchange 2000 organization and would like to connect his Routing Groups with connectors. His friend suggested using the Routing Group connector but Bill would like to try a connector originally designed for an off-the-shelf email system used in his previous company. Is this a recommended practice?

- ○ a. No, you can use only the RGC or the SMTP connector to connect Routing Groups.
- ○ b. Yes, most connectors can be used to connect various Routing Groups.
- ○ c. No, the X.400 connector should be used for limited-bandwidth connections.
- ○ d. No, connectors designed for third-party email systems cannot connect Routing Groups.

Question 39

You have a remote server connector that resembles the Internet Mail Service from a legacy Exchange server in your organization. You also want to define transport layer security and other security parameters for your end users. Ideally, which connector should you configure for your Exchange server?

- ○ a. A Routing Group connector, because it is the easiest way to connect Routing Groups.
- ○ b. The X.400 connector, because it guarantees delivery over low-bandwidth connections.
- ○ c. An SMTP connector, because it is most compatible with the IMC from legacy versions.
- ○ d. All connectors would provide similar functionality and similar levels of security in this case.

Question 40

You are configuring a Lotus Notes connector on your Exchange 2000 server named Phantom. You have just installed the Notes client version 4.6. What should you do now before starting a connection between your Notes server and your Exchange server?

- ○ a. Install the Notes client on the Exchange connector server.
- ○ b. Create an ID file for the connector in your Notes environment.
- ○ c. Create a notes.ini file for the connector in your Notes environment.
- ○ d. Create a Mail Router database associated with your Exchange server.

Question 41

Sylvia is running an MS Mail Post Office version 3.2. She wants to incorporate a new Exchange 2000 server and hopes the two mail systems can coexist. She installs an MS Mail connector and is now looking for the connector directory on her Exchange server. Where can she find this directory?

○ a. \Exchsrvr\Conn\MSMail

○ b. \Exchsrvr\conndata\dxamex

○ c. \exchsrvr\conndata\dxams

○ d. \Exchsrvr\Connect\Msmcon

Question 42

Mike is concerned about secure email and is considering using both session-based and message-based security. He knows that a PKI can verify and authenticate the validity of all parties involved in an electronic exchange. What component actually establishes a PKI?

○ a. Windows 2000 Certificate Services

○ b. Exchange 2000 KMS

○ c. Outlook 2000 Professional client

○ d. Exchange 2000 enterprise KMS

Question 43

BigBooks.com hosts its own root CA, and both external and internal email clients send and receive secured email. The manager, Danny, wants to use a commercial root CA so that trust relationships will be simplified. What will happen to his existing issuing CA?

○ a. There will be more administrative overhead in archiving root CA certificates.

○ b. The issuing CA will become subordinate to the commercial root CA.

○ c. There will be minimal dependency on external organizations.

○ d. The Windows 2000 issuing CA becomes equal to the commercial root CA.

Question 44

When comparing the IM service with the Chat Service in Exchange 2000, how would you classify meeting styles versus meeting structures for the two services?

○ a. Both the IM and Chat Service have a semistructured, open-forum meeting style.

○ b. IM has an open-forum meeting style, whereas Chat Service is closed forum.

○ c. IM has a closed-forum meeting style, whereas Chat Service is open forum.

○ d. IM is semi-structured, whereas Chat Service is more immediate.

Question 45

You have just installed and configured IM on your single Exchange server. However, you just discovered that one of your users is sending inappropriate material using his IM client. How can you disable this user's access to the IM service without using the Exchange Task Wizard?

○ a. Find the user's folder in AD Users and Computers, select Properties, and disable all services on the IM tab.

○ b. Find the user's folder in AD Sites and Services, select the IM container, choose Properties, and then select Disable IM Services.

○ c. You have to create a DWORD Registry entry called **IMDisable** and set the value to 1.

○ d. Use the Exchange Features tab of the user's Properties sheet and click on the Disable button.

Question 46

Which tool in Exchange Server is considered the primary tool used to monitor the health or status of your network?

○ a. The MTA Check utility

○ b. Eseutil.exe

○ c. The Notifications and Status interface

○ d. The Monitoring and Status tool

Question 47

You have just configured a new Exchange server and would now like it to log a critical state when the System Attendant stops running. You would also like your new server to send you a notification via email to alert you when it crosses a certain threshold. How can Exchange be configured to do this by default?

○ a. Open the server's Properties sheet, click on Detail on the Notifications tab, and then click on Add to configure an email address for notification.

○ b. Exchange 2000 cannot be configured by default to alert you via notifications; you have to configure this manually through the Notifications or Status interfaces.

○ c. Notifications are usually configured by default but mostly for default services such as SMTP or the WWW Publishing Service.

○ d. From the server's Properties sheet, click on Add on the Monitoring tab, select a resource, and then configure the resource with either a Warning State Threshold or Critical State Threshold.

Question 48

Peter is having trouble monitoring the SMTP queues on his Exchange 2000 server. He wants to use System Manager to monitor the X.400 queues as well as the SMTP queues. Areas of concern include message age and the total number of messages in these queues. He notices a backlog in the Local Delivery queue. What could this indicate?

○ a. It most probably indicates a problem with the Web Storage System.

○ b. It points to problems with Active Directory lookups.

○ c. It indicates broken connections to all domain controllers within the organization.

○ d. It means there are problems with Message Transfer Agent connections.

Question 49

You are checking your hard drive for the location of your newly created Storage Group called Tech Storage Group. You have placed two mailbox stores and three public folder stores in this Storage Group. How many transaction logs now exist on your hard drive for the Tech Storage Group?

- ○ a. One transaction log for your mailbox stores and one transaction log for your public folder stores
- ○ b. Five transaction logs, one for each individual store
- ○ c. One transaction log for all stores within the Tech Storage Group
- ○ d. Two transaction logs for your mailbox stores; public folder stores do not require transaction logs

Question 50

You have an existing Exchange 5.5 site with an organization name of Crest. You just purchased a new Exchange 2000 server and are in the process of installing and configuring it. However, you chose not to install the new server into your existing Exchange 5.5 site. How can you now replicate your original organization name into Active Directory and make it the Exchange 2000 organization name?

- ○ a. You have to choose another organization name for your Exchange 2000 server because it was not installed into your original site.
- ○ b. You can use Exchange System Manager to associate your organization with your new server.
- ○ c. You have to use the ADC after installation to associate your organization name with the new Exchange 2000 server.
- ○ d. The Exchange 5.5 server was not upgraded to Exchange 2000 first, so you cannot use the original organization name.

CHAPTER NINETEEN
Answer Key

1. b
2. a
3. b, c
4. d
5. d
6. b
7. c
8. a
9. a, b, c
10. a
11. b
12. a
13. c
14. b
15. c
16. a
17. b
18. d
19. a
20. c
21. b
22. b, c
23. a
24. d
25. b
26. c
27. a
28. b
29. c
30. a
31. a, c
32. d
33. d
34. a
35. a
36. c
37. b
38. d
39. c
40. b
41. d
42. a
43. b
44. c
45. d
46. d
47. b
48. a
49. c
50. a

Question 1

Answer b is correct. Simple Mail Transfer Protocol (SMTP) is the native transport used in Exchange 2000. Answers a, c, and d are incorrect because these protocols are not the *default transport protocol* that Exchange 2000 uses. These protocols are used in conjunction with SMTP to provide a total messaging solution.

Question 2

Answer a is correct. Exchange 2000 stores all native content in an STM file. Answers b, c, and d are incorrect because there are no such file extensions within Exchange 2000.

Question 3

Answers b and c are correct. The Installable File System (IFS) lets you use Exchange as a file repository for any application and makes it possible to map Exchange folders and mailboxes as a shared drive. Answer a is incorrect because this is a direct function of the inetinfo.exe process. Answer d is incorrect because it describes an incorrect function of the IFS.

Question 4

Answer d is correct. A default server installation contains one public folder store, which, in turn, contains one public folder hierarchy. Answer a is incorrect because there is only one store by default. Answer b is incorrect because one hierarchy is contained within one store by default. Answer c is incorrect because one store *is* enabled by default.

Question 5

Answer d is correct. All Exchange 2000 protocols are now hosted within the Internet Information Server (IIS) process. Answers a and b are incorrect because they describe incorrect locations within the Exchange Server architecture for all protocols. Answer c is incorrect because the inetinfo.exe process, not the first available process, now hosts all protocols.

Question 6

Answer b is correct. The EXchange InterProcess Communication (EXIPC) layer helps facilitate the transfer of data between the Internet Information Server (IIS) process and the Web Storage System process. Answer a is incorrect because this is a result of the Web Storage System process alone. Answer c is incorrect because IIS now naturally processes Simple Mail Transfer Protocol (SMTP) communication and not because of the EXIPC. Answer d is incorrect because this is a natural consequence of using the SMTP service with Exchange and has nothing to do with the EXIPC layer.

Question 7

Answer c is correct. The focus of new products from Microsoft, including Exchange 2000 Server, revolves around its new more encompassing .NET initiatives. Answer a is incorrect because Microsoft does not want to emphasize services over products. Answer b is incorrect because concentrating on just messaging services is too narrow a focus for Microsoft. Answer d is incorrect because other products besides Exchange Server help organizations achieve some measure of "five 9" reliability.

Question 8

Answer a is correct. The Microsoft Distributed InterNet Applications Architecture (Windows DNA) model has only three correct components: a user interface, business logic, and data services. Answer b is incorrect because the DNA model does not use loosely coupled applications; rather, it uses tightly coupled ones. Answer c is incorrect because the DNA model is not protocol independent. Answer d is incorrect because it is too general and does not specifically refer to a combination of user interfaces, business logic, or data services.

Question 9

Answers a, b, and c are correct. Customer, broker, and supplier are the three components of the Generic Architecture for Information Availability (GAIA) architecture. Answer d is incorrect because a helper component is independent of and complementary to the role of the broker. The other three components are *required*.

Question 10

Answer a is correct. It describes the principal focus for the Microsoft Operations Framework (MOF) model. Answers b and c are incorrect because they pertain to Generic Architecture for Information Availability (GAIA) transactions as performed by a broker. Answer d is incorrect because this statement is the function of the Microsoft Distributed InterNet Applications Architecture (Windows DNA) distributed–services architecture.

Question 11

Answer b is correct. Microsoft (MS) Mail used a shared-file system to host mailboxes for each user, and Exchange Server has been a client/server messaging system from the beginning. Answer a is incorrect because Exchange Server is not a shared-file system. Answer c is incorrect because the General Post Office (GPO) used in MS Mail had no active role in managing message flow; also, the System Attendant (SA) in Exchange is not directly responsible for message flows. Answer d is incorrect because both MS Mail and Exchange are asynchronous processes.

Question 12

Answer a is correct. The attachment is the part of an email message that provides a method for transferring both documents and infectious viruses. Answer b is incorrect because a signature usually identifies only the sender of a message. Answer c is incorrect because the body is the actual payload that contains the message itself, independent of additional documents that will be sent to the recipient. Answer d is incorrect because the message header displays only information about the email message to the recipient.

Question 13

Answer c is correct. Connectors are software that provide gateway services between separate Routing Groups or other email systems. Answer a is incorrect because Administrative Groups are simply collections of servers that share common administrative functions. Answer b is incorrect because Routing Groups describe collections of servers in terms of network connectivity. Answer d is incorrect because Message Stores describe where messages are kept on a system and have no bearing on communication with foreign mail systems.

Question 14

Answer b is correct. The X.500 model provides a framework for developing a single namespace of users. Answer a is incorrect because X.500 is defined by a single, unified global directory. Answer c is incorrect because the Directory User Agent (DUA), not the Directory System Agent (DSA), interacts specifically with the X.400 Message Transfer Agent (MTA). Answer d is incorrect because DUAs actually request services through their local DSA. The DSA, in turn, references a larger Directory Information Tree (DIT).

Question 15

Answer c is correct. LISTSERV is now part of the Exchange 2000 feature set. Answer a is incorrect because it describes an older method of transferring text messages using the ASCII character set. Answer b is incorrect because it refers to a Unix utility used to transmit non-ASCII binary files. Answer d is incorrect because it refers to a storage technology that provides an interface using Component Object Model (COM) and relates to Microsoft's digital nervous system (DNS) initiatives.

Question 16

Answer a is correct. The standalone version known simply as Exchange 2000 Server provides messaging and collaboration for Small Offices/Home Offices (SOHOs) and is limited to a 16GB database per server with automatic installation and configuration. Answer b is incorrect because it is designed for businesses that require unlimited message storage and multiple stores per server. Answer c is incorrect because it describes a fictitious version of Exchange Server. Answer d is incorrect because this type of server exclusively provides data-conferencing and multicast video-conferencing services in addition to a "regular" Exchange server.

Question 17

Answer b is correct. The private Information Store (IS) was called a Message Store (MS) in the X.400 specification. Answers a, c, and d are incorrect because even though they represent essential elements of the Exchange 5.x architecture, none of them relates directly to the concept of an MS as the private IS does.

Question 18

Answer d is correct. In a single-server site, the Message Transfer Agent (MTA)'s sole function is to expand distribution lists (DLs). Answer a is incorrect because this event occurs when you are routing messages to other messaging systems. Answers b and c are incorrect because they represent functions of the Information Store (IS).

Question 19

Answer a is correct. Key Management Service (KMS) is now the center of communication among the administrator, Certificate Services, the Exchange System Attendant (SA), and the cryptographic service provider (CSP). Answer b is incorrect because a Certificate Authority (CA) is a trusted entity that issues certificates to other entities. Answer c is incorrect because the Microsoft Management Console

(MMC) is the management interface that replaces the Exchange Administrator program used in previous versions of Exchange. Answer d is incorrect because there is no official Microsoft Directory Synchronization Service (MSDSS).

Question 20

Answer c is correct. The messaging transport architecture in Exchange 2000 now uses Simple Mail Transfer Protocol (SMTP) for native communications and the X.400 connector for mixed-mode connections. Answer a is incorrect because Exchange 2000 uses the X.400 Message Transfer Agent (MTA) as a protocol engine to connect to earlier Exchange servers. Answer b is incorrect because other connectors may or may not be needed; however, nothing can guarantee connectivity. Answer d is incorrect because the X.400 MTA is needed only for mixed-mode environments, and other connectors may still be needed.

Question 21

Answer b is correct. The Message Transfer Agent (MTA) managed routing and message delivery, whereas the Information Store (IS) handled message storage. Answer a is incorrect because the System Attendant (SA) monitored servers and connections as well as replicated directory information. Answer c is incorrect because the Directory Store (DS) controlled access to the Message Store (MS) as well as replicated remote directory services. Answer d is incorrect because the IS performed local delivery, and the MTA was responsible for remote delivery.

Question 22

Answers b and c are correct. Service management issues in Exchange 2000 include scalability and reliability. These measures help ensure that your solution delivers promised features at agreed service levels. Answer a is incorrect because your collaborative solutions are inherently linked to the network operating system (NOS) directory object itself. Answer d is incorrect because protocol services and directory services are now separate functional areas within the Exchange architecture.

Question 23

Answer a is correct. The first step of an installation plan includes creating a deployment plan based on corporate objectives and user needs. Answer b is incorrect because deploying the structural aspects of the network operating system (NOS) is the second step of an installation plan. Answer c is incorrect because it describes the final step of the installation plan—a changeover from Microsoft Solutions Framework (MSF) to Microsoft Operations Framework (MOF). Answer d is incorrect because it describes the third stage of a successful installation plan.

Question 24

Answer d is correct. You use the **mmc path/filename.msc /a** command to create a new console frame in Author Mode. Answers a, b, and c are incorrect because they all describe incorrect variations in the syntax used to create a new console frame explicitly in Author Mode.

Question 25

Answer b is correct. All snap-ins conform to the multidocument interface (MDI) specification. Answer a is incorrect because only standalone snap-ins function without additional support. Answer c is incorrect because snap-ins enforce a design standard that minimizes training and *reduces* total cost of ownership (TCO). Answer d is incorrect because some snap-ins do not open in Author Mode by default.

Question 26

Answer c is correct. Different Simple Mail Transfer Protocol (SMTP) addresses could use recipient policies to control the conditions under which one address or another will be used. Answer a is incorrect because it refers indirectly to system policies, not recipient policies. Answer b is incorrect because *recipient policies* control email address generation. Answer d is incorrect because the default policy in the Recipients Policies container does not prohibit multiple SMTP addresses.

Question 27

Answer a is correct. Membership in one Administrative Group does not prevent membership in a Routing Group in another Administrative Group. Answers b, c, and d are incorrect because they are all true statements. In native mode, you can uncouple Administrative Groups from Routing Groups to gain more flexibility in your environment.

Question 28

Answer b is correct. Exchange 2000 with the Web Storage System and the Installable File System (IFS) helps users publish HTML documents stored in public folders. Answer a is incorrect because Instant Messaging (IM) does not help end users with Web publishing directly. Answer c is incorrect because this would help users *locate* messages stored in public folders. Answer d is incorrect because this describes an administrative requirement, not an end-user requirement.

Question 29

Answer c is correct. Clients query Domain Name System (DNS) to locate the nearest Global Catalog (GC) servers. GC servers are represented as SRV records in DNS, and clients query these records to locate domain controllers when they first log on to a domain. Clients are also referred to GC servers for address book lookups. Answer a is incorrect because legacy versions of Exchange used Windows Internet Naming Service (WINS) as their preferred naming service. Answer b is incorrect because Exchange servers use only DNS to locate other Exchange servers. Answer d is incorrect because you should be running bind 8.1.2 or later.

Question 30

Answer a is correct. The Exchange Global Access List (GAL) can display users from only a single forest. Answer b is incorrect because the GAL displays users from only one forest at a time. Answer c is incorrect because it is totally irrelevant to the question. Answer d is incorrect because the GAL is not part of the configuration partition of Active Directory (AD).

Question 31

Answers a and c are correct. Generally, you don't run ForestPrep if all Exchange servers are in one domain, the domain contains the schema master, all users are in the domain, and the account installing Exchange has Enterprise Admin and Schema Admin rights. Answer b is incorrect because it describes a step needed to prepare Active Directory (AD) for mixed-mode environments. Answer d is incorrect because the Windows 2000 LDAP viewer support tool known as ldp.exe or LDP is used to enable Lightweight Directory Access Protocol (LDAP) operations and has nothing to do with the ForestPrep utility.

Question 32

Answer d is correct. The Active Directory Connector (ADC) must be installed whenever you upgrade an existing legacy Exchange organization before running ForestPrep. Answer a is incorrect because DomainPrep is run after ForestPrep. Answer b is incorrect because you run setup after everything else is done. Answer c is incorrect because it is not necessary to configure connection agreements before you run ForestPrep.

Question 33

Answer d is correct. To open a mailbox using Outlook Web Access (OWA), you type "http://*servername*/exchange/*userid*" in a browser window. Answers a, b, and c are incorrect because they display incorrect syntax to access a user's mailbox using OWA and a Web browser.

Question 34

Answer a is correct. The Lightweight Directory Access Protocol (LDAP) server is the only component that needs to be changed *only if* the Exchange 2000 server is not a Global Catalog (GC) server. Answer b is incorrect because the incoming and outgoing server fields remain intact after the upgrade. Answer c is incorrect because not every setting remains the same after an upgrade. Answer d is incorrect because, as stated, you need to change the LDAP server.

Question 35

Answer a is correct. Creating multiple recipient containers makes moving mailboxes a difficult process. Answer b is incorrect because organizational units (OUs) are used in Exchange 2000. Answer c is incorrect because it involves fictitious information. Answer d is incorrect because it describes a tool used in Exchange 2000, not Exchange 5.5.

Question 36

Answer c is correct. Mailboxes can be moved whether or not user objects are moved in Active Directory (AD). Answers a and b are incorrect because user objects don't have to be moved in AD. Answer d is incorrect because mailboxes are not moved between Routing Groups, only between mailbox stores or between servers.

Question 37

Answer b is correct. Administrative and Routing Group interfaces are disabled by default. Answer a is incorrect because Administrative Group views are disabled by default. Answer c is incorrect because you can select View configurations in mixed mode as well as native mode. Answer d is incorrect because administrative views are configured using an organization's Properties sheet, not **regedt32** and the Microsoft Management Console (MMC).

Question 38

Answer d is correct. You cannot use connectors designed for third-party systems to connect Routing Groups. Answer a is incorrect because you can also use the X.400 connector. Answer b is incorrect because certain third-party connectors may not work. Answer c is incorrect because you are not limited to only the X.400 connector in this case.

Question 39

Answer c is correct. Use the Simple Mail Transfer Protocol (SMTP) connector whenever transport layer security (TLS) or other security is involved in your organization. Answer a is incorrect because the Routing Group connector (RGC) is equivalent to the site connector used in legacy Exchange servers. Answer b is incorrect because low-bandwidth connections are not an issue here. Answer d is incorrect because not all connectors provide similar functionality or security in a given situation.

Question 40

Answer b is correct. You create an ID file in your Notes environment before starting a connection. Answer a is incorrect because you have already installed the Notes client. Answer c is incorrect because a notes.ini file should already exist in *%system%*\notes.ini after you install the Notes client. Answer d is incorrect because this is configured after a connection is made.

Question 41

Answer d is correct. The Microsoft (MS) Mail connector directory on the Exchange server is in \Exchsrvr\Connect\Msmcon. Answers a, b, and c all represent incorrect or fictitious directory locations for the MS Mail connector. Answer b actually indicates a directory used by the Lotus Notes connector for directory synchronization.

Question 42

Answer a is correct. Windows 2000 Certificate Services establishes a Public Key Infrastructure (PKI). Answers b, c, and d are incorrect because these components do not actually *establish* the PKI. In fact, the Exchange 2000 Key Management Service (KMS) assists you in deploying a Secure MIME (S/MIME) client.

Question 43

Answer b is correct. The internal root Certificate Authority (CA) will become subordinate to any commercial root CA that takes over. Answer a is incorrect because there is less administrative overhead with a commercial CA. Answer c is incorrect because there is more dependency on external factors for a commercial root CA. Answer d is incorrect because the Windows 2000 CA becomes subordinate to the commercial CA.

Question 44

Answer c is correct. Instant Messaging (IM) has a closed-forum meeting style and an immediate meeting structure. Chat has a semi-structured open-forum meeting style. Answer a is incorrect because IM is a closed, not open, forum. Answer b is incorrect because IM is a closed-style service, whereas Chat is an open-style service. Answer d is incorrect because IM is immediate/ad hoc, whereas Chat is semi-structured.

Question 45

Answer d is correct. This is one way of disabling a user's access to Instant Messaging (IM) services other than using the Exchange Tasks Wizard. Answers a, b, and c are all incorrect and fictitious methods of disabling a user's access to IM services in Exchange.

Question 46

Answer d is correct. This tool, located in the Tools folder in System Manager, is primarily used to monitor the health of your servers. Answer a is incorrect because it is a command-line tool that tries to fix all MTA message queues and the messages within those queues. Answer b is incorrect because Eseutil.exe is an offline tool that defragments databases while the Information Store (IS) is not running. Answer c is incorrect because it describes interfaces for the Monitoring and Status tool, not the actual tool itself.

Question 47

Answer b is correct. Exchange 2000 is not configured *by default* to send notifications. Answer a is incorrect because there is no Notifications tab in a server's Properties sheet. Answer c is incorrect because notifications are not configured by default; they are manually configured through an interface. Answer d is incorrect because it describes how to add a resource to Exchange Server, not how to configure notifications.

Question 48

Answer a is correct. A backlog in the Local Delivery queue indicates a problem with the Web Store. Answer b is incorrect because another queue manages Active Directory (AD) issues. Answer c is incorrect because the Messages Awaiting Directory Lookup queue indicates problems contacting domain controllers (DCs). Answer d is incorrect because it is not relevant to this question.

Question 49

Answer c is correct. There is only one set of transaction logs for all five of these stores. Answer a is incorrect because mailbox stores and public folder stores all share the same set of transaction logs. Answer b is incorrect because each store does not require a separate transaction log. Answer d is incorrect because public folder stores use transaction logs just like mailbox stores.

Question 50

Answer a is correct. The existing organization name will be replicated to Active Directory (AD) as an Exchange 2000 name if you install the new server into your original site. Answer b is incorrect because this snap-in is not used to replicate organizational names. Answer c is incorrect because the Active Directory Connector (ADC) is not used to replicate the organizational name. Answer d is incorrect because the original server does not need to be upgraded; the new server has to be installed into the original site.

Appendix A
Answers to Review Questions

Chapter 1 Solutions

1. **a, c, d.** Identity management, directory services, and the network operating system (NOS) are all mutually dependent.

2. **a, b, c.** Microsoft software will continue to support a common screen interface library (MMC), consolidated directory services, and common dynamic link library (COM+) objects.

3. **a.** E-commerce is forcing interoperability; the other answers provide interoperability. Commercial businesses also force interoperability.

4. **c.** Total cost of ownership (TCO) is correct.

5. **b.** Microsoft collectively refers to a network of personal computer–based services as digital nervous system.

6. **d.** Networking essentials is correct.

7. **d.** There is no such thing as the X.4000 standard. If the question had asked about X.400, the correct answers would be a and b, Message Transfer Agent (MTA) and Message Store (MS).

8. **a.** Microsoft.NET is the new Microsoft initiative that promises to create a universal canvas on client workstations.

9. **c.** SMTP (Simple Mail Transfer Protocol) plays the most significant role in messaging services.

10. **a, c.** Both decentralized management and a single namespace are X.500 specifications.

11. **d.** Network protocols do not depend on AD directory services.

12. **b.** MAPI (Messaging Application Programming Interface) provides an interface for messaging.

13. **d.** API (application programming interface) does not provide a solution to identity management; it provides support for software development.

14. **a, b.** LDAP (Lightweight Directory Access Protocol) and MAPI (Messaging API) interface with the Exchange Directory Store (DS).

15. **a.** The basic components of Microsoft Repository are a storage engine and COM interface.

16. **c.** AD can be best described as consolidation of identity management.

17. **a.** MSF (Microsoft Solution Framework) is especially useful when you are planning a project.

18. **c.** MSF (Microsoft Solution Framework) is a milestone-driven methodology that focuses on quality assurance through repeated testing.

19. **d.** You do not conduct a goals analysis as part of preparing a new installation; you conduct a needs analysis.

20. **b.** Installing Exchange 2000 in a mixed-mode environment will disable many of the important features associated with lowering TCO.

Chapter 2 Solutions

1. **c.** Directory services has been "outsourced" to Windows 2000.

2. **d.** Microsoft Windows 2000 interfaces provide extensibility.

3. **d.** You cannot install Exchange 2000 in NT 4 because NT 4 does not support AD.

4. **d.** Maintenance, support, and capital investments all contribute to TCO.

5. **b.** HML does not interoperate with Exchange 2000. HML does not stand for anything.

6. **c.** Good toolbars provide instrumentation that simplifies administration.

7. **a, c.** SA (mad.exe) and IS (store.exe) are part of the X.400 specifications.

8. **a.** X.400 connector helps the MTA.

9. **d.** Either synchronization (foreign mail systems) or replication (Exchange servers within an organization) updates directory ISs.

10. **d.** Key Management is an optional service that provides both DES and S/MIME encryption services.

11. **a.** DRAS provides asynchronous dial-up capability.

12. **c.** Storage services distinguish Exchange 5.5 from earlier versions; the size of the database was unlimited as compared to an earlier maximum size of 16GB.

13. **a.** SMTP was supported in Exchange version 4.

14. **b, d.** The MTA does not manage local messages nor does SA replicate messages.

15. **c.** Exchange focuses on messaging; Notes focuses on sharing data.

16. **d.** It is not true that SA is run only when it is necessary to perform housekeeping. SA is also the loader for all other Exchange services.

17. **c.** DS (Directory Services) is redundant and can be outsourced to AD.

18. **c.** ADC (Active Directory connector) would be the tool used to synchronize legacy version 5.5 with Exchange 2000 while you are upgrading mail systems.

19. **d.** Load balancing provides increases in performance but not reliability.

20. **a, c.** Both Exchange Enterprise Server 5.5 and Enterprise Server 2000 support some form of clustering.

Chapter 3 Solutions

1. **c.** The Web Storage System enhances administration because one repository unifies shared storage space.

2. **a, b, d.** The functional services are protocol, directory, and storage services.

3. **a.** Legacy message stores differ from the stores in Exchange 2000 in that legacy message stores were based on one database.

4. **b.** Win32 interfaces cannot read/write to **http://hostserver/username**.

5. **a, b, c, d.** The Web Store provides exposure to both mailboxes and public folders, retrieval of data based on queries, access to CDOs, and access to traditional MAPI objects.

6. **e.** None of the above; all the services listed are solution services.

7. **c, d.** Data requests from MAPI clients are sometimes converted; non-MAPI client data is never converted.

8. **b, c.** The two EXIFS formats are *.edb and *.stm.

9. **d.** None of the above; EXIFS creates folders by default on the M: drive.

10. **a, b.** Each object in EXIFS has a URL, and you can stop and start EXIFS from the command line only.

11. **d.** None of the above. EXIFS integrates with IIS; WebDAV is a set of HTTP extensions.

12. **b, c, d.** WebDAV provides read access to unstructured content in EXIFS over HTTP, write access to all EXIFS data stores, as well as server-side synchronization.

13. **a.** Administration is performed using an MMC snap-in.

14. **a, d.** The Web Store provides both Win32 and ADO programming support.

15. **a, b, c, d.** All four file types listed are collected: rich text (*.edb), streaming (*.stm), site replication services (*.srs), and key management services (*.kms).

16. **c.** SIS has the greatest impact on capacity because it stores a copy of a message only once in a database.

17. **c.** The maximum log size is 5MB.

18. **b.** Data is converted to RTF when a MAPI client modifies and saves data.

19. **a.** A transaction must create a new data state or return data to the state it was before a transaction is applied.

20. **b, c.** A full-text search applies different endings to the same base word through the stemming process.

Chapter 4 Solutions

1. **a, b, c, d, e.** Directory services has changed, so identity and permission management has changed. Exchange 2000 runs on only Windows 2000, whereas Exchange 5.5 ran on NT 4 or mixed mode Windows 2000. Finally, there has been a change in emphasis from X.400 and MAPI to SMTP protocols.

2. **b.** Both TCO and ROI are financial metrics that top-level management use to help evaluate the general performance of an Exchange administrator.

3. **c, d.** Both Microsoft Operations Framework (MOF) and CCTA's IT Infrastructure Library (ITIL) provide support and maintenance methodologies.

4. **a, b, c.** All three of these areas—hardware maintenance, application support, and user support—impact TCO.

5. **a, b, c, d.** The design of management instrumentation is unique to every installation and is based on deployment of Exchange services, NOS services, AD directory services, and the fundamental objectives of the corporation.

6. **a, b, d.** Application software solutions, network connectivity, and user management can all be typical parts of an administrator's job description.

7. **d.** A key to TCO reduction is to include MOF team members in the MSF phase of deployment.

8. **d.** None of the above; the MMC runs on Windows 2000, NT 4, and Windows 9x and can be distributed in author mode.

9. **a, b.** You can use both the AD Service Interface (ADSI) Editor and AD Users and Computers to manage users and permissions.

10. **d.** Legacy distribution lists have been replaced in Exchange 2000 by mail-aware groups.

11. **a.** The Exchange 2000 namespace is based on the multimaster model of Windows 2000.

12. **d.** There is not enough information supplied to decide. Any of the three recipient models will conform to legacy or Exchange 2000. However, messaging group administration is the best choice if you choose to maintain a legacy organizational structure.

13. **c.** The correct answer is adminpak.msi in \I386 on the Windows 2000 Installation CD-ROM root directory.

14. **a, b.** TSA provides remote control of any Exchange server in remote administration mode. Access to up to two Terminal Services clients is available by default.

15. **a.** ldp.exe does not require Mailbox Manager rights to operate.

16. **b.** The distributed management model is appropriate in a mixed-mode architecture.

17. **c.** If you disable the Administrative Group option after populating a group with servers, the servers are returned to the default server grouping.

18. **b.** You can assign servers only to Routing Groups independent of administrative group membership in Windows 2000 native mode.

19. **a.** The Exchange Administration Delegation Wizard assigns Read Only, Read/Write, and Read/Write/Change permissions to the Exchange Administrator group just like attributed roles in Exchange 5.5.

20. **a.** ADC synchronizes legacy DLs with AD universal distribution groups but does not provide access control to Public Folder trees.

Chapter 5 Solutions

1. **a, c, d.** Exchange 2000 specifically interacts with Active Directory partitions or naming contexts, GC servers, and groups.

2. **a, b, d.** The three key areas are organizational, user, and administrative support.

3. **b.** Active Directory is based on a multimaster model.

4. **b.** DNS resolves host names specifically to IP addresses.

5. **c.** Windows 2000 uses Active Directory, which relies on DNS to resolve AD object names to IP addresses.

6. **a, c.** A Windows 2000 enterprise can be organized as a tree, a forest, and a domain.

7. **b.** The AD name component is compatible with NetBIOS.

8. **c.** The key to planning a namespace is efficient name resolution.

9. **b.** It is recommended for security reasons that you use different naming conventions for your internal and external namespaces.

10. **c.** Exchange 2000 on IIS 5, which is actually a dedicated server, is the best configuration for an Exchange 2000 server.

11. **b.** Exchange 2000 stores configuration information in the Configuration naming context.

12. **c.** LDAP Data Interchange Format files are imported as part of the installation of the first Exchange 2000 server and extension of the AD schema.

13. **c.** Deploying an Exchange server close to a GC server is a best practice recommendation.

14. **a, b, d.** Naming conventions, group size, and ownership are all relevant factors to consider when you are planning AD groups.

15. **b.** You should use universal groups when there is network connectivity among domains.

16. **a, b, d.** Clustering, front/back-end servers, and load balancing are all examples of horizontal scaling, in which many machines provide the same services.

17. **d.** When you are planning public folder storage and replication, the number of trees, the number of branches, and the replication patterns are all relevant.

18. **b.** Public folder affinities do not consume more network bandwidth than replication.

19. **d.** Processor, memory, network connectivity, and disk system all contribute to a standalone server's performance.

20. **c.** Uptime performance, sometimes described as "five 9" reliability, is the most relevant measure of system accessibility.

Chapter 6 Solutions

1. **b.** Exchange System Manager is particularly useful in the area of storage management.
2. **a, b, c.** TS runs any software, manages an Exchange server over slow dial-up connections, and runs better than an Exchange 5.5 administrative program over a dial-up connection.
3. **a.** Dynamic DNS is an installation prerequisite for Exchange 2000 Server.
4. **d.** Exchange 2000 has added conferencing to Exchange's range of features.
5. **b, c.** Exchange 2000 Server for the SOHO environment and Exchange 2000 Enterprise Server for all environments require a good deployment plan.
6. **b.** A backup is recommended before installation and after verification.
7. **a.** Confirming the NetBIOS name of the server targeted for Exchange installation is necessary when you are preparing an environment for an Exchange installation.
8. **d.** It is not necessary to run either ForestPrep or DomainPrep before installing Exchange 2000 Server in a single-domain environment.
9. **a, b, c.** The EnterpriseAdmin, SchemaAdmin, and DomainAdmin group memberships need to be assigned.
10. **b.** 128MB is the minimum memory requirement for Exchange 2000.
11. **a.** You should stay current with service packs.
12. **a, c.** The Exchange server can be installed on a Windows 2000 DC with AD GC and must be able to access other servers using Dynamic DNS.
13. **d.** When you install the first Exchange server in a domain, an organization, an Administrative Group, and a Routing Group are created.
14. **b.** Transaction logs are best written to duplexed drives.
15. **d.** Message information stores are best written to RAID 5 disk subsystems.
16. **d.** Collaborative Services and System Management Tools are missing from a Minimum Mode installation.
17. **b.** The setup.ini file is used to automate the installation of Exchange 2000 Server.
18. **a.** Exchange Server Setup Progress.log records the details of every operation during installation.

19. **a, b, d.** Checking client access to mailboxes, creating mailboxes, and creating server policy regarding default address generation are considered post-installation tasks that are part of the verification process.

20. **c.** TS client and Computer Management snap-in are both tools that allow you to verify services running on a remote Exchange Server.

Chapter 7 Solutions

1. **b.** Schedule+ is an add-in component that provides compatibility between Schedule+ and the Outlook Calendar.

2. **a.** Office 2000 comes in Small Business, Standard, Professional, Premium, and Developer's editions, but not "Advanced Server" Edition.

3. **b.** Outlook 97 cannot publish calendars as Web pages, but Outlook 2000 can. All other answers hold true for both Outlook 97 and Outlook 2000.

4. **c.** No E-Mail mode allows you to use only the contact-, task-, and schedule-management features of Outlook.

5. **c.** The Internet Only option allows you to use messaging in addition to Outlook's contact-, task-, and schedule-management features.

6. **d.** By default, users will see the Outlook Today page displayed when they start Outlook 2000 for the first time.

7. **a.** Support for email within Outlook Express is similar to that of the Internet Mail Only option in Outlook.

8. **b.** When Outlook Express interacts with Exchange 2000 Server for retrieving messages, it does so over either the POP3 or IMAP4 protocol.

9. **c.** You need version 3 or later browsers to support any functionality required by HTML 3.2, such as frames or Java.

10. **a, d.** OWA is not intended to replace the Outlook client for 16-bit Windows or Macintosh operating systems.

11. **b.** Personal Address Books are not available in OWA because they are stored locally on your workstation.

12. **b.** There is no real Outlook client for the Unix operating system, so Unix users can use either a third-party Internet mail client or OWA to connect to an Exchange 2000 server.

13. **d.** You can customize the setup of Outlook by using switches, and most switches involve using a Microsoft Installer package file or MSI file.

14. **a.** The **/I *MSI file path*** switch specifies the name of the MSI file to be used during installation; it cannot be used with the **/a** switch.

15. **c.** To view or create additional profiles in Outlook, you right-click on the Outlook icon on your desktop and choose Properties from the shortcut menu. From there, you can click on the Show Profiles button to view the current profile that your client is using.

16. **a, b, c.** Outlook Express, Outlook, and Telnet are sufficient software for sending mail via SMTP.

17. **c.** The MIME specification provided SMTP with the ability to manage binary file attachments.

18. **c.** By default, OWA passes security credentials to the Web server for authentication of users.

19. **c.** If your Outlook client is configured only for Internet mail, go to the Mail Delivery page under Tools|Options and reconfigure mail support.

20. **d.** Answer d is false; DAV is a protocol that extends HTTP functionality, not an OWA application programming interface.

Chapter 8 Solutions

1. **a, b, c, d, e.** All the listed objects are valid Exchange 2000 recipient types.

2. **a, b.** Contacts, which are mail-enabled users, correspond to an Exchange 5.5 custom recipient.

3. **b.** A decentralized model is best when network connections are slow.

4. **c.** Recipient Update Service creates the proxies and the mailbox.

5. **b.** It is marked for deletion and can be recovered on the system until a cleanup is performed.

6. **c.** Mail-enabled users, otherwise known as contacts, both hold addresses and apply rules to redirect messages.

7. **c.** The contents of the group inherit the attribute changes, but these changes may be overridden at the object level.

8. **d.** Distribution groups can have rules applied to them.

9. **b.** All the information in the General tab, including the Web page URL, appears in the GAL.

10. **b, c.** Both alias and delivery restrictions in the subpanel of the Exchange General tab can be changed.

11. **d.** None of the above; there is no E-Mail panel or Properties sheet. Delivery restrictions have their own dialog box when you select them from the Exchange General tab.

12. **b.** An NDR is a special message generated when an incoming or outgoing message triggers a predetermined threshold or condition.

13. **c, d.** Four default alternative addresses are generated: cc:Mail, Microsoft Mail, Simple Mail Transfer Protocol (SMTP), and X.400.

14. **d.** None of the above; the feature is in the Exchange Advanced tab.

15. **b.** The Exchange Advanced tab has a button that activates the Custom Attributes dialog box.

16. **a, b.** Neither Storage Limits nor Managed By are featured attributes of a contact recipient object.

17. **c.** Profile is not a featured attribute of a group recipient object.

18. **d.** None of the above; the LDAP query is displayed in the General tab of the specific policy.

19. **c.** Removal of the policy is the least preferred way to prevent the future use of that policy because it creates orphaned attributes.

20. **c.** ESENTUTIL is a maintenance tool that performs low-level operations specifically on ESE datastores. Both AD and Exchange use the Extensible Storage Engine.

Chapter 9 Solutions

1. **c.** The false statement is: RPC and SMTP work efficiently under native-mode Exchange 2000.

2. **a, b, d.** Low-speed connectivity, loosely defined connections, and low-quality connections limit the use of RPCs in an enterprise environment.

3. **b.** Loosely defined connections limit the usefulness of X.400 in an enterprise environment.

4. **c.** MIME provides more complex data types when combined with SMTP.

5. **d.** None of the answers is correct. Although pipelining and chunking have effects on network overhead and speed, neither feature applies to X.400; they apply to enhanced SMTP. Chunking involves passing an argument to the receiving server specifying the length of the message at the start of the transmission. The message can be processed more efficiently because the receiving

server anticipates a specific amount of data in advance. Pipelining similarly avoids network overhead by minimizing the number of acknowledgments passed during a transmission.

6. **a.** The true statement is: Windows 2000 supports the extended SMTP feature set.

7. **a.** A major difference between IMS in Exchange 5.5 and SMTP in Exchange 2000 is the use of sockets.

8. **b.** When you are working with Exchange 2000 and SMTP, reload Exchange 2000 after reinstalling SMTP services.

9. **b, c, d.** The AQ, Categorizer, and Routing Engine are components of the Transport Core.

10. **a, b.** Domain and link queues handle outbound messages.

11. **d.** There is no change in throughput when a second SMTP virtual server is added.

12. **c, d.** MAPI messages are converted to TNEF and may be converted to MIME.

13. **c.** In Exchange 2000 native mode, the MTA is used for X.400 connectors.

14. **a, b, c.** The Categorizer performs address resolution, verification of message formats, and handling of multiple message copies.

15. **b.** Mailbox recipient information is stored in AD directory services.

16. **b.** Directory services handle the replication of link state information.

17. **a, c.** Exchange Server information is found in the AD and the A DNS record.

18. **b.** The most important role of the RGM is broadcasting the LST to members of the Routing Group.

19. **a.** To change an RGM, select the Set As Master feature in the context menu of the specific computer under the Member node.

20. **c.** Answers a and b are correct.

Chapter 10 Solutions

1. **a, b, c.** The site concept includes Administrative Groups, Routing Groups, and physical sites where machines are located.

2. **d.** None of the selections is correct. At a minimum, Exchange 2000 provides Routing Group, SMTP, and X.400 connectors. The latter use a TCP protocol stack.

3. **a.** X.400 connectors can be configured on an RAS protocol stack.

4. **b.** SMTP connectors support SSL.

5. **b.** SMTP connectors provide a variety of authentication methods.

6. **a.** The format of the foreign mail system determines address space.

7. **a.** Assigning any cost measure over 50 to both machines would balance a service load across two servers.

8. **b.** Assigning a cost measure under 50 to one server and over 50 on another server would create a fail-over relationship between two servers.

9. **b.** If more than one server has an RGC, it can act as a fail-over bridgehead server.

10. **b, d.** To install a connector, you need to have at least two Routing Groups. Deploy servers to different Routing Groups that have similar connectivity characteristics.

11. **d.** None of the selections is correct. Answer b should read SMTP (Simple Mail Transfer Protocol).

12. **d.** Cost values are no longer used.

13. **a, b, c, d.** Because Exchange 2000 has virtual SMTP servers, SMTP connectors have replaced IMS connectors in Exchange 2000. IMS connectors were bound to TCP port 25. An Exchange 2000 SMTP virtual server can be assigned any TCP port, but by default, it is assigned TCP port 25. The combination of SMTP protocol and TCP port is called a socket.

14. **b.** An SMTP virtual server refers to the Mail Exchange record first to determine message routing.

15. **b.** SMTP is best when bandwidth is specified between 16Kbps and 64Kbps.

16. **c.** SMTP includes smart card support through the transport layer security (TLS) authentication protocol.

17. **b, c.** Both TCP - X.400 and X.25 - X.400 provide for the scheduling of mail flows.

18. **e.** All the connectors listed—RGC, TCP - X.400, X.25 - X.400, and SMTP—can restrict content.

19. **a, b, c, d.** All the conditions must be met. Gateway Service for NetWare and Client Service for NetWare must be installed, NetBIOS and SAP must be configured, and NetWare frame types or NWLink must be configured. IIS must be running for Exchange 2000 to function correctly.

20. **a, c.** Both the Mail connector Post Office and the Mail connector (PC) MTA are valid MS Mail components. The Mail connector Interchange is the missing third component.

Chapter 11 Solutions

1. **d.** The recommended setting for RUS when users do not use email address proxies is Never Run.

2. **d.** None of the above is correct; you use ADE to internally synchronize cc:Mail post offices.

3. **a, b.** You can create new Windows accounts and new Windows accounts that are disabled.

4. **a, b.** Both import.exe and export.exe are additional components on the foreign mail system that are critical when you install the cc:Mail connector.

5. **a.** The dynamic link library that is installed with the Notes client is required on the local Exchange server for the Notes connector to function correctly.

6. **a, c.** Exchange 2000 includes cc:Mail and Notes (as well as MS Mail and Novell GroupWise) connectors.

7. **b.** The Import Container tab allows you to filter objects before they are added to the directory listings.

8. **d.** The Delivery Restrictions tab is common among cc:Mail, Notes, and GroupWise connectors.

9. **d.** The General tab in the Novell GroupWise connector controls message sizes and delivery order.

10. **b.** Linking a single connector to a post office without mailboxes is the recommended best practice when you are configuring an Exchange cc:Mail connector.

11. **d.** Another feature (the option box that allows ADE to propagate synchronized entries) on the Post Office tab enables you to synchronize directory objects.

12. **b.** The Advanced tab in the Notes connector can reduce the size of the Notes database.

13. **b, d.** The Notes connector converts Notes Doc Links to a URL shortcut or an OLE link (and an RTF attachment).

14. **a.** The conndata subdirectory holds the text-based mapping files for Exchange connectors.

15. **b, d.** Adding the name of the domain in the text box on the Address Space tab writes ★ @ **mydomain.tch** to the system and configures that particular connector to receive all mail for mydomain.tch.

16. **b.** Dirsync specifically handles the directory synchronization of the Notes address book.

17. **c.** The default name of the Notes address book is names.nsf.

18. **d.** None of the above is correct. When you configure the Novell GroupWise connector, the NetWare account name is typically a member of the NTGateway Group.

19. **c.** The Import Container tab in the Novell GroupWise connector configures the filtering of imported directory entries.

20. **b.** The false statement is: SNADS can connect to any Exchange server in a mixed-mode environment. It cannot connect to an Exchange 2000 server.

Chapter 12 Solutions

1. **a, b, c.** Interference, interception, and impersonation could all compromise a DNS server.

2. **b.** Penetration is typically facilitated when system defaults are used to install software.

3. **d.** All the phases in a hacking episode—discovery, penetration, and control—are intentional and are therefore considered a serious breach in corporate rules.

4. **c.** Accessibility is the security control affected by the hacking discovery phase.

5. **a, b, d.** A security audit includes risk analysis, baseline analysis, and a physical analysis. Another main component is threat analysis.

6. **d.** NSlookup provides you with a listing of MXs.

7. **b.** Telnet is an online utility that can be used to impersonate or spoof an SMTP server.

8. **c, d.** A firewall can be a combination of various technologies that separate public from private networks, or a packet filter.

9. **a, b.** A firewall typically has logging capabilities and packet-filtering features. It also has alarm features.

10. **a, b, c, d.** Firewall technologies can be categorized by two classes of rules: allow traffic to pass unless specifically denied, and deny traffic unless specifically allowed. This is the same as saying specify what traffic can pass, and specify what traffic cannot pass.

11. **d.** A proxy server maps a publicly known IP address with a private, internal IP address.

12. **a, b, c, d.** All answers are correct. A circuit-level gateway transfers a packet from one IP address to another at the network level; an application-level

gateway can read the contents of a packet, transfers a packet from one IP address to another at the network level, and is slower than a circuit-level gateway.

13. **a, c, d.** A packet-filtering router; a screened, multihomed host; and a screened subnet can all use separate IP ranges.

14. **b, c.** Both the three-pronged and the midground screened subnets have multiple firewalls and multiple zones.

15. **a.** Port 80 must be allowed to pass packets when you are running OWA over an unsecured channel.

16. **c.** Port 443 must be allowed to pass packets when you are running OWA over a secured channel.

17. **d.** KMS provides all the security controls listed: integrity, confidentiality through encryption, and authentication through encryption.

18. **c, d.** Digital certificates include the issuer's unique ID and are issued by a CA.

19. **c.** The default lifetime of a root CA certificate is two years.

20. **c.** Key recovery is the one vital function that KMS performs.

Chapter 13 Solutions

1. **c.** Exchange 2000's Chat Service is based on the IRC protocol.

2. **a.** Data conferencing allows prearranged electronic conferences where users can share multimedia information.

3. **d.** A registered channel is created by a system administrator and is considered permanent.

4. **a, c.** A channel host and sysop can monitor and control a chat community's dynamic channels and registered channels.

5. **b, c.** Dynamic channels and registered channels have channel hosts.

6. **a.** A cloneable channel is a registered channel that automatically duplicates itself when a member limit has been reached.

7. **c.** Right-click on the Classes folder under Chat Communities in the Exchange System snap-in and choose New|Class.

8. **d.** All IM communication occurs over the RVP protocol in Exchange 2000.

9. **a, c.** They can obtain presence information and RVP notifications.

10. **b.** This user class is composed of all users who originate from a ".net" domain.

11. **c.** An IM home server is responsible for maintaining presence information for any user assigned to it.

12. **b.** The user's computer queries DNS for an SRV record.

13. **a.** You have to enter an address record for every IM server into DNS.

14. **a, b, c, d.** An identity mask for configuring member scope includes the username, domain, nickname, and IP address fields.

15. **c.** Kerberos protocol version 5 is considered the default protocol for authentication in Windows 2000.

16. **a.** Passwords must be stored in a reversible encrypted format.

17. **a, b, c.** #, &, and %# are valid IRC channel prefixes.

18. **b.** MCU is used to describe Conferencing Server.

19. **c.** The false statement is: IM servers talk to IM servers.

20. **a.** The digest authentication method is one method used by IM clients to authenticate to their home servers.

Chapter 14 Solutions

1. **a.** Three main logs are used in Event Viewer: Application, Security, and System. Each log is 512K by default.

2. **c.** All logs in Event Viewer start out as 512K logs, but they can be configured to be larger than this.

3. **b.** A logging level of 1 corresponds to a Minimum level of logging.

4. **b.** You can use a server monitor to check the status of services on a Windows 2000 machine and provide alerts when critical states are reached.

5. **d.** System Monitor is part of the Performance Console, which can chart the performance of system parameters in Windows 2000.

6. **c.** The System State folder in ntbackup.exe allows you to specify whether the AD, the Registry, or the SysVol folder will be backed up.

7. **b.** The Exchsrvr folder contains critical information that exists within the file system.

8. **a.** An archive bit that is set to OFF implies the file has been backed up.

9. **a.** A normal backup backs up all files, regardless of their archive bit setting.

10. **b.** The General tab for a Storage Group's Properties sheet indicates if circular logging has been turned on or off.

11. **b.** A set of personal folders exists as a single file with a .pst extension.

12. **c.** An Outlook 98 user will find the scanpst.exe program in the \ProgramFiles\ Common Files directory.

13. **a.** The **eseutil /r** command restores broken links in your databases.

14. **c.** The filever.exe utility displays versions of EXE or DLL files on an Exchange 2000 server.

15. **b.** System Monitor is a Windows 2000 snap-in; performance monitoring is what you do using System Monitor.

16. **a.** Throughput is the amount of work performed within a given amount of time.

17. **d.** Memory\Pages/sec shows statistics on how fast pages are read from or written to disk to resolve a hard page fault.

18. **b.** Inadequate memory increases the Processor\Interrupts/sec counter.

19. **b.** Windows 2000 enables PhysicalDisk counters (but not LogicalDisk counters) by default.

20. **c.** Both warning and error messages are logged with the Minimum logging level.

Chapter 15 Solutions

1. **d.** Using multiple Routing Groups for geographically dispersed locations can help you manage network bandwidth consumption better than a single Routing Group.

2. **a.** GCs can help reduce client lookup traffic within a Routing Group.

3. **b.** Developing includes prototype testing and BE implementation.

4. **a.** POP3 uses port 110, and IMAP4 uses port 143.

5. **c, d.** Distributing the functionality results in improved response times and reduced downtimes.

6. **a.** The DNS service is one key component you need for a successful Exchange 2000 implementation.

7. **b.** Organizational unit structure influences the logical structure of AD.

8. **a, c.** OUs delegate administration and hide certain objects from administrators.

9. **b.** Horizontal scalability refers to adding several servers that all perform the same task.

10. **c.** All combination servers can host mailbox stores for MAPI clients.

11. **d.** All FE servers use RPCs to communicate with BE servers running AD.

12. **d.** The store.exe service has to be running, and at least one private IS has to be mounted.

13. **a, b.** RAID 0 is less expensive than RAID 5, and RAID 1 is more expensive than RAID 0.

14. **a.** Not enough disks are used in this scenario because at least two disks will be mirrored.

15. **c.** Top-level public folders are created on the home server of the user who created them.

16. **d.** Outlook 2000 is more integrated with Windows 2000 than Outlook Express is because it can directly query AD using DSProxy.

17. **a.** Clients contact DSProxy and receive referrals informing them that GC servers will handle all future requests.

18. **a.** Exchange 2000 establishes LDAP connections to nearby DCs and GCs.

19. **d.** The DSAccess cache allows all Exchange services to cache a directory lookup without querying a GC server.

20. **c.** Additional Public Folder trees are viewable only by NNTP and Web clients, not MAPI clients such as Outlook 2000.

Chapter 16 Solutions

1. **b.** All servers within an Exchange 5.x site communicated with each other using RPCs.

2. **c.** Legacy servers replicated information between each other using LDAP.

3. **b.** The Windows 2000 IIS service now hosts all transport protocols for Exchange 2000.

4. **a, b, d.** Every successful upgrade to Exchange 2000 relies on AD, DNS, NNTP, and SMTP being installed in Windows 2000.

5. **a.** At least one server in a domain must provide name-resolution services with the ability to perform dynamic updates.

6. **a, c.** To install Exchange 2000, you must belong to the Enterprise Admins and Schema Admins security groups.

7. **b.** It creates the actual organization object in the configuration-naming context.

8. **a, c, d.** ForestPrep requires Enterprise Admins, Schema Admins, and local Administrator privileges to run.

9. **a.** Some components such as the IBM Office Vision connector are not upgraded to Exchange 2000 features.

10. **b.** The ADC moves custom recipients over to AD, where they become contacts.

11. **c.** If users do not exist in AD, they are found in the deleted items location of the message store.

12. **c.** Exchange 2000 uses universal security groups to assign permissions to public folders.

13. **a.** Public folder affinity is transitive only for Exchange 2000, not Exchange 5.x servers.

14. **d.** Circular logging is disabled by default in Exchange 2000 and aids in the recovery of a failed server.

15. **d.** OWA uses the Web Storage System to render and retrieve data in Exchange 2000 Server.

16. **a.** Exchange 2000 turns on message tracking once for the entire server after the upgrade is completed.

17. **c.** Preparing the Windows 2000 forest schema precedes the installation of the ADC.

18. **b.** One instance of the ADC can be used to define multiple connection agreements, with each agreement going from AD to a different Exchange 5.x site.

19. **a.** User agreements are created with the ADC and replicate recipient objects and their data.

20. **c.** ConfigCA is a read-only connection agreement for two-way communication between SRS and AD.

Chapter 17 Solutions

1. **c.** You can transform XML to HTML using XSL.

2. **d.** You can write scripting code that modifies the appearance rather than the content of information with both HTML and XSL.

3. **a, b, d.** The three layers are Presentation, Data, and Business Logic.

4. **b.** In OWA architecture, IIS authenticates users.

5. **b.** ISAPI determines the proper response form to a service request.

6. **c.** The browser client communicates with IIS when requesting data services.

7. **a, b, c, d.** DHTML, HTML, XML, and XSL can all be involved in rendering responses when OWA returns a request to an IE5 browser.

8. **d.** Both HTTP and LDAP are used when OWA proxies service requests to BE servers.

9. **a, c, d.** A single namespace, more efficient SSL encryption/decryption services, and easier deployment of security measures are benefits provided by an FE/BE architecture.

10. **a, b.** Database services and file system services are key SMFAs built into the Web Store.

11. **b.** Support of Win16 applications is not a key feature of the Web Store.

12. **a.** OWA provides policy-based management with significantly less overhead than the full-featured Outlook application.

13. **a, c, d.** IE5 renders forms for IE5 browser clients using HTML and XML in both IE4 with add-on XML parser software and IE5, which has a built-in XML parser.

14. **a, d.** Concurrency control and extensibility are features provided with WebDAV extensions that are not found in HTML alone.

15. **d.** Backward compatibility with HTML is not an objective of XML language design.

16. **a.** HTML, not DTD, defines how elements are displayed.

17. **a, b, d.** The most significant XML characteristics are that documents are well formed, valid, and standardized.

18. **d.** The XSL processor is located on both the client and server side.

19. **d.** IE5 uses HTC files rather than C++ and Java compiled code.

20. **d.** You can configure IE4 or later browsers using an XML processor plug-in; IE5 reads XML code directly.

Appendix B
Objectives for Exam 70-224

Installing and Upgrading Exchange 2000 Server	Chapter(s)
Install Exchange 2000 Server on a server computer.	6
Diagnose and resolve failed installations.	14
Upgrade or migrate to Exchange 2000 Server from Exchange Server 5.5.	2, 16
Diagnose and resolve problems involving the upgrade process.	16
Manage coexistence with Exchange Server 5.5.	2, 16
• Maintain common user lists.	16
• Maintain existing connectors.	11, 16
• Move users from Exchange Server 5.5 to Exchange 2000 Server.	16
• Configure the Exchange 2000 Active Directory Connector to replicate directory information.	16
Diagnose and resolve Exchange 2000 Active Directory Connector problems.	14
Perform client deployments. Clients include Microsoft Outlook 2000, Outlook Web Access, POP3, IMAP4, and IRC.	7
• Configure Outlook Web Access.	7, 17
• Configure client access protocols.	10

Configuring Exchange 2000 Server. Types of servers include mailbox, public folder, gateway, virtual, Chat, and Instant Messaging.	Chapter(s)
Configure server objects for messaging and collaboration to support the assigned server role.	13
• Configure information store objects.	4
• Configure multiple storage groups for data partitioning.	3
• Configure multiple databases within a single storage group.	3
• Configure virtual servers to support Internet protocols.	9
• Configure Exchange 2000 Server information in the Windows 2000 Active Directory.	4
• Configure Instant Messaging objects.	13
• Configure Chat objects.	13
Create and manage administrative groups.	4
Configure separate Exchange 2000 Server resources for high-volume access. Resources include stores, logs, and separate RAID arrays.	3, 15
Diagnose and resolve Exchange 2000 Server availability and performance problems.	14
• Diagnose and resolve server resource constraints. Resources include processor, memory, and hard disk.	14
• Diagnose and resolve server-specific performance problems.	14
Configure Exchange 2000 Server for high security.	1, 12
• Configure Exchange 2000 Server to issue v.3 certificates.	1, 12
• Enable Digest authentication for Instant Messaging.	1, 12
• Configure Certificate Trust Lists.	1, 12
• Configure virtual servers to limit access through firewalls.	10
• Configure Key Management Service (KMS) to issue digital signatures.	12

(continued)

Configuring Exchange 2000 Server. Types of servers include mailbox, public folder, gateway, virtual, Chat, and Instant Messaging (continued).	Chapter(s)
Create, configure, and manage a public folder solution.	13, 15
• Configure the Active Directory object attributes of a public folder.	13
• Configure the store attributes of a public folder.	13
• Configure multiple public folder trees.	13
Configure and manage system folders.	13

Managing Recipient Objects	Chapter(s)
Configure a user object for messaging.	8
• Configure a user object for email.	8
• Configure a user object for Instant Messaging.	13
• Configure a user object for Chat.	13
Manage user and information store association.	4
• Configure user information stores.	5
Diagnose and resolve problems that involve user and information store placement. Problems include security, performance, and disaster recovery.	10, 15
Create and manage address lists.	8
• Create security groups.	8
• Create distribution groups.	8
Diagnose and resolve Recipient Update Service problems.	8

Monitoring and Managing Messaging Connectivity	Chapter(s)
Manage and troubleshoot messaging connectivity.	14
• Manage Exchange 2000 Server messaging connectivity.	10
• Manage connectivity to foreign mail systems. Connectivity types include X.400, SMTP, and Internet messaging connectivity.	10, 11
• Diagnose and resolve routing problems.	9, 11
• Diagnose and resolve problems reported by nondelivery report messages.	9
Manage messaging queues for multiple protocols.	9
Monitor link status.	14
• Monitor messages between Exchange 2000 Server computers.	14
• Monitor messages between Exchange 2000 systems and foreign systems.	14
Configure and monitor client connectivity. Clients include Outlook 2000, Outlook Web Access, POP3, IMAP4, and IRC.	7, 17
Diagnose and resolve client connectivity problems. Problems include DNS structure, server publishing structure, DS Proxy/DS Access, address resolution, Instant Messaging clients, various connection protocols, and non–Windows 2000 environments.	11, 14
Manage public folder connectivity.	4
• Configure and monitor public folder replication.	4
• Diagnose and resolve public folder replication problems.	4

Managing Exchange 2000 Server Growth	Chapter(s)
Monitor services use. Services include messaging, Chat, public folder access, Instant Messaging, and calendaring.	14
• Monitor the Information Store service.	14
• Monitor server use by configuring server monitors.	14
• Monitor Instant Messaging by using System Monitor.	14
Manage growth of public and private message store databases.	5, 15

(continued)

Managing Exchange 2000 Server Growth (continued)

	Chapter(s)
Manage growth of user population and message traffic.	5, 15
Monitor the growth of client use. Clients include Outlook 2000, Outlook Web Access, POP3, IMAP4, and IRC.	14
Manage recipient and server policies.	8
Diagnose and resolve problems that involve recipient and server policies.	14
Optimize public folder and mailbox searching.	17
• Configure the public folder store or mailbox store for full-text indexing.	17
• Perform full-text indexing.	17

Restoring System Functionality and User Data

	Chapter(s)
Apply a backup and restore plan.	3
Diagnose and resolve backup and restore problems.	3
Restore user data and System State data.	3
• Recover deleted mailboxes.	14
• Recover deleted items.	14
Restore information stores.	3
Configure a server for disaster recovery. Configurations include circular logging, backup, and restore.	3
Diagnose and resolve security problems that involve user keys.	1, 12

Appendix C
Study Resources

Books

Gerber, Barry. *Mastering Microsoft Exchange 2000 Server*. Alameda, CA: Sybex, 2001. ISBN 0-7821-2796-7. The book is divided into sections that define Exchange's basic features, architectural components, installation, administration, and interoperability through Internet services and the Outlook client. It concludes these comprehensive sections with the management of applications through Outlook Forms Designer.

Glenn, Walter J., and Bill English. *Microsoft Exchange 2000 Server Administrator's Companion*. Redmond, WA: Microsoft Press, 2000. ISBN 0-7356-0938-1. This is a comprehensive overview of Exchange that covers planning and deployment, as well as issues of functionality, from an administrator's perspective.

Goncalves, Marcus. *Exchange 2000 Server Black Book*. Scottsdale, AZ: The Coriolis Group, 2000. ISBN 1-57610-641-1. This text provides concise and specific answers as well as immediate solutions to real-world problems. It covers design and configuration issues that relate to core components, deployment, and maintenance of Exchange 2000.

Ivens, Kathy, and Kenton Gardinier. *Windows 2000: The Complete Reference*. New York, NY: Osborne/McGraw-Hill, 2000. ISBN 0-07-211920-9. This is a comprehensive reference book on the network operating system (NOS) that supports Exchange 2000. It has specific areas describing Internet and intranet functionality that are useful in understanding how protocol services are provided in an Exchange organization.

Joshi, Kent, et al. *Using Microsoft Exchange 2000 Server Special Edition*. Indianapolis, IN: Que, 2000. ISBN 0-7897-2278-X. This large text covers Exchange Server core components and planning, the Web Store, and AD. It has individual chapters on various examples of external connectivity and associated methods for troubleshooting their operations, in addition to entire sections on the Outlook client and collaborative tools.

Microsoft Exchange 2000 Server Resource Kit, Microsoft Press, Redmond, WA, 2000. ISBN 0-7356-1017-7. This is two guides: the Enterprise Deployment Guide and the Resource Guide. The discussions in these guides are probably the best source of information specifically for the Microsoft exam, such as the sections on backbone configuration and tuning, as well as external connectivity.

Nielsen, Morten Strunge. *Windows 2000 Server Architecture and Planning, 2nd Edition*. Scottsdale, AZ: The Coriolis Group, 2001. ISBN 1-57610-607-1. The text offers detailed explanations regarding the design of Active Directory (AD) and the planning of functional and structural components of a Windows 2000 enterprise. This background information is useful for when you are managing recipient objects in an Exchange organization.

Redmond, Tony. *Microsoft Exchange Server for Windows 2000: Planning, Design and Implementation*. Woburn, MA: Digital Press, 2000. ISBN 1-55558-224-9. The author has extensive experience with Exchange Server products and provides in easy-to-understand terms the theory behind design, as well as specific information about how to implement an Exchange organization. The book covers all aspects of the product, including maintenance and troubleshooting, recipient management, and future software developments.

Stanek, William R. *Microsoft Exchange 2000 Server Administrator's Pocket Consultant*. Redmond, WA: Microsoft Press, 2000. ISBN 0-7356-0962-4. This pocket-size book is organized so that you can quickly retrieve concise information related to fundamentals in administration (such as managing recipients) as well as information about AD, data stores, and group administration.

Online Resources

www.examcram.com is a great resource for industry news, study tips, practice questions, and test information.

www.exchangesoftware.com is an excellent site sponsored by **Msexchange.org** with a comprehensive list of tools and news features. It also provides a mailing list for news, tutorials, and other Exchange-related information.

www.microsoft.com/exchange/ is the Microsoft Exchange Server Web site. This official Microsoft site offers evaluation software and service packs in addition to technical papers that are published online.

www.microsoft.com/TechNet/exchange/prodfact/ex2kinfo.asp is a brief article that outlines how the Exchange platform brings users closer to knowledge through messaging and collaborative objects.

www.microsoft.com/TechNet/exchange/prodfact/platinum.asp is a product overview from July 1999 that describes general features and benefits of Exchange.

www.microsoft.com/TechNet/exchange/prodfact/umvision.asp defines Microsoft's mission in providing a unified messaging platform to knowledge workers through access anytime, anywhere, and through any physical medium.

www.microsoft.com/TechNet/sql/levrep.asp discusses the Microsoft Repository and strategies for warehousing data. It is a good article for background information about the Web Store and how other BackOffice products like SQL Server 7 have managed data.

www.microsoft.com/TechNet/win2000/introch1.asp provides background information about Microsoft Windows 2000 architecture and the Server kernel or microcode. This article is the first chapter from *Introducing Windows 2000 Server*, published by Microsoft Press (Redmond, WA, 1999).

Glossary

access control entry (ACE)
A statement within an object that determines who can access that object and the type of access it possesses.

Access Control List (ACL)
A security mechanism that controls access to domain objects via access control entries (ACEs). A default ACL is applied to every object you create in a directory. An ACL cannot cross domains.

Active Directory (AD)
A namespace within Windows 2000 that adds new features to the traditional Windows 2000–based directory service. These features include a brand-new domain model and hierarchical namespace, which make it easier to manage large quantities of information. AD is a unified and distributed database of objects that uses one replication mechanism. Exchange 2000 now uses AD as a primary means of data storage.

Active Directory Connector (ADC)
A service that runs on a Windows 2000 domain controller (DC) and allows for synchronization and replication between directories, specifically between an Exchange 5.5 directory and a domain naming partition in Windows 2000. ADC is required in a mixed-mode setting with legacy Exchange servers to synchronize such information as distinguished names. There are two distinct versions of this service: The Windows 2000 ADC replicates objects in an Exchange 5.5 site, whereas the Exchange 2000 ADC also replicates configuration information to Active Directory (AD).

Active Directory Migration Tool (ADMT)
A tool used in conjunction with Active Directory Connector (ADC) to migrate user accounts and domains to Windows 2000. It helps you synchronize an upgrade to Exchange 2000 with an upgrade or migration from the Windows NT 4 operating system (OS) to a Windows 2000–based environment. When users are migrated before Windows 2000 is fully deployed, ADC creates a disabled user account. The ADMT can migrate accounts into the domain that contains disabled user accounts and merge duplicate accounts during the migration.

Active Directory Services Interfaces (ADSI)
A Windows-based interface for high-level network directory services that consolidates information from various network operating environments. It uses the features of directory services from multiple network providers to present one directory service interface so that network objects can be effectively managed. You can use ADSI to update user information and browse Active

Directory (AD) across multiple operating systems (OSs). ADSI consists of client-side DLL files that provide a set of directory-management functions and services, and you can access these functions from any Windows operating environment.

ActiveX Data Object (ADO)

A programming interface that provides a method of accessing Microsoft BackOffice data, independent of which application the data is stored in. Developers use ADO to query and sort Exchange Server data, so they can write applications that use data found in the Web Storage System. They can also append dynamic objects to static Web pages using ADO.

Administrative Group

Defines the administrative topology for a company and represents a collection of objects grouped together for management purposes. It facilitates the management of permissions and rights. In a mixed-mode environment with Exchange 5.5 servers, it is functionally equivalent to a site. You also use an Administrative Group to separate the management of system policies and Routing Groups. You can apply system policies from any Administrative Group to all Exchange servers in the domain tree.

ADSI Edit

A Windows 2000 Resource Kit utility that installs as a Microsoft Management Console (MMC) snap-in and views objects in Active Directory (AD), including schema and configuration data. You use it to view and modify objects such as Administrative Groups, manage how permissions are inherited from their configuration contexts, and set Access Control Lists (ACLs) on objects.

asymmetric cipher

Allows you to calculate keys for deciphering encrypted text and solves the key management problem of symmetric key encryption. Two keys are used: one for encryption and the other for decryption. By using an asymmetric cipher, a sender and a recipient do not have to agree on a key before sending their data. See also *cipher* and *symmetric cipher*.

block cipher

A method of encrypting text in which a cryptographic key and algorithm are applied to a block of data at once as a group, instead of 1 bit at a time. The alternative to a block cipher is a stream cipher. Cipher text is applied from one encrypted block to the next block in sequence so that identical blocks of text do not get encrypted the same way in a message (which makes it easier to decipher the cipher text). A block cipher uses shared-key encryption and breaks a message into fixed-length blocks, each 64 bits long. Most modern ciphers are block ciphers and use a combination of a key and an algorithm. See also *cipher* and *stream cipher*.

bridgehead server

A server with multiple connectors that connected two sites in legacy Exchange Server. A bridgehead server replicated mail and directory information between sites. Exchange 2000 uses bridgehead servers, but the Global Catalog (GC) now replicates directory information. You can also use a bridgehead server to connect two Exchange 2000 Routing Groups, with one primary and one secondary bridgehead server per Routing Group connection.

CAST

A 64-bit symmetric block cipher that encrypts one block of data at a time, instead of the whole byte of data. It is similar to Data Encryption Standard (DES) and supports keys ranging from 40 to 128 bits long. See also *block cipher*, *cipher*, and *Data Encryption Standard (DES)*.

cipher
A method of encrypting text or concealing its readability or meaning. This term is also sometimes used to refer to the encrypted text message itself. A cipher uses mathematical functions to encrypt and decrypt messages. Using a cipher, you can readily convert clear text data to an unreadable version known as cipher text. There are four types of ciphers: asymmetric, block, stream, and symmetric. Ciphers work by realigning the alphabet or manipulating text in a consistent manner. Most modern ciphers are block ciphers and use a combination of a key and an algorithm. All ciphers require that the key be kept in a secure and controlled area. See also *asymmetric cipher*, *block cipher*, *CAST*, *stream cipher*, and *symmetric cipher*.

clear item
A message represented as clear text that anyone can read.

Collaborative Data Objects (CDO) 1.21
Also known as Active Messaging and Object Linking and Embedding (OLE) Messaging, a technology based on the Component Object Model. The Microsoft OLE messaging library provides an interface to Messaging Application Programming Interface (MAPI) and allows you to add mail and messaging functionality to your applications. To use the OLE messaging library, you must have MAPI installed. The messaging library contains many objects made up in a hierarchy. The top-level object is the Session object, and all other objects (such as the Folder object) are referenced via this object. Using OLE, you can embed a fully functional Excel spreadsheet within an email message.

Collaborative Data Objects (CDO) for Exchange 2000
A technology that creates messaging applications based on the Component Object Model. Exchange 2000 adds an extensive set of CDO objects for Exchange objects and provides a larger set of objects than the Windows 2000 CDO. This provides objects for email, voicemail, fax, and even resource booking. Exchange 2000 CDO works with ActiveX Data Objects (ADOs) and Object Linking and Embedding for Databases (OLE DB) to perform general data-access functions such as queries.

Collaborative Data Objects (CDO) for System Management
Formerly known as Exchange Management Objects (EMO), an interface that allows an administrator to access certain types of management information within Exchange 2000 Server, including databases and Storage Groups.

Collaborative Data Objects (CDO) for Windows 2000
A Simple Mail Transfer Protocol (SMTP)-based library that provides a messaging feature and comes preinstalled with Windows 2000 Professional and Windows 2000 Server. It is an application programming interface (API) that establishes interfaces and functions for accessing messaging data. You can use CDO for applications that will provide Multipurpose Internet Mail Extensions (MIME) creation and management. It also integrates with ActiveX Data Object

(ADO) components to give access to both the Web Storage System and Active Directory (AD).

Conference Technology Provider (CTP)
A service that integrates with Conference Management Service (CMS) and supports application sharing, chat, and multiparty video conferencing over Internet Protocol (IP) multicasts. CTP supports both T.120-compatible programs and H.323 protocol clients.

Conferencing Management Service (CMS)
Simplifies the administration of conferencing services within Exchange 2000 by displaying one interface for meetings of various types. It allows administrators to regulate the number of conferences that an organization would like to schedule simultaneously. Users take advantage of Exchange 2000 Conferencing Server to schedule meetings using the Outlook 2000 Calendar function.

Configuration Connection Agreement (Config CA)
A connection agreement created by the Site Replication Service (SRS) when Exchange 2000 is installed into an existing Exchange 5.5 organization. The name of this agreement takes the form of Config CA_AdministrativeGroupName_Exchange2000ServerName. The Exchange 2000 Active Directory Connector (ADC) creates it to transfer two-way configuration information between an Exchange 5.5 site and the configuration naming partition of Active Directory (AD).

connection agreement
Defines a relationship between an existing Exchange site and the Windows 2000 Active Directory (AD). You use a connection agreement in conjunction with the Active Directory Connector (ADC); it helps you replicate direction information between the Exchange site and AD. A connection agreement contains such information as the name of the server being contacted for replication and the object classes being replicated. You can establish multiple connection agreements for one Active Directory Connector (ADC). There are two types of connection agreements: a user connection agreement, which replicates recipient objects and their data, and a configuration agreement, which replicates configuration information specific to Exchange Server.

contact
An object that results when you use the Active Directory Connector (ADC) to move a custom recipient, or a recipient address external to your Exchange organization, to Active Directory (AD). All contacts in AD are not immediately specified with an email address because you can do this later. A contact helps you reference mailboxes in a foreign messaging system and helps make common email addresses more available in the Global Access List (GAL) within Exchange 2000.

Data Encryption Standard (DES)
A widely used method of data encryption that uses a private key. You can use 72 quadrillion or more possible encryption keys. For each given message, the key is chosen at random from among this enormous number of keys. Both the sender and the receiver must know and use this same private key. DES applies a 56-bit key to each 64-bit block of data. Although this itself is considered strong encryption, many organizations now use triple DES and apply three separate keys in succession. DES was created at IBM in 1977 and

adopted by the United States Department of Defense. It is also specified as an American National Standards Institute (ANSI) X3.92 standard.

domain controller (DC)
A server that manages security interactions for users and domains. It helps centralize administration because you create user accounts only once. To qualify as a DC, a computer has to be configured with Windows 2000 Server, Windows 2000 Advanced Server, or Windows 2000 Datacenter Server. All DCs store a copy of the local domain database and replicate this information to other DCs within the same forest.

domain mode
One of two modes of any Active Directory (AD) domain you create: mixed mode or native mode. By default, all domains run in mixed mode, which emulates the conditions and limits of most Windows NT 4 networks. A mixed-mode domain can interoperate with all pre–Windows 2000 domain controllers (DCs), called *down-level DCs*. All clients that use the Windows NT 4 directory service authenticate to a Windows 2000 domain using mixed mode. In contrast, native mode prevents any support for down-level replication, forcing you to remove any DCs not running Windows 2000 servers. There is no domain master in a native-mode domain because all DCs become peers with each other. You can change from mixed mode to native mode at any time, but this change is not reversible.

Domain Name System (DNS)
The primary domain naming and location service that Active Directory (AD) uses. It helps resolves user-friendly names into Internet Protocol (IP) addresses and is based on the Request for Comments (RFC) 1035 standard. You can use either Transmission Control Protocol (TCP) or User Datagram Protocol (UDP) to transport DNS protocol messages, which connect to server port 53 for either. You can make ordinary DNS requests with TCP, although it is customary to use UDP for normal operations. You must use TCP in certain situations, such as zone transfers, however, because records may be lost if you use an unreliable protocol such as UDP. Exchange servers use DNS to locate other similar servers; therefore, it is best to put all Exchange 2000 servers in a DNS zone that is created on a Windows 2000 DNS server.

domain tree
A group of multiple Windows 2000 domains that allow resource sharing between domains. Although a tree can consist of one domain, it is best to join multiple domains in a hierarchical structure by creating a large and contiguous namespace. For example, you could create a parent domain of Toys.com and a child domain of South.Toys.com. In this case, both domains would belong to one domain tree and would function as one unit. Each domain contains portions of the directory database that are specific to users in that domain. All domains in a tree share a common schema and a common Global Catalog (GC).

DSAccess cache
Allows all Exchange services to cache or store directory lookups without querying a Global Catalog (GC) server. This feature of Exchange helps increase the performance of servers that run the Active Directory (AD) service. All types of directory access (except for address book searches) utilize

DSAccess from a Messaging Application Programming Interface (MAPI) client or certain parts of Simple Mail Transfer Protocol (SMTP) outbound routing. The default cache consists of no more than 4MB of entries cached for five minutes.

DSProxy

The Exchange 2000 service that sends directory requests on behalf of Messaging Application Programming Interface (MAPI) clients to Active Directory (AD) through a Name Service Provider Interface (NSPI). The NSPI forwards MAPI directory system calls to a Global Catalog (GC) server. The System Attendant (SA) uses Domain Name System (DNS) to find the closest AD server at startup and then passes this name to the DSProxy process, or dsproxy.dll. DSProxy works using Transmission Control Protocol/Internet Protocol (TCP/IP) and Internetwork Packet Exchange (IPX), but does not work using NetBIOS.

encryption/decryption

The conversion of data into a form called cipher text, which unauthorized users cannot easily understand. Decryption implies converting encrypted data back into its original form, so anyone can understand its context. You use a decryption key or algorithm to recover the contents of an encrypted signal. The more complex the encryption algorithm, the harder it is to eavesdrop on private communications between a sender and a recipient. This form of security is becoming very important in wireless communications because this form of communication is easier to break into than hard-wired circuits. A form of encryption known as *strong encryption* refers to the use of ciphers that are virtually unbreakable unless the appropriate decryption key is present. See also *cipher*.

enterprise

An overall organization. See also *forest*.

EPOXY

See *EXchange InterProcess Communication layer (EXIPC)*.

Event Service

A service used by Exchange Server 5.5 that allowed developers to write programs that would process an event in a public folder or mailbox.

event sink

Allows a user to write code to obtain access to Network News Transfer Protocol (NNTP) and Simple Mail Transfer Protocol (SMTP) stacks. You build an event sink by creating a DLL file using tools such as Microsoft Visual Basic or Visual C++. An event sink can take the form of a Protocol event, Web Storage System event, or Transport event. A Protocol sink extends the features of SMTP, such as rejecting mail from certain recipients. A Web Storage System event consists of synchronous, asynchronous, or system events. A Transport event helps track basic functions of Exchange 2000 Server while SMTP requests are being completed (for example, attaching a standard message to all outgoing mail).

Exchange Conferencing Services (ECS)

An Exchange service that allows users to host virtual meetings by using video, audio, and chat services. Server-side components perform conference management and session coordination services, allowing users to schedule online meetings or reserve meeting rooms using the Outlook 2000 client and the T.120 protocol. ECS contains a resource reservation agent and a conference controller.

EXchange InterProcess Communication layer (EXIPC)
Formerly known as the EPOXY layer, a shared area in memory to which the store.exe process and all Internet Information Server (IIS) protocols in Exchange 2000 can read and write. This layer allows information to be switched rapidly between the IIS protocols running inside the inetinfo.exe process and the store.exe process. It is best to use the EXIPC layer for small packet transfers because of the shared memory used to communicate between the two processes that is involved. Exchange 2000 Server also uses the Central Queue Manager (CQM) for queue cleanup if a failure in one of the two processes occurs. EXIPC consists of a protocol DLL file that implements a binding facility and a shared memory heap.

Exchange Virtual Server (EVS)
The unit of failover found in an Exchange cluster group. Exchange 2000 now supports active/active clusters, so that you can manage two or more nodes as one system. If one node fails, the other nodes of the cluster take over its clients. The cluster supports one or more Exchange virtual servers, and each virtual server runs on one of the nodes. Multiple virtual servers can exist on one node. See also *virtual server*.

Extensible Storage Engine (ESE)
Also known as Joint Engine Technology (JET), the database technology on which Exchange Server 2000 is based. It is also part of the Microsoft Web Storage System. ESE uses a B-tree structure (or "balanced-tree" structure) to store its data, and every page in the database file is a node in the B-tree structure. One ESE database can hold up to 16 terabytes of information, whereas the Active Directory (AD) database, which also uses ESE technology, can hold up to 32 terabytes of data. An ESE database can perform online defragmentation but does not reduce the size of the database involved. The ESE DLL file (esent.dll) uses a transacted database system with log files to guarantee that all committed transactions are stable. See also *Joint Engine Technology (JET)*.

forest
Also known as an enterprise, a group of one or more domain trees. A forest allows different divisions to operate independently while at the same time communicating with other domains. All domain trees in a forest share a common schema and procedures on how domain objects communicate with each other. All domains in the forest share the same Global Catalog (GC) and configuration information. There is a direct relationship between an Exchange 2000 organization and an Active Directory (AD) forest. The Exchange 2000 Server Global Access List (GAL) can display users from only one forest.

front-end/back-end (FE/BE)
A method of separating client access from client data for non–Messaging Application Programming Interface (MAPI) clients using Exchange 2000 Server. These include Post Office Protocol 3 (POP3) clients and clients using Outlook Web Access (OWA). An FE/BE architecture allows you to use one group of servers as data servers and one group as protocol servers. The data servers handle the actual message stores and are sometimes referred to as "information store servers," whereas the protocol servers service the Hypertext Transport Protocol

(HTTP) and POP3 protocols and allow clients to connect directly to a BE server that hosts client mailboxes or public folders. This type of architecture allows for a more unified namespace than you get with normal administrative designs because users do not have to know the name of every server they have to log on to. It also helps to isolate BE servers from being attacked. You can also use FE/BE architecture to reduce the overhead involved in Secure Sockets Layer (SSL) encryption.

Global Catalog (GC)

A storage location for attributes of any object created in Active Directory (AD). It is the central storehouse of information regarding objects in a domain tree or forest. AD produces content for the GC through the normal replication process between the domains that are part of the master directory. You use the attributes stored in the GC for common search operations (such as first name, last name, and so on). Use the GC to find objects in your network without having to fully replicate all information between domain controllers (DCs).

group

A collection of user accounts that helps you centralize administration by allowing you to assign permissions to a specified group rather than individually to each user in the group. A user object can belong to multiple group objects. Windows 2000 Server uses either a security group or a distribution group. The type of group determines how you will use it. The Windows 2000 operating system (OS) uses only security groups to assign permissions to resources. Applications use distribution groups for functions unrelated to security. Only programs that work with Active Directory (AD) services can successfully use distribution groups.

hash function

Provides message integrity checks and digital signatures. A hash function is generally faster than an encryption or digital signature algorithm. A hash function H is a transformation that takes an input m and returns a fixed-size string called the hash value h. These functions have a variety of computational uses. The inputs can be of any length, and the outputs have a fixed length. A hashing algorithm is one way, meaning that you can create a hash from a document but you cannot re-create the document from a hash. A hash is not an encryption of the document. Most importantly, it's very difficult to find two documents with the same hash.

hosted organization

Also known as a virtual server or virtual organization, a scenario where multiple companies are hosted in one Exchange 2000 environment. In this case, both Active Directory (AD) and the Web Storage System must be partitioned correctly so that one company's data is not accessible to other company. All companies can be hosted in one forest within one domain, where organizational units (OUs) partition each company's users. Alternatively, each company can be hosted in a separate forest, so that each company's users can contain a distinct AD schema. Each separate company requires its own unified namespace, such as **www.baseball-for-me.com**.

HTTP-DAV

See *Web Distributed Authoring and Versioning (WebDAV)*.

Information Store service

An important component of Exchange 2000 that maintains a repository or storehouse of user data, such as e-mail. The Store.exe process divides user data into mailbox stores and public stores. It can be found in the \Exchsrvr\Bin directory by default on any Exchange 2000 server.

Installable File System (IFS)
See *Web Storage System*.

Instant Messaging (IM)
A service that allows users to see presence information (such as online, offline, or busy) for other users. Users can send instantaneous communications to each other using components found at both the client and the server. The IM server is part of the inetinfo.exe process and is implemented as an Internet Information Services API (ISAPI) extension. All IM communication uses the Rendezvous Protocol (RVP), which is a subset of Hypertext Transport Protocol (HTTP). You must use an IM client (which consists of a client user interface, the Microsoft Network (MSN) provider, and support for RVP) to log on to IM servers.

Instant Messaging Presence Protocol (IMPP)
The protocol that clients use when connecting to an Instant Messaging (IM) server. It is more formally known as the Microsoft Rendezvous Protocol (RVP) (it will become known as IMPP in a future ratified standard). All IM activity occurs over Hypertext Transport Protocol (HTTP) and port 80, so IMPP (or RVP) allows you to transmit presence information (such as online, offline, or busy) and instant messages over the Internet between dissimilar networks or domains.

Internet Message Access Protocol 4 (IMAP4)
A protocol used to access email or bulletin board messages that are kept on a mail server. It allows a client email program to access remote message stores as if they were local. IMAP's ability to access messages from more than one computer has become extremely important as reliance on electronic messaging has increased. IMAP can also do offline processing, but its special strength is in online and disconnected operations. It is more advanced than *Post Office Protocol 3* (POP3).

Joint Engine Technology (JET)
The underlying database technology used in Exchange Server 4 and 5. This technology has been replaced by the Extensible Storage Engine (ESE) structure of Exchange Server 5.5 and Exchange 2000 Server. It also lies at the core of the Microsoft Access database system and provides functionality and structure to many other applications, including the File Replication Service and Windows Internet Naming Service (WINS).

Lightweight Directory Access Protocol (LDAP)
A client-server protocol used to access directory services. It was initially used as a front end to the X.500 directory service standard, but it is usually used with other types of directory servers. It does not require the upper layers of the Open Systems Interconnection (OSI) models and is a simple protocol to implement for clients accessing a directory-based operating system (OS). The LDAP model is based on information about objects in the form of attributes, which have values associated with a certain type.

link state algorithm (LSA)
Also known as a propagation protocol, an algorithm, new to Exchange 2000 Server, that was first developed by Edsger Dijkstra in 1959. It forms the foundation of the Open Shortest Path First (OSPF) protocol, used by many routers today. LSA propagates the current state of the system in realtime to every server in the organization, which helps eliminate message loops or bounces between

servers. This link-propagation protocol has replaced the Gateway Address Table (GWART) used in Exchange Server 5.5.

mail-based replication (MBR)
A method of moving directory-related information between sites in Exchange Server 5.5 organizations by placing this information in a mail message and using the Message Transfer Agent (MTA) to deliver the data. Active Directory (AD) also uses this mechanism to replicate directory information within Exchange 2000 Server using the Simple Mail Transfer Protocol (SMTP) transport protocol.

Message Database Encapsulated Format (MDBEF)
A database format implemented in Exchange Server. Exchange 2000 Server uses MDB files to represent database files found within Storage Groups. Each server can have multiple database files residing within multiple Storage Groups.

Message Digest 5 (MD5) algorithm
Takes a message of arbitrary length and produces a 128-bit fingerprint or message digest of the input. It is not possible to produce two messages with the same message digest. The MD5 algorithm, developed by Professor Ronald Rivest of MIT, is intended for digital signature applications where a large file must be compressed in a secure manner before it is encrypted with a private key. MD5 is a way to verify data integrity and is much more reliable than checksum or other commonly used methods.

Message Transfer Agent (MTA)
A part of Exchange Server used for addressing and transporting messages. Legacy versions of Exchange based the MTA on the X.400 standard, which supported multiple transport mechanisms, including Transmission Control Protocol/Internet Protocol (TCP/IP) and X.25. Exchange 2000 Server still uses an X.400-based MTA but only to establish a route between two Routing Groups, or between a Routing Group and an external X.400 messaging system.

Messaging Application Programming Interface (MAPI)
Developed by Microsoft and other companies to allow Windows-based applications to access a variety of messaging systems, including Microsoft (MS) Mail and Novell's Message Handling System. MAPI also allows mail-aware applications to exchange both mail and data with others on a network. MAPI consists of a standard set of C language functions stored in a DLL file. Developers who use Active Server Pages (ASP) access the MAPI library by using Collaborative Data Objects (CDO). Visual Basic developers can access MAPI functions through a translation layer.

metabase
Meta means "an underlying definition or description" as well as "more comprehensive or fundamental." Thus, a metabase is a database where Internet Information Server (IIS) stores most of the Internet site configuration information within Windows 2000. Applications can manipulate this metabase via a distributed Component Object Model (COM) interface and through an Active Directory Service Interface (ADSI) provider.

metabase update service
A service in Exchange 2000 that reads data from Active Directory (AD) and places it in the Internet Information Server (IIS) metabase. It facilitates making configuration changes to remote systems.

metadata
Meta means "an underlying definition or description" as well as "more comprehensive or fundamental." Thus, *metadata* is a definition or description of data. This term describes the structure of data within a process such as the Web Storage System.

mixed-mode site
Also known as a mixed-vintage site, a legacy Exchange 5.x site that also consists of Exchange 2000 servers.

Multipoint Control Unit (MCU)
Also known as Multipoint Conferencing Server (MCS), the central connection for a multipoint videoconferencing session. It provides connection points to clients and manages the distribution of video and audio streams. It also provides the necessary transport services for data and application sharing.

Name Service Provider Interface (NSPI)
A component of DSProxy that sends directory requests to Active Directory (AD) on behalf of Messaging Application Programming Interface (MAPI) clients. It forwards all MAPI requests to a Global Catalog (GC) server without opening any remote procedure call (RPC) packets in the process.

namespace
Usually refers to the Domain Name System (DNS) namespace established within a Windows 2000 forest. It is a distributed database organized as a hierarchical tree. Every node of the tree is referred to as a *domain*. A forest is usually represented by a contiguous namespace of parent and child domain hierarchies. An example of such a namespace is a parent domain of baseball.com and a child domain of east.baseball.com.

naming context
A section of Active Directory (AD) with its own properties, including replication configuration information. You use a naming context to define the boundary for information contained with the AD database. The units of replication in AD are found within the domain-naming context, the schema-naming context, and the configuration-naming context. Exchange 2000 stores most of its information in the configuration-naming context, which is replicated to every domain controller (DC) within a Windows 2000 forest.

native mode
An environment consisting only of Exchange 2000 servers. Any servers running earlier versions of Exchange are not permitted to join a native Exchange 2000 organization.

Network News Transfer Protocol (NNTP)
Described by Request for Comments (RFC) 997, the primary protocol that clients and servers use to manage information posted on a Usenet newsgroup. It replaced the original UUCP protocol. (UUCP, the Unix-to-Unix Copy Protocol, described a set of Unix programs used to send files between different Unix systems or commands to be executed on another system.) An NNTP server manages the global network of Usenet newsgroups and includes the server at your Internet Service Provider (ISP). An NNTP client is included as part of a standard Web browser, or you may use a separate client program called a *newsreader*.

Object Linking and Embedding for Databases (OLE DB)
Microsoft's low-level application programming interface (API) used to access a variety of data sources. OLE DB includes

the SQL capabilities of the Microsoft-sponsored Open Database Connectivity (ODBC) interface as well as access to data other than SQL data. OLE DB uses a set of routines for reading and writing data. The "Object" in OLE DB consists of a data source object, a session object, and a command object.

Outlook Web Access (OWA)
A way of accessing email using a standard HTTP port and a standard Web browser. You install OWA when you first install Exchange 2000 Server. It requires Microsoft Internet Explorer 3 (IE3) or later or Netscape Navigator 3 or later. These versions support Hypertext Markup Language (HTML) features such as frames and Secure Sockets Layer (SSL). Users have access to functionality for email, calendars, group scheduling, and basic public folders. This application cannot replace the full-featured Outlook client for 16-bit Windows operating systems (OSs) or Macintosh. Two features that are *not* available when you use OWA are personal address books (which are stored locally on your workstation) and the spell checker.

policy
A group of settings applied to the same class of objects within Active Directory (AD). For example, recipient policies can control email address generation and are more flexible than the legacy site addressing features found in Exchange Server 5.5 sites. You can use filters to regulate which recipients the policies will apply to.

Post Office Protocol 3 (POP3)
The most recent version of an Internet-standard protocol for receiving email messages. It is a client-server protocol where an Internet access provider receives and holds mail. It is built into the Netscape and Internet Explorer (IE) browsers. POP3 is considered a store-and-forward service that uses a conventional Transmission Control Protocol/Internet Protocol (TCP/IP) port number of 110 to receive email. POP3 works best using one computer and offline message access, where messages are downloaded and then deleted from the mail server. The offline mode of access that POP3 supports effectively ties the user to one computer for message storage and manipulation. POP3 is often contrasted with Internet Messaging Access Protocol 4 (IMAP4), which is more of a remote file server.

protocol farm
A grouping of protocol virtual servers that can operate together to provide one protocol service for redundancy purposes. It can even span multiple computers and serve as a primary connection point for users in an organization. Users can access information without having to know its physical location.

public folder connection agreement (PFCA)
A connection agreement that replicates public folder objects between an Exchange 5.5 directory and Active Directory (AD). Each PFCA is configured as a two-way connection agreement and replicates between the site naming context in the Exchange 5.5 site and the appropriate System Objects container in AD.

Public Folder tree
Also known as a public folder root or top-level hierarchy, it represents an arrangement of public folder objects in a tree-like structure. In previous versions of Exchange Server, organizations contained only one root-level public folder named All Public Folders. Exchange 2000 Server creates

multiple root-level public folders or Public Folder trees that appear in addition to the All Public Folders tree. Every public folder hierarchy you configure has its own database in the Web Storage System. Multiple public stores run under one process. The default All Public Folders tree is available to all Messaging Application Programming Interface (MAPI), Network News Transfer Protocol (NNTP), and Hypertext Transport Protocol (HTTP) clients. Other Public Folder trees are available only to NNTP and Web clients, not to Outlook 2000 clients.

RC2
A conventional secret-key block encryption algorithm considered as a replacement for Data Encryption Standard (DES). The input and output block sizes are each 64 bits long, and the key size is variable, ranging from 1 through 128 bytes. The current implementation of RC2 uses 8 bytes. This algorithm is easier to implement on 16-bit microprocessors and runs almost twice as fast as the DES standard on IBM Advanced Technology (AT) hardware.

RC4
A stream cipher algorithm that uses variable-length keys. It was developed in 1987 by Ronald Rivest of MIT for RSA Data Security and was proprietary until 1994. The keystream is independent of the plain text used in the message. Each entry in the algorithm is a permutation of the numbers 0 through 255, and the permutation is itself a function of the variable-length keys. See also *cipher* and *stream cipher*.

Recipient Update Service (RUS)
Generates Simple Mail Transfer Protocol (SMTP) and proxy addresses for users. It checks if any object in the forest has the same address; if it does, it appends a number to this duplicate address to make it unique. Every domain that contains objects with Exchange settings requires one server running RUS. It is a good idea to create separate domain controllers (DCs) dedicated to running this service.

remote procedure call (RPC)
Also known as a function call or subroutine call, a protocol that one program uses to request a service from a program located in another computer without understanding all the network details involved. RPC uses the client/server model, where the requesting program is the client and the service-providing program is the server. RPC is a synchronous operation, meaning that the requesting program is suspended until all results from the remote procedure have been returned. This protocol covers both the Transport layer and the Application layer in the Open Systems Interconnection (OSI) model of network communications. It allows development of applications, including multiple programs distributed in a network.

Rendezvous Protocol (RVP)
A subset of the HTTP-DAV protocol, which is itself an extension to Hypertext Transport Protocol (HTTP) 1.1. All Instant Messaging (IM) communication occurs using RVP. It uses existing network technologies to allow notifications within an organization and allows an entity known as a *watcher* to obtain presence information (such as online, offline, or busy) regarding users in an organization. It also allows instant messages to be sent to instant message inboxes inside the current Windows 2000 domain. This protocol is related to work that is currently being done by the Instant Messaging and Presence

Protocol Working Group (part of the IETF) in developing a new implementation of RVP known as Instant Messaging and Presence Protocol (IMPP). RVP merely provides an existing implementation of this soon-to-be-ratified standard.

resource
An object that represents facilities in Active Directory (AD). In the context of collaboration, you use this object for data or videoconferences using components such as Instant Messaging (IM) or Chat.

resource mailbox
An object in the Windows 2000 Active Directory (AD) directory service that references a resource that can receive messages. No matter where this resource resides, it has a recipient object in AD. A resource mailbox in Exchange 2000 must exhibit a direct one-to-one correspondence with a Windows 2000 security principal.

Routing Engine (RE)
One of the three primary components of Exchange Server, the others being the Information Store (IS) service and the System Attendant (SA). The RE service coordinates the transfer of messages between Exchange servers. If this particular service shuts down, Exchange can no longer move messages throughout your network. It directs messages to their intended destinations as well as makes sure that all messages arrive intact.

Routing Group
A group of servers that communicate with each other over a high-speed local area network (LAN) connection. Exchange 2000 uses Routing Groups instead of Exchange sites. Information between servers in the same Routing Group flows immediately using the Simple Mail Transfer Protocol (SMTP) protocol, not a connector. A Routing Group helps you lay out the physical network topology of your connected servers. To be included in a Routing Group, all Exchange servers must belong to the same Windows 2000 forest and have a permanent SMTP connection to one another.

Routing Group connector (RGC)
A Simple Mail Transfer Protocol (SMTP)–based connector that is functionally equivalent to the Exchange 5.5 site connector. It allows servers in a Routing Group to act as routing servers and allows you to choose multiple servers in the Routing Group as bridgehead servers for either end of the connector. An RGC provides fault tolerance if one of the servers in the Routing Group fails for any reason. Multiple bridgeheads help you control which servers can send or receive messages between Routing Groups. You can use an RGC to connect to prior versions of Exchange configured with the site connector, which uses remote procedure calls (RPCs).

routing object
An object used to program Exchange Server's Routing Engine (RE) behavior. This object allows you to create *process definitions*, which define the series of states to be tracked by the RE. Exchange Server 5.5 included routing object libraries or helper objects for creating document routing applications. These were designed for Messaging Application Programming Interface (MAPI)–based email applications. Exchange 2000 Server is fully compatible with routing objects and other MAPI applications. You use a routing object in applications that are modeled as business processes.

routing service
Uses a link state table to find the shortest path between two Routing Groups. Any server that cannot find a route for a message using the link state table cannot attempt to deliver that message.

schema
The part of Active Directory (AD) that contains definitions of all objects, such as computers and users stored in AD. These definitions define classes of objects contained in AD, as well as the types of attributes each object can have. It is possible to add components within the schema, but you cannot delete unused components (they are deactivated). You can modify the schema by using the Microsoft Management Console (MMC) or by installing software that changes the schema indirectly. When Exchange 2000 is installed, the AD schema is extended with attributes that start with *ms-Exch-*.

Scripting Agent
Allows server-side scripts to be run if certain events, such as posting or deleting a message, occur.

Secure Hash Algorithm-1 (SHA-1)
Specified in the Secure Hash Standard (SHS), developed by NIST and published as a federal information processing standard (FIPS PUB 180), SHA-1 was a revision to SHA that was published in 1994. The revision corrected an unpublished flaw in SHA. Its design is very similar to the Message Digest 4 (MD4) family of hash functions developed by Professor Ronald Rivest of MIT. The algorithm takes a message of fewer than 264 bits long and produces a 160-bit message digest. It is somewhat slower than MD5, but the larger message digest makes it more secure against brute-force attacks.

Secure Sockets Layer (SSL)
A protocol that provides privacy and reliability between two communicating applications. It contains the SSL Record Protocol, used to encapsulate upper-layer protocols such as HTTP and Telnet found within the Open Systems Interconnection (OSI) model of network communications. An example of an encapsulated protocol used by SSL is the Handshake protocol, which allows the server and client to authenticate each other and negotiate an encryption algorithm before the application protocol transmits or receives any data. SSL is application protocol independent and provides connection security where each connection is private and reliable.

security principal
An object that can log on to a Windows 2000 domain and access some or all of that network's resources. With respect to Exchange 2000, a security principal is a mailbox-enabled user that can access network resources as well as send and receive mail. A non-security principal cannot access network resources and has email sent to an external address.

Simple Authentication and Security Layer (SASL)
Defined in Request for Comments (RFC) 2222, adds authentication support to connection-based protocols. To use this feature, a protocol includes a command for identifying and authenticating users to a server. A security layer is usually inserted between the protocol and the connection.

Simple Mail Transfer Protocol (SMTP)
The heart of Exchange 2000 transport services. It is the Internet standard for transporting messages and is based on Requests for Comments (RFCs) 821 and

822. When you install Microsoft Windows 2000, a basic SMTP service is automatically installed as part of the inetinfo.exe process. This basic service supports many of the Extended SMTP (ESMTP) commands such as **helo**, **mail**, and **data**. Although there is only one SMTP service, you can configure multiple virtual SMTP servers on every Exchange 2000 server in your organization. Exchange 2000 enhances the delivery functions of the SMTP service that comes preinstalled with Windows 2000.

sink
See *event sink*.

site
A range of Internet Protocol (IP) subnets. Active Directory (AD) uses this concept to establish boundaries for replication traffic. A site also helps clients in a remote site to locate their domain controller (DC) for validation purposes. Exchange 5.5 Server used this concept to describe a logical group of servers that could be referenced without consideration of their physical location.

Site Consistency Checker (SCC)
Also known as the Site Knowledge Consistency Checker (SKCC), runs within the Site Replication Service (SRS), which is responsible for replicating Exchange 5.x site and configuration information to the configuration-naming partition of Active Directory (AD). This allows an Exchange 2000 server to be represented in the Exchange 5.5 site list so that earlier versions of Exchange Server can send messages to the Exchange 2000 server. The SCC is an improved version of the Knowledge Consistency Checker (KCC) from Exchange Server 5.5 and ensures that knowledge consistency is kept for sites and Administrative Groups when they coexist between Exchange Server 5.5 and Exchange 2000 Server.

Site Replication Service (SRS)
A component that maintains two versions of the Exchange server directory during mixed-mode operation. An instance of SRS is installed on the first Exchange 2000 server that is introduced into an Exchange 5.5 site and allows directory replication between the two versions of Exchange. It effectively transforms the Active Directory (AD) version of an Exchange directory into an Exchange 5.5 site and allows an Exchange 2000 server to resemble an Exchange 5.5 server. The SRS is displayed in the Exchange 5.5 Administrator program as the Exchange 5.5 Directory Service.

Storage Group
A representation of a fixed database layout within Exchange 2000 Server. It corresponds to an instance of the Extensible Storage Engine (ESE) with its own set of transaction log files. Up to four Storage Groups per server are supported in Exchange 2000. Each Storage Group supports up to five databases, which can be either a mailbox store or a public folder store. All transactions for all databases in one Storage Group are in one set of log files. You can restore a database within a Storage Group without affecting the other databases in the same Storage Group.

store
The name given to the storage structure on an Exchange server. Each store is found in a Storage Group. There are two kinds of stores: a mailbox store for messages and a public folder store for public folder use. Each store consists of both EDB and STM files. You cannot create a store until you have created the Storage Group. Upon

installation of Exchange 2000 Server, you see a default Storage Group named First Storage Group, which contains one mailbox and one public folder store.

stream cipher
A symmetric encryption algorithm designed to be much faster than a block cipher. A block cipher operates on large blocks of data, whereas a stream cipher typically operates on smaller units of text. A stream cipher generates a *keystream* and provides encryption by combining the keystream with the plain text, using the bitwise **XOR** operation (an "Exclusive Or" logical Boolean operation applied to each byte of data you wish to encrypt). If the generation of the keystream does not depend on the plain text or cipher text, the result is a synchronous stream cipher. Most stream cipher designs are for synchronous stream ciphers. See also *block cipher* and *cipher*.

symmetric cipher
A form of data encryption in which one key encrypts and decrypts a message. Although effective, this form of encryption makes it difficult to securely share the key between the sender and recipient. The sender has to be able to securely communicate the shared key. See also *cipher*.

System Attendant (SA)
One of the three key services in Exchange 2000, the others being the Information Store (IS) service and the Routing Engine (RE) service. The SA is considered to be the background manager for key Exchange system services because it helps maintain link state tables used for message delivery as well as monitors the connections between servers. It monitors many behind-the-scenes activities that are vital to an optimal configuration of Exchange Server.

T.120
This standard addresses realtime data conferencing and covers the document conferencing and application sharing portion of a multimedia teleconference. It is a comprehensive specification that resolves complex technological issues and was established by the International Telecommunications Union (ITU-T). Many major vendors, including Microsoft, MCI, and Cisco Systems, are implementing T.120-based products. For example, this protocol is used with Exchange Data Conferencing and Video Conferencing together with the Microsoft NetMeeting client. The T.120 infrastructure can work with both unicast and multicast data packets simultaneously, providing a flexible solution for a mixed multicast-unicast network.

user
An object that can log on to a domain and gain access to network resources or log on to a computer and gain access to resources on that computer. Windows 2000 supports domain users, local users, and built-in user accounts. Users who can access network resources can be either mail enabled or mailbox enabled, depending on where their email is sent.

user principal name (UPN)
A friendly name for a user. It is shorter than the distinguished name, which represents a collection of attributes in a directory information tree (DIT). It is a combination of the username and Domain Name System (DNS) name of the domain where the user resides. For example, if Ted Smith resides in the baseball.com domain tree, his UPN would be TedSmith@baseball.com. The UPN does not depend on the distinguished name, so Ted Smith could be

moved to another domain without disrupting his logon. A UPN is an attribute of a security principal object.

virtual root
A shortcut to a physical storage location that may reside anywhere on the network. Internet Information Server (IIS) uses it to display the resources of a Web server. A virtual root allows users to connect to resources by using a user-friendly path instead of a strict and complex navigation hierarchy.

virtual server
Allows you to support users with different configuration needs, such as message formats. You create a virtual server for each instance of a default protocol that comes installed with Exchange 2000 Server. For example, a default Hypertext Transport Protocol (HTTP) protocol server is created during installation, but you can configure multiple HTTP virtual servers based on this default protocol server, using configurations for authentication or message formats. A unique Internet Protocol (IP) port number and address specify each virtual server defined for each protocol. You can create a protocol virtual server for file transfer protocol (FTP), Hypertext Transport Protocol (HTTP), Internet Message Access Protocol 4 (IMAP4), Network News Transfer Protocol (NNTP), Simple Mail Transfer Protocol (SMTP), and Post Office Protocol 3 (POP3).

Web Distributed Authoring and Versioning (WebDAV)
Also known as HTTP-DAV, a set of extensions to Hypertext Transport Protocol (HTTP) that allows users to collaboratively manage files on remote Web servers. It came about because of the need to create, remove, and query information about Web pages, and to link pages of any media type to related pages. WebDAV provides multiple management features, including namespace management, which allows users to receive a listing of pages at a particular hierarchy level (similar to directory listings in a file system), and version management, which supports collaboration by allowing multiple authors to work on the same document in parallel tracks.

Web Storage System
A technology that provides local and remote users with access to Exchange Server's file systems. It is a hierarchical database that manages documents and email messages. Every Web Store exists as a folder on the local machine so applications can store files in this store from either local or remote locations. The folder can be seen under a default M: drive that is given the share name of BackOfficeStorage. Any user can access any data in this store, including messages and documents, by using a Uniform Naming Convention (UNC) name within a Web browser. The Web Store also includes an indexing feature that allows users to rapidly discover Web Store content. Developers can access this system using a programming language that supports the Component Object Model (COM).

X.509
A standard published by the International Telecommunications Union (ITU-T) in 1988 as part of the X.500 directory recommendations. It defines a standard certificate format. The Internet Privacy Enhanced Mail Request for Comments (RFC), published in 1993, included specifications for a Public Key Infrastructure (PKI) based on these X.509 certificates.

Index

Bold page numbers indicate sample exam questions.

A

Access control, public folders, 130–131
Access Control Lists. *See* ACLs.
Account management, 240–244
ACLs, 78, 218
Across-the-wire upgrade, 549
Actions, 11, 407
Active Client, 489, 582–583
Active Directory. *See* AD.
Active Directory Connector. *See* ADC.
Active Directory Installation Wizard, 153
Active Directory Services Interface. *See* ADSI.
Active Server, 582–583, 589
Active Server Pages. *See* ASP.
ActiveX, 581, 589
ActiveX controls, 581
ActiveX Data Object. *See* ADO.
ActiveX scripting, 581
ActiveX Server, 53
AD, 20, 26, 57, 174, **606**
  AD-dependent services, 21
  directory services, 20, 40, 150
  domains, 152–154
  functions of, 286, 293, 503
  GC server, 147, 156–157
  groups, 157–158
  IIS, 293
  KMS and, 390–398
  logical structure, 149–155
  namespace, 19, 150–151, 482
  naming contexts, 155–156
  naming partitions, 537
  .NET services, 110
  Novell GroupWise, 353
  optimizing capacity, 500
  planned upgrade to Exchange 2000, 515
  planning, 149–155
  populating before migrating to Windows 2000 Server, 543
  transitive trusts, 154–155, 166
AD Administration Tool, 122
ADC
  functions of, 16, 115, 359
  installation, 524–525
  in legacy systems, 361
  mixed-mode environment, 175, 356, 357, 537, 538
  MSDSS and, 58 upgrading to Exchange 2000, 515, 524–527, 550
adclean.exe, 544
AD Delegation of Control Wizard, 122–123, 135
AD Delegation Wizard, 135
AD Domains and Trusts snap-in, 61, 118, 135, 175
Address book, 27
  Lotus Notes, 350
  mixed-mode environment, 542
Addressing, preparing to upgrade legacy system to Exchange 2000, 514
Address lists, 259–262
Address list server, 181
Address resolution, Categorizer, 280–281, 282, 285, 293
Address space, 302
Address Space tab
  Lotus cc:Mail connector, 343, 344
  Lotus Notes connector, 349
  Novell GroupWise connector, 354
  SMTP connector, 307
  X.400 connector, 315
ADE, 341, 360
Administration, 14, 42–43, 101–136
  collaborative services management, 115
  of distribution groups, 130
  domain structure, 119–120
  legacy issues, 121
  needs, 115–118
  Outlook Web Access (OWA), 220–221

671

performance management, 132–134
permission management, 122–124
policies, 124–125
public folders, 130–131
recipient management, 118–124, 135
security, 154
security groups, 130
server management, 125–129, 135
storage services, 73–74, 115
Administrative Groups, 128, 326, **603**, **606**
Administrative models
    account management, 240
    recipient management, 120–121, 135
    server management, 126–127, 135
Administrative roles, account management, 240–241
Administrative services, planning, 175
Administrative tools
    installing, 176–177
    for performance management, 133–134
    for recipient management, 121–122, 135
    for server management, 128–129, 135
Administrator, changing role of, 2
ADO, 41, 79, 584
AD schema, extending, 178–181
ADSI, 17, 58, 118, 585
ADSI Edit, 265
AD Sites and Services snap-in, 61, 118, 135, 175
AD Users and Computers snap-in, 49, 61, 240, 242, 264
    functions of, 118, 122, 176, 353
    mixed-mode environments, 175
Advanced Queuing. *See* AQ.
Advanced tab
    Lotus cc:Mail connector, 343, 344
    Lotus Notes connector, 352–353
    SMTP connectors, 307
    X.400 connector, 315–317
Agent, 10
All Public Folders folder, 76, 100
API, 17, 583–585, 589
Application-level gateways, 380
Application log, 451
Application programming interface. *See* API.
AQ, 50, 51, 280, 282, 286, 293
Archive bit, 464
ASP, 53, 221, 584
Assets, 371–372
Asymmetric encryption, 377
Asymmetric keys, 383, 398
Asynchronous communication, 408
Asynchronous messaging system, 15
Asynchronous process, 14

Asynchronous protocol, 420
Atomicity, of transaction, 83
Atomic transactions, 60
Attribute fields, 91
Auditing
    audit logs, 450–451
    for monitoring, 450–451
    for planning, 335–336
    for security, 375–376
Audit logs, 450–451
auth command, 279
Authentication
    client configuration, 221–222
    defined, 376
    digest authentication, 422, 423
    with ESTMP, 279
    Kerberos, 221–222
    SAS, 222
    simple authentication, 387
    with SMTP connectors, 306
    SSO, 222
    strong authentication, 387
Authorization, 376, 377
Automatic Directory Exchange. *See* ADE.

B

Backbone layered topology, 288, 289
Back-end servers. *See* BE servers.
Backups, 84, 459, 460
    scheduling, 465
    types of, 464
    using Windows 2000, 461–465
Backup tab, of ntbackup.exe, 466, 467
BadMail directory, 284
Bandwidth rule, 307
Baseline analysis, auditing, 375–376
Bastion, 380, 381
BDAT, 278
BE servers
    configurations for, 496
    functions of, 485, 503
    hardware requirements for, 494
"Big Iron," 4
Binary Data Transfer. *See* BDAT.
BizTalk Server 2000, 41, 370
BP-14, 315–316
BP-15, 315, 316
Bridgehead servers, 303, 304, 307, 378
Brokers, 11, 12, **597**
B-tree indexing, 83
Business objectives, 41–43

C

CA, 384–385, 387–390, 394, **608**
Cache Size counter, 85
Canonical record, 421
Capacity, 504
   client traffic and, 498–499
   factors affecting, 496–498
   optimization, 499–501
   troubleshooting, 501–502
Capacity planning, 132, 495–502
CAPI, 41
Capture filters, 449
Cascading Style Sheets. *See* CSS.
CAST-40, 48
CAST-60, 48
Categorization, 285–286
Categorized Message Queue, 282
Categorizer, 280–281, 282, 285–286, 293
cc:Mail connector. *See* Lotus cc:Mail connector.
CCITT, 17
CCTA, 13, 111
CDO, 17, 80, 221, 280, 293, 585
CDO 2, 280, 281, 293
CDO 3, 281
CDOEX, 280, 281, 293
Central Computer and Telecommunications Agency. *See* CCTA.
Centralized administration
   recipient management, 120
   server management, 126–127
Centralized model, account management, 240
Certificate authority. *See* CA.
Certificates, 398
Certificate Services, **608**
   components of, 387–388
   installing, 387, 388–389, 398
CFML, 581
CGI scripts, 579–580, 582, 589
Channels, 408, 413–414
Character-based searches, 92
Chat client, 417–418
Chat community
   creating, 413–417
   removing, 415
Chat room, 408
Chat servers, 159
Chat services, 409–419, 424–425, **609**
   administrative controls for, 409–412
   Chat client, 417–418
   creating a chat community, 413–417
   ejecting a member, 417–418
   functions of, 33, 53, 189
   restricted list, 416
Checkpoint file, 84, 101
Checksum, 85
*.chk file, 84, 101
Chunking, 278
Circular logging, 84–85, 101, 460–461
Client. *See* Clients.
Client access, planning, 164–165
Client applications
   Exchange client, 203, 207
   Macintosh clients, 208
   Outlook 2000, 203–206, 212–216
   Outlook Express, 206–207
   Schedule+, 203, 207–208
   Unix clients, 208, 217, 230
Client configuration
   authentication, 221–222
   Exchange client, 203, 207
   legacy features, 227–230
   Macintosh clients, 208
   Outlook 2000, 203–206, 212–216
   Outlook Express, 206–207
   Outlook Web Access (OWA), 218, 220–221
   OWA, 26, 53, 165, 216–217
   Schedule+, 203, 207–208
   Unix clients, 208, 217, 230
   WebDAV protocol, 32, 77, 100, 217–218
   Web Store, 48, 72, 75, 100, 219–220
Clients, 10, 202–203. *See also* Client applications, Client configuration.
Chat client, 417–418
   instant messaging and, 424
Client/server architecture, two-tier, 15
Client Service for NetWare, 320
Client-side scripting, 582
Cloneable chat room, 409
Clustering, planning, 164
Clusters, 87, 88
Cluster Service, 63, 164
CMIS, 9–10, 34, 55
CMOT, 9
CNAME record, 421
Coexistence, 536, 549. *See also* Mixed-mode environment.
ColdFusion, 581
Collaboration, 406–426
   Chat Service, 33, 53, 189, 408–419
   instant messaging, 33, 159, 189, 252, 419–424
   Intranet technologies, 418
   Knowledge-Management Paradigm, 407

674   Collaboration Data Objects

Collaboration Data Objects. *See* CDOs.
Collaboration services
   Microsoft Exchange Messaging And Collaboration Services, 189, 301
   Web Store, 48, 72, 75, 100, 219–220, 561
Collaboration tools, 407
Collaborative Data Objects. *See* CDOS.
Collaborative services management, administration, 115
Collaborative workspace, 80–83
COM, 581
COM-based frame, 117
Combination server, 485
Comité Consultatif International Téléphonique et Télégraphique. *See* CCITT.
Common gateway interface scripts. *See* CGI scripts.
Common Management Information Services. *See* CMIS.
Component Object Model. *See* COM.
Component Selection screen, installation, 187–188, 190
Computer Associates ArcServeIT, 460
Computers, history of, 4
Computers and System Manager, 49
Confidentiality, security, 377
ConfigCA, 531, 538
Configuration subspace, 156
Configuring
   connection agreements, 525–527
   firewalls, 379
   MS Mail, 322–324
   Novell clients, 320
   public folders, 161–162
   remote mail, 229, 231
   scheduled connections, 229–230, 231
   X.400 connectors, 308, 311–318
Conformance, X.400, 316
Connected Routing Groups tab, X.400 connector, 317, 318
Connection agreements
   ConfigCA, 531, 538
   configuring, 525–527
   nonprimary agreement, 538
   primary agreement, 538
Connectivity, 334–361. *See also* Connectors.
   generic deployment, 342–343
   strategic planning, 334–339, 359
Connector mailbox, 348
Connector Manager, 282
Connector MTAs tab, MS Mail, 323
Connector Properties sheets, MS Mail, 322–323

Connectors, 300–318, 360, **598**, **607**
   address space, 302
   audit, 337
   coexistence with legacy Exchange, 544–548
   cost of, 303
   function of, 16, 51–52
   installing, 301–302
   legacy Exchange 5.5 site connectors, 364–365
   Lotus cc:Mail connector, 52, 189, 339, 360, 361
   Lotus Notes connector, 52, 189, 319, 340, 347–353, 360–361, **607**
   migration of, 544–548, 550
   mixed-mode environment, 544–548
   MS Mail connector, 189, 309, 321, 322, 323, 339, 340
   Novell GroupWise connector, 52, 189, 340, 353–356, 361
   properties of, 302–303
   RGCs, 51, 163, 303, 304, 305, **607**
   site connectors, 304–305
   SMTP connectors, 51, 163, 303, 305–307, 326
   strategic planning, 335–336, 359
   X.400 connectors, 49, 51, 163, 275, 304, 307–318
Connector scope, 307
Connector servers, 159
Consistency
   of databases, 94–99, 101
   of transaction, 83
Console tree, MMC, 116
Consumers, 11
Contact, 239
Contact attributes, 255, 257
Contact management, 243
Contact object, 337
Content class, 561
Content format, recipient settings, 245
Content Restrictions tab, X.400 connector, 317
Context menu, 118
Counters, 443–444
Cryptographic API. *See* CAPI.
Cryptographic service provider. *See* CSP.
CSP, 383, 388
CSS, 576
Custom Installation Wizard, 212, 231
Custom recipient, 239, 337

D

DASL protocol, 217
Databases
   consistency, 94–99, 101
   defragmentation of, 95, 437

ESEFILE, 98–99
ESEUTIL, 96
file types, 81–83, 100
ISINTEG, 97–98
message databases, 61
mounted, 88
multiple message databases, 31
number of databases supported, 101
soft recovery, 95, 96
in Storage Groups, 86–87
tips for using, 95
transaction log file, 460
unmounted, 88
Web Store, 564–565
Database services, Web Store, 48, 72, 75, 100, 561
Data conferencing servers, 159
Data Conferencing Service. See DCS.
Data Encryption Standard. See DES.
Data-Processing Paradigm, 4
data statements, 278
Data storage, 32, 59–60
Data store, 27
DAV. See WebDAV.
DAV Searching and Locating protocol.
 See DASL protocol.
DBA, 45, 85
DCF GML, 574
dcpromo.exe, 153
DCS, 159, 424–425
Decentralized model, account management, 240
Default recipient policies, 262
Defragmentation, 95, 437, 451–452, 469
Delegated administration, 120
Delivery Options tab, SMTP connectors, 306–307
Delivery reports, 258
Delivery restrictions, recipient settings, 246, 247, 249
Delivery Restrictions tab
 Lotus cc:Mail connector, 344, 345
 Lotus Notes connector, 350
 Novell GroupWise connector, 354–355
 X.400 connector, 318
Delivery Status Notification. See DSN.
DES, 48
Design
 assessing project risk, 481
 FE/BE design. See FE/BE design.
 FE server, 493–495
 hardware considerations, 481–483
 mixed-mode environment, 542–543
 MSF Infrastructure Deployment Process Model, 479–481, 503

 preparing to upgrade legacy system to Exchange 2000, 514, 548
 RAID design configurations, 90, 186, 193, 444–445, 483, 490–493
 server sizing issues, 490–495
 troubleshooting, 501–502
Details tab
 Lotus cc:Mail connector, 346–347
 Lotus Notes connector, 353
 Novell GroupWise tab, 356
 X.400 connector, 317
DHCP, 175
DHTML, 562, 578
Diagnostic logging, 455–456, 469
Dial-up network. See DUN.
Dial-Up Networking tab, Outlook 2000, 229
Digest authentication, 422, 423
Digital certificates, 386, 387
"Digital dashboard," 26, 47–48
Digital Equipment Corporation (DEC), 4
Directory, 16
Directory-enabled networks, 292
Directory Information Tree. See DIT.
Directory Requestor Post Office, 324
Directory Server Post Office, 324
Directory Service lookups, Outlook Express, 207
Directory services, 40, 46–47, 59–61
 defined, 175
 metadirectories, 22, 64, 585
 planning, 146–147, 175
 preparing to upgrade legacy system to Exchange 2000, 514
Directory Store. See DS.
Directory synchronization
 Lotus cc:Mail, 339, 341, 342, 343
 Lotus Notes, 340, 347
 mixed-mode environments, 359
 MS Mail, 324–325, 339
 Novell GroupWise, 340, 355
 strategic planning, 336, 359, 360
Directory synchronization agent, 324
Directory System Agent. See DSA.
Directory User Agent. See DUA.
dir.edb, 98
Dirsync Options tab, Lotus Notes connector, 350
Dirsync Schedule tab, Novell GroupWise connector, 355
Dirsync synchronization, 325
Disaster planning, 165–167, 459–468
 backups, 84, 459, 460
 restore process, 461, 466–468

Disk counters, 443–444
Disk Defragmenter snap-in, 451–452
diskperf -? command, 444
diskperf -yv command, 443–444
dispatch.exe, 45, 325
Display filters, 449
Distributed management, server management, 127
Distributed services, 55–63
Distributed-services architecture, 12, 99–100
Distribution groups, 130, 157
Distribution lists. *See* DLs.
DIT, 19
DLs, 226, 239, **599**
DMZ, 380, 381
DNS, 25, 286, 294, **604**
  instant messaging and, 420–421
  security and, 377
  troubleshooting, 436
DNS namespace, planning, 151
DocLinks, 347, 349
Document Composition Facility Generalized Markup Language. *See* DCF GML.
Document Object Models. *See* DOMs.
Document sizes, strategic planning, 336
Domain Name System. *See* DNS.
DomainPrep, 178, 181, 193, 528
/DomainPrep switch, 181
Domain queues, 282
Domains, 153
  defining first domain, 153
  designing, 483
  planning, 152–154
Domain structure, administration of, 119–120
Domain subspace, 155
DOMs, 562
DOS, 10
DRAS connector, 52
DS
  AD and, 57
  changes to, 153
  functions of, 46, 54, 64
DSA, 19
DSAccess, 47
DSAccess API, 500–501
dsmain.exe, 46, 64
DSN, 278, 580
DSProxy, 47, 500
DUA, 19
DUN, 228, 304
Duplexing, 186
Durability, of transaction, 83

Dynamic buffer allocation. *See* DBA.
Dynamic channel, 409
Dynamic data, 462
Dynamic DNS, 175, 377
Dynamic Host Configuration Protocol. *See* DHCP.
Dynamic HTML. *See* DHTML.

E

EAI, 41
E-commerce, 25
*.edb file, 76, 81, 83, 100, 101
edb.log, 81, 82
edbtemp.log file, 82
EDK, 49
ehlo command, 277, 279, 307
8-bit clean, 278
Electronic message, 15. *See also* Messaging systems.
Email
  attachment, 16, **598**
  body, 16
  components of container object, 15–16
  header, 15
  history of, 24
  Outlook Express, 206
  signature, 16
Email addresses, 17
  recipient policy, 338–339
  recipient settings, 245
E-Mail Addresses tab, Exchange 2000, 251–252
Empty tags, 576
Encryption, 382
  asymmetric, 377, 398
  keys, 277, 398
  public key encryption, 382, 383–384
  SMTP connectors, 306
End users, 73
Enterprise application integration. *See* EAI.
Enterprise root CA, 384, 388–390
Enterprise subordinate CA, 385
Entities, 574
Entry module, Certificate Services, 387
EPOXY, 50, 99, 216–217, **596**
Error control, 13
error.exe, 436
ESE, 52, 83–91
  circular logging, 84–85, 101
  memory management, 85–86
  SGs, 61–62, 74, 86
  single instance, 86
  SRS, 537
  system-related file types, 84, 101

ESEFILE, 98–99
ESENTUTIL, 265
ESEUTIL, 96, 436–437, 468
eseutil.exe, 436–437, 468
ESMTP, 19, 274, 277
   eturn command, 307
   features of, 278–279, 293
ETRN, 279
eturn command, 307
Event Viewer. *See* Windows 2000 Event Viewer.
Exchange 4, 44
   comparing versions, 53–54
   X.400 and, 27–28, 34, 44
Exchange 5, 34
   architecture, **600**
   comparing versions, 53–54
   Internet and, 28
   transport protocols, 309
Exchange 5.5, **605**, **606**
   ADC, 16
   architecture, 49, **600**
   collaboration, 407
   comparing versions, 34, 53–54
   components of, 44
   data type, 83
   features of, 21, 28, 34
   KMS, 386–387
   legacy Exchange 5.5 site connectors, 364–365
   MDBEF, 76
   organizational topology, 151
   recovering after failed upgrade, 532–535
   SMTP services in, 274, 276
   store.exe, 87
   transport protocols, 309
   upgrading to Exchange 2000, 512–535
   user organization, 129
Exchange 2000, 6
   account management, 240–244
   administration, 14, 42–43, 110–136
   administrative models, 120–121
   APIs, 583–585
   architecture, 41–42, 55–63, 99–100, 110, 238
   backup, 84
   backups, 84, 459, 460, 461–465
   capacity planning and assessment, 132, 495–502
   clients, 202–203
   collaboration, 406–426
   connectivity. *See* Connectivity.
   connectors. *See* Connectors.
   database file types, 81–83
   data storage, 59–60
   design issues, 479–495
   design of, 41–42
   directory services. *See* Directory services.
   disaster recovery planning, 165–167, 459–468, 469
   distributed services, 55–63
   expanded functionality of, 31–32
   features of, 31–33
   FE/BE design, 12, 55, 63, 100, 483–490, 493–495, 503, 571–572
   functions of, 14
   hardware requirements for, 183, 493, 514–515, 516–517
   installation of, 114, 174–193
   interoperability, 299–326
   as KM information broker, 28–33, 34, 47, 73, 174
   legacy systems, 42, 43–55
   license agreement, 521
   licensing, 190
   mailbox management, 242–243
   markup languages, 560, 572–578, 588
   memory management, 85–86
   memory requirements for, 493–494
   as messaging service provider, 25–28
   minimum requirements for, 183–184
   mixed-mode configuration, 115, 356–359, 536–548
   monitoring, 86, 434, 440–459, 468
   native mode, 356, 540, 541, 550
   .NET framework, 585–587
   optimization, 159–160, 184–185, 434
   physical structure, 158–160
   planning. *See* Planning.
   protocol services, 56, 61–63
   Query Processor, 93
   recipient management. *See* Recipient management.
   relationship with Windows 2000, 75, 185
   removing, 534–535
   requirements for, 183–187, 193, 493
   restore process, 461, 466–468
   routing management. *See* Routing management.
   security, 370–398
   SMTP services in, 276–277
   snap-ins, 42
   storage services. *See* Storage services.
   System Management Tools, 49, 121, 189, 393
   transport protocols, 309
   transport services, 49–53
   troubleshooting, 435–440, 468, **610**
   upgrading to, 512–535
   Web forms, 579, 589
   Web Services, 566–572
   Web solutions, 579–583

Web Storage System, 76–79, 81–82, 91–92, 560–566, 587
Web support, 32–33
Exchange 2000 Enterprise Server (Exchange Server), 6, 27, 29–30, 34, **601**
Exchange 2000 Monitoring and Status Tool, 133, 452–455, 469, **609**
Exchange 2000 Server, 29–30, 34, **599**
   deploying, 113–115
   ESEFILE, 98
   Internet protocols, 187
   KM and, 47
Exchange 2000 Setup utility, 178, 182
Exchange 2000 System Management Tools, 49, 121, 189, 393
Exchange Administration Delegation Wizard, 123–124, 135–136
Exchange Advanced tab, Exchange 2000, 252–256, 258–259
Exchange Chat Service, 409–419, 424–425, **609**
   administrative controls for, 409–412
   Chat client, 417–418
   creating a chat community, 413–417
   ejecting a member, 417–418
   functions of, 33, 53, 189
   restricted list, 416
Exchange Client, 203, 207, 230
Exchange Conferencing Server, 31, 34, 418–419
Exchange connectors. *See under* individual connectors.
Exchange Development Kit. *See* EDK.
Exchange Features tab, Exchange 2000, 252
Exchange General tab, Exchange 2000, 247–251
Exchange GroupWise Directory Update Schedule, 355
Exchange H.323 Videoconferencing Bridge, 419
Exchange Installable File System. *See* EXIFS.
EXchange InterProcess Communication layer. *See* EPOXY.
Exchange Server 5.5 Service Pack 3, 98
Exchange Server Migration Wizard, 544, 550
Exchange Server monitors, 456–459
Exchange Server Post Office tab, 343
Exchange System Attendant, 191
Exchange System Manager, 31, 322, 340, 390, 395, 466
Exchange T.120 MCU, 419
Exchange Task Wizard, 242–243
EXIFS. *See also* Web Store.
   function of, 72, 73, 76, 78, 79, 100, 281
   Internet standards and, 80
   restarting, 76
EXIPC. *See* EPOXY.

Exit module, Certificate Services, 387
Expansion server, 258
EXPN, 279
Export Containers tab, 361
   Lotus cc:Mail connector, 346
   Lotus Notes connector, 351–352
   Novell GroupWise tab, 356
Extended IRC. *See* IRCX.
Extended SMTP. *See* ESMTP.
Extensible Hypertext Markup Language. *See* XHTML.
Extensible Markup Language. *See* XML.
Extensible Storage Engine. *See* ESE.
Extensible Style Language. *See* XSL.
External connectivity. *See* Connectivity.
external.exe, 45

F

Fault tolerance, 164
   defined, 31, 75, 302
   SGs, 75, 87
Favorites tab, MMC, 116
FE/BE design, 12, 483–490, 503, 571–572
   benefits of, 486–487, 588
   BE servers, 485
   fault tolerance, 63
   FE servers, 484–485, 488, 490, 493–495, 503
   firewalls, 486
   issues to monitor, 490
   limitations of, 489
   load balancing, 63, 100
   single namespace, 486, 503, 571–572
   when to use, 487–488
FE servers, 159, 484–485, 503
   component design issues, 493–495
   OWA, 494, 495
   protocols, 490
   security, 488, 572, 588
File system objects, 582
File system services, Web Store, 75, 561
filever.exe, 436
Filtered synchronization, 228, 229
find command, 263
Finger, 20
Firewalls, 370, 378–382
   configuration, 379
   defined, 378
   FE/BE design, 486
   integration with Exchange 2000, 382
   topologies, 380–381
   types of, 379–380

Foreign systems, **598**. *See also* Interoperability.
   auditing, 335–336
   connectors. *See* Connectors.
   interoperability with, 318–325, 334
      Lotus cc:Mail, 52, 189, 319, 339, 341, 342, 343, 360, 361
      Lotus Notes, 52, 55, 189, 319, 340, 347–353, 360–361
   mixed-mode environments, 356–359
   naming conventions, 336
   Novell GroupWise, 45, 189, 320, 340, 353–356
   physical audit, 335
   recipient policy, 338–339
ForestPrep, 178–181, 193, **605**
   installation of Exchange 2000, **604**
   upgrading to Exchange 2000, 515–516, 520–523, 549
Forms, 49, 407, 579, 589
FQDN, 150, 348
Fragmentation, 437
Frame type, 320
Front-end/back-end distributed-services structure. *See* FE/BE design.
Front-end servers. *See* FE servers.
Full duplex network connections, 494
Full mesh topology, 288
Full-text indexing, 32
Full-text search, 32, 92–94
Fully qualified domain name. *See* FQDN.

G

GAIA, 11–12, 34, 55, 407, 566, **597**
GAL, **604**
   accessing, 360
   AD and, 47, 156, 239
   function of, 252, 338
   groups and, 243
Gateway, 19, 45, 52
Gateway Address Routing Table. *See* GWART.
Gateway Service for NetWare, 320
GC
   functions of, 47, 110, 336, 360
   strategic planning, 338
GC server, 147, 156–157
GDI, 317
Generalized markup languages, 573–574
General Post Office. *See* GPO.
General Properties sheet, SMTP connectors, 306
General Purpose Trees, 77
General tab
   Exchange 2000, 247, 255, 257, **606**
   Lotus Notes connector, 348–349
   Novell GroupWise connector, 354
   X.400 connector, 311, 312
Generic Architecture for Information Availability. *See* GAIA.
get command, 570
Global Access List. *See* GAL.
Global Catalog. *See* GC.
Global Catalog Servers, 241, 286
Global Domain Identifier. *See* GDI.
Globally Unique Identifier. *See* GUID.
GPO, 15, 27
Group attributes, 257–259
Group management, 243–244
Group Policy, 262
Groups, 147, 157–158
Groupware, 55
GroupWise. *See* Novell GroupWise.
*.gthr, 94
gthrlog.vbs utility, 94
GUID, 287, 460
GWART, 53, 274, 291, 294

H

Hacking, 374–375. *See also* Security.
HAL, 41
"Hanging attach" records, 96
Hard coding, 574
Hard disk monitoring, Disk Defragmenter snap-in, 451–452
Hardware
   capacity and, 496–497
   design considerations, 481–483
   preparing to upgrade legacy system to Exchange 2000, 514–515, 516–517
   requirements for Exchange 2000, 183
Hardware abstraction layer. *See* HAL.
Hardware Compatibility List. *See* HCL.
HCL, 184, 462, 463, 516
Header, email message, 15
Heap, 99
helo command, 307
Home server, 421–422
Hop, 286
Horizontal scalability, 484, 490, 504
Host server, messaging services, 15
Hot fixes, 184
HTML, 28, 562, 574–575, 577, 588
HTTP, 28, 42, 490, 561, 569, 588
HTTP-DAV, 99
Hub and spoke configuration, 287–288

Hypertext Markup Language. *See* HTML.
Hypertext Transfer Protocol Distributing Authoring and Versioning. *See* HTTP-DAV.
Hypertext Transport Protocol. *See* HTTP.

I

IANA, 277
IBM Systems Network Architecture Distribution Services. *See* SNADS.
ICANN, 46
IE protected store, 386
IIS, 220, 221, 293, **596**
IIS Metabase, 52
ILS, 253
IMAIL process, 76
IMAP, 99
IMAP4, 224, 486, 490, 572
Impersonation, 373
Import Container tab
   Lotus cc:Mail connector, 345–346
   Lotus Notes connector, 350–351
   Novell GroupWise connector, 355–356
IMS, 52, 53, 303
IMS connector, 276
Inbound Queue, 281
Inbox Repair Tool, 436, 438–439, 468
Incident control, 13
Incoming messages, routing of, 283–285
Indexing, 91–94, 101
inetinfo.exe, 55, 99, **596**
Information-management models
   CMIS, 9–10, 34
   GAIA, 11–12, 34
   X.400 message handling system, 17–19, 34, 44
   X.500 directory services, 19–20
Information model, defined, 22
Information-Sharing Paradigm, 4, 11
Information Store. *See* IS.
Information Store Integrity Checker. *See* ISINTEG.
Information technology, paradigm shifts in, 2–7, **596**
INI files, 211
In-place upgrade, 529–531
Installable File System, 595, **603**
Installation, **602**, **611**
   Active Directory Installation Wizard, 153
   ADC, 524–525
   administrative tools, 176–177
   of Certificate Services, 387, 388–389
   Component Selection screen, 187–188, 190
   of connectors, 189, 301–302, 360–361

   Custom Installation Wizard, 212, 231
   deployment, 174–175, 182–187
   of Exchange 2000, 114, 174–193
   hardware requirements, 183–184
   Installation Wizard, 187, 188, 190, 339, 340
   of instant messaging, 421–423
   of KMS, 393–398
   of Lotus cc:Mail connector, 189, 360
   Lotus Notes connector, 189, 360–361
   Microsoft MS Mail connector, 189
   migrating legacy features, 114–115, 550
   Network Monitor Tools, 449
   of Novell GroupWise connector, 189
   of Outlook 2000 client, 208–212
   of Outlook Web Access (OWA), 217
   Setup Wizard, 301
   SOHO installations, 29, 61, 182
   upgrading legacy system to Exchange 2000, 512–535
Installation Wizard, 187, 188, 190, 339, 340
Instant messaging, 419–424, **609**
   activating, 252
   benefits of, 420
   clients and, 424, 425, 426
   domain name system (DNS) and, 420–421
   function of, 33
   installing, 421–423
   Microsoft Exchange Instant Messaging Service, 159, 189, **609**
Instant messaging servers, 159, 423–424
Instant Messaging Service, 159, 189, **609**
Instant Messaging Virtual Servers Wizard, 422
INSTMSG, 422
Interception, 373
Interference, 373
Internal links, 574
International Telecommunication Union. *See* ITU.
Internet
   Exchange 5 and, 28
   history of, 5, 23
Internet access components, 53
Internet Assigned Number Authority. *See* IANA.
Internet Corporation for Assigned Names and Numbers. *See* ICANN.
Internet Explorer 5, 577–578, 589
Internet Information Services API. *See* ISAPI.
Internet Locator Service. *See* ILS.
Internet Mail connector, 53, 306
Internet Mail Service. *See* IMS.
Internet News Service, 53
Internet protocols, Outlook Web Access (OWA), 222–227

Legacy systems   681

Internet Relay Chat. *See* IRC.
Internet Service Manager snap-in, 423
Interoperability, 299–326. *See also* Foreign systems.
   connectors. *See* Connectors.
   Lotus cc:Mail, 52, 189, 319, 339, 341, 342, 343,
      360, 361
   Lotus Notes, 52, 55, 189, 319, 340, 347–353, 360–361
   mixed-mode environments, 356–359
   MS Mail, 321–325
   Novell GroupWise, 45, 189, 320, 340, 353–356
   Novell NetWare, 320
   strategic planning, 334–339, 359, 360
Intersite communication, 300–301
Intranet, 418
IPCONFIG /all command, 187
IPSec, 25
IPX/SPX, 320
IPX/SPX drivers, 55
IRC, 24, 408
IRCS, 408
IRC servers, 159
IRCX protocol, 414
IS, 18, 19, 45, 54, 64, 74, **601**
ISAPI, 26
ISINTEG, 97–98, 436, 439–440, 468
isinteg.pri, 97
isinteg.pub, 97
Isolation, of transaction, 83
ITIL, 12, 111
IT Infrastructure Library. *See* ITIL.
ITU, 17–18, 44

J

JavaScript, 581
JDBC, 581, 589
JET, 22, 52, 59
JET Blue, 22
JET Red, 22, 83
Joint Engine Technology. *See* JET.
JScript, 581

K

KCC, 530
Keep alive, 582
Kerberos, 25, 152, 221–222, 382–383, 386
Key Management Server files, 81, 100
Key Management Service. *See* KMS.
Key pair, 384

KM, 7, 47, 55
   collaboration, 406
   Exchange 2000 and, 28–33, 34, 47, 73, 174
   idealized KM system, 40
KM Database, 386
KM information broker, Exchange 2000 as, 34
KMS, 187, 189, 385–398, **600**
   AD and, 390–398
   certificate authority, 387–390
   installing, 393–398
   legacy KMS, 386–387
KM Security Dynamic Link Library (DLL), 386
*.kms file, 81, 100
Knowledge, defined, 7, 8
Knowledge Consistency Checker. *See* KCC.
Knowledge-Management Paradigm, 2, 5–7, 11, 12,
   40, 407
Knowledge Management. *See* KM.
Knowledge objects, 564
Knowledge workers, 29, 72

L

Layered backbone topology, 342
LDAP, 26, 46, 207, **605**
LDAP Data Interchange Format. *See* LDIF.
LDIFDE, 265
LDIF files, 156
Leapfrog method, 519–520
Legacy Exchange, 53
Legacy issues, administration, 121, 136
Legacy Microsoft Mail connector, 52
Legacy systems, 42, 43–55, 177, **601**
   ADC, 16, 58, 115, 175, 356, 357, 359, 361, 515,
      524–527, 550
   administrative services, 176
   Chat client, 417
   connectors, 52
   directory services, 46–47
   DS, 46
   Exchange key management, 48
   Internet access components, 53
   IS, 45
   KMS, 386–387
   legacy Exchange 5.5 site connectors, 364–365
   migrating during 2000 installation, 114–115, 550
   mixed-mode environments, 115, 356–359, 536–548
   MS services, 47
   MTA, 45–46, 301
   remote mail, 227, 228–229, 231

SA, 44
scheduled connections, 229–230, 231
Store service failure, 88
system management, 48–49
upgrading to Exchange 2000, 512–535
workflow of, 54–55
License agreement, 521
Lightweight Directory Access Protocol. *See* LDAP.
Link monitors, 519
Link queue, 280, 294
Link state algorithm. *See* LSA.
Link state routing, 291–292
Link State Table. *See* LST.
list command, 409, 415
LISTSERV, 24, **599**
List server, 226
Load balancing
    capacity and, 496
    defined, 62, 302
    FE/BE design, 63, 100
Local delivery queue, 286
Local Postoffice tab, MS Mail, 323
Locking controls, WebDAV, 570
*.log file, 84, 101
Log files, 84
Logging, 450–451, 455–456, **610**
    circular logging, 84–85, 101, 460–461
    diagnostic logging, 455–456, 469
Logging levels, 455–456
Logical grouping, for server management, 128
Logical organization, recipient management, 122
Logical structure, directory services, 146–147
Logon dialog box, 222
Log Transaction Redo, 96
Lotus cc:Mail, 319
    directory synchronization, 339, 341, 342, 343
Lotus cc:Mail connector, 52, 339, 360
    installation of, 189, 360
Lotus cc:Mail Post Office, 342
Lotus Notes, 55, 347
    directory synchronization, 340, 347
Lotus Notes connector, 52, 319, 340, 347–353, **607**
    installation of, 189, 360–361
LSA, 294
LST, 288–289, 290

M

M: drive, 74
Macintosh clients, 208
mad.exe, 44, 64

mail.box, 352
Mailbox-enabled recipient, 239, 265, 341
Mailboxes, 239
    managing, 242–243
    moving, 538–540, **606**
Mailbox folder, 76
Mailbox servers, 159
Mail connector interchange, 321, 322
Mail connector MTA, 321, 322
Mail connector post office, 321
Mail-enabled AD group, 239
Mail Exchange records. *See* MX records.
Mailing lists, 226
Mainframe computers, 4
Mainframe environments, directory synchronization, 359
Maintenance, 435
Managed By tab, Exchange 2000, 257, 258
Management Agent tool, 359
Management services, 12
MAPI, 17, 41, 59, 293, 585
MAPI Clients Tree, 77, 100
MAPI Directory Service. *See* MAPI DS.
MAPI DS, 47
MAPI messages, message routing, 284–285, 293
mapmex.tbl, 347
mapnotes.tbl, 347, 348
Markup languages, 560, 572–578, 588
    defined, 573
    generalized, 573–574
    HTML, 28, 562, 574–575, 577, 588
    Internet Explorer 5, 577–578, 589
    specific, 573
    XHTML, 575
    XML, 8, 26–27, 42, 77, 570, 575–577
    XSL, 576, 577, 588–589
MBX subfolder, 74, 76, 100
MCU, 419
MDBEF, 76, 83
Member Of tab, Exchange 2000, 255, 256
Members tab, Exchange 2000, 257
Memory allocation, monitoring, 86
Memory management, 85–86
Memory requirements, for Exchange 2000, 493–494
Message Database Encapsulated Format. *See* MDBEF.
Message databases, 61
Message Digest 5, 389
Message format, Categorizer, 280–281, 282, 285, 293
Message Handling System. *See* MHS.
Message hash, 85

Message routing, 274. *See also* Routing management.
   categorization, 285–286
   connectors. *See* Connectors.
   foreign systems. *See* Foreign systems.
   incoming messages, 283–285
   MAPI messages, 284–285, 293
   in mixed-mode environment, 357–358
   multiple copies, 286
   outbound mail, 286
   queues, 282, 293
   Routing Groups, 128, 282, 287–291
   routing topology, 287–289
   Transport Core, 280–281, 283, 293
Message size, in Lotus cc:Mail, 343
Message Store. *See* MS.
Message tracking, upgrading to Exchange 2000, 519
Message Tracking Center, 134
Message Transfer Agent. *See* MTA.
Message Waiting Directory Lookup queue, 294
Message Waiting To Be Routed queue, 294
Messaging API. *See* MAPI.
Messaging systems, 14–17
   characteristics of, 14–15
   Exchange 2000 as provider, 25–28, 32
Metabase Editor (MetaEdit) 2, 52
Metadirectories, 22, 64, 585
Metadirectory services, 26, 58, 359, 360
Metalanguage, 574
MHS, 44
Microsoft
   "Information at Your Fingertips" (IAYF), 3–4
   paradigm shift by, 5–7, **596**
Microsoft Active Platform, 581–583, 589
Microsoft Chat 2, 425
Microsoft Cryptographic API. *See* CAPI.
Microsoft Directory Synchronization Services.
   See MSDSS.
Microsoft Distributed InterNet Applications
   Architecture. *See* Windows DNA.
Microsoft Exchange 2000 Server Resource Kit, 440, 465, 499
Microsoft Exchange 2000 Wizard, 523
Microsoft Exchange. *See under* Exchange.
Microsoft Exchange eseutil.exe utility, 96, 436–437, 468
Microsoft Exchange Inbox Repair Tool, 436, 438–439, 468
Microsoft Exchange ISINTEG utility, 97–98, 436, 439–440, 468
Microsoft Exchange Messaging And Collaboration Services, 189, 301
Microsoft Hardware Compatibility list, 184
Microsoft Joint Engine Technology. *See* JET.
Microsoft Management Console. *See* MMC.
Microsoft Metadirectory Services, 26, 58, 359, 360
Microsoft model, 372
Microsoft MS Mail. *See* MS Mail.
Microsoft.NET. *See* .NET.
Microsoft NetMeeting, 31, 408, 419
Microsoft Office 2000 Resource Kit, 212
Microsoft Office Custom Installation Wizard, 212, 231
Microsoft Operations Framework. *See* MOF.
Microsoft Outlook 2000, 203–206, 499
   dial-up connection to Exchange Server, 229
   features of, 204–205
   installing, 208–212
   Internet protocols, 204
   multiple mailbox access, 214–216
   multiple profiles in, 214
   profiles, 212–216
   remote mail, 227, 228–229, 231
   service options, 205–206
   uses of, 230
Microsoft Outlook Express, 206–207, 230
Microsoft Readiness Framework. *See* MRF.
Microsoft Repository, 22–23, 59
Microsoft Search service, 92, 93
Microsoft Solutions Framework. *See* MSF.
Microsoft TechNet, 440
Migration
   of connectors, 544–548, 550
   Exchange Server Migration Wizard, 544, 550
   OWA, 567
Migration file, 544
MIME, 24, 50, 225, 274, 277, 278, 293
Mirrored disk array, 491
Mirroring, 186
Mixed management, server management, 127
Mixed-mode environment, 240, 356–359, 536–548, 549–550, **601**
   ADC, 356, 357, 537, 538
   connectors, 544–548
   design, 542–543
   directory synchronization, 359
   message routing in, 357–358
   Move Mailbox Utility, 538–540
   offline address book, 542
   public folder replication, 543
   routing masters, 542
   site replication service (SRS), 537–538
MMC, 116–118, **602**

MMC snap-in tools, 42, 61, 117, 192, **602**
   AD Domains and Trusts, 61, 118, 135, 175
   AD Sites and Services, 61, 118, 135, 175
   AD Users and Computers, 49, 61, 118, 122, 135, 175, 176, 239, 240, 242, 264
   Certificate Authority, 394
   System Manager, 48, 77, 239, 264, 409–410, 413
MOF, 12–14, 111, 112–115
Monitoring, 434, 440–459, 468
   dedicated machines for, 443
   Exchange 2000 tools, 452–459
   Exchange Server monitors, 456–459
   memory allocation, 86
   Windows 2000 utilities, 441–452
Mounted databases, 88
Move Mailbox Utility, 538–540
MRF, 13
MS, 16, 18, 27, 47–48, 74
MSDSS, 58
MSF, 13, 111, 478, 479, 503
MSF Infrastructure Deployment Process Model, 479–481, 503
MSI files, 212
MS Mail, 206, 321–325, 340, **598**
   configuring, 322–324
   Connector Properties sheets, 322–323
   directory synchronization, 324–325, 339
   history of, 27
MS Mail connector, 309, 339, 340
   components of, 321
   configuring, 322
   directory synchronization, 339
   installation of, 189
   Interchange tab, 322, 323
MS Mail Post Office, 321, **608**
MST files, 212
MTA, 18, 50, 52, 54, 64, **600**, **601**
   frequency of checks, 323
   legacy systems, 45–46, 301
   mail connector MTA, 321
   role of, 50, 274, 292
   X.400, 276, 292
mtacheck.exe, 530, 549
MTA-In, 51
MTA transport stack, creating, 310
MTS-Out, 51
Multihomed firewall, 380, 381
Multipoint Control Unit. *See* MCU.
Multipurpose Internet Mail Extensions. *See* MIME.
MX records, 294, 377

N

Named objects, identifying, 337–338
Name resolution, 25, 50
Name Service Provider Interface. *See* NSPI.
names.nsf, 350
Namespace
   AD, 19, 150–151, 482
   defined, 19
   defining, 150–151, 166
Naming, standards of, 160–161
Naming contexts, 147, 155–156
NAS, 61
Native mode, 356, 540, 541, 550, **603**
NDRs, 246, 283, 284, 285
NDS, 20, 26
NetBIOS, 320
.NET, 26, 80
   Microsoft.NET Management Services, 5
   .NET framework, 585–587
   .NET platform, 5–7, **596**
   .NET servers, 5, 6, 30, 40, 110, 589
NetMeeting. *See* Microsoft NetMeeting.
NETNEWS, 24
NetWare. *See* Novell NetWare.
Network administration, 26
Network Attached Storage. *See* NAS.
Network Load Balancing Service. *See* NLBS.
Network Monitor. *See* Windows 2000 Network Monitor.
Network Monitor agent, 449
Network Monitor Tools, 449
Network News Transfer Protocol. *See* NNTP.
Network resources, 371
Network topology, new paradigm, 25
Newsgroups, 206, 226
Newsreaders, 206
New User Wizard, 242
NLBS, 484
NNTP, 17, 28, 77, 99, 206, 226–227, 230
NNTP protocol stack, 187
Nondelivery Reports. *See* NDRs.
Nonprimary connection agreements, 538
NOS, 10, 22, 111
Notes Database Maintenance Schedule option, 352
Novell Client32, 320
Novell Directory Services. *See* NDS.
Novell GroupWise, 45, 320
   directory synchronization, 340, 355
Novell GroupWise API gateway, 353

Novell GroupWise connector, 52, 340, 353–356, 361
   installation of, 189
Novell NetWare, 320
nslookup command, 377
NSPI, 47
NTBACKUP, 265, 464, 466, 467, 469
ntbackup.exe, 464, 466, 467, 469
NTDSUTIL, 265
NT File System. *See* NTFS.
NTFS, 83
NT LAN Manager. *See* NTLM.
NTLM, 59
NTLM authentication protocol, 386
NTLM security, 421

O

Object content, 91
Object Linking and Embedding. *See* OLE.
Object Linking and Embedding Database.
   See OLEDB.
Object properties, 91
ODBC, 41, 580, 589
ODI LAN drivers, 44
Offline address book, mixed-mode environment, 542
Offline defragmentation, 95, 437
Offline folders, Web Store, 564
Offline synchronization, 228
OIM, 22
OLAP databases, 22
OLE, 322
OLEDB, 79, 584
On-demand conversion, 82
Online analytical processing databases.
   See OLAP databases.
Online defragmentation, 95, 437
Online meetings, 419
OnSubmission queue, 283
Open Database Connectivity. *See* ODBC.
Open Data-Link Interface. *See* ODI.
Open Information Model. *See* OIM.
Open message transfer system, 226
Open Shortest Path First. *See* OSPF.
Operating system (OS), preparing to upgrade legacy
   system to Exchange 2000, 514
Optimization, 434
   capacity, 499–501
   Exchange 2000 installation and, 184–185
   of servers, 159–160
Organization, 19
Organizational grouping, 32

Organizational units. *See* OUs.
Organization names, 160
Organization tab, Exchange 2000, 247, 248
OSI Address panel, X.400 connector, 313, 314
OSI Reference Model, 25, 26, 62, 372
OSPF, 291
OST files, 438
OUs, 119–120, 122
   account management, 241
   defined, 338
   for server management, 128
Outbound mail, message routing, 286
Outlook 2000. *See* Microsoft Outlook 2000.
Outlook Express. *See* Microsoft Outlook Express.
Outlook Forms Converter, 579
Outlook Web Access. *See* OWA.
Out-of-office messages, 258
Override tab, X.400 connector, 314–315
OWA, 53, 165, 216–217, **605**
   administration, 220–221
   advantages of, 218, 270
   architecture, 567
   authentication protocols, 383
   choosing, 230
   displaying objects, 568–569
   FE servers, 494, 495
   forms, 407–408, 579, 589
   functions of, 26, 588
   HTTP and, 569, 588
   Internet mail protocols supporting, 222–223
   memory requirements for, 494
   migration of, 567
   minimum requirements for, 218
   missing features of, 219
   request and delivery of service, 568
   server access, 569
   upgrading to Exchange 2000, 519
   WebDAV and, 569–571

P

Package files, 212
Packet filtering, 379, 380, 381
Packet switching, 24
Paradigm, 3
Paradigm shifts, in information technology, 2–7,
   33–34, **596**
Parity, 492
Password, 393, 397
Patch files, 84, 101, 464
*.pat file, 84, 101, 464

PDP-1, 4–5
PDP-11, 5
Penetration, hacking, 374
perfmon.exe tool, 442
Performance management, 132–134.
  See also Monitoring.
  administrative tools, 133–134
  capacity planning, 132, 495–502
  RAID technology, 492
Performance management tools, Windows 2000, 134
Performance Monitor, 134, 442
Performance optimization. See Optimization.
Performance tab, Task Manager, 447, 448
Permission management
  AD Delegation of Control Wizard, 122–123
  Exchange Administration Delegation Wizard, 123–124
  public folders, 162
  recipient management, 122–124
Physical plant, 116, 148
Pipelining, 278
PKI, 152, 377, 398, **608**
Planning, 146–159, 175–176
  AD logical components, 155
  AD logical structure, 149–155
  assessing project risk, 481
  capacity planning, 132, 495–502
  client access, 164–165
  clustering, 164
  corporate objectives, 147–149
  Directory Service components, 146–147
  disaster recovery planning, 165–167, 459–468, 469
  domain structure, 152–154
  for legacy system upgrade to Exchange 2000, 513–520
  MSF Infrastructure Deployment Process Model, 479–481, 503
  namespace, 150–151, 166
  physical structure, 158–160
  recipient management, 152–157
  server configuration, 164–165
  SGs, 90–91
  strategic planning, 334–339, 359, 360
  trees, 154
  trust relationships, 154–155, 166
PLATINUM technology, Inc., 23
Policies, recipient management, 124–125, 262–265
Policy-based management, 336
Polling frequency, 323
Polling interval, 349
POP2, 223–224

POP3, 28, 93, 99, 490, **596**, **605**
Port number
  chat community, 408
  SRS, 538
Post Office Database, 319
Post Office Protocol. See POP2 and POP3.
Post Office tab, Lotus cc:Mail connector, 341–342, 360
Pre-Categorizer queue, 285, 293
Presentation Service Access Point. See PSAP.
Presentities, 420
Primary connection agreements, 538
Principal account, 238–239
Private keys, 388
priv.edb, 99
Problem control, 13
Processes tab, Task Manager, 447
Professional Office System. See PROFS.
Profiles
  defined, 212
  Outlook 2000, 212–216
PROFS, 45, 357, 358, 361
PROFS connectors, 358, 517
Programmability, 32
Property promotion, 78–79, 91–92
PROSPERO, 24
Protocols, 230
  Outlook Web Access (OWA), 222–227
Protocol services, 56, 61–63
  distributed architecture, 99–100
  EPOXY, 50, 99
Protocol settings, recipient settings, 246
Protocol stub, 99
Proxy server, 379
PSAP, 313
PST files, 438
pub.edb, 99
Public folder affinities, 131, 136, 162–163
Public folder replication, mixed-mode environment, 543
Public folders, 26, 49, 239, **596**
  access control, 130–131
  administration of, 130–131, 136
  configuring, 161–162
  hierarchies, 162
  inability to view, 543
  replication, 163
Public folder servers, 159
Public folder support, 77–78
Public Folder tree, 77
Public Folder trees, number of, 161
Public key, 383

Public key encryption, 382, 383–384
Public Key Infrastructure. *See* PKI.
Published information, recipient settings, 246

Q

Query Processor, 93
Queues, 282, 293
Queue Viewer, 133

R

RAID, 90, 444–445, 483, 496, 504
RAID 0, 186, 491–493, 496
RAID 0+1, 491
RAID 1, 186, 193, 491–493
RAID 3, 492
RAID 5, 186, 492, 493, 496
RE, 281
Realtime collaboration, 33
Realtime collaboration servers, 159
Realtime collaborative services. *See* RTCs.
Recipient management, 118–124, 135, 238–266
    account management, 240–244
    address lists, 259–262
    administrative tools for, 121–122
    contact attributes, 255, 257
    contact management, 243
    group attributes, 257–259
    group management, 243–244
    logical organization, 122
    mailbox management, 242–243
    permission management, 122–124
    planning, 152–157
    policies, 124–125, 262–265
    recipient settings, 245–262
    user attributes, 246–255
Recipient names, 161
Recipient policies, 124–125, 262–263, 266, 338–339
Recipients, 16, 129, 238–240
Recipient settings, 245–262
    address lists, 259–262
    contact attributes, 255, 257
    content format, 245
    delivery restrictions, 246, 247, 249
    email addresses, 245
    group attributes, 257–259
    protocol settings, 246
    published information, 246
    storage limits, 246, 249, 251
    user attributes, 246–255
Recipient Update Service. *See* RUS.

Recovery
disaster recovery planning, 165–167, 459–468, 469
recovering Exchange 5.5 server after failed upgrade, 532–534
restore process, 461, 466–468
Redundancy, 459
Redundant Array of Independent Disks. *See* RAID.
Registered channel, 409
Relative ID. *See* RID.
Reliability, 164
Remote mail, 227, 228–229, 231
Remote procedure calls. *See* RPCs.
Rendezvous Protocol. *See* RVP.
Replication, 45, 46, 161, 163
Request for Comments. *See* RFCs.
res1.log, 87
res2.log, 87
Resource Monitor, 63
Response time, 445
Restore process, 461, 466–468
Return on investment. *See* ROI.
RFCs, 224
RGC, 51, 163, 303–305, 326, **607**
RGM, 290–291, 294
Rich-text files, 59, 81, 82, 100
RID, 281
Risk analysis, auditing, 376
ROI, 111, 112
Rollback procedures, 96, 529–531, 549
Routable domains, 352–353
Routing Engine. *See* RE.
Routing Group connector. *See* RGC.
Routing Group Master. *See* RGM.
Routing Groups, 287–291, 326
    capacity and, 497
    creating, 287, 289
    link state information, 292
    names, 160
    RGM, 290–291, 294
    for server management, 128, 282
    topologies, 287–289
Routing management, 274–294
    ESMTP, 19, 274, 277–279, 293
    link state routing, 291–292
    MIME, 24, 50, 225, 274, 277, 278, 293
    S/MIME, 48, 274, 277, 293
    SMTP. *See* SMTP.
Routing masters, mixed-mode environment, 542
Routing and Remote Access Service. *See* RRAS.
Routing server, 422
Routing topologies, 287–289

RPC Ping Client, 436
RPC Ping Server, 436
RPCs, 49, 177, 274–275, 301
RRAS, 304
RTCs, 115, 419, 424
RTF/HTML converter, 82
RUS, 242, 260, 261–263, 266, 339
RVP, 420, 425, 426

S

SA, 44, 54, 64, 191
SANs, 61, 90
SAP, 320
SAS, 222
Scalability, 74, 75, 484, 490, 494, 495, 504, **601**
scanpst.exe, 436, 438, 439
Schedule+, 203, 207–208
Schedule+ Free/Busy connector, 339
Scheduled connections, 229–230, 231
Schedule tab, X.400 connector, 312, 313
Schema, 515
Schema subspace, 156
Screened-host firewall, 381
Screened-subnet firewall, 381
Scripting language, 26, 560, 562–563, 572–578, 589
Script kiddie, 374
sd_iis.dll, 50
sd_store.dll, 50
Secret key, 383
Secure chat room, 409
Secure Hash Algorithm-1. *See* SHA-1.
Secure MIME. *See* S/MIME.
Secure Sockets Layer. *See* SSL.
Security, 370–398, **608**
    administration of, 154
    auditing, 375–376
    authentication, 221–222, 279, 306, 376, 377
    authorization, 376, 377
    bridgehead servers, 303, 304, 307, 378
    confidentiality, 377
    control concepts, 376–377
    defined, 371
    DNS considerations, 377–378
    encryption, 277, 306, 377, 382, 383–384, 398
    Exchange key management, 48
    FE server, 488, 572
    firewalls, 370, 378–382
    hacking, 374–375
    integration, 377
    Kerberos, 25, 152, 221–222, 382–383, 386

    KMS, 187, 189, 385–398
    nonrepudiation, 377
    password, 393, 397
    Public Key Infrastructure (PKI), 152, 377, 398, **608**
    threats to, 371, 373–375
Security Attention Sequence. *See* SAS.
Security groups, 130, 157
Security log, 451
Security policy, 370–371
Security protocols, 371
Security Support Provider Interface. *See* SSPI.
SendQ folder, 284
Server configuration, planning, 164–165
Server management
    administration of, 125–129, 135
    administrative models, 126–127
    system policies and groups, 129
    tools for, 128–129
Server message block architecture.
    See SMB architecture.
Server monitors, 519
Server names, 161
Servers, 159. *See also* Server management.
    address list server, 181
    BE servers, 485, 494, 496, 503
    bridgehead servers, 303, 304, 307, 378
    chat servers, 159
    combination server, 485
    connector servers, 159
    data conferencing servers, 159
    FE server, 493–495
    GC server, 147, 156–157
    home server, 421–422
    .NET servers, 5, 6, 30, 40, 110, 589
    optimization of, 159–160
    proxy server, 379
    RGMs, 290–291, 294
    Routing Groups, 290
    routing server, 422
    sizing issues, 490–495
    SMTP virtual server, 276
    standard server, 485
    video conferencing servers, 159
    virtual servers, 63, 276, 277
Server-side components, 582
Server-side objects, 582
Server-side scripting, 582
Service accounts, creating, 181–182
Service Advertising Protocol. *See* SAP.
Service call referral, 47

Service-level agreements. *See* SLAs.
Service options, 205–206
Service packs, 184
Service providers, 11
Session Service Access Point. *See* SSAP.
setup.exe file, 520, 524
setup /r, 535
SGML, 574
SGs, 61–62, 74, 86, **611**
    managing, 87–89
    planning, 90–91
SHA-1, 389
Shadow, 321
SharePoint Portal Server, 29, 370
Shortcut menu, 118
Simple authentication, 387
Simple Mail Transfer Protocol. *See* SMTP.
Simple Network Management Protocol. *See* SNMP.
Simple Object Access Protocol. *See* SOAP.
Single homed firewall, 381
Single-Instance Store. *See* SIS.
Single-master primary DC model, 119
Single namespace
    FE/BE design, 486, 571–572
    X.500 directory services, **599**
Single Sign On. *See* SSO.
Singletons, 576
SIS, 81, 82, 101
Site, 301
Site addressing, preparing to upgrade legacy system to Exchange 2000, 514
Site connectors, 304–305
Site design, preparing to upgrade legacy system to Exchange 2000, 514, 548
Site Replication Service. *See* SRS.
Site Replication Service files, 81, 100
size command, 279
SLAs, 111–112
Small Office/Home Office installations. *See* SOHO installations.
Smart host, 306
SMB architecture, 83
SMFAs, 9–10, 58, 264
S/MIME, 48, 274, 277, 293
SMP configuration, 493
SMTP, 224–226, **595**, **596**, **601**, **603**, **605**
    components of, 50
    defined, 19, 222, 274
    functions of, 52, 278
    MTA and, 301
    naming convention, **605**
    turn command, 307
    X.400 and, 275–277, 284, 292
SMTP connectors, 51, 163, 303, 305–307, 326, **607**
SMTP queues, **610**
SMTP services
    categorization, 285–286
    incoming messages, 283–285
    outbound mail, 286
    Routing Groups, 287–291
    Transport Core, 280–281, 283, 293
SMTP virtual servers, 276
SNADS, 45, 357, 358, 361
SNADS connectors, 358, 517
SNMP, 9
SOAP, 8, 576
Soft recovery, 95, 96
Software patches, 184
SOHO installations, 29, 61, 182
Source extractors, 544
Specific management functional areas. *See* SMFAs.
Specific markup languages, 573
SRS, 537–538, 549
srs.edb, 537
*.srs file, 81, 100
SSAP, 313
SSL, 303, 495, 572
SSL/TLS, 386
SSO, 152, 222, 372
SSPI, 41
Stack tab, X.400 connector, 312–313
Standalone root CA, 385
Standalone subordinate CA, 385
Standard Generalized Markup Language. *See* SGML.
Standard server, 485
Static data, 461, 462
Stemming process, 92
*.stm file, 76, 81, 83, 100, **595**
Storage Area Networks. *See* SANs.
Storage Groups. *See* SGs.
Storage limits, recipient settings, 246, 249, 251
Storage services, 56–58, 59–60, 72–101, 175
    administration of, 73–74, 115
    collaborative workspace, 80–83
    database file types, 81–83
    design, 73–80, 100
    Extensible Storage Engine (ESE), 52, 83–91
    indexing, 91–94, 101
    installable file system features, 76–80
    property promotion, 78–79, 91–92

protocol services, 99–100
public folder support, 77–78
streaming data support, 78
Web-based support, 76–77
Store driver, 283, 284
store.exe, 45, 55, 64, 85, 87, 99
Strategic planning, 334–339, 359, 360
   auditing, 335–336
   Global Catalog, 338
   named objects, 337–338
   recipient policy, 338–339
   RUS, 339
Streaming data support, 78
Streaming files, 81, 83, 100
Streaming store, Web Store, 564
Striped disk array, 491
Stripe sets, 186
Strong authentication, 387
Sun JDBC, 581, 589
Symmetric keys, 398
Symmetric Multi-Processor configuration. *See* SMP configuration.
Synchronization, 46, 324. *See also* Directory synchronization.
Synchronous collaboration, 33
Synchronous communication, 408
Sysop, 409, 425
System Attendant. *See* SA.
System log, 451
System management, legacy systems, 48–49
System Management Tools, 49, 121, 189, 393
System Manager MMC snap-in, 48, 77, 239, 264, 409–410, 413
System Monitor Performance Logs and Alerts, 442, 445–446
System policies
   recipient management, 124
   server management, 129
Systems Network Architecture Distribution Services. *See* SNADS.
SYSVOL, 462

T

Tags, 573
Task Manager. *See* Windows 2000 Task Manager.
TCO
   administration objectives and, 112
   client applications and, 203
   design and, 41–42, 64, 90, 111
TCP/IP protocol suite, 187

Terminal Services. *See* TS.
Terminal Services Architecture. *See* TSA.
Threat analysis, auditing, 376
Three-pronged screened subnet, 381
TLDs, 150, 153
tls command, 279
TNEF, 284, 293
Top-level domains. *See* TLDs.
Total cost of ownership. *See* TCO.
Transaction, 83–85
Transaction logs, 84, 101, 460, 537, **611**
Transform files, 212
Transitive trusts, 154–155, 166
Transport Core, 280–281, 283, 293
Transport Neutral Encapsulated Format. *See* TNEF.
Transport protocols, 309, 372
Transport Service Access Point. *See* TSAP.
Transport services, 49–53, 175
Transport stack, creating, 310
Trees, planning, 154
Tree tab, MMC, 116
Troubleshooting, 435–440, 468, **610**
   capacity, 501–502
   design and, 501–502
   eseutil.exe, 96, 436–437, 468
   Inbox Repair Tool, 436, 438–439, 468
   ISINTEG, 97–98, 436, 439–440, 468
Trust relationships, planning, 154–155
TS, 176–177, 192
TSA, 113
TSAP, 313
turn command, 279, 307
Two-tier client/server architecture, 15

U

UA, 18
UML, 22
Unified Modeling Language. *See* UML.
Uniform Resource Locator. *See* URL.
Universal canvas, 26, 47–48, 78
Universal Data Access architecture, 582–583
Universal device interface, 48
Universal storage, 48
Unix clients, 208, 217, 230
Unix-to-Unix Copy. *See* UUCP.
Unmounted databases, 88
update /r, 535
Upgrading to Exchange 2000, 549–550, **603**
   ADC, 515, 524–527, 550
   checking for successful upgrade, 532

DomainPrep, 528
failed upgrade, 532–535
ForestPrep, 520–523, 549
hardware requirements, 514–515, 516–517
mixed-mode configuration, 536–548
performing the upgrade, 531
post-upgrade procedures, 532–535
preparation for, 513–520
rollback procedures, 529–531, 549
URL, 150, 561
Usenet, 24, 53, 226
User Agent. See UA.
User attributes, 246–255
User bans, 409, 412
User classes, 409, 425
User object, 337
User profile, capacity and, 498
UUCP, 24
UUEncode/UUDEcode, 24

V

VBScript, 581
VCS, 159
Veritas BackUpExec, 460
Vertical scalability, 484, 504
Video conferencing servers, 159
Video Conferencing Services. See VCS.
Virtual servers, 63, 276, 277
Visual Studio, 80
Voice messaging, 252
VRFY, 279
Vulnerability, 371, 373–375

W

WANs
history of, 23–24
routing topology, 287–289
WAP, 48
Watcher, 420
WBEM, 43
Web-Based Enterprise Management. See WBEM.
Web Client, 230
WebDAV, 32, 77, 100, 217–218, 282
    OWA and, 569–571, 588
Web Distributed Authoring and Versioning.
    See WebDAV.
Web forms, 579, 589
Web markup languages, 574–575, 588
    HTML, 28, 562, 574–575, 577
    Internet Explorer 5, 577–578, 589

XHTML, 575
XML, 8, 26–27, 42, 77, 570, 575–577
XSL, 576, 577, 588–589
Web Services, 566–572, 588
Web Storage System, 76, 77, 78, 560–566, 587, **596**, **610**
    Exchange 2000 database, 81–82
    property promotion, 78–79, 91–92
    streaming data support, 78
Web Store, 48, 72, 219–220, 560–566, 587–588, **603**
    database management, 564–565
    defined, 75
    events, 565–566, 588
    HTML support, 562, 588
    knowledge objects, 564
    Microsoft Win32 support, 563
    offline folders, 564
    scripting support, 562–563
    services of, 75, 100
    streaming store, 564
Whois, 20
Wickets, 573
Wide area networks. See WANs.
Win32, 79
window.print() function, 578
Windows 2000
    backups with, 461–465
    Disk Defragmenter snap-in, 451–452
    DNA model, **597**
    domain topology of, 152–153
    legacy KMS, 386–387
    monitoring utilities, 441–452, 468
    performance management tools, 134
    trust relationships, 154, 166
Windows 2000 AD Account Cleanup Wizard, 544
Windows 2000 Administration Tools, 121
Windows 2000 Advanced Server, 61
Windows 2000 Advanced Server System Monitor,
    442–446
Windows 2000 Datacenter Server, 61
Windows 2000 Event Viewer, 134, 450–451, 469
Windows 2000 Internet Protocol Security. See IPSec.
Windows 2000 Network Monitor, 447–450, 469
Windows 2000 Performance Monitor, 134
Windows 2000 Professional, 121
Windows 2000 Server Resource Kit, 52, 265
Windows 2000 Server System Monitor, 442–446
Windows 2000 System Monitor, 442
Windows 2000 Task Manager, 446–447
Windows 2000 Terminal Services, 121
Windows CE, 48

Windows DNA, 8–14, 12
Windows Explorer ACL editor, 78
Windows Internet Name Service. *See* WINS.
Windows Management Instrumentation. *See* WMI.
Windows NT 4, domain topology of, 152–153
Windows NT, Performance Monitor, 442
Windows NT Key Manager Service, 386
WINS, 175
Wireless Application Protocol. *See* WAP.
Wireless Markup Language. *See* WML.
WMI, 43
WML, 48
World Wide Web, history of, 5
"Write-ahead" strategy, 85

X

X.400
 addressing method, 307–308
 MTA, 276
 SMTP and, 275–277, 284, 292
X.400 connectors, 49, 51, 163, 275, 304, 307–318
 configuring, 308, 311–318
 disadvantages of, 308
X.400 message handling system, 17–19, 34, 44, 285
X.400 queues, **610**
X.500 directory services, 19–20, **599**
XHTML, 575
XML, 8, 26–27, 42, 77, 570, 575–577
XSL, 576, 577, 588–589

Coriolis introduces

EXAM CRAM INSIDER™

A FREE ONLINE NEWSLETTER

Stay current with the latest certification information. Just visit ExamCram.com and sign up to receive the latest in certification and training news for Microsoft, Java, Novell, A+, and more! Read e-letters from the Publisher of the Exam Cram and Exam Prep series, Keith Weiskamp, and certification experts about future trends in IT training and education. Access valuable insider information on exam updates, new testing procedures, sample chapters, and links to other useful, online sites. Take a look at the featured program of the month, and who's in the news today. We pack all this and more into our *Exam Cram Insider* online newsletter to make sure *you* pass your next test!

To sign up for our twice monthly newsletter, go to www.ExamCram.com and click on "Become a Member" and sign up.

EXAM CRAM INSIDER – Another reason Exam Cram and Exam Prep guides are *The Smartest Way To Get Certified*.™ And it's free!

CORIOLIS™
Certification Insider Press

ExamCram.com

The leading resource for IT certification!

This groundbreaking, e-learning Web destination for test preparation and training incorporates an innovative suite of personalized training technologies to help you pass your exams. Besides providing test preparation resources and an array of training products and services, ExamCram.com brings together an extensive community of professionals and students who can collaborate online.

ExamCram.com is designed with one overriding philosophy in mind—great access!

Review industry news, study tips, questions and answers, training courses and materials, mentor programs, discussion groups, real-world practice questions, and more.

Practice Exams: *Take a FREE practice exam for the certification you choose.*

Questions of the Day: *Study questions are posted every day. Or, sign up to have them emailed to you daily.*

Exam Cram Study Center: *Get the facts on an exam, review study resources, read study tips, and more.*

OTHER HIGHLIGHTS:

Ask the Mentors: Ask questions and search the archives for answers.

Certification Planner: Discover the variety of certification programs offered.

Open Forum: Post your thoughts on weekly topics and see what others think.

Certification Resource Centers: Quickly find out about the newest certification programs.

Join the thousands who have already discovered ExamCram.com. Visit ExamCram.com today!

CORIOLIS
Certification Insider Press

The Smartest Way to Get Certified

What's on the CD-ROM

The *MCSE Exchange 2000 Administration Exam Prep*'s companion CD-ROM contains the testing system for the book, which includes 50 questions. Additional questions are available for free download from **ExamCram.com**; after registering, simply click on the Update button in the testing engine. You can choose from numerous testing formats, including Fixed-Length, Random, Test All, and Review.

Note: The following software is required to complete the real-world projects:

- Exchange 2000 Server Enterprise Edition
- Windows 2000 Advanced Server
- Windows 2000 Service Pack 1
- Internet Explorer version 5.x or higher

If you plan to build or test external connectors, you will need additional computers properly installed with the foreign mail systems and connected to a private network to which you have appropriate administrative rights.

System Requirements

Software

- Your operating system must be Windows 98, NT 4, or 2000.
- To view the practice exams, you need Internet Explorer 5.x.

Hardware

- An Intel Pentium, AMD, or comparable 100MHz processor or higher is recommended for best results.
- 32MB of RAM is the minimum memory requirement.
- Available disk storage space of at least 10MB is recommended.

Software developed by Dreamtech Software, India